Rethinking Hanslick

Eastman Studies in Music

Ralph P. Locke, Senior Editor
Eastman School of Music

Additional Titles of Interest

August Halm: A Critical and Creative Life in Music
Lee A. Rothfarb

Beethoven's Century: Essays on Composers and Themes
Hugh Macdonald

European Music and Musicians in New York City, 1840–1900
Edited by John Graziano

Good Music for a Free People: The Germania Musical Society in Nineteenth-Century America
Nancy Newman

Liszt's Transcultural Modernism and the Hungarian-Gypsy Tradition
Shay Loya

Variations on the Canon: Essays on Music from Bach to Boulez in Honor of Charles Rosen on his Eightieth Birthday
Edited by Robert Curry, David Gable, and Robert L. Marshall

Verdi in America: "Oberto" through "Rigoletto"
George W. Martin

Wagner and Venice
John W. Barker

Wagner and Venice Fictionalized: Variations on a Theme
John W. Barker

Wagner and Wagnerism in Nineteenth-Century Sweden, Finland, and the Baltic Provinces: Reception, Enthusiasm, Cult
Hannu Salmi

A complete list of titles in the Eastman Studies in Music series
may be found on our website, www.urpress.com.

Rethinking Hanslick

Music, Formalism, and Expression

Edited by Nicole Grimes,
Siobhán Donovan, and Wolfgang Marx

UNIVERSITY OF ROCHESTER PRESS

Copyright © 2013 by the Editors and Contributors

All Rights Reserved. Except as permitted under current legislation, no part of this work may be photocopied, stored in a retrieval system, published, performed in public, adapted, broadcast, transmitted, recorded, or reproduced in any form or by any means, without the prior permission of the copyright owner.

First published 2013
Reprinted in paperback 2015

University of Rochester Press
668 Mt. Hope Avenue, Rochester, NY 14620, USA
www.urpress.com
and Boydell & Brewer Limited
PO Box 9, Woodbridge, Suffolk IP12 3DF, UK
www.boydellandbrewer.com

ISSN: 1071-9989
hardcover ISBN: 978-1-58046-432-1
paperback ISBN: 978-1-58046-522-9

Library of Congress Cataloging-in-Publication Data

Rethinking Hanslick : music, formalism, and expression / edited by Nicole Grimes, Siobhán Donovan, and Wolfgang Marx.
    pages cm. — (Eastman studies in music, ISSN 1071-9989 ; v. 97)
  Includes bibliographical references and index.
  ISBN 978-1-58046-432-1 (hardcover : alkaline paper) 1. Hanslick, Eduard, 1825–1904. 2. Music—19th century—Philosophy and aesthetics. 3. Musical criticism—History—19th century. I. Grimes, Nicole, editor. II. Donovan, Siobhán, 1966– editor. III. Marx, Wolfgang, 1967- editor. IV. Series: Eastman studies in music ; v. 97.
  ML423.H25R48 2013
  720.973—dc23

2012048300

A catalogue record for this title is available from the British Library.

This publication is printed on acid-free paper.
Printed in the United States of America

Contents

Foreword by Mark Evan Bonds — vii

Acknowledgments — xi

Abbreviations — xii

Chronology — xiii

Introduction — 1
Nicole Grimes

Part One: Rules of Engagement

1. Negotiating the "Absolute": Hanslick's Path through Musical History — 15
   James Deaville

2. Hanslick's Composers — 38
   Fred Everett Maus

3. Hanslick, Legal Processes, and Scientific Methodologies: How Not to Construct an Ontology of Music — 52
   Anthony Pryer

4. Otakar Hostinský, the Musically Beautiful, and the *Gesamtkunstwerk* — 70
   Felix Wörner

Part Two: Liberalism and Societal Order

5. Hanslick on Johann Strauss Jr.: Genre, Social Class, and Liberalism in Vienna — 91
   Dana Gooley

6. Waltzing around the Musically Beautiful: Listening and Dancing in Hanslick's Hierarchy of Musical Perception — 108
   Chantal Frankenbach

7. "Poison-Flaming Flowers from the Orient and Nightingales from Bayreuth": On Hanslick's Reception of the Music of Goldmark — 132
   David Brodbeck

8 German Humanism, Liberalism, and Elegy in Hanslick's
   Writings on Brahms   160
   Nicole Grimes

   Part Three: Memoirs and Meaning in Social Contexts

9 The Critic as Subject: Hanslick's *Aus meinem Leben* as a
   Reflection on Culture and Identity   187
   Lauren Freede

10 "Faust und Hamlet in Einer Person": The Musical Writings of
   Eduard Hanslick as Part of the Gender Discourse in the
   Late Nineteenth Century   212
   Marion Gerards

11 Body and Soul, Content and Form: On Hanslick's Use of the
   Organism Metaphor   236
   Nina Noeske

   Part Four: Critical Battlefields

12 Hanslick and Hugo Wolf   261
   Timothy R. McKinney

13 Battle Rejoined: Hanslick and the Symphonic Poem in the 1890s 289
   David Larkin

14 On "Jewishness" and Genre: Hanslick's Reception of Gustav Mahler 311
   David Kasunic

   Selected Bibliography   339

   List of Contributors   345

   Index   351

Foreword

Any serious account of musical criticism or aesthetics in the nineteenth century has to confront Eduard Hanslick at some point. For more than forty years, he was the leading music critic in Vienna, one of Europe's cultural capitals, and his brief treatise on aesthetics, *Vom Musikalisch-Schönen*, remains the central document in the history of the concept known as "absolute music," the idea of music as a wholly self-referential art of pure form.

But music was about more than music in Hanslick's Vienna, as he himself well knew. It was a cultural battlefield that pitted defenders of the city's musical past—Haydn, Mozart, and Beethoven, or at least the Beethoven of the first eight symphonies—against the advocates of the "Music of the Future," who considered Beethoven's Ninth the fountainhead for the new music of Wagner and Liszt. Both as a critic and as an aesthetician, Hanslick was on the front line of battle, leading a war of words against those who considered the forms of the past superseded and inadequate to the demands of the present. *Vom Musikalisch-Schönen* provided traditionalists with a philosophical argument by which to justify their rejection of the "Music of the Future" on the basis of something more than merely personal dislike of the new music or resistance to change in general. By the same token, *Zukunftsmusiker* could now attack their opponents on grounds that went beyond the charge of garden-variety conservatism, for Hanslick's treatise claimed philosophical standing in the world of ideas. The fact that Hanslick could issue no fewer than ten different editions of the book during his lifetime speaks to the power of its ideas. Critics who differed with him were still issuing book-length rebuttals to his theories in the 1880s and 1890s. By the time of the work's last authorial edition (1902), it had been translated into Spanish (1865), French (1877), Italian (1883), Danish (1885), Russian (twice, in 1885 and 1895), English (1891), and Dutch (1892).[1] It has never been out of print.

To pigeonhole Hanslick simply as a conservative, however, is to miss the richness of his thought. The controversy that surrounded his writings transcended the narrow world of musical aesthetics and criticism because his treatise and concert reviews together went to the heart of two long-standing issues about all the arts, not just music. The first was the relationship between form and content. As the least material and most abstract of all the arts, music had long been recognized as fundamentally different in kind. Unlike a poem, a drama, a novel, a painting, or a sculpture, a work of purely instrumental music did not have to be "about" anything other than itself. (If a composer chose to provide some verbal clue as to a work's import, as for example in the case of Beethoven's *Pastoral* Symphony, that information was not actually heard in performance and could therefore be considered as standing apart from the work itself, not *in* what audiences actually heard.) Philosophers and critics had always recognized form as a category of central importance in art, but the idea that an art might consist exclusively of form posed a conceptual challenge. In an era when the term "abstract art" did not yet exist, only music offered the possibility of an art of pure form. But commentators were slow to accept the consequences of such a high degree of abstraction and for the most part continued to describe it in terms of an emotional content expressed through the agency of form. Only gradually did critics begin to recognize music's lack of content as the key to understanding not just music but all the arts, and in time the advocates of absolute music advanced to the forefront of those who saw form as the defining element of the aesthetic experience. By 1877, the novelist and literary critic Walter Pater could famously declare that "all art constantly aspires towards the condition of music"—that is, an art in which form and content were one and the same.[2]

Hanslick's writings also spoke to the central issue of art's role in society. Because of music's fundamentally self-referential nature, he argued, it could not represent or engage with the external world; this in turn allowed music to provide a refuge of pure beauty from the realm of the mundane. Hanslick's motives were at least partly political: in the wake of the Revolutions of 1848/49, he wanted to provide a theoretical justification for insulating music from the turmoil of social and political change. In this sense, his attitude toward music was actually far more radical than that of Wagner, who considered music (and art in general) as a means of revolution. But Wagner's idea was scarcely novel: the socially disruptive potential of music had been recognized long before by Socrates, who in Plato's *Republic* affirms Damon's observation that "the modes of music are never disturbed without unsettling of the most fundamental political and social conventions."[3] Hanslick's view of music as a self-sufficient, self-contained art, by contrast, would figure prominently in several currents of modernist aesthetics in the early twentieth century, most notably formalism and objectivity. Seen from a distance, then, it is Hanslick and not Wagner who emerges as the more unconventional and even radical of the two, though not in ways that Hanslick himself could have anticipated. It is with good reason that Jean-Jacques Nattiez has called *Vom Musikalisch-Schönen* a text "fundamental to musical modernity."[4]

The time is right for a thorough reevaluation of Hanslick's work, both as an aesthetician and as a critic: Dietmar Strauß's invaluable synoptic edition of *Vom Musikalisch-Schönen* now allows us to trace in revealing detail the shifts and refinements of Hanslick's thought over the years, and Strauß's ongoing critical edition of Hanslick's journalistic criticism is bringing to light reviews their author suppressed or altered in later years for one reason or another. The essays in *Rethinking Hanslick: Music, Formalism, and Expression* move beyond the polemics and labels that have shadowed Hanslick's writings from the start. This is the first English-language book devoted entirely to Hanslick in more than sixty years, and its fourteen authors offer an unparalleled diversity of perspectives. It is also one of the very few books in any language to approach Hanslick's philosophical treatise, his critical writings, and his rich autobiography as a comprehensive whole. These essays have much to tell about Hanslick's attitudes toward (among other things) dance, the body, issues of gender, issues of faith, politics, musical perception, the sciences, his legal training, his own critics, and above all the music he wrote about, from Johann Strauss waltzes to Richard Strauss tone poems. *Rethinking Hanslick: Music, Formalism, and Expression* helps us appreciate the breadth and complexity of one of the most influential writers on music in the nineteenth century.

Mark Evan Bonds

Notes

1. I am grateful to Olga Panteleeva for calling my attention to the two Russian translations.

2. Walter Pater, "The School of Giorgione," *Fortnightly Review* 22 (October 1877): 528.

3. Plato, *Republic*, trans. Paul Shorey, in *The Collected Dialogues of Plato*, ed. Edith Hamilton and Huntington Cairns (Princeton, NJ: Princeton University Press, 1961), 424c.

4. Jean-Jacques Nattiez, "Hanslick: The Contradictions of Immanence," in his *The Battle of Chronos and Orpheus: Essays in Applied Musical Semiology*, trans. Jonathan Dunsby (New York: Oxford University Press, 2004), 105.

Acknowledgments

This volume began with a conference, "Eduard Hanslick: Aesthetic, Critical, and Cultural Contexts," that took place at University College Dublin (UCD) in June 2009. As a collection of essays, it has grown and developed since then. But its debt to the many participants of the conference endures. The conference was generously supported by the UCD School of Music, and UCD School of Languages and Literatures. A number of our colleagues provided warm support and encouragement for the project during and since that time. At the UCD School of Music, we thank Harry White, Thérèse Smith, Julian Horton, and Melissa Devereux. At the UCD School of Languages and Literatures, we thank Jean-Michel Picard and Bronwyn Salmon. We are grateful to David Brodbeck at the Department of Music of the University of California, Irvine, and owe special thanks to Kerry Houston at the Dublin Institute of Technology. We are also indebted to the Austrian Ambassador to Ireland, His Excellency Dr Walter Hagg.

The production costs for the book were offset by an award from the Seed Funding Scheme of University College Dublin. Part of Nicole Grimes's work toward this volume was carried out under the auspices of a Marie Curie International Outgoing Fellowship within the Seventh European Community Framework Program. We gratefully acknowledge all of this financial assistance.

At the University of Rochester Press, we thank most warmly Suzanne Guiod, Ralph Locke, Ryan Peterson, Julia Cook, Carrie Crompton, and Tracey Engel. Two anonymous reviewers provided insight and advice at a level of detail that bespeaks their exceptional knowledge and commitment to Hanslick Studies. Their input and close engagement with the text has significantly strengthened the volume. Kevin C. Karnes and Mark Evan Bonds gave of their time to read these essays and were gracious and generous with their advice and encouragement. Angela R. Mace helped in locating sources in Berlin at a time when none of us could be there. We also thank Peter Maurice Tuite for his ongoing support and practical assistance.

Every volume of collected essays represents a collective effort. We wish to thank all of the contributors whose lively and stimulating engagement with Hanslick and the constellation of ideas orbiting around him made this book conceivable in the first place. The patience, positive attitude, and commitment of all the authors throughout the editing process has made it a joy and a privilege to work with each of them.

Abbreviations

AML	Eduard Hanslick, *Aus meinem Leben*, 2 vols. (Berlin: Allgemeiner Verein für Deutsche Litteratur, 1894).
AML/W	Eduard Hanslick, *Aus meinem Leben*, ed. and with an afterword by Peter Wapnewski (Kassel: Bärenreiter, 1987).
OMB	Eduard Hanslick, *On the Musically Beautiful*, trans. Geoffrey Payzant (Indianapolis: Hackett, 1986).

Sämtliche Schriften 1/1, 1/2, 1/3, 1/4, 1/5, 1/6, 1/7, respectively for:

Sämtliche Schriften: Historisch-kritische Ausgabe, vol. 1/1, *Aufsätze und Rezensionen 1844–1848*, ed. Dietmar Strauß (Vienna: Böhlau, 1993).
Sämtliche Schriften: Historisch-kritische Ausgabe, vol. 1/2, *Aufsätze und Rezensionen 1849–1854*, ed. Dietmar Strauß (Vienna: Böhlau, 1998).
Sämtliche Schriften: Historisch-kritische Ausgabe, vol. 1/3, *Aufsätze und Rezensionen 1855–1856*, ed. Dietmar Strauß (Vienna: Böhlau, 1998).
Sämtliche Schriften: Historisch-kritische Ausgabe, vol. 1/4, *Aufsätze und Rezensionen 1857–1858*, ed. Dietmar Strauß (Vienna: Böhlau, 2000).
Sämtliche Schriften: Historisch-kritische Ausgabe, vol. 1/5, *Aufsätze und Rezensionen 1859–1861*, ed. Dietmar Strauß (Vienna: Böhlau, 2005).
Sämtliche Schriften: Historisch-kritische Ausgabe, vol. 1/6, *Aufsätze und Rezensionen 1862–1863*, ed. Dietmar Strauß (Vienna: Böhlau, 2008).
Sämtliche Schriften: Historisch-kritische Ausgabe, vol. 1/7, *Aufsätze und Rezensionen 1864–1865*, ed. Dietmar Strauß (Vienna: Böhlau, 2011).

VMS	Eduard Hanslick, *Vom Musikalisch-Schönen: Ein Beitrag zur Revision der Ästhetik der Tonkunst*, ed. Dietmar Strauß, vol. 1 (Mainz: Schott, 1990).
VMS/2	Dietmar Strauß, *Vom Musikalisch-Schönen: Ein Beitrag zur Revision der Ästhetik der Tonkunst*, vol. 2 (Mainz: Schott, 1990).
WS	*Wiener Salonblatt*.

Chronology

1825	September 11, born in Prague to mother Karolina Katharina Hanslik (née Kisch, daughter of non-Orthodox Jews who converted to Catholicism upon her marriage) and father Joseph Adolph Hanslik (Catholic), who at that time lived in house no. 459 in the *Altstadt*.
1833	The Hanslik family moved with Karolina Katharina's parents to house no. 780 in *Neustadt* (*Rossmarkt*, today known as *Wenzelsplatz*). Here Hanslick's maternal grandparents played a central role in his life, and nourished his interests in scholarly pursuits and French literature, a subject further enriched for him by his mother. Hanslick and his siblings were home-schooled by their father, from whom Hanslick inherited his intellectual preoccupation with philosophy and aesthetics. Both German and Czech (his father's native tongue) were spoken in the home, which was frequented by eminent figures in Czech cultural circles such as Václav Hanka (1791–1861), librarian of the Bohemian Museum; the historian František Palacký; and physiologist Jan Evangelista Purkyně.
1839	From autumn 1839 Hanslick took private music lessons with Václav Jan Tomášek.
1840	Successfully passed his Abitur exams. Thereupon, he enrolled for two "philosophical years" (*philosophisches Obligatsstudium*) at Prague University. His subjects were Religion, Theoretical Philosophy, Mathematics, Latin, and Natural History.
1843	Began his university studies, from which he was to graduate with great success. His subjects included Natural Law, Criminal Law, Statistics of European States, and Statistics of the Austrian Empire. According to Hanslick's autobiography, his mother died at this time.

In addition to Hanslick's own writings, the sources for this timeline include Jitka Ludvová, "Einige Prager Realien zum Thema Hanslick," in *Eduard Hanslick zum Gedenken: Bericht des Symposiums zum Anlass seines 100. Todestags*, ed. Theophil Antonicek, Gernot Gruber, Christoph Landerer (Tutzing: Hans Schneider, 2010), 163–180; Geoffrey Payzant, "Translator's Preface," in Eduard Hanslick, *On the Musically Beautiful*, trans. Geoffrey Payzant (Indiana: Hackett Publishing, 1986), xi–xvii. Note that the spelling of the family name as "Hanslik" is not an error. Hanslick later changed his name to the more Germanic "Hanslick."

1844   Published first article as a music critic, under the pen name of "Ed-d": "Zweites Konzert des Cäcilienvereins am 15. Dezember," *Beiblätter zu Ost und West*, no. 203 (December 19, 1844). Hanslick continued to write occasional pieces for this paper. At this time, the family moved to Prague II, no. 985.

1846   From his address in Prague, Hanslick moved to Vienna to complete his final year of study in law. During this year, he also began to write music reviews for the *Wiener Allgemeine Musik-Zeitung* (including the famous 1846 review of Wagner's *Tannhäuser*).

1848   Hanslick's lied "Liebeslied unter'm Vyšehrad" was performed at the *Ständetheater*, Prague, on January 9. This lied remained in the repertoire until the 1870s. It was later recomposed as a piano transcription (*Transcription de Salon sur un Air Bohême de Dc Ed. Hanslick pour le piano Op. 692*) by a composer using the pseudonym François Behr, and published by the Prague Publishing House Hoffmann in 1896. From 1848 Hanslick also began to write music criticism for the *Wiener Zeitung*, the *Sonntagsblätter*, and other journals and papers both in and outside of Vienna.

1849   Graduated from the University of Vienna, as a Doctor of Philosophy in Law.

1850–52   Took up a temporary position at the State Finance Office in Klagenfurt.

1851 (?)   Hanslick's father died.

1852   Transferred to the Finance Ministry in Vienna upon promotion, and soon thereafter moved to another position in the Ministry of Education.

1853   Another of Hanslick's lieder with the bilingual title "Der böhm'sche Musikant—Český houslista" was included on a recital program by Cecilie Soukop-Botschon at the *Ständetheater* Prague.

1854   Publication of the first edition of *Vom Musikalisch-Schönen*, which was recognized as his *Habilitationsschrift* in 1856 by the University of Vienna.

1855   Began writing music criticism for the Viennese newspaper *Die Presse*, which would in 1864 become the *Neue Freie Presse*.

1856   Appointed to an external, unpaid lectureship on the History and Appreciation of Music, at the University of Vienna.

1861	Appointed Associate Professor of the History and Aesthetics of Music at the University of Vienna (a salaried post).
1864	Appointed permanent music critic for the Viennese liberal daily newspaper *Neue Freie Presse*.
1869	Began to publish his critical writings in book form, beginning with *History of Concert Life in Vienna*.
1870	Appointed Full Professor at the University of Vienna, and awarded the doctorate *in honoris causa*.
1876	Married the singer Sophie Wollmuth (b.1856).
1884	Invited to contribute to the *Kronprinzenwerk* (Crown Prince's Œuvre) in Vienna, which saw twenty-four volumes appear under the official title *Die österreichisch-ungarische Monarchie in Wort und Bild* from 1885 to 1902. This invitation catapulted Hanslick to the highest level of society, where he made many valuable contacts. He devoted an entire chapter of his autobiography to this episode in his life.
1894	Published his autobiography, *Aus meinem Leben*.
1895	Retired from professional life, yet continued to write reviews on important works and premières for the *Neue Freie Presse* until his death, but with less frequency as the years continued.
1904	Died in Baden on August 6.

Introduction

Nicole Grimes

Eduard Hanslick is celebrated today primarily for his seminal publication in the field of music aesthetics—*Vom Musikalisch-Schönen: Ein Beitrag zur Revision der Ästhetik der Tonkunst.* Upon its initial publication in Leipzig in 1854, this small book elicited controversy and heated debate. The nine subsequent editions published throughout Hanslick's lifetime—between 1858 and 1902[1]—ensured that the text remained the focus of debate on musical aesthetics well into the twentieth century.

Vom Musikalisch-Schönen, as Geoffrey Payzant reminds us, was directed against the aesthetics of feeling prevalent in eighteenth- and nineteenth-century writings on music, and sought to "clear away the rubble of obsolete prejudices and presuppositions" and to "mark out the foundations upon which a new theory might be built."[2] In writing his memoirs in the winter of his life, Hanslick acknowledged that the reception of the book was fraught with divisive reaction. He accepted some responsibility for this. Confronting directly the issue that had provoked the most controversy, and anticipating the concern that would continue to confound Hanslick scholarship, he conceded that it was misleading to speak of a "lack of content" (*Inhaltslosigkeit*) with regard to instrumental music. The fundamental issue he had tried to address was how musical form imbued with spirit (*beseelte Form*) was to be differentiated philosophically from empty form (*leere Form*).[3]

With a mixture of self-deprecation and self-assurance, Hanslick viewed his 1854 *Büchlein*[4] as little more than a sketch or foundation whose negative, polemic aspects towered above its positive, systematic ones. He felt that a comprehensive, methodical *Ästhetik der Musik* was what was required to come to terms with this fundamental issue, a task that demanded an undivided capacity for work, and complete concentration of thought.[5] Although Hanslick hinted at carrying out such a project in his 1861 letter of application for the position of Professor of the History and Aesthetics of Music at the University of Vienna (which he successfully secured), he became frustrated in his efforts to identify objective criteria by which to judge musical beauty and deviated from his original path, turning instead—as Kevin Karnes has recently shown—to writing a cultural and "living history" of Viennese concert life.[6]

It was in his capacity as a music critic for the *Neue Freie Presse*, Austria's leading liberal daily, that Hanslick was at once celebrated and feared throughout Europe for more than four decades.[7] From the 1860s onward, he collated his writings and began publishing volume after volume of collected criticisms, supplemented in 1894 by an extensive autobiography, *Aus meinem Leben*. These writings are as rich for their musical insights as they are for their penetrating and multifaceted exploration of the cultural, sociopolitical, and religious contexts in which the reviewed works were composed, performed, and received. Hanslick was as fascinated by the composers he critiqued and the relationship between their lives and works, as he was curious about his fellow audience in Vienna. He was writing for a well-educated, liberal-minded readership, the Viennese *Bildungsbürgertum*, who were conscious of tradition and their place within Viennese society.

Scholarship on Hanslick, from the mid-nineteenth century until recent decades, has tended to focus predominantly on the aesthetic monograph. Given the provocative nature of this text, discussion of Hanslick and musical aesthetics tends to be framed in terms of a series of binary oppositions: form/expression; absolute/program music; objectivity/subjectivity; formalism/hermeneutic criticism. In more recent years, there has been a growing recognition of the fertile middle ground that lies between such polarities, with Mark Evan Bonds having paved the way by recognizing the centrality of the spiritual and philosophical aspects of Hanslick's monograph. This is best articulated in the last paragraph, which was cut from all but the first edition:

> This spiritual content thus combines, in the soul of the listener, the beautiful in music with all other great and beautiful ideas. He does not experience music merely as bare and absolute through its own beauty, but simultaneously as a sounding image of the great movements in the universe. Through deep and secret relationships to nature the meaning of tones is heightened far beyond the tones themselves, and allows us always to feel the infinite even as we listen to the work of human talent. Just as the elements of music—sound, tone, rhythm, strength, weakness—are found in the entire universe, so man rediscovers in music the entire universe.[8]

Bonds asserts that "the significance of this passage—and its subsequent deletion—can scarcely be overestimated. This was not merely one of many pronouncements buried deep within *Vom Musikalisch-Schönen*, but rather the ringing culmination of Hanslick's entire treatise."[9] Subsequently, Nicholas Cook clarified that "Hanslick did not say that music does not, cannot, or should not convey feelings, moods or emotions.... There should never have been any doubt as to what his basic thesis was—that the objective properties of music, rather than people's subjective responses to it, constitute the proper concern of musical aesthetics."[10] Mark Burford would go one step further by arguing that Hanslick negotiated a "middle ground between idealism and materialism." Burford's key insight is his claim that "in his attempt to characterize music's essence, Hanslick did not so much reject musical metaphysics as, to a certain extent, reconceptualize it by arguing that the ideal content of music is a product of a human spirit, not a transcendent one."[11]

Until very recently, however, scholarly investigation into Hanslick's critical writings lagged far behind the advances made in research on *Vom Musikalisch-Schönen*. This absence of scholarly study devoted to the critical writings is matched by the paucity of English translations of this material, with Henry Pleasants's volume of 1950 continuing to stand alone in this regard.[12] Until the end of the twentieth century, Hanslick's reviews tended to be drawn upon either in an attempt to better understand the aesthetic treatise, or as excerpts to bolster perceived views on certain composers. It is difficult to account for this disparity in the treatment of the aesthetic and critical writings in Hanslick studies, although we might do well to consider the turn that musicological writings took in West Germany and Anglo-America in the Cold War era and its aftermath.

As Celia Applegate points out, the reign of objective musical analysis and documentary studies in this period, with its emphasis on musical positivism, "meant the exclusion of what Joseph Kerman calls 'criticism,'—that is the consideration of aesthetic criteria and extra-musical meanings in a work."[13] Broadly speaking, musicology in West Germany in the Cold War years can be understood as identifying certain modes of thought (such as sociopolitical readings of musical works) as extramusicological and thereby outside the concerns of musicological discussion. In this climate, music was considered to be a "socially functionless, non-authoritarian discourse."[14] East German musicology during this period can be understood as "theorizing music as social discourse."[15] Anne Shreffler sees the Marxist musicology of East Germany as anticipating the tenets of the North American "New Musicology" promoted by commentators such as Joseph Kerman and Lawrence Kramer. For Marxist music historians, the priority was to reconnect music with society. As Shreffler argues, "East German musicology was concerned with the need to find out how music communicates, between whom and in what contexts, how it did so in the past, what is communicated and for what purpose, and finally how the 'message' of a work changes, if it does, over time."[16] The fact that this East German discourse was carried out under a Marxist banner meant that it could be rejected out of hand by West Germans, as they did not accept its basic premise.[17]

The writings from postwar, divided Germany that have had the greatest impact on Anglo-American scholarship are those of Carl Dahlhaus. As James Hepokoski reminds us, "At the heart of the Dahlhaus project was an effort to keep the Austro-German canon from Beethoven to Schoenberg free from aggressively socio-political interpretations."[18] During these Cold War years, it was "Dahlhaus's intention to shelter the German Romantic canon"—with which Hanslick was largely preoccupied—"from ideology critique."[19] Hanslick's hermeneutic descriptions of music—be they poetic, sociopolitical, or even nationalistic—fit less comfortably in this system than a discussion of the formalist aspects of *Vom Musikalisch-Schönen*.

With the end of the Cold War in 1989 came the translation of much of Dahlhaus's output into English, and the establishment of the field of "New Musicology." In the wake of these seismic shifts, a host of scholars were intent on finding ways in which to reconnect the Germanic repertoire of the long nineteenth century with its social context, and to forge alternatives to the Dahlhaus system. Susan McClary was one of Dahlhaus's sharpest critics, observing a disparity in his output. In *The Idea of Absolute Music*, she writes, Dahlhaus "painstakingly delineates [a] history whereby a social discourse was appropriated and redefined first by romantic mystics and then by objectivists." Yet in his *Nineteenth Century Music*, she claims, he continues to respect the prohibitions of that tradition of objectivity, in that "he practices only structural analysis on instrumental music and scorns those who would venture into hermeneutic studies of symphonies."[20]

McClary ascribes this disparity to a philosophy that in 1993 still regulated "much of musicology, blocking all but the most formalistic approaches to criticism."[21] Yet her own writings at that point continued to be regulated by the very philosophy to which she referred: on the one hand she rescues Brahms from his reputation as a composer of absolute music, and on the other she disregards Hanslick's own hermeneutic discussion of Brahms's compositions, instead labelling him the "chief polemicist for the absolutists."[22] McClary goes one step further than Dahlhaus here: where Dahlhaus envisaged Hanslick's concept of "absolute musical art" to be dissolved "from functions, texts, and programs as pure instrumental music," McClary interpreted it, via Dahlhaus and Roger Scruton, to be "self-contained, innocent of social or other referential meanings."[23]

Constantin Floros shared this disinclination to allow Hanslick's writings be understood and interpreted on their own terms. The hermeneutic bent of Floros's writings is all the more pronounced when pitted against Hanslick's "doctrine of Brahms as a prototype of the 'absolute' musician."[24] Floros charges Hanslick with "simply ignor[ing] the considerable share of the poetic and autobiographic in the work of [Brahms]."[25] Although Anne Shreffler's analysis of East and West German musicological writings during the Cold War is sharp and lucid, she too promotes only a formalist reading of Hanslick's aesthetic output, grouping him with a number of German theorists who have little in common with Hanslick's critical œuvre: "From Hanslick to Riemann, many theorists, including Schenker, have sought to reduce the content of music to the relationships between notes, labelling its expressive content as something 'external.'"[26] The trajectory of Hanslick studies in the late twentieth and early twenty-first century, therefore, is such that it charts Hanslick from being the opponent of program music, to being opposed to extramusical adjuncts, to one who conceives of music being hermetically sealed off from its expressive content and cultural context.

Winding the clock back three decades to Patricia Carpenter, a former pupil of Schoenberg, hers seems like a lone—if sage—voice in the wilderness. She is one of the few critics of *Vom Musikalisch-Schönen* to recognize both Hanslick's intellectual debt to German Idealism and the expressive resonance of his book in her warning that "inconsistencies in Hanslick's dogma are enhanced if it is forced into a formalist mold; for him, art is expressional. Music is mere form, but not only form; it is also expressive of musical ideas."[27]

Rethinking Hanslick: Music, Formalism, and Expression introduces a paradigm shift to Hanslick studies. Taking its cue from Carpenter, it aims to redress the manifold misreadings of Hanslick outlined above. Such an approach would not be possible without the pioneering work of a number of scholars over the past three decades. Geoffrey Payzant has had a profound impact on how we understand Hanslick's thought, both through his revised translation of *Vom Musikalisch-Schönen* and in his numerous essays.[28] Dietmar Strauß continues apace with the crucial task of publishing the *Sämtliche Schriften*, which follows on his pivotal publication of a scholarly, annotated edition of the aesthetic monograph.[29] Without this vital endeavor, current Hanslick scholarship would be severely impoverished. David Brodbeck's analysis of the nuances and complexities of liberalism in Vienna in the closing decades of the nineteenth century is incisive, and his teasing out of changing conceptions of German identity, from something rooted in culture to something rooted in ethnicity, provides a much-needed critical frame of reference for future studies related not only to Hanslick, but also to a range of German and Czech artists.[30] Kevin C. Karnes's 2009 monograph gives cogent consideration to Hanslick's role in the formative stages of the discipline of musicology in *fin-de-siècle* Vienna, a topic that is profitably taken up again in Nicholas Cook's *The Schenker Project*.

The present volume aims to build on the scholarship published in recent years, and to forge an avenue in Hanslick studies that considers not only his aesthetic monograph, but also the critical and autobiographical writings. The essays contained in this volume embrace ways of thinking about Hanslick's writings that are outside of the polarities that marked earlier discussion of his work. This book encompasses the variety of political, cultural, social, and musical issues that may have influenced Hanslick's aesthetic judgment; it seeks to investigate how Hanslick's critical writings document aspects of the changing social context of *fin-de-siècle* Vienna; it probes the nature of the relationship between Hanslick's critical writings and his aesthetic theory; it examines the extent to which Hanslick reveres expression in music; and it traces the legacy of nineteenth-century German philosophy in his critical writings.

The essays in this volume are arranged thematically. Part 1 analyses Hanslick's rules of engagement with a musical work. James Deaville conducts an investigation into the reception history of Hanslick's aesthetic and critical writings, providing a comprehensive assessment of Hanslick's changing role as a music critic and aesthetician in German-speaking Europe from the mid-nineteenth century to the present. Fred Everett Maus negotiates the intricacies of Hanslick's complex theories on the art of listening by comparing Hanslick's approach in the 1854 monograph to that in his critical writings, arguing for a fourfold relation between composer, music, Hanslick as listener, and the reader of his essay. Felix Wörner's close analysis of the 1877 response to *Vom Musikalisch-Schönen* by Ottakar Hostinský is one of the first English-language considerations of the work of this important figure. Wörner attempts to reconcile Hanslick's position concerning the beautiful in music with Richard Wagner's concept of the "Gesamtkunstwerk," and Hostinský's concomitant attempt to reshape the dichotomy between form and content in music. Anthony Pryer broaches the ontological quagmire surrounding the concepts of form and content in music by assessing the influence Hanslick's legal training had on his aesthetic judgment, concluding that this training impinged strongly on Hanslick's views about what might be counted as admissible evidence in a debate on musical beauty.

Part 2 is concerned with issues surrounding liberalism in Vienna and the shifting goalposts of societal order. Margaret Notley has described elsewhere the basic aspects of the liberal worldview as "pro-German sentiment, antagonism toward the Catholic Church, and profound distrust of anti-intellectual trends."[31] Viennese liberalism also shared common traits with European liberalism of the time such as a belief in progress and the promotion of scientific methods.[32] Hanslick, Brahms, Theodor Billroth, Max Kalbeck, and Gustav Dömpke were among the intellectual elite of Viennese liberalism, with Hanslick and Ludwig Speidel serving as music and theatre critics respectively for the *Neue Freie Presse*. In their writings, these figures both constituted and contested liberalism, each providing their own individualized response to it. This section teases out the nature of Hanslick's response in this regard. Both Dana Gooley and Chantal Frankenbach explore the role of dance in Hanslick's aesthetics in relation to his liberal outlook. Gooley embarks on an exploration of the overlap between art-genre, social hierarchy, and liberal ideology in Hanslick's reviews and essays on Johann Strauss Jr. (Strauss II), whose compositional trajectory both mirrors and challenges the liberal ideology that underpins Hanslick's criticism. Chantal Frankenbach's discussion of Hanslick's response to dance forms and their changing generic designations extends beyond the Strauss family to the work of Johannes Brahms. She juxtaposes Hanslick's attitude to dance in *Vom Musikalisch-Schönen* and in the critical writings, uncovering incongruous attitudes on women, the relationship between pleasure and reason, and the triumph of appearance over reality, all of which she sets against the backdrop of Vienna as a *fin-de-siècle* city of paradoxes. David

Brodbeck and Nicole Grimes both investigate Hanslick's reviews of the composers who inhabited the same German liberal circles as the critic in Vienna. Brodbeck explores Goldmark's reception by Hanslick across a range of genres. In particular, he considers the issue of "Jewish Orientalisms" in Goldmark's music, which made it difficult for Hanslick, at times, to hear the composer's music as fully German, as the output of one who was fully acculturated. Brodbeck offers us a means of understanding the paradox created when one German liberal describes the music of another in terms of non-German ethnic essentialism. Grimes turns to Hanslick's writings on Brahms, the composer he considered to be quintessentially German. She suggests that it was their shared German liberal values that made Hanslick amenable to understanding the cultural, religious, and political context of Brahms's "musical elegies," a group of works composed between 1868 and 1883—a period coinciding with the ascendancy of a modern form of liberalism in Vienna—that are intimately connected to the turn-of-the-century New Humanism espoused by a group of early nineteenth-century German poets including Goethe, Schiller, and Hölderlin.

Issues of Germanness and *Bildung* extend to literary, gender, and social contexts in Part 3. Here, the merits of Hanslick's autobiography—which has too often been read solely for its personalized impressions of individual composers—are reassessed by Lauren Freede in relation to their rich cultural context. In describing the cultural life around him in nineteenth-century Vienna, Hanslick was also describing the process whereby a national view of music developed that married a belief in music as sublime and apolitical with the conviction that it simultaneously manifests a politically constructed nation. Freede argues, therefore, that Hanslick's *Aus meinem Leben* contributes to a wider dialogue about the centrality of music to Austro-German society, and charges Hanslick with recognizing the contribution of music toward the establishment of a national identity and culture. Bound up with this is a social discourse on gender. Marion Gerards contends that the movement for women's emancipation was one of the most socially and politically rousing topics debated in Vienna in the latter part of the nineteenth century. Although Hanslick never overtly acknowledged this movement in his writings, Gerards suggests that the pervasiveness of these debates was such that they impacted on writings and reflections on music, and went hand in hand with a controversial discussion about "natural" gender qualities. She explores Hanslick's understanding of music in the context of this social discourse, and examines the implications this had for his position on the role of music in the nation. Nina Noeske focuses her analysis of Hanslick's gender designations on the organism metaphor. As such, she addresses the broader question of the metaphorical connections between the "healthy" and the "unhealthy" organism in writings on music. Noeske argues that Hanslick viewed the musically beautiful as a healthy—and preferably male—organism, and understood physicality and feelings to be feminine attributes. She shows that, according to Hanslick, it is not only women who are less well suited to genuine artistic activity (on account of their naturally weaker constitution), but also the representatives of the so-called New German School.

While Hanslick is today best remembered for his role in the aesthetic struggles around the "New German School"—particularly concerning Liszt, Wagner and Brahms—his career as a critic spanned more than half a century. He lived well into the Viennese *fin-de-siècle* with its explosive mixture of grandeur and decadence, encountering a younger generation of composers. This period of Hanslick's life, which has hitherto received scant attention, is addressed in Part 4. Timothy R. McKinney explores the reciprocal, if fraught, relationship that existed between Hanslick and Hugo Wolf, who both pursued careers as critics and composers. McKinney takes as the centerpiece of his study Wolf's setting of Eduard Mörike's *Abschied*—an irony-soaked account of an encounter between artist and critic—and traces the interaction between the critical mood of the authorial voice (Wolf's) and the voice of the critic (Hanslick's). David Larkin turns to the compositions of Richard Strauss and Dvořák who, partly by renewing the genre of program music, prompted a return to Hanslick's earlier critical battlefields. Theorizing Hanslick's response to program music, Larkin considers the disparity in Hanslick's responses not only to the work of these two composers, but also to their various categories of program music. Ultimately, it is the treatment of tonal syntax that Larkin deems to be central to Hanslick's judgment of their symphonic poems. By comparison, David Kasunic finds that Hanslick treated his one-time student Gustav Mahler's early music with surprisingly indulgent consternation. Although Mahler would seem an unlikely candidate for Hanslick's critical forbearance, Kasunic reveals that in his reviews of Mahler's orchestral songs and First Symphony in 1900, Hanslick grapples with the aesthetic, generic, and formal challenges that these works pose, rather than dismissing them out of hand. He argues that Hanslick sought to carve out a distinctly non-Wagnerian aesthetic space for Mahler, and explores the kinship of composer and critic in the context of the anti-Semitic outbursts in Vienna around 1900.

Together these essays speak to the significance of Hanslick's contribution not only to studies in music, but also to the aesthetics and philosophy of music, as well as looking anew at broader sociopolitical issues. It is hoped that the volume will provide readers with an engaging and deepened understanding of the work of this powerful figure in nineteenth-century musical life. Geoffrey Payzant wrote with wonderful wit of the categories of creatures whose response to music Hanslick considered to be inadequate. These included "elephants, spiders, enthusiasts, women and Italians."[33] As was the case with Hanslick's output, *Rethinking Hanslick: Music, Formalism, and Expression* proposes to challenge and provoke, yet also to enrich and enlighten. It is aimed at audiences and listeners, readers and thinkers, connoisseurs and amateurs. In the spirit of Hanslick, we encourage all who read these pages to take leave of the company of elephants and spiders and, along with the authors contained herein, "to be agreeably led astray."³⁴

Notes

1. For full details of the various editions, and a definitive version of the text that collates all of the changes, see Eduard Hanslick, *Vom Musikalisch-Schönen: Ein Beitrag zur Revision der Ästhetik der Tonkunst*, vol. 1, ed. Dietmar Strauß (Mainz: Schott, 1990) (hereafter cited as *VMS*).

2. Geoffrey Payzant, "Translator's Preface," in Eduard Hanslick, *On the Musically Beautiful*, trans. Geoffrey Payzant (Indianapolis: Hackett, 1986), xiii (hereafter cited as *OMB*).

3. "Das Wesen der Musik ist aber noch schwerer in philosophische Kategorien zu bannen als das der Malerei, weil die entscheidenden Begriffe 'Form' und 'Inhalt' in der Musik nicht standhalten wollen, der Trennung sich widersetzen. Will man der reinen Instrumentalmusik einen bestimmten Inhalt vindizieren, (—in der Vokalmusik liefert ihn das Gedicht und nicht die Musik—) so müßte man die kostbarsten Perlen der Tonkunst über Bord werfen, denen niemand einen von der Form trennbaren 'Inhalt' nachzuweisen oder auch nur herauszufühlen vermag. Anderseits ist es, wie ich wohl einsehe, ein mißverständlich Ding schlechtweg von der 'Inhaltlosigkeit' der Instrumentalmusik zu sprechen, was auch meiner Schrift die meisten Gegner erweckt hat. Wie ist in der Musik beseelte Form von leerer Form wissenschaftlich zu unterscheiden?" Eduard Hanslick, *Aus meinem Leben*, ed. and with an afterword by Peter Wapnewski (Kassel: Bärenreiter, 1987), 155 (hereafter cited as *AML/W*).

4. Ibid., 150.

5. "Ich hatte natürlich die Absicht, meine Abhandlung 'Vom Musikalisch-Schönen'" mit der Zeit zu einer eigentlichen Ästhetik der Tonkunst zu erweitern und auszuführen. Daß jene Schrift nur eine Art Skizze oder Unterbau bedeute, war mir ebenso klar, als daß ihr negativer polemischer Teil den positiven, systematischen an Umfang und Schärfe überrage. Aber eine vollständige, systematische Ästhetik der Musik—das ist ein Unternehmen, welches ungeteilte Arbeitskraft und unzersplitterte Konzentration des Denkens erfordert." Ibid., 153.

6. For details, see Kevin C. Karnes, *Music, Criticism, and the Challenge of History: Shaping Modern Musical Thought in Late Nineteenth-Century Vienna* (New York: Oxford University Press, 2008), 58.

7. Although Hanslick resigned from the *Neue Freie Presse* in 1895, he wrote occasional reviews right up until the time of his death.

8. "Dieser geistige Gehalt verbindet nun auch im Gemüth des Hörers das Schöne der Tonkunst mit allen andern großen und schönen Ideen. Ihm wirkt die Musik nicht blos und absolut durch ihre eigenste Schönheit, sondern zugleich als tönendes Abbild der großen Bewegungen im Weltall. Durch tiefe und geheime Naturbeziehungen steigert sich die Bedeutung der Töne hoch über sie selbst hinaus und läßt uns in dem Werke menschlichen Talents immer zugleich das Unendliche fühlen. Da die Elemente der Musik: Schall, Ton, Rhythmus, Stärke, Schwäche im ganzen Universum sich finden, so findet der Mensch wieder in der Musik das ganze Universum." Hanslick, *VMS*, 171. Cited in Dahlhaus, *The Idea of Absolute Music*, trans. Roger Lustig (Chicago: University of Chicago Press, 1989), 28.

9. Mark Evan Bonds, "Idealism and the Aesthetics of Instrumental Music at the Turn of the Nineteenth Century," *Journal of the American Musicological Society* 50, nos. 2–3 (1997): 415. See also, Bonds, *Music as Thought: Listening to the Symphony in the Age of Beethoven* (Princeton, NJ: Princeton University Press, 2006).

10. Nicholas Cook, *The Schenker Project: Culture, Race and Music Theory in Fin-de-Siècle Vienna* (New York: Oxford University Press, 2007), 50. Along similar lines, see Charles Youmans, *Richard Strauss's Orchestral Music and the German Intellectual Tradition: The Philosophical Roots of Musical Modernism* (Bloomington: Indiana University Press, 2005), 11.

11. Hanslick, *VMS*, 171.

12. Eduard Hanslick, *Vienna's Golden Years of Music*, trans. Henry Pleasants (New York: Simon and Schuster, 1950).

13. Celia Applegate, "What Is German Music? Reflections on the Role of Art in the Creation of the Nation," *German Studies Review* 15 (1992): 21–32.

14. James Hepokoski, "The Dahlhaus Project and Its Extra-Musicological Sources," *19th-Century Music* 14, no. 3 (1991): 222.

15. Anne Shreffler, "Berlin Walls: Dahlhaus, Knepler, and Ideologies of Music History," *Journal of Musicology* 20, no. 4 (2003): 500.

16. Ibid., 504.

17. Ibid.

18. Hepokoski, "The Dahlhaus Project," 222.

19. Ibid., 225.

20. Susan McClary, "Narrative Agendas in 'Absolute' Music: Identity and Difference in Brahms's Third Symphony," in *Musicology and Difference: Gender and Sexuality in Music Scholarship*, ed. Ruth Solie (Berkeley: University of California Press, 1993), 327–28.

21. Ibid., 327.

22. Ibid.

23. Ibid. McClary acknowledges Dahlhaus here, and not Scruton, although her conception of "absolute music" has much in common with the latter. For an excellent analysis of the use of the term "absolute music" throughout music history, and of the disproportionate weight that has been attached to this term in relation to Hanslick's writings, see Sanna Pederson, "Defining the Term 'Absolute Music' Historically," *Music and Letters* 90, no. 2 (2009): 240–62.

24. Constantin Floros, *Johannes Brahms, "Free but Alone—A Life for a Poetic Music,"* trans. Ernest Bernhardt-Kabisch (Frankfurt/M: Peter Lang, 2010), 202.

25. Ibid.

26. Shreffler, "Berlin Walls," 513–14. The suggestion that Hanslick was a theorist crops up again in McClary's *Conventional Wisdom*, where she writes, "Theorists since the nineteenth-century critic Eduard Hanslick have generally solved the split [between the question of form versus content] by redefining everything as structure—thus the institutional prestige of our graphs, charts, and quasi-mathematical explanations of music." Susan McClary, *Conventional Wisdom: The Content of Musical Form* (Berkeley: University of California Press, 2001), 6.

27. Patricia Carpenter, "Musical Form and Musical Idea: Reflections on a Theme of Schoenberg, Hanslick, and Kant," in *Music and Civilization: Essays in Honor of Paul Henry Lang*, ed. Edmond Strainchamps and Maria Rika Maniates in collaboration with Christopher Hatch (New York: Norton, 1984), 408.

28. In addition to *OMB*, see Geoffrey Payzant, "Hanslick, Sams and Gay, and 'Tönend Bewegte Formen,'" *Journal of Aesthetics and Art Criticism* 40, no. 1 (1981): 41–48; "Hanslick, Heinse and the 'Moral' Effects of Music," *Music Review* 49, no. 2 (1988): 126–33;

"Hanslick on Music as Product of Feeling," *Journal of Musicological Research* 9, no. 2–3 (1989): 133–45; *Eduard Hanslick and Ritter Berlioz in Prague: A Documentary Narrative* (Calgary, AB: University of Calgary Press, 1991); *Hanslick on the Musically Beautiful: Sixteen Lectures on the Music Aesthetics of Eduard Hanslick* (Christchurch, NZ: Cybereditions, 2002).

29. The publication of the critical writings is an ongoing project with Böhlau in Vienna. See the list of abbreviations at the outset of this book for details of the volumes available at the time of writing. Strauß's edition of *Vom Musikalisch-Schönen* is referred to as *VMS* throughout this volume. His second volume, charting the historic-critical response to it, is referred to as Strauß, *VMS/2*.

30. See David Brodbeck, "Dvořák's Reception in Liberal Vienna: Language Ordinances, National Property, and the Rhetoric of *Deutschtum*," *Journal of the American Musicological Society* 60, no. 1 (2007): 71–132; and "Hanslick's Smetana and Hanslick's Prague," *Journal of the Royal Musical Association* 134, no. 1 (2009): 1–36.

31. Margaret Notley, *Lateness and Brahms: Music and Culture in the Twilight of Viennese Liberalism* (Oxford: Oxford University Press, 2007), 15.

32. Ibid., 16–17. See also Carl Schorske, "Politics and the Psyche: Schnitzler and Hofmannsthal," in *Fin-de-Siècle Vienna: Politics and Culture* (New York: Vintage Books, 1981), 5–10.

33. Geoffrey Payzant, "Elephants, Spiders, Enthusiasts, Women and Italians: Some Byways of Hanslick Research (1982)," in *Sixteen Lectures on the Musical Aesthetics of Eduard Hanslick* (Christchurch, NZ: Cybereditions, 2003), 17–27. Payzant's list refers broadly to those whom Hanslick considered to respond pathologically, as opposed to intellectually, to music. As many of the essays in this volume attest, we do not endorse Hanslick's inclusion of the last two categories in this list.

34. *OMB*, 64.

Part One

Rules of Engagement

Chapter One

Negotiating the "Absolute"

Hanslick's Path through Musical History

James Deaville

Introduction: The Path to Hanslick

Hanslick's name barely appears in current popular or everyday culture—and yet, most musicians do recognize "Hanslick," albeit with an unmistakable bias in their reception. When performers, students, or even certain music historians and musicologists describe him, they most often provide an unflattering portrayal of a conservative, formalist aesthetician of absolute music on the one hand,[1] a fearsome yet eminent critic with gigantic blind spots on the other.[2]

Music appreciation texts—the sources of knowledge for thousands of undergraduates and their instructors in North America since they began appearing in the 1960s—have perpetuated the topos of Hanslick as the champion of absolute music. For example, the definitive text by Grout, Palisca, and Burkholder, *A History of Western Music* (2006), characterized Hanslick as "the most articulate proponent of absolute music."[3] To substantiate this claim, the book juxtaposes a brief one-hundred-word passage from section 3 of *Vom Musikalisch-Schönen* with a longer paragraph from Liszt's essay on the *Harold Symphony*.[4]

Regarding the other popular perception of Hanslick, as an errant purveyor of vitriol, the researcher could consider the writings of *New Yorker* critic and blogger Alex Ross—unofficial arbiter of taste for Generation X.[5] Ross's blog *The Rest Is Noise* has consistently presented Hanslick as a critic whose conservative bias led him to misjudge contemporary composers, most notably in his "mistaken" reviews of Wagner and of Tchaikovsky's violin concerto. For example, in a comment on critic Paul Bowles's denunciation of Duke Ellington's *Black, Brown, and Beige*, Ross writes: "That's one of the stupidest reviews in the history of criticism, right up there with Hanslick on Tchaikovsky and Virgil Thomson on Sibelius."[6]

Composer and critic Nicholas Slonimsky had facilitated such a use of Hanslick through his 1953 *Lexicon of Musical Invective*,[7] which, as an ostensibly amusing collection of passages from the work of critics who reviled "great" composers, effectively assigned Hanslick's critical work to the role of source material for malevolent bon mots. The fourteen excerpts include his well-known polemics against Bruckner, Liszt, Richard Strauss, Tchaikovsky, and Wagner, which have served as fodder for reviewers and program annotators since Hanslick's time. Slonimsky's introductory tongue-in-cheek essay "Non-Acceptance of the Unfamiliar" unfortunately contributes to the negative image of Hanslick by presenting some of the most striking excerpts from his reviews without reference to cultural or historical contexts.[8]

Slonimsky himself was not original in this approach to music criticism in general and Hanslick in particular: as he admitted, the prominent forerunner, even model,[9] was Wilhelm Tappert's 1877 *Wagner-Lexikon: Wörterbuch der Unhöflichkeit* (Wagner-Lexicon: Dictionary of Rudeness, Containing Coarse, Mocking, Scathing, and Defamatory Expressions Which Have Been Used by Enemies and Mockers of and against Master Richard Wagner, His Works, and His Followers),[10] which cites Hanslick contra Wagner eighteen times. The goal of Tappert was to expose the tactics of contemporary critics who far overstepped the bounds of propriety in their literary castigation of Wagner. His own strategy, however, was to subject these individuals similarly to public ridicule by publishing their most outrageous linguistic excesses and misjudgments out of context.[11] It was this opposition of Hanslick (and his aesthetically conservative colleagues) to the so-called New German School of Wagner and Liszt that not only inspired Tappert to anthologize these words, but also—two decades earlier—caused the progressive composers, performers, and critics around Liszt to take up the pen against Hanslick.[12]

That which had brought Hanslick to their attention, and indeed, had quickly catapulted the little-known Viennese critic to international prominence, was the publication of his aesthetic tract *Vom Musikalisch-Schönen* in 1854.[13] Hanslick's reviewing activity prior to the book's publication may have attained more than local notoriety in Vienna; his aesthetic reflections on setting texts that were not suited for composition appeared in the *Rheinische Musik-Zeitung* of 1852,[14] and the 1853 Viennese season report in the *Oesterreichische Blätter für Literatur und Kunst* was reprinted in the *Neue Berliner Musikzeitung*.[15] Nevertheless, the occasional nature of his musico-literary production in the 1840s and early 1850s resulted in a limited dissemination and knowledge of that body of work—Liszt and colleagues in Weimar and Leipzig appear not to have taken notice of Hanslick before 1854.

This essay aims to trace Hanslick's path through musical history beginning with that momentous publication, which created an internationally recognized name for the aesthetician-critic and caused him to enter into the annals of musicology. We shall chronologically follow the warp and woof of his reputation and legacy through the intervening generations of reception that have held up a mirror to the culture of their times. In doing so, we will discover that Hanslick's travels through time took some unexpected and disputatious turns.

The Book and the "War"

There can be no doubt that *Vom Musikalisch-Schönen* exploded like a bomb in the central European book market, and nowhere more so than in the Weimar of Liszt and the Leipzig of Franz Brendel.[16] Almost overnight Hanslick became a figure of note, whether for approbation or for condemnation; so while his friend Robert Zimmermann published the first favorable review—the first response to the book altogether—in the *Oesterreichische Blätter für Literatur und Kunst* on November 20, 1854,[17] Liszt's circle set to work immediately to meet what they considered a powerful challenge to their aesthetic position. Their initial public reaction to Hanslick's treatise, however, has been overlooked by both Hanslick and Liszt scholarship: in the *Neue Zeitschrift* of December 8, 1854, Peter Cornelius published a modest statement of Weimar's position, tucked away in the final pages of a review of an unimportant symphony by Richard Würst:[18]

> This question still divides the musical world in two parties. For the one music is a fanciful playing with notes according to rules of euphony and aesthetic principles.... According to them music should have its effect in and of itself without any mediating extramusical ideas.... The other party regards the music passed on to it by the great masters as a poetically developed language.... It wants to determine form every time on the basis of the poetic thought; only this shall give it justification.[19]

In the absence of supporting documents from Weimar or the press, one could speculate that Cornelius inserted this incongruous passage at the instigation of Liszt or Brendel. Nevertheless, what we observe here is a summary of the two parties' positions without heated polemics or detailed refutation, yet clearly biased toward Liszt and Wagner. This surface calm in the face of Hanslick undoubtedly resulted more from Cornelius's general nonconfrontational manner and elevated style than from any directive from Liszt or Wagner, since the literary productions emanating from the progressive party at this time were quite partisan and polemic.[20]

More circumstantial responses, for and against, followed in due course. Although this substantial literature has yet to be gathered and analyzed,[21] several contemporaries did attempt their own surveys of the "battlefield." In his own monograph-length critique of *Vom Musikalisch-Schönen* from 1859, New German writer Ferdinand Peter Graf von Laurencin listed other authors who had opposed Hanslick in print: "Ambros, Brendel, Carrière, Th. Vischer und A. Kullak, thus by far the most brilliant opponents to Dr. Hanslick's theorems....

Only J. C. Lobe... was the person who... considered Hanslick's publication."[22] Arthur Seidl himself provided an overview of the literature from the "war" three decades later,[23] which is plainly marked by his own pro-Wagner position in the questionable assignment of aestheticians to the opposition to Hanslick, as listed below.[24]

In Opposition:
A. W. Ambros, *Die Grenzen der Musik und Poesie* (Leipzig, 1856)
Fr. Th. Vischer and K. Köstlin, *Aesthetik der Musik* (Stuttgart, 1857)
Ad. Kullack, *Das Musikalisch-Schöne* (Leipzig, 1858)
Fr. Th. Vischer, *Über das Verhältnis von Inhalt und Form in der Kunst* (Zurich, 1858)
F. P. Graf Laurencin, *Dr. Hanslick's Lehre vom Musikalisch-Schönen. Eine Abwehr* (Leipzig, 1859)
M. Carrière, *Aesthetik* (Leipzig, 1859)
E. Krüger, *System der Tonkunst* (Leipzig, 1866)
K. Köstlin, *Aesthetik* (Tübingen, 1869)
Fr. Stade, *Vom Musikalisch-Schönen* (Leipzig, 1870)
C. Fuchs, *Praeliminarien zu einer Kritik der Tonkunst* (Leipzig, 1871)
R. Wagner, *Gesammelte Schriften* (Leipzig, 1873)
O. Liebmann, *Zur Analyse der Wirklichkeit* (Strassburg, 1876)
O. Hostinský, *Das Musikalisch-Schöne und das Gesammtkunstwerk* (Leipzig, 1877)
Fr. v. Hausegger, *Musik als Ausdruck* (Vienna, 1885)

In favor:
R. Zimmermann, review in *Oesterreichische Blätter für Literatur und Kunst* (1854)
H. Lotze, review in *Göttinger Gelehrte Anzeigen* (1855)
M. Lazarus, *Leben der Seele* (Berlin, 1857)
R. Zimmermann, *Geschichte der Aesthetik* (Vienna, 1858)
H. v. Helmholtz, *Lehre von den Tonempfindungen* (Braunschweig, 1862)
H. Lotze, *Geschichte der Aesthetik* (1868)
R. Zimmermann, *Studien und Kritiken zur Philosophie und Aesthetik* (Berlin, 1870)
H. A. Köstlin, *Aesthetik der Tonkunst* (Stuttgart, 1879)
H. Ehrlich, *Die Musik-Aesthetik in ihrer Entwicklung von Kant bis auf die Gegenwart* (Leipzig, 1881)
E. v. Hartmann, "Idealismus und Formalismus in der Musikaesthetik," in *Auserwählte Werke* (Berlin, 1886)

While high-profile aestheticians of the New German School produced extended critical essays and book-length *Gegenschriften*,[25] Hanslick's supporters tended to incorporate his ideas into their own aesthetic writings. The first years were arguably the most productive for the debates, since the discussions were fresh and they generated novel ideas on both sides of the dispute. Some of Hanslick's points may have arisen in the pre-1854 rhetoric aimed against Wagner and Liszt,[26] but it was *Vom Musikalisch-Schönen* that—by virtue of its clarity and brilliance—sparked the broad contestation of the seemingly polarized aesthetic positions.[27]

Liszt staked out his own leading role within the opposition to Hanslick—and thus also within the "progressive" movement of the early 1850s—by publishing his aesthetic manifesto in the *Neue Zeitschrift* from July and August of 1855, in the form of the *Harold in Italy* essay.[28]

Although the absence of documentary evidence precludes an empirical determination of whether the appearance of Hanslick's book impacted on the timing and content of Liszt's own statement of artistic beliefs, the publication of his key essay on *Harold in Italy* within nine months of *Vom Musikalisch-Schönen* strongly suggests a connection. Cornelius's review essay from November 1854 then takes on a new potential meaning from this perspective: it could have served as a "notice of action" from the New Germans while Liszt was preparing his circumstantial statement for release.

In all of this, the movement around Liszt and Wagner was at a distinct disadvantage: Hanslick had publicly set the agenda for discussion, Liszt and colleagues then reacted in prose, and Hanslick's supporters either responded to them in turn or—in the case of the aestheticians—simply adopted his ideas into their own constructions. Thus the New Germans were pressed into a defensive position in the literary realm (and that with quite limited publication vehicles at their disposal).[29] Moreover, *Vom Musikalisch-Schönen* forced a shift in the partisan activity of the critics around Liszt: in 1854, only two of the thirty-odd *Neue Zeitschrift* feature articles dealt with orchestral music. In 1855–56, however, we find two of the three coryphaei of the progressive movement turning to the issue of program music in major contributions to the *Neue Zeitschrift* and the "spin-off" journal *Anregungen für Kunst, Leben und Wissenschaft*, with Liszt's *Harold in Italy* article series in the former, followed by Brendel's extended reflections on *Programmmusik* in the latter.[30]

It is interesting to observe how Hanslick could be positioned here as a force for reform, in other words, as "Hanslick the Progressive." After all, his book's purpose was to revise (i.e., correct) prior aesthetic thought, drawing upon the philosophical advances of his day.[31] Thus in a quite positive review of October 1855, *Neue Berliner Musikzeitung* editor and critic Otto Lange took up Hanslick's words and stressed the book's role as foundation "for a revision of previous aesthetics of music."[32] The unnamed reviewer in the 1855 *Leipziger Repertorium der deutschen und ausländischen Literatur*, in contrast, regarded *Vom Musikalisch-Schönen* unfavorably, since the treatise introduced an unwelcome "*new* direction and understanding" into musical aesthetics.[33]

Furthermore, a reversal of anticipated positions is revealed by an examination of the New German responses to Hanslick and his supporters.[34] Brendel justifies the music and thought of Wagner and Liszt ultimately as continuing the directions initiated by Beethoven, rather than striking off along new paths. These tactics, taken up by Richard Pohl, Hans von Bronsart, and other New German apologists in the late 1850s, show them adopting defensive postures as Hanslick's concepts found application above all in reviews of the symphonic poems of Liszt, which tended to decry those pieces as excessive in novelty and contrary to the spirit of Beethoven.[35]

Despite the critical "spin" provided by Liszt, Brendel, and their colleagues (Wagner remained largely aloof from the polemic debates of the 1850s) and by Alan Walker in more recent times,[36] Hanslick seems to have maintained the upper hand in all of this. In fact, his book provided the nexus for uniting the disparate oppositional voices to Wagner, Liszt, and associates throughout Germany and Austria (Vienna, Berlin, and Cologne, among other cities).[37] Hanslick himself did not take up the pen in defense of his *Büchlein*,[38] but rather calmly produced new editions of the book at periodic intervals, each typically evoking *Gegenschriften* by the New Germans, as represented in the list below. Intentionally or not, the new editions seemed to serve as challenges to his opponents, for whom a successful refutation of *Vom Musikalisch-Schönen* came to attain the status of *non plus ultra*—they rose to the bait, and were replaced by new contenders when the next version appeared. Thus upon publication of the book's second edition in early 1858, we find responses in monographs by Adolf Kullak and Ferdinand Peter Graf Laurencin, to be followed by Hostinský's book (1877) dealing with the fourth edition (1874), and then by monographs by Arthur Seidl and Friedrich von Hausegger responding to the contents of the seventh edition (1885). So Hanslick's *Büchlein* "remained a focus of debate over a long period," as Nicholas Cook asserts[39]—indeed, Robert Hirschfeld and Hausegger entered into a serious dispute over the latter's critical review of the seventh edition.[40] Specific editions of *Vom Musikalisch-Schönen* were the subject of monograph *Gegenschriften* as listed below:

First edition (1854)
A. W. Ambros, *Die Grenzen der Musik und Poesie* (Leipzig, 1856)
Second edition (1858)
Adolph Kullack, *Das Musikalisch-Schöne* (Leipzig, 1858)
F. P. Graf Laurencin, *Dr. Hanslick's Lehre vom Musikalisch-Schönen. Eine Abwehr* (Leipzig, 1859)
Fourth edition (1874)
Ottokar Hostinský, *Das Musikalisch-Schöne und das Gesammtkunstwerk* (Leipzig, 1877)
Seventh edition (1885)
Friedrich von Hausegger, *Musik als Ausdruck* (Vienna, 1885)

Arthur Seidl, *Vom Musikalisch-Erhabenen. Prolegomena zur Aesthetik der Tonkunst* (Regensburg, 1887)

Yet none of these writings delivered a serious blow to *Vom Musikalisch-Schönen*—the New Germans could not produce the decisive refutation, nor did they publish their own aesthetic theory that could compete with Hanslick's in perceived quality, popularity, and dissemination. *Vom Musikalisch-Schönen* was recognized by friend and foe alike as a brilliant, logically argued, and organized piece of aesthetic writing. Here is what New German ideologue Laurencin wrote about it in 1859, sounding more like a Hanslick proponent than a begrudging commentator:

> Hanslick's work contains many clever, even felicitous details, in particular concerning the heap of one-sided virtuosi, of inflexible contrapuntists, in general concerning those who indulge in extramusical purposes. For all of them there is quite beneficial teaching [in the book]. If we consider it from a stylistic perspective, Hanslick's little book is a masterpiece in miniature: it is impossible to express oneself more flowingly and, from the viewpoint of scientific method, more satisfactorily than Herr Dr. Hanslick has accomplished here.[41]

"Zwei Seelen": A Divided Life

While engaging in the ongoing revision and republication of *Vom Musikalisch-Schönen*, Hanslick carried on his critical activities in Vienna, above all for the liberal daily *Neue Freie Presse* (1864–1939) where he served as critic between 1864 and 1895 (from 1855 to 1864 he had reviewed for *Die Presse*). This work at one of the leading Viennese newspapers attracted attention from beyond the boundaries of the city, especially as the writings began to appear in the collections primarily published by Albert Hoffmann in Berlin.[42] Interestingly, Hanslick never again published an aesthetic treatise other than new editions of *Vom Musikalisch-Schönen*, while he collected and produced volumes of critical writings. Commentators on Hanslick have tended to conflate his work as music critic for Viennese papers of liberal political persuasion with his role as author of *Von Musikalisch-Schönen*, with the latter positioned as driving the former.[43] Most recently, Nicole Grimes has convincingly argued that this linkage requires unpacking, since friends and foes alike have unwittingly used it to justify reading his critical writings through the lens of the book, and at the same time to draw upon the more polemic reviews to disprove the validity of the 1854 publication.[44] The search of the popular press for easily quotable, outrageous bon mots—e.g., those published by Slonimsky—and musical scholarship's continuing single-minded pursuit of aesthetic meaning and truth have resulted in a general neglect of Hanslick's activities and creations as music critic, which in matters of style and even content seem to contradict *Vom Musikalisch-Schönen*. It did not help the Hanslick-*Rezeption* that in attempting to sort out this amalgamation, Robert Hirschfeld identified his mentor's "two souls" (*zwei Seelen*), unfavorably comparing the "glib" (*schlagfertig*) and "stylistically graceful" (*stylistisch anmuthig*) writings of the critic (Hanslick the panderer to public appeal) with what Kevin C. Karnes translates as the "dignified and scholarly approach" of the professor (Hanslick the aesthetician).[45]

The past and present reductionist reading of Hanslick the critic has favored presenting and discussing his adverse critical writings about Wagner, Liszt, Bruckner, and Tchaikovsky, and his panegyrics to Brahms. In this regard, it is curious that nineteenth-century scholarship has revealed itself willing to ascribe the excesses of Hugo Wolf vis-à-vis Brahms and Liszt to style,[46] while observers have attributed Hanslick's immoderate statements to flaws in his judgment, another consequence of merging the aesthetician with the feuilletonist. Such facile assessments of his critical activities have overlooked important issues such as Hanslick's critical-political engagement,[47] his development as literary stylist,[48] his critique of compositional styles such as late nineteenth-century Italian opera,[49] and his support of composers other than Brahms (including Dvořák and Humperdinck).[50] The superficial treatment of Hanslick the critic has also led to his devolution to the status of an adjective, whether the "feared critic" as assessed by detractors,[51] or the "brilliant writer about music" in the words of supporters.[52] These diametrically opposing evaluations reflect the divided opinion of his day on Hanslick's activities as music critic: it was too easy for New Germans to conflate Hanslick the critic with Hanslick the author of *Vom Musikalisch-Schönen*, whereby they could dismiss his opinions.[53] However, it should be noted that the *Gegenschriften* to the *Büchlein* exclusively treat the aesthetician Hanslick, and that only as revealed in the treatise. Hanslick's supporters were not without their own biased, reductive rhetoric; an unnamed author of an appraisal in *Signale* wrote in 1864: "The music reviewer of *Die Presse*, Dr. Hanslick, has resigned from that paper and is said to be generally disposed toward writing no more journal reports. We would truly regret this in the interest of the good cause, since Herr Hanslick is not only a fine, sage critic, but he also always made it a practice of delivering an equally humane and correct judgment in musical matters."[54]

However, among late-nineteenth-century Hanslick respondents, none stands out like Wagner, whose responses—actual, possible, and mythical—have become canonic in the Hanslick literature.[55] Hanslick's association with Beckmesser in *Die Meistersinger* was already well established in the nineteenth century, as the critic himself notes in his 1894 autobiography: "The Wagnerians have applied to me the sobriquet 'Beckmesser' and thereby proven how they do not understand their master and his most understandable figure . . . I have never attacked Wagner for the sake of petty details, never sought individual departures from the rules in his works. . . . On the contrary, just those

Wagnerians appear to me to have much in common with Beckmesser. There are also Beckmessers of admiration."[56] Despite Hanslick's denial of the designation's appropriateness and his attempt to turn the tables, applying it to the Wagnerians, the association between him and Beckmesser served as one of the primary topoi in the Hanslick-*Rezeption*,[57] which took on particular vehemence as Jewish characteristics were mapped onto the character of Beckmesser.[58] Of course, Wagner's dismissal of *Vom Musikalisch-Schönen* in the 1869 edition of *Das Judentum in der Musik* reinforced the anti-Semitic rhetoric that was read into *Die Meistersinger*, since Wagner rejected the *Büchlein* on the basis of its author's Judaism.[59]

Wagner's narrative in *Mein Leben* about the tearful Hanslick seeking reconciliation at a party of Frau Luise Dustmann enjoyed less circulation: "My good mood made it very easy for me to treat Dr. Hanslick that evening like a superficial acquaintance, until he took me to the side for an intimate conversation. There he assured me, with tears and sobs, that he no longer could bear to see himself misjudged by me."[60] Among others, Thomas Grey has questioned the story,[61] yet the image of the contrite critic persisted well into the twentieth century, finding credence even with an authority like Ernest Newman.[62]

There can be little doubt that the critic Hanslick exerted considerable sway in Vienna at the end of the century, as studies by Sandra McColl and Karnes, among others, have established.[63] Still, McColl has also noticed how his influence waned at least in the last decade,[64] due to what can be put forward as a complex web of factors: (1) Hanslick's own aging and attendant withdrawal from the music criticism scene; (2) the growing field of music criticism in Vienna, as accompanied by the inevitable displacement of the older generation; (3) the gradual acceptance of Wagner's music as an unavoidable, if not welcome, force in the cultural landscape of central Europe; and (4) an increasing recognition of Hanslick's old-fashionedness and irrelevance to *Jahrhundertwende* culture.

Before leaving the nineteenth century, we should cast a quick glance at his reception beyond German-speaking territory. This is indeed terra incognita for Hanslick research, one example from the New World will suffice to illustrate how widely Hanslick's writings had found dissemination during that century. *Dwight's Journal of Music* appeared in Boston between 1852 and 1881,[65] and its editor, John Sullivan Dwight, privileged Central European musical taste while spurning the New Germans. As a result, it was almost inevitable that his journal would prominently feature translations of Hanslick's reviews from the *Neue Freie Presse*. This reprint activity began in the mid-1860s and increased during the course of the 1870s. It represents the first point of contact with Hanslick for Americans, since *Vom Musikalisch-Schönen* would not be available in English translation until 1891, and the other books did not appear in translation until even later.[66] As such, then, the musical Northeast of the 1860s and 1870s—Dwight's readership base—became familiar with and received a favorable impression of Hanslick, which coincided with their conservative taste that rejected Wagner and Liszt during those decades.[67] Comments by Alexander Wheelock Thayer in 1863 reflect Dwight's own support for what he regarded as the unbiased opinion of Hanslick the critic, while at the same time reinforcing his journal's bias toward German *Kulturgut*: "This morning's *Presse* (May 5) has an article by Hanslick on a certain Mad. Fabbri-Mulder, in which truth is spoken without fear or favor. People who are so sensitive at home, if a notice of them does not make them compounds of Lind, Sontag, Alboni, Malibran, Patti, and all the other great singers, may think themselves lucky that they have no Eduard Hanslick to tell them plain truths."[68]

A Troubled Legacy

Hanslick's death in 1904 elicited a host of articles of varying tenor, the most favorable originating, of course, in Vienna. For example, both Julius Korngold and Guido Adler published warm and respectful eulogies in the *Neue Freie Presse*.[69] Korngold's concluded: "In Eduard Hanslick we bury a proselytizer for music-aesthetic perception, a master of style, an adornment of criticism, a pride of this paper. His name will live on."[70] Another eulogist, writing in *Der Kunstwart* of 1904, was not so kind—in fact, was not kind at all: "And thus, despite the dazzling outer garb [of his writings], Hanslick represented in reality a low point of musical judgment."[71] Needless to say, the *Bayreuther Blätter* maintained silence over his passing, perhaps less out of hostility than out of a simple lack of concern, a tacit recognition of his irrelevance for that journal's project. It should not surprise us that the press from other parts of Europe and the world did take note of Hanslick's death, given his notoriety: for example, in New York, which was riding the crest of the wave of the city's Wagner mania,[72] the following passage appeared in an obituary from the *New York Times*: "He was one of the most bitter opponents of Wagner and one of the last critics to recognize the possibilities of the new style of opera."[73]

Death may have silenced his voice in the press, may have ceased his editing of *Vom Musikalisch-Schönen* (with the tenth edition of 1902),[74] but Hanslick's legacy—more accurately expressed, legacies—carried on, with an exponential intensification of the bifurcation. On the one hand, the ideas of *Vom Musikalisch-Schönen* influenced some of the leading figures in early twentieth-century Austrian and German musical aesthetics: Arnold Schoenberg, Heinrich Schenker, and Theodor Wiesengrund Adorno. On the other, only one of the collections of Hanslick's criticisms underwent further publications posthumously, *Suite* appearing again in 1910.[75] The next edition of Hanslick's critical writings did not appear until 1947, with Heinrich Kralik's *Aus Eduard Hanslicks Wagner-Kritiken*.[76] The absence of reprints in the first decades of the century reflects the widespread disdain for his critical writings, not for their style but rather their (mis)pronouncements on important figures like Wagner and Bruckner.

The first attempt to provide a new general collection of Hanslick's music criticisms did not appear until 1950, and then (surprisingly) in English translation, by the American music critic Henry Pleasants.[77]

Space does not permit an extended discussion of Hanslick's role in the aesthetic landscape of Central Europe during the first decades of the twentieth century. Although Cook well positions Hanslick within *Jahrhundertwende* Vienna,[78] a comprehensive study of his influence upon early twentieth-century music aesthetics in German-speaking Europe is still lacking.[79] Still, recent research has led to a better understanding of how important his thought was for certain key composers and aestheticians of the period; his influence on Schoenberg, Schenker, and Adorno has been well documented by Patricia Carpenter, Nicholas Cook, and Max Paddison, respectively.[80] Yet the esteem that these and associated thinkers brought to Hanslick's aesthetic work remained largely isolated, considering the ongoing appeal of the *Musik als Ausdruck* ideology—for example, among the epigones of Strauss and the New German School, who continued producing large-scale tone poems and philosophical systems rooted in program music well into the twentieth century.[81] One important exception was Rudolf Schäfke, whose brief 1922 dissertation about Hanslick represented the first scholarly German-language monograph about his aesthetics,[82] and the only one before Werner Abegg's book in 1974.[83]

In general, however, the late nineteenth-century, Wagner-based critique of Hanslick predominated, as we can observe in the Hanslick entry of Bruno Schrader's 1905 edition of *Bremers Handlexikon der Musik*: "Hanslick . . . issued . . . above all the aesthetic *Vom Musikalisch-Schönen* . . . the ultraconservative avowal of formalism in music, which was immobilized by A. Kullak's text *Das Musikalich-Schöne* (1858). H. still declared Wagner's *Lohengrin* to be unmusical in 1900."[84] Here we find most components of the unfavorable Hanslick appraisal: the conservative formalist aesthetician who—by implication—advocated absolute music and whose critical writings rejected Wagner and—again by implication—the progressive direction in music. Add the critic's "exclusive" support of Brahms among contemporary composers and one has constructed the topos that dominated Hanslick-*Rezeption* during the rest of the twentieth century.

That his legacy would eventually become involved in the politics of the Third Reich stands to reason: on the one hand, he was Jewish by virtue of his mother; on the other, he had opposed composers favored by the Nazis. Needless to say, he received extended treatment in the *Lexikon der Juden in der Musik* by Stengel and Gerigk.[85] For most of the musical commentators of the Third Reich, however, Hanslick simply had not existed—after all, he was a critic, one of the professions of "intellectual piracy" that Josef Goebbels had replaced with *Kunstbetrachtung*.[86] And Hanslick could more easily be written out of music history altogether than figures like Mendelssohn and Schoenberg, the omission of whose historical contributions to music was more difficult (although not impossible) because of their importance.[87]

Needless to say, it was in the context of his opposition to the "great" German composers Wagner and Bruckner that Hanslick's name did arise in the music literature from the Nazi period. Max von Millenkovich-Morold reflects the party's animosity toward the critic Hanslick when he writes: "I can attest from long-term personal observation that the Wagner enmity in Austria, and beyond that among the all-German 'intelligentsia,' was awakened by Hanslick, fed by Hanslick, again and again flogged by Hanslick."[88] The vehement Nazi partisan Robert Scherwatzky made clear the reason for Hanslick's opposition to Bruckner: "Then, however, a hostile, invidious press began to embitter his life. Under the leadership of the totally uncomprehending, maliciously wise-cracking half-Jew Hanslick. . . ., it viciously tore apart his creations or was simply silent about them."[89] These complaints against Hanslick's general antipathy toward the two composers were by no means new, but now they were informed by the racial politics of the Third Reich, according to which his Jewishness was responsible for Hanslick's critical positions—he had become a racially flawed character incapable of rendering correct judgments.

Another Nazi propagandist who drew public attention to Hanslick was Goebbels himself. On the occasion of the International Bruckner Festival in Regensburg in June 1937, the *Reichspropagandaminister* gave a speech to the Bruckner-Gesellschaft; members of the *Reichsmusikkammer*; and high-level Nazi functionaries, including Hitler. In this propaganda on behalf of the "Aryan" Bruckner, Goebbels blamed the Jewish element for the composer's difficulties, mentioning Hanslick by name and quoting from one of his reviews (alongside unidentified reviews by Gustav Doempke):

> A hostile, journalistic branch of criticism, with its incessant torments, embittered him [Bruckner] to his rich life of work. . . . It is with reluctance and disdain that we turn our attention today to these intellectual carpet-baggers, who in Bruckner's day misused their esteemed station as judges in order to set down sentences such as this one about his music, whose form-creative innovation they simply could not understand: "We truly shudder before the scent of mould that assaults our noses from the discords of this putrefactive counterpoint" [Gustav Doempke]. Or: "It is not impossible that the future belongs to this dream-distorted, hung-over style [*traumverwirrten Katzenjammerstil*]—a future which, for that reason, we do not envy" [Eduard Hanslick].[90]

Goebbels also cited the widely disseminated statement "I destroy whomever I wish to destroy," which he put into the mouth of Hanslick during an encounter with Bruckner. Julian Horton effectively situates this speech in the context of Nazi Bruckner-*Rezeption*,[91] but we can just as easily position it within the Wagnerian critique of Hanslick, which was initiated by Wagner himself and subsequently taken up by Tappert and carried further by the Bayreuth circle of Hans von Wolzogen, Houston Stewart Chamberlain, and Carl Friedrich Glasenapp: "In the battle against the greatest German artist, no means appeared too base and too corrupt. A fictitious letter [arose] from one of the main camps of poisoned animosity, the Viennese *Neue Freie Presse*, the headquarters of Herr Hanslick."[92]

Hanslick the aesthetician also came in for severe criticism from the ideologues of the Third Reich, all the more because of Wagner's aforementioned critique of *Vom Musikalisch-Schönen* that centered the pamphlet's problems on its author's Judaism. In contrast with the formulation of Wagner's aesthetics as "music as expression," the system of Hanslick was identified as pure and simple formalism,[93] which helped Nazi writers about music to position him with Jewish creators and their unnatural, *entartete* productions. Paul Ehlers articulated the differences of the two *Weltanschauungen* in the following comparison of Hanslick's book with Friedrich von Hausegger's *Die Musik als Ausdruck* (1887): "There the formalistic principle as the embodiment of the nature and effect of music—here the inner spirit of the creative artist as the womb and shaping force of music."[94] According to this assessment, Hanslick's incomprehension of Wagner and Bruckner resulted from his Jewish, formalist aesthetic system, which led to serious error in his critical judgments.

Hanslick "in Rehab"

Given the historical weight of this German propaganda against Hanslick, it might not surprise us that the first voices vigorously raised in defence of Hanslick during the twentieth century originated outside Central Europe, specifically in Great Britain. Indeed, Stewart Deas provocatively entitled his 1940 book on Hanslick *In Defence of Hanslick*.[95] We may today regard Deas's approach to Hanslick's life, work, and standing as imbalanced, yet he attempted to restore a damaged reputation by bringing the critic again into public discourse. In many ways he set the stage for the eventual revival, also finding support in Henry Pleasants's 1950 edition of critical texts.[96] However, unlike Deas, who devoted considerable space to *Vom Musikalisch-Schönen*, Pleasants solely addresses Hanslick as critic.[97] It is ironic but understandable that this English translation would represent the first broad collection of Hanslick's critical writings, when we consider the turmoil in musicology and music criticism in Central Europe during and just after the war.

Despite Pleasants's work, Germany—both East and West—became the site for work about and around Hanslick in the decades after the war. Hiroshi Yoshida has observed how Friedrich Blume's article "Hanslick" in *Die Musik in Geschichte und Gegenwart* from 1956 attempts to destigmatize and Germanize the aesthetician-critic and his "musical contribution."[98] The same type of rehabilitation of Hanslick takes place in music histories, including those of Nazi partisans among musicologists like Hans-Joachim Moser, in whose *Musikgeschichte in Hundert Lebensbildern* of 1958 Hanslick occupies a benign position.[99]

Through the aestheticization of the Cold War, however, Hanslick again became a figure of contestation, although free from the vituperations of the Wagnerians and the Third Reich. The concepts of musical autonomy and absolute music were fought by musicologists across the internal German border, as we read in studies by James Hepokoski,[100] Anne Shreffler,[101] and Sanna Pederson.[102] In his critique of the methods of leading West German musicologist Carl Dahlhaus, Hepokoski established the basic opposition between East German Marxist readings of musical history and Dahlhaus's attempt to construct an anti-Marxist musical epistemology. While Dahlhaus invested heavily in the cause of absolute music, Marxist ideologue Georg Knepler opposed this ostensibly antisocialist ideology, as Shreffler summarizes:

> Music scholarship since the mid 19th century, has, according to Knepler, attempted to separate music from its semantic, communicative function and to replace it with a purely "syntactical" one (by this he means an internally consistent, "musical" one). From Hanslick to Riemann, many theorists ... have sought to reduce the content of music to the relationships between notes, labeling its expressive content as something "external." Knepler believes that to deny music's communicative, semantic function means to exclude its emotional impact and correspondingly, its aesthetic value. ... The problems begin for Knepler when the "element of syntax is taken as an absolute, when the relative autonomy of musical processes is taken to be absolute autonomy."[103]

Of course, the battle drew in *Vom Musikalisch-Schönen* and Hanslick himself, whose thought became the subject of a campaign by Dahlhaus—as Pederson argues—to establish a myth of absolute music in his "ideological battle against Marxist musicology and his East Berlin counterpart Georg Knepler."[104] Knepler himself openly rejected the aesthetic principles of absolute music as espoused by Dahlhaus most clearly in *Die Idee der absoluten Musik*.[105] Thus in his 1961 *Musikgeschichte des XIX. Jahrhunderts*,[106] the East German musicologist actually expressed support for Hanslick's critical work, noting that some of his writings contradict the book's fundamental ideologies. In a fascinating development in Hanslick-*Rezeption*, it appears that the German Democratic Republic became the place for cultivating Hanslick the critic, since it was in Leipzig that the first German-language collection of his *Musikkritiken* appeared in print, in 1972.[107] This occurred even as Dahlhaus was solidifying his position on Hanslick's formal and aesthetic concepts in the late 1970s. Werner Abegg published his aforementioned *Musikästhetik und Musikkritik bei Eduard Hanslick* in 1974, which aestheticized the criticisms as a means to get to the aesthetics. In the intervening years up to the end of the Cold War in 1989, further publications of Dahlhaus and other musicologists of the Federal Republic of Germany reinforced the image of West Germany and Austria as a hotbed for the study of Hanslick's thought.[108] This is not to deny the value of the scholarly work that grappled with his position in Central

European traditions of Kant, Hegel, and Schopenhauer interpretation,[109] but rather to argue for the broader musico-political context for these discussions.

Yet it may be indicative that some of the greatest advances in understanding were accomplished by a Canadian professor of philosophy named Geoffrey Payzant (1926–2004).[110] He not only produced the first reliable English translation of *Vom Musikalisch-Schönen*,[111] but also shed light on Hanslick's formative years in Prague,[112] the aesthetic influences he received from J. F. Herbart,[113] and his lifelong friendship with Robert Zimmermann.[114] It may not be an exaggeration to identify Payzant as the scholar who contributed most to the the aesthetic and historical research on Hanslick in the 1980s, especially by extending the philosophical discussion beyond Kant and the traditional German idealist thinkers.

He also influenced Dietmar Strauß, whose contributions to our understanding of Hanslick as aesthetician and critic have been crucial for Hanslick scholarship since 1990. With his successive publications of scholarly critical editions of *Vom Musikalisch-Schönen* in 1990 and the critical writings beginning in 1993,[115] Strauß gave a strong impetus to Hanslick research by introducing a solid scholarly basis for interpreting Hanslick's overall importance for and specific contributions to musical thought and life in the second half of the nineteenth century. Certainly the type of work that Markus Gärtner and Nicole Grimes have recently accomplished with the aesthetics and the critical writings, respectively,[116] would have been much more difficult without Strauß's editions and their valuable commentary.

But there remains much serious scholarship ahead for Hanslick: the critical edition of the writings awaits continuation and completion;[117] we possess no critical edition of his letters, which remain scattered throughout Central Europe; *Aus meinem Leben* requires a contextual study of its own; we have yet to position him within the politics of his time; we need to compare style and content of his critical writings with those of his day, both favorable and from the New German side; someone needs to gather and study the various reviews of *Vom Musikalisch-Schönen*, especially the *Gegenschriften*; and there remain many unresolved aesthetic questions. While it might seem that the aesthetic side is underrepresented in this list of Hanslick desiderata, the whole history of his path through musical history has been filled with such studies, to the exclusion of other topics that would assist the researcher come to terms with the figure and work of Hanslick. May the current collection serve as an important step in coming to a fuller understanding of Hanslick's historical position, cultural context, and contribution to music criticism and aesthetics.

Notes

For their generous assistance in the preparation of this essay, I extend special thanks to Nicole Grimes, Mark Evan Bonds, and Fred Maus. All translations are my own unless otherwise stated.

1. For example, Leon Botstein seems to adopt this position when he writes: "According to Hanslick's theory, which became widely popular, music was an essentially formalist art." *The Compleat Brahms: A Guide to the Musical Works of Johannes Brahms* (New York: Norton, 1999), 23.

2. About Hanslick as "feared critic," see for instance Peter Gay, *Pleasure Wars: The Bourgeois Experience. Victoria to Freud* (New York: Norton, 1998), 102.

3. J. Peter Burkholder, Donald J. Grout, and Claude V. Palisca, *A History of Western Music*, 7th ed. (New York: Norton, 2006), 727.

4. Ibid.

5. Born in 1968, Ross has arguably become the best known and most read commentator on "classical music" in the United States. He has served as music critic at *The New Yorker* since 1996, and his book *The Rest Is Noise: Listening to the Twentieth Century* (New York: Farrar, Straus & Giroux, 2007) garnered several awards.

6. Alex Ross, "Black Brown & Beige," in *The Rest Is Noise* (October 26, 2004), at http://www.therestisnoise.com/2004/10/index.html (accessed November 12, 2012).

7. Originally published in 1953 by Coleman-Ross in New York, the book was reprinted by Norton in 2000.

8. Nicholas Slonimsky, "Prelude: Non-Acceptance of the Familiar," in *Lexicon of Musical Invective: Critical Assaults on Composers Since Beethoven's Time* (New York: Coleman-Ross, 1953), 3–33.

9. Ibid., 32.

10. The full title is *Ein Wagner-Lexikon: Wörterbuch der Unhöflichkeit, enthaltend grobe, höhnende, gehässige und verleumderische Ausdrücke, welche gegen den Meister Richard Wagner, seine Werke und seine Anhänger von den Feinden und Spöttern gebraucht worden sind. Zur Gemüthis-Ergötzung in müssigen Stunden gesammelt von Wilhelm Tappert* (Leipzig: E. W. Fritzsch, 1877).

11. Samples of Hanslick's vitriolic language as presented by Tappert include the following: "Alliterationsgestotter" (stuttering of alliteration) about the text of *Das Rheingold* (2), "Fanatiker der Melodielosigkeit" (fanatic of unmelodiousness) regarding Wagner in *Lohengrin* (13), and "eine trostlose Musik" (desolate music) for the Prelude to *Tristan und Isolde* (39). Among composers, Anton Bruckner feared Hanslick above all, as is evident from his failed attempt of 1886 to get Emperor Franz-Joseph to forbid the critic from writing "so schlecht" about him. See Hans Commenda, *Geschichten um Anton Bruckner* (Linz: Muck, 1946), 126.

12. As Liszt established himself in Weimar during the early 1850s, he attracted a circle of pupils and associates around him, composers and performers like Joachim Raff and Hans von Bülow, who would advocate the new direction of Liszt and Wagner in print, above all in the *Neue Zeitschrift für Musik*. Journal editor Franz Brendel (1811–68)—Schumann's successor at the *Neue Zeitschrift*—had himself begun promoting the cause of Wagner and Liszt at the beginning of the 1850s. These critics came to regard Hanslick as an opponent to the progressive movement and its leading figures. About this promotional activity, see James Deaville, "The Controversy Surrounding Liszt's Conception of Programme Music," in *Nineteenth-Century Music: Selected Proceedings of the Tenth International Conference*, ed. Jim Samson and Bennett Zon (Aldershot, UK: Ashgate, 2002): 98–124.

13. Eduard Hanslick, *Vom Musikalisch-Schönen. Ein Beitrag zur Revision der Ästhetik der Tonkunst* (Leipzig: Rudolph Weigel, 1854). Dietmar Strauß has published a text-critical edition: Eduard Hanslick, *Vom Musikalisch-Schönen: Ein Beitrag zur Revision der Ästhetik der Tonkunst*, vol. 1, ed. Dietmar Strauß (Mainz: Schott, 1990) (cited hereafter as *VMS*) and

Dietmar Strauß, *Vom Musikalisch-Schönen: Ein Beitrag zur Revision der Ästhetik der Tonkunst*, vol. 2 (Mainz: Schott, 1990) (cited hereafter as *VMS/2*).

14. "Aesthetische Betrachtungen über Composition sogenannter unmusikalischer Texte—veranlasst durch Hoven's Composition der 'Heimkehr' von H. Heine," *Rheinische Musik-Zeitung* 2, no. 15 (October 11, 1851): 529–31; and no. 16 (October 18, 1851): 541–43.

15. Regarding the original publication in the *Oesterreichische Blätter für Literatur und Kunst*, see Dietmar Strauß, "Vom Davidsbund zum ästhetischen Manifest: Zu Eduard Hanslicks Schriften 1844–1854," in Hanslick, *Sämtliche Schriften* 1/1(Vienna: Böhlau, 1993), 290. The reprint appeared as "Die Wiener Concertsaison in ihrer künstlerischen Bedeutung," *Neue Berliner Musikzeitung* 7, no. 20 (June 15, 1853): 157–58.

16. With the designation "war," I am drawing upon Alan Walker's terminology for the musico-aesthetic dispute between "progressive" and "conservative" forces that dominated central Europe in the second half of the nineteenth century. However, Walker calls it the "War of the Romantics," which is misleading since it did not necessarily involve what we might call musical romantics. Moreover, the designation "war" simplifies the dispute into a binary opposition of diametrically opposing forces, which does not permit the continuum of positions that were occupied by participants. Walker, *Franz Liszt: The Weimar Years, 1848–1861* (New York: Knopf, 1989).

17. Zimmermann, "Zur Aesthetik der Tonkunst: Vom Musikalisch-Schönen," *Oesterreichische Blätter für Literatur und Kunst* 47 (November 20, 1854): 313–15.

18. Peter Cornelius, "Concertmusik. Klavierauszüge zu vier Händen. Richard Würst, Op. 21. Preis-Symphonie . . . ," *Neue Zeitschrift für Musik* 41, no. 24 (December 8, 1854): 258–59.

19. "Diese Frage theilt noch heute die musikalische Welt in zwei Parteien. Der einen ist die Musik ein phantastisches Spiel in Tönen nach Regeln des Wohllautes und ästhetischen Gesetzen. . . . Nach ihr soll die Musik durch sich selbst wirken ohne vermittelnde Nebengedanken. . . . Die andere Partei betrachtet die ihr von den großen Meistern überlieferte Musik als eine poetisch ausgebildete Sprache. . . . Sie will aus dem poetischen Gedanken heraus seine jedesmalige Form bedingen, nur dieser soll ihr die Berechtigung verleihen." Ibid.

20. See Deaville, "Die neudeutsche Musikkritik: Der Weimarer Kreis," in *Liszt und die Neudeutsche Schule*, ed. Detlef Altenburg (Laaber: Laaber-Verlag, 2006), 55–76, for a detailed discussion of progressive music criticism around Liszt in the early 1850s.

21 Despite Strauß's careful and thorough research for his scholarly edition of *Vom Musikalisch-Schönen*, a reception history of this central book has yet to be undertaken.

22. "Ambros, Brendel, Carrière, Th. Vischer und A. Kullak, also die weitaus geistvollsten Schwertführer wider Dr. Hanslick's Theoreme . . . Nur J. C. Lobe . . . war es, der . . . Hanslick's Schrift in das Auge gefaßt hat." Ferdinand Peter Graf von Laurencin, *Dr. Hanslick's Lehre vom Musikalisch-Schönen: Eine Abwehr* (Leipzig: Heinrich Matthes, 1859), viii–x.

23. Arthur Seidl, *Vom Musikalisch-Erhabenen. Prolegomena zur Aesthetik der Tonkunst* (Regensburg: M. Wasner, 1887), 2–3.

24. The separation of writers into camps "opposed" and "in favor" represents a tabular distillation of Seidl's comments on those pages of his book.

25. The term *Gegenschrift* is taken from legal terminology, here referring to the various literary attempts to counter Hanslick's book.

26. See Deaville, "The Controversy Surrounding Liszt's Conception of Programme Music," for excerpts from this early oppositional literature.

27. In attempting to draw clear lines of demarcation between the aesthetic positions, scholars like Walker have failed to take into account the diversity of opinions on both sides that militate against black-and-white representations of the dispute.

28. Franz Liszt, "Berlioz und seine Haroldsymphonie," *Neue Zeitschrift für Musik* 43, no. 3 (July 13, 1855): 25–32; 4 (July 20): 37–46; 5 (July 27): 49–55; 8 (August 17): 77–84; and 9 (August 24): 89–97. A form of that article series, however, was ready for publication before November 1854, prior to Hanslick's publication. See Deaville, "The Controversy Surrounding Liszt's Conception of Programme Music," 105.

29. Above and beyond the *Neue Zeitschrift*, the *Berliner Musik-Zeitung Echo* revealed itself willing to publish favorable articles about Wagner and Liszt, and J. C. Lobe's *Fliegende Blätter für Musik* (1855–57) adopted at times a supportive position toward the New Germans, but no other music journal of the 1850s consistently espoused the cause.

30. Franz Brendel, "Programmmusik," *Anregungen für Kunst, Leben und Wissenschaft* 1 (1856): 82–92. Brendel and Pohl established this journal to provide an alternative publication venue to the *Neue Zeitschrift*, for the "insiders" of their circle.

31. His subtitle was *Eine Revision der bisherigen Ästhetik der Tonkunst*.

32. Otto Lange, "Musik-Literatur: Dr. Eduard Hanslick, Vom Musikalisch-Schönen...," *Neue Berliner Musikzeitung* 9, no. 42 (October 17, 1855): 330.

33. "neue Wendung und Fassung." "Schöne Künste. [21] Vom Musikalisch-Schönen...," *Leipziger Repertorium der deutschen und ausländischen Literatur* 13, no. 1 (January 1854): 38.

34. See Deaville, "The Controversy Surrounding Liszt's Conception of Programme Music."

35. These works were the first major musical manifestations of the progressive party, taking place outside of Weimar and Thuringia first in 1855. Keith Johns collected and translated various German-language reviews of the symphonic poems from the 1850s in his *The Symphonic Poems of Franz Liszt*, ed. Michael Saffle (Stuyvesant, NY: Pendragon Press, 1997), 86–138.

36. See his chapter "War of the Romantics" in *Franz Liszt*, 338–67.

37. Passages from *Vom Musikalisch-Schönen* appeared, for example, in Ludwig Bischoff's *Niederrheinische Musik-Zeitung*, the belletristic Leipzig journal *Die Grenzboten*, and even in *Dwight's Journal of Music* from Boston.

38. He used the diminutive to designate both its size and its limited scope.

39. Cook, *The Schenker Project: Culture, Race, and Music Theory in Fin-de-Siècle Vienna* (New York: Oxford University Press, 2007), 48.

40. Ibid.

41. "Im Einzelnen enthält Hanslick's Werk viel Geistreiches, ja sogar Treffendes, namentlich in Bezug auf die Schichten der einseitigen Virtuosen, starren Contrapunctisten und überhaupt auf Jene, die außermusikalischen Zwecken fröhnen. Diesen Allen gibt es sehr heilsame Lehren. Stylistisch betrachtet, ist aber Hanslick's Werkchen ein Meisterstück im Kleinen. Denn es ist nicht möglich, sich leichtfließender und doch dem Scheine von Wissenschaftlichkeit genügender auszusprechen, als es Herrn Dr. Hanslick hier gelungen ist." Ferdinand Peter Graf von Laurencin, *Dr. Hanslick's Lehre*, 226–27.

42. In all, thirteen "anthologies" of his criticism appeared, nine of them under the aggregate title *Die moderne Oper*.

43. This applies both to members of the popular press and scholars, ranging from Alex Ross to Carl Dahlhaus and Werner Abegg.

44. See Nicole Grimes's dissertation, "Brahms's Critics: Continuity and Discontinuity in the Critical Reception of Johannes Brahms" (PhD diss., Trinity College [University of Dublin], 2008).

45. The source for these passages is the 28-page pamphlet of Hirschfeld entitled *Das kritische Verfahren Ed. Hanslick's* (Vienna: R. Löwit, 1885), 6–7. Karnes's translation appears in his *Music, Criticism, and the Challenge of History: Shaping Modern Musical Thought in Late Nineteenth-Century Vienna* (New York: Oxford University Press, 2008), 68.

46. See, for example, Walker, *Franz Liszt: The Weimar Years, 1849–1861*, 353, or Hans-Hubert Schönzeler, *Bruckner* (London: Marion Boyars, 2003), 67.

47. Exceptions include David Brodbeck's extensive study "Dvořák's Reception in Liberal Vienna: Language Ordinances, National Property, and the Rhetoric of Deutschtum," *Journal of the American Musicological Society* 60, no. 1 (2007): 71–131 and Margaret Notley's monograph *Lateness and Brahms: Music and Culture in the Twilight of Viennese Liberalism* (New York: Oxford University Press, 2007), especially 207–11.

48. Sandra McColl's *Music Criticism in Vienna 1896–1897: Critically Moving Forms* (Oxford: Clarendon Press, 1996) does compare a variety of critics, also from a stylistic viewpoint, but her study limits itself to one year.

49. Arthur Groos and Roger Parker, "Three Early Critics and the Brothers Mann: Aspects of the *La bohème* Reception," in *Giacomo Puccini: "La bohème"* (Cambridge: Cambridge University Press, 1986), 129–41.

50. The aforementioned article by Brodbeck does look at Dvořák reception in the broader Viennese context, including Hanslick's reviews and activities on his behalf.

51. For example, Liszt supporter A. W. Gottschalg called Hanslick a "gefürchteter Kritiker" in his review of Robert Hirschfeld's booklet *Das kritische Verfahren Ed. Hanslick's* (Vienna: Löwitz, 1885); "Notizen," *Urania: Musik-Zeitschrift für Orgelbau, Orgel- und Harmoniumspiel* 42, no. 9 (1885): 142.

52. This particular phrase appears as "[es giebt] keine geistreicheren Schriftsteller über Musik" in the review "Zwei musikalische Feuilletonisten" by the conservative writer Gustav Dömpke in *Im neuen Reich* 1(1881): 442.

53. This was the case with the response to Hanslick's review of *Les Préludes* in *Die Presse* of March 12, 1857. See Deaville, "The Controversy Surrounding Liszt's Conception of Programme Music," 119–22.

54. "Der Musikreferent der Presse, Dr. Hanslick, ist von diesem Blatt zurückgetreten und soll überhaupt gesonnen sein, keine Journalberichte mehr zu schreiben. Wir würden dies im Interesse der guten Sache aufrichtig bedauern, da Herr Hanslick nicht nur eine feine, geistvolle Feder ist, sondern auch immer ein eben so humanes als richtiges Urtheil in musikalischen Dingen zu fällen pflegte." Anon., "Wiener musikalische Skizzen," *Signale für die musikalische Welt* 22, no. 34 (August 18, 1864): 550.

55. One finds this already in Stewart Deas, *In Defence of Hanslick* (London: Williams & Norgate, 1940). However, given the paucity of literature about Hanslick, it stands to reason that the Wagner side of the relationship is better represented in the secondary literature.

56. "Die Wagnerianer haben mir den Beinamen 'Beckmesser' aufgebracht und damit bewiesen, daß sie ihren Meister und dessen verständlichste Figur nicht verstehen. . . . Ich habe Wagner nie um Kleinigkeiten willen angegriffen, niemals einzelne Regelwidrigkeiten in seinen Werken aufgespürt. . . . Hingegen scheinen mir gerade die Wagnerianer viel Ähnlichkeit mit Beckmesser zu haben. Es gibt auch Adorations-Beckmesser." Hanslick, *Aus meinem Leben*, ed. and with an afterword by Peter Wapnewski (Kassel: Bärenreiter, 1987), 357–58 (hereafter abbreviated as *AML/W*). Elsewhere in the passage, he uses the term "Beckmesserei," which had normalized itself in the German language by the end of the century.

57. An interesting coinage along these lines, which would find some dissemination, was that of Hanslick as the "Wiener Beckmesser." The Wagnerian Jan van Santen-Kolff can take credit for its first occurrence, in the article "'Ja, ja, der Merker!' . . . ," *Musikalisches Wochenblatt* 14, no. 19 (May 3, 1883): 241. (Ellipsis in original.)

58. See Thomas Grey, "The Jewish Question," in *The Cambridge Companion to Wagner*, ed. Thomas Grey (Cambridge: Cambridge University Press, 2008), 203–18; and above all, the articles in *Wagner's Meistersinger: Performance, History, Representation*, ed. Nicholas Vazsonyi (Rochester, NY: University of Rochester Press, 2003).

59. Richard Wagner, *Das Judenthum in der Musik* (Leipzig: J. J. Weber, 1869), 47.

60. "Meine gute Laune machte es mir sehr leicht, an jenem Abende Hanslick so lange als oberflächlich Bekannten zu behandeln, bis er mich zu einem intimen Gespräch bei Seite zog, in welchem er unter Thränen und Schluchzen mir versicherte, er könne es nicht ertragen sich von mir länger verkannt zu sehen." Richard Wagner, *Mein Leben*, 2 vols. (Munich: F. Bruckmann, 1911), 2: 818–19.

61. Grey, "Masters and Their Critics," 170.

62. Ernest Newman, *The Life of Richard Wagner*, vol. 3: 1859–1866 (New York: Knopf, 1941), 198.

63. McColl, *Music Criticism in Vienna*; Karnes, *Music, Criticism, and the Challenge of History*.

64. McColl, *Music Criticism in Vienna*, vii.

65. About Dwight and his journal, see Ora Frishberg Saloman, *Beethoven's Symphonies and J. S. Dwight: The Birth of American Music Criticism* (Boston: Northeastern University Press, 1995).

66. Until Geoffrey Payzant's translation of *Vom Musikalisch-Schönen* in 1986 (as *On the Musically Beautiful*), that of Gustav(e) Cohen from 1891 (*The Beautiful in Music*), published by Novello in London, would remain standard and unique as a complete English translation. Selections from the critical writings were available in English translation by Henry Pleasants in 1950, as *Vienna's Golden Years of Music, 1850–1900*.

67. For a discussion of Liszt's critical reception in the New World, see Deaville, "'Westwärts zieht die Kunstgeschichte': Liszt's Symphonic Poems in the New World," in *Kulturelle Praktiken und die Ausbildung von Imagined Communities in Nordamerika und Zentraleuropa*, ed. Susan Ingram, Markus Reisenleitner, Cornelia Szabó-Knotik (Vienna: Turia & Kant, 2001), 223–43.

68. Alexander Wheelock Thayer, "Paragraphs from Vienna," *Dwight's Journal of Music* 23, no. 7 (June 27, 1863): 55.

69. Julius Korngold, "Eduard Hanslick," *Neue Freie Presse*, Abendblatt (August 8, 1904): 1–4; and Guido Adler, "Eduard Hanslicks Lebenswerk," *Neue Freie Presse*, Morgenblatt (August 9, 1904): 1–3.

70. "Wir begraben in Eduard Hanslick einen Lehrer musikästhetischen Erkennens, einen Meister des Stils, eine Zierde der Kritik, einen Stolz dieses Blattes. Sein Name wird leben." Ibid., 4.

71. "Und so bedeutete Hanslick ungeachtet der blendenden äußeren Form dem Gehalte nach in Wahrheit einen Tiefstand des musikalischen Urteils." Anon., "Eduard Hanslick," *Der Kunstwart* 17 (1904): 488.

72. See Joseph Horowitz, *Wagner Nights: An American History* (Berkeley: University of California Press, 1994), for an exhaustive discussion of Wagner's role in late nineteenth-century America.

73. Anon., "Dr. Eduard Hanslick Dead: Austrian Musical Critic Once Was a Bitter Opponent of Wagner," *New York Times* (August 8, 1904): 7.

74. Like the editions since the fourth of 1874, this one was published in Leipzig by the press of Johann Ambrosius Barth.
75. First published in 1884 by Teschen/K. Prochaska in Vienna. Prochaska reissued it in 1910.
76. Heinrich Kralik, *Aus Eduard Hanslicks Wagner-Kritiken* (Vienna: Europa-Verlag, 1947).
77. Eduard Hanslick, *Vienna's Golden Years of Music, 1850–1900*, ed. and trans. Henry Pleasants (New York: Simon and Schuster, 1950).
78. Cook, *The Schenker Project*.
79. Kevin Karnes's study *Music, Criticism, and the Challenge of History* carries the aesthetic discussions forward into the twentieth century with Schoenberg and Ernst Kurth, and even references Hanslick's influence on the Second Viennese Circle in passing, yet he does not significantly bring Hanslick into the twentieth century.
80. Patricia Carpenter and Severine Neff, *Schoenberg's Philosophy of Composition: Thoughts on the "Musical Idea and Its Presentation"* (Berkeley, CA: University of California Press, 1997); Cook, *The Schenker Project*; Max Paddison, "Music as Ideal: The Aesthetics of Autonomy," in *The Cambridge History of Nineteenth-Century Music*, ed. Jim Samson (Cambridge: Cambridge University Press, 2002), 318–42.
81. With Richard Strauss as its progenitor, the so-called Munich School of the first decades of the twentieth century followed his compositional paths as epigones, with symphonic poems like Alexander Ritter's *Erotische Legende* and *Kaiser Rudolfs Ritt zum Grabe*, Max von Schillings's *Meergruß* and *Seemorgen*, and Siegmund von Hausegger's *Dionysische Phantasie, Barbarossa* and *Wieland der Schmied*.
82. Rudolf Schäfke, *Eduard Hanslick und die Musikästhetik* (Leipzig: Breitkopf & Härtel, 1922).
83. Werner Abegg, *Musikästhetik und Musikkritik bei Eduard Hanslick*, in *Studien zur Musikgeschichte des 19. Jahrhunderts*, vol. 44 (Regensburg: Bosse, 1974).
84. "Hanslick . . . gab . . . vor allem das ästhetische 'Vom Musikalisch-Schönen' . . . , das ultrakonservative Bekenntnis des Formalismus in der Musik heraus, das durch A. Kullaks Schrift 'Das Musikalisch-Schöne' (1858) paralysiert wurde. H. erklärte noch 1900 Wagners 'Lohengrin' für unmusikalisch." Bruno Schrader, "Eduard Hanslick," in *Bremers Handlexikon der Musik* (Leipzig: Reclam, 1905), 176.
85. *Lexikon der Juden in der Musik*, ed. Theo Stengel and Herbert Gerigk (Berlin: Bernhard Hahnefeld, 1940): cols. 101–4.
86. About his introduction of the designation, see Cornelia Schmitz-Berning, *Vokabular des Nationalsozialismus* (Berlin: Walter de Gruyter, 2000), 365.
87. For example, Ernst Bücken's *Musik der Deutschen: Eine Kulturgeschichte der deutschen Musik* (Cologne: Staufen-Verlag, 1941), does not mention Hanslick at all, despite an extended discussion of the New Germans Liszt and Wagner and their aesthetics (275–89). Music historians of the period tended to substitute Robert Schumann, but also Albert Lortzing and Heinrich Marschner, for the non-Aryan Mendelssohn.
88. "Ich kann es aus langjähriger eigener Beobachtung bezeugen, daß die Wagner-Feindschaft in Österreich und darüber hinaus in der gesamtdeutschen 'Intelligenz' von Hanslick geweckt, von Hanslick genährt, von Hanslick immer wieder ausgepeitscht [worden ist]." Max von Millenkovich-Morold, *Vom Abend zum Morgen: Aus dem alten Österreich ins neue Deutschland* (Leipzig: Philipp Reclam, 1940), 62.
89. "Dann begann aber eine feindselig-gehässige Presse ihm das Leben zu vergällen. Unter Führung des völlig verständnislosen, hämisch-witzelnden Halbjuden Hanslick . . . zerpflückte sie in boshafter Weise Bruckners Schöpfungen oder schwieg

sich einfach über sie aus." Robert Scherwatzky, *Die großen Meister deutscher Musik in ihren Briefen und Schriften*, 3rd ed. (Göttingen: Deuerlichsche Verlagsbuchhandlung, 1942), 310.

90. John Michael Cooper, trans., "Joseph Goebbels's Bruckner Address in Regensburg (June 6, 1937)," *Musical Quarterly* 78, no. 3 (1994): 606–7.

91. Julian Horton, *Bruckner's Symphonies: Analysis, Reception and Cultural Politics* (Cambridge: Cambridge University Press, 2004), 64–67.

92. "Bei der Bekämpfung des größten deutschen Künstlers erschien kein Mittel zu gemein und zu schlecht. Von einem der Hauptlager giftiger Feindschaft, der Wiener 'Neuen freien Presse,' dem Stammsitze des Herrn Hanslick aus, ging . . . ein fingierter Brief." Carl Friedrich Glasenapp, *Das Leben Richard Wagners*, vol. 5, 4th ed. (Leipzig: Breitkopf & Härtel, 1907), 18.

93. See, for example, Franz Rühlmann, *Richard Wagners theatralische Sendung: Ein Beitrag zur Geschichte und zur Systematik der Opernregie* (Braunschweig: H. Litolff, 1935), 110.

94. "Dort das formalistische Prinzip als Inbegriff des Seins und der Wirkung der Tonkunst—hier das Innere des schaffenden Künstlers als Urschoß und formgebende Kraft der Musik." Paul Ehlers, "Zu Friedrich von Hauseggers 100. Geburtstage," *Zeitschrift für Musik* 104 (1937): 666.

95. See note 55.

96. Hanslick, *Vienna's Golden Years of Music*.

97. Pleasants's collection of almost forty writings attempted to provide a representative sampling of the reviews, which indeed range over Hanslick's entire career and include a variety of essays—not just the major Wagner and Brahms reviews.

98. Hiroshi Yoshida, "Eduard Hanslick and the Idea of 'Public' in Musical Culture: Towards a Socio-Political Context of Formalist Aesthetics," *International Review of the Aesthetics and Sociology of Music* 32, no. 2 (2001): 180.

99. See, for example, Hans-Joachim Moser, *Musikgeschichte in hundert Lebensbildern* (Stuttgart: Reclam, 1958), 521.

100. James Hepokoski, "The Dahlhaus Project and Its Extra-Musicological Sources," *19th-Century Music* 14, no. 3 (1991): 221–46.

101. Anne Shreffler, "Berlin Walls: Dahlhaus, Knepler, and Ideologies of Music History," *Journal of Musicology* 20, no. 4 (2003): 498–525.

102. Sanna Pederson, "Defining the Term 'Absolute Music' Historically," *Music and Letters* 90, no. 2 (2009): 240–62.

103. Shreffler, "Berlin Walls," 513–14.

104. Pederson, "Defining the Term 'Absolute Music,'" 262.

105. Carl Dahlhaus, *Die Idee der absoluten Musik* (Kassel: Bärenreiter, 1978).

106. Georg Knepler, *Musikgeschichte des XIX. Jahrhunderts*, 2 vols. (Berlin: Henschelverlag, 1961).

107. Eduard Hanslick, *Musikkritiken*, ed. Lothar Fahlbusch (Leipzig: Philipp Reclam, 1972).

108. For West German aesthetic discussions of Hanslick, 1974–89, see above all Detlef Altenburg, "Franz Liszts Auseinandersetzung mit der Musikästhetik E. Hanslicks," in *Ars musica, musica scientia: Festschrift Heinrich Hüschen*, ed. Altenburg (Cologne: Verlag der Arbeitsgemeinschaft für Rheinische Musikgeschichte, 1980), 1–9; Carl Dahlhaus, "Über die 'verottete Gefühlsästhetik,'" in *Beiträge zur musikalischen Hermeneutik* (Regensburg: Bosse, 1975), 159–64, repr. in *Klassische und romantische Musikästhetik* (Laaber: Laaber, 1988), 329–35; Dahlhaus, *Die Idee der absoluten Musik* (Kassel: Bärenreiter, 1978;

Eng. trans., 1989); Bernd Sponheuer, "Zur ästhetischen Dichotomie als Denkform in der ersten Hälfte des 19. Jahrhunderts: eine historische Skizze am Beispiel Schumanns, Brendels, und Hanslicks," *Archiv für Musikwissenschaft* 37 (1980): 1–31; Sponheuer, *Musik als Kunst und Nicht-Kunst: Untersuchungen zur Dichotomie von "hoher" und "niederer" Musik im musikästhetischen Denken zwischen Kant und Hanslick* (Kassel: Bärenreiter, 1987); Wolfgang Suppan, "Franz Liszt zwischen Eduard Hanslick und F. von Hausegger: Ausdrucks- contra Formästhetik," *Studia musicologica Academiae Scientiarum Hungaricae* 24 (1982): 113–31; and Norbert Tschulik, "Neues zur Ästhetik und Kritik Eduard Hanslicks," *Österreichische Musik-Zeitschrift* 34 (1979): 601–10.

109. See all the philosophical/aesthetic contributions of Tschulik, Sponheuer, and Suppan in note 108.

110. About Payzant, see the detailed entry by Clifford Ford in *The Canadian Encyclopedia*, at http://www.thecanadianencyclopedia.com/articles/emc/geoffrey-payzant (accessed November 12, 2012).

111. Geoffrey Payzant, *On the Musically Beautiful* (Indianapolis: Hackett, 1986). Payzant's edition and translation takes Gustav(e) Cohen's translation from 1891 to task, most notably for consistently rendering the German word *Ton* as "sound" rather than "tone" (96–102).

112. *Eduard Hanslick and Ritter Berlioz in Prague: A Documentary Narrative* (Calgary, AB: University of Calgary Press, 1991).

113. Geoffrey Payzant, "Hanslick on Music as Product of Feeling," *Journal of Musicological Research* 9, no. 2–3 (1989): 133–45.

114. Geoffrey Payzant, "Eduard Hanslick and Robert Zimmermann: A Biographical Sketch," January 28, 2001, http://www.rodoni.ch/busoni/cronologia/note/hanslick.pdf (accessed November 12, 2012).

115. *VMS* and *VMS/2*; Eduard Hanslick, *Sämtliche Schriften*, ed. Dietmar Strauß (Vienna: Böhlau, 1993–).

116. Markus Gärtner, *Eduard Hanslick versus Franz Liszt, Aspekte einer grundlegenden Kontroverse* (Hildesheim: Georg Olms, 2005); Nicole Grimes, "Brahms's Critics: Continuity and Discontinuity in the Critical Reception of Johannes Brahms."

117. At the time of writing (2012), seven volumes have appeared in print.

Chapter Two

Hanslick's Composers

Fred Everett Maus

Readers usually interpret Eduard Hanslick's famous treatise *On the Musically Beautiful* in light of its memorable statements and arguments that articulate a "formalist" position, that is, an account of self-sufficient musical art, purely musical beauty, and an appropriate contemplative mode of listening. In this standard interpretation, Hanslick's treatise remains, to the present, the most prominent example of formalism in musical aesthetics.

However, Hanslick's detailed music criticism, addressing specific compositions in the context of Viennese concert life, does not typically stay within the limits of this aesthetic position. The apparent discrepancy between Hanslick's treatise—a brief, early text—and the other writings that took up much of his life is well-known.[1] Even more interestingly, Hanslick's treatise itself offers heterogeneous statements and implications about music and music perception.

In this paper, I indicate the complex, unresolved character of Hanslick's thought, especially in the treatise, with regard to a particular topic, the role of the composer in musical experience. This emphasis departs from the more usual focus on ideas about emotion and expression. I shall be pointing to some confusion in Hanslick's thinking; however, I regard this confusion as evidence of a praiseworthy, if not fully self-aware, openness to musical experience.

The Style of Hanslick's Treatise

The treatise *On the Musically Beautiful* maintains a briskly confident manner, and Hanslick is not gentle with people who differ from him in aesthetic beliefs or musical practices.

For example, Hanslick writes sarcastically about the existing state of music aesthetics:

> "Music has to do with feelings," we are told. This expression "has to do" is a characteristically vague utterance of previous musical aesthetics. In what the connection between music and feelings (specific feelings connected with specific pieces of music) might consist, according to what natural laws music

might work, and according to what laws of art it might be shaped—about all this the people who "have to do" with it leave us entirely in the dark.[2]

According to Hanslick, he must begin by clarifying the views of his opponents, something they have not bothered to do, before going on to rebut them. For not only are his antagonists wrong, they are also intellectually slovenly; they mix up the claims that music causes feelings and that music represents feelings. Hanslick proceeds to distinguish these positions and argue against the aesthetic relevance of each one. His account of prevalent traditions in discourse about music shows little curiosity about why other writers wrote as they did; once he has diagnosed confusion and errors, the earlier texts hold no interpretive challenges for him. His crisp, unsympathetic dismissal may be read as bracing and vigorous, or as stinging.

Hanslick also writes sarcastically about listeners carried away by feelings: "Slouched dozing in their chairs, these enthusiasts allow themselves to brood and sway in response to the vibrations of tones, instead of contemplating tones attentively."[3] Hanslick does not invite us to imagine the experiences of these languorous listeners—experiences that might be quite pleasant. Rather, he places us outside the listeners, as though we are looking at their bodies from a distance, and invites us to visualize their bad posture and uncontrolled movements as they indulge in the pleasures of bodily stimulation by sonic vibration. Apparently, Hanslick hopes that a voyeuristic glimpse of slumping, rocking bodies will inspire disgust or, at least, reluctance to identify with such unseemly sensualists. In similar passages throughout the treatise, Hanslick's ideas gain extra force from his impatient, aggressive style, and his unsympathetic, sometimes punitive treatment of opponents.

In another conspicuous quality of its style, the treatise is not only polemical, but also strives for demonstration through logical reasoning. The book includes passages of genuinely shrewd argumentation, recognized as such by generations of subsequent philosophers. In particular, Hanslick's argument that music cannot represent specific feelings (or emotions) has earned respectful discussion. Hanslick reasons that the individuation of feelings requires specific thought-content, and that music has no way to communicate the relevant thoughts, and therefore no way to individuate feelings. While one may seek ways to disagree with the conclusion, Hanslick's formulation of a clear argument is helpful in thinking about the issue.[4]

It is possible to bring these two qualities—confident advocacy and logical reasoning—together in a single image of the book. Hanslick's position, one might say, is the product of careful reasoning, which has led the author to strongly held and firmly expressed convictions on matters of personal importance.

But neither an emphatic style nor the appearance of logic should necessarily inspire trust. Either quality may cover the reality of confusion, tending to hide the author's unresolved intellectual and experiential tensions from readers and from the author himself. Overt logical reasoning seems to assure readers of the author's rational control over content, an appearance that may coexist with unacknowledged confusion. And a firm, sometimes harsh rejection of opponents creates exciting images of interpersonal opposition between the author and other people: perhaps, in a fine example of the psychic mechanism of projection, such images of external conflict may distract attention from internal tensions within Hanslick's own thought.

One important area of complexity in Hanslick's thought, hidden beneath his confident, logical tone, concerns the role of the composer in musical experience. Several questions about this topic concern Hanslick in the treatise. When a listener contemplates music in an aesthetically appropriate way, does she or he direct attention purely to sounds and their relationships, separating those sounds from their origin in a composer's activity? Or do thoughts about the composer enter into an appropriate musical experience in some way? If so, how is the composer properly imagined or conceived, within an experience of musical art? What are the continuities and distinctions among the composer as he figures in listening experience, the composer as a subject of musical and intellectual history, and the composer as a subject of biographical study?

These questions are of demonstrable interest to Hanslick, since he offers various answers to them. However, he never formulates them as explicitly as I have just done, and his thoughts on these issues are disorganized and discrepant. Thus, the topic of the composer, apparently somewhat difficult for Hanslick, invites careful rereading of his treatise, setting aside Hanslick's own brisk, rational style in order to seek evidence of his more complex and unresolved thoughts and experiences.

Juxtaposition of Two Passages by Hanslick

In the Preface to the 1891 edition of the treatise, Hanslick summarizes his main positive claim about musical beauty: "The beauty of a piece is specifically musical, i.e., is inherent in the tonal relationships without reference to an extraneous, extramusical context."[5] In stating this, Hanslick gives a warning to music lovers: irrelevant contexts may distract one from proper thinking about music, or proper listening to music. Someone who wants to hear the beauty in music should contemplate the relationships among tones. There, and only there, will musical beauty be found. Presumably, too, a music critic who wishes to guide listeners to an appreciation of beauty should write in a way that helps them concentrate on "specifically musical" qualities.

Hanslick's summary, in the sentence quoted, conforms to a widespread conception of Hanslick's aesthetic formalism, and there are many similar passages in his treatise. Hanslick is the historical author most strongly associated with the position that, in musical experience, only musical sound and relationships within musical sound are aesthetically relevant objects of attention, and only the contemplation of sound and sonic relationships is an aesthetically relevant activity. According to this position, extramusical information or "contexts" have no bearing on aesthetic appreciation of music.

While many passages in Hanslick's treatise maintain and elaborate this position, Hanslick has other ways of relating to music. To show this unmistakably—even dramatically—I shall juxtapose a second passage by Hanslick to the one I just quoted.

Hanslick's review of the 1865 première of Schubert's *Unfinished* Symphony describes the beginning of the performance:

> When, after the few introductory measures, clarinet and oboe in unison began their gentle cantilena above the calm murmur of the violins, every child recognized the composer, and a muffled "Schubert" was whispered in the audience. He had hardly entered, but it seemed that one recognized him by his step, by his way of opening the door. And when, after this nostalgic cantilena in the minor, there followed the contrasting G major theme of the violoncellos, a charming song of almost *Ländler*-like intimacy, every heart rejoiced, as if, after a long separation, the composer himself were among us in person.[6]

This wonderful report moves back and forth between description of music and an image of Schubert himself, entering a room to a joyous reception by the audience. The description does not encourage readers to distinguish sharply between the musical qualities and the evocation of Schubert; rather, the music—gentle, murmuring, nostalgic, charming—merges into the story of a beloved man who has returned after a long absence. The listeners recognize him by the sounds he makes, his footfall, his way of opening a door. These sounds, unlike the self-sufficient tones of pure music, index the proximity of a familiar body and its individual style of habitual movement. It seems that the space Schubert enters, where his way of opening the door is so easily recognized, is domestic, rather than a public space like a large concert hall; Schubert's entrance has transformed the space surrounding the listeners, making it feel like a home to which Schubert has returned. Intimacy pervades Hanslick's description, suggesting friendship, family, and erotic love.

This affectionate communal hallucination of Schubert's bodily presence goes well beyond the narrow focus on "tonal relationships" that Hanslick's treatise often recommends.

Composers in Hanslick's Criticism

The première of one of Schubert's most important compositions, decades after his death, is a significant event, and it is not surprising that Hanslick's review responds with special warmth. However, this vivid evocation of Schubert is part of a pattern: Hanslick, in his concert reviews, routinely writes about the composers of the music he has heard. Often, qualities of the music are, at the same time, perceptible qualities of the composer himself, and music criticism becomes a kind of portraiture.

For example, according to Hanslick, "the qualities which attract the public and interest the musician in Liszt's symphonic poems do not flow from the pure fountain of music; they are artificially distilled."[7] This statement links the defects of Liszt's music to a psychological limitation in his process of creation. Listening to Liszt's music, one is brought into contact with the composer's mental processes. Again, of Brahms's First Symphony, Hanslick writes that "Brahms's tendency to veil or dampen anything which might have the appearance of 'effect' makes itself felt . . . to a questionable degree."[8] Here, a personal aesthetic preference of Brahms seems to limit the range of one of his compositions. Listening to the music, one experiences Brahms's characteristic actions of veiling and dampening, and through those actions, one aspect of Brahms's personality: a recurring aversion to showy effects.

To different degrees, these comments about Liszt and Brahms are negative, connecting limitations in the music to personal limits of the composer. In view of these examples, one might wonder whether the composer's presence becomes more conspicuous when his music has failed in some way. Perhaps, when a composer succeeds, one hears only beautiful music; but when a composer's skill has lapsed, one hears the symptoms of human effort and human weakness.

However, the materialization of Schubert, brought about through his *Unfinished* Symphony, was a sign of the effectiveness of the music, and other musical successes also turn Hanslick's attention to the composer himself. Hanslick links the success of the *St Matthew Passion* to Bach's personal traits: "That Bach was able, without anxious effort, to exclude all sensuous and worldly elements and still absorb the listener in an area of human feeling so rigorously circumscribed is the supreme testimony of the strength of his genius and of his feeling."[9] The success of Bach's *Passion*, a composition that Hanslick admires despite its "gloomy, constrained piety," brings Hanslick into contact with Bach's individual sensibility.

Of Beethoven's *Missa Solemnis*, Hanslick writes that "the Mass in D and the Ninth Symphony stand unique and alone. . . . It is no more possible to build upon them than to find Beethoven's genius, with all its personal convictions, conflicts, and destinies, all its psychological and pathological prerequisites, repeated in another human being."[10] Hanslick's statement identifies a parallel between the unique individuality of Beethoven's music and of Beethoven himself, and yet Hanslick implies something more than parallelism. Surely the unrepeatable achievements of these compositions result from, and display, Beethoven's genius; and then it seems that all the personal qualities that Hanslick finds in Beethoven's genius are present, somehow, in the music itself.

In describing the individual movements of the *Missa Solemnis*, Hanslick emphasizes a transformation as the piece reaches its second movement, the "Gloria." In this movement, according to Hanslick, "overpowering grandeur of conception tears the composer from convention and carries him along with it."[11] According to Hanslick's description, at a certain point in the Mass one hears something happening to Beethoven, as though an event in Beethoven's life is perceptible in the present moment of listening: hearing the "Gloria," one hears Beethoven being overpowered by the grandeur of his own conception. Subsequently, the "Credo" brings an additional transformation: "The further he [Beethoven] goes, the more the walls of the cathedral seem to fall back before him. Everything becomes higher and broader."[12] As in the description of Schubert, it seems that the composer's presence transforms the nature of the performance space. This time, the musically conjured space is not domestic. Rather, Hanslick describes it as a cathedral—already an act of imagination, since he bases his article upon a performance in Vienna's Redoutensaal, a glamorous entertaining and performance space in the Hofburg Palace—and he imagines the cathedral as magically expanding in response to Beethoven's forward motion. Immediately after, the musical sound, flowing in waves like a liquid, seems to escape the cathedral setting and its audience: "The waves of tone are directed no longer at the church and its community; they seem, rather, to flow back to the origin of being."[13] After these surreal images, Hanslick drops back to a more literal style to assert the transparency with which the *Missa Solemnis* displays Beethoven's religious and ethical character: "The consecration of a lofty and liberal religiousness and the earnestness of an unbending morality are discernible as a principle in all of his life and works."[14] This is a firm assertion of the presence of the composer's personal traits in the music.

The Elimination of Composers in Hanslick's Treatise

A strong emphasis on composers, their identities, personalities, their presence in musical experience—ongoing in Hanslick's reports of concert life—is not what one might expect from a reading of some of the most famous formulations in Hanslick's treatise on musical beauty. For example, at one point Hanslick writes that "in pure contemplation the hearer takes in nothing but the piece of music being played."[15]

The one extended description of music in the treatise, the analysis of a passage from Beethoven's "Prometheus" Overture, follows through on this restricted account of musical experience. In stating "what the attentive ear of the music lover hears," Hanslick describes rising and falling melodic motion, rhythmic punctuation, and a combination of symmetry and variation. The description includes brief flourishes of metaphor, with references to the rising and falling of water in a fountain, and to the "lights and shadows" of the instrumentation. There is no indication, however, that the listener is aware of a human creative force.[16]

One passage, while acknowledging the composer as creator of the music, seems to insist upon the separateness of the composition and the composer. "The composer shapes something autonomously beautiful. The limitlessly expressive ideal material of the tones permits the subjectivity of his inner formative process to make its mark upon the products of his shaping. . . . Once they have been absorbed out of the artistic process into the product, however, these characteristics are of interest as musical determinations, i.e., as the character of the composition, not of the composer."[17] This statement seems particularly clear and emphatic: what is left at the end of the creative process is a separate, autonomous composition. The attributes of the composer may figure in a causal explanation of the attributes of the composition, but it is only the composition that is aesthetically interesting. A listener may be aware, in some intellectual way, of the composer's role in creating the music, but aesthetic experience forgets the composer and contemplates the music itself. It is difficult to reconcile this position with the evocations of Schubert and Beethoven that I have quoted from Hanslick's criticism.

Another passage in the treatise describes the composition as an organically self-generating entity. Here, Hanslick places the observation of creative activity within the listener's experience, but at the same time, displaces the causal role of the composer, replacing the composer with an alternative creative agency:

> Since the composition follows formal laws of beauty, it does not improvise itself in haphazard ramblings but develops itself in organically distinct gradations, like sumptuous blossoming from a bud. This bud is the principle theme, the actual material and content (in the sense of subject matter) of the whole tonal structure. Everything in the structure is a spontaneous continuation and consequence of the theme, conditioned and shaped by it, controlled and fulfilled by it.[18]

Similarly, at another point Hanslick states that "the auditory imagination . . . enjoys in conscious sensuousness the sounding shapes, the self-constructing tones, and dwells in free and immediate contemplation of them."[19] The image of "self-constructing tones" seems to block any vivid awareness of the actual composer's role.

According to the passages just cited, a listener should attend to musical sound and relationships within it. The composer has a causal relation to this musical sound, but appropriate listening involves an awareness of the music, as distinct from the composer. The sense of creative agency one may experience in listening can be heard as the music constructing itself, perhaps growing out of the shaping influence of the musical theme.

This position is clear and internally consistent. However, not only does it fail to account for the emphasis on composers in Hanslick's critical writing: numerous passages in Hanslick's treatise itself seem to counter an exclusive focus on self-creating musical sound, instead giving the composer a prominent role in musical experience. In fact, *On the Musically Beautiful* offers several different ways of placing the composer within the listener's experience.

The Presence of Composers in Hanslick's Treatise

I shall distinguish six different conceptions of the composer's role for listeners. Of these, the first three concern different ways of making the composer relevant to the composition, and therefore implicitly bringing the composer into a listener's experience of music. The other three address, more explicitly, a relationship between the composer and the listener, formed within the activity of listening.[20]

First conception: The composition is heard as emanating from, or shaped by, an artistic mind.

Hanslick ends his treatise by stating that "in each composition, the content derives from its particular tonal structure as the spontaneous creation of mind out of material compatible with mind."[21] At this summarizing point in the book, Hanslick suggests a duality, but also a compatibility, between mind and material. Musical sound, the center of attention for a listener, seems to be the material with which a mind can create. Elsewhere, in two important analogies introduced to show how music can be beautiful without being representational, Hanslick compares the experience of music to the viewing of an arabesque or of the patterns created in a kaleidoscope. In both cases, he concludes his analogy by indicating the special role in music of artistic creativity; this marks an important contrast with the arabesque and especially with the mechanical kaleidoscope. Writing of the arabesque, he asks readers to imagine that the visible lines "come into being in continuous self-formation before our eyes." This analogy offers another image of music as self-creating, but, to conclude, Hanslick adds: "Let us think of this living arabesque as the dynamic emanation of an artistic spirit."[22] That is, one does not only imagine the arabesque as self-creating, but also one experiences it as brought to life by the contribution of an "artistic spirit," who is felt to act in the present to maintain the liveliness of the image. Similarly, Hanslick specifies that music, unlike the images of a kaleidoscope, is "the direct emanation of an artistically creative spirit."[23] It is interesting that these references to an "artistic spirit" do not directly mention the composer as such; perhaps, at these moments, Hanslick wishes to evoke a composer-like entity that is somehow immanent in the composition—as the actual concrete, embodied composer is not. Nonetheless, such passages point toward a certain kind of musical experience: listening to music, one hears the interaction between a creative spirit and the sonic material that this spirit creates or shapes.

Second conception: An artistic mind is present in the musical composition, where listeners may perceive it.

According to this second idea, the "creative spirit" is not only a source or shaper of the music, but seems to be somehow caught up within the music. My formulation of this second role of the artistic mind is somewhat obscure, but it is clearer than some of the original passages that I am trying to summarize. For example: "The forms which construct themselves out of tones are not empty but filled; they are not mere contours of a vacuum but mind giving shape to itself from within."[24] In this sentence Hanslick seems to resist the distinction he sometimes uses between musical material and the external mind that shapes and controls it. Though Hanslick briefly evokes an image of tonal forms as containers, "not empty but filled," he also wants to affirm that the mind, presumably the composer's mind, is identical to the forms created from tones. Elsewhere, Hanslick connects the composer's thoughts and feelings to those in the musical composition. "The spiritual energy and distinctiveness of each composer's imagination make their mark upon the product as character. Accordingly, as the creation of a thinking and feeling mind, a musical composition has in high degree the capability to be itself full of ideality and feeling."[25] Here, a causal relation between the composer's thought and feelings and those in the music merges ambiguously into a different relationship, through a kind of transfer of the composer's mental qualities into those of the music.

Third conception: The composer's thoughts and feelings are in the composition like blood in a beautiful body.

According to Hanslick: "Thoughts and feelings run like blood in the arteries of the harmonious body of beautiful sounds. They are not that body; they are not perceivable, but they animate it."[26] Elsewhere, Hanslick's references to an "artistic, creative spirit" disembody the composer, who is present in the music only as *Geist*. The present passage, though, brings an image of the composition as a beautiful body, in which the creator figures not as mind, but as pulsing blood. The emphatically bodily language is haunting. Perhaps it goes a bit far for Hanslick, who immediately shifts to less material language: "The composer composes and thinks. He composes and thinks, however, at a remove from all objective reality, in tones."²⁷ The notion of "thinking in tones" or "thinking in music" is interesting in itself; but in context, Hanslick's recourse to such thinking also reads as an abrupt, defensive turn away from a more carnal image of music.

In general, Hanslick is wary of embodiment as a potential distraction from appropriate musical experience. Not only does he typically disembody the composer, but also, in his discussion of "pathological" listening, he consistently warns against bodily responses to musical sound. It is intriguing, then, that he sometimes admits an attractive figure of embodied music into his discourse. The discussion of arabesque, similarly, ends with a reference to blood: "Let us think of this living arabesque as the dynamic emanation of an artistic spirit who unceasingly pours the whole abundance of his inventiveness into the arteries of this dynamism."²⁸ Perhaps, in such passages, Hanslick gives a somatic, somewhat eroticized form to the sensuousness of music, his imagery acknowledging aspects of musical experience that he more often sets aside.²⁹

Fourth conception: In musical listening, the creative mind merges with that of the listener.

According to Hanslick, "The 'specifically musical' part of a composition is the creation of the artistic spirit, with which the contemplating spirit unites in complete understanding."³⁰ Rather than mentioning the actual empirical composer, Hanslick refers to an "artistic spirit," now matched and united with a "contemplating spirit." This is a strong statement of musical listening as an intersubjective communion, or perhaps even a temporary identity, between two "spirits" or "minds."

Fifth conception: A listener follows the events of a composition as though following the present actions of the composer, and tries to anticipate what the composer will do next.

This claim gives specificity and temporal eventfulness to the interaction between the listener's and composer's minds. According to Hanslick, "the most significant factor in the mental process [*Seelenvorgang*] which accompanies the comprehending of a musical work and makes it enjoyable" is this: "the mental satisfaction which the listener finds in continuously following and anticipating the composer's designs, here to be confirmed in his expectations, there to be agreeably led astray."³¹ This passage refers to the composer as such. In this conception of listening, the composer is present, moment-to-moment, in the listener's experience. The actual musical sound seems to lose some of its exclusive importance, becoming the medium through which two minds interact. Unlike the third conception, which suggested unification through complete understanding, this account maintains separation between the composer and listener. The listener tries to occupy the composer's perspective and anticipate the composer's choices, but part of the pleasure comes from a power differential: the composer may do as he wishes, and the listener can only try to guess what that will be.

Sixth conception: The listener follows and enjoys the creator's power over musical materials.

In one passage, Hanslick places strong emphasis on the composer's power over musical materials, and assigns the listener a role as admiring witness of that power: "It is a splendid and significant thing to follow the creative spirit as it magically opens up before us a new world of elements, coaxes them into all imaginable relationships with one another, and thus builds up, demolishes, produces, and destroys, controlling the entire wealth of a domain which elevates the ear into the subtlest and most highly developed of the sense organs."[32] Here, Hanslick distinguishes between the composer or "creative spirit" and the materials of music with particular clarity. Elsewhere in the treatise, Hanslick does not depict the "creative spirit" as omnipotent and potentially destructive, but here he does so with vigor. Listening, which Hanslick elsewhere describes as an act of intersubjective alignment with the composer's mind, becomes an imaginative attention to, perhaps participation in or identification with, the composer's power.

Interpreting and Evaluating Hanslick's Writing

On the basis of the quotations I have discussed, I suggest that Hanslick's aesthetics of music not only celebrates a contemplative relation between listener and composition; it also explores relationships between composer and listener, mediated by the musical composition. The latter part of Hanslick's thought is continuous with his critical writing, which often includes sharply observed character sketches of composers as they reveal themselves through their music. In the treatise, though, the role of the composer in musical experience, while a recurring topic, is not the direct, sustained focus of Hanslick's aesthetic theorizing. As a result, his claims about the composer are intermittent, varied, discrepant, and inadvertently revealing, and in these ways different from discourse that has been more consciously disciplined.

I began by commenting on a review of Schubert's *Unfinished* Symphony. Here is the last part of the passage I quoted, along with its continuation: "Every heart rejoiced, as if, after a long separation, the composer himself were among us in person. The whole movement is a melodic stream so crystal clear, despite its force and genius, that one can see every pebble on the bottom. And everywhere the same warmth, the same bright, life-giving sunshine!"[33] After welcoming Schubert back—quite tenderly—Hanslick suddenly takes his readers into an appealing, but apparently uninhabited, scene of nature. Where did Schubert go? How did we move from the intimate space in which we heard Schubert's footsteps, his hand on the door, to a sunlit stream? Hanslick brings the composer and the performance of his music close together, and then separates them again. This beautiful and intriguingly discontinuous description reflects, vividly, yet indirectly, Hanslick's ongoing, intense, multifaceted concern for the role of the composer in musical experience.

To summarize: *On the Musically Beautiful*, sometimes read for its austere advocacy of a strictly limited account of music, may be read instead as an indecisive rumination that ranges between two accounts, one in which music is sheer patterned sound, another in which music conjures human presence or *Geist*. And Hanslick's treatise, even setting aside the provocative further evidence of his criticism, shows uncertainty about the role of the composer or creative agency in the experience of listeners.

As mentioned, Hanslick responds impatiently to theoretical unclarity, in particular the apparent confusion of previous theorists of musical feeling. Hanslick's response to their theoretical uncertainty is to distinguish two positions, one about music as the cause of feeling, one about music as a representation of feeling, and discuss each position separately. But when writers seem to run ideas together, there may be good reasons; perhaps writers who fail to separate different relations between music and feeling are, in fact, expressing something important about musical experience. Recent work by the philosopher Kendall Walton, for example, places the expressive content of music in very close relation to the feelings that music causes in its listeners, and indicates why listeners may find it difficult to know whether certain feelings belong to the music or to themselves.[34]

Similarly, there may be good reasons for Hanslick's complex presentation of ideas about the composer. Indeed, issues about the role of the composer, or the composer-like creative agency, or other anthropomorphisms, within the experience of instrumental concert music have not gone away. These issues resurface in two of the most ambitious mid-twentieth century contributions to musical aesthetics. Stanley Cavell's essays on music in *Must We Mean What We Say?* ask many related questions, including, memorably, "why it is we treat certain objects, or how we *can* treat certain objects, in ways normally reserved for treating persons."[35] Edward T. Cone, in *The Composer's Voice*, responds to similar questions by developing a complex account of personas and virtual agents; despite Cone's energy and ingenuity, his work still leaves puzzles about the role of the composer.[36] Similar concerns have shaped much of the subsequent literature on dramatic and narrative qualities of instrumental music.[37] Hanslick's unresolved, apparently marginal discourse about the role of composers in musical experience points to an important, and persistently challenging, area of reflection.

Notes

1. Some writers note that expressive language appears in Hanslick's journalism, apparently in contradiction to the treatise, and explore this apparent contradiction between theory and practice. See Peter Kivy, "On Hanslick's Inconsistency," in *New Essays on Musical Understanding* (Oxford: Oxford University Press, 2001), 39–43; and Robert W. Hall, "On Hanslick's Supposed Formalism in Music," *Journal of Aesthetics and Art Criticism* 25, no. 4 (1967): 433–36. In a fascinating brief essay, Kevin C. Karnes suggests that, for much of his career, Hanslick regarded his work as historical, thus as a departure from the philosophical emphasis of the treatise. Kevin C. Karnes, "Eduard Hanslick's History: A Forgotten Narrative of Brahms's Vienna," *American Brahms Society Newsletter* 22, no. 2 (2004): 1–5.

2. Eduard Hanslick, *Vom Musikalisch-Schönen: Ein Beitrag zur Revision der Ästhetik der Tonkunst*, vol. 1, ed. Dietmar Strauß (Mainz: Schott, 1990), 25 (hereafter cited as *VMS*); Eduard Hanslick, *On the Musically Beautiful*, trans. Geoffrey Payzant (Indianapolis: Hackett, 1986), 3 (hereafter cited as *OMB*).

3. *VMS*, 129; *OMB*, 59.

4. For an excellent discussion of Hanslick's argumentation, see Malcolm Budd, *Music and the Emotions: The Philosophical Theories* (London: Routledge, 1985), 16–36.

5. *VMS*, 17; *OMB*, xxiii.

6. This review first appeared as Ed. H. [Eduard Hanslick], "Concerte" in the *Neue Freie Presse* (December 20, 1865): 1–3, three days after the première of the work. (Because Hanslick signed his byline in the *Neue Freie Presse* as "Ed. H.," it will be retained here in citations of his articles from that newspaper.) Hanslick subsequently included it in his collected works in *Aus dem Concertsaal: Kritiken und Schilderungen* (Vienna: Braumüller, 1870), 350–51. This translation is taken from Eduard Hanslick, *Vienna's Golden Years of Music, 1850–1900*, trans. and ed. Henry Pleasants (New York: Simon and Schuster, 1950), 104.

In discussing Hanslick's criticism, I have drawn a few examples from Henry Pleasants's widely available selection of translations. This is an alternative procedure to the careful, thorough studies of Hanslick's thought by specialist scholars that are now the norm (in this volume, for example). There are two significant traditions of Hanslick scholarship, one dealing with Hanslick as a historical figure, drawing potentially on all available evidence from his writings and contextual material; another treating Hanslick, and the treatise especially, in a nonspecialist way as a part of philosophical aesthetics. This essay belongs to the second tradition. My main interest is in the musical and philosophical claims of the treatise, and my references to Hanslick's criticism are meant to open up the topic of the composer's role in a vivid way, preparatory to my central discussion of the treatise's references to compositional agency.

7. Eduard Hanslick, "Les préludes," *Die Presse* (March 12, 1857), *Sämtliche Schriften* 1/4, 51–52; trans. from Pleasants, *Vienna's Golden Years of Music*, 49.

8. Hanslick, "Brahms's Symphony No. 1" (1876), trans. from Pleasants, *Vienna's Golden Years of Music*, 177.

9. Eduard Hanslick, "Die 'Matthäus-Passion' von Joh. Seb. Bach, 18.4.1862," *Sämtliche Schriften* 1/6, 89; trans. from Pleasants, *Vienna's Golden Years of Music*, 100–101; translation modified.

10. Eduard Hanslick, "Beethoven's große Festmesse," *Sämtliche Schriften* 1/5, 341; trans. from Pleasants, *Vienna's Golden Years of Music*, 69–70.

11. Ibid., 341; 70.

12. Ibid., 342; 71.

13. Ibid., 342; 71.

14. Ibid., 343; 72–73.

15. VMS, 29; OMB, 4–5.

16. VMS, 49–50; OMB, 12–13.

17. VMS, 106; OMB, 47.

18. VMS, 167–68; OMB, 81.

19. VMS, 77; OMB, 30.

20. Since I am quoting from Geoffrey Payzant's translation of the treatise, it is important to realize that in the passages that I quote, Payzant often translates the word *Geist* as "spirit," but sometimes instead as "mind." In quoting and discussing, I shall use both terms.

21. VMS, 171; OMB, 83. The phrase *geistfähige[s] Material*, translated as "compatible with mind," is present in editions from 1865 on.

22. VMS, 75; OMB, 29.

23. VMS, 76; OMB, 29.

24. VMS, 78; OMB, 30.

25. VMS, 80; OMB, 31.

26. VMS, 169; OMB, 82.

27. VMS, 169; OMB, 82.

28. VMS, 75; OMB, 29.

29. For a discussion of Hanslick's relation to embodiment and eroticism, see Fred Everett Maus, "Hanslick's Animism," *Journal of Musicology* 10, no. 3 (1992): 273–92.

30. VMS, 131–32; OMB, 60. This sentence was a relatively late addition to the treatise from 1874 on.

31. VMS, 138; OMB, 64.

32. VMS, 137–38; OMB, 64.

33. Ed. H., "Concerte," *Neue Freie Presse* (December 20, 1865): 1; trans. from Pleasants, *Vienna's Golden Years*, 104.

34. To put it simply, Walton suggests that music causes feelings in listeners; listeners project these feelings onto the music, as musical attributes; and then listeners imagine that their own feelings are the result of empathy or contagion. Kendall Walton, "Projectivism, Empathy, and Musical Tension," *Philosophical Topics* 26, no. 1–2 (1999): 407–40.

35. Stanley Cavell, *Must We Mean What We Say? A Book of Essays*, updated ed. (Cambridge: Cambridge University Press, 2002), 189.

36. Edward T. Cone, *The Composer's Voice* (Berkeley: University of California Press, 1974).

37. For surveys of this literature, see Fred Everett Maus, "Narratology, narrativity," in *New Grove Dictionary of Music and Musicians* (New York: Oxford University Press, 2001); and Fred Everett Maus, "Classical Instrumental Music and Narrative," in *A Companion to Narrative Theory*, ed. James Phelan and Peter Rabinowitz (Oxford: Blackwell, 2005), 466–83.

Chapter Three

Hanslick, Legal Processes, and Scientific Methodologies

How Not to Construct an Ontology of Music

Anthony Pryer

Hanslick's Dilemma: The Ingredients of Music

As Hanslick himself tells us, his treatise *On the Musically Beautiful* contains both a positive thesis and a negative one.[1] The positive thesis is concerned with what music *is*—the content of music consists solely of tonally moving forms, and musical beauty is of a special kind found only in music. The negative thesis is concerned with what music *is not*—distinct emotions are not part of the content of music, nor are the feelings conveyed by the composer or the performer, or felt by the listener. Curiously, the book has much more to say about the negative thesis than the positive one, and this essay will attempt to establish exactly why this should be so, and what consequences that imbalance has for Hanslick's views about the nature of music. Moreover, it should be noted that we will follow (at least initially) the usual line here by tacitly implying that his arguments explore directly the issue of the "ontology" of music. Technically, however, they seem to have more to do with the identifying characteristics of music and the individuation of particular works, than with how music "exists" as an entity in the universe, as it were. We will return to aspects of this issue in the final section.

Hanslick approaches his positive thesis—what music actually *is*—by appealing to what he thought of as the methods of scientific investigation. However, what these methods eventually produced was a list of ingredients of music that seem to be hopelessly disconnected and diverse. Some items are austerely reductionist in relation to the "content" of music (tones and forms alone), others oddly idealist in terms of the "substance" attributed to music ("substance" as a distinct concept appears miraculously only on the two final pages of his treatise),[2] and the whole is somewhat undertheorized in terms of how a "sonic" object might be distinguished from a "musical" one, or how "beautiful" musical works might be distinguished from merely pleasant and well-crafted ones (as some might be tempted to describe Hanslick's own surviving compositions).[3]

Having created this ontological quagmire, Hanslick then makes various attempts within the treatise itself to reconnect with real musical experiences. He eventually suggests, for example, that the bonds between musical elements are not in fact open to scientific investigation,[4] that the content of music can be grasped only musically, but never graphically,[5] that performance coaxes an electric spark out of some "obscure secret place,"[6] and that musical forms are filled rather than empty.[7]

To understand what is happening here, we need to take one or two steps backward. After all, it is rather too easy to assume that Hanslick is writing his treatise as a philosopher in the modern sense, proceeding with a specific proof focused on his positive thesis. However, he does not quite do this, since most of his actual "proofs" are in support of his negative thesis, and although his work contains commentaries upon philosophical notions—for example, he alludes to the ideas of Vischer, Herbart, Zimmermann, Kant, Hegel, and others—we may doubt that these commentaries are Hanslick's most important contribution to the subject. In the first place, it seems likely that he took some of his central ideas from the philosopher Robert Zimmermann and the Prague journalist Bernhard Gutt.[8] And secondly, there are some indications that Hanslick himself thought that his special contribution was likely to be his forensic skill in laying out the evidence, and his scientific objectivity in dealing with it. Thus we need to look at his legal and scientific agendas in this paper and their effects on his attempts to talk coherently about the ontology of music. When that is done, we can then turn to Hanslick's own observations on musical experience and musical performance to see if they contain within them the seeds of a new approach to the ontology of music.

Legal Methodologies

We should remember that when Dr. Hanslick wrote his treatise, he was a doctor neither of music nor of philosophy as such, but of law. He obtained his doctorate in Vienna in 1849, and immediately began his work on the subject of the musically beautiful. He was attached for a time to the "Landesgericht"—a Provincial Court or Assize Court—where he specialized in criminal law,[9] and there are many references to legal concepts in Hanslick's treatise, including his major statement on the status of evidence. He tells us: "Apart from all interpretation, it is the work itself which is under consideration. And as the jurist pretends that whatever is not in the evidence is not in the world, so for aesthetic judgment nothing is available which is not in the work of art."[10]

This ground rule for admissible evidence is not quite as helpful as it may seem, partly because it is easier to say what is materially relevant to a legal case than it is to control exactly what is encompassed within the limits of a work of art. After all, if what a musical work is stands "apart from all interpretation," then that is going to make it rather hard to take into account all of the relevant aesthetic attributes of compositions such as Mozart's *Musical Joke*, or those connected with irony, such as those found "in" some of the Shostakovich symphonies. And it is going to make it equally difficult to include among our legitimate aesthetic responses those that find their basis in the thrill of originality and innovative insight, since those qualities must rely (implicitly or explicitly) on historical comparison and a knowledge of traditions for their full emergence and appreciation.

Hanslick's statement on juridical standards of evidence comes at the end of a sustained passage of argument (in chapter 3) concerning what is to be analyzed in relation to the aesthetic effects of music, and how those things are to be analyzed. Curiously enough, those intense investigations receive answers that are not so much scientific as quasi-legal. The reason for this is that Hanslick makes it his business to focus on the *causes* of aesthetic effects, and those causes turn out to be so complex in relation to individual, particular responses to specific works, that no "universal," one-stop scientific law could be found to cover all of the cases. But this is to get ahead of the argument, and to appreciate the nature of the outcome we need to take a closer look at the contributing details.

Hanslick's first attempt to discuss causation in relation to aesthetic effect is as follows: "the powerful effect of a theme comes not from the supposed augmentation of anguish in the composer but from this or that augmented interval, not from the trembling of his soul but from the drumstrokes, not from his yearning but from the chromaticism."[11] This first step turns out to be crucial since it excludes from the causal arena not only the composer's feelings, but also anything from the personal, cultural, or historical situation that might conceivably incline the musical events to be construed one way rather than another. A few pages later, Hanslick elaborates on this view: "To compare differences in world view between Bach, Mozart and Haydn and then go back to the differences between their compositions may count as a very attractive and meritorious exercise, yet it is infinitely complicated and will be more prone to fallacies, the stricter the causal connection it seeks to establish."[12] Clearly Hanslick knows that music has effects, and he wants to know what causes them; but he does not want to know so much about their ultimate origins or their attendant webs of influence that he (and his methods) become overwhelmed and his judgments inconclusive. His solution to this dilemma is to stick to the technical features of music which, with deliberate care, he describes as the "proximate determining cause" (*nächste[n] bestimmende[n] Ursache*) of those effects.[13]

The term "proximate cause"—the cause closest to the effect—is in fact a legal notion designed precisely to prevent judgments being overwhelmed by endless causal chains of circumstance. For example, if A shoots and injures B, then A's action is what lawyers call the "cause-in-fact" of those injuries to B which result solely from the shooting. If, however, while being wheeled into hospital, B is struck by lightning, A is not responsible for the additional injuries caused in that way (it is the lightning that is taken to be the "proximate cause" of those), despite the fact that B would not have been in that place but for A's action. In other words, in legal terms, the notion of proximate cause acts as a convenient mechanism for limiting admissible causes-in-fact—a proximate cause is deemed to be a new intervention that breaks an established causal chain.[14]

Just how convenient for Hanslick's argument this legal notion is, it is not hard to imagine. It allows him to concentrate on the immediately encountered sonic ingredients of what he can now refer to as "the music itself" in preference to what he characterizes as the more distant and therefore—as he submits in a quasi-legal way—irrelevant intentions of the composer, or the communications of the performer, or the culturally-informed preparedness that allows listeners to access and richly experience music of different kinds. Some have been ready to take this "ring-fencing" of particular types of cause to be equivalent to the empirical, focused objectivity striven for in scientific treatments of causation,[15] but we should be more cautious. Not only is Hanslick's notion of proximate cause essentially a legal and pragmatic one, but the process of applying it to the arts gives it a decidedly unscientific orientation.

The supporting arguments for this view are complex, but they can be briefly characterized with the aid of an example. When Isaac Newton (so the story goes) sat under his tree and was hit by an apple, he came up with some "universal" laws of gravitation that demonstrated (among other things) that smaller objects are attracted to larger ones. However, if he had been attempting to demonstrate why that particular apple fell on his particular head in the particular year of 1666 in that particular location, he would still be at his calculations. This is because science cannot provide *one-stop* laws that explain the circumstantial "coming into being" of very particular complex events or effects.[16] But these are precisely the types of explanation we have tended to seek in relation to artworks; we have traditionally been less interested in why human beings write symphonies in general than (say) in whether Beethoven's *Eroica* specifically bears the imprint of having been written in Vienna with the character of Napoleon in mind, because it is the latter question that seems the more likely to impinge upon our aesthetic pleasures and understanding. And for similar reasons, we have been less interested in asking why, in general, people feel emotions in relation to music (which may be an interesting psychological, biological, or cultural question) than why a particular person X feels a particular emotion Y in the presence of a particular passage of music Z.

Unfortunately, such specific events arise not from single causes but from complex webs of causation, and we should not be surprised that science cannot provide "a single ... law" to cover them.[17] even if that fact made Hanslick despair. However, we should be clear that the lack of a single covering law does not make the connection between music and emotion arbitrary or "unscientific." It only means that (for us, in our current state of knowledge) each such specific emotive effect is rather unpredictable. Moreover, the crucial point here is that the word "unpredictable" in that statement does not mean "undeterminable" by scientific laws, it only means "complexly determinable by many specific and interacting neurological, physiological, personal and cultural factors" only some of which we are fully able to understand or investigate. By contrast, legal systems, because of their need for everyday applicability to complex particular cases, cut through this difficulty and come up with compromise "laws" (they are actually "rulings") that allow judgments to be made. But legal "laws" have an entirely different intent, status, and effect from scientific ones, and by falling back on the severely restricted "proximate determining causes" familiar from the legal domain, Hanslick did not advance toward the general ("universal") all-encompassing laws of science, but rather retreated from them.

It seems unlikely that Hanslick recognized this maneuver as a retreat, since later on in chapter 3 he tells us that a philosophical foundation of music cannot be constructed until the connection between each musical element and its determinant (singular!) has been established. Moreover, he insists that to discover such connections requires a double approach consisting of "a strictly scientific framework and the most elaborate casuistics."[18]

At first glance this seems to be a somewhat odd moment in the development of Hanslick's "method." Given his frequent appeals to science, the reference to a scientific framework is hardly surprising, but the use of the term "casuistics" (*Casuistik*) is very intriguing. In its common usage "casuistry" is usually taken to be a derogatory term implying the kind of clever but false reasoning often associated with legal, moral, or religious debates. It would be odd in the extreme were Hanslick to be openly using the word in that sense. It seems far more likely that he intended to use it rather in a technical sense to refer to a method of solving conflicts of principle on a case-by-case basis. (The root of the word is the Latin for "case," *casus*.) This is certainly its normal application in the legal field, and Hanslick's aesthetic treatise was unusual in its time for testing its philosophical ideas against a string of specifically identified musical "cases"— Beethoven's *Prometheus Overture*,[19] Gluck's "Che farò senza Euridice,"[20] Handel's *Messiah*,[21] and so on. There is, however, something interesting about the way in which he uses his specific cases, and to understand exactly what that is, we need to take a brief detour into the Austrian legal system.

When Hanslick trained as a lawyer, the Austrian system had already benefited from the eighteenth-century reforms under Maria Theresa and the new codification of laws in the *Allgemeines Bürgerliches Gesetzbuch* (General civic code of law) of 1812. However, the basis of that system was still Roman Law. This was because jurists were trained in Catholic universities where Canon Law was at the centre of instruction, and Canon Law was essentially based on Roman law. The impact of the Roman system on the German-speaking lands from the sixteenth century onward did not so much modify their ancient laws as overwhelm them.[22] For our purposes, however, the most important distinction between the ancient Germanic law and the Roman-law systems lies in their respective attitudes to previous, similar legal cases. In the former (as in English law), precedence was important, and earlier rulings would provide the mould, as it were, for judgments in similar cases. There might be some discussion (some "descriptive interpretation," as it is sometimes called) concerning precisely what was intended by the wording of the original judgment, but the rule was to follow precedent whenever possible.[23] By contrast, in systems based on Roman law it is the laws and edicts which provide the only bedrock of judgments (not the individual case rulings), and it is specifically the job of jurists to apply them afresh to each new case.[24]

We can perhaps see now how the Roman jurist system might relate to the organization of Hanslick's treatise. When he assembles his string of specific music examples (Beethoven, Gluck, Handel, etc.), he is not doing it to establish a pattern, or to establish an evolving body of "case-law" in his judgments; rather he is attempting to test and apply his philosophical principles afresh to each varying case and examine each example on its own merits. And when he investigates previous discussions by known authorities (such as Spitta on Bach,[25] or Rochlitz on Mozart[26]) he shows no sign of treating their judgments as guiding precedents. Indeed he does his best to discredit them as "witnesses"—a process, incidentally, which he later puts into reverse when assembling his list of "eminent people"[27] who will be wheeled out to support his notion that music does not have a "content." This indifference to constructing a case-law system with an emphasis on precedence is exactly what one would expect from a lawyer trained in Austria at that time.

Also, there seems to be another reason why Hanslick is interested in testing his ideas on a succession of single-case investigations, and it is a crucial one for his theory. The attention to particular instances provides a useful way in which he can prevent notions of musical beauty being handed down from on high, as it were, from general theories of beauty applicable to all the arts. He tells us: "The subjectless formal beauty of music does not preclude its productions from bearing the imprint of individuality. The manner of artistic treatment, like the invention of this or that particular theme, is *in each case unique*: it can never be dissolved into a higher unity, but remains an individual."[28] This statement seems to be suggesting that, not only is there a specifically musical kind of beauty (an innovative claim long credited—perhaps wrongly—to Hanslick), but also that each beautiful musical work has its own particular type of beauty (a more interesting, problematic, and underexplored assertion). Either way, as in the Austrian legal system, it is the general laws that must be tested anew in each case, rather than prior rulings being handed down to cover general classes of case by default.

However, the legal dimension has a greater significance for Hanslick's treatise than this, and to understand that significance we need to think about the difference between defending a philosophical premise and defending a client in the criminal courts. The crucial point is this: in legal systems, the method of "proof" is not really to demonstrate that a defendant is *by nature* innocent—pure as the driven snow, as it were; rather it is to show that certain accusations are false, certain witnesses are incompetent or malicious, certain types of evidence are inadmissible, and that therefore the defendant is not guilty *as charged* (even though he or she might be guilty in some other respect). In other words, the whole process is largely based on negative rebuttal, and a favorable verdict, should it come, is still cast in the form of "not guilty" rather than "entirely innocent." This is precisely how Hanslick's thesis, for the most part, is organized: it does not produce a complete set of arguments to establish exactly what music by nature is (though it makes some assertions), but rather focuses on demonstrating that the imputations of previous theorists as to its nature are false. In other words, Hanslick's treatise proceeds exactly like a courtroom drama, and that is what makes it so readable. We should note, though, that the legal-proceedings model, with its strong focus on transgressive aspects of behavior rather than on the essential "nature" of the person involved (whether saintly or evil), is fundamentally "anti-ontological."

These aspects by no means exhaust the many references to legal practices in Hanslick's book. We see, for example, that he also draws upon the notion of proximate cause to explain why, in those cases where music has a text, the text may seem to be the cause of the expression. He says: "Only in a logical (we almost said juridical) sense is the text the main thing and the music a mere accessory."[29] His point is that although the text may be the immediate spur for the expression in the work, it is the musical ingredients that actually bring that expression directly into being; they are its true proximate cause. And his further (unstated) point seems to be that we need to treat the notion of proximate cause with subtlety in relation to aesthetic effects by drawing a distinction between mere instigation and actual production. (Had Hanslick fully grasped that distinction he might have extended it to highlight in a sophisticated way the differences between the causal effects of the musical ingredients of a written work and the causal effects of its performances perceived through particularized, persuasive sound patterns, as we shall see in the final section.) Continuing the legal theme, Hanslick also insists that the idea that there is a necessary link between particular passages of music and particular emotions has no more subtlety than a "police order,"[30] and whenever he emphasizes the need for proof he seems to show a preference for using the verb *beweisen* (to prove) or one of its cognates (invoking the notion that one has "to present legal evidence of a fact) rather than, for example, *erproben* (to put to the test) or *prüfen* (to check).[31] But now it is time to turn to a more established source for Hanslick's methodologies—the world of nineteenth-century science.[32]

Scientific Methodologies

Hanslick's book opens with a sustained appeal to scientific methods. The most important aspect of this approach is that it allows him (at least at first) to characterize music as an "object" that can be examined dispassionately and empirically in relation to its material form alone—that is, aside from all feeling, culture, or presentational skill. He tells us that music is "first and foremost objective structure,"[33] and it is this approach that leads most obviously to what some have called the "extreme formalism" of Hanslick's views,[34] notwithstanding the modicum of metaphysics that, for complicated reasons, he felt obliged to introduce.

In keeping with these views, Hanslick begins by telling us that we can only gain "objective" knowledge about music by "getting alongside the thing itself."[35] There are many references in the treatise to the "music itself," or some near equivalent,[36] and Hanslick seems confident that music, as an object, can be observed neutrally in a manner that he describes as being "apart from all interpretation"[37]—that is, as if music were a scientifically definable object, rather like a piece of gold or a polar bear.

But it is unlikely that this approach will help matters. After all, gold and polar bears are what philosophers call "natural kinds,"[38] the identities of which are determined by atomic or genetic structures, criteria open to independent standards of verification that guarantee their claims to be particular things. By contrast, music is what some philosophers call an "artificial kind" (such as a clock or a chess set), the identity or "being" of which is not directly defined by physical characteristics alone, but by contextually emergent sets of rules or functions or perceptions that govern its use—in other words, by things that certainly cannot be read straight off the object itself. Science can enable us to distinguish between "gold" (a yellow precious metal) and "fool's gold" (a yellowish iron pyrite) since, despite their similar appearances, the former is an element with the atomic number 79, and the latter is a mineral with the chemical formula FeS_2. But we cannot confidently, or analogously, distinguish "music" from "fool's music," though some might feel that we can easily identify "music for fools," which is a rather different matter since "music for fools" is, in some senses, still "music."

At one point Hanslick himself clearly asserts that the laws governing music are not "natural" but rather arise from "culture."[39] But, nonetheless, he continues to insist that his scientific examination of music will be done only with "objective data," never with a supposed "state of mind,"[40] and he emphasizes that we should recognize that "the laws of beauty proper to each particular art are inseparable from its distinct material and technique."[41]

The references to "material" and "technique" here are interesting. They are—it seems to Hanslick (at least initially)—directly observable, and verifiable as being part of the artwork itself and therefore admissible as evidence. Indeed, they are the chief means by which he attempts to maintain the notion that music is simply an "object." However, as the book progresses, many concepts that were treated initially as concrete pieces of empirical data—"material," "form," "melody," etc.—gradually acquire metaphysical attributes. This seems to be part of a developing attempt to include within the work aesthetic and spiritual characteristics that, it becomes apparent, are gradually seen as necessary to distinguish artworks from sonic structures, real music from mere notational schemes and beautiful music from trivial music.

Many of the concepts that Hanslick introduced to effect the metaphysical turn of his treatise—"idea," substance," "form," and so on—had already accrued complex pedigrees within the German philosophical tradition. Recently, several illuminating studies have appeared which attempt to situate the treatise among, for example, the ideas of Ludwig Feuerbach and the Young Hegelians, or the gathering skepticism toward Idealist philosophy, or the new scientific viewpoints as exemplified by Ludwig Büchner's widely read *Kraft und Stoff*, published in 1855, which championed a kind of mechanical materialism (and which provoked an intense campaign against "vulgar" materialism from Karl Marx and Friedrich Engels, amongst others).[42] In parallel with these investigations, much attention has been paid to the final paragraph of the first edition of *Vom Musikalisch-Schönen* (removed from later versions), which reveals rather too blatantly that Hanslick has failed to free himself from a metaphysical backdrop in spite of his adoption of new scientific methods. In his final, excised paragraph, Hanslick tells us that the spiritual content of music "combines, in the soul of the listener" with "all other great and beautiful ideas," and "through deep and secret relationships to nature, the meaning of tones" allows us "to feel the infinite even as we listen to the work of human talent."[43] The crucial imputation of remarks such as these is that music is not only organizationally, but somehow *mysteriously* different from mere sound—and the fact that musicians and theorists have been nervous of losing that imputation perhaps accounts for some of the philosophical difficulties that we, together with Hanslick, have found ourselves in.

Interesting as recent studies have been in documenting and exposing Hanslick's own views as to what he thought the contemporary challenges were, they rarely chart the exact philosophical confusions that impede his theories as to the ingredients of music. Take, for example, the notion of "material." It begins in chapter 1 as something observable and subject to "research."[44] In chapter 3 we are told that in music the concept of form is "materialized,"[45] and we are later assured that this same musical form consists of "concrete tonal structures" (*concrete Tonbildungen*).⁴⁶ But in chapter 4 we find a more ambitious version of "material" in play specifically in relation to "tones," since we read that the ideas of the composer are made manifest in "the limitlessly expressive ideal material [*geistige[r] Stoff*] of the tones"⁴⁷—a phrase that is likely to give an empirical scientist a headache. Moreover, it is not easy to discover how this material gets these extra meanings into the tones, or even exactly how "tones" acquire their musical qualities. The following passage, for example, comes in chapter 6, and appears thus in Payzant's translation: "We receive from mother nature only material for material; this latter is the pure, measurable tone, determined according to height and depth of pitch. It is the prime and indispensable requisite of all music. *It forms itself* into melody and harmony, which are the two principal factors of music."⁴⁸

From this description we glean that nature provides sounds ("material for material"), which then mysteriously become tones (musical material), which then mysteriously form *themselves* into melody and harmony, which (as we have been told) are the proximate causes of what we experience in relation to music. In fact the German of the final sentence—"Diese gestaltet ihn zu Melodie und Harmonie, den zwei Hauptfactoren der Tonkunst"—makes Hanslick's thoughts a little clearer because the word "diese" (feminine) suggests that it is referring back to the feminine noun "Musik" in the previous sentence, and so it is music that transforms tones into harmony and melody, and not the tones themselves by virtue of some mysterious self-reflexive activity of their own. Even so, this produces a peculiar kind of tautology wherein music (as a mysterious active agent) itself produces harmony and melody out of tones, which therefore suggests that tones are both musical and not quite fully musical until that transforming operation of "music" has taken place. Moreover, this is not quite the end of the story, since the sentence following the quotation tells us that it is not "music" that has transformed tones into melody and harmony after all; rather these last two "are creations of the human spirit."⁴⁹

As with much (semi-)Idealist writing, it might be possible to construct a system of thought in which Hanslick's various opaque notions could find an "implicative" function, but it seems unlikely that that would help much to clear the fog that lies just below the surface. What Hanslick is doing here and elsewhere is gradually assimilating metaphysical attributes to empirical ones in an aesthetic maneuver he seems to think of as "embodiment" (*Verkörperung*)⁵⁰—a catch-all term frequently found in aesthetic writings, but which has almost no explanatory force, and which often seems to combine the physical and metaphysical in ways as puzzling as the mind-body problem.⁵¹ After all, "embodiment," despite its corporeal associations, is ultimately a metaphysical concept, so it is no wonder that Hanslick fairly quickly gives up attempting to unite the physical and metaphysical aspects into a coherent theory of ontology. Indeed, as early as chapter 3, he simply resigns himself to saying: "Despite the inscrutableness of the ultimate ontological grounds, there is a multitude of proximate causes [*näherliegender Ursachen*— the word "näherliegender" was added in the 1874 edition] with which the ideal expression of a piece of music is in precise correlation."[52]

What is clear is that Hanslick's ontology of music quickly begins to fall between several different stools. He cannot take account of musical emotions or variable cultural understandings of music because he cannot directly observe them or formulate general laws about them. He cannot include the effects of musical performance because they are too unpredictable and subjective, and therefore cannot be part of a fixed object. And he cannot rely just on empirical descriptions of tones and structures for, as he says, they "follow laws entirely different in their artistic application from the laws of their effects as isolated phenomena."[53] What then is to be done? One possible way forward is to look not at what Hanslick has to say about the content and identity of music, but at what he implies about the "musicness" of music, especially in his odd remarks about performance. In the final section I shall briefly attempt to sketch a new approach to the ontology of music based on remarks from within Hanslick's treatise itself.

The "Musicness" of Music

For much of the treatise, Hanslick is so busy treating compositions as scientific objects that only in passing does he comment upon the nature of what we might call their "musicness." This hesitation is perhaps understandable for someone trying to use scientific methods to capture the essence of music. After all, even Western notated musical scores contain instructions that leave an unsettling element of freedom for the performer (*cadenza, espressivo, rubato,* etc.) alongside those that do not (certain pitch and rhythm indications for example). Additionally, it is normative in Western performance traditions for performers to impose their own, sometimes unique, patterns of emphasis and intensity on the work in what we refer to as "interpretations."

As Hanslick sensed, two particular ontological difficulties arise from this complex situation. The first is how we are going to link the variations that arise in performance with a concept of the fixed identity of the artwork. The second is how we are going to claim that the aesthetic qualities displayed through the performance are indeed those of the artwork and not merely those of the (perhaps uniquely whimsical) performance. These are deep questions and all that can be done here is to use the hints that are already present in Hanslick's treatise to sketch out (somewhat speculatively) a possible reconfiguration of the issues for further investigation.

What we find throughout Hanslick's argument is that he is anxious to protect himself from the endless possibilities of variation in performance and listener response by fixing all relevant meanings within the tones themselves.

To achieve this, as we have seen, he falls back on the notion of some kind of embodiment: "The impression of feeling inheres in the physical substratum of the tones."[54] And if we should ask exactly how we might gain access to these embodied elements contained "in" the tones, Hanslick explains that "the content of a musical work can be grasped only musically, never graphically: i.e., as that which is *actually sounding in* each piece."[55]

This is a rather telling formulation, and it is one that is clearly mirrored in his journalist musical criticism. For example, he says of Wagner's *Rienzi* and *The Flying Dutchman* that they should not be judged by "the mere study of cold notes," for such a study "can receive its ultimate completion and confirmation only through the actual sensual conception," and that, furthermore, the critic "may, on other occasions, in actual performance, often recognize as mere paper effect something that had struck him as particularly promising in his study."[56] In other words, it is performance that seems, in Hanslick's system, to do the work of "embodiment," conjuring up the metaphysical out of the physical. At one point he even goes so far as to tell us that performance is in any case essential from the beginning of the artistic endeavor: "An inner singing, not a mere inner feeling, induces the musically gifted person to construct a musical artwork."[57] In fact it is hard to avoid the impression that what we might call a "performance postulate" underpins much of his work. Whenever Hanslick is analyzing the inner content of music he also seems, by aesthetic default, to be calling to mind a particular real or imagined performance.[58]

These constant references to latent performance should give us pause, but we will then need to consider exactly how we might theorize performances within the work-concept. Most attempts to do this run into the difficulty that it seems to be impossible to integrate the fixed identity of the work with the variant identities of the resultant sound-structures—and, moreover, the former have an inconvenient tendency to possess aesthetic attributes that the latter cannot easily acquire (works can be "Liszt-influenced," for example, in a way that performances of them rarely are).[59] There has been a recent move to circumvent these issues by characterizing the musical work as a "script" (after the theatrical model) rather than as a "text."[60] But although this formulation captures the open-endedness of performances, it does not explain how actual performances could be the most important signifiers of the identity of the work. For one thing, there is the uneasy implication that the work does not exist as a clear entity until all the performances are known—but what then happens if some performances actually contradict others, or if the final performance is canceled?[61] And for another, there is a difficulty with saying that these performances are displaying "interpretations" at all, since it would be rather difficult to say what they were interpretations "of," if the identity of the work were not fixed until the final performance had taken place. In other words, the problem of fixing the artistic identity of a written score has simply been transferred (without much benefit) to the problem of fixing the identity of the "relevant" class of performances, and we cannot easily say what "relevant" means in this situation without falling back on some shadowy prior notion of the "work itself," which the whole system is designed to exclude.

It seems possible that these problems will always arise when we attempt to link performance only to the issue of the *specific identity of works*, rather than to the *type of artefactuality* (and concomitant experience) that the category of "music" implies. Hanslick's treatise, notwithstanding its metaphysical contortions, amounts to an ongoing demonstration that attempts to compress the essence of "music" into the essence of "the identity of a specific work" are bound to lead to trouble. This is because one can imagine that it would be possible to define the uniqueness of a notated page or an intended soundscape by mere description (as it were), as if they were not really artworks at all—as if they were respectively (say) no more than an eccentric type of wallpaper, and a specially contrived sonic signaling device. An alien visitor from space might easily pick up their uniqueness without knowing that they were music, or without knowing what music was. Even for us, such a process of definition could not confirm their membership of the category "music" without some (real or imagined) demonstration that the appropriate attributes of musical performances and responses (meaningful phrasings, coherent patterns of intensity, the evocation of musical experiences, and so on) could arise from engagement with those objects.

If Hanslick had separated the conditions of "unique identity" from the "musical-in-nature" condition of the general kind of object we take a work to be, he might have been able to make some headway with the two ontological problems mentioned at the beginning of this section. First, variations in performance could have been accommodated theoretically because the ways of turning a set of notes into a generic thing called "music" are infinitely more varied than the ways of conveying the identity of a particular piece. And second, such a move would have absolved him from the burden of having to demonstrate that all the relevant aesthetic qualities of the performance must, in some sense, be sanctioned by the artwork "itself"—and he would no longer have to claim that performance was the mere "reproduction of a musical work" as he put it.[62] Of course a specific musical composition, as a "strategy" for producing aesthetic experiences, would still control those qualities associated solely with the work—the unique structure, the harmonic rhythm, the specific melodic shapes, and other such ingredients made manifest in performance. In that controlling sense, the initiating strategy (the score, the scheme of notes) is potentially an artwork. But a second set of attributes—more general aesthetic qualities—still needs to be contributed by the performance in the service of "musicness." And, as we know, performances employ a varied range of techniques to evoke the generic type "music," since in that facet of their activity they have to be faithful only to the type, not to the particular work.[63] There are many ways in which one can give the impression that something is music, but only a few in which one can confirm that something is a particular, identifiable work.[64]

Hanslick's text on several occasions suggests that he is struggling to make this distinction between the describable ingredients of a specific work and the generalized uplifting artistic and musical attributes. In his central treatment of musical beauty (chapter 3), for example, he felt constrained to point out that "what makes a piece of music a work of art and raises it above the level of physical experiment is something spontaneous, spiritual and therefore incalculable."[65] Again, in chapter 4, his remarks oscillate somewhat unnervingly between insisting that the composed work is "the completed artwork" of which the performance is mere "reproduction,"[66] and telling us that the real "moment of fulfillment" occurs in performance, since the "reproductive act . . . coaxes the electric spark out of its obscure secret place and flashes it across to the listener."[67]

These attempts to compress the attributes of musicality into those of specific identity seem to lie at the heart of Hanslick's tendency to fall back on the opaque notion of "embodiment"—and given his historical situation he was almost bound to construe that notion in Idealist terms. Moreover, he was more interested in musicality than in identity, and that is another reason his book is so lopsided: it has much more to say about all of those things (emotional expression, the distracting charm of melodies, the appropriate representation of texts, etc.) that were not, according to his ontological theory, "in" the work, than those that were. It is only to be regretted that he did not fully theorize the role of performance and its task of transforming an inanimate schematic ("scientific") notational object into a valuable musical experience, though he clearly alluded to that role in many different ways. Even within the terms that Hanslick does discuss it, music seems to require a special *double* type of ontological treatment—one for the work, and another for the "musicness"—which would be incompatible with models derived from science or the law. This is because science and the law tend to be concerned with causes of events, not reactions to events. The Morning Star and the Evening Star may elicit different responses from us, but science is interested in their single cause (the planet Venus); and in law, the injured victim and the perpetrator may arouse distinct emotions and sympathies, and yet still (in cases of negligence, for example) arise from the same person, the same legal "cause-in-fact." By contrast, "musicness" is not a cause, but a response to an initiating cause (the schematic work), and a response that has its own further causes (grounded in cultural, intellectual, and emotional understanding) beyond the reach of the specific work. Hanslick's heroic attempts to assert that these two types of cause are in fact the same one have a lot to answer for, not only in terms of his theory, but historically, in terms of the ways in which we have construed the art form of music ever since.

Notes

My thanks to those participants of the Hanslick Conference at University College Dublin, June 2009, who provided interesting comments on an earlier version of this paper, especially: Mark Evan Bonds, Dana Gooley, Franz Michael Maier, and Fred

Maus. I am also especially grateful to Peter Kivy who kindly discussed with me a much earlier draft of the final section of this paper, to Barbara Eichner who helped to clarify the nuances of some of the more obscure passages in Hanslick's German, and to the lawyer Kate Denholm who patiently discussed the legal arguments with me.

1. Eduard Hanslick, *On the Musically Beautiful*, trans. Geoffrey Payzant (Indianapolis: Hackett, 1986), xxii–xxiii (hereafter *OMB*). For the original German, see the critical, synoptic edition that records the changes to the various editions of the treatise as issued in Hanslick's lifetime: *Vom Musikalisch-Schönen: Ein Beitrag zur Revision der Ästhetik in der Tonkunst*, vol. 1, ed. Dietmar Strauß (Mainz: Schott, 1990), 7–18 (hereafter *VMS*).

2. By "substance" Hanslick seems to mean "spiritual substance" (*geistige[r] Gehalt*), and this is only clearly distinguished from "content" (*Inhalt*) in the final chapter (*OMB*, 82; *VMS*, 169). Hence Payzant translates the one earlier reference to *geistige[r] Gehalt* (in chapter 3) as "ideal content" (*OMB*, 30; *VMS*, 78), and the chapter 3 reference does not appear in the index under "Substance." For Payzant's discussion of this issue, see *OMB*, 114–15, n. 9. For a succinct account of the rather different and more complex notion of "Substance" (*Substanz*) in Hegelian philosophy, see Michael Inwood, *A Hegel Dictionary* (Oxford: Blackwell, 1992), 285–87.

3. *Lieder aus der Jugendzeit von Eduard Hanslick* (Berlin: Simrock, 1882). There is a copy in the British Library, shelfmark F.424.g. For a brief discussion of the songs, see Eric Sams, "Eduard Hanslick, 1825–1904: The Perfect Anti-Wagnerite," *Musical Times* 116 (October 1975): 867–68.

4. *OMB*, 31; *VMS*, 79.
5. *OMB*, 81; *VMS*, 167.
6. *OMB*, 49; *VMS*, 110.
7. *OMB*, 80; *VMS*, 166.
8. See, for example, the discussion in Geoffrey Payzant, *Eduard Hanslick and Ritter Berlioz in Prague* (Calgary, AB: University of Calgary Press, 1991), 107–15.
9. Eduard Hanslick, *Aus meinen Leben* (Berlin: Allgemeiner Verein für Deutsche Litteratur, 1894), 2 vols, vol. 1, 158 (hereafter cited as *AML*).
10. *OMB*, 37; *VMS*, 89. The word that Payzant translates as "interpretation" is *Commentar*.
11. *OMB*, 33; *VMS*, 82–83.
12. *OMB*, 39; *VMS*, 93.
13. *OMB*, 33; *VMS*, 82. Payzant translates *nächste[n] bestimmende[n] Ursache* only as "proximate causes" (in the plural). The categorization of types of causes goes back at least to Aristotle's *Physics* and *Metaphysics*, but Hanslick seems not to have had these sources directly in mind at this point.
14. For the legal notion of proximate cause, see Herbert Hart and Tony Honoré, *Causation in the Law* (Oxford: Clarendon Press, 1985), 90, 95–96.
15. See, for example, the assessment of Hanslick in Nicholas Cook, *The Schenker Project: Culture, Race and Music Theory in Fin-de-Siècle Vienna* (New York: Oxford University Press, 2007), 50.
16. For a comparison of the formation of causal laws in the humanities and in science, see Karl Popper, *The Poverty of Historicism* (London: Routledge & Kegan Paul, 1957). The example of Newton and his apple is discussed on pages 117–25.
17. *OMB*, xxii; *VMS*, 16.
18. "eines streng wissenschaftlichen Geripps und einer höchst reichhaltigen Casuistik." *OMB*, 35; *VMS*, 85.
19. *OMB*, 13; *VMS*, 49–50.
20. *OMB*, 17; *VMS*, 56–57.

21. *OMB*, 19; *VMS*, 59.

22. Nigel Foster, *Austrian Legal System and Laws* (London: Cavendish Publishing Limited, 2003), 10–11, 13–14. The standard sourcebook for the legal history of Austria is *Quellensammlung zur Österreichischen und Deutschen Rechtsgeschichte*, ed. Rudolf Hoke and Ilse Reiter (Vienna: Böhlau, 1993).

23. For an interesting discussion of the role of "descriptive interpretation" in law, and its apparent contrast with "evaluative interpretation" in the arts, see Ronald Dworkin, "Law as Interpretation," in *The Politics of Interpretation*, ed. William J. T. Mitchell (Chicago: University of Chicago Press, 1983), 249–70.

24. For a useful, brief summary of the tasks of jurists under systems based on Roman law, see *Justinian: The Digest of Roman Law*, ed. and trans. Colin Kolbert (London: Penguin Books, 1979), 21–37.

25. *OMB*, 14n; *VMS*, 52.

26. *OMB*, 7n; *VMS*, 33–34.

27. *OMB*, 77; *VMS*, 160.

28. *OMB*, 83; *VMS*, 170. Emphasis added.

29. *OMB*, 16n; *VMS*, 56.

30. *OMB*, 5; *VMS*, 29.

31. For examples of *beweisen* usage see, for example, *OMB*, 14, 22, 25, and 29; *VMS*, 51, 65, 70, and 76. Payzant variously translates this concept as "prove," "test" or "show"—words which do not clearly capture the legal overtones.

32. Hanslick was not the only Viennese music theorist to be influenced by legal studies. Wayne Alpern has demonstrated their profound effect on the thinking of Heinrich Schenker. However, it should be noted that Schenker seems to have been less interested in courtroom procedures than in wider issues of philosophical jurisprudence. He discusses, for example, the relation of the over-arching "Divine Law" to the laws of the Austro-Hungarian Empire and, in turn, its relation to the freedoms of its satellite states (for which read the hierarchical layers of Schenkerian analysis and their subservience to the "primordial law"—*Urgesetz*—which later became modified into the notion of *Ursatz*), and to the tensions between the constraints of the legal system and the freedom of individuals (for which read the constraining "laws" of the tonal system and their effects on individual creativity). See Wayne Alpern, "Music Theory as a Mode of Law: The Case of Heinrich Schenker," *Cardozo* Law Review 20 (1999): 1459–1511; and Alpern, "Schenkerian Jurisprudence: Echoes of Schenker's Legal Education in his Musical Thought" (PhD diss., City University of New York, 2010). See also the many references to Alpern's work in Cook, *The Schenker Project*, as indicated in the index to that volume.

33. *OMB*, 47; *VMS*, 106.

34. For a discussion of "extreme formalism" and "enhanced formalism" in relation to Hanslick, see Peter Kivy, *Antithetical Arts: On the Ancient Quarrel between Literature and Music* (New York: Oxford Clarendon Press, 2009), 60–64, and 66–67.

35. "den Dingen selbst an den Leib zu rücken." *OMB*, 1; *VMS*, 22.

36. For example, see *OMB*, 1, 33, 37, 39, 45, and 66; *VMS*, 22, 83, 89, 93, 103, and 142.

37. "ohne allen Commentar." *OMB*, 37; *VMS*, 89.

38. See, for example, Saul Kripke, *Naming and Necessity* (Oxford: Blackwell, 1981), 116–44.

39. *OMB*, 70; *VMS*, 148.

40. *OMB*, 33; *VMS*, 83.

41. "die Schönheitsgesetze jeder Kunst untrennbar sind von den Eigenthümlichkeiten ihres Materials, ihrer Technik." *OMB*, 2; *VMS*, 23.

42. For these wider perspectives in relation to Hanslick, see, for example: Christoph Landerer, "Ästhetik von oben? Ästhetik von unten? Objectivität und 'naturwissenschaftliche' Methode in Eduard Hanslicks Musikästhetik," *Archiv für Musikwissenschaft* 61, no. 1 (2004): 38–53; Mark Evan Bonds, *Music as Thought: Listening to the Symphony in the Age of Beethoven* (Princeton, NJ: Princeton University Press, 2006), 104–15; Mark Burford, "Hanslick's Idealist Materialism," *19th-Century Music* 30, no. 2 (2006): 166–81; Kevin C. Karnes, *Music, Criticism and the Challenge of History: Shaping Modern Musical Thought in Late Nineteenth-Century Vienna* (New York: Oxford University Press, 2008), 21–75; and Cook, *The Schenker Project*, 48–62. On the relation between philosophy and science in the period, see Frederick Gregory, *Scientific Materialism in Nineteenth-Century Germany* (Dordrecht: Reidel, 1977); and Herbert Schnädelbach, *Philosophy in Germany, 1831–1933*, trans. Eric Matthews (Cambridge: Cambridge University Press, 1984).

43. "Dieser geistige Gehalt verbindet nun auch im Gemüth des Hörers das Schöne der Tonkunst mit allen andern großen und schönen Ideen. Ihm wirkt die Musik nicht blos und absolut durch ihre eigenste Schönheit, sondern zugleich als tönendes Abbild der großen Bewegungen im Weltall. Durch tiefe und geheime Naturbeziehungen steigert sich die Bedeutung der Töne hoch über sie selbst hinaus und läßt uns in dem Werke menschlichen Talents immer zugleich das Unendliche fühlen." *VMS*, 171. The passage does not occur in the Payzant or Cohen translations, which are based on later editions. For discussions of, and quotations from, this paragraph, see, for example, Carl Dahlhaus, *The Idea of Absolute Music*, trans. Roger Lustig (Chicago: University of Chicago Press, 1989), 28 (from which I quote in the body of the article); Bonds, *Music as Thought*, 109; Kivy, *Antithetical Arts*, 66; and Karnes, *Music, Criticism and the Challenge of History*, 33.

44. *OMB*, 2; *VMS*, 23.

45. *OMB*, 30; *VMS*, 78.

46. *OMB*, 60; *VMS*, 132.

47. *OMB*, 47; *VMS*, 106.

48. *OMB*, 68–69; *VMS*, 146. Emphasis added.

49. "Beide finden sich in der Natur nicht vor, sie sind Schöpfungen des Menschengeistes." *VMS*, 146.

50. *OMB*, 8, 11, 20, and 40n; *VMS*, 42, 47, 62, and 95.

51. It may be indicative of the problematic nature of the term that not one of the following recent guides to aesthetics even attempts an article on "embodiment": *Encyclopedia of Aesthetics*, ed. Michael Kelly (New York: Oxford University Press, 1998), 4 vols; *The Oxford Handbook to Aesthetics*, ed. Jerrold Levinson (New York: Oxford University Press, 2003); *The Blackwell Guide to Aesthetics*, ed. Peter Kivy (Oxford: Blackwell, 2004); *The Routledge Companion to Aesthetics*, ed. Berys Gaut and Dominic McIver Lopes (Abingdon, UK: Routledge, 2005); *A Companion to Aesthetics*, ed. Stephen Davies et al. (Oxford: Wiley-Blackwell, 2009). Nor does the term occur in the indexes to those books, or in standard guides to metaphysics such as *A Companion to Metaphysics*, ed. Jaegwon Kim and Ernest Sosa (Oxford: Blackwell, 1995).

52. "bei aller Unerforschlichkeit der letzten, ontologischen Gründe,—doch eine Anzahl näherliegender Ursachen gibt, mit welchen der geistige Ausdruck einer Musik in genauem Zusammenhang steht." *OMB*, 32; *VMS*, 82.

53. "Es folgen jedoch diese Elemente (Töne, Farben) in ihrer künstlerischen Verwendung ganz anderen Gesetzen, als jener Ausdruck ihrer isolirten Erscheinung." *OMB*, 12; *VMS*, 48.

54. "die Gefühlswirkung, der Materie des Tons innewohnt und zur guten Hälfte physiologischen Gesetzen folgt." *OMB*, 60; *VMS*, 132.

55. "So kann also der Inhalt eines Tonwerks niemals gegenständlich, sondern nur musikalisch aufgefaßt werden, nämlich als das in jedem Musikstück concret Erklingende." *OMB*, 81; *VMS*, 167. Emphasis added.

56. Eduard Hanslick, *Music Criticisms, 1846–99*, trans. and ed. Henry Pleasants (Harmondsworth, UK: Penguin Books, 1963), 36.

57. "Ein inneres Singen, nicht ein inneres Fühlen treibt den musikalisch Talentirten zur Erfindung eines Tonstückes." *OMB*, 47; *VMS*, 106.

58. Indeed, when Hanslick attempts to undermine Gluck's setting of "Che farò senza Euridice," he pointedly supports his argument by adding without comment (in the early editions) the ludicrous performance indication: "Vivace con disperazione." In the 1874 edition this was modified to "Vivace" alone: *OMB*, 17; *VMS*, 57. Gluck's original marking (for the 1762 Italian version) was "Andante espressivo," which might well be among the earliest uses of the term "espressivo" in relation to music. "Espressivo" seems to imply a style or attribute of the performance itself, in contrast to "con espressione" which invites the performer to display a particular element of the composition in a particular way. The instruction "espressivo" is extremely rare before the nineteenth century, when certain kinds of music became primarily pretexts for performer display.

59. See, for example, Jerrold Levinson, "What a Musical Work Is," *Journal of Philosophy*, 77 (1980): 5–28, and the discussion of Levinson's ideas in Lydia Goehr, *The Imaginary Museum of Musical Works: An Essay in the Philosophy of Music* (Oxford: Clarendon Press, 1992), 44–55. For a recent survey of ontological theories of music (with a Platonist conclusion), see Julian Dodd, *Works of Music: An Essay on Ontology* (New York: Oxford University Press, 2007).

60. See, for example, Nicholas Cook, "Music as Performance," in *The Cultural Study of Music: A Critical Introduction*, ed. Martin Clayton, Trevor Herbert, and Richard Middleton (New York: Routledge, 2003), 204–14.

61. See Cook, "Music as Performance," 207: "Historically privileged texts . . . do not exhaust the work's identity [which is] something existing in the relation between its notation and the field of its performances."

62. *OMB*, 48; *VMS*, 109.

63. This probably explains why the notion of "the music itself" persists so strongly in spite of demonstrations that the meanings of works are derived from their specific location in time and place. What really persists is not "the music itself" but the notion of "musicness itself": this, too, changes over time, but much more slowly than the specific meanings encoded in particular works.

64. For further discussion of these issues, see my "Performance as the Bermuda Triangle of Musical Ontology: Identity versus Variety, and the Persistence of the 'Text,'" on the official website of the international conference "The Embodiment of Authority: Perspectives on Performances" held at the Sibelius Academy, Helsinki in 2010, at http://www.siba.fi/fi/web/embodimentofauthority/proceedings/pryer (accessed November 15, 2012).

65. "Was eine Musik zur Tondichtung macht, und sie aus der Reihe physikalischer Experimente hebt, ist ein Freies, Geistiges, daher unberechenbar." *OMB*, 42; *VMS*, 97.

66. "das fertige Kunstwerk . . . und Reproduction." *OMB*, 48; *VMS*, 109.

67. *OMB*, 49; *VMS*, 110.

Chapter Four

Otakar Hostinský, the Musically Beautiful, and the Gesamtkunstwerk

Felix Wörner

Introduction

Most of the reactions to Eduard Hanslick's monograph *Vom Musikalisch-Schönen* during the author's lifetime have either a decidedly polemical or a flattering ring to them. The result is that Hanslick's theories on musical aesthetics are often abbreviated to handy catch-phrases, a practice that attests to the ideological prejudice of many of his contemporaries, and that has subsequently prevented an objective and substantive dialogue with his aesthetic theory. Despite avoiding such a polemical tone, *Das Musikalisch-Schöne und das Gesammtkunstwerk vom Standpunkte der formalen Ästhetik*,[1] published by Otakar Hostinský (1847–1910) in 1877, was poorly received and is largely forgotten today. The Czech aestheticiaṇ's critical musings on Hanslick's theories were intended to give a philosophical justification for a redefinition of the relationship between the two most important trends in music aesthetics of the late nineteenth century. As the title of his book indicates, Hostinský is at pains to draw together the category of the musically beautiful coined by Hanslick and the idea of the *Gesamtkunstwerk* as advocated by Wagner in his theoretical writings.

The poor reception of Hostinský's text can be ascribed, in part, to this conciliatory approach. Hanslick himself, in later editions of *Vom Musikalisch-Schönen*, accused Hostinský of distorting his original argument and drawing misguided and conflicting conclusions.[2] Hanslick's appraisal of Hostinský is echoed in the works of authors such as Rudolf Schäfke, Bojan Bujić, and Carl Dahlhaus, who grappled with Hostinský's text in the twentieth century. Without exception, these writers characterized Hostinský's book as an unsuccessful or, at least, problematic attempt to synthesize contrary aesthetic positions.[3] The aim of this essay is to reassess Hostinský's aesthetics of music through a new critical reading of his treatise. It is concerned first with Hostinský's account of late nineteenth-century aesthetic discussion; second with a reconstruction of his concept of a "theory of a connection of the arts" [*Theorie der Verbindung der Künste*]; and third with an analysis of his notion of *Stimmung*. In order to come to an appropriate understanding of Hostinsky's aesthetic position, it is necessary to situate his thinking in its biographical context and in the cultural context of his work.

Hostinský: Biographical Background

Hostinský was born in Bohemia in 1847 and received his education at Prague and Munich universities, studying aesthetics, art history, archaeology, and music history. In 1883, shortly after the establishment of the Czech campus of the Charles University in Prague, he was appointed to the chair of aesthetics.[4] This was a prestigious position; after Vienna, Prague was one of the most important cultural and intellectual centers in the Austro-Hungarian Empire during the late-nineteenth century. His influential writings on the history of music (especially Czech-related) and on music theory led to his reputation as the founding father of Czech musicology.[5] Hostinský also raised his influential voice on cultural matters outside the academic world. His concerns often overlapped with or conflicted with those of his colleague Guido Adler at the German-speaking campus of the Charles University. In public discourse both scholars emphasized, independently of one another, the outstanding role played by music in the formation of national identity, and referred in particular to the cultural inheritance of their respective Czech and German national traditions.[6] Comparable debates on the role of art in nation building, a role that was strengthened as the national movements intensified, were common in central Europe in the late nineteenth century. Hostinský, therefore, entered into an ongoing public debate about the cultural functions of music in identity formation, especially in relation to opera. In his three articles—"Art and Nationality" (1869),[7] "Wagnerianism and Czech National Opera" (1870),[8] and "On Program Music" (1873)[9]—he made the case that it is only truly possible for a composer to evoke the psychological core of a nation in art through the dramatic setting of vernacular texts.

The Czech philosopher Miloš Jůzl has shown that these three early essays already contain the main principles of Hostinský's aesthetics, which can be summarized by means of binary oppositions. In his reconstruction Jůzl juxtaposes the categories "progress" and "conservatism"; "nationalism" and "cosmopolitanism"; "music drama" and "opera"; "dramatic perspective" and "purely musical perspective"; "dramatic flow" and "closed musical numbers"; "[dramatic] realism" and "formalism"; "content" and "virtuosity, formality"; "[unity of] style" and "eclecticism"; "[musical] stylization" and "naturalism"; "natural expression" and "unnatural expression."[10] That Hostinský favored the former in each case demonstrates how far removed his concept of musical aesthetics was from Hanslick's at this early stage. Among other objectives, Hostinský's aesthetic categories aimed, at ennobling the operatic music of Bedřich Smetana, who was celebrated in his native land as a champion of national Czech culture following his operas *Prodaná nevěsta* (*The Bartered Bride*, 1866, rev. 1870) and *Dalibor* (1867, rev. 1870). Hanslick, however, regarded Smetana's music from the perspective of the liberal Viennese *Bürgertum*, who perceived the works of Austro-German musical culture as quasi-transnational cultural assets, and as the zenith and measure of contemporary music production. Therefore the instrumental works of Bohemian composers were acceptable only if they could be categorized independently of any national elements (such as were unavoidable in the native-language operas of this time).[11] Whereas in his early writings, Hostinský implicitly distanced himself from Hanslick's aesthetic categories, he later engaged explicitly with Hanslick's position in *Das Musikalisch-Schöne und das Gesammtkunstwerk vom Standpunkte der formalen Ästhetik*, which characterizes Hanslick's quest for the establishment of the musically beautiful in pure instrumental music as one-sided, and consequently, intended to aesthetically distinguish a subset of only one certain musical culture. Hostinský's treatise is the first full-scale critical examination of Hanslick's book that expands on particular aspects of Hanslick's thought by extending more balanced consideration of art forms such as the musical drama.

Hostinský's Aesthetic Theory in the Context of Hanslick's Aesthetic Thought

Hostinský opens *Das Musikalisch-Schöne und das Gesammtkunstwerk vom Standpunkte der formalen Ästhetik* with a summary of Hanslick's criteria for the "musically beautiful," which separate the beauty specific to music from that of other types of art such as painting, architecture, or poetry. In drawing up this inventory, Hostinský pursues two goals. First, he strives to clearly distinguish Hanslick's position and aesthetic foundation from the views of the advocates of an expressive aesthetic and to strengthen Hanslick's—in his opinion—argumentative superiority. Hostinský discusses the counterarguments put forward by Hanslick's prominent critics, in particular Friedrich Theodor Vischer,[12] Wilhelm A. Ambros,[13] Adolf Kullak,[14] Count Laurencin,[15] and F. Stade.[16]

The second aspect of his introductory chapter is, however, more important for an evaluation of Hostinský's own contribution to music aesthetics and his elucidation of the principles of philosophical formal aesthetics. Here, Hostinský aims for a clarification of the relationship between Hanslick's music aesthetics and the principles of formal aesthetics upon which his own philosophical position is built.

After the collapse of idealist aesthetics, a formal aesthetic was developed as the leading direction in philosophical aesthetics of nineteenth-century Austria and, from the mid-century onward, was publicized as the official position of the Austrian Ministry of Education.[17] The fundamental principles of formal aesthetics were established at the beginning of the nineteenth century by the philosopher Johann Friedrich Herbart (1776–1841). Although Herbart did not publish an independent work on aesthetics, he frequently discussed the problems of philosophical aesthetics in his publications. Furthermore, his reflections exhibited sufficient consistency for the main tenets of his theory to be later developed by his students and formulated into a system.[18] His writings attained notoriety in the second half of the nineteenth century, primarily due to two monographs published by his influential pupil Robert Zimmermann (1824–98), *Geschichte der Ästhetik* (1858) and *Allgemeine Ästhetik als Formwissenschaft* (1865).[19]

Zimmermann's works exerted such an influence that his view of formal aesthetics soon overshadowed Herbart's original conception.[20] Hostinský, who had published two papers on Herbart's aesthetic theory and engaged critically with Zimmermann's interpretation of Herbart's philosophy, was also considered a renowned expert on Herbart's writings.[21] The basic conception of Hostinský's aesthetic theory can be read as a close extrapolation of Herbart's philosophical principles; Hostinský postulates a contradiction between the basic principles of Hanslick's treatise *Vom Musikalisch-Schönen* and the basic principles of Herbartian philosophy. Hostinský's close proximity to Herbart lends weight to his claim that "one cannot regard Hanslick to have proceeded from the same philosophical stance as Herbart."[22] Yet even as he distances Hanslick's thought from that of Herbart, Hostinský emphasizes the strong influence of Hegel and Vischer on Hanslick. And truly, it was only in later editions of *Vom Musikalisch-Schönen* that Hanslick moderated the influence of these figures on his aesthetic thinking.[23]

Hostinský's study of the differences between Herbart's philosophical aesthetics and Hanslick's concept of the musically beautiful opens with an analysis of the fundamental tenets of Herbart's philosophical aesthetics: "Everything that is beautiful ... is a construct. However, wherever this construct affects our aesthetic taste, it is not its individual elements as such, that is, its 'material,' but rather and much more the mutual relation of these elements to one another, i.e., their 'form.'"[24] Each aesthetic object consists of many elements. The aesthetic judgment, Herbart argues, is not based on the contemplation of these individual elements, but rather on the complex relationship between these elements. It is this relationship that determines the aesthetic form of the work of art. Based exclusively on this principle of formal aesthetics, however, music cannot be said to have content, to describe feelings, or to express poetic thoughts.[25] The principles of formal aesthetics are extraneous to the thesis rejected by Hanslick, namely, that music is emotional or can express feelings, as formal aesthetics do not address these issues in the first place. Rather,

Hostinský categorizes such issues as psychological and thus isolates them from formal aesthetics. Hanslick's opposition to the legitimacy of the aesthetics of feeling, according to Hostinský, is based on psychology, rather than on formal aesthetics.[26] Formal aesthetics judge the beauty of a work of art on the basis of its formal disposition, that is, on the basis of the aesthetic quality of the individual elements and their mutual relations within the work, without taking the potential content of the work into consideration.[27] This position does not clarify, one way or the other, whether music has the ability to express or arouse emotions; Hostinský merely stresses that aesthetic judgments are independent of content and feelings.

Before Hostinský strives for a subtle separation of aesthetic judgments, that is, between judgments of taste and subjective impression,[28] he dissociates himself from Hanslick in two important ways. The first concerns the relationship between notated score and the performance of the musical artwork; the second concerns identifying the relation of music and other art forms that underlies Hostinský's concept of *Kunstverein*.[29]

Contrary to Hanslick, who holds that a musical work is finalized in the score,[30] Hostinský argues that the performance itself, the acoustic realization of the notation, is a fundamental component of the final musical work and is, accordingly, a necessary component of an aesthetic judgment. He describes the correlation between written notation (objects fixed by the composer) and performance (sound that is perceptible by the senses) as follows: the traditional musical notation remains inadequate, despite ever-greater specificity in various respects. In particular, moments integral to the interpretation (e.g., agogics, tone colors, articulation, etc.) are at best sketchily fixed by the score.

The accomplished musician, therefore, faces not a purely reproductive task, but rather a task of production. From this perspective, composer and interpreter should ideally form "one single artistic personality,"[31] even though they are often spatially and temporally removed from one another. Hostinský assigns the interpreter the task of realizing the musical work in accordance with the intentions of the composer. This goal allows for an appropriate reconstruction and addition of certain unnotated aspects of the score (although Hostinský does not specify how this requirement should be met by the interpreter); in this way the interpreter is promoted to a "representative" of the composer. Hostinský regards performance as a necessary condition for the completion of the "objective artwork,"[32] thereby confirming the importance of sonic realization for aesthetic judgment. Hostinský therefore conceives of the aesthetics of production and reproduction as complementary—close to one another and serving the realization of the objective work of art.

As a corollary of this concept of complementarity, Hostinský later advanced a vision of the *Gesamtkunstwerk* as a unity of different arts.[33] Contrary to traditional aesthetics, in which the different art forms are treated as strongly distinct from one another, in Hostinský's concept of *Gesamtkunstwerk*, the different art forms are so close and interdependent that they assume an inextricable unity. As Hostinský demonstrates more precisely later in his treatise, the interaction of different kinds of art in the *Gesamtkunstwerk* (e.g., poetry, music, drama, and dance) can be seen as analogous to the collaboration of the composer and interpreter during the representation of the "objective work of art."

Hostinský's most pointed criticism of Hanslick is directed at the latter's evaluation of the relationship between text and music in opera. Hanslick establishes the primacy of instrumental music by asserting that "of what *instrumental music* cannot do, it ought never be said that *music* can do it, because only instrumental music is music purely and absolutely."[34] This assertion is inextricably bound up with Hanslick's definition of the musically beautiful, and his fundamental principle that opera is a genre subordinate to pure instrumental music follows directly from it. Hostinský is opposed to this view and considers a definition of the musically beautiful based on a firm hierarchy of musical forms (e.g., absolute music, vocal music, dramatic music) to be utterly unfounded. Rather, he argues that different art forms such as music and poetry should be understood and aesthetically appraised independently, according to principles appropriate to each art form. As soon as different art forms, for instance, are combined in a work of dramatic art, a "new kind of art" is developed that follows its own artistic principles.[35] Hostinský does not rule out the possibility of aesthetic conflict between different art forms such as music and poetry. He does criticize Hanslick's thesis, however, of music as the leading principle *per se* for aesthetic judgment, calling it unfounded and untenable—an "arbitrary act" [*willkuerlichen Akt*]—[36], as it ignores the demands of text and reigns supreme. Aesthetic judgments are based exclusively on the "*Ton*formen und *Ton*verhältnisse" of a musical composition, and therefore not on the "what," or to put it another way, its content, but rather on the "how," that is, the specific musical form: "In a musical work of art . . . there are only forms and relations which are carried by tones; they cannot be judged other than as *Tonformen, Tonverhältnisse*."[37] Hostinský qualifies this Hanslickian view with an analysis of Ambros's remarks on the relationship between poetry and music: "[Music] is, on the one hand, an architecturally formal art; on the other hand, an art of poetical ideas—indeed, up to a limit to be determined farther on, of given materials. The architectonic form and the poetical idea must pervade it—though the one or the other element can, to be sure, more or less decidedly predominate."[38] Hostinský's thesis, which can be developed on the basis of this quotation, is as follows: If within some areas of art (such as drama and poetry) the organization of the form is affected by the "given material" and the "poetic idea," then the possibility of a close cooperation of different arts (such as poetry and music) and their relevance for the aesthetic judgment must be examined, at least for those kinds of music in which several kinds of art meet. What is the nature of the poetic idea, however, if music, unlike language, cannot express a certain idea? Both Ambros and Hostinský fall back on the concept of *Stimmung* to clarify this problem, yet each draws on different aspects of it. Whereas Ambros interprets the *Stimmungen* produced by music as certain psychological emotions or feelings that are dictated to us by music, the concept of *Stimmung* obtains a new dimension with Hostinský. He refers to "mood" in contrast to "feeling," due to the absence of a certain imaginative content [*Vorstellungsinhalt*]. Rather, he asserts, it "actually refers to a certain state of our inner soul [*einen gewissen Zustand unseres Inneren*]."[39] It evokes a *Stimmung*, that is, a psychic disposition, whose "certain aural impressions, as such, are bound up with the musical tonal feelings and their multifarious combinations."[40]

These *Stimmungen*, or "emotions" [*Gemüthsbewegungen*] are pure aesthetic feelings and possess "immediate, necessary, objective and fixed" qualities as long as they are not bound to other concepts,[41] while other thoughts released by the musical impression are "indirect, accidental, subjective and vague."[42] *Stimmungen*, therefore, are part of an aesthetic judgment under certain conditions. "The feeling awakened in us through music is only aesthetic as long as it is objectively fixed to the music, that is, to the *sensations of tone*."[43]

The History of the Term *Stimmung*

The use and conceptual range of the term *Stimmung*, for which there is no sufficiently complex equivalent in the English language, has undergone a fundamental change within aesthetic theory since the late eighteenth century. In his investigation into the history of the term, David Wellbery identifies three aspects that are relevant to its use.[44] First, *Stimmung* indicates an emotive quality and is directly related to "the first person," a phenomenon that can be paraphrased as the "quality of the self." Its relative uncertainty is a characteristic of the concept of *Stimmung*, which becomes particularly clear in comparison with the specific, intentional quality of *Gefühle* (emotions) directed toward an object. *Stimmung* can be connected with the entire range of our experience, without fixing itself to a certain object. The complexity of *Stimmungen* is such that it is difficult to capture the way *Stimmung* affects experience. Second, when we speak of *Stimmung*, we speak of an "atmosphere," an integrative potential, a unifying power which results in many different elements flowing together into a uniform experience. As a third and last aspect, Wellbery describes the "communicative dimension" of *Stimmung*, through which a large group of people can be affected (as in a "political mood"). This criterion is not relevant to Hostinský's concept of *Stimmung*.

During the second half of the eighteenth century, the concept of *Stimmung* was usually discussed in relation to its music-theoretical dimension (the tuning of instruments). Kant gives the *Stimmung* metaphor a decidedly aesthetic formulation in his *Critique of Judgment* when he writes:

A presentation that, though singular and not compared with others, yet harmonizes with the conditions of the universality that is the business of the understanding in general, brings the cognitive powers into that proportioned attunement [*proportionierte Stimmung*] which we require for all cognition and which, therefore, we also consider valid for everyone who is so constituted as to judge by means of understanding and the senses in combination (in other words, for human beings).[45]

Irrespective of the Kantian problem of "proportioned attunement" between the powers of imagination and understanding (and considered necessary as a condition of the suggested general communicability of aesthetic judgments), it is crucial to the history of the term that Kant designates *Stimmung* exclusively as a relation between two powers.[46] The connotation of "self-reference" that best characterizes *Stimmung* in its current usage was first suggested in Hegel's *Lectures on Aesthetics* (1818), designating it as one of the characteristic moments of the lyric genre, "the single mood [*Stimmung*] or general reflection aroused poetically by the external stimulus" which "forms the centre determining ... the plan and connection of the poem as a work of art."[47] According to Wellbery, Fichte was the first to effect a crucial change in the development of the aesthetic concept of *Stimmung*. Fichte complements Hegel's definition with two aspects characteristic of the early romantics. First, he extends the concept of *Stimmung* to include "the passage to the unconscious" [*den Bezug zum Unbewußten*] and, second, he observes a "hermeneuticizing of *Stimmung*."[48] The first indicates that *Stimmung* withdraws from representation and finds expression in the conceptions in an indefinable way. With the second aspect Wellbery shows how the early romantic artists were at pains to share their *Stimmung*. "*Stimmung* became the content of the communication [*Mitteilung*], only the *Stimmung* is no content, rather the movement pattern of the artist's utmost subjectivity, i.e., self-directed autonomy."[49] The work of art splits into the outer form and the inner *Stimmung*, the latter being indefinable.

Hostinský refers on the one hand to the early romantic concept of *Stimmung*. On the other hand, his differentiation between "fixed" and "vague" emotions—taking up a definition from Robert Zimmermann's aesthetics[50]—allows him to interpret the category *Stimmung* as a formal aspect of aesthetics (in contrast to Ambros, who viewed *Stimmung* in terms of content). *Stimmungen* are generated for the listener by music; they are the result of a psychological process which is released by "the *Tonempfindungen* entering the consciousness."[51] If we associate a more or less specific impression of feelings with music-evoked *Stimmung*, then we as listeners subjectively relate music to certain perceptions (after we have been transported by the *Tonempfindungen* into a *Stimmung*). This act, however, already lies beyond the "objectivity of the work of art";[52] therefore the perceptions released by instrumental music are different in kind from those that would be evoked by a poem. The connection posited by Hostinský between *Tonverhältnissen*, *Tonempfindungen* und *Stimmungen* makes it possible for him to append the latter to aesthetic judgments. All "impressions" that the music causes in the listener stand in contrast to this, as they are deemed to count as subjective feelings and therefore are not established in the work of art.[53]

Hostinský, the *Kunstverein*, and the *Gesamtkunstwerk*

As we have already seen, no preference for a certain type of art may be deduced from the principles of formal aesthetics. The merging of different art forms into certain genres calls into question a fundamental principle of Herbartian aesthetics, namely the demand for a "purity of style."[54] In order to rescue this principle, Hostinský develops a "theory of unification of the arts,"[55] as the theoretical basis for the so-called Society of Arts [*Kunstverein*], that is, of the *Gesamtkunstwerk*.[56] If one takes the view that "opera is not the work of one single art, but rather is the collaboration of all arts,"[57] then this poses the question of hierarchy and the relationship between the different artforms. According to Hostinský, the *Gesamtkunstwerk* is based on the organic interaction of the participating arts in an "organic whole." He discusses three instances where the different arts try to participate in this ideal harmony: (1) the "content" or "material," later characterized as "logical principle";[58] (2) the "form of appearance" as the aesthetic form—temporal or spatial—of the arts involved;[59] and (3) the psychological harmony of *Stimmung*.[60] Hostinský comments on the three aspects as follows:

1. The material element of poetry, that is, its "content," frequently finds a correspondence in the fine arts, sculpture or painting, yet not in music. Likewise a connection between the fine arts and music is lacking at this level.
2. Following a distinction between *Malerei* and *Poesie* established by Gotthold Ephraim Lessing in his "Laokoon,"[61] Hostinský divides the external forms (of appearance) of art into the categories of temporal art and spatial art. In principle, the two categories are not organically connected; so, for example, the temporal art of music [*Zeitkunst Musik*] and the spatial fine arts [*Raumkunst, bildende Kunst*] are unconnected and form no synthesis. This barrier between the fine arts in the broadest sense and the temporal arts of music and poetry (only the latter being close to the fine arts, at least materially, as mentioned in point 1), can only be waived if there is motion in spatial art, that is, a temporal development. Such a dynamicization of spatial art can be found in scenic art, which is connected organically with poetry in the dramatic genre.[62] Music and the fine arts draw near only in ballet, where Hostinský differentiates between "dramatic" ballet (pantomime) and "absolute" ballet (formal dance). The proviso for the organic synthesis of different art

types presupposes the same external forms and, with the exception of music, a frame of reference. Both categories belong to an "objective unity of the artwork."[63]

3. The objective unity of the work of art is supplemented by the demand for a "harmony of moods" [*Einklang der Stimmung*], which possesses the potential to combine materially dissociative arts (such as poetry and music). This criterion represents a subjective instance rooted in perception; this is part of the theory of art [*Kunstlehre*].[64] Here again, Hostinský refers closely to the aesthetic theory of Herbart, which reads as follows: "That affect, which the work can generate by its own internal, aesthetic conditions, is not to be denied it; this applies also to the converging of expressions where different arts collaborate, and mutually illuminate one another. . . . The unity of a work of art is rarely an aesthetic unity; and one would be misguided if one were to generally regard it as such."[65]

In order to proceed to Hostinský's later deliberations, it is of crucial importance to bear in mind the difference between the aspects in points 1 and 2. It is only then that one can evaluate a finished work of art according to the criteria of formal aesthetics, as opposed to the aspects in point 3 for the theory of art [*Kunstlehre*], that is, for the genesis of the work of art. Formal aesthetics rely on numerous opinions regarding the elementary conditions found in the work of art, which, according to the theory, are independent and equally valid considerations in the overall judgment.[66] Only the individual perception of each recipient—which is influenced by factors such as talent, training, and momentary disposition—succeeds in weighting the partial judgments accordingly and differentiating which opinions are more or less relevant for the overall judgment. A comparable hierarchy between the participating arts emerges from a contemplation of the *Gesamtkunstwerk*. Although Hostinský assumes an organic whole even in his contemplation of the *Gesamtkunstwerk*, a hierarchical structure of several partial arts nevertheless grows out of that whole, and is expressed in the organization of (organic) form. Hostinský refers here not to a gradation of aesthetic priority, but rather to a differentiation of the psychological meaning for the "shaping" [*Formgebung*] of the whole. The creation of a work of art (i.e., in the domain of art theory) has very different requirements than the aesthetic evaluation of the work. Hostinský therefore argues that the subject matter does not play a role in the evaluation of an artwork, but does factor into the conception of artworks where materiality (i.e., content) is relevant. It follows that in art forms such as painting or poetry, it is the subject matter that determines which form or shape is appropriate to that particular work. Hostinský grants a prominent role to poetry in the *Gesamtkunstwerk*—in contrast to Hanslick. The form of the materially-shaped art of poetry is influenced by its content.[67] Hostinský describes the problem from two perspectives.

First, a text frequently expresses a certain *Stimmung*. Hostinský in fact agrees with Hanslick that for "the aesthetic of pure music, i.e., absolute instrumental music," feelings and moods are irrelevant for aesthetic judgment.[68] Already Kant argued in the *Critique of Judgment* that "all music not set to words" was to be assigned to "free beauty (*pulchritudo vaga*)";[69] this "does not presuppose a concept of what the object is [meant] to be."[70] The "accessory beauty" (*pulchritudo adhaerens*) is certainly to be differentiated from the "free beauty," as it concerns a "judgment of taste, whereby an object is defined as beautiful under the concept of a particular purpose." It is hence characterized by Kant as "not pure."[71]

We may accept Hanslick's premise that no *Stimmungen* are expressed in the musically beautiful in such a way as to be relevant for our aesthetic judgment, yet, according to Hostinský, the situation changes as soon as music and text form a unity. Hostinský claims that in the so-called union or society of arts [*Kunstverein*] the specific *Stimmung* expressed by the text influences our perception of the music. In addition, *Stimmung* was considered only as a subjective experience in pure instrumental music, and this experience has to be related to the mood experienced by the text. This relation, however, transcends the subjective impression and becomes part of the (objective) aesthetic judgment. Hostinský claims that this relation is part of our aesthetic judgment about the "society of arts"; therefore, our aesthetic judgment about the society of arts may be classified as "*pulchritudo adhaerens*." The only additional requirement specified by Hostinský at this point is that the music must not question the *Stimmung* expressed by the text, as this would contradict the principle of aesthetic unity.

Second, if we endorse this statement, Hanslick's argumentation needs revising. It is no longer plausible to transfer the principles derived from pure instrumental music to vocal music or to music that is part of a *Kunstverein*. Instead, the "materiality" or the content of the text, including the emotional content, affects the entire work of art, including the music. In this way Hostinský amends Hanslick's principles of the musically beautiful by invoking the ability of art to create *Stimmungen*, and therein recognizes the standardizing principle of the *Gesamtkunstwerk*. This definition leads to an overall distancing from Hanslick's position. Hostinský explains that under certain conditions, subjective impressions in the form of *Stimmungen* occupy a key role in his theory of *Gesamtkunstwerk*. This means that the level of congruence between text and music is based on *Stimmungen* and is therefore best left to the realm of psychology.

While Hanslick completely denies the relevance of *Stimmung* in his monograph *Vom Musikalisch-Schönen*,[72] the concept has a crucial function in Hostinský's proposed theory of *Kunstverein* as the synthesis of different types of art. Hostinský attributes to the unity of *Stimmung* the ability to set different material elements in a relationship with one another. Where vocal musical drama is concerned, this concept of *Stimmung* complements and revises Hanslick's criteria of the musically beautiful that are not sufficient to understand the different types of art (music and poetry). The similarity of *Stimmung* to the comparable *Gestimmt-Sein* ("being in tune with each other") is necessary for the integration of different art forms into an organic whole.

The differentiation between the theories of aesthetics and art is also relevant to Wagner's stipulation that "in the *Gesammtkunstwerk* drama is the purpose, the music is but a means of expression."[73] Hostinský followed Hanslick's view in the evaluation of opera, namely that the musical and dramatic aspects are equal. If one judges their relationship from the perspective of the theory of art, then this balance shifts: the drama moves into the foreground as the aspect determining content and form. This analysis is confirmed by the inclusion of *Stimmung* as a factor shaping our perception. Based on the demand for the unity of the artwork, music (which is materially indefinite) follows the materially bound art form poetry in its *Stimmung*, which Hostinský designates "the determining and the conditional."[74] This difference between instrumental music and vocal music leads of necessity to a different classification within the system of categories for aesthetics. Whereas instrumental music is understood as "purely formal, objectless art," vocal music (and naturally, also musical drama) is a "*Kunstverein*, whose form-giving principle is no longer absolute music, but rather the material-giving factor: poetry."[75]

The fact that Hostinský's work on aesthetics in the twentieth century was more or less consigned to oblivion outside the Czech-speaking region can be attributed to an unfortunate combination of several different factors. First, his treatise *Das Musikalisch-Schöne und das Gesammtkunstwerk vom Standpunkte der formalen Ästhetik* was strongly criticized by both Hanslick and the "New German School." Second, in later years Hostinský became more preoccupied with national Czech themes than with aesthetics, and published almost exclusively in Czech following his appointment at the Czech University; therefore, his scholarship was not really noticed outside of the Czech-speaking lands.[76] While these factors had a negative impact on the broader reception of his writings, the significance of Hostinský's treatise is unquestionable.

Hostinský's critique of, and response to, Hanslick's position was motivated by the fact that he considered the one-sided aesthetic ennoblement of so-called absolute instrumental music to be inadequately judged. The enlargement of Hanslick's concept of music with the aim of incorporating vocal music and music drama as equals to instrumental music required bridging the traditional gap in aesthetics between different art forms, and realizing that the unification of different art forms resulted in a new, integrated, and independent art form. The overcoming of this separation of different art forms, long established in aesthetic tradition, achieved for Hostinský's theory an aesthetic reevaluation of the concept *Stimmung*, to which he assigned a primary, integrative function. The *Stimmung* into which we are transposed by a work of art must be considered to belong to the domain of psychology. This notwithstanding, Hostinský values the unity of *Stimmung* as outstanding for aesthetic legitimacy and for our understanding of works that unite different forms of art. This philosophical reevaluation of the concept of *Stimmung*, by which Hostinský justifies the concept of *Kunstverein* as being on an equal footing in aesthetic theory to separate art forms, modifies the traditional system of aesthetic categories and forms the nucleus of Hostinský's individual contribution to philosophical aesthetics. Although Hostinský never managed to produce a differentiated or systematic analysis of how *Stimmungen* concretely influence our evaluation of works of art, his new interpretation of the concept of *Stimmung*—which stemmed from Hanslick's *Vom Musikalisch-Schönen*—pointed toward a topic that would become *en vogue* only a few decades later, around 1900. Then a part of psychological aesthetics, it would finally be given a radical new meaning with Martin Heidegger's ontological analysis in *Sein und Zeit*.[77]

Translated by Nicole Grimes

Notes

The author would like to thank Ben Haas and the two anonymous reviewers for their comments and feedback on an earlier draft of this essay. All translations are by Nicole Grimes unless otherwise stated.

1. Ottokar Hostinský, *Das Musikalisch-Schöne und das Gesammtkunstwerk vom Standpunkte der formalen Ästhetik* (Leipzig: Breitkopf & Härtel, 1877).

2. "A paradoxical exception is found in the interesting and diligent study by O. Hostinský ... who appears to agree completely with my premise in the first part of his book, yet when dealing with the concept of 'Kunstverein,' he limits, turns, and interprets my thoughts in such a way that he reaches exactly the opposite conclusions as me." For the original German, see Eduard Hanslick, *Vom Musikalisch-Schönen: Ein Beitrag zur Revision der Ästhetik der Tonkunst*, vol. 1, ed. Dietmar Strauß (Mainz: Schott, 1990), 15 (hereafter *VMS*).

3. Schäfke characterizes the outcome of Hostinský's effort to connect Hanslick and Wagner by means of formal aesthetics as an "unhappy, 'eclectic compromise.'" Rudolf Schäfke, *Eduard Hanslick und die Musikästhetik* (Leipzig: Breitkopf & Härtel, 1922), 34, and see also 54; Bojan Bujić discusses Hostinský under the heading "The Eclectic Tendency," in *Music in European Thought: 1851–1912*, ed. Bojan Bujić (Cambridge: Cambridge University Press, 1988), 132–51; Dahlhaus deals with Hostinský's text in *The Idea of Absolute Music* in chapter 2, "The History of the Term and Its Vicissitudes." Here he is critical of Hostinský's simplified dichotomy: "Hostinský compares 'absolute, purely formal, objectless' music with architecture and ornamentation on the one hand, and 'representative, content-laden, objective' music with sculpture and painting on the other in order to demonstrate that there exists not one 'pure musical art' but rather two possibilities of a 'pure style' in music. However, Hostinský recognizes the distortion in the accusation that Wagner had 'shattered' the musical forms; this recognition disturbs the simplicity of his esthetic system." Carl Dahlhaus, *The Idea of Absolute Music*, trans. Roger Lustig (Chicago: University of Chicago Press, 1989), 35–36. See also Dahlhaus, *Die Idee der absoluten Musik* (Kassel: Bärenreiter, 1978), 40–42. Recently, Lothar L. Schneider has given a more sympathetic evaluation of Hostinsky's work: Lothar L. Schneider, "*Form*

versus *Gehalt*. Konturen des intellektuellen Feldes im späten 19. Jahrhundert," in *Eduard Hanslick zum Gedenken. Bericht des Symposiums zum Anlass seines 100. Todestages*, ed. Theophil Antonicek, Gernot Gruber, and Christoph Landerer. Wiener Veröffentlichungen zur Musikwissenschaft 43 (Tutzing: Hans Schneider, 2010), 39–54, particularly 47–49.

4. For a history of the Charles University in Prague, see *Dějiny Univerzity Karlovy: 1802–1918*, ed. Jan Havánek (Prague: Charles University, 1997), 183–330.

5. See in particular Hostinský, *Die Lehre von den musikalischen Klängen: Ein Beitrag zur aesthetischen Begründung der Harmonielehre* (Prague: H. Dominicus, 1879).

6. Kevin Karnes explores the relationship between Adler's positivist scholarship and the German national overtones in his work. See Kevin C. Karnes, *Music, Criticism, and the Challenge of History: Shaping Modern Musical Thought in Late Nineteenth-Century Vienna* (Oxford: Oxford University Press, 2008), 167–80.

7. "Umění a národnost," *Dalibor* (1869): 1 (1–2), 2 (10–11), 3 (17–18).

8. "Wagnerianismus a Česká národní opera," *Hudební listy* 1 (1870): 5, 6, 8, 11, 12.

9. "O hudbě programní," *Dalibor* (1873): 35, 36, 37, 38, 41, 42, 43, 44, 47.

10. The most comprehensive study on Hostinský's work remains Miloš Jůzl, *Otakar Hostinský* (Prague: Melantrich, 1980), 46. For a brief sketch of the aesthetic debate on Czech opera in English, see Brian S. Locke, *Opera and Ideology in Prague* (Rochester, NY: Rochester University Press, 2006), 14–35.

11. See the detailed study by David Brodbeck on this topic, "Hanslick's Smetana and Hanslick's Prague," *Journal of the Royal Musical Association* 134, no. 1 (2009): 1–36.

12. Hostinský, *Das Musikalisch-Schöne und das Gesammtkunstwerk*, 9.

13. Ibid., 12–28. August Wilhelm Ambros, *Die Grenzen der Musik und Poesie: Eine Studie zur Ästhetik der Tonkunst* (Leipzig: H. Matthes, 1856, repr. 1872), is central to Hostinský's critique.

14. Hostinský, *Das Musikalisch-Schöne und das Gesammtkunstwerk*, 28.

15. Ibid., 29–30.

16. Ibid., 30–31.

17. See Geoffrey Payzant, "Hanslick und Zimmermann," in *Hanslick on the Musically Beautiful: Sixteen Lectures on the Musical Aesthetics of Eduard Hanslick* (Christchurch, NZ: Cybereditions, 2002), 129–42, especially 130–37.

18. See Wolfhart Henckmann, "Über die Grundzüge von Herbarts Ästhetik," in *Herbarts Kultursystem: Perspektiven der Transdisziplinarität im 19. Jahrhundert*, ed. Andreas Hoeschen and Lothar Schneider (Würzburg: Königshausen & Neumann, 2001), 231–58.

19. Robert Zimmermann, *Geschichte der Ästhetik als philosophischer Wissenschaft* (Wien: Braumüller, 1858; Repr. New York: Johnson, 1972); and *Allgemeine Ästhetik als Formwissenschaft* (Wien: Braumüller, 1865; repr. New York: Johnson, 1972).

20. On Zimmermann's *Wirkungsgeschichte*, see Lambert Wiesing, "Formale Ästhetik nach Herbart und Zimmermann," in *Herbarts Kultursystem*, ed. Hoeschen and Schneider, 283–96.

21. For Hostinský's publications on Herbart, see *Herbarts Ästhetik in ihren grundlegenden Teilen quellenmäßig dargestellt und erläutert* (Hamburg: Leopold Voss, 1891); and *Ueber die Bedeutung der praktischen Ideen Herbart's für die allgemeine Aesthetik* (Prague: Pr. řivnáŕČ, 1883 [first in Czech 1881]).

22. Hostinský, *Das Musikalisch-Schöne*, 5 and 8 respectively, as note 1. Hanslick's relationship to Herbartianism is a controversial topic and has been variously assessed. The most recent summary is in Christoph Landerer, *Eduard Hanslick und Bernard Bolzano: Ästhetisches Denken in Österreich in der Mitte des 19. Jahrhunderts* (Sankt Augustin: Academia, 2004), 11–22.

23. Along with Strauß's critical commentary in Dietmar Strauß, *Vom Musikalisch-Schönen: Ein Beitrag zur Revision der Ästhetik der Tonkunst*, vol. 2 (Mainz: Schott, 1990), see Schäfke, *Eduard Hanslick und die Musikästhetik*; and Dahlhaus, "Eduard Hanslick und der musikalische Formbegriff," *Musikforschung* 20 (1967): 145–53.

24. "Alles, was schön ist, . . . ist ein Zusammengesetztes. Das aber, wodurch dieses Zusammengesetzte auf unseren ästhetischen Geschmack wirkt, sind nicht seine einzelnen Elemente als solche, also sein 'Stoff,' sondern vielmehr die gegenseitigen Beziehungen und Verhältnisse dieser Elemente zu einander, also seine 'Form.'" Hostinský, *Das Musikalisch-Schöne*, 6–7.

25. Ibid., 7. Hostinský argues that it is at least conceivable that "musical tones . . . can be interpreted as symbols of feelings and impressions of thoughts."

26. "Wenn also Hanslick gegen die Bejahung dieser Frage [dass die musikalischen Töne Gedanken und Gefühle ausdrücken, somit zu einem wirklichen Sprachmittel werden] entschiedenen—jedenfalls berechtigten—Protest einlegt, so thut er dies offenbar nur im Namen der Psychologie, nicht aber im Namen der formalen Aesthetik. . . . Die formale Ästhetik lässt für ihre Zwecke das inhaltliche, das Culturmoment der Kunst bei Seite und fordert vor Allem Schönheit. Ihr gilt jede Kunstschöpfung für ästhetisch vollberechtigt, die eben ein Schönes ist, mag sie nun dies oder jenes—oder auch gar nichts—darstellen. Sie schreibt dem Künstler nicht vor, was er uns bieten soll, sondern verlangt nur, dass das, was er uns bietet, schöne Formen habe; den Stoff, den Gegenstand der Darstellung, berücksichtigt sie nur insofern, als er auf die ästhetische Gestaltung des Kunstwerkes selbst Einfluss übt, also nur in den speciellen Kunstlehren, dem angewandten Theile der Aesthetik." Ibid., 7–8.

27. In order to prevent misunderstandings, Hostinský specifies that aesthetic form is not identical to "the concept of art form," the specifically musical form (in the sense of a theory of form). See Hostinský, *Das Musikalisch-Schöne*, 13. Hostinský summarizes this aspect of formal aesthetics: "To meet its own needs, formal aesthetics leaves content, the cultural element of art, to one side and demands beauty above all. It legitimizes every artistic creation as fully qualified aesthetically, as long as it is beautiful whether it represents this or that—or nothing at all. It does not prescribe the artist what he should offer us, but requires only that what he offers has beautiful form; he considers the material, the object of representation, only in so far as it exerts an influence on the aesthetic organization of the artwork, that is, only in the special theory of art, the applied part of the aesthetic." Ibid., 155.

28. See Hostinský, *Das Musikalisch-Schöne und das Gesammtkunstwerk*, 32–57.

29. Hostinský is referring to the concept of a "Vereinigung aller Künste" in the Wagnerian sense, without using the Wagnerian term. *Kunstverein* was also often used after 1800 to designate liberal societies supporting ideas of modern art in Germany.

30. "The act in which the direct emanation of a feeling in tones can take place is not so much the fabrication as the reproduction of a musical work. That, philosophically speaking, the composed piece, regardless of whether it is performed or not, is the completed artwork ought not to keep us from giving consideration to the division of music into composition and reproduction, which is one of the most special features of our art, wherever this division contributes to our understanding of a musical phenomenon." Eduard Hanslick, *On the Musically Beautiful*, trans. Geoffrey Payzant (Indianapolis: Hackett, 1986), 48–49, hereafter referred to as *OMB*. Original German in *VMS*, 109.

31. Hostinský, *Das Musikalisch-Schöne und das Gesammtkunstwerk*, 68.

32. "Only once the final chord of a new composition has faded away in an actual performance has one the right to say the piece is absolutely 'complete' as an objective work of art." Ibid., 61.

33. "The whole, regardless of its complexity (it being a synthesis of the most disparate elements) should be understood as a perfect artistic unit, and only in this context can one recognize the sensuous present, i.e., the flawlessly performed drama as the complete work of art." "Das ganze wenn auch noch so complicirte, aus den buntesten Factoren zusammengesetzte Werk als eine vollkommen künstlerische Einheit aufzufassen bestrebt ist und im Zusammenhange damit auch erst das sinnlich gegenwärtige, d. h., tadellos aufgeführte Drama für das vollendete Kunstwerk ansieht." Hostinský, *Das Musikalisch-Schöne und das Gesammtkunstwerk*, 70–71.

34. Cited in Hostinský, *Das Musikalisch-Schöne und das Gesammtkunstwerk*, 71. The original is in chapter 2 of *Vom Musikalisch-Schönen*. The passage reads: "This is only for the reason that whatever can be asserted of instrumental music holds good for all music as such. If some general definition of music be sought, something by which to characterize its essence and its nature, to establish its boundaries and purpose, we are entitled to confine ourselves to instrumental music. Of what *instrumental music* cannot do, it ought never be said that *music* can do it, because only instrumental music is music purely and absolutely. Whether, for its value and effects, one prefers vocal or instrumental music, . . . one will always have to grant that the concept 'music' does not apply strictly to a piece of music composed to a verbal text. In a piece of vocal music, the effectiveness of tones can never be so precisely separated from that of words, action and ornamentation as to allow strict sorting of the musical from the poetical. Where it is a matter of the 'content' of music, we must reject even pieces with specific titles or programs. Union with poetry extends the power of music, but not its boundaries." *OMB*, 15–16; *VMS*, 52–53.

35. Hostinský, *Das Musikalisch-Schöne und das Gesammtkunstwerk*, 71.

36. Ibid., 74–75.

37. "In einem musikalischen Kunstwerk . . . liegen nur Formen und Verhältnisse vor, die von Tönen getragen werden; sie können mithin auch nicht anders beurtheilt werden, denn als *Tonformen, Tonverhältnisse*." Ibid., 51. (Emphasis in original.) See also 11.

38. "[Musik] ist einerseits eine architektonisch-formelle Kunst, andererseits eine Kunst poetischer Ideen—ja bis zu einer, weiterhin näher zu bestimmenden Grenze, gegebener Stoffe. Die architektonische Form und die poetische Idee müssen sich in ihr durchdringen—allerdings aber kann das eine oder das andere Element mehr oder minder entschieden vorwalten." Ambros, *Die Grenzen der Musik und Poesie*, 20. This translation is from Ambros, *The Boundaries of Music and Poetry: A Study in Musical Aesthetics*, trans. J. H. Cornell (New York: Schirmer, 1893), 20.

39. Hostinský, *Das Musikalisch-Schöne und das Gesammtkunstwerk*, 23.

40. Ibid., 45.

41. Ibid., 46.

42. Ibid.

43. Ibid., 47.

44. David E. Wellbery, "Stimmung," in *Ästhetische Grundbegriffe: Historisches Wörterbuch in sieben Bänden*, ed. Karlheinz Barck et al, vol. 5 (Stuttgart: J. B. Metzler, 2005), 703–33.

45. "Eine Vorstellung, die als einzeln und ohne Vergleichung mit anderen dennoch eine Zusammenstimmung zu den Bedingungen der Allgemeinheit hat, welche das Geschäft des Verstandes überhaupt ausmacht, bringt die Erkenntnisvermögen in die proportionierte Stimmung, die wir zu allem Erkenntnisse fordern, und daher auch für jedermann, der durch Verstand und Sinne in Verbindung zu urteilen bestimmt ist (für jeden Menschen), gültig halten." Immanuel Kant, *Kritik der Urteilskraft*, § 9, ed. Karl Vor-

länder (Hamburg: Felix Meiner, 1924), 57–58. This translation taken from Kant, *Critique of Judgment*, trans. Werner S. Pluhar (Indianapolis: Hackett, 1987), 63–64.

46. For a detailed analysis of the Kantian use of the metaphor of *Stimmung*, see Wellbery, "Stimmung," 707–10.

47. G. W. F. Hegel, *Vorlesungen über die Ästhetik*, ed. Hermann Glockner, vol. 14 (Stuttgart: F. Frommann, 1927), 424.

48. Wellbery, "Stimmung," 714–15.

49. Ibid., 715.

50. Hostinský, *Das Musikalisch-Schöne und das Gesammtkunstwerk*, 47.

51. Ibid., 24.

52. Ibid., 26.

53. Ibid., 56. Hostinský speaks in this context of the "subjective impression of the objective artwork itself."

54. Following Herbart, Hostinský characterizes "purity of style" as a "rule of art" and writes: "Each art must, above all, retain the rigor and purity of its style." Ibid., 2.

55. Ibid., 76.

56. In his introduction to the term *Gesammtkunstwerk*, Hostinský refers to the fact that he uses the word in the "simplest manner and with no ulterior motive." For a history of the term, see Dieter Borchmeyer, "Gesamtkunstwerk," in *Die Musik in Geschichte und Gegenwart*, 2nd ed., Sachteil (Kassel: Bärenreiter, 1994–99), Col. 1282–89.

57. Hostinský, *Das Musikalisch-Schöne und das Gesammtkunstwerk*, 77; Robert Zimmermann, *Studien und Kritiken zur Philosophie und Aesthetik*, Bd. I: *Zur Philosophie* (Vienna: Wilhelm Braumüller, 1870), 245.

58. Hostinský, *Das Musikalisch-Schöne und das Gesammtkunstwerk*, 81; See also 111–21 for a detailed discussion of this in relation to poetics and music.

59. Ibid., 81; for a detailed discussion of this in relation to poetics and music, see ibid., 121–28.

60. Ibid., 89; see 128–37 for a detailed discussion of this in relation to poetics and music. See also Bujic, *Music in European Thought*, where he writes that "unity of mood of music and poetry is what is primarily meant by 'dramatic expression' in the *Gesamtkunstwerk*," 140.

61. Gotthold Ephraim Lessing, "Laokoon: oder über die Grenzen der Malerei und Poesie" [Berlin, 1766], in *Werke*, Bd. 6, *Kunsttheoretische und kunsthistorische Schriften* (Munich: Carl Hanser, 1974), 7–187.

62. Hostinský, *Das Musikalisch-Schöne und das Gesammtkunstwerk*, 85.

63. Ibid., 88.

64. "It is not the 'poetic content' of the music with which the poetic content of the text must agree. . . . That is completely impossible, because music has no such 'content,' and thus cannot enter into an aesthetic relationship with the poetic content of a poem; furthermore as Hanslick aptly remarks, the union with poetry can certainly 'extend the power of music, but not its boundaries.' The harmony of word and music in this regard is, strictly speaking, not aesthetic, but rather a psychological rule of art, albeit a no less relevant one." Hostinský, *Das Musikalisch-Schöne und das Gesammtkunstwerk*, 79–80.

65. "Derjenige Affect, welchen das Werk durch seine eigenen, inneren ästhetischen Verhältnisse erregen kann, ist ihm nicht zu missgönnen; auch nicht das Zusammentreffen des Ausdrucks, wo verschiedene Künste zusammenwirken, und sich gleichsam gegenseitig beleuchten. . . . Die Einheit eines Kunstwerkes ist nur selten eine ästhetische Einheit; und man würde in sehr falsche Speculationen gerathen, wenn man sie

allgemein dafür halten wollte." Johann Friedrich Herbart, *Schriften zur Einleitung in die Philosophie*, ed. Gustav Hartenstein (Leipzig: Leopold Voss, 1850), 164.

66. "Each work of art consists of a larger or smaller quantity of individual elementary *relationships*, to which just as many aesthetic *judgments* correspond. Each of these judgments [of the elementary *relationships*] however, is completely independent and remains independent of the rest; because each one is equally original and unmediated, none *more or less worthy* than the other, all are equally justified, and thus *any kind of* ranking *according to* aesthetic *relationships* and judgments is to be rejected from a purely aesthetic standpoint." [Jedes dieser Urteile [über die elementaren Verhältnisse] ist aber ganz selbständig und von den übrigen unabhängig; denn jedes ist eben ursprünglich und unmittelbar, keines höher oder niedriger, als ein anderes, alle sind gleich berechtigt, eine wie immer geartete Rangordnung unter den ästhetischen Verhältnissen und Urtheilen ist daher vom rein ästhetischen Standpuncte aus zu verwerfen.] Hostinský, *Das Musikalisch-Schöne und das Gesammtkunstwerk*, 90–91.

67. "The poetic basis, the text, is relatively speaking the most independent, because here the form grows directly out of the specific content of the art." Hostinský, *Das Musikalisch-Schöne und das Gesammtkunstwerk*, 98.

68. Ibid., 78.

69. Kant, *Kritik der Urteilskraft*, § 16, 70. The translated Kant excerpts are from Kant, *Critique of Judgment*, trans. Pluhar, 76.

70. Ibid., § 16, 69; this translation modified from Kant, *Critique of Judgment*, trans. Pluhar, 76.

71. Kant, *Kritik der Urteilskraft*, § 16, 69, Pluhar, 76.

72. Hanslick considers *Stimmung*, a term he rarely uses, to be a subcategory of *Gefühl*. At the same time, he deplores the vague use of the terms *Gefühl*, *Stimmung*, *Affekt*: "Without separating 'feeling' [*Gefühl*] from 'sensation' [*Empfindung*], we cannot investigate the varieties of the former: sensuous and intellectual feelings, with their chronic manifestation in temperament and their acute manifestations in affect, preference, and passion . . . are indiscriminately flung together, and music is declared to be the art that arouses feeling." *OMB*, 5; *VMS*, 29–30. Later, *musikalische Stimmung* is named as an instance that guarantees the organic unity of a multimovement composition: "It is the unity of musical impression [*musikalische Stimmung*] which characterizes the four movements of a sonata as organically unified, not the connection with objects thought of by a composer." *OMB*, 37; *VMS*, 89.

73. Hostinský, *Das Musikalisch-Schöne und das Gesammtkunstwerk*, 143. Hostinský refers to Wagner's famous dictum, "Der Irrtum in dem Kunstgenre Oper bestand darin, daß ein Mittel des Ausdruckes (die Musik) zum Zwecke, der Zweck des Ausdruckes (das Drama) aber zum Mittel gemacht war." Richard Wagner, *Oper und Drama*, Einleitung, in *Gesammelte Schriften und Dichtungen*, vol. 3, ed. Wolfgang Golther (Berlin: Deutsches Verlagshaus Bong, 1913), 231.

74. Hostinský, *Das Musikalisch-Schöne und das Gesammtkunstwerk*, 100.

75. Ibid., 143. This theoretical distinction leads Hostinský in the last instance to follow Hanslick's description of orchestral music in the *Gesamtkunstwerk* as "an accessory [and] decorative," as something that ceases "to have an effect as pure art." Ibid., 146.

76. Hostinský's main work on aesthetics was edited posthumously from his unpublished papers. See *Otakara Hostinského Esthetika I*, ed. Zdeněk Nejedlý (Prague: J. Laichter, 1921).

77. Martin Heidegger, *Sein und Zeit*, 16th ed. (Tübingen: Max Niemeyer, 1986).

Part Two

Liberalism and Societal Order

Chapter Five

Hanslick on Johann Strauss Jr.

Genre, Social Class, and Liberalism in Vienna

Dana Gooley

In his review of Johann Strauss Jr.'s 1881 operetta *Der lustige Krieg*, Hanslick critiqued the current state of Viennese operetta as follows: "This is what makes most of our Viennese operettas so intolerable: they earnestly ape Verdi and Meyerbeer. Your Sepperl and Leni sing like Raoul and Valentine, so that every squabble at the inn becomes a St. Bartholomew's Night. At any moment, naturally, the composer can leap down from his tragic throne into the most trivial yodeling; Raoul and Valentine get transformed back into Sepperl and Leni, the Huguenots into tailor's apprentices; and the rest of us get seasick from this miserable swinging back and forth."[1] Hanslick's comment tightly binds aesthetic and social categories: the aesthetic problem of Viennese operetta is a mismatch of musical registers—the importation of the grand dramatic manner of French *grand opéra* (here indexed by Meyerbeer's *Les Huguenots*) into the light, naïve, conversational atmosphere of *Singspiel*. Such blending of registers gives rise to a grotesque stage spectacle: the rapid metamorphosis of characters of low social status—simple unpretentious folk like "Leni and Sepperl"—into heroic and highborn characters like Raoul and Valentine. Hanslick's discomfort with the mixing of high and low musical genres goes hand in hand with social commentary. Musical and theatrical genres ought to stay true to their "natural," established boundaries and limits. When they don't, they might give over to the disorienting, perhaps even nausea-inducing spectacle of social mobility, where peasants become noblemen overnight, and vice versa. The good news, in this rather bleak assessment of Viennese operetta, is that at least one composer avoids the trap: "Strauss avoids (a few fleeting moments excepted) dragging the pathetic style of grand opera into the *Singspiel*."[2]

In this essay I explore this overlap between genre and social hierarchy in Hanslick's reviews and essays on the music and operettas of Johann Strauss Jr. (Strauss II), and consider their relation to the culture and politics of liberalism. In many writings Hanslick shows a drive to categorize, arrange, and sort the phenomena he discusses into orderly sequences, series or hierarchies. When surveying a composer's œuvre or a historical period, for example, he tends to break down the whole into components—genres, phases of development, style periods, institutions, etc.—and then rank their relative importance or aesthetic quality. This tendency stems not from some suspicious mania for taxonomy or analytic control, but from a desire to diversify the criteria that are invoked in acts of aesthetic judgment, rather than dogmatically apply a single set of criteria that would have relevance for all musical phenomena. A musical work, Hanslick appears to believe, should be judged not by artificially imposed external criteria, but by the criteria of the class of things to which it appears to belong. He demands that musical works clearly invoke the genre to which they belong, because without such reference points, aesthetic judgment is impossible. That, anyway, is the philosophical justification. But Hanslick's references to genre in his criticism are also suffused with an almost moralistic tone. He suggests that genres represent a "natural" sorting or sifting of music into distinct types; that each musical work ought to respect and behave in accordance with its generic boundaries; and that the moment a work calls forth criteria from another genre it ceases, in a sense, to be true to itself. This conception of genre, articulated with remarkable consistency in his critical œuvre, reveals its social, ethical, and political subtexts when Hanslick extends it to composers, performers, and stage characters. He demands that these figures respect their natural boundaries and behave in a way that is "true" to their given constitution or temperament.

To Hanslick, who was accustomed to defending the integrity and separateness of genres, the music and career of Johann Strauss Jr. provided a unique confrontation and challenge. Not only did the younger Strauss expand the boundaries of the waltz and polka forms he inherited from his father's generation, and "cross over" into concert hall music, but after 1870 he abandoned the dance orchestra milieu altogether and initiated a productive career as an operetta composer. Strauss's stylistic evolution enacted a socially loaded "upward" move from the world of *volkstümlich* music to the more prestigious world of operetta. Moreover, operetta was a "modern" genre, having made its way from Paris to Vienna in the late 1850s and 1860s by way of Offenbach, and its conventions were in flux in the 1860s and 1870s. Hanslick watched the genre closely as its history unfolded, sometimes policing its "proper" boundaries, at other times welcoming their expansion. While he was generally positive about Offenbach, his views on Strauss were more ambivalent. Hanslick was sensitive to a certain unmediated duality in Strauss's operettas: on the one side, the familiar melodiousness and melodic charm of the Viennese dances, on the other, the witty, conversational tone of comic opera as derived from Offenbach (and to a lesser degree Lortzing and Suppé). Unlike Offenbach's works, Strauss's operettas pulled the spectator in two different directions, putting the warm, nostalgic feeling of Viennese dances side by side with the ironic, satirical, sometimes cynical tone of Offenbach's Paris. Hanslick questioned whether the symmetrical, self-enclosed phrasings of Viennese dance music could be developed into a convincing musico-dramatic language, and he critiqued Strauss with this problem in mind.

The social subtext of this aesthetic question was the relationship of the middle and lower classes to the bourgeois elite in the "golden age" of Viennese political liberalism, the 1860s and 1870s. Recent studies by Margaret Notley, David Brodbeck, and Kevin C. Karnes have demonstrated that Hanslick's intellectual perspective was strongly allied with post-1848 liberalism, a perspective characterized by optimism, support for free economic enterprise, devotion to the leadership of educated elites, faith in rational governance, and a commitment to free expression in the public sphere.[3] Political liberalism arrived at a peak in the 1860s with the establishment of a constitution, and gradually lost its parliamentary power through a series of challenges and setbacks starting with the stock market crash of 1873. The decline of parliamentary influence, however, did not kill off liberalism as a force in Viennese politics and society. Liberal assumptions and practices had already become deeply sedimented in Vienna's political and cultural life. Historian Pieter Judson has articulated this point most forcefully in a series of revisionist studies. Challenging Carl Schorske's influential narrative of liberal "crisis" and "decline" toward the fin de siècle, Judson argues that "if the liberals lost several battles to preserve their political predominance, they may have won the war in their efforts to maintain a political culture based on much of their world view."[4]

Liberals like Hanslick aspired to educate and elevate, through culture and schooling, the *Volk* whose social position had remained so static during *Vormärz*. They wanted to integrate into the public sphere the social classes that had been excluded from political participation under absolutist rule. Strauss's operettas promised to emblematize the social progress of the people by audibly incorporating folk culture—the sounds of the waltz and polka—and giving it expression on the public theater stage. The refraction of Viennese folk music through the opera stage would demonstrate that Austrian society had made room in its public sphere for the voice of the people(s). Through operetta the formerly disenfranchised populace might actually gather up consciousness of, and celebrate, its own evolution under political liberalism.

Social and political ideas of this sort infiltrate Hanslick's commentary on Strauss as an operetta composer. He is particularly attuned to the question whether Strauss had truly transcended his dance music roots and mastered the more "elevated" art of dramatic composition. Yet Hanslick's views on Strauss are not consistent. He sometimes supports the composer's impulse to extend generic boundaries, but at other times insists that the composer stay within traditional generic boundaries. Around 1850 he is skeptical about the younger Strauss's pretentions to transcend the dance-music sphere, and this skepticism filters into his response to the first operettas. But in the mid-1880s Hanslick changes his tack and writes an essay warmly celebrating Strauss's crossover to the operetta stage. Toward the end of the century, as Wagnerism gains influence over composers and audiences, Hanslick reverts to an image of Strauss as an icon of Viennese *Volkstümlichkeit*. Hanslick's shifts of position on the operetta genre, transmitted to the liberal readership of the *Neue Freie Presse*, reflect the shifting grounds of the liberal perspective as it negotiated various challenges: neoabsolutism, the "downward" expansion of the urban middle classes, and the antiliberal opposition parties that came to the fore in the 1880s and 1890s.

The Rule of "Natural" Boundaries

Long before Strauss Jr. turned to the composition of operetta, Hanslick had voiced positions on Viennese dance music that brought questions of generic boundaries to the fore. In the aftermath of the ultimately unsuccessful revolution of 1848, whose reforms he openly supported, Hanslick published two articles concerning dance music: (1) an obituary of Johann Strauss Sr. (1849); and (2) a review article on the dance music of the sons of Lanner and Strauss (1850). Together these articles make two major points that are difficult to reconcile, and point to a curious ambiguity in the waltz as a genre. First, Hanslick eloquently defends the Viennese waltz against detractors. In the obituary of Strauss I (1849) he describes the waltz as "a genre that composers and critics usually look down on with sovereign condescension."[5] In the 1850 essay on the children of Strauss I and Lanner, he chides Eduard Krüger, a writer associated with Leipzig's *Neue Zeitschrift für Musik*, for dismissing the dance music of the present as evidence of musical decline. In favor of the waltz, Hanslick points out that genius manifests itself in small forms as well as large, and that the quality of a musical work depends more on "how" it is handled than "what" is handled. In a phrase bearing an interesting trace of neoabsolutist ideology, he writes, "Great talent also moves in small forms, and it is especially this—the divine radiance—before which we bow."[6] In addition to this note of Christian egalitarianism, Hanslick introduces an idea that will remain constant through all his future commentary on the Viennese waltz: its embodiment of a distinctive Austrian sensibility with a *volkstümlich* color: "It has always been Vienna where dance music was cultivated with the most brilliant talent. No European capital can hold its own with the Austrian one in this domain. Though undoubtedly a subordinate genre, Vienna can indeed claim to have represented it at its most perfect."[7]

With the qualifying phrase "undoubtedly a subordinate genre," Hanslick reinstates a hierarchy of value, and thus oddly undermines his defense of the Viennese waltz. In the very course of asserting the "equality" of small and large forms and the international stature of the waltz, he demotes it to a lower, secondary rank. This is no accidental slip, for he does something similar in the Strauss I obituary: "From a purely artistic standpoint dance music appears nevertheless to be of subordinate rank."⁸ The second-rate status of this music, in Hanslick's view, is a consequence of its integral tie to the dance function, which excludes it from the "higher" realm of the aesthetic. Hanslick credits Strauss I with initiating (but not completing) the emancipation of the waltz from its functionality through an intensification of "aesthetic" qualities. Strauss's themes possess "an often striking autonomy and *potential for* further development . . . a premonition of that higher shaping of the waltz form."⁹ But what Strauss I initiates, or anticipates, fails to reach its potential. His well-invented melodies lack the form that would bring them to full realization. The serial, potpourri-like form, where one melody or motif succeeds another without development, inhibits the progress of the genre: "The present form of waltz music presents a great obstacle to its artistic development and to every composer who brings to it a better endowment of talent or knowledge."¹⁰ Hanslick devotes a remarkable amount of space to this issue, hoping that eventually "the most appropriate form would emerge, at best an expanded rondo form, or a two-part form with both parts repeated and a coda."¹¹ Hanslick's message on Johann Strauss I, then, is a mixed one: on the one hand, the waltz music merits full admiration for its invention, charm, and authentic expression of Viennese *volkstümlich* spirit; but on the other, the waltz's strict, unrevised formal boundaries inhibit its entry into "higher" music. The waltz is simultaneously better than most critics think, and not good enough. It is beautiful in its naïveté, but too naïve for "higher" beauty.

This contradiction replays, at the level of aesthetic discourse, a basic problem in the liberal political ideology that Hanslick absorbed and espoused—namely, its ambivalent stance toward the lower social orders: the *Kleinbürgertum*, laborers, and peasantry. Pre-1840 liberalism in Vienna had been concerned primarily with restraining monarchical power, and had relied on an imagined unity of interests among the various middle classes and lower classes. In liberalism's "second phase," from 1840 to 1870, the disunity of the people it claimed to represent began to show. The upper strata of the middle classes, the *Bildungsbürger* and *Wirtschaftsbürger*, came into a closer alliance with one another and took increasing distance from the *Kleinbürgertum*.¹² The political sympathies of the lower classes departed from liberalism and gravitated toward radical democracy and socialism, the main agents of revolution in 1848–49.¹³ As a defense against this fracture, liberals relied on rhetoric that included the lower classes in the concept of "civil society," while simultaneously implying that those classes should submit to the "natural" leadership of the elite, educated bourgeoisie. The liberal ideal was to harmonize bourgeois society by elevating the lower orders both politically and aesthetically (through art and *Bildung*). Hanslick demands something similar of the Viennese waltz after Strauss I: it should transcend its *volkstümlich* frame, whose static form entraps its potential, and elevate itself to an autonomous, "higher" order emancipated from its functionality. Recall that, in Hanslick's view, Strauss I's music already bears the seeds of an impetus to advance aesthetically, but lacks the necessary formal means. This idea parallels the liberal elite's conception of its own role in civil society: a handmaiden to the social and political emancipation of the people, not an "imposition" from above. Through its superior vision and insight, the liberal elite makes the lower classes conscious of their own aspirations and destiny. Hanslick's prescriptions for the formal development of the waltz are offered in precisely this spirit. The aspiration of liberals to unify the social divisions within the middle classes, however, proved unrealistic, for as Kocka puts it, "in order to take part in the game of culture and to obey its rules, such conditions had to be fulfilled which were beyond the reach of the majority.... The bourgeois status of most of the petty bourgeoisie was highly precarious and questionable."[14]

Because dance music is closely tied to social life, Hanslick's aesthetic critique of the waltz exposes its social correlates. In his obituary of Strauss I, for example, he celebrates the composer's significance for the ballroom culture and for youthful courtship. But he immediately proceeds to distance himself from that world: "If there were nothing further to praise, Strauss's passing would concern only the dance world, *whose advocate I can hardly say I felt summoned to become.* To the musician, Strauss would only have significance if his dances, divorced from their function—that is, outside the ballroom—possessed sufficient content to create musical interest."[15] This strong dichotomy between the musician's interest in the waltz and the dancer's interest in the same is made entirely at the expense of the dancer. Hanslick's eagerness to mark his distance from the culture of the ballroom, with the condescending joke about his inability to become its "advocate" (*Anwalt*), subtly exposes the issue of social class. The word *Anwalt* most commonly meant "lawyer"—a member of the same class, the *Bildungsbürgertum*, to which Hanslick belonged as a university-educated civil servant and writer. As a music critic—an aesthetic "judge"—Hanslick has no desire to defend the world of danced waltzes, which he will leave to the lower social orders.

A similar logic informs the passing reference to the waltz in *Vom Musikalisch-Schönen* (1854): "J. Strauss [I] set down charming, even inspired music in his better waltzes—it ceases to be brilliant the moment they are merely danced to in time."[16] The larger context of this passage is relevant to the social subtext. It comes from chapter 5, "Musical Perception: Aesthetic Versus Elemental," where Hanslick distinguishes between "aesthetic" and "elementary" listening. "Aesthetic" listening is active and contemplative, whereas "elementary" listening is passive and physical. Hanslick explicitly associates the "elementary" response with the layman and the "aesthetic" response with the educated artist. His proposal that "elementary" response to a Strauss waltz automatically shuts down "aesthetic" response suggests an insurmountable boundary between the sensibilities of the layperson and that of the educated person (or at least a rejection of the layperson's relation to music). It is all the more striking that, as Bernd Sponheuer has shown, the converse does not hold true in *Vom Musikalisch-Schönen*: although the dancer is incapable of hearing the waltz aesthetically, the educated listener *does* reap the sensual benefits of "elementary" response alongside his "aesthetic" response, as though the aesthetic redeems the elementary.[17]

While the main point of the Strauss I obituary is that composers need to expand the traditional waltz form, Hanslick's review of waltzes by Strauss II, published less than a year later, censures the son for expanding too far. Hanslick recognizes Strauss II as the fully legitimate inheritor of his father's talent and legacy, but criticizes recent compositions where the son uses modern compositional techniques—advanced harmonies, instrumentation, and above all, elements of dramatic or contrasting pathos—that transgress the proper boundaries of the waltz genre. Hanslick is especially emphatic about the importation of compositional techniques from genres such as opera and symphony: "An art-genre is enriched neither in form nor content when a pathos is forced on it that contradicts its essence."[18] The essence referred to here is the overarching cheerful tone of the traditional waltz, which apparently can tolerate no contradiction or dialectical complement. By introducing passages in a contrasting serious tone, the younger Strauss seems to be forcing the genre, and the audience cannot respond with "the healthy cheers that sound when a waltz by the old Strauss or Lanner is heard."[19] Strauss II was clearly treating the genre progressively, but not according to Hanslick's standard of progress. Thus his injunction to the young composer: "I cannot suppress the wish that the best waltz composer of the present might abandon this false path, which he may be pursuing only momentarily."[20]

Hanslick's attitude toward Strauss II in this article might be described as quietistic: it favors gradual progress within established channels and invalidates progress achieved through the experimental, "revolutionary" infringement of traditional boundaries. Published in 1850, the article may reflect the chastened tone of liberalism of the years immediately after 1849, which had to make accommodations to "neoabsolutist" reaction. In light of the failure of revolutionary strategy, which had sought a radical overturning of class hierarchies, a liberal reaffirmation of the "naturalness" of social boundaries seemed in order. Indeed, Hanslick concluded his article with a stern, almost antirevolutionary message: "Therefore let each keep to his pure limits and avoid dragging things in from foreign places: to the educated sense for beauty, the polka-izing of opera style and the hero-ification of dance music stand on the same level."[21] Hanslick, the *Bildungsbürger* in possession of an "educated sense of beauty," claims insight into the destiny of the waltz genre that Strauss II (less musically educated) cannot see, and he appoints himself to the task of guiding the genre along its correct evolutionary path.

Operetta: Elevating the Waltz

Hanslick was still watching carefully for the proper observance of generic boundaries twenty-one years later, when Strauss's first operetta, *Indigo*, had its première (1871). As he knew well, Strauss's move to operetta was part of a gradual evolution that began with his freer treatment of the traditional waltz, continued with his increasing devotion to concert performances, and culminated in performances at the *Gesellschaft der Musikfreunde,* Vienna's home for symphonic music and oratorios, in 1869–70.[22] Strauss's transition to the still more public sphere of operetta with *Indigo* was one Hanslick looked upon with some trepidation: "I openly admit to the worry with which I awaited Strauss's first opera. A painter of still-life and genre pictures who suddenly becomes a history painter, or a poet-specialist in epigrams or sonnets who attempts a drama, could scarcely have a rougher transition or more unfavorable situation."[23] Hanslick's ultimate judgment of *Indigo* was similar to that of the next two operettas, *Der Karneval in Rom* (1873) and *Die Fledermaus* (1874), and he compiled the three reviews in an essay, "Johann Strauss Jr. als Opernkomponist" (ca. 1875). Here Hanslick judges Strauss's music to be uniformly inventive and fresh. In the case of *Indigo*, he even credits the music with rescuing a poor libretto. But the libretti are judged miserable, and Hanslick highlights a basic mismatch between Strauss's talent and the dramatic genre. Of the three operettas, Hanslick prefers *Indigo* because it includes the longest stretches of uninterrupted dance music, where Strauss (he argues) is most at home. He expresses his relief at Strauss's compositional modesty with a revealing social metaphor: "Strauss deserves the most honest praise for not imitating either Wagner or Meyerbeer, not seeking to stretch out artistically with fussy modulations and dissonances but rather treating things as *a naturally feeling, good musical person of proper middle-size.*"[24] Hanslick adds that Strauss's early operettas, considered as dramatic music, offer very little of interest, and pale beside the theatrical flair of Offenbach and Lecoq: "Thus we see in the three Strauss operettas an unquestionably brilliant talent outside his proper sphere."[25] Hanslick concludes that the true measure of Strauss's talent is his dance music, and encourages readers to look there for the composer's real ability. This judgment, sending Strauss back home where he belongs, might be expected from the critic who had earlier tried to talk Strauss out of writing more complex waltzes and polkas.

Hanslick's reserved opinion of Strauss's early theater works was not a consequence of any snobbish bias against operetta as a genre. On the contrary, he took a keen interest in operetta from the moment Offenbach's work penetrated into Vienna's theater culture in the late 1850s. His perspective on Offenbach and the operetta genre, articulated in a retrospective essay published shortly after the composer's death, centers on the question of genre and its limits. French operetta, in his view, emerged as a reaction to the *opéra comique* of the 1850s, which was slowly gravitating toward the scale and pomp of *grand opéra*. Offenbach developed the small-scale operetta to preserve, in undiluted form, the dialogic pace and satiric bite that were getting stamped out of the *opéra comique* genre: "To the musical tragedy and the higher musical comedy, Offenbach added a third, well-justified category: the musical farce."[26] Hanslick felt that Offenbach's short farces of the 1850s, as contrasted with the larger-scale works of the 1860s and 1870s, represented the best in Offenbach because they were firmly devoted to a clearly bounded aesthetic tone of humor and wit. Although Offenbach's musical language was modern, the satirical impetus was traditional, established, and "true," thus preferable to self-conscious, "modern" mixtures of the pathetic and farcical. The moment Offenbach introduced strains of pathos, Hanslick felt, he strained the basic cheerful tone of the genre and crossed a boundary: "It was always at his expense that Offenbach left his most personal domain."[27] Hanslick does not chastise Offenbach for submitting to the demand for more expanded and developed multi-act operettas in the 1860s. But he argues that these larger works "sacrifice the earlier simplicity, more or less, to become partly frivolous-grotesque, partly puffed-up stories."[28] With both Offenbach and Strauss II, then, Hanslick demands operettas that stay true to their "low" social register by using simple means, sustaining an atmosphere of good cheer, and resisting the diluting influence of grand opera gestures. He demands this partly on aesthetic grounds, partly on the basis of what he considers the composer's "natural" temperament, which should not be forced against itself.

Ten years after his not-very-positive assessment of Strauss's three early operettas, Hanslick had quite dramatically changed his opinion, and wrote about it in an essay on the Strauss *Jubiläum* of 1884—the fortieth anniversary of Strauss II's dance orchestra. The laudatory tone of this essay can be attributed in part to the festivity of the occasion, but the *Jubiläum* essay also offers a significant shift in argumentation and perspective. Over the course of the intervening decade, Strauss had written five new operettas, in which Hanslick detected considerable progress in the handling of the through-composed elements of dramatic composition. Strauss's librettists, moreover, were providing better material, notably in *Der lustige Krieg* (1881). The *Jubiläum* essay begins with a paean to Strauss I, Lanner, and the traditional Viennese waltz, a genre he firmly equates with the Austrian land and the spirit of its people. But instead of presenting Strauss II as heir to and continuer of the waltz tradition, as he had ca. 1849–50, Hanslick now emphasizes a break with the past. The world of *Alt-Wien*, where the waltz bloomed, was on the wane: "The time of childish pleasure was over with the events of the year 1848. . . . Gone, gone forever! Let us not be deceived, even the waltz period in Vienna is dying out."[29] But this was no occasion for nostalgia, for the young Strauss had transformed the traditional material with his operettas: "In his operettas the irresistible dance composer is given back to us renewed and rejuvenated. This is where we see the son far outstripping the father: in the elevation to a higher, much more ambitious sphere of art."[30] The technical advances to the waltzes that Hanslick earlier censured are here reappraised as the product of a necessary evolution: "That he abandoned the father's musical simplicity, greatly extended rhythmic periods as well as individual waltz sections, and gradually emphasized the piquant and complex in harmonization and orchestration—these things lie in the passing of time."³¹ The *Jubiläum* essay thus establishes Strauss II as an icon of gradual, unforced progress, and of the successful crossover from dance music to light opera. The younger Strauss inherits his father's musical vocabulary without overturning it in a spirit of "revolution." With operettas he evolves the waltz out of its static, *volkstümlich* limitations and elevates it to the stage, where the public can see its own reflection and admire its own presence in the public sphere.

Hanslick's change of perspective in the *Jubiläum* essay is informed by the ideology and optimism of Viennese liberalism. The political subtext emerges with rare transparency in a single phrase: "Fortunately Strauss did not completely abdicate as 'King of the Waltz' when he laid down his conductor's baton about fourteen years ago [i.e., the year *Indigo* was premièred]; he only extended his kingdom and limited the triple meter with a constitution."³² With the metaphor of the constitution that productively restrains power, Hanslick invokes the great political achievement of *Nachmärz* liberalism: the constitution established in 1862 to limit the powers of the Austrian monarch, itself only one step toward the climax of "high liberalism" in the years 1867–74.³³ Hanslick's sympathy with the high liberal cause had found pronounced expression in his *Geschichte des Concertwesens in Wien* of 1869. The *Geschichte* draws a stark contrast between pre-1848 and post-1848 political conditions, and links these conditions directly to their aesthetic counterparts. The year 1848, he wrote, marks the "boundary between old and new Austria—not only in political and social terms, but also with respect to literary and artistic life."³⁴ The political dispossession of the people in *Vormärz* had its counterpart in the relative lack of distinguished music or of serious musical attitude, and perhaps also in the stagnant evolution of the waltz genre.³⁵ Strauss II's successful crossover to operetta, Hanslick wrote in the *Jubiläum* essay, symbolized the transcendence of the *Vormärz* past that Hanslick had so openly celebrated in the *Geschichte*: "Our Johann Strauss marks music history as the only professional waltz composer to turn to dramatic music after years of uninterrupted activity as a ball conductor.... Old Strauss and Lanner would never have dared to dream of such an advancement [*Avancement*]."³⁶ Strauss's operettas were distinctively Viennese, sophisticated, and popular. More than contemporary symphonies, which lacked popularity, they could convincingly be presented as aesthetic manifestations of liberal political achievement.³⁷

Reclaiming Simplicity: The Threat of Wagnerism

Toward the end of the century, as Strauss continued to feed the demand for new operettas, Hanslick's enthusiasm for the composer's "progress" cooled down, and he began accenting the virtues of Strauss's authentic "folk" tone.

Part of the problem was that Strauss, like other composers of operetta and comic opera, was coming under the influence of Wagnerian music drama, an influence Hanslick rarely viewed positively (although he did sometimes say positive things about Wagner's music). Hanslick always preferred comic theater in its undiluted form, with no admixture of pathos, melancholy, or grandeur. It was this that made him prefer early Offenbach to later Offenbach, and to criticize sharply the act 2 finale of Strauss's *Zigeunerbaron*, with its unexpectedly dark turn of events. In the 1860s and 1870s, the greatest threats to the "purity" of operetta were the conventions of French *opéra comique* and *grand opéra*—the Lenis and Sepperls singing like Raoul and Valentine, as mentioned earlier. But by the later 1880s and 1890s, as Camille Crittenden has shown, Wagnerian influence had become pervasive enough in Vienna to pose a new threat, and Hanslick began shoring up the boundaries of operetta against "progressive" compositional trends.[38] In 1898 he praised Richard Heuberger's *Der Opernball* because its composer "completely fulfilled his goal . . . inasmuch as he held this goal always before him: keeping the boundaries of the true Viennese operetta pure. Heuberger lapsed into neither of the most popular mistakes around here: one is called false pathos and the other unfeigned commonness."[39] Around 1900 Hanslick increasingly championed the simplicity and unpretentious naïveté of *Vormärz* genres as benchmarks for comic opera. He greeted the revival of comic operas by Lortzing and Haydn with open arms: "We would not and cannot do without Lortzing today; though no great master, he is the last naïve opera composer among Germans"; the style of these antiquated comic operas provides "welcome refreshment after the outrages of the Nibelung's song and the Iliad."[40] The Illiad reference alludes to Goldmark's opera *Achilles*, which Hanslick had recently seen and criticized for its Wagnerism.[41]

This late-century reclamation of comic purity also shapes Hanslick's views on later operettas of Strauss II. The clearest examples of Wagnerian infiltration in Strauss were *Simplicius* (1887), with its unmistakably Wagnerian libretto, and *Ritter Pásmán* (1892), Strauss's one and only *opéra comique*. In the *Ritter Pásmán* review, Hanslick congratulates the composer for negotiating with success the "upward" transition from operetta to *opéra comique*, but then qualifies his praise: "Who would have guessed Strauss could do it! Nevertheless, in my opinion the older form of comic opera, with spoken dialogue (as in Lortzing) or light recitatives supporting the conversational tone (as in Flotow) is the most suited of all to his unique talent, preserved for so many years in steady, even practice. . . . What we miss is our dear old Johann Strauss."[42] Hanslick follows this nostalgic comment with an unusual request: since the best music in *Ritter Pásmán* is the ballet music, Strauss should compose a complete ballet for the Viennese public. A ballet from Strauss would be most appropriate because "he is from the inside, and in his entire being, an 'absolute' musician, i.e., his musical imagination is not at home when tied to words."

This yearning for a simpler, nonoperatic Strauss marks a dramatic reversal of the position Hanslick had taken in the *Jubiläum* essay of 1884. While that essay had celebrated Strauss's progress from ballroom to concert hall to theater, Hanslick now balks at Strauss's "progress" from operetta to *opéra comique*. Indeed, by insisting on Strauss as fundamentally an "absolute" musician, he retracts his earlier validation of the composer's transition to operetta. In the *Jubiläum* essay Hanslick had dismissed *Vormärz* waltzes as "childish pleasures" (his words) of a superseded past. Now he asks Strauss to return to those *Vormärz* conventions—to the folksy tone and modesty of Flotow and Lortzing. In the optimism of the *Jubiläum*, Hanslick had been able to praise Strauss for embracing modern musical elements "without turning back to the paradisiacal innocence of our *Vormärz* composers, *which is gone forever*."[43] Now, in the presence of the Wagnerian threat, he hopes Strauss will revisit that paradise.

Hanslick's cooler attitude toward Strauss in the 1890s, and the more polemical, anti-Wagnerian framework of the discussion, betrays a loss of the confidence he had shown in the *Jubiläum* essay. This may reflect the more splintered and defensive character of liberalism as it evolved in the 1880s and 1890s. The liberal perspective had to change its tack because, as Kocka puts it, "there was a gradual weakening of the belief in progress which had been typical of the *Bürgertum* in its progressive-emancipatory phase."[44] From the mid-1870s forward the unity of the middle classes, which *Nachmärz* liberals had tended to idealize, began to shatter in the face of organized pressure from the working classes, non-German nationals, and anti-Semites. Like many liberals who grew up in the 1840s, Hanslick had difficulty accepting the particularist claims of these groups, and did not adjust his thought patterns to the more differentiated, contestatory civil society they were bringing into being. As Brodbeck and Notley have shown, his music criticism often expressed resistance to recent social and political changes.[45] The adjustments liberals were making later in the century reflected Vienna's rapidly changing demographics, which were directly affecting the social character of operetta audiences. As Moritz Csáky has shown, the city's gradual incorporation of its outlying districts between 1848 and 1900 shifted the balance within the middle classes by bringing in an unprecedented number of *Kleinbürger*, who proceeded to weaken the dominance of the liberally oriented *Großbürger*.

> This new urban middle class, while also bourgeois but consisting mainly of members of light industry, laborers, and traders, distinguished itself in both social membership and mental orientation from the already established, liberal urban bourgeoisie, who ... found in the economic arrivistes of the bourgeoisie their principal competition. This new middle class also certainly contributed to the fall of political liberalism, for its social and political goals did not align with those of the already saturated bourgeoisie.[46]

In a society where the "natural" leadership of the liberal elite was being called into question and dismantled from all sides, Hanslick longed for the Strauss II of earlier times—not the upward-striver, but the Strauss who accepted his modest boundaries and worked brilliantly within them.

To conclude, the evolution of Johann Strauss Jr. as composer and cultural figure made him a uniquely attractive object for the social and political investments of liberalism in its optimistic and emancipatory phase. He was the inheritor and preserver of a distinctively Viennese cultural tradition of dance music, a tradition rooted in folk expression but developed by Strauss I and Lanner into an internationally recognized form of urban dance music. At the same time, Strauss II embraced change and developed the music he had inherited in a progressive fashion. Having started from the simple dance forms of his father, he moved to more complex, expanded versions of the waltz, then crossed over into operetta and, by the end of the century, *opéra comique*. This gradual "upward" social movement, combined with the authenticity of his Viennese folk roots, which never left his music through all its transformations, made Strauss a seductive image for liberal ideals, which aspired to a comparable reconciliation of organic tradition and modern change—monarchical authority and democratic self-determination. I have argued here that Hanslick's critiques of Strauss II, from the dance music to the operettas and *Ritter Pásmán*, address the problem of social reconciliation in the guise of an aesthetic discussion of generic difference and generic boundaries. Hanslick struggles to rein in the most troubling contradiction of liberal ideology: the presupposition that the interests of the elite upper bourgeoisie (*Bildungsbürger* and *Wirtschaftsbürger*) would stand for the interests of all of middle-class society. It is this that makes him waver between praise of and condescension toward the *volkstümlich* character of the Viennese waltz; and it is this that makes him alternate between celebration and disapproval of Strauss's attempts at "higher" forms of composition. The trajectory of Viennese liberalism in the post-1848 era—rising to a confident high point in the early 1870s and becoming more defensive toward the fin de siècle—found its echo in Hanslick's ambivalence about the possibilities and limits of Strauss's dance music and operettas.

Notes

All translations are my own unless otherwise stated.

1. "Ihre Sepperl und Leni singen wie Raoul und Valentine, und jeder Wirthshausstreit wird zur Bartholomäusnacht. Natürlich springt der Componist von seinem tragischen Throne jeden Augenblick in die trivialste Jödlerei hinab, Raoul und Valentine verwandeln sich wieder in Sepperl und Leni, die Hugenotten in Schneidergesellen, und wir Anderen werden von diesem grausamen Geschaukel seekrank." Eduard Hanslick, "'Das Spitzentuch der Königin' und 'Der lustige Krieg,'" in *Aus dem Opernleben*

der Gegenwart: neue Kritiken und Studien (Berlin: Allgemeiner Verein für Deutsche Litteratur, 1889), 101.

2. "Strauß vermeidet es (wenige flüchtige Momente etwa ausgenommen), den pathetischen Styl der großen Oper in das Singspiel zu verschleppen." Ibid., 101.

3. Margaret Notley, *Lateness and Brahms: Music and Culture in the Twilight of Viennese Liberalism* (Oxford: Oxford University Press, 2007); David Brodbeck, "Dvořák's Reception in Liberal Vienna: Language Ordinances, National Property, and the Language of *Deutschtum*," *Journal of the American Musicological Society* 60, no. 1 (2007): 71–132; David Brodbeck, "Hanslick's Smetana and Hanslick's Prague," *Journal of the Royal Musical Association* 134, no. 1 (2009): 1–36; Kevin C. Karnes, *Music, Criticism, and the Challenge of History: Shaping Modern Musical Thought in Late Nineteenth-Century Vienna* (Oxford: Oxford University Press, 2008).

4. Pieter Judson, "Rethinking the Liberal Legacy," in *Rethinking Vienna 1900*, ed. Steven Beller (New York: Berghahn Books, 2001), 74. See also his book *Exclusive Revolutionaries: Liberal Politics, Social Experience, and National Identity in the Austrian Empire, 1848–1914* (Ann Arbor: University of Michigan Press, 1996). Balancing his emphasis on the strength and continuity of liberalism toward the fin de siècle, Judson argues for the relative continuity of liberalism across the 1848 divide. Even in the "neoabsolutist" 1850s, the liberalism that had taken shape in associations of the 1840s continued to follow its regular course. On the need for an alternative to the Schorske paradigm, see Benjamin M. Korstvedt, "Reading Music Criticism beyond the *Fin-de-siècle* Vienna Paradigm," *Musical Quarterly* 94, no. 1–2 (2011): 156–210, especially 161–69.

5. Eduard Hanslick, "Johann Strauss [I]" (1849), repr. in *Aus dem Concert-Saal: Kritiken und Schilderungen* (Vienna: Braumüller, 1897), 11.

6. Ibid.

7. "Es ist doch allezeit Wien, wo die Tanzmusik mit glänzendster Begabung cultivirt wurde. Keine europäische Hauptstadt kann hierin mit der österreichischen in die Schranken treten. Ist diese Kunstgattung auch zweifellos eine untergeordnete, so kann sich Wien doch rühmen, gerade sie am vollkommensten repräsentirt zu haben." Eduard Hanslick, "Tanzmusik und die Söhne von Strauss und Lanner" (1850), in Hanslick, "Johann Strauss [I]," 28.

8. Hanslick, "Johann Strauss [I]," 12.

9. Ibid., 14. Emphasis added. In formulating these ideas about the evolution of dance music beyond its mere function, Hanslick seems to be borrowing from an article by Philipp Fahrbach, "Geschichte der Tanzmusik seit 25 Jahren," *Wiener allgemeine Musik-Zeitung* 7 (1847): 138. Fahrbach (1815–85) was a dance-orchestra leader and associate of Strauss I who had a prolific career but was overshadowed by the fame of Strauss II.

10. Hanslick, "Johann Strauss [I]," 12.

11. Ibid., 15.

12. Jürgen Kocka, "The European Pattern and the German Case," in *Bourgeois Society in Nineteenth-Century Europe*, ed. Jürgen Kocka and Allan Mitchell (Oxford: Berg Publishers, 1993), 16–17.

13. *Bourgeois Society in Nineteenth-Century Europe*, 41.

14. Kocka, "The European Pattern," 8.

15. Hanslick, "Johann Strauss [I]," 13. Emphasis added.

16. "J. Strauss hat reizende, ja geistreiche Musik in seinen bessern Walzern niedergelegt,—sie hört auf es zu sein, sobald man lediglich dabei im Tact tanzen will." *VMS*, 142.

17. Bernd Sponheuer, *Musik als Kunst und Nicht-Kunst: Untersuchungen zur Dichotomie von 'hoher' und 'niederer' Musik im musikästhetischen Denken zwischen Kant und Hanslick* (Kassel: Bärenreiter, 1987), 88. It is worth noting that in *Vom Musikalisch-Schönen* Hanslick also associates the "elementary" or "pathological" response not with the uneducated alone, but also with certain educated-bourgeois types, most notably in his satirical vignettes of the opium-drenched aesthete and the demonstratively enthusiastic music dilettante. In the second edition (Leipzig: Weigl, 1858), Hanslick inserted a footnote on page 82 to distinguish such indulgent, degraded bourgeois pleasure from the more innocent, natural sensual pleasure of the uneducated: "This type of musical listening is not identical with the joy that, in every art, the naïve public experiences in art's merely sensory aspect" (Es ist diese Art des Musikhörens nicht identisch mit der in jeder Kunst vorkommenden Freude des naiven Publicums an dem blos sinnlichen Theil derselben).

18. "Eine Kunstgattung wird weder im Inhalt noch in der Form bereichert, wenn man ihr ein Pathos aufzwingt, dem ihr Wesen widerstrebt." Hanslick, "Tanzmusik und die Söhne von Strauss und Lanner," 31.

19. Ibid.

20. Ibid.

21. "Halte darum Jeder die Grenzen rein und verhüte Verschleppungen aus fremdem Gebiet: vor dem gebildeten Schönheitssinn steht die Verpolkung des Opernstyls und die Heroification der Tanzmusik auf einer Stufe." Ibid.

22. Andreas Ballstaedt, "Die Walzer von Johann Strauss (Sohn)—Gebrauchsmusik oder Werk?" in *Johann Strauß. Zwischen Kunstanspruch und Volksvergnügen*, ed. L. Finscher and A. Riethmüller (Darmstadt: Wissenschaftliche Buchgesellschaft, 1995), 83.

23. "Ich bekenne unverhohlen die Besorgniß, mit welcher ich Strauss' erster Oper entgegensah. Ein Schilderer von Stilleben und Thierstücken, der plötzlich Historienmaler wird, eine Dichter-Specialität im Epigramm oder Sonnett, welche sich ans Drama wagt: sie haben schwerlich einen grelleren Uebergang, eine schwierigere Stellung." Ed. H. [Eduard Hanslick], "Johann Strauss als Operncomponist," in *Die moderne Oper: Kritiken und Studien* (Berlin: Allgemeiner Verein für Deutsche Litteratur, 1885), 334–35. Review originally published as Ed. H., "Indigo und die vierzig Räuber," *Neue Freie Presse* (February 12, 1871): 1–2. (Because Hanslick signed his byline in the *Neue Freie Presse* as "Ed. H.," it will be retained here in citations of his articles from that newspaper.)

24. Hanslick, "Johann Strauss als Operncomponist," 337. Emphasis added.

25. Ibid., 340.

26. "Zur musikalischen Tragödie und dem höheren musikalischen Lustspiel fügte Offenbach eine dritte wohlberechtigte Kategorie hinzu: die musikalische Posse." Eduard Hanslick, "J. Offenbach," in *Aus dem Opernleben der Gegenwart: Neue Kritiken und Studien* (Berlin: A. Hofmann, 1884), 269. On this point, Hanslick follows Offenbach's own defense of the genre, "Concours pour une operette en un acte," in *Revue et gazette musicale de Paris* (July 20, 1856). The text is contextualized in Mark Everist, "Offenbach: Music and Image" in *Music, Theater, and Cultural Transfer, Paris 1830–1914*, ed. Annegret Fauser and Mark Everist (Chicago: University of Chicago Press, 2009), 72–98. I am grateful to Gabriela Cruz for this reference.

27. Hanslick, "J. Offenbach," 279.

28. Ibid., 272.

29. Eduard Hanslick, "Zum Strauss-Jubiläum," in *Musikalisches Skizzenbuch: Neue Kritiken und Schilderungen* (Berlin: Allgemeiner Verein für Deutsche Litteratur, 1896), 212. Ellipsis in original.

30. Ibid., 213.

31. "In the *Zigeunerbaron* the composer demonstrates a new step forward in the command of larger forms, and in the refined, characteristic treatment of the dramatic" ("Im Zigeunerbaron offenbart sich ein neuer Fortschritt des Componisten in Bewältigung grösserer Formen, in feiner und characteristischer Behandlung des Dramatischen"). Ibid., 214. Hanslick continues to offer a favorable opinion of Strauss's technical progress in composition a year later in his review of *Der Zigeunerbaron* (1885). Hanslick, *Musikalisches Skizzenbuch*, 98.

32. "Zum Strauss-Jubiläum," 212–13.

33. William J. McGrath gives a precise summary of the progression of liberalism between 1848–74 in *Dionysian Art and Populist Politics in Austria* (New Haven, CT: Yale University Press, 1974), 4–13. The key turning points are 1859, when military defeat made the neoabsolutists concede to liberalism, and 1867, when a more modern form of liberalism less tied to the Josephinian form came to its peak.

34. "Das Jahr 1848 bildet die Grenzscheide zwischen dem alten und neuen Oesterreich—nicht blos im politischen und socialen, auch im literarischen und künstlerischen Leben. Vom Jahre 1848 dürfen wir den Umschwung der musikalischen Verhältnisse in Oesterreich datiren." Eduard Hanslick, *Geschichte des Concertwesens in Wien*, 2 vols. (Vienna: W. Braumüller, 1869), 1:368. On this issue see Hiroshi Yoshida, "Eduard Hanslick and the Idea of 'Public' in Musical Culture: Towards a Socio-political Context of Formalist Aesthetics," *International Review of the Aesthetics and Sociology of Music* 32, no. 2 (2001): 191. See also Dana Gooley, "Hanslick and the Institution of Criticism," *Journal of Musicology* 28, no. 3 (Summer 2011): 292–93 and 305–6.

35. Hanslick's view of the relationship of the waltz to the mentality of the *Vormärz* public is indicated in this passage from his autobiography: "Cut off from all public affairs, the Vienna public threw itself into the cult of the plainly distracting and entertaining in art. . . . For lack of political media, people read with amazing seriousness the 'Theaterzeitung,' the 'Humorist' etc. In musical matters Italian opera, virtuosity, and waltzes dominated." (Von allen grossen geistigen Interessen abgesperrt, warf sich das Wiener Publikum auf den Kultus des schlichtweg Zerstreuenden, Unterhaltenden in der Kunst. . . . In Ermangelung politscher Organe las man mit wunderlicher Wichtigkeit die 'Theaterzeitung,' den 'Humorist' usw. Auf musikalischem Gebiet herrschte die italienische Oper, das Virtuosentum, der Walzer.) Hanslick, *AML*, 1:118.

36. "Unsern Johann Strauss verzeichnet die Musikgeschichte als den einzigen Walzercomponisten von Fach, der nach vieljähriger, ununterbrochener Thätigkeit als Balldirigent sich der dramatischen Musik zugewendet hat . . . Alt-Strauss und Lanner hatten für sich ein solches Avancement nie zu träumen gewagt." "Zum Strauss-Jubiläum," 213.

37. On the difficulties advancing the symphony genre as an emblem of liberal politics, see Notley, *Lateness and Brahms*, 150–56. The basic problem was that the symphony genre had never achieved "popularity." Crittenden cites a travel guidebook from 1892 claiming that "the majority of Viennese musical families practice dance music at home rather than classical music, since understanding the latter is something reserved for the very few." See Camille Crittenden, *Johann Strauss and Vienna: Operetta and the Politics of Popular Culture* (Cambridge: Cambridge University Press, 2000), 38.

38. On operetta and the influence of Wagner, see chapter 7 of Crittenden, *Johann Strauss and Vienna*, entitled "Waltzing Brünnhilde: *Zukunftsmusik* and Viennese Operetta."

39. Eduard Hanslick, *Am Ende des Jahrhunderts* (Berlin: Allgemeiner Verein für Deutsche Litteratur, 1899), 110–11. Cited in Crittenden, *Johann Strauss and Vienna*, 43.

40. Eduard Hanslick, *Aus neuer und neuester Zeit: Musikalische Kritiken und Schilderungen* (Berlin: Allgemeiner Verein für Deutsche Litteratur, 1900), 26.

41. For a discussion of Hanslick's reception of Goldmark, see David Brodbeck, "'Poison-Flaming Flowers from the Orient and Nightingales from Bayreuth': On Hanslick's Reception of the Music of Goldmark," in the current volume. —Eds.

42. "Trotzdem bleibt meines Erachtens für sein eigenartiges und in so langjährig gleichmässiger Praxis festgehaltenes Talent die ältere Form der komischen Oper mit gesprochenem Dialog (wie bei Lortzing) oder mit leichten, den Konversationston streifenden Recitativen (wie bei Flotow) die allergeeignetste ... was uns abgeht, ist unser lieber alter Johann Strauss." Hanslick, "Ritter Pásmán," in *Fünf Jahre Musik* (Berlin: Allgemeine Bibliothek für Deutsche Litteratur, 1896), 19.

43. "'Das Spitzentuch der Königin' und 'Der Lustige Krieg,'" 108. Emphasis added.

44. Kocka, "The European Pattern," 19.

45. See Brodbeck, "Dvořák's Reception," and Notley, *Lateness and Brahms*.

46. Moritz Csáky, "Der soziale und kulturelle Kontext der Wiener Operette," in *Johann Strauß*, 40.

Chapter Six

Waltzing around the Musically Beautiful

Listening and Dancing in Hanslick's Hierarchy of Musical Perception

Chantal Frankenbach

Hanslick's 1854 treatise *Vom Musikalisch-Schönen* entered the canon of musical aesthetics as an essentially negative formulation of musical beauty, claiming more what beautiful music *is not* than what it *is*. Thus, in order to demonstrate what he could not clearly posit in terms of pure sound, Hanslick employed a theory of musical perception as a more substantive criterion of judgment, drawing on various manifestations of listening to describe the *effects* of musical beauty. This approach led Hanslick to examine the incompetent musical listener as thoroughly as he did the competent listener, the true disciple of the beautiful. As Nicholas Cook puts it, Hanslick's aesthetics was, more than anything else, "a polemic against what he saw as the inadequate manner in which most people listen to music."[1] Taking his place among a series of critics who discuss the listener's responsibility for musical meaning, Hanslick proposed a hierarchy of listening types that contrasts the intellectual nature of "true listening" with a less admirable, "pathological" type of listening.[2] He refers to the primitive elements of music—sound and motion—as "elemental," and further brands listeners who are satisfied with a merely sensual relationship to these elements as "enthusiasts." Their sensitivity is the direct opposite of rational, pure contemplation, "which alone is the true and artistic method of listening."[3] Offering a model of perception that required educated, attentive listening, Hanslick's treatise contributed to a standard for musical experience that upholds—even to the present—a uniquely suspicious attitude toward human movement.

Although the carefully observed immobility of Western concert audiences is now accepted as axiomatic to "serious" musical understanding, its emergence out of the dance-infused traditions of baroque and classical music bears investigation.[4] Hanslick's treatise expresses a nearly uniform disapproval of dance, yet many of his reviews and essays written for the press bring more conflicted opinions to light; here Hanslick often expresses genuine affection for the waltz, both as a musical tradition and as a vibrant element of Viennese social life. In this essay, I examine Hanslick's writing on dance music to assess his view of dance as an impediment to musical listening.[5]

In nineteenth-century Vienna, the waltz was a beloved pastime that formed a potent counterpoint to the emerging standard of immobility required in the theater or concert room. Several caricatures from the Viennese press illustrate the tension between dancing and seated listening among the audiences of Johann Strauss Jr. The first is a comic depiction of the Viennese audience's incapacity to sit quietly through an operetta in the presence of Strauss's music (see fig. 6.1).

Another image appearing seven years later declares that Strauss, as a member of a fictional "rescue squad," will not be called to save people from fire or flood, but from a far worse fate in the theater. "For example in the Theater an der Wien, when a very boring piece has been played . . . he must rush to the orchestra, reach for his baton, begin a waltz, and then play his repertoire until ten. Everything comes alive, everyone cheers, they push the chairs aside to dance and when they leave, they shout out: We have never been so entertained!" (see fig. 6.2) The extreme postures of cramped stillness (and drooping inattention in the boxes) during an operetta, compared with the physical exuberance of dancing, amply demonstrate this audience's preference for waltzing over listening. Figure 6.3, which compares Strauss Sr. in the ballroom with his son in the theater, further suggests that the restriction of movement in the theater was broadly felt—even among the educated elite—as a betrayal of the Viennese love for dancing. The words *piano* and *moderato* written on the subdued Strauss's score in the second image contrast soberly with the flying tails and broken fiddle strings of the first. In addition to the musicians, the "listeners" in the background—waltzing in the first image, sitting (and leaving) in the other—tell a tale of longing for physical engagement regardless of venue, genre, or class.[6]

Because the waltz was popular among all strata of Viennese society, its practice threw a wrench in Hanslick's hierarchy of listening types, which linked the musical elite with cerebral listening and the lay listener with movement.[7] In the Viennese ballroom physical engagement with music crossed barriers of both class and education, proving especially resistant to the paradigm of intellectual musical enjoyment favored by Hanslick. Charlotte Moscheles, wife of the famous composer and pianist Ignatz Moscheles, writes in 1873 that the effect of Strauss's music was not easy to suppress and persisted even among seated concert listeners:

Figure 6.1. *Kikeriki,* January 7, 1877. "In the Carltheater, the audience, during the performance of Strauss's new Operetta, has only a single wish: that the seats be moved out of the way." Reproduced with permission from the Department of Special Collections and University Archives, W. E. B. Du Bois Library, University of Massachusetts Amherst.

> Where he fiddles, all dance—dance they must. In the concerts which he gives with his small orchestra, people dance as they sit; at Almack's, the most fashionable of all the subscription balls, aristocratical [*sic*] little feet hop to his tunes, and we too the other night at a party had the good fortune to dance to his fiddling, and, old married folk as we are, felt ourselves young again.[8]

It is to be expected that dance music would induce many listeners to dance in a ballroom, yet critics offer further evidence of this broadly felt impulse among theater and concert audiences as well. From a review of Strauss Sr.'s concert tour to Leipzig in 1834, we learn that his audiences were deeply susceptible to the physical pull of his music: "Voices were raised from those who felt that with Strauss's departure they saw the disappearance of the highest

Johann Strauß erhielt anläßlich seines 40jährigen Jubiläums neben zahllosen anderen Auszeichnungen auch das Diplom eines Ehrenmitgliedes vom Lebensrettungs= Verein.

Nun, mit dem Retten von Menschen aus Feuer= oder Wassergefahr wird sich der nervöse, schwächliche Komponist wohl nicht befassen, aber in anderer Beziehung kann er doch im Sinne des Rettungsvereines arbeiten;

so zum Beispiel im **Theater an der Wien**, wenn wieder einmal ein recht langweiliges Stück gegeben wird, welches schon durch seinen ersten Akt das gesammte Publikum einschläfert,

da soll er als Rettender Hinsinkende erheben, indem er in's Orchester eilt, den Taktirstock ergreift, einen Walzer dirigirt und dann bis 10 Uhr sein Repertoir abspielt und Alles wird, erwacht, jubeln, zum Leben erweckt sein, die Sperrsitz' wegräumen, zu tanzen anfangen und beim Fortgehen ausrufen: „So hab'n wir uns noch nie unterhalten!"

Figure 6.2. *Kikeriki*, October 23, 1884. Reproduced with permission from the Department of Special Collections and University Archives, W. E. B. Du Bois Library, University of Massachusetts Amherst.

Figure 6.3. *Kikeriki,* January 5, 1879. "While Strauss Sr. found satisfaction and happiness in charming the Viennese people with native melodies, his son is convinced that the Viennese idiom should be denied. He seeks refinement in an operetta which reminds the Viennese of anything but their wonderful homeland." Reproduced with permission from the Department of Special Collections and University Archives, W. E. B. Du Bois Library, University of Massachusetts Amherst.

musical pleasure their legs had ever experienced. His electrifying bowing had penetrated deep into their bodies, where they would otherwise never see this light." The soul of this orchestra "is Strauss, whose spirit controls the bodies of everyone who participates.... No one who actually carries true music in his body can stand pure dance rhythms for hours without dancing to them, or watch dancing without at least eating or drinking."[9] Confirming the physical responses evoked by Strauss's music in the concert hall, a reviewer by the name of Joseph Oppenheim wrote in the *Neue Freie Presse*:

> In the front rows of the lower seats, some people who are too close to the magician start to jerk up as if electrified. The musical current infects others very quickly. People unwillingly beat the time with their hands and feet, and before they know it the entire house wants to rise up, sing along, dance, fly, and float, and the theater becomes a ballroom and everyone screams: "Strauss! Strauss!"[10]

According to Oppenheim, only a very few are not affected in this way. As Strauss threw out one waltz after another, "even the forehead of the strictest judge would gladly have relaxed its frown. And if he didn't dance with this music himself, at least he observed the electric effects of the [music] with a hearty laugh."[11]

The waltz-crazed atmosphere of Vienna, where Strauss Jr. was arguably the last European composer to regularly inhabit both the ballroom and concert hall, gave Hanslick abundant opportunities to consider the relationship of listening and dancing. His often contradictory responses to dance indicate that he struggled to reconcile his philosophical position on aesthetic listening with the milieu of dance that surrounded him. Yet a careful examination of Hanslick's writings on dance reveals that throughout his life he ultimately dismissed the physical experience of dance in favor of intellectual listening.

Kevin C. Karnes's study of Hanslick's career—and the shifts in critical values that drove it—suggests that Hanslick's early effort to employ the methods of the natural sciences to the aesthetics of music led to his adoption of a paradigm for listening that privileged a rational, intellectual approach to music available only to a select group of initiated listeners.[12] Karnes chronicles a series of methodological "epiphanies" Hanslick experienced that dramatically altered the tone of his writing over his long career.[13] Hanslick reversed his position on formalist musical aesthetics in the mid-1860s, turning briefly from aesthetic to historical modes of inquiry, and then devoting the remainder of his career to journalistic criticism.[14] While many modern scholars have accepted his initial treatise as his most important work, contemporary accounts of Hanslick indicate that his true passion was, in fact, for the work that came after the treatise: the criticism that allowed him to embrace the values of a *feuilletonist*, reviewing the musical life of Vienna from the basis of his own tastes and setting down his opinions of Viennese concert life for posterity.[15] Hanslick's views on dance music—in which delight in the genre as a cornerstone of Austrian music consistently accompanies scorn for its failure to meet his formalist aesthetic standards—are not adequately explained by the methodological shifts Hanslick experienced over the course of his career. I suggest that they are better understood when viewed within a hierarchy of musical perception that contrasted the intellectual with the pathological as manifested in listening and dancing.

The priority given to objective inquiry in Hanslick's academic milieu emerged along with a change in modes of musical contemplation, which encouraged concert listeners to bring their own intellectual apparatus to bear on the music they heard.[16] Earlier rubrics for musical experience had obliged a listener only to react in conventionally appropriate ways to a musical stimulus: pastoral themes induced calm; minor modes produced melancholy; and dance music impelled people to dance. In the context of an emerging public awareness of musical listening as a specialized skill, however, dancing represented the antithesis to listening. Indeed, to the extent that Hanslick's treatise aimed to improve "listening," it also aimed to denounce dancing.

Hanslick's Early Criticism of Dance Music

Vom Musikalisch-Schönen is the only work in which Hanslick's disdain for dance is undiluted. His abundant critical writings (later collected and published in eleven volumes) present a more complicated stance on the value of dance music Hanslick's first publication to include a significant discussion of dance is found in an obituary for Johann Strauss Sr.[17] This document, written in 1849, five years before the treatise, expresses keen enthusiasm for dance and dance music. Hanslick begins the article with a defense of the genre, which he says critics and composers have treated with unjust contempt. He argues for a broad view of musical form, noting that "even in small forms, great talent is proven, and it is this talent, this divine spark, which we honor first."[18] Hanslick reminds his readers that even the most erudite mass, if poorly composed, cannot surpass the artistic worth of a charming waltz. How much better, he says, to be great in a small genre, than to be meager in a large one.[19] Hanslick's tribute to Strauss becomes, in fact, a tribute to dance music. He asserts dance music's potential to surpass the "elemental" requirements of dancing and to attain a higher plane of artistic meaning:

> The worth of each art form either rises or falls with the demands that are brought to it. Our request to dance music goes as such: that it not just keep the stamping beat of the dancers, but that it understand their souls, interpret their feelings and passions, and elevate and make these noble. The lowest level of dance music is only concerned with the feet, but on a higher level it should speak to fantasy, feeling, and spirit.[20]

After this gesture of support for the genre of dance music, Hanslick calls for the dance composer to craft his music to dance's highest potential. This requires a modification of raw physicality to a more elevated plane of cultural life:

> In order to command this higher level, it will certainly be necessary that the composer should raise his understanding of a merely gymnastic view of the dance to one that relates to a social meaning. In our highly civilized society, dance has already been lifted from its original meaning to bloom at a much higher one. If we only wanted to see dance as a physical exercise, then it would be practiced in gymnastic schools. Our present-day dance amusements, as often as they may be caricatured, are and remain the consecrated asylums of tender needs and goals.[21]

Although the association of "feeling" with physicality in this tribute is consistent with Hanslick's position on dance music in *Vom Musikalisch-Schönen*, the warmth he conveys for dance could not be further from the tone of the treatise that was to appear five years later.

Yet Hanslick's obituary to Strauss is not an unalloyed encomium to dance. Just when it seems that Hanslick is calling for music and dance to be joined in a blissful, artistic union, he abruptly draws back. Hanslick accomplishes this turn of opinion by drawing a distinction between dancers and musical connoisseurs: a distinction founded on the way each of them listens to music:

> Up to now we have viewed Strauss's dance music only insofar as it serves the dance and its interests; if there were nothing else to praise, Strauss's passing would affect only the dance world.... For the musician, Strauss could have meaning only if his dances, loosened from their purpose, still had enough of a musical foundation to interest a connoisseur.... Strauss never failed to present musical richness in rhythm, harmonization, and instrumentation, which the careful ear of the musician would listen to while the dancer became drunk on the sweet fire of the melody.[22]

This is but one of Hanslick's many characterizations of dancers as sensuously intoxicated and musicians as rational and deliberate. By separating the attentive listeners from the inebriated dancers, so to speak, Hanslick gives himself a platform from which to further criticize the formal frame of the waltz:

> The form of the waltz presently acts as a hindrance to artistic development and to every composer who brings a talent or knowledge to it. The small, tightly closed framework of the waltz doesn't allow for even the smallest development of a melody, which must end without a trace to make room for a second and third, and so forth, until all five waltzes are rolled out like an incoherent set of images in a peep show.... This is an unartistic waste which the most gifted mind must soon tire of.[23]

Hanslick's concern with principles of musical coherence and development now overrides any amiable sentiments he may have for dance. He turns to the formal characteristics of the waltz in order to clarify his view that dance music cannot participate in the rational, organic processes that are the mark of true art music. The parade of themes, each left "undeveloped," offends Hanslick's sense of music as an intellectual endeavor in which the elaboration of a musical idea over time is the highest achievement of musical art:

> The waltz as a composition (as opposed to the individual waltz) should not be composed of five independent pieces strung together, each motive swallowed by the next. Instead it should form one complete, coherent, closed-off whole.

One or two main themes would be enough; these would have the freest musical development within the limits of dance. . . . Only through a unified form can the composer escape the double evil of inventing half a dozen new motives in order to waste them. Only through its form can the waltz develop artistic value and content and receive a character of its own.[24]

After shifting incrementally toward a condemnation of the formal inadequacy of dance music, the obituary ends with an apology for the genre's failure to engage the musical mind. Hanslick's praise of the waltz is difficult to reconcile with his criticism of its formal simplicity. This review clearly demonstrates, however, that by 1849 he already had the solid belief in a hierarchy of physically and mentally opposed listening types that he would articulate in the treatise.

In November of 1853, Hanslick published a review of Strauss Jr.'s waltzes in which he touches on many of the themes from the 1849 obituary. Although it offers exuberant praise for the waltz as the quintessential music of Vienna, the review is fraught with contradictions. Hanslick claims that the waltz is both a "subordinate genre" and a "blank sheet" that offers composers freedom to write music of spirit and power.[25] Again demonstrating his belief in a dual system of listening—in which one set of listeners can be pleased with the elemental aspects of Strauss's music and another will require more rigorous forms of musical beauty—Hanslick makes explicit the two levels upon which dance music may be considered: "Naturally we think beyond the simplistic technique that is needed for dance music to its poetic soulfulness and independent musical beauty. From this standpoint we do not wish to judge the waltz as dance movement, but to listen to it in tranquil pleasure as music, a satisfaction we have gained with each composition of the older and the younger Strauss."[26] Regardless of the fact that Strauss's waltzes were intended for a dancing audience, Hanslick turns them toward an immobile listening experience. With the phrase "to listen to it in tranquil pleasure as music," he implies that to listen to this music while dancing would lower its status as music. Hanslick continues: "A beautiful waltz is one of the many easy things that not everybody can execute. The tight frame and the strict conditions that exist in its music require the waltz composer to invest the first downbeat with invention, to throw his invention away without having used it, and then again and again to create and discard. He who has few ideas cannot produce a waltz."[27] Hanslick grants the dance composer originality and fertility of ideas, but with a clear warning that this is not enough for the serious listener.

Dancing and Listening in *Vom Musikalisch-Schönen*

Hanslick fully articulates his theory of listening in *Vom Musikalisch-Schönen* where he separates music as an agent of emotion from music as an aesthetic phenomenon. Admitting that music has the potential to operate either way, he puts the burden of this determination on the listener, who must direct his mental powers to the correct level of intellectual engagement:

> *Mental* activity is a necessary concomitant in every aesthetic enjoyment and often varies considerably in several individuals listening to one and the same composition. In the case of the sensual and emotional natures it may sink to a minimum, whereas in highly intellectual persons it alone may turn the scale.... To become intoxicated, nothing but weakness is required, but truly *aesthetic listening* is an *art* in itself.[28]

In Hanslick's theory of listening, emotional responses to music are closely linked with physicality. He states that with the feelings aroused by music "there always co-exists a strong physical agitation."[29] Both responses—the emotional and the physical—inhabit a category of musical enjoyment that obviates intelligent listening. According to Hanslick, "The more overpowering the effect is in a physical—i.e., in a pathological—sense, the less it is due to *aesthetic* causes."[30]

Hanslick believes music's power to excite physical movement is an unfortunate by-product of musical perception: not the object of music but, nonetheless, an undeniable phenomenon. Seeking to explain the pathological listeners' affinity for dancing, he questions whether pleasant memories of dancing might compel them to maintain their association of music with movement, but concludes that this does not fully explain the phenomenon: "We cannot, without being one-sided, dispute the *physiological* action of martial or dance music, and attribute its effect solely to a psychological association of ideas.... The feet do not move because it is dance-music, but we call it dance-music because the feet move."[31] Hanslick candidly abandons his attempt to explain how music can inspire movement, claiming that the physiological sciences are not and never will be able to demonstrate such an effect: "All this lies beyond the mysterious bridge which no philosopher has ever crossed. It is the one great problem expressed in numberless ways: the connection between mind and body."[32] Lacking a scientific explanation for the connection between listening and moving, Hanslick, like many European thinkers in the Cartesian tradition of mind-body dualism, prefers to operate on the basis of their separation.

In a curious twist of terms, Hanslick describes the physically moved listener as passive, reserving "activity" for the mental agitations of listeners who approach music intellectually. In this exchange of connotations, a dancer whirling to a waltz experiences musical "passivity" while an individual sitting still in a concert becomes "active." Of the physically moved listeners, Hanslick says: "While in a state of passive receptivity they suffer only what is elemental in music to affect them, and thus pass into a vague 'supersensible' excitement of the senses, produced by the general drift of the composition. Their attitude towards music is not an observant but a *pathological* one. They are, as it were, in a state of waking dreaminess."[33] Often using terms of diminished sensory awareness for passive listeners, Hanslick refers to their intoxication, their desire to be lulled, even to the clouded state of the near-dead, and coyly suggests some recently developed medical anaesthetics as a foil to aesthetic listening: "To recent times, by the way, we owe a discovery of the greatest moment for such listeners as merely wish their feelings to be played upon to the exclusion of their intellect, the discovery of a far more potent factor than music. We are alluding to ether and chloroform. There is no doubt that these anaesthetics envelop the whole organism in a cloud of delightful and dreamlike sensations."[34] In Hanslick's view, the passive, "anaesthetic" listener is the most easily satisfied member of the audience and the one who lowers the dignity of music, lacking "the criteria of intelligent gratification."[35] Geoffrey Payzant concludes that "elemental" responses to music are, for Hanslick, "unmediated by intelligence. Tapping the foot or nodding the head in response to musical rhythm is for Hanslick a reflex similar to the kick of a dead frog's legs in a saline solution with the administration of an electric current."[36]

Hanslick's depiction of elemental listeners compares their musical pleasures to such things as a warm bath, a fine cigar, and a fondness for wine. This category of sensual pleasures also includes dancing. In *Vom Musikalisch-Schönen*, he frankly illustrates his distrust of dance with an anecdote about a debtor who induces his creditor to forgive his entire debt by plying him with music, which affects him, according to Hanslick,

> in the same manner as one who by the tune of a waltz is suddenly roused from repose and impelled to dance.... Neither of them acts of his own free will, neither of them is overwhelmed by a superior mind or by moral beauty, but simply in consequence of a powerful nervous stimulus. Music loosens the feet or the heart just as wine loosens the tongue. But such victories only testify to the weakness of the vanquished. To be the slave of unreasoning, undirected, and purposeless feelings, ignited by a power which is out of all relation to our will and intellect, is not worthy of the human mind. If people allow themselves to be so completely carried away by what is elemental in art as to lose all self-control, this scarcely redounds to the glory of the art, and much less to that of the individual.[37]

Hanslick notes that among those most susceptible to dancing are youth, who have not learned to control their physical impulses. In the presence of dance music they experience "a twitching of the whole body, and especially of the feet."[38] Animals and "savages" are also vulnerable to the stimulus of dance music. The impulse to dance, in fact, grows in proportion to the crudeness of mind and character: the lower the level of culture, the more potent the effect. "It is well known that the action of music is most powerful of all in the case of savages."[39] To those who would claim music's effect on animals as proof of its power to move the emotions, Hanslick responds: "It is true that the sound of the trumpet inspires the horse with courage and an eagerness for the battle, that the fiddle tempts the bear to waltz, and that both the nimble spider and the clumsy elephant move to its fascinating strains. But is it, after all, so great an honour to be a musical enthusiast in *such* company?"[40]

Hanslick's listening categories are based, in part, on broad determinations of cultural development. The advanced state of musical understanding among northern Europeans, he says, gives them a heightened capacity for musical understanding. He maintains that contemplative listening, "demands, in fact, the keenest *watching* and the most untiring *attention*. In the case of intricate compositions, this may even become a mental exertion. Many an *individual*, nay, many a *nation* undertakes this exertion only with great reluctance."[41] Among the "nations" that are less fit for musical understanding, Hanslick includes any "primitive" culture, generally invoking the figure of the "savage" to represent non-European cultures. Claiming that "our infants in the cradle sing better than adult savages," he writes of European musical advances as "slowly gained triumphs of the human mind."[42] In Hanslick's view, the evolution of European musical culture rests on the special emphasis placed on melody, harmony, and the system of major and minor modes and equal temperament: the material ingredients of "tonally moving forms."[43]

Hanslick further justifies his Eurocentric view of intellectual listening on the grounds that rhythm is, of all the elements in music, the only one present in nature. For this reason he assigns it the lowest level of musical sophistication: "When the South Sea Islanders rattle with wooden staves and pieces of metal to the accompaniment of fearful howlings, they are performing natural music, that is, no music at all."[44] Thus by separating the "natural" element of rhythm from the more culturally developed elements of melody and harmony, Hanslick implicitly distances music from dance and fortifies his argument for an immobile manner of listening.

Attitudes toward Dance in Hanslick's Coterie

Thus far, Hanslick's reviews and his writing on dance in the treatise reveal very mixed attitudes to the value of dance in music and in Viennese society. The opinions of his contemporaries further point out the apparent conflicts in Hanslick's tastes, where his love for the waltz seems to collide with his professional commitment to serious music. Given the denunciations of dance found in the treatise, it is surprising to learn that Hanslick was known to be thoroughly susceptible to the pleasures of dance. His autobiography contains enthusiastic reminiscences about both theater and ballroom dance. In one poignant example, Hanslick describes an evening at a gathering where the aged former ballerina Fanny Elssler was present. Impressed by her ineffable grace and beauty and her legendary fame, the assembled guests persuaded Elssler to dance for them. Upon her request, Hanslick himself played the piano while she demonstrated the "Cacchucha" for the guests. Hanslick remarks on his good fortune that the music was simple enough for him to play at the piano without taking his eyes off Elssler: "It was a sight that I cannot forget. Fanny Elssler lifted her dress a little and danced, or rather floated, two or three times through the big room, up and down with such graceful, expressive bending and tilting of the head and upper body, with such round, undulating movements of the arms, that I understood for the first time the true ideal of dance."[45] Despite Hanslick's comments on the "simplicity" of the music, his impassioned description of Elssler is difficult to accord with the indictment of dance in his treatise.

Even more surprising is the fact that Hanslick and his circle of friends, which included Brahms and Theodor Billroth, were avid players of four-hand waltz music and that this genre was considered Hanslick's forte.[46] From a reminiscence of his friendship with the singer Adelina Patti, whom he befriended during her stay in Vienna in 1863, we learn that Hanslick enjoyed dancing as well. "After meals, I would play waltzes by Strauss and Lanner, which she loved to hear. Sometimes she would impulsively push tables and chairs aside, Strakosch [her brother-in-law] would take over at the piano, and we would dance as a single, enraptured couple around the room."[47]

Contemporary descriptions of Hanslick also call into question the sincerity of his aesthetic prescription for pure contemplative listening and of his interest in autonomous formal procedures in "serious" music. Richard Specht recalls attending one of Hanslick's lectures on music at the University of Vienna. Noting that Hanslick's course was delivered without luster until he played his musical examples at the piano, Specht writes:

> It was amusing to see his short, quick fingers scurry across the keys and quite comical to see him tickle out of the keyboard . . . a strongly rhythmic, hopping polka or a merry, spruce little piece from a French comic opera, which he did with visible gusto, contentedly and coquettishly skipping with the music. . . . He loved tid-bits better than the sublime and grandiose in music. When he spoke of a Bach Passion or of Beethoven's late period, one had the impression that he had to spur himself on. . . . Those he loved were composers like Auber, Rossini and Johann Strauss.[48]

Specht's belief that Hanslick was most comfortable with simple, entertaining music is borne out by several incidents in Hanslick's relationship with Brahms. The most telling involves the single dedication Brahms granted to the critic: the op. 39 waltzes for four hands, published in 1865. Brahms wrote to Hanslick, explaining the dedication and the choice of genre:

While writing the title of the four-hand waltzes, which are to appear shortly, your name came to me spontaneously. I don't know why, I thought of Vienna, of the beautiful girls with whom you play four-hand music, of you yourself, a connoisseur of these and a good friend. Suddenly I felt the necessity of dedicating it to you. If it is all right with you that it remains thus, then I thank you most obediently; if, however, you for any reason do not desire the things, then give word and the engraver receives a contrary order. They are two books of little innocent waltzes in Schubertian form—if you do not want them and would prefer your name on a proper, four-movement work, then "Give the command, and I will follow."[49]

Brahms calls attention to Hanslick's musical tastes by calling him a "connoisseur" of four-hand music, likely implying the waltz genre Hanslick was known to love. Brahms biographer Max Kalbeck addresses the difficulty of interpreting these cryptic remarks in his discussion of the op. 39 dedication. He notes that "gifts from Brahms always had their clever connotation, which often times remained hidden from the receiver. What the dedication of his Op. 39 meant . . . couldn't possibly escape the addressee. Hanslick was a passionate four-hand player and waltz-playing was his particular strength."[50] On the surface, Brahms's gift to Hanslick was a lovely set of pieces in a genre he loved. Hanslick's contemporaries, however, suggest that the dedication carried a message: the waltzes were more suitable for Hanslick than "a proper, four-movement work."[51] According to Max Graf, "Brahms dedicated to Hanslick, not one of his weighty works, but his *Liebeslieder* [sic] waltzes, as if he meant to say, 'Waltzes—that is your music, my friend!' The great composer was malicious even in his dedications."[52]

Brahms seems also to have doubted Hanslick's opinion of his own compositions, confessing to Specht just before his death "his belief that Hanslick never had any real feeling for his music."[53] As a guest at Hanslick's seventieth birthday celebration, during a long speech in praise of Hanslick's embrace of the history of music from Bach to Brahms, Brahms was heard to grumble: "You must mean Offen-Bach!"[54] When it was Brahms's turn to speak in Hanslick's honor, he commended Hanslick's cleverness and discernment, yet noted their "pronounced tendencies to take different paths—so little do many things interest him that please me, and vice versa."[55]

These anecdotes suggest that Hanslick's colleagues accepted a clear division between the merits of dance music and serious music and held Hanslick accountable for them as well. Yet while they seem to disparage Hanslick for the breadth of his tastes, they may tell us more about his fellow critics' attitudes to dance than about Hanslick's or even Brahms's sentiments toward the waltz. David Brodbeck has convincingly shown Brahms's high regard for the waltz, his pride in its place in the musical life of Vienna, and his deep admiration for the dances of both Schubert and Johann Strauss.[56] Andrew Lamb offers further compelling evidence of Brahms's admiration for Strauss's waltzes, his efforts to aid Strauss in his career, and their intimate friendship as fellow composers.[57] The subtle beauties Brahms employed in the op. 39 waltzes further indicate that he had every faith in the genre's potential for complex and nuanced musical sophistication. As for Hanslick, his reviews indicate that he believed any perceived antagonism between music and dance was generated as much by manner of apprehension as by genre. Hanslick believed, as we will see in his later reviews of Strauss Jr., that the waltz could absorb the harmonic and textural depth of serious music. He turned, rather, to its uses—whether for listening or for dancing—for judgments of musical quality, often switching from one to the other in the same review. His genuine love for the waltz, combined with his belief in true musical listening as an activity reserved for a "thoughtful"—and hence, immobile—musical elite, suggests that Hanslick wrote for two kinds of listener at once. And while Hanslick himself seems to belie the distinction by eagerly inhabiting both groups, he invariably upholds a hierarchy that ranks the moving dancer below the contemplative listener.

The Waltz and the Music of the Future

Several of Hanslick's reviews from the 1850s demonstrate how his attitudes to dance and serious music were tested by Johann Strauss Jr. Hanslick's principal complaint about Strauss Sr. was the "narrow" formal scope of his waltzes. Yet when Strauss Jr. tampered with the harmonic and timbral conventions of the Viennese waltz, Hanslick reacted with alarm. In 1854, Hanslick wrote of the "worrisome path" Strauss Jr. had taken:

> In his new waltzes one can often find a misplaced pathos that does not belong in dance music and has an almost disturbing effect on the listener. . . . All spice must find its measure most of all in good taste and, beyond that, in the requirements of the genre. The deplorable chord progressions pushed out by the trombones, which form the second half of No. 1 of the "Schallwellen," would be most at home in an opera finale . . . In a waltz they are offensive. . . . Not everything that plays in three-quarter-time is a waltz.[58]

Hanslick reminds his reader that the waltz requires a lightness and charm that is spoiled by the heavy instrumentation and confusing harmonic digressions of Strauss's newest compositions. An unfamiliar defensiveness creeps into his writing as he negotiates this threat to the waltz by calling for a clear division of musical genres. This view appears to be in keeping with the listening categories established in the treatise, except that now the tables are turned and Hanslick seeks to protect the dancer's simple pleasures from the influence of progressive art music: "A genre will not be enriched in either its content or form if one forces a pathos onto it that goes against its essence. Even though artificial magnificence is cheered everywhere, it will be the ruin of the lightly exhilarating pieces that exist to provide beautiful dancers with happiness, fun, and grace. May everyone then keep the boundaries pure, and try to prevent abductions from foreign territories."[59] The "foreign territories" refer to the New German School, but the "boundaries" also divide "beautiful dancers" from serious listeners and enforce a distinction between physical and cerebral responses to music. Whether Hanslick is praising or reproving, dancers are not to be confused with musical connoisseurs.

In 1858 Hanslick published a review in *Die Presse* that extended his argument for "pure boundaries" and clarified his intolerance for mixtures of dance with serious music. Here again, Hanslick admonishes Strauss Jr. for incorporating "symphonic" elements into his waltzes, the very element he denounced them for lacking in previous reviews. Describing Strauss's "enrichment" of the waltz as a compositional vindication of sorts, Hanslick suggests that the waltz composer is attempting to restore a balance that was lost when the symphony was "popularized" with dance motives in the late eighteenth century:

> Strauss has apparently taken an act of great historic retribution as his goal. When, around the end of the last century, orchestra music became popular through the systematic lowering of the Haydnesque style, Pleyel, Wranitzky, Hoffmeister, Gyrowetz and Rosetti... went so far as to make the "merriest" Ländler the motives of their symphonies. Johann Strauss apparently wants to compensate for this disgrace of his Viennese ancestors, and he decorates his waltzes with motives that would rightly have their place of honor in the symphonies of the newest schools.[60]

Once again, whether dance impulses invade the genre of the symphony, or symphonic techniques adorn the music of dances, Hanslick objects to their mixture on the basis of temporally correct listening. Dancing, which incapacitates the listener's attention to the unfolding of musical ideas over time, requires music that makes no such demands. Hanslick believes that Strauss's inclusion of a forward-looking ethos in his waltzes overlooks this relationship on both an individual listening level and an overarching historical one. Alluding to the "endless melody" of Wagner and his school, Hanslick writes that Strauss has calculated his newest waltzes "more for the Weimar 'Court of Muses' than for Vienna":

> In fact I have also noticed in Strauss's new works the sharp, prickly aroma that wild game gives off when it is past its prime and that music gives off when it smells of the future.... Those of his waltzes which sound fresh and natural without "forward-looking" originality are still much better dance music

than those outspread motives whose endless periods combine with the most sought-after harmonization in order to confuse ears and feet.[61]

While Hanslick frequently contrasts the "ear" of the musician with the "feet" of the dancer as a way of distinguishing between aesthetic and physical listening types, in this review he implies that both the musician's ear and the dancer's feet are offended by Strauss's innovations. Most significant in this response to Wagner is Hanslick's defensive integration of the interests of the musical connoisseur with those of the dancer; each, he claims, is justifiably disturbed by Strauss's mixture of physical stimulus with elite listening.

Hanslick's Later Criticism

The issue of listening as a cerebral exercise in conflict with the physical pleasures of dancing remains in Hanslick's criticism to the end of his career. Hanslick's 1869 volume *Geschichte des Concertwesens in Wien* contains a chapter titled "Charakter der Vormärzlichen Concertepoche" that describes the musical life of Vienna before the uprisings of 1848 and records Hanslick's interpretation of that era from a point almost two decades after the publication of the treatise. Of particular interest in this work is the distinction, still intact, between intellectual and physical listeners. Hanslick praises the charm and "poetic life" of the waltz that could both "interest the musician" and "please the dancers." Yet in the same paragraph, he reports: "It is clear that this sweet, numbing, three-four time, which dominated all heads and feet, necessarily pushed the great serious music into the background and made the audience more and more incapable of mental effort."[62] In order to counterbalance the appeal of the waltz to its devotees, Hanslick reiterates his criterion for ranking the two listening types: mental effort. In spite of his obvious delight in the genre of dance music, Hanslick the formalist is never far from view.

As if finally to account for his protean opinions of dance music, in 1884 Hanslick printed a remarkably thoughtful reflection on his attitude toward dance over the course of his career. First noting the audacity of Strauss Jr.'s endeavor to bring dance music into the concert hall, he directly confronts the clash of values between functional dance and seated listening: "Soon after his Vienna debut, he dared to embark on a grand tour with his orchestra. In this new undertaking, he was preceded by his father: the first to my knowledge, to venture on tours with dance music and to play his waltzes not in a dance hall for ball guests but in concert halls for a listening audience."[63] Hanslick takes advantage of the physical displacement of genre and venue—the music of functional dance played in a setting that expressly discourages movement— to consider the inherent contradictions in this arrangement and his own views on dancing and listening, first confessing his early apathy for Strauss's waltz music: "In the mid-forties, Strauss played with his orchestra in my hometown of Prague at the municipal theater. I was a passionate young music lover, but I felt no interest for it and I only visited one Straussian production because of the overtures of Beethoven and Weber which graced the program. I barely paid attention to the waltzes. To me one seemed like the other."[64]

Hanslick attributes his early indifference to dance music to his youthfulness, a topic he mentions often in his discussions of dance.[65] Writing as an older man, Hanslick reflects on young people's alertness to pathos and their tendency to dismiss what is not grand and majestic:

> This pathetic sentiment brought all of us young people in those days to thirst after the plays of Schiller or the tragedies of Shakespeare, while it never occurred to us to go and see a comedy. In music it was Beethoven's symphonies, Mendelssohn's overtures. . . . They were the objects of our delight, our yearning. What were comic operas . . . that only had melody and temperament? Oh, this childish "only"! What importance could music have that was only for dancing?[66]

From this candid reflection on the maturation of his tastes, it appears that the denunciation of dance in the 1854 treatise might have grown from his youthful fascination with the pathos of serious music and the specialized listening it required. Looking back on a lifetime of experience, Hanslick now allows, however, that a certain insight is also needed to appreciate what is possible in smaller forms and to understand the beauty of the miniature. The mature critic, he says, "finally understands that genius is in fact possible in dance music and that there is room on the narrow rose petal of a waltz for a clever and lovely thought."[67] But then, as he has so many times before, Hanslick circles back to listening. "I learned only later to listen to dance music not with the impatient ear of someone who wants to dance, but with the alert ear of the musician."[68] In the end, the question of dance music doesn't really rest with its value as music but with the act of listening. While a musician can learn to listen for the truly artistic in dance music, a dancer will continue to be guided by an "impatient ear": an ear not willing to listen over time for the formal developments that the aesthetic listener seeks. As the treatise generally relied on a hierarchy of musical perception for second-hand evidence of musical beauty, listening competence also forms the rubric for Hanslick's particular judgments on the merits of dance music.

Hanslick is not generally known or remembered for his confessions of fondness for the waltz. Nor is he remembered as a critic who wrote warmly of dance music while simultaneously questioning its value as art music. Instead, his treatise—which relegated dance to a category of inadequate listening—became his twentieth-century legacy, effectively serving the streams of thought that shaped musical modernism and its attendant listening norms. From his writing for the press, we learn that the prescription for elite listening established in the treatise subtly but tenaciously persisted in his thought and prevailed in his critical voice, even over his delight for the dance culture that enveloped him in Vienna. Hanslick's struggle with the competing values of listening and moving—which Strauss manipulated so powerfully among the Viennese public—offers fascinating insights into a social milieu where popular and serious music were still caught up with one another and an audience that had not yet accepted hard boundaries between physical and intellectual genres of music. Hanslick himself waltzed brilliantly over these very boundaries that he, as much as any other critic, helped to establish.

Notes

All translations are my own unless otherwise indicated. I thank Marcella Livi for assistance with the translations.

1. Nicholas Cook, *Music, Imagination, and Culture* (Oxford: Clarendon Press, 1990), 15.

2. On the emergence of this listening paradigm, which Bonds traces to E. T. A. Hoffmann, see Mark Evan Bonds, *Music as Thought: Listening to the Symphony in the Age of Beethoven* (Princeton, NJ: Princeton University Press, 2006), 6-10.

3. Eduard Hanslick, *The Beautiful in Music*, trans. from the 7th ed. by Gustav Cohen (1891; repr. New York: Da Capo Press, 1974), 134. While the Payzant translation is used throughout this volume, I have chosen the Cohen translation for its clarity on the topic of physical movement and for its more fluid syntax overall.

4. Meredith Little and Natalie Jenne have demonstrated the wide scope of functional dance values in music of the early eighteenth century in *Dance and the Music of J. S. Bach* (Bloomington: Indiana University Press, 1991). Wye Allanbrook further points out the persistent residue of dance as a topical presence in music of the later eighteenth century in *Rhythmic Gesture in Mozart: Le Nozze di Figaro and Don Giovanni* (Chicago: University of Chicago Press, 1983).

5. Material from this paper was presented at the conference "Eduard Hanslick: Aesthetic, Critical, and Cultural Contexts," University College Dublin, 2009, and at the annual meeting for the American Musicological Society, 2010. A more extended discussion of attitudes toward dance in music criticism may be found in the author's forthcoming dissertation, "Disdain for Dance, Disdain for France: Choreophobia in German Musical Modernism" (PhD diss., University of California, Davis, 2012).

6. Dana Gooley points out elsewhere in this volume that a divergence of musical genres—in this case between functional dance and operetta—is associated with a corresponding divergence of social class. Gooley understands Hanslick's concern with genre boundaries as a manifestation of his allegiance to the liberal ideals of the educated, elite Viennese bourgeoisie. This explanation for Hanslick's contradictions on dance relies on perceptions of the waltz as a social practice imbued with the values of the *Volk*. While the waltz did originate as a dance of the folk, I allow a wider social sphere for the waltz as it came to be practiced in Vienna—including the educated elite as practicing dancers—in my interpretation of its impact on Viennese musical life. For further discussion of the "elevation" of the waltz into "higher" genres, see David Brodbeck, "Primo Schubert,

Secondo Schumann: Brahms's Four-Hand Waltzes, Op. 39," *Journal of Musicology* 7, no. 1 (1989): 58-80.

7. Karl Kobald writes: "Whether poor or rich, young or old, peasant or nobility, washerwoman or duchess, prince or worker, Bohemian or German, Hungarian or Croat, all swayed and turned, forgetting sorrows and life in the dance." Karl Kobald, *Johann Strauss* (Vienna: Österreichischer Bundesverlag, 1925), 8. Cited in Camille Crittenden, *Johann Strauss and Vienna: Operetta and the Politics of Popular Culture* (Cambridge: Cambridge University Press, 2000), 34.

8. Charlotte Moscheles, *Recent Music and Musicians as Described in the Diaries and Correspondence of Ignatz Moscheles* (1873; repr. New York: Da Capo Press, 1970), 248.

9. "Ja, es erhoben sich Stimmen, die mit Strauss den höchsten musikalischen Genuß scheiden sahen, den ihre Beine je empfunden, denen sein electrischer Bogenstrich so recht bis in's Innerste gedrungen war, wo es sonst nie Licht ward.... Die Seele davon ist Strauss, dessen Geist die Körper aller Mitwirkenden beherrscht; ... Uebrigens kann Keiner, der wahre Musik im Leibe hat, reine Tanzrhythmen, ohne darnach zu tanzen oder tanzen zu sehen, oder wenigstens behaglich dabei zu essen und zu trinken." "Strauss im Norden," *Neue Leipziger Zeitschrift für Musik*, No. 78 (December 29, 1834): 309-310.

10. "In den vorderen Parterrebänken beginnen einige Menschen, die zu nahe dem Zauberer sitzen, wie elektrisirt emporzuzucken, das musikalische Fluidum theilt sich blitzrasch den Anderen mit, man schlägt unwillkürlich den Tact mit Händen und Füßen, und alsbald will das ganze Haus sich erheben und mitsingen und mittanzen und fliegen und schweben, das Theater wird zum Ballsaal und Alles ruft: Strauss! Strauss!" *Neue Freie Presse* (March 3, 1875), 7. Joseph Oppenheim (1839-1900) was a journalist and satirist. Born in Darmstadt-Arheiligen, he came to Vienna in the 1860s and went to work for the *Neue Freie Presse* in 1872.

11. Da mochte auch die Stirn des strengsten Richters sich wohlgefällig entrunzeln, und wenn er nicht selber mittanzte, so hat er wenigstens mit herzlichem Lachen die elektrischen Wirkungen der specifisch wienerischen Operette an den Anderen beobachtet. *Neue Freie Presse* (March 3, 1875): 7.

12. Kevin C. Karnes, *Music, Criticism, and the Challenge of History: Shaping Modern Musical Thought in Late Nineteenth-Century Vienna* (Oxford: Oxford University Press, 2008), 21-75. Dana Gooley discusses the conflict this created for the critic who strove to educate the public without alienating himself from the "average" listener. See Dana Gooley, "Hanslick and the Institution of Criticism," *Journal of Musicology* 28, no. 3 (Summer 2011): 289-324.

13. Karnes, *Music, Criticism, and the Challenge of History*, 34.

14. Ibid., 48–75.

15. For discussion of the *feuilleton* and its implications in nineteenth-century Viennese music criticism, see Sandra McColl, *Music Criticism in Vienna 1896–1897: Critically Moving Forms* (Oxford: Clarendon Press, 1996), 1–4.

16. See Bonds, *Music as Thought*, 5-28.

17. Strauss died on September 25, 1849. The review appeared on October 6, 1849, in the *Beilage zum Morgenblatte der Wiener Zeitung*.

18. "Als Componist hat er bekanntlich die Tanzmusik gepflogen, eine Gattung, auf welche Tonsetzer und Kritiker gewöhnlich mit souveräner Verachtung herabsehen. Mit Unrecht. Auch in der kleinen Form bewährt sich das große Talent, und dieses, als der göttliche Funke, ists, vor dem wir uns zuerst beugen." Hanslick, *Sämtliche Schriften* 1/2, 124.

19. Der simpelste Dorfschullehrer, der einen contrapunktischen Cursus mitgemacht hat, bringt es dahin, eine Messe zu componiren, in welcher mehr sogenannte Gelehrsamkeit steckt, als in Strauss's sämmtlichen Werken zusammen,—aber in alle Ewigkeit wird der schöne Walzer mehr Kunstwerth haben, als die schlechte Messe." Ibid., 124.

20. "Der Werth jeder Kunstgattung aber steigt oder fällt mit den Anforderungen, die man ihr stellt. Unsre Anforderung an die Tanzmusik geht dahin, daß sie nicht blos das Stampfen der Tänzer im Takt erhalte, sondern deren Seelenleben verstehe, ihre Gefühle und Leidenschaften interpretire, steigere, veredle. Der unterste Grad der Tanzmusik hat nur mit den Füßen zu thun, auf höherer Stufe spricht er zur Phantasie, zum Gefühl, zum Geist." Ibid., 124.

21. "Um diese höhere Stufe zu behaupten, wird freilich nöthig sein, daß sich der Componist von einer blos gymnastischen Anschauung des Tanzes zu dessen geselliger Bedeutung erhebe. In unserer allerhöchst civilisirten '*bonne société*' ist der Tanz von seiner ursprünglichen Bedeutung längst zu einer höheren gediehen. Wollte man in demselben nur körperliche Uebung sehen, so würde man ihn in Turnschulen pflegen. Unsere heutigen Tanzunterhaltungen, so oft sie auch zur Carricatur herabgewürdigt werden mögen, sind und bleiben die geweihten Asyle zärtlicherer Bedürfnisse und Bestrebungen." Ibid. 124–25.

22. "Wir betrachteten bisher noch immer die Strauss'sche Tanzmusik nur insofern sie dem Tanze und dessen Interessen dient; wäre nichts weiter an ihm zu loben, so träfe Straussens Verlust lediglich die Tanzwelt.... Für den Musiker konnte Strauss nur dann Bedeutung haben, wenn seine Tänze, abgelöst von ihrem Zwecke, also außer dem Ballsaal, noch musikalischen Fond genug gehabt, um den Kenner zu interessiren ... Strauss erwies sich in der Ausarbeitung seiner Musikstücke als ein feiner, künstlerischer Geist, dem Alles Rohe und Dilettantenhafte fern lag.... verfehlte er doch nie, im Rhythmus, im Periodenbau, und namentlich in der Harmonisirung und Instrumentation eine Fülle von Zügen niederzulegen, welchen das bedächtige Ohr des Musikers lauschte, während der Tänzer an den süßen Feuer der Melodie sich einen Rausch trank." Ibid., 125–26.

23. "Wie die Form der Walzermusik noch gegenwärtig beschaffen ist, erscheint sie als das größte Hemmniß für deren künstlerische Entwicklung, und für jeden Componisten, der ihr eine bessere Mitgift von Talent oder Kenntniß zubringt. Der kleine, festgeschlossene Rahmen des Walzers läßt auch die kleinste Entwicklung einer Melodie nicht zu, welche deshalb, so wie sie zu Ende gekommen, auch spurlos verloren geht, um einer zweiten und dritten u.s.f. Platz zu machen, bis alle 5 Walzer wie eine unzusammenhängende Bilderreihe in einem Guckkasten abgerollt sind.... Es ist dies eine unkünstlerische Verschwendung, welche die begabteste Productionskraft bald erschöpfen muß." Ibid., 126.

24. "Der Walzertanz (zum Unterschiede vom einzelnen Walzer) solle nicht aus fünf selbstständigen, zusammenhanglos aneinander gereihten Stücken bestehen, deren jedes 1 oder 2 neue Motive verschlingt, sondern er solle ja Ein abgeschlossenes, zusammenhängendes Ganze bilden. Dazu würden 1 oder 2 Hauptthemen hinreichen, denen (innerhalb der Grenzen der Tanzbarkeit) die freieste musikalische Entwicklung gegönnt und geboten wäre.... Nur durch die einheitliche Form kann der Componist dem doppelten Uebel entgehen, ein halb Dutzend neue Motive erfinden, und sie nutzlos vergeuden zu müssen, nur durch sie kann der Walzer als Musikstück sich zu künstlerischen Werth und Inhalt entwickeln, nur durch sie endlich kann er einen Charakter erhalten." The persistence of Hanslick's application of the values of absolute music to genres of dance music in modern scholarship is discussed further in my forthcoming dissertation, "Disdain for Dance, Disdain for France." Ibid., 127.

25. "eine untergeordnete [Kunstgattung]," "ein weißes Blatt." Ibid., 267.
26. "Natürlich haben wir damit nicht die bloße Technik im Auge, die für Tanzmusik leicht genug erworben wird, sondern gerade deren poetische Beseelung, und selbstständig musikalische Schönheit. Dieser Standpunkt wünscht also nicht, den Walzer im Tanzesflug zu erproben, sondern in beschaulichem Genuß ihn als Musik anhören zu können, eine Befriedigung die uns in jeder Produktion von Alt- oder Jung-Strauss geworden ist, welcher wir beiwohnten." Ibid. This review appeared in the *Österreichische Blätter für Literatur und Kunst*, November 28, 1853.
27. "Ein schöner Tanz gehört zu den vielen leichten Dingen, die nicht Jedermann trifft. Der engste Rahmen und die unerbittlichsten Bedingungen, die es in der Musik gibt, heißen im Walzer den Komponisten mit dem ersten Taktschlag die volle Erfindung einsetzen, sie alsdann ohne fruchtbare Benützung frisch gepflückt wegwerfen, und so immer wieder neu gewinnen und vergeuden. Wem nichts einfällt, der kann keinen Walzer machen." Ibid.
28. Hanslick, *The Beautiful in Music*, 136–37.
29. Ibid., 115.
30. Ibid., 122.
31. Ibid., 117.
32. Ibid., 119.
33. Ibid., 124.
34. Ibid., 126.
35. Ibid., 125.
36. Geoffrey Payzant, "Hanslick, Heinse and the 'Moral' Effects of Music," *Music Review* 49, no. 2 (1988): 132.
37. Hanslick, *The Beautiful in Music*, 128–29. David Gramit discusses this passage in "Between Täuschung and Seligkeit: Situating Schubert's Dances," *Musical Quarterly* 84 (2000): 221-37.
38. Hanslick, *The Beautiful in Music*, 117.
39. Ibid., 130.
40. Ibid., 130.
41. Ibid., 136.s42. Ibid., 147.
43. Geoffrey Payzant, *Hanslick on the Musically Beautiful: Sixteen Lectures on the Musical Aesthetics of Eduard Hanslick* (Christchurch, New Zealand: Cybereditions, 2003), 29.
44. Hanslick, *The Beautiful in Music*, 146.
45. "Aber es war ein Anblick, den ich nicht vergesse. Fanny Elssler hatte ihr Kleid ein wenig geschürzt und tanzte, oder vielmehr schwebte zwei- bis dreimal den geräumigen Saal auf und nieder mit so graziösem, ausdrucksvollen Beugen und Neigen des Hauptes und Oberkörpers, mit so runden, welligen Bewegungen der Arme, daß mir zum erstenmal klar wurde, was ein idealer Tanz sei." Hanslick, *Aus meinen Leben* (Berlin: Allgemeiner Verein für Deutsche Litteratur, 1894), 2 vols, vol. 1, 224.
46. Max Kalbeck, *Johannes Brahms*, vol. 2 (Berlin: Deutsche Brahms-Gesellschaft 1908), 189. On Hanslick's enjoyment of the waltz in the context of Viennese society, Max Graf notes: "Hanslick was Viennese to the core. He loved the facile sensuousness of Italian arias, the wit of the French *opéra comique*, the melodious stream of Strauss's waltzes and Offenbach's operettas, just as the careless, pleasure-seeking, brilliant, and elegant society of Vienna did.... One must have met the little old gentleman at parties, have seen him joking, paying compliments to the lovely Viennese ladies, retailing the latest witticisms, and finally, after a good meal, to which he did justice like a connoisseur, sitting down at the piano and playing Strauss waltzes; then one could realize that

he belonged to Viennese society in heart and mind and soul." Max Graf, *Composer and Critic: Two Hundred Years of Musical Criticism* (New York: W. W. Norton, 1946), 246-47.

47. Eduard Hanslick, *Hanslick's Music Criticisms*, trans. Henry Pleasants (New York: Simon & Schuster, 1950), 170.

48. Richard Specht, *Johannes Brahms*, trans. Eric Blom (New York: E. P. Dutton, 1930), 171-72.

49. I use the translation in David Brodbeck, "Brahms as Editor and Composer: His Two Editions of Ländler by Schubert and His First Two Cycles of Waltzes, Opera 39 and 52" (PhD diss., University of Pennsylvania, 1984), 183. See Kalbeck, *Johannes Brahms*, 2: 190 for original German text.

50. Kalbeck, *Johannes Brahms*, 2:189.

51. Ibid., 2: 190, this translation from Brodbeck, "Brahms as Editor and Composer," 183.

52. Graf, *Composer and Critic*, 247.

53. Specht, *Johannes Brahms*, 172.

54. Ibid., 172.

55. Cited in Ian Swafford, *Johannes Brahms: A Biography* (New York: Vintage Books, 1997), 601. Swafford comments on Brahms's toast: "For history above all, he wanted to commend his friend and their friendship, and at the same time to distance himself from his best champion." Brahms had in fact communicated his dissatisfaction with Hanslick's views early in his life when, after reading over *Vom Musikalisch-Schönen*, he wrote to Clara Schumann that he had "found such a number of stupid things on first glance that [he] gave it up." *Clara Schumann, Johannes Brahms: Briefe aus den Jahren 1853-1896*, ed. Berthold Litzmann (Hildesheim: Georg Olms Verlag, 1970), 62.

56. David Brodbeck, "Primo Schubert, Secondo Schumann," 59–61.

57. Andrew Lamb, "Brahms and Johann Strauss," *Musical Times* 116, no. 1592 (October 1975): 869–71.

58. "In seinen neuen Walzern findet sich häufig ein falsches Pathos eingeschmuggelt, das in der Tanzmusik gänzlich ungehörig, beinahe verstimmend auf den Hörer wirkt. . . . Allein jede Würze muß ihr Maß finden, vor allem im guten Geschmack, dann überdies in den Bedingungen der bestimmten Kunstgattung. Die von Posaunen herausgestoßene klägliche Akkordenfolge, welche den zweiten Theil von Nr. 1 der 'Schallwellen' bildet, fände allenfalls Anwendung bei Opernfinalen, worin es besonders blutig zugeht; in einem Walzer ist sie abscheulich. . . . Nicht alles, was im Dreivierteltakt spielt, ist darum ein Walzer." Hanslick, *Sämtliche Schriften* 1/2, 380–81. This review originally appeared in the *Österreichische Blätter für Literatur und Kunst*, October 6, 1854. The "Schallwellen" waltz was Strauss's op. 148, written in 1854.

59. "Eine Kunstgattung wird weder im Inhalt noch in der Form bereichert, wenn man ihr ein Pathos aufzwingt, dem ihr Wesen widerstrebt. Ist aber erkünstelte Großartigkeit überall von Uebel, so wird sie geradezu Ruin für jene leicht beschwingten Tonwesen, deren Bestimmung es ist, schöne Tänzerinnen mit Frohsinn, Scherz und Anmuth zu umklingen. Halte darum Jeder die Grenzen rein und verhüte Verschleppungen aus fremdem Gebiet." Hanslick, *Sämtliche Schriften* 1/2, 381.

60. "Strauss hat sich offenbar einen Act großartiger historischer Vergeltung zum Ziel gesetzt. Als gegen Ende des vorigen Jahrhunderts die Orchestermusik durch systematische Verflachung des Haydnschen Styls populär gemacht wurde, gingen die Herren Pleyel, Wranitzky, Hoffmeister, Gyrowetz und Rosetti . . . die 'fidelsten'Ländler zu Motiven ihrer Symphonien und Quartetten zu machen. Johann Strauss will offenbar diese Schmach seiner Wiener Vorfahren durch Compensation tilgen, und schmückt

seine Walzer mit Motiven, deren Ehrenplatz von rechtswegen die Symphonien der neuesten Schule wären." Hanslick, *Sämtliche Schriften* 1/4, 235. See chapter 5 in this volume for further discussion of Hanslick's desire to regulate genre boundaries.

61. "Strauss scheine die neuesten Walzer mehr für den Musenhof von Weimar als für Wien berechnet zu haben. In der That bemerkte auch ich in Strauss' neueren Werken jenen scharf prickelnden Duft, den das Wildpret ausströmt, wenn es nach Vergangenheit, und die Musik, wenn sie nach Zukunft riecht.... Diejenigen seiner Walzer, welche ohne vorstechende Originalität wenigstens frisch und natürlich klingen, sind noch immer weit bessere Tanzmusik als jene gespreizten Motive, deren endlose Perioden sich mit der gesuchtesten Harmonisirung verbünden, um Ohren und Füße in Verwirrung zu bringen." Hanslick, *Sämtliche Schriften* 1/4, 235.

62. "Das dieser füß betäubende Dreivierteltact, der sich aller Köpfe und Füße bemächtigt hatte, nothwendig die große, ernste Musik in den Hintergrund drängte und die Zuhörer zu einer geistigen Anstrengung immer unfähiger machte, begreift sich." Hanslick, *Geschichte des Concertwesens in Wien*, 2 vols. (1869; repr. Farnborough: Gregg, 1971), 1:365. An augmented version of this review is repr. in Hanslick, *AML*, 119.

63. "Bald nach seinem Wiener Debut wagte er schon wiederholte große Kunstreisen mit seinem Orchester. In diesem ganz neuen Unternehmen war ihm sein Vater vorangegangen—meines Wissens der Erste, der es gewagt, mit Tanzmusik auf Kunstreisen zu gehen, seine Walzer nicht in einem Tanzlocale für Ballgäste, sondern im Concertsaale vor einem zuhörenden Publicum zu produciren." Hanslick writes on the occasion of the fortieth anniversary of Strauss Jr.'s debut at Domeyer's in 1844. *Neue Freie Presse*, October 15, 1884, repr. in *Musikalisches Skizzenbuch* (Berlin: Allgemeiner Verein für Deutsche Litteratur, 1896), 209.

64. "Um die Mitte der Vierziger Jahre spielte Strauss mit seinem Orchester in meiner Vaterstadt Prag, im ständischen Theater. Leidenschaftlicher junger Musikfreund, fühlte ich doch dafür gar kein Interesse und besuchte eine einzige Strausssche Production wegen der Ouvertüren von Beethoven und Weber, die das Programm zierten. Auf die Walzer achtete ich kaum; sie kamen mir einer wie der andere vor." Hanslick, *Musikalisches Skizzenbuch*, 209.

65. It was young people, we may recall, who were most susceptible to the nervous impulses of dance in *Vom Musikalisch-Schönen*, and the young again, in the obituary to Strauss Sr., who were in need of the sustenance dance could provide for their "inner life." Hanslick, *Sämtliche Schriften* 1/2, 124.

66. "Es ist derselbe pathetische Zug, der uns junge Leute damals nach allen Aufführungen Schillerscher oder Shakespearescher Tragödien lechzen machte, während es uns nicht einfiel, zu einem Lustspiel ins Theater zu gehen. In der Musik waren Beethovens Symphonien, Mendelssohns Ouvertüren.... Gegenstand unseres Entzückens, unserer Sehnsucht. Was sollten uns komische Opern, ... die nur Melodie und Temperament hatten? O, über dies kindische 'nur'! Was sollte uns vollends Tanzmusik, außer um dazu zu tanzen?" Hanslick, *Musikalisches Skizzenbuch*, 210.

67. "Er kommt endlich dahinter, daß auch in der Tanzmusik Genialität möglich und auf dem schmalen Rosenblatt eines Walzers Raum ist für einen sinnigen und liebenswürdigen Gedanken." Ibid.

68. "Es gehört eben auch für die Kleinkunst, für die Miniaturschönheit eine gewisse Heranbildung; ich wenigstens lernte erst später Tanzmusik nicht mit dem ungeduldigen Ohr des Tanzlustigen, sondern mit dem aufmerksamen des Musikers anhören." Ibid.

Chapter Seven

"Poison-Flaming Flowers from the Orient and Nightingales from Bayreuth"

On Hanslick's Reception of the Music of Goldmark

David Brodbeck

> The distinctive qualities of this most deeply serious of composers are well known—the hot-bloodedness, passion, his decisive characteristics, which dominate his feelings, sometimes at the expense of beauty, but never at the expense of truth, or of that which seems true to him.
>
> —Eduard Hanslick

> Hanslick was always more disapproving than approving in his judgment toward me. [He] attacked my mind, not the work.
>
> —Carl Goldmark

On May 18, 1900, the Vienna Court Opera celebrated the seventieth birthday of Carl Goldmark with a performance of the composer's *Die Königin von Saba* (*The Queen of Sheba*), a grand opera in four acts on a libretto by Salomon Hermann

---

All translations are my own unless otherwise stated.

The first epigraph is from one of Hanslick's reviews: "Man kennt die eigenthümlichen Vorzüge dieses tiefernsten Tondichters: das Heißblütige, Leidenschaftliche, einschneidend Charakteristische, das mitunter auf Kosten der Schönheit, aber nie auf Kosten der Wahrheit oder desjenigen, was ihm als wahr erscheint, seine Empfindungen beherrscht." Ed. H. [Eduard Hanslick], "Hofoperntheater. Concerte," *Neue Freie Presse* (December 7, 1880): 2; repr. in Eduard Hanslick, *Concerte, Componisten und Virtuosen der letzten fünfzehn Jahre 1870–1885* (Berlin: Allgemeiner Verein für Deutsche Litteratur, 1886), 283. Hereafter I will retain Hanslick's characteristic byline in the Neue Freie Presse (Ed. H.) in citations of his articles from that newspaper.

The second epigraph is from Goldmark's memoir: "Hanslick war in seinem Urteil stets gegen mich mehr ablehnend als zustimmend. . . . [Er hat] mein Gemüt—nicht das Stück—getroffen." Karl Goldmark, *Erinnerungen aus meinem Leben* (Vienna: Rikola Verlag, 1922), 98; English translation from Carl Goldmark, *Notes from the Life of a Viennese Composer*, trans. Alice Goldmark Brandeis (New York: Albert and Charles Boni, 1927), 175 (from which here and throughout I have adapted my own translations).

Mosenthal. Although he would miss this celebratory performance, Eduard Hanslick, the semi-retired music critic for the *Neue Freie Presse*, made sure to mark the day with a *feuilleton* in which he paid friendly tribute to a composer whose works had long been a fixture in Vienna's operatic and concert bills.[1] Hanslick had always harbored certain misgivings about Goldmark's music, but he was careful not to allow those to cloud the day. Moreover, he admired Goldmark's solid character and was genuinely fond of the man, with whom he had been friendly for many years.[2] And so the critic begins by graciously extolling Goldmark's ascent to a hard-won place at the very center of Vienna's musical culture:

> Well, could it be seventy already? How immeasurably long this distance seems to us in our younger years, and yet how incredibly quickly we turn up there one day! For Goldmark the first half of this journey was difficult and troublesome. "Ich hatte viel Bekümmernis" [I had much affliction], he sang with Sebastian Bach. But whoever bravely struggles through a forest of hindrances to artistic heights and indisputable worth is to be celebrated with redoubled heartiness. The long sad period of hardship did not embitter our jubilarian; the fame finally achieved neither blinded him nor made him aloof. He is always ungrudgingly appreciative of external successes. His goodwill, his fairness can be counted on. . . . Hand in hand with the high estimation for Goldmark the artist goes a general sympathy for the man himself. How publicly and splendidly both were expressed ten years ago when Goldmark's sixtieth birthday was celebrated together with the one-hundredth performance of his "Queen of Sheba!" And all day today the omniscient cricket on the hearth will chirp loudly and cheerfully over the masses![3]

By the time of this notice, Goldmark had produced an extensive catalogue of works, including several operas as well as solo vocal, choral, piano, chamber, and orchestral compositions. Although Hanslick pays all this music its due, it is Goldmark's first opera, *The Queen of Sheba*, to which he devotes the bulk of his attention. This was not only the work whose première on the same stage a quarter century earlier had paved the way for the great international reputation that Goldmark once enjoyed, but also the one that, more than any other, shaped Hanslick's essential understanding of the composer's style.

Notably, both Hanslick and Goldmark came of age during the revolutionary year of 1848 and then followed their own paths (often intertwined, to be sure) to become cultural pillars of Liberal Vienna.[4] Liberals of this generation espoused a set of "democratic" principles aimed at dismantling privilege by birth, encouraging free enterprise, reducing the power of the church, and so on, but they did so within a framework of strict German chauvinism. The obvious contradiction raised by this project in the context of the polyglot, multinational Austrian state—with eleven officially recognized nationalities and as many local languages—was glossed over by an almost religious devotion to the idea of "culture."[5] Thus *Deutschtum* and bourgeois cultural values such as property ownership and education were treated as though they were one and the same: to be liberal was to be German; to be German was to be liberal. The idea of race (or what we would now term ethnicity) had little to do with this particular construction of social identity. Liberal culture was (at least theoretically) to be open to all people, but German identity was the price of admission.[6]

Hanslick's music-critical writing reflects key tenets of this liberal nationalism. We can see this, for example, when Hanslick—the Prague-born grandson of a Czech-speaking farmer from small-town Bohemia—writes about the music of Bedřich Smetana and Antonín Dvořák, not in terms of Czech nationalism, but as embodiments of the same German culture that he himself had so firmly embraced.[7] It was the same liberal nationalist project that had enabled Goldmark, the son of a Jewish cantor in small-town Hungary, to rise to his illustrious artistic position in the imperial capital. Yet it appears that Hanslick could never fully convince himself concerning Goldmark's own German credentials— and this despite Goldmark's decided self-perception as a German composer (an identity that neither Smetana nor Dvořák would ever have embraced).[8] In what follows I explore this discrepancy between Hanslick's Goldmark and Goldmark's Goldmark. I begin with Hanslick's earliest writings on Goldmark's music, for already there can be found mention of certain "troubling" aspects of Goldmark's style that would come into focus for Hanslick only later on with the appearance of *The Queen of Sheba* and would forever inhibit a full-throated approval of his friend's music.

Adumbrations of Hanslick's Goldmark

In a *feuilleton* of January 15, 1857, Hanslick glances back at the Viennese concert season to date, noting the odd fact that "not a single celebrity" had yet graced the public with an appearance. Instead, as he observes, "our concert announcements give only honorable names from the Viennese address book: Bondy, Kukaseder, Goldmark, Gall, Weidner, Tobisch, Rappoldi, etc."[9] With this witty passing remark, Hanslick makes mention for the first time of the otherwise unheralded Goldmark, who was then toiling away in obscurity as a twenty-six-year-old violinist in Vienna's *Carltheater*. The second mention comes four months later, in a retrospective of the now completed season: "A unique new class of concert-givers were the composers. Messrs. Gall, Langwara, Goldmark tested the youthful wings of their inspiration, so it seemed, to the great satisfaction of their friends and themselves."[10]

Hanslick refers here to the self-produced concert by which Goldmark made his Viennese début as a composer. Occurring on March 12, 1857, this included a Psalm setting, a piano quartet, two songs, and an overture. Hanslick left no review and may well not have been in attendance; his attention was focused on Liszt's symphonic poem *Les Préludes*, heard in the concert of the *Gesellschaft der Musikfreunde* on March 8, and the subject of an important review to which we shall return. He had, nevertheless, played a crucial role behind the scenes in bringing Goldmark's music to public attention. The composer's concert had originally been scheduled for December 26, 1856, but was called off at the last moment.[11] (This explains why Hanslick mentioned it already in January.) In need of additional funding to make a second attempt, Goldmark offered to provide one unnamed potential patron with expert testimony of his talent from two recognized experts—Josef Dachs, a piano instructor at the Vienna Conservatory (who ultimately performed in the concert), and "Professor Hanslick," recently appointed as an unpaid lecturer at the University of Vienna. "I was sure of Dachs," Goldmark later recalled. "But Hanslick I was not acquainted with." He continues: "So I sent him my overture, wrote him what was involved, and asked for his opinion. He wrote to my Maecenas: 'The work shows talent but is still immature.' My patron thereupon took fifty seats, which helped me greatly. Not only were my expenses covered, but I had gotten an audience as well, a far more important matter."[12]

Goldmark did not appear again as a composer in Vienna until the beginning of the next decade. In a second self-produced Viennese concert, given in January 1861, he hired the newly founded Hellmesberger Quartet to perform his String Quartet, op. 8, and Piano Trio, op. 4 (with pianist Julius Epstein); sharing the stage was Goldmark's young piano student Caroline Bettelheim, who performed six numbers from the composer's *Sturm und Drang*, op. 5, a cycle of character pieces for piano.[13] In a brief notice, Hanslick acknowledges that this selection of new chamber and piano compositions gave "undeniable proof of a talent that ... augurs well." Yet, he adds: "Tranquility and clarity are still missing. Very favorable outlines are stifled in their effect by the rhapsodic parceling out of the form, by the bizarre rhythm, finally by the characteristically churning restlessness. We dare hope that the fermenting must will in due course become wine."[14]

Hanslick's review of the String Quintet, op. 9, heard in a concert given by the Hellmesberger Quartet in December 1862, is more uniformly favorable. Claiming to know "next to nothing" (*so gut wie nichts*) by the composer, the critic reports that Goldmark has "up to now avoided the public, not forced himself upon it," and he adds encouragingly: "The newest quintet ... may persuade him conclusively of the groundlessness of this modesty. This work is marked by a mood that is worthy, of strong character, although perhaps all too serious, and gives evidence of an energetically striving spirit and excellent musical technique."[15] In light of this favorable report, it is not entirely surprising to discover that Hanslick saw to it in the following year, that from among fifteen applicants, Goldmark was selected as the first composer to be awarded an Austrian state stipend in support of talented artists of limited means.[16]

Hanslick's earlier equivocation about the composer's music resurfaced in his review of the Suite for Piano and Violin, op. 11, introduced by Caroline Bettelheim and Joseph Hellmesberger in January 1865. The critic describes the work as "skillful, ingenious, but somewhat gloomy and reflective." Especially notable is his comment about the second movement, an Andante in C-sharp minor. This he describes as "a melancholic, long-drawn-out lament whose melody and harmonization are reminiscent of Oriental tunes." Still, he notes that overall, "the composer has thrown off a good deal of his earlier muddled state and brooding subjectivity [and] become clearer, freer, more concise in his form," and he concludes by expressing the hope that the composer would continue to break free of those earlier disturbing characteristics, especially with respect to melody, and so might continue as a forward-striving artist. In that case, he writes, Goldmark's "most noble, serious . . . music will then also not be without universal effect."[17]

The critic recognizes something of this hoped-for development in the *Sakuntala* Overture, heard in a concert given by the Vienna Philharmonic on December 26, 1865. Hanslick is pleased to report that this essay in Indian local color, based on a dramatization of part of the *Mahabharata* by the eminent Sanskrit poet Kālidāsa, was no symphonic poem in disguise (notwithstanding the inclusion in the score of a synopsis of the drama). "Whatever the relationship of the composition to the famous Indian drama," he writes, "it is not dependent in the ambiguous sense of descriptive music. As a piece of music that is fully understandable and independent in and of itself, it takes from the subject only the poetic stimulus, the general mood and local color, at most the simplest main features of the dramatic peripeteia."[18] Clearly, *Sakuntala* had passed Hanslick's acid test, laid out eight years earlier in his review of Liszt's *Les Préludes*, that "music be based on its own laws and remain specifically musical, thus making, even without the program, a clear, independent impression."[19] Moreover, Hanslick writes, the work is "fresh and characteristic in its invention, of clear outline and fine detail," and indeed "shows a decisive clarification of Goldmark's earlier somewhat confused and wallowing talent," with "only a few passages reminding us of the former love of dissonance and solemn obscurity."[20] This last pronouncement might seem to embody the hope that Goldmark had at last begun to turn in a stylistic direction that Hanslick would find more congenial and fitting, but that was decidedly not to be.

Behind the Scenes at the *Hofoper*

The long genesis of *Die Königin von Saba* can be traced back to this same period. Here the brief biblical tale of the Queen of Sheba's visit to the court of King Solomon is merely the point of departure for a tragic love story in which the courtier Assad, betrothed to the High Priest's daughter, Sulamith, is seduced and eventually destroyed by the Queen, an exotic *femme fatale* whom Hanslick, in his review of the opera's opening, describes as "a kind of Egyptian Messalina" (*eine Art egyptischer Messalina*).[21] Hanslick evidently had it on the composer's word that he had originally imagined "the young Bettelheim girl" in the title role. That, of course, would be Caroline Bettelheim, who made her début at the Vienna Court Opera in 1862. (Hanslick describes her as "the excellent young pianist who had become an even more outstanding singer.")[22] If Goldmark is to be believed, he sketched a scenario for the work in 1863 and then turned to Caroline's regular tutor for help in working out the dramatic details. At all events, it is clear that no real progress was made on the project until early 1866, when Goldmark commissioned Mosenthal to write a proper libretto. Composition of the first two acts seems to have gone fairly smoothly, but the score was not completed in its original three-act form (with *lieto fine*) until November 1871. The composer submitted this to the management of the Vienna Court Opera several months later, but even then he would have to wait through nearly three years of frustration and dashed hopes before the work—revised in December 1874 as a four-act opera with a tragic conclusion—was finally put on the boards.[23]

As Hanslick later explains: "For ten years the meticulous composer was occupied with the score. When happily the end was reached, he stood only at the beginning of almost incalculable difficulties and hindrances."[24] The critic knew of what he wrote. In January 1873, he had received a letter from the composer in which Goldmark voiced his suspicion that his work had been passed over for performance solely because the Intendant General of the Court Theaters, Count Eugen Wrbna-Freudenthal, was "anxious and mistrustful" on account of certain earlier "failures by native composers."[25] Goldmark urged the critic, who, he wrote, had been "entrusted by the state with the noble honor of promoting art and artistic interests," to come to the assistance of his fellow Austrian, concluding: "I appeal to this lofty mission of yours!"[26]

Goldmark was not being entirely forthcoming here concerning the person whom he held responsible for keeping the work off the stage. In a revealing letter of March 20, 1873, to his brother Joseph, he makes it clear that he considers his main obstacle to obtaining a performance to be, not Wrbna, but Johann Herbeck, Director of the Court Opera, whom Goldmark had long suspected of artistic jealousy.[27] The same letter also gives evidence that Goldmark now held out little hope of winning Hanslick's support:

> I spoke with Hanslick. I found him to be unfavorably disposed toward my thing. He thought I should first seek out a small stage in Germany, after which it would go easily here. He also wants to become familiar with my work before doing anything. The real reason for his behavior is this: he is doing all he can to bring about a performance of [Ambroise] Thomas's *Hamlet* (a miserable work).[28]

Goldmark thereupon reports that his meeting with Hanslick had taken place in the midst of negotiations for a forthcoming performance of *Sakuntala*, heard in the subscription concerts of the Vienna Philharmonic on January 26, 1873, and that the press had used this occasion to "clamor ardently and unanimously" for a performance of *The Queen of Sheba*, as well. "Yet," as Goldmark explains, "that has—at least for the time being—made things worse." He continues:

> Hanslick, even more upset over having been pre-empted in the matter and that such a significant public pressure is being exerted, [and] also worried about the performance of his *Hamlet*, is now completely against me and lets me feel it. How far the affair with Hanslick goes you may gather from the following facts. The enclosed article "German Music in Italy," as I have found out, was first delivered to the *Neue Freie Presse*. The paper wanted to publish it as [something] very interesting. Hanslick suppressed it. Unidentified friends of mine have interceded with [Michael] Etienne, the editor of this paper, to do something on my behalf. [Etienne] is sending one of his employees to one of my closer friends in order to inform himself about the situation regarding the matter of my opera—but for decency's sake Hanslick should be asked.[29]

I have been unable to identify the article in question, and what is preserved of Goldmark's letter breaks off at this tantalizing point, leaving us to guess at the continuation. Somewhat disingenuously—and perhaps with a guilty conscience as well—when Hanslick looked back on the episode nearly thirty years later, he recalled only how Goldmark's "appeal to my rather doubtful influence turned out to be unnecessary [since] the only authoritative advocates in this matter"—Herbeck and his colleague on the conducting staff, Otto Dessoff—"had expressly recommended Goldmark's opera and in Prince Hohenlohe, Wrbna's successor, had found a receptive ear."[30]

Whatever Hanslick's actions may have been with regard to the opera when he was asked for support in 1873—and Goldmark claimed in this context that the critic's "influence behind the scenes was much stronger and more dangerous than in front"—he did nevertheless later lend the still-unperformed work at least tepid support.[31] Consider his response to the Queen's Entrance March from act 1, which was included in a gala concert held at the *Gesellschaft der Musikfreunde* on January 11, 1874.[32] Although Hanslick expresses skepticism about the "strong orientalizing melodic style" (which "can only find its full justification within the opera itself"), he does not hesitate to pronounce the music "ingeniously conceived, genuinely dramatic, and unusually brilliantly orchestrated."[33] This observation scarcely justifies Goldmark's claim that Hanslick had characterized the march as the only piece in the opera worthy of being performed and given a hearing, nor does it provide any evidence of the lesson he claims to have learned from the occasion of "what I had to expect from that quarter."[34] A few months later, moreover, Hanslick took additional steps on Goldmark's behalf. In a *feuilleton* of September 30, 1874, entitled "Von der Oper" (Concerning opera), he urges the theater management to schedule some new productions in the forthcoming season, including, among his list of worthy possibilities, *The Queen of Sheba* (which, in a sign that he had taken Goldmark's appeal to his patriotic duty to heart, he recommends in particular because it was "the work of a respected, home-grown composer").[35] These urgings were not without their effect, and several weeks later, following Wrbna's resignation, the opera was at long last accepted, put into rehearsal, and scheduled for production later that season. After some additional delays and significant last-minute cuts made following the dress rehearsal, *The Queen of Sheba* finally opened on March 10, 1875, to great popular acclaim.

How German a Composer?

Hanslick's critical response was an altogether different matter. "I was not prepared for the kind of thing I was to hear from Hanslick," as Goldmark recalls. "It was simply annihilating. Ridicule, lies, contempt!"[36] Hanslick held a low opinion of the libretto, and he places the responsibility for this state of affairs squarely on Goldmark's shoulders:

> We know Mosenthal as much too experienced a theatrical poet to think him capable of deluding himself about the weaknesses of this libretto. He anticipated them and pointed out the meagerness of the material to the composer. But Goldmark wanted to compose nothing other than a "Queen of Sheba," the ideal embodiment of which he envisioned . . . in his beautiful, brilliantly witty student Caroline Bettelheim. He placed less weight on "plot" and all the more on "mood," and in fact the latter prevails so strongly that the second half of the opera frays out into nothing but simple moods of a predominantly lamenting tone.[37]

Yet the critic is kinder—at least at first—to the musical setting. "Goldmark's score is an imposing work," he writes, "which in certain places reveals a powerful and singular talent. Its strength lies in the passionate expression of feelings and the splendor of the [tone] painting, the distinctiveness of the Jewish-Oriental character."[38] Hanslick assigns the opera to a stylistic space lying somewhere between Meyerbeer and early Wagner. He acknowledges the presence of certain Wagnerian reminiscences (particularly in the overture) but distances the work from the "Wagnerian School" (by which he means "the most recent Music of the Future").[39] On the contrary, the opera "is independently created, and in its ensemble numbers leans on the architecture of the older school. These broadly developed and powerfully climactic vocal movements vaguely recall the magnificent Andante from the second finale of *Tannhäuser*.

These are forms that belong to an earlier period and have long since been outlawed by today's Wagner."[40] Turning his attention from musical structure to musical style, Hanslick notes that here, too, Goldmark recalls both Meyerbeer and early Wagner, which can be seen not only in "the passionate singing, the massed effects, the orchestral splendor," but also "unfortunately [in] the profusion of all three things."[41]

This point marks a turn in Hanslick's critical take on the music, and what follows makes plain his dissatisfaction with the work as a whole: "[Goldmark] insists on the heights of pathos and exaltation almost without interruption, and many beauties fail to make their full effect because he gives us no rest."[42] Hanslick evidently finds a precedent—but no satisfying artistic justification—for this tendency toward unbridled intensity in the parallelism that is the basic rhetorical device found in the Psalms and the prophetic literature of the Old Testament, whereby the idea expressed in the first half line of verse is repeated for emphasis in the second. (For example, "They will beat their swords into ploughshares and their spears into pruning hooks," from Isaiah.) Thus he observes how: "Even in subordinated moments, Goldmark's tone, like that of Hebraic poetry, is altogether solemn, which at once proclaims what it says as something momentous. 'Heaven shall hearken to the oration, and earth shall listen intently to the words!'"[43]

For Hanslick, this solemnity—this retention of Hebraic rhetoric, so to speak—is not a good thing in a modern opera, and he finds entirely too much of it in the work at hand, in the pathos of the singing and in the numerous orchestral interludes, which "so frequently interrupt the singing and, as it were, emphatically punctuate the singer's every phrase." This is to be regretted especially because it impedes the dramatic flow. More than that, it seems lacking in good taste: "In the affective moments Goldmark pushes passion to the extreme; the straining of the voices in the highest register, and the chromatic storm in the orchestra—with its thunderous timpani and trombones and the lightning raging downward in the strings—is scarcely to be outdone."[44]

It is within this context that Hanslick now declares the most prominent feature of all Goldmark's music to be its "Jewish-Oriental character." He acknowledges that this style had left an "interestingly exotic but artistic imprint" on several earlier works—recall his remarks about the composer's "characteristically churning restlessness," "brooding subjectivity," "solemn obscurity," "lamenting, whining tunes," and all the rest—and he recognizes that its appearance was to some degree justifiable in *The Queen of Sheba* as *couleur locale* (since the opera "parades a Jewish subject on its own ground").[45] Nevertheless, it is evident that Hanslick finds something about the whole enterprise unsatisfying:

> Perhaps it is the one-sidedness of my taste, but I confess that this kind of music can only be tolerated in small doses—as a starter, but not the main

course. Goldmark has settled down in this preference for Oriental music, with its lamenting, whining tunes, augmented fourths and diminished sixths and the disagreeable fluctuation between major and minor, its heavily growling basses above which thousands of dissonant and small tones are crossing.[46]

Hanslick acknowledges that the composer made effective use of this mode in the opera's religious scenes and national dances, that is, in those places in which the drama seems to demand it, but he complains that "this so quickly tiring and ever exotic manner" also appears in passages wherein nothing specifically "Jewish" but rather something "universally human" is to be expressed.[47] What is implied, here, of course, is a binary opposition between "Jewish-Oriental" music and what, later in the review, he calls "European-Occidental" music.[48] For Hanslick, one place in which the latter is required comes in the garden scene in act 2. The passage opens with a wordless *Lockruf* (or siren song) by the Queen's Mooress slave Astaroth, who lures Assad to a romantic encounter with her sovereign by means of an exotic vocalise (ex. 7.1).

Surely this music is intended to signify sultry, dangerous, Near Eastern female sexuality.[49] But in a striking misreading of the dramatic moment, Hanslick draws attention instead to Salomon Sulzer, the famous *hazzan* at Vienna's *Stadttempel* and the compiler and composer of *Schir Zion* (*Song of Zion*), a significant anthology of music for the Jewish liturgy (published in two volumes in 1840 and 1865): "How strange the song without words . . . ! Those are sounds that call devout Jews into the synagogue but no lover to a rendezvous; old Sulzer in soprano clef!"[50]

In a recent article, Peter Stachel observes that this and other locutions found in Hanslick's review anticipate discourse that would later clearly be understood as anti-Semitic, although he seems hesitant—rightly, in my view—to attribute anti-Semitic intent to Hanslick himself.[51] We would do better to interpret the negative shading of Hanslick's criticism as a reflection of German liberal ideology, which, in Habsburg Austria, countenanced, indeed sought to encourage, ambitious Bürger from all the Monarchy's "non-German" social groups, not least the Jews from the Eastern provinces, to identify as Germans (in the sense of embracing bourgeois German cultural values). Clearly, Goldmark's retention of "Jewish-Orientalisms"—as Hanslick heard the music—could not easily be reconciled with this liberal nationalist project. Put differently: the critic struggled at times to hear the composer's music as fully German, one might say, fully acculturated.[52]

This was true, not only of *The Queen of Sheba*, but of other works as well. Consider Hanslick's review of Goldmark's second opera, *Merlin* (1886), written to a libretto by Siegfried Lipiner based on Arthurian legend. Although the harmonic language in this later opera was too Wagnerian to meet with Hanslick's wholehearted approval, the composer's rejection of the structural

Example 7.1. Goldmark, *Die Königin von Saba*, entrance march, act 2, scene 2, m. 49

compositional principles of the music drama and his reliance on lyrical melody and traditional vocal forms came in for praise. Likewise appealing to the critic was that in this work Goldmark did without those "Jewish-Oriental melodies, whose sickly moaning [had] spoiled [for him] the undeniable beauties of [*The Queen of Sheba*]."[53] Yet even here Hanslick cannot help wondering whether the "pregnant national character" of the earlier opera is not somehow "more original, more 'Goldmarkian,'" since "the Oriental, with its passion and colorful display, but also with its unrest, intensity, and exalted solemnity, does not lie merely within the subject matter of *The Queen of Sheba*, but within our composer himself, who grew up under a doubly Oriental influence, the Jewish and the Hungarian."[54]

Seen in this essentializing light, those features of Goldmark's style that offended the critic's sensibilities appear to be those that might have suggested a lack of identification with the secular religion of *Bildung*, that characteristic Enlightenment ideology involving "culture, education, manners, cultivation, self-formation, reason, aesthetic taste, and moral individuality," as Marsha Rozenblit has put it, that for ambitious Jews like Goldmark provided the means by which to assimilate into bourgeois German culture.[55] Is it any wonder that Goldmark bristled at the "ridicule, lies, contempt" that he read into the critic's comments? By emphasizing the putatively "Jewish-Oriental" aspects of the composer's style, Hanslick was striking at the very heart of Goldmark's self-perception as a German composer.[56]

Goldmark and the Limits of Program Music

Over the next quarter-century, Goldmark's music was a familiar presence in Vienna's musical life—and, as such, a subject for Hanslick of continual critical discussion. We cannot consider the critic's writings on Goldmark in their entirety, but by sampling his reviews of the composer's concert and dramatic overtures, we can not only gauge the degree to which his understanding of Goldmark's music remained guided by a sense of its supposed Jewish-Oriental character, but also gain some insight into his thinking about one of the leading aesthetic issues of the day, program music.

Hanslick begins his review of the overture to Kleist's *Penthesilea*, performed by the Vienna Philharmonic on December 5, 1880, by recalling his experience of playing through the four-hand arrangement of the work ahead of time with his friend Theodor Billroth: "At the first two chords we felt as though we had fallen off the bench. In our long experience with dissonances, which are increasing in number by every year, we never imagined that anyone would blurt out such a thing. It sounds like a sharp whiplash along with the victim's scream; Wagner's Valkyries gallop in more considerately than these Amazons of Goldmark."[57] If this overture thus offers immediate proof of what Hanslick understood as Goldmark's abiding love of dissonance, its piercing (*grell*) tone, as the critic had to acknowledge, was at least true to the drama. As he explains:

> The poetry of the horrific—that is certainly what a composer wants to bring and should bring to the task of making a musical setting of Kleist's famous tragedy.... In truth, a composer of a *Penthesilea* overture must gather together all the hideous things that can be forced from music—that "cheerful art," as it was known in the Middle Ages—if he wants to at least approximate the frightful impression of Kleist's drama.[58]

Although Hanslick obviously has his doubts about using "the cheerful art" toward an unbeautiful end, he grants that Goldmark did so out of his own inner necessity.[59] But inasmuch as the work "is conceived and structured more poetically than musically," *Penthesilea* falls short in Hanslick's estimate, as the critic looks in vain for what Beethoven had achieved in his *Egmont* and *Coriolan* overtures, which, even with their "most pregnant dramatic characteristics, flow, universally understandable, unified, and in an uninterrupted musical stream."[60]

Hanslick was more favorably disposed toward the concert overture *Im Frühling*, introduced by the Vienna Philharmonic on December 1, 1889. Perhaps recalling his experience of *Penthesilea*, he approached the work with a degree of wariness and puzzlement. What, after all, was he to expect from music by a composer of Goldmark's temperament that carried the title *In the Spring*?

> The inscription put us in a hopeful and yet at the same time somewhat anxious mood.... Will Goldmark, the powerful King of Dissonances, take leave of his most piercing chords for the sake of May? Will he glorify spring without at the same time making opposition to it? Will he not bring us poison-flaming flowers from the Orient and nightingales from Bayreuth? These were the concerns that were spoken under the breath. Goldmark has subdued them in a most delightful manner.[61]

Im Frühling meets with Hanslick's approval in part because of the way in which its descriptive title energizes the listener's fantasy without stifling it—and without trumping purely musical considerations.[62] Thus the first and second themes offer what Hanslick describes as "favorable and ingeniously used motives" for an extensive development that is animated in the most natural way by "the songs of finches and skylarks."[63] Goldmark is, however, unable to leave well enough alone (we might imagine Hanslick thinking) and instead soon pays "a visit to 'Wahnfried.'" This occasions some of the critic's finest purple prose:

> Wagnerian harmonies, at first diffident and scattered, later plunge downward from the mountaintops like a wild chase; syncopated chromatic sixth chords in the strings and woodwinds against which the basses and trombones invoke a gruesome procession of rising diminished seventh chords. This is not the obligatory spring weather we had counted on but rather a little preliminary run-through of Armageddon, in which rivers, forests, mountains tumble about and all the bowels of the globe threaten to rupture.[64]

One wonders just how seriously to take all this. In any case, the Wagnerian outburst is over soon enough, and the "delightful bird concert" (*herziges Vogelkonzert*) returns to bring the work to an exultant close. "So warmly felt and so freshly painted" (*so warm empfunden und so frisch gemalt*), this music—a fine display of "the cheerful art"—tugged at Hanslick's heartstrings in a way that perhaps none of the composer's earlier works had managed to do.

Hanslick was even more favorably impressed by the overture to Aeschylus's *Der gefesselte Prometheus* (*Prometheus Bound*), performed by the Vienna Philharmonic on March 23, 1890.[65] Once again, he had his doubts going in. After all, the subject of Prometheus offered nothing in the way of the easily understandable musical allusions such as was afforded, for example, by the subject of spring: "Would the loathsome vulture that pecks at Prometheus's liver not also simultaneously bite at our ears? Instead of the hero, would not his brother Epimetheus appear, causing to emanate from Pandora's box everything music has to offer from its arsenal of evil biting house flies?"[66] Yet once again Hanslick could happily report that his concerns had been unfounded. Indeed, there was "virtually nothing repulsive or ugly" in the music, despite the "incisive tragedy of the composition, glowing red-hot in the fire of the most vigorous orchestra."[67]

Whereas in the similarly tragic *Penthesilea* Goldmark is faulted for placing the poetic element before the musical, this time he is praised for turning matters around: in *Prometheus Bound* the "burning energy of expression" is coupled with "musical content and lucid form."[68] This is, of course, the key element for Hanslick, who has no tolerance for music that aims to be understood as "a dramatic copying" (*eine dramatische Nachmalerei*) of a literary work, and so serves as nothing more than a "brilliantly illustrated marginal notation."[69] What follows is worthy of quotation at some length:

> The Overture begins likes a solemn quiet sea with an Adagio in C minor; this gradually builds into more vigorous motion, which comes into full flow in the

Allegro (likewise in C minor). Following the defiant, sharply marked main theme is a second theme in C major of a noticeably gentle, almost idyllic expression.... Many shall take umbrage at the peaceful tone of this second theme. Whether it signifies the recollection of earlier happiness or the hope for salvation I will leave to the masters of exegesis [*Auslegekünstlern*] to decide. It seems to me, however, to be a credit to the composer that he interrupts and pacifies the agonies of torment of the bound Prometheus, that he allows him and us to catch our breath. This contrast was musically necessary; in an orchestral piece we first want music and only then tragedy, insofar as it can be explained in the former.[70]

Here Hanslick applauds Goldmark's decision to put musical considerations first in composing his C-major theme, and he makes no attempt to hide his contempt for anyone who would seek to explain the music in terms of a detailed program. That same contempt is evident at the end of the review as well; in a passage in which Goldmark is praised for steering clear of the dangers of strict program music, Hanslick pointedly turns a disparaging eye toward a composer who, in his view, had showed none of Goldmark's good judgment: "Goldmark's merit is that he does not lose himself in pedantic depictive details, but instead has always kept his eye on the larger whole and created a musical artwork from his dangerous material. In order to properly understand what is meant by these words, one needed only to stay on a bit at the Philharmonic concert after Goldmark's overture and have a listen to Liszt's *Dante* Symphony."[71]

Hanslick was clearly let down after this by Goldmark's *Sappho* Overture, performed by the Vienna Philharmonic on November 26, 1893. His description of the work as "genuine Goldmark, Goldmark in monumental size; a fiery sea of passion, a primeval forest of dissonances; more intellectually stimulating than beautiful, more shocking than enjoyable, altogether 'frightfully interesting,' as the Berliners say," is not meant to be complimentary.[72] And even less so is his suggestion that Goldmark had sketched the love's grief of the protagonist with such an intensity that what he produced would be sufficient to depict "three Sapphos with enough left over for a Medea or an abandoned Ariadne."[73] As with *Prometheus Bound*, he fears that Goldmark's choice of dramatic subject will only give license to the "exegetes" to practice their dubious art: "Once an instrumental work is inscribed 'Sappho,' it is not hard to make out Phaon, Melitta, Sappho's jealousy, and her plunge from the Leukadian Cliffs. The acumen of the exegete and attributor [*Aus- und Unterleger*] operates easily with a fixed itinerary. I have often fought against these interpretive feats, which are based on the false assumption that pure instrumental music is capable of precise expression."[74]

Like Smetana's symphonic poem *Vyšehrad*, which the Philharmonic players had performed two weeks earlier, Goldmark's *Sappho* Overture—presumably composed with Grillparzer's tragedy from 1818 in mind—sets out with a harp solo that evokes an ancient bardic quality appropriate to its poetic content.[75] Taking note of the similarity between the two recently heard works, Hanslick

Example 7.2. Goldmark, *Sappho* Overture, mm. 1–4

Example 7.3. Goldmark, *Sappho* Overture, mm. 29–37

complains that, whereas "Smetana's grey harpist, despite his sadness, begins with a pure E-flat major triad," Goldmark, composing in the dark key of E-flat minor, opens with a dissonant chord (ex. 7.2). This not only was a surprising decision, Hanslick writes, but a questionable one as well, "something like beginning a lyrical poem with the word 'nevertheless.'"[76]

This *bon mot* was followed by a peculiar account of the new lyrical theme in the oboe that soon enters above a repetition of the harp's opening music: "Judging by the lamenting triplet figures, augmented fourths, and diminished sixths, the Greek poetess might have been a niece of "Sakuntala" and frequently in Palestine as well."[77] We are familiar with the critic's linking of augmented fourths and diminished sixths to "Jewish-Oriental music," of course, but the theme in question contains neither (ex. 7.3).

Nor does Hanslick's characterization of "lamenting triplets"—a well established trope for music associated with the Jews—seem quite right in the case at hand, since, with the exception of one quintuplet, the music flows freely and evenly in compound duple meter.[78] It is as though Hanslick has simply recycled a set of locutions that had originally been used to describe, say, the sultry theme played by the English horn and bass clarinet in the Entrance March from *The Queen of Sheba* (ex. 7.4).

But what does the sound world of that exotic milieu have to do with the ancient Grecian setting of Grillparzer's tragedy? Elsewhere I have argued that in his review of *Vyšehrad*, Hanslick downplays the symphonic poem's status as an expression of Czech nationalism and indeed writes about Smetana as though he were a German.[79] This only makes the critic's incongruous posting of *Sappho* to the East all the more telling. By hearing Eastern-tinged harmonic intervals and "Jewish triplets" where none seem to exist, Hanslick reverts to an essentializing mode with respect to the Jewish composer, questioning Gold

Example 7.4. Goldmark, *Die Königin von Saba*, act 1, scene 7 (Queen's Entrance March), mm. 199–207

mark's status as a German composer at a time when Goldmark was as much a part of the Viennese cultural establishment as Brahms and Hanslick himself.

The Cricket on the Hearth and Hanslick's "Eternal Truth"

By way of conclusion, let us return to the genre of opera and consider Hanslick's response to a work that was, in many respects, unimaginably far removed from "genuine Goldmark"—and so closer to the critic's heart than most. In *Das Heimchen am Herd* (1896), based on A. M. Willner's adaptation of Dickens's Christmas story *The Cricket on the Hearth*, Hanslick was delighted to discover that Goldmark had found a most unexpected muse: "Goldmark (*un chercheur*, as the French say), who in his earlier works liked to seek out the singular, the unusual, to whom every strong feeling was easily converted into ectasy, every stimulus, into caustic shrillness, this same Goldmark finds in *The Cricket* the charming, modest tone of the domestic piece and knows not to let go of it, even with happy detours into comedy."[80]

With its old-fashioned alternation of strophic songs, arias, duets, and choruses, this fairy-tale opera counts, for Hanslick, as a "renunciation" of Wagnerian music drama. And in place of "sickly moaning" we find wholesome melodies that are "singable and simple" and regular in their periodical rhythm—qualities that, as we have seen, Hanslick had too often found missing in Goldmark's music. Here "the voices rule, the orchestra accompanies." Goldmark's *Cricket* thus "preaches the eternal truth"—and this is, of course, Hanslick's own sermon— "that music cannot exist without the laws of form and symmetry, lest it degenerate into a mere pathological stimulation of the senses."[81]

Still, Hanslick is not unstinting in his praise. He questions the novelty and originality of the composer's melodic invention, for example, even as he lauds the "rosy-cheeked wholesomeness" (*rotwangige Gesundheit*) of the individual numbers as a welcome contrast to the "threatening shadows of the young Goldmark" (*drohende Schatten des jungen Goldmark*). And he extols the effective orchestration but then, with his next breath, cries out: "The harsh modulations, the nesting in chromatic and enharmonic passages, especially the up and down chase of the chromatic chord progressions!" Even in this modest piece, then, Hanslick has no trouble making out the "'Court Composer to the Queen of Sheba,' the attending cricket on Goldmark's hearth, which reports *anytime* something happens, merry *or* poignant."[82]

More than twenty years after its première, then, the "Jewish-Oriental" *Queen of Sheba* remained for Hanslick the touchstone of Goldmark's style. But the critic does not end with this coded reference to all those traits in the composer's manner that had always left him cold; instead he moves to a gracious conclusion: "Our joy over Goldmark's latest success is strong and sincere," he writes. "It is directed not only at the distinguished artist but as much at the man, whose personality, full of character and inimical to publicity in such a large extent, enjoys universal respect and sympathy."[83] Anticipating the sentiments that Hanslick would express three years later, on the occasion of the composer's seventieth birthday, these lines also suggest something about a *Goldmark-Bild* that was forty years in the making. Admiring Goldmark the *Mensch* came easier to Hanslick than praising his "frightfully interesting" music. As a proud acculturated German composer, Goldmark must have hoped for better than this from the most important critical voice in the rich musical world in which he lived.

Notes

1. Ed. H., "Karl Goldmark (Zum 18. Mai 1900)," *Neue Freie Presse* (May 18, 1900): 1–2; this essay carries the dateline "Karlsbad, May 15, 1900." The *feuilleton* was reprinted later that year, with slight emendations, under the title "*Die Königin von Saba*: Festvorstellung zu Goldmarks 70. Geburtstag [18. Mai 1900]," in Eduard Hanslick, *Aus neuer und neuester Zeit (der modernen Oper IX. Teil): Musikalische Kritiken und Schilderungen* (Berlin: Allgemeiner Verein für Deutsche Litteratur, 1900), 10–17.

2. The relationship between Goldmark and Hanslick is briefly considered in Harald Graf, "Carl Goldmark: Beziehungen zu den Zeitgenossen," *Studia Musicologica Academiae Scientiarum Hungaricae* 38 (1997): 373–83. Graf's discussion is weakened somewhat by his uncritical use of Goldmark's memoirs, which, as we shall see, are not always reliable.

3. It appears that at the time of writing, Hanslick was under the impression that it was not *The Queen of Sheba*, but rather *Das Heimchen am Herd* (*The Cricket on the Hearth*), a more recent opera from 1896, that had been scheduled for performance on Goldmark's birthday. "Also auch schon Siebzig? Wie unabsehbar lang dünkt uns in jüngeren Jahren diese Strecke, und doch wie unheimlich schnell finden wir eines Tages und dort angelangt! Die erste Hälfte der Wanderung verlief für Goldmark sorgen- und mühevoll. 'Ich hatte viel Bekümmerniß,' sang er mit Sebastian Bach. Wer aber durch einen Wald von Hindernissen sich muthig durchgekämpft zu künstlerischer Höhe und unbestrittener Geltung, den feiern wir glückwünschend mit verdoppelter Herzlichkeit. Die lange trübe Zeit der Entbehrungen hat unsern Jubilar nicht verbittert, der endlich erlangte Ruhm ihn weder geblendet, noch erkältet. Immer sehen wir ihn neidlos anerkennend bei fremden Erfolgen. Auf sein Wohlwollen, seine Gerechtigkeit kann man bauen.... Hand in Hand mit der Hochschätzung für den Künstler Goldmark geht die

"POISON-FLAMING FLOWERS FROM THE ORIENT" 149

allgemeine Sympathie für den Menschen. Wie laut und festlich kam Beides zum Ausdruck, als vor zehn Jahren Goldmark's sechzigster Geburtstag zugleich mit der hundertsten Aufführung seiner 'Königin von Saba' gefeiert wurde! Und vollends heute wird das allwissende Heimchen am Herd über die Maßen stark und fröhlich zirpen!" Ed. H., in *Neue Freie Presse* (May 18, 1900): 1. In Hanslick, *Aus neuer und neuester Zeit*, 10–11, the last sentence was adapted to read simply: "Und vollends heute!"

4. For a succinct discussion of the general cultural earmarks of Liberal Vienna, see David S. Luft, *Eros and Inwardness in Vienna: Weininger, Musil, Doderer* (Chicago: University of Chicago Press, 2003), 14–22. Liberal musical culture in Vienna, and Brahms's leading position within it, is the focus of Margaret Notley, *Lateness and Brahms: Music and Culture in the Twilight of Viennese Liberalism* (Oxford: Oxford University Press, 2007).

5. I have borrowed this neat formulation from Scott Spector, "Another Zionism: Hugo Bergmann's Circumscription of Spiritual Territory," *Journal of Contemporary History* 34 (1999): 87–108 (89n).

6. Among the many seminal writings of Pieter M. Judson that explore this idea, see his "Rethinking the Liberal Legacy," in *Rethinking Vienna 1900*, ed. Steven Beller (New York: Berghahn, 2001), 57–79.

7. See David Brodbeck, "Dvořák's Reception in Liberal Vienna: Language Ordinances, National Property, and the Rhetoric of *Deutschtum*," *Journal of the American Musicological Society* 60, no. 1 (2007): 71–132; see also Brodbeck, "Hanslick's Smetana and Hanslick's Prague," *Journal of the Royal Musical Association* 134, no. 1 (2009): 1–36.

8. Among other references, see Goldmark's letter to Franz von Holstein of April 18, 1877, in which he describes himself and Holstein as "poor German composers" (*arme deutsche Komponisten*), quoted in Adolph Kohut, *Berühmte israelitische Männer und Frauen in der Kulturgeschichte der Menschheit: Lebens- und Charakterbilder aus Vergangenheit und Gegenwart*, 2 vols. (Leipzig: A. W. Payne, 1900–1901), 1:19.

9. "Seltsam bleibt es, daß die Saison, deren erste größere Hälfte wir nun vorüber haben, noch keine einzige Celebrität herbeigebracht hat. . . . Immer nennen unsere Concertanzeigen nur ehrenwerthe Namen aus dem Wiener Adressenbuch: Bondy, Lukaseder, Goldmark, Gall, Weidner, Tobish, Rappoldi u.s.f." Ed. H., "Musik," *Die Presse* (January 15, 1857): 1; repr. in Hanslick, *Sämtliche Schriften* 1/4, 17–18.

10. "Eine eigene, neue Classe von Concertgebern waren in der verflossenen Saison die Componisten. Die Herren Gall, Langwara, Goldmark prüften die jugendlichen Schwingen ihrer Begeisterung, wie es schien, zu ihrer und ihrer Freunde großer Zufriedenheit." Ed. H., "Die Wiener Concert-Saison 1856–57," *Die Presse* (May 21, 1857): 2; repr. in Hanslick, *Sämtliche Schriften* 1/4, 107.

11. The concert bills for this aborted concert and the concert that finally took place on March 12, 1857, are preserved in the manuscript collecion of the National Széchényi Library, Budapest (Goldmark-IV/8 and Goldmark-IV/9, respectively).

12. Goldmark, *Erinnerungen*, 54–58; *Notes from the Life*, 97–104. The composer errs in this report by giving the date of the concert as March 12, 1858, but there is no reason not to accept his recollection of this initial interaction with Hanslick at face value. For a review of Goldmark's concert, see Carl Debrois van Bruyck, "Musikalisches," *Wiener Zeitung* (March 20, 1857): 258.

13. In his seventieth-birthday tribute, Hanslick erroneously places this concert in the year 1860; see Hanslick, *Aus neuer und neuester Zeit*, 11.

14. "Der junge Tonsetzer lieferte in einer Reihe größerer und kleinerer Compositionen unleugbar Beweise eines Talentes, das, von würdigem Streben und einer nicht geringen technischen Fertigkeit getragen, Gutes verspricht. Ruhe und Klarheit feh-

len noch. Sehr glücklich Aperçus werden durch rhapsodische Zerstücklung der Form durch bizarre Rhythmik, endlich durch einen eigenthümliche wühlende Unruhe in ihrer Wirkung erstickt. Wir dürfen hoffen, der gährende Most werde seinerzeit guter Wein werden." Ed. H., "Musik," *Die Presse* (January 17, 1861): 2; repr. in Hanslick, *Sämtliche Schriften* 1/5, 292. The Hellmesberger Quartet took the string quartet into its own repertoire and repeated it at the end of the year, on December 15, in one of its own concerts; Hanslick, who was ill, did not attend.

15. "Herr Goldmark . . . hat sich als Componist bisher der Oeffentlichkeit eher entzogen, als aufgedrängt. Sein neuestes Quintett . . . darf ihn füglich von dem Ungrund dieser Bescheidenheit überzeugen. Eine charaktervolle, würdige, nur vielleicht allzuernste Haltung trägt dies Werk, das von einem energisch strebenden Geist und von tüchtigster musikalischer Technik Zeugniß gibt." Ed. H., "Musik," *Die Presse* (December 18, 1862): 2.

16. Hanslick, *Aus neuer und neuester Zeit*, 10–11. The date of this stipend is incorrectly given as 1857 in Clemens Höslinger, "Karl Goldmark (1830–1915): Der Komponist der 'Königin von Saba,'" in *Vergessen: Vier Opernkomponisten des 19. Jahrhunderts* (Vienna: Der Apfel, 2008), 58. Twenty years later, Goldmark would join Hanslick and Brahms on the selection committee for this award.

17. "Um so ehrenvoller der Erfolg, den die tüchtige, geistreiche, aber etwas trübe und reflectirte Composition errang . . . Der zweite [Satz ist] ein breit ausgeführtes Andante in Cis-moll, eine düstere, langgezogene Klage, deren Melodik und Harmonisirung an orientalische Weisen anklingt . . . Der Komponist hat einen guten Theil seiner früheren Verworrenheit und grübelnden Subjectivität von sich geworfen, er ist klarer, freier, in der Form conciser geworden. Wir hoffen, er werde in dieser Befreiung, besonders nach melodischer Seite hin, noch einen Schritt weiter thun; seine von edelstem, ernstem Sinn getragene Musik wird dann auch der allgemeinen Wirkung nicht entbehren." Ed. H., "Concerte," *Neue Freie Presse* (January 10, 1865): 2.

18. "Was das Verhältniß der Composition zu dem berühmten indischen Drama 'Sakuntala' betrifft, so ist es kein abhängiges in dem mißverständlichen Sinne der descriptiven Musik. Als Musikstück an und für sich vollkommen verständlich und selbstständig, nimmt sie von dem Gegenstand nur die poetische Anregung, die allgemeine Stimmung und Localfarbe, allenfalls die einfachsten Grundzüge der dramatischen Peripetie." Ed. H., "Concerte," *Neue Freie Presse* (December 30, 1865): 2; trans. adapted from Paul A. Bertagnolli, *Prometheus in Music: Representations of the Myth in the Romantic Era* (Aldershot, UK: Ashgate, 2007), 322.

19. Ed. H. "Les préludes," *Die Presse* (March 12, 1857): 1–3; repr. in Hanslick, *Sämtliche Schriften* 1/4, 47–53; trans. as "Liszt's Symphonic Poems," in *Vienna's Golden Years of Music 1850–1900*, ed. and trans. Henry Pleasants (New York: Simon and Schuster, 1950), 47. As Nicole Grimes has argued, the critic did not oppose all music with extramusical associations (as is still too often assumed), but rather only that which seeks to be understood in terms of a detailed program rather than its musical content; see Nicole Grimes, "Brahms's Critics: Continuity and Discontinuity in the Critical Reception of Johannes Brahms" (PhD diss., Trinity College, University of Dublin, 2008), 160–69 (and passim). We shall explore this matter further below with regard to Goldmark's later overtures.

20. "Frisch und charakteristisch in der Erfindung, von klarer Anlage und feinem Detail, zeigt die Ouvertüre eine entschiedene Klärung des früher etwas wirren und wühlenden Talentes Goldmark's. Nur wenige Stellen erinnern an seine ehemalige Disso-

nanzen-Liebe und pathetische Unklarheit." Hanslick, in *Neue Freie Presse* (December 30, 1865), 2; trans. adapted from Bertagnolli, *Prometheus in Music*, 322.

21. Ed. H., "Die Königin von Saba," *Neue Freie Presse* (March 12, 1875): 1; repr. in Eduard Hanslick, *Musikalische Stationen (der "Modernen Oper" II. Theil)* (Berlin: Allgemeiner Verein für Deutsche Litteratur, 1885), 300. Hanslick's reference to the sexually insatiable wife of Emperor Claudius was no doubt prompted by the recent success at the Hoftheater of Adolf Wilbrandt's play *Arria und Messalina* (1874). Hanslick clearly is using "Egyptian" as a broad-brush descriptor for the East; the ancient kingdom of Sheba seems to have been located at the southern end of the Arabian Peninsula, perhaps extending over the Red Sea into parts of present-day Eritrea or Ethiopia. In any case, in the opera the Queen is described as "the Star of Arabia."

22. "Goldmarks Phantasie hatte ihm anfangs die Bettelheim als ideale Königin von Saba vorgegaukelt, war doch aus der trefflichen jungen Pianistin eine noch vorzüglicher Sängerin geworden." Hanslick, *Aus neuer und neuester Zeit*, 15. In 1867 Caroline married the Austrian notable Julius von Gomperz and largely retired from the operatic stage, never to sing the role that she had inspired.

23. The extant documentary evidence belies Goldmark's own account of this complex story (Goldmark, *Erinnerungen*, 114–29; *Notes from the Life*, 205–32). For a thorough study, see Thomas Aigner, "Die Bestimmung der Skizzen, Entwürfe und Frühfassungen der Oper *Die Königin von Saba* von Carl Goldmark—Grundlagen zur Geschichte der Entstehung des Werks" (thesis: University of Vienna, 2006); I am grateful to Dr. Aigner for sharing a copy of this work with me. The unpublished correspondence from Goldmark to his older brother Joseph, some of which I discuss below, likewise allows us to elaborate on and correct certain details in Goldmark's recollection. This correspondence is preserved in box 1 of the Goldmark Family Papers, Rare Book and Manuscript Library, Columbia University (hereafter Goldmark Family Papers). Some of the letters are autograph manuscripts; others, typewritten transcripts.

24. "Zehn Jahre lang war der peinlich gewissenhafte Komponist mit der Partitur beschäftigt. Damit glücklich zu Ende gelangt, stand er aber erst am Anfang fast unübersehbarer Schwierigkeiten und Hindernisse." Hanslick, *Aus neuer und neuester Zeit*, 13–14.

25. "Ich habe Grund zu glauben, daß unsere Direktion durch einige vaterländische Mißerfolge ängstlich und mißtrauisch wurde." Goldmark's letter to Hanslick is quoted at length in Hanslick, *Aus neuer und neuester Zeit*, 14; and (slightly abridged) in Goldmark, *Erinnerungen*, 122–24; *Notes from the Life*, 220–23.

26. "Sie sind vom Staate mit dem schönen Ehrenamte betraut, die Kunst und die künstlerischen Interessen zu fördern—welches zum Teile auch darin bestehen, den Künstlern in ihren Nöten beizustehen. Ich appelliere an diese Ihre schöne Mission!" Hanslick, *Aus neuer und neuester Zeit*, 15.

27. Typewritten partial transcript of an unpublished letter to Joseph Goldmark of March 20, 1873, Goldmark Family Papers, box 1.

28. "Ich sprach mit Hanslick, ich fand ihn nicht günstig für meine Sache gestimmt. Er meinte, ich sollte doch zuerst eine kleine Bühne in Deutschland aufsuchen, dann ginge es hier leicht. Auch wolle er zuerst mein Werk kennenlernen, bevor er was tue. Der wahre Grund seines Verhaltens ist: er setzt alles daran, Hamlet von Thomas (ein erbärmliches Werk) hier zur Aufführung zu bringen." Ibid. Hanslick got his wish: *Hamlet* opened at the Court Opera on July 14, 1873, and ran for eight performances. For Hanslick's review, see Ed. H., "Hamlet," *Neue Freie Presse* (July 17, 1873): 1–3.

29. "Da fällt mitten in die Unterhandlungen die Aufführung meiner Sakuntala. Notizen haben schon früher über die Sache in den Zeitungen kursiert. Jetzt wird

die Gelegenheit von dem Blättern benützt und *alle* verlangen stürmisch und einhellig die Aufführung meiner Oper. Ich schicke Dir einige davon. Doch das hat die Sache—momentan wenigstens—noch verschlimmert. Hanslick, darüber noch mehr verstimmt, dass man ihm in der Angelegenheit zuvorgekommen und eine so bedeutenden öffentlich Pression ausübt, auch in Sorge um die Aufnahme seines Hamlet ist nun ganz gegen mich und lasst es mich auch fühlen. Wie weit die Geschichte mit Hanslick geht, magst Du aus folgenden Tatsachen entnehmen. Der mitfolgende Artikel 'Deutsche Musik in Italien' war, wie ich in Erfahrung gebracht, zuerst der N.Fr. Presse übergeben. Das Blatt hätte ihn als sehr interessant gern gebracht. Hanslick hat ihn unterdrückt. Mir unbekannte Freunde haben sich bei Etienne, Redakteur desselben Blattes, verwendet, doch in meiner Sache etwas zu tun. Dieser schickt einen seiner Mitarbeiter zu einem meiner näheren Freunde, um sich über den Stand der Opernsache zu informieren—doch müsse Hanslick anstandshalber gefragt werden" (typewritten partial transcript of an unpublished letter to Joseph Goldmark of March 20, 1873, Goldmark Family Papers, box 1).

30. "Der Appell an meinen sehr zweifelhaften Einfluß erwies sich als unnötig; hatten doch Herbeck und Dessoff, in diesem Fall die einzig berufenen Anwälte, Goldmarks Oper nachdrücklich empfohlen und bei Wrbnas Amtsnachfolger, dem Fürsten Hohenlohe, ein geneigtes Ohr gefunden." Hanslick, *Aus neuer und neuester Zeit*, 15. See also Ed. H., "Hofoperntheater," *Neue Freie Presse* (March 27, 1897): 2. As Lord Chamberlain (*Erster Oberhofmeister*), Prince Konstantin Hohenlohe-Schillingsfürst was not Wrbna's replacement, but rather his superior. Hanslick is correct in identifying Hohenlohe and Dessoff among the opera's supporters, but, on the basis of an undated letter from Goldmark to his brother that was written in early 1874 (Goldmark Family Papers, box 1), we can conclude that Herbeck remained opposed.

31. "Der Einfluß Hanslicks war aber hinter den Kulissen viel stärker und gefährlich als vor denselben" (Goldmark, *Erinnerungen*, 121–22; *Notes from the Life*, 218–19).

32. Goldmark discusses the events surrounding this performance in his undated letter to his brother from early 1874 (Goldmark Family Papers, box 1).

33. "Das Tonstück, dessen stark orientalisirende Weise allerdings erst in Oper selbst seine volle Rechtfertigung finden kann, ist geistreich concipirt, echt dramatisch angelegt und mit ungewöhnlichem Glanz instrumentirt." Ed. H., "Das Liszt-Concert im großem Musikvereinssaale," *Neue Freie Presse* (January 13, 1874): 2.

34. Goldmark, *Erinnerungen*, 126; *Notes from the Life*, 226.

35. "Die dritte vorgeschlagene Novität, Goldmark's 'Königin von Saba,' hätte, als das Werk eines geachteten einheimischen Componisten, jedenfalls Berücksichtigung verdient." Ed. H., "Von der Oper," *Neue Freie Presse* (September 30, 1874): 1.

36. Goldmark, *Erinnerungen*, 130; *Notes from the Life*, 234. Goldmark does acknowledge that the critic softened as the years went by, writing, "Hanslick expressed himself far less severely in his book, *The Modern Opera*, which appeared somewhat later. Twenty years later he had changed completely; he wrote an outstanding article about the work at the time of its one-hundredth performance at the Vienna Court Opera." Although Goldmark overstates the extent to which Hanslick ameliorated his tone when he revised the review for inclusion in *The Modern Opera* (i.e., Hanslick, *Musikalische Stationen*, 298–305), there are a few passages in which this does hold true to some extent. In those cases, I will quote from the review as it originally appeared in the *Neue Freie Presse*. For the "outstanding article" occasioned by the one-hundredth Viennese performance, see Hanslick, in *Neue Freie Presse* (March 27, 1897): 2.

37. "Wir kennen Mosenthal als viel zu bewährten Theaterdichter, um ihm eine Selbsttäuschung über die Schwächen dieses Textbuches zuzutrauen. Er hat sie vorausgesehen und dem Componisten die Dürftigkeit des Stoffes zu bedenken gegeben. Goldmark wollte aber gerade nur eine 'Königin von Saba' componiren, für welche ihm damals als ideale Verkörperung seine schöne, geistvolle Schülerin Caroline Bettelheim vorgeschwebte. Er legte wenig Gewicht auf 'Handlung,' desto mehr auf 'Stimmung,' und in der That überwiegt letztere so stark, daß die zweite Hälfte der Oper sich fast in lauter simple Stimmungen, vorwiegend klagenden Tones, zerfasert." Hanslick, in *Neue Freie Presse* (March 12, 1875): 1; the passage was softened slightly when the review was reprinted in Hanslick, *Musikalische Stationen*, 300.

38. "Goldmark's Partitur ist eine achtunggebietende Arbeit, die in einzelnen Partien ein starkes und eigenthümliches Talent verräth. Die Stärke zeigt sich in der Leidenschaftlichkeit des Gefühlsausdruckes und dem Glanz der Malerei, die Eigenthümlichkeit in dem jüdisch-orientalischen Charakter der Musik." Hanslick, *Musikalische Stationen*, 301.

39. "Sie gehört, trotz einzelner Reminiszenzen an Wagner, keineswegs zur neuesten Zukunftsmusik." This remark appears, not in Hanslick's opening night review for the *Neue Freie Presse*, but in his retrospective take on the recent season for the Berlin journal *Deutsche Rundschau*; see Eduard Hanslick, "Die musikalische Saison in Wien 1874–1875," *Deutsche Rundschau* 3 (April–June 1875): 313.

40. "Goldmark's Stil hält ungefähr die Mitte zwischen Meyerbeer und dem früheren Wagner (*Tannhäuser*). Bei aller mittelbaren Einwirkung Wagner's und trotz einzelner Reminiszenzen an ihn (gleich in der Ouvertüre) gehört 'Die Königin von Saba' doch nicht zur eigentlichen Wagner-Schule. Sie ist selbstständig erfunden und lehnt in den Ensemble-Nummern an die Architektonik der älteren Schule. Diese sich breit entfaltenden und mächtig steigernden Vokalsätze erinnern in ihrem Bau ungefähr an das prachtvolle Andante im zweiten Finale des 'Tannhäuser.' Das sind Formen welche früheren Epoche angehören und die von dem heutigen Wagner längst geächtet sind." Hanslick, *Musikalische Stationen*, 302.

41. "Von Meyerbeer und Wagner hat Goldmark die Leidenschaftlichkeit des Gesanges, die Masseneffecte, den Orchesterprunk, leider auch das Uebermaß in diesen drei Dingen." Ibid.

42. "Er beharrt fast ununterbrochen auf der Höhe des Pathos und der Exaltation, läßt manche Schönheiten nicht zur vollen Wirkung kommen, weil er uns keine Ruhepunkte gönnt." Ibid.

43. "Selbst in untergeordneten Momenten ist der Ton Goldmark's, wie der der hebräischen Poesie, ein durchaus feierlicher, der, was er sagt, sofort als etwas Wichtiges ankündigt. 'Die Himmel sollen der Rede horchen, und die Erde soll den Worten lauschen!'" Hanslick, *Musikalische Stationen*, 302. Here Hanslick is paraphrasing the discussion of this aspect of Hebraic poetry found in Karl Rosenkranz's *Die Poesie und ihre Geschichte* (*Poetry and Its History*) (1855), right down to the use of the same illustrative pseudo-biblical verse: "[Because of its use of] parallelism] the tone of Hebraic poetry is . . . essentially solemn. It proclaims what it says at once as something momentous that deserves attention. Heaven shall hearken to the oration, and earth shall listen intently to the words." (Der Ton der Hebräischen Poesie wird dadurch im Wesentlichen ein feierlicher. Er kündigt, was er sagt, sofort als etwas Wichtiges an, das der Aufmerksamkeit werth sei. Die Himmel sollen der Rede horchen und die Erde soll den Worten lauschen.) Karl Rosenkranz, *Die Poesie und ihre Geschichte: Eine Entwicklung der poetischen Ideale der Völker* (Königsberg: Gebrüder Borntrāger, 1855), 337–38.

44. "Das drückt sich nicht nur in dem Pathos seines Gesanges, sondern auch in den zahlreichen Orchester-Zwischenspielen aus, welche den Gesang so häufig unterbrechen und gleichsam jede Phrase des Sängers nachdrücklich unterstreichen. Das retardirt oft empfindlich den dramatischen Fortgang. In Momenten des Affects treibt Goldmark die Leidenschaftlichkeit auf die äußerste Spitze; da ist die Anstrengung der Singstimmen in höchster Lage, da ist der chromatische Sturm im Orchester mit seinem Pauken- und Posaunendonner und den wie rasend herabfahrenden Blitzen der Streichinstrumente kaum mehr zu überbieten." Hanslick, *Musikalische Stationen*, 302.

45. "Als hervorstechendste Eigenthümlichkeit der Goldmark'schen Musik bezeichnete ich oben ihren orientalisch-jüdischen Charakter. Er macht sich schon in Goldmark's früheren Werken (Ouvertüre zu 'Sakuntala,' Violin Suite, etc.) mehr oder minder geltend und gab ihnen ein interessant-fremdartiges, aber künstliches Gepräge. In der 'Königin von Saba,' welche einen jüdischen Stoff auf eigenstem Grund und Boden vorführt, nimmt der Componist natürlich das Recht zur breitesten Entfaltung dieser Musikweise in Anspruch." Ibid., 302–3.

46. "Vielleicht ist es eine Einseitigkeit meines Geschmackes, aber ich gestehe, diese Art Musik nur in sehr mäßigen Dosen vertragen zu können; als Reizmittel, aber nicht als Nahrung. Mit dem Eigensinn eines geistreichen Mannes hat sich Goldmark eingenistet in diese Vorliebe für orientalische Musik, mit ihrer klagenden, winselnden Melodik, ihren übermäßigen Quarten und verminderten Sexten, ihrem unerquicklichen Schwanken zwischen Dur und Moll, ihren bleischwer fortbrummenden Bässen, über welchen sich tausend dissonirende Töne und Tönchen kreuzen." Ibid., 303. In the continuation of this passage, Hanslick dwells briefly on—and with evident distaste for—what he sees as Goldmark's predilection for "piercing discords (*schneidende Mißklänge*)." Ibid.

47. "Wo in der 'Königin von Saba' orientalische Musikweise als Totalfarbe gefordert ist, da wirkt Goldmark ebenso charakteristisch als effectvoll. Dies ist der Fall erstens bei allen religiösen Scenen der Handlung, sodann in den nationalen Tänzen. . . . Diese so schnell ermüdende und immer fremdartig bleibende Manier nimmt aber in Goldmarks Oper einen zu großen Raum ein, sie herrscht auch an manchen Stellen, wo nichts Jüdisches, sondern nur allgemein Menschliches auszusprechen ist." Ibid., 303–4.

48. "Da sehnen wir uns denn manchmal nach einem herzhaften Schluck klarer europäisch-abendländischer Melodie." Ibid., 304.

49. See, for example, the discussion of this passage in Ralph P. Locke, "Cutthroats and Casbah Dancers, Muezzins and Timeless Sands: Musical Images of the Middle East," *19th-Century Music* 22, no. 1 (1998): 47–48.

50. "Wie wunderlich klingt das Lied ohne Worte, mit welchem Astaroth den Assad zur Königin lockt! Das sind Klänge, mit welchen man fromme Juden in die Synagoge, aber keinen Liebhaber zum Rendezvous treibt; der Alte Sulzer im Sopranschlüssel!" Hanslick, in *Neue Freie Presse* (March 12, 1875): 3. Hanslick cut the last phrase, with its direct reference to Sulzer, when adapting the review for *Musikalische Stationen*, 304. For Hanslick's admiring tribute to Sulzer, see Ed. H., "Salomon Sulzer," *Neue Freie Presse* (March 13, 1866): 1; repr. in Eduard Hanslick, *Aus dem Concertsaal* (Vienna: Wilhelm Braumüller, 1870), 401. For a brief discussion and partial translation of this *feuilleton*, see Eric Werner, *A Voice Still Heard . . . : The Sacred Songs of the Ashkenzic Jews* (University Park, PA: Pennsylvania State University Press, 1976), 216–17 (ellipsis in original). That Hanslick was deeply moved by Sulzer's synagogal song and singing is not, of course, to say that he saw any place for such a style in the concert hall or opera theater, apart from providing occasional local color.

51. Peter Stachel, "Eine 'vaterländische' Oper für die Habsburgermonarchie oder eine 'jüdische Nationaloper'? Carl Goldmarks *Königin von Saba* in Wien," in *Die Oper im Wandel der Gesellschaft: Kulturtransfers und Netzwerke des Musiktheaters in Europa*, ed. Sven Oliver Müller, Gesa zur Nieden, Philipp Ther, and Jutta Toelleden (Munich: Oldenbourg, 2010), 215–16. This article came to my attention when work on my own article was largely completed; I am grateful to Dr. Stachel for sharing a copy of his article with me in advance of publication.

52. Many of the attributes that Hanslick assigns to Goldmark's "Jewish-Oriental" music recall those used pejoratively by Wagner in "Das Judentum in der Musik." Jens Malte Fischer, *Richard Wagners "Das Judentum in der Musik": Eine kritische Dokumentation als Beitrag zur Geschichte des Antisemitismus* (Frankfurt/M: Insel, 2000). But Hanslick by no means accepted Wagner's racialist claim that Jewish composers could never write genuine German music (or that of any other Western nation). On the contrary, Hanslick's take might better be seen as one of exasperation that this particular Jewish composer, for whatever reason, did not always seem to heed the liberal imperative to overcome difference but rather seemed to insist on writing in a style redolent of his Jewish heritage.

53. "Mit aufrichtigem Vergnügen vermisse ich im Merlin ein vorstechendes Kennzeichen der Königin von Saba: die orientalisch-jüdischen Weisen, deren krauses Gewimmer uns die unleugbaren Schönheiten dieser Oper stark verleidet hat." Ed. H., "Merlin," *Neue Freie Presse* (November 21, 1886): 2; repr. in Hanslick, *Musikalisches Skizzenbuch (der "modernen Oper" IV. Theil): Neue Kritiken und Schilderungen* (Berlin: Allgemeiner Verein für Deutsche Litteratur, 1888), 81.

54. "Ob man aber nicht gerade wegen dieses prägnant nationalen Charakters die Königin von Saba origineller, 'goldmarkischer' finden wird, als den Merlin? Es wäre möglich und nicht gerade unbegründet. Das Orientalische mit seiner Gluth und Farbenpracht, aber auch mit seiner Unruhe, Heftigkeit und exaltirten Feierlichkeit liegt nicht blos im Stoff der Königin von Saba, es liegt auch von Haus aus in unserm Componisten, der unter doppelt orientalischem Einfluß, dem jüdischen und ungarischen, aufgewachsen ist." Hanslick, *Musikalisches Skizzenbuch*, 81. This notion of a "doubly Oriental influence" was borrowed from Ludwig Speidel's review of *The Queen of Sheba*; see sp. [Ludwig Speidel], "Hof-Operntheater," *Fremden-Blatt* (March 12, 1875): 5.

55. See Marsha Rozenblit, *Reconstructing a National Identity: The Jews of Habsburg Austria during World War I* (Oxford: Oxford University Press, 2004), 24, and the references cited there.

56. It seems never to have occurred to Hanslick that *Die Königin von Saba* might have been conceived as an *Orientalist* opera, written from the point of view of a *German* composer, a possibility I have explored in "Essentialism, Orientalism, and Musical Identity in Goldmark's *Queen of Sheba*" (paper read at the annual meeting of the American Musicological Society, Indianapolis, IN, November 2010).

57. "Wir hatten zuvor neugierig die Unvorsichtigkeit begangen, das Werk in vierhändigem Arrangement durchzuspielen, eine Operation, die wir jedermann erst nach der Orchester-Aufführung empfehlen möchten. Gleich bei den ersten zwei Accorden glaubten wir vom Stuhle zu fallen, denn kaum war es uns in unserer langen, mit jedem Jahre dissonanzenreicheren Praxis vorgekommen, daß jemand mit einer solchen Thür ins Haus fällt. Es klingt wie ein scharfer Geißelhieb sammt dem dazugehörigen Aufschrei des Getroffenen; Wagners Walküren sprengen rücksichtsvoller herein, als diese Goldmarkschen Amazonen." Ed. H., "Hofoperntheater. Concerte," *Neue Freie Presse* (December 7, 1880): 2; repr. in Hanslick, *Concerte, Componisten und Virtuosen der letzten*

fünfzehn Jahre 1870–1885 (Berlin: Allgemeiner Verein für Deutsche Litteratur, 1886), 282; trans. adapted from Bertagnolli, *Prometheus in Music*, 324.

58. "Doch bekennen wir gerne, das dieser gefürchtete Auftakt im Orchester weniger schmerzlich klingt, und da er ein Tongemälde einleitet, welches zwar grell, aber bedeutungsvoll und poetisch wirkt. Die Poesie des Entsetzlichen—das ist's ja, was ein Componist hervorbringern will und soll, der Kleists berühmte Tragödie nachzumusicieren unternimmt. . . . Der Componist einer 'Penthesilea'-Ouvertüre muß fürwahr alles Gräßliche sammeln, was sich der Musik—dieser 'heiteren Kunst,' wie sie das Mittelalter nannte—nur abzwingen läßt, will er den furchtbaren Eindruck des Kleistschen Dramas zur Noth erreichen." Ibid., 282–83.

59. See the quotation from this review given as my first epigraph.

60. "Man sieht, daß Goldmarks Composition mehr poetisch als musikalisch gedacht und geformt ist; dies ist der wesentlichste Vorwurf, der sie mit so vielen anderen ihrer verwandten Ouvertüren trifft, im Gegensatz zu Beethovens 'Egmont-' oder 'Coriolan-Ouvertüre,' welche bei prägnantester dramatischer Charakteristik doch allgemein verständlich, einheitlich und in ununterbrochenem musikalischen Fluß dahinströmen." Ibid., 284.

61. "'Im Frühling' betitelt Goldmark seine neue Ouvertüre. Die Aufschrift hat uns hoffnungsvoll und doch zugleich etwas ängstlich gestimmt. . . . Wird Goldmark, der gewaltige Dissonanzen-König, es über sich gewinnen, dem Mai zuliebe seine schneidendsten Akkorde zu verabschieden? Wird er den Frühling verherrlichen, ohne ihm zugleich Opposition zu machen? Wird er uns nicht giftflammende Blüthen aus dem Orient herüberbringen und Nachtigallen aus Bayreuth? So ungefähr flüsterten unsere Besorgnisse. Goldmark hat sie auf da liebenswürdigste und beinahe vollständig besiegt." Ed. H., "Concerte," *Neue Freie Presse* (December 8, 1889): 1; repr. in Hanslick, *Aus dem Tagebuche eines Musikers (der 'Modernen Oper' VI. Theil)* (Berlin: Allgemeiner Verein für Deutsche Litteratur, 1892), 270.

62. Here I am paraphrasing a position that Hanslick takes in criticizing Rimsky-Korsakov's *Scheherazade*. Ed. H., "Musik," *Neue Freie Presse* (February 10, 1898): 1; repr. in Hanslick, *Am Ende des Jahrhunderts 1898–1899 (der "Modernen Oper," VIII. Teil)* (Berlin: Allgemeiner Verein für Deutsche Litteratur, 1899), 289. The importance of this review in articulating Hanslick's views on program music is discussed in Grimes, "Brahms's Critics," 162–63.

63. "Ohne alles Präludiren setzt seine 'Frühlings-Ouvertüre' mit einem jubelnden Thema in A-dur ein, das nach einigen beschwichtigenden Takten sich in As-dur, dann mit aller Kraft in C-dur wiederholt, um endlich in ein zweites Thema von idyllischer Harmlosigkeit einzulenken. Beide Themen bieten günstige und geistreich verwendete Motive für die ziemlich umfangreiche Durchführung; Finkenschlag und Lerchentriller, wie man sie natürlicher nicht wünschen kann, liefern dazu den lieblichsten Aufputz." Hanslick, *Aus dem Tagebuche eines Musikers*, 271.

64. "Ganz und gar ohne Besuch in 'Wahnfried' geht es freilich nicht ab: Wagnerische Harmonien, anfangs schüchtern und vereinzelt, stürzen später als wilde Jagd von den Bergesgipfeln hernieder; synkopirte chromatische Sextakkorde der Geigen und Holzbläser, gegen welche Bässe und Posaunen eine schauerliche Procession von aufsteigenden verminderten Septimakkorden ins Feld führen. Das ist nicht das obligate Frühlingswetter, auf das man gerechnet hatte; eher eine kleine Vorprobe des Weltunterganges, wobei Flüsse, Wälder, Gebirge durcheinanderpurzeln und alles Eingeweide des Erdballes zu platzen droht." Ibid.

65. "Die Prometheus-Ouvertüre bedeutet eine weitere bewusste Klärung von Goldmarks starkem, aber turbulentem Talent; erfreuliche Anzeichen waren schon in der 'Frühlings-Ouvertüre . . . wahrzunmehmen.'" Ed. H., "Concerte," *Neue Freie Presse* (March 28, 1890): 1; repr. in *Aus dem Tagebüche eines Musikers*, 299.
66. "Wird der scheußliche Geier, der an Prometheus' Leber hackt, sich nicht zugleich in unsere Ohren verbeißen? Wird nicht statt des Helden unversehens sein Bruder Epimetheus auftauchen und aus der berüchtigten Büchse der Pandora alles auffliegen machen, was die Musik an bösen Stechfliegen besitzt?" Hanslick, *Aus dem Tagebuche eines Musikers*, 299; trans. adapted from Bertagnolli, *Prometheus in Music*, 325.
67. "Nichts von alledem ist geschehen. Trotz der einschneidenden, im Feuer des stärksten Orchesters heißgeglühten Tragik dieser Composition habe ich geradezu Abstoßendes, Häßliches nicht darin bemerkt." Hanslick, *Aus dem Tagebuche eines Musikers*, 299; trans. adapted from Bertagnolli, *Prometheus in Music*, 325.
68. "Die 'Ouvertüre zum Gefesselten Prometheus des Aeschylos,' eine der besten, reifsten Compositionen Goldmarks, reizt nicht bloß durch die heiße Energie des Ausdrucks, sie hat auch musikalischen Gehalt und übersichtliche Form." Hanslick, *Aus dem Tagebuche eines Musikers*, 298.
69. The first quotation is from Hanslick, *Aus dem Tagebuche eines Musikers*, 298; the second, from Hanslick, "Liszt's Symphonic Poems," 46.
70. "Die Ouvertüre beginnt wie feierliche Meeresstille mit einem Adagio in C-moll; dasselbe drängt allmählich zu der heftigeren Bewegung, die in dem Allegrosatz (gleichfalls in C-moll) in vollen Fluß geräth. Auf das trotzige, scharf markirte Hauptthema folgt ein zweites in C-dur von auffallend sanftem, fast idyllischem Ausdruck. . . . Mancher soll Anstoß genommen haben an dem friedlichen Ton dieses Seitenmotives. Ob es die Erinnerung an früheres Glück oder die Hoffnung auf Erlösung andeute, überlasse ich den Auslegekünstlern. Mir aber scheint es geradezu ein Verdienst des Componisten, daß er die Folterqualen des angeschmiedeten Prometheus vorübergehend unterbricht und beschwichtigt, ihn und uns gleichsam Athem schöpfen läßt." Hanslick, *Aus dem Tagebuche eines Musikers*, 298–99.
71. "Aber Goldmarks Verdienst ist es, daß er sich nicht in kleinlich ausmalendes Detail verloren, sondern stets das große Ganze im Auge behalten und aus seinem gefährlichen Stoffe ein musikalisches Kunstwerk geschaffen hat. Um vollkommen zu verstehen, was mit diesen Worten gemeint ist, brauchte man im Philharmonischen Concert nur noch ein Weilchen nach Goldmarks Ouvertüre sitzen zu bleiben und sich die 'Dante-Symphony' von Liszt anzuhören." Ibid., 300.
72. "Die neue Ouvertüre ist echter Goldmark, Goldmark in Überlebensgröße; ein Feuermeer von Leidenschaft, ein Urwald von Dissonanzen; mehr geistreich als schön, mehr aufregend als erfreulich, im ganzen 'furchtbar interessant,' wie die Berliner sagen." Ed. H., "Concerte," *Neue Freie Presse* (November 28, 1893): 1; repr. in Eduard Hanslick, *Fünf Jahre Musik [1891–1895] (der "Moderne Oper" VII. Teil)* (Berlin: Allgemeiner Verein für Deutsche Litteratur, 1896), 291–32.
73. "Mächtig packt uns die um Schönheit unbekümmerte Energie, mit welcher Goldmark das Liebesleid der Sappho schildert; ich glaube, es würde diese Musik für drei Sapphos ausreichen und bliebe noch etwas übrig für eine Medea oder eine verlassene Ariadne." Hanslick, *Fünf Jahre Musik*, 233.
74. "Die Ausleger finden da fröhlich Arbeit. Wenn einmal ein Instrumentalstück 'Sappho' überschrieben ist, dann fällt es nicht allzu schwer, den Phaon, die Melitta, Sapphos Eifersucht und ihren Sturz vom leukadischen Fels herauszufinden. Der Scharfsinn der Aus- und Unterleger operirt leicht bei also gebundener Marschroute. Mit ern-

sten Gründen habe ich oft gegen diese Interpretations-Kunststücke gefochten, welche auf der falschen Voraussetzung einer exacten Ausdrucksfähigkeit reiner Instrumentalmusik fußen." Hanslick, in *Neue Freie Presse* (November 28, 1893): 1; Hanslick, *Fünf Jahre Musik*, 233 (where the last sentence is dropped).

75. We know that Hanslick assumed that Goldmark's source was Grillparzer, since it was the Austrian dramatist who had invented the character of Melitta, Sappho's slave.

76. "Sie beginnt ganz stoff- und zeitgemäß mit einem breit ausgeführten Harfen-Solo. Daß die Harfe gleich mit einem dissonierenden Akkord einsetzen werde, dürfte freilich nicht jedermann vermutet haben; beginnt doch selbst Smetanas greiser Harfenist am Wyssehrad, trotz seiner großen Traurigkeit, mit dem reinen Es-Dur-Dreiklange. Ein gefühlvolles Andante mit einem dissonierenden Akkord anzufangen, ist immer bedenklich—etwa so, als begänne man ein lyrisches Gedicht mit dem Worte 'Nichtsdestoweniger.'" Hanslick, *Fünf Jahre Musik*, 231–32.

77. "Über den Moll-Akkorden der Harfe erhebt sich dann ein Gesangsthema der Oboe. Nach diesen klagenden Triolenfiguren, übermäßigen Quarten und verminderten Sexten zu schließen, dürfte die griechische Dichterin ein Geschwisterkind der 'Sakuntala' und auch häufig in Palästina gewesen sein." Hanslick, *Fünf Jahre Musik*, 231–32.

78. Fifteen years earlier, in his review of Anton Rubinstein's opera *The Maccabees*, Hanslick had made more fitting use of this trope. There, describing the scene near the beginning of the third act in which the Jews, struck down by hunger, war, and pestilence, gather outside Jerusalem to "lament and pray," Hanslick draws attention to "the well-known Oriental unison melodies, with their dragged eighth notes and wailing triplets." (Der dritte Act . . . führt uns auf einen Platz vor Jerusalem, wo das Volk . . . klagt und betet. Wir hören wieder die bekannten orientalischen Unisono-Melodieen mit ihren geschleiften Achteln und jammernden Triolen.) Ed. H., "Die Makkabäer," *Neue Freie Presse* (February 26, 1878): 3; repr. in Hanslick, *Musikalische Stationen*, 328. This trope can be traced back in association with Goldmark to Ludwig Speidel's review of *Die Königin von Saba*, the same review from which Hanslick borrowed the "doubly Oriental" trope; see Speidel, in *Fremdenblatt* (March 12, 1875): 5.

79. Brodbeck, "Hanslick's Smetana and Hanslick's Prague," 25–32.

80. "Was uns an Goldmarks neuer Oper zunächst erfreut und noch Tausende erfreuen wird, ist der natürliche Ausdruck der Empfindung. Goldmark, welcher ("un chercheur," wie die Franzosen sagen) in seinen früheren Werken gern auf die Suche nach Apartem, Ungewöhnlichem ausging, dem jedes starke Gefühl leicht in Ektase, jedes Reizmittel in ätzende Schärfe überschlug, derselbe Goldmark findet im "Heimchen" den liebenswürdigen, maßvollen Ton des Familienstückes und weiß ihn, sogar mit glücklichen Abstechern ins Komische, festzuhalten." Ed. H., "Hofoperntheater," *Neue Freie Presse* (March 22, 1896): 2; repr. in Hanslick, *Am Ende des Jahrhunderts*, 15.

81. "Was die neue Oper auf den ersten Blick auszeichnet, ist ihre Abkehr vom modernen 'Musikdrama,' von dem angeblich alleindramatischen und alleinseligmachenden System Wagners. Im 'Heimchen' wechseln Strophenlieder, Arien, Duette und Chöre; freie Parlandosätze flechten sich in die Kantilene; Liebende und Eheleute genieren sich nicht, in Terzen zu singen; einzelne Wörter und Sätze werden ohne weiters wiederholt, mitunter sogar . . . sehr oft. Die Melodien, meistens sangbar und einfach, bewegen sich in faßlichen Rhythmen und Perioden; die Singstimmen herrschen, das Orchester begleitet. So predigt denn das 'Heimchen' die nie veraltende Wahrheit, daß Musik ohne die Gesetze der Form und Symmetrie nicht existieren kann, soll sie nicht

zu bloßem pathologischen Nervenreiz herabsinken." Hanslick, *Am Ende des Jahrhunderts*, 14–15.

82. "Immerhin erkennen wir an einzelnen Manieren (und Goldmark hat deren wie jeder Künstler) den 'Hofkomponisten der Königin von Saba,' wie er einmal einem Freunden vorgestellt wurde. Die scharfen Modulationen, das Nisten in chromatischen und enharmonischen Gängen, insbesondere die auf- und niederrauschende Jagd chromatischer Accordfolgen! Diese Figur ist das teilnehmende Heimchen am Goldmarkschen Herd, das sich jederzeit meldet, wenn etwas los ist, Frohes oder Schmerzliches." Ibid., 16; emphasis added.

83. "Unsere Freude über Goldmarks neuesten Erfolg ist stark und aufrichtig. Sie gilt nicht nur dem ausgezeichneten Künstler, sondern ebenso sehr dem Manne, dessen charaktervolle, jeder Reklame abholde Persönlichkeit in so hohem Grade die allgemeine Achtung und Sympathie genießt." Hanslick, *Am Ende des Jahrhunderts*, 17.

Chapter Eight

German Humanism, Liberalism, and Elegy in Hanslick's Writings on Brahms

Nicole Grimes

> I could almost envy [Hanslick] his power of expressing himself, if not exhaustively, yet with an intuitive sympathy, which not only provides an outlet for his own feelings but helps others who have no command of words to express theirs.
> —Elisabet von Herzogenberg to Brahms, January 3, 1882

Eduard Hanslick's reviews of the works of Johannes Brahms span from 1862, when he announced "the appearance before the Viennese public of this blond, St. John visage of a composer,"[1] to the year of Hanslick's death, 1904. Composer and critic struck up a close and lifelong friendship following their meeting in 1862, a friendship they shared with the Austrian surgeon and amateur musician Theodor Billroth—the three being on intimate *du* terms and forming the "closest musical threesome."[2] Hanslick was the music correspondent for the *Neue Freie Presse*, Austria's leading liberal daily newspaper.[3] It was here that he published his abundant and multifarious writings on Brahms. Not only are Hanslick's Brahms reviews musically perceptive and insightful, they can also be understood as a cultural commentary on the musical world of Vienna in the late nineteenth century, and they illuminate the cultural, religious, and political context in which Brahms's works were composed and received.

Hanslick's output on Brahms is vast and, therefore, I have chosen here to focus only on one aspect of this output: a selection of the reviews of Brahms's choral and orchestral works composed between 1868 and 1883, an output that for reasons made clear below I refer to as Brahms's "musical elegies." This period coincided with the ascendancy of a modern form of liberalism in Vienna to which both Hanslick and Brahms subscribed. The works I will explore in this essay are either settings of, or are closely related to the poetry of Goethe, Schiller, and Hölderlin. They are, therefore, inextricably linked to the turn-of-the-century New Humanism espoused by these poets. My discussion of Hanslick's reading of these works is cognizant of his own humanist inclinations. My findings are informed by the recent work of Mark Burford, among others, who argues that Hanslick's goal in his aesthetic treatise was not to "deny idealism, but rather to renegotiate a middle ground between idealism and materialism," that is, to renegotiate the nexus between spirit and matter. Invoking the literature of what he refers to as "optimistic messianic humanism," Burford both critiques Hanslick's writings in the context of German idealism and outlines continuity in humanist writings from Ludwig Feuerbach through Ludwig Büchner to Hanslick.[4] Building on the work of Mark Evan Bonds, Burford argues that Hanslick "took Hegel's aesthetic and clung to the metaphysical premise of the 'Idea' or 'Spirit' in music, though in a newly interpreted sense." Burford's key insight is his claim that "in his attempt to characterize music's essence, Hanslick did not so much reject musical metaphysics as, to a certain extent, reconceptualize it by arguing that the ideal content of music is a product of a human spirit, not a transcendent one."[5]

In this essay I will explore Hanslick's reviews of Brahms's "musical elegies" as outlined in table 8.1 in relation to the composer's complex and multifaceted engagement with poetry and extramusical texts. I aim to show that Hanslick was in a unique position among Brahms's critics—as one who was within his circle of confidants, and was therefore privy to the private musical meaning of many of his works, and as one who shared Brahms's liberal outlook—to convey the rich and complex meaning of these works to his liberal readership. Moreover, I argue that these reviews form an integral part of the reception history of Brahms's music that has been largely overlooked in the literature on Hanslick and Brahms in favor of a discussion of the 1854 monograph *Vom Musikalisch-Schönen*.

From German Humanism to Viennese Liberalism

The period 1867 to the mid-1890s witnessed the ascendancy of a modern form of liberalism in Vienna before it was quelled at the hands of the Christian Social demagogue Karl Lueger. Following the creation of the Dual Monarchy (Austria Hungary) in 1867, Emperor Francis Joseph's Constitutional Edict of 1869 granted a number of significant civic and social reforms, including the appointment of Austria's first parliamentary cabinet or *Bürgerministerium*, and the availability of Austrian citizenship for the first time. Hereby all citizens were guaranteed equal legal rights, leading to a greater degree of ethnic tolerance (particularly for the Jewish communities); the displacement of Christianity (specifically: Catholicism) in favor of rationalism and science; and the primacy of German culture, which was celebrated further following Prussia's victory

Table 8.1. Brahms's musical elegies: timeline of compositions and reviews

Work	Date of composition	Poem	Date of poem	Date of Hanslick's review
Schicksalslied, op. 54	1868–71	Hölderlin, "Hyperions Schicksalslied"	1797–98	1872
Alto Rhapsody, op. 53	1869	Goethe, "Harzreise im Winter"	1777	1875 (reviewed with the *German Requiem*)
[Brahms, Symphony No. 1 in C minor, Op. 68 premiered on 4 November 1876]				
Tragische Ouvertüre, op. 81	1880	—	—	1880
Nänie, op. 82	1881	Schiller, "Nänie"	1799	1882
Gesang der Parzen, op. 89	1882	in Goethe, *Iphigenie auf Tauris*	1779–87	1883

over France in 1871.[6] As Pieter Judson neatly encapsulates it, "this bill of rights allowed freedom of belief and public worship and granted to every citizen the same civil rights no matter what the individual's religious beliefs."[7] The law also recognized the autonomy of individual religions to administer their own internal affairs and—in a clause pointed toward the hitherto privileged Catholic Church—stated that "no citizen who did not wish to could be compelled to take part in a public religious function." In the thirty-five years that Brahms resided in Vienna (1862–97), this liberalism experienced a steady and dramatic decline before the city was engulfed in what Carl Schorske refers to as a "Christian Social tidal wave" in the 1890s that witnessed a rise in anti-Semitism and an alliance with the Catholic Church.[8]

Modern Viennese liberalism shared traits with European liberalism of the time, such as a belief in progress and the promotion of scientific methods, with Viennese liberalism appealing largely to the *Bildungsbürgertum*: the educated, culturally formed German and Jewish-German middle and upper middle classes.[9] Brahms, Hanslick, Billroth, Max Kalbeck, Gustav Dömpke, and Ludwig Speidel were among the intellectual elite of Viennese liberalism, with Hanslick and Speidel being music and theater critics, respectively, for the *Neue Freie Presse*. Leon Botstein has asserted that "Brahms's reputation among the Viennese in the 1880s was seen as linked to the older liberal elite,"[10] and his music of this period "was part of an older conception of *Bildung*, in which music, literature and painting were capable of cultivating a sensibility at odds with the vulgarities of modern mass intolerance and hatred."[11]

It was during this very period, between 1868 and 1883, that Brahms produced four one-movement works for choir and orchestra, *Alto Rhapsody*, op. 53; *Schicksalslied*, op. 54; *Nänie*, op. 82; and *Gesang der Parzen*, op. 89. These works are settings of texts by three of Germany's most eminent poets from the turn of the nineteenth century: Johann Wolfgang Goethe (1749–1832), Friedrich von Schiller (1759–1805), and Johann Christian Friedrich Hölderlin (1770–1843); and the texts of three of the poems, opp. 54, 82, and 89, are based on legends of classical antiquity.

Brahms's engagement with these poetic texts was, in turn, an engagement with the turn-of-the-century New Humanism of Humboldt, Goethe, Schiller, and their contemporaries. This "humanistic 'new learning'" entailed "a 'Renaissance' or rebirth of Greco-Roman civilization and its associated values."[12] These quintessentially German values are neatly encapsulated by J. A. Symonds for his English readership in the 1898 text *The Renaissance in Italy*, where he explains that "the essence of humanism consists in a new and vital perception of the dignity of man as a rational being apart from theological determinations and in the further perception that classic literature alone displayed human nature in the plenitude of intellectual and moral freedom."[13] Such a humanistic bent is also akin to the spirit and ethos of the classical German elegy as developed by Goethe, Schiller, and their contemporaries. Schiller is regarded as having provided the most sophisticated theory of the elegiac mode in *Über naïve und sentimentalische Dichtung* (1795–96) in describing it as a "modern, sentimental state of mind inspired by the disjunction between imperfect reality and ideal, which embodies some sort of 'moral harmony.'"[14] This romantic sensibility epitomizes what Svetlana Boym categorizes as "reflective nostalgia"—a fascination with the present and a longing for another time or set of values—that becomes a "driving force for the human condition."[15] Brahms's fixation on a poetic and poetical world that existed close to a century before he penned these works betrays signs of such a nostalgic element. On account of the ideological kinship between the classical German elegy and the Brahms works explored in this essay, I propose to call these works Brahms's "musical elegies."

The Hellenic ideal espoused by this "humanism" belonged to the future of "modern Germany [that these poets] were engaged in building."[16] The values of rationality and belief in human progress central to this endeavor focused on "the cultivation of the individual, a process seen as imperative if the society were to receive any collective benefits from its educational system."[17] The classicist Ludwig Curtius wrote of German humanism: "This 'pure humanity' was not a pale abstract theory, but a moral command, directed at each individual, for the reconstruction of his personal life."[18] This intense moralistic reflection espoused by these poets resonates with the values that were central to Viennese liberalism. For Brahms, for whom "cultural standards, love of learning and humanism seemed unquestionably allied in [his] mind,"[19] these texts by Goethe, Schiller, and Hölderlin surely gave powerful expression to his own liberal view of the world.

Common to Brahms's "musical elegies" are endings that respond to their preceding texts, functioning either to extend the text or to reverse its meaning. Hanslick's reviews recognize that these works are interrelated and that they bear comparison with Brahms's *German Requiem*. According to Schiller's dictum, "'tender softness and melancholy' . . . did not suffice if they failed to lead up to the energetic principle of *Bildung*, or spiritual harmony meant to transcend the poem's despondency."[20] This also held true for Hanslick, for whom it was not the poetry, but rather Brahms's response to the poetry in his music that he considered to fulfill this energizing and spiritual role. Hanslick attributes numerous qualities to Brahms's compositions that are in keeping with liberal values: the displacement of Christianity in favor of a secularized (usually, Greek) outlook on the world; an aspiration toward *Bildung*; a devotion to one's task; strength; masculinity; an ethical character; and an indifference to external opinion.[21] A reading of Hanslick's reviews of these works uncovers a continuity between the humanist revival in German education from Goethe to Burckhardt, to the moral and ethical dimension these pieces share with the humanism of the idealist period (including the works of Beethoven), and finally to that of Viennese liberalism.[22]

From Poetry's Object of Sorrow to Music's Object of Joy

Since the première of Brahms's *Schicksalslied*, critical opinion has been divided on account of the orchestral postlude. His choice to end a choral work with a purely instrumental orchestral section perplexed critics as much then as it does now.[23] The work opens with a 28-measure orchestral introduction in E-flat major, with a performance direction of "Langsam und sehnsuchtsvoll" (slow and full of longing), an unusual tempo designation for Brahms. The postlude uses all of the same musical material as the introduction, but it is transposed down a minor third to C major, evoking the traditional musical topos for light and sunrise. The tempo designation is now "Adagio."

This work is a setting of Hölderlin's poem of the same title, which ends in hopelessness, with suffering humanity being hurled into an abyss of uncertainty. The majority of critics at the time of the work's first performances saw an "imaginary continuation of the contents of the poem" in this final, instrumental movement and sensed the effect of comfort and reconciliation.[24] Several critics, however, understood the *Nachspiel* to be at odds with Hölderlin's poetic message. Some understood the music to have conquered or subjugated the words of the poem, while others lamented the fact that composers of the day ventured near texts of such high poetic quality.[25]

Unlike those who see the postlude in Brahms's setting of Hölderlin's "Schicksalslied" as being either in congruence with or in contradiction to the poem, Hanslick is concerned with the expressive potential of pure instrumental music, which he understands here to express that which cannot be seized in words. He outlines the stark contrast between Brahms's setting of the first two strophes, an Adagio in E-flat major describing "the blessed peace of the Olympic gods who 'breathe aloft in the light of immortality,'"[26] and the setting of the third, an Allegro in C minor that "describes the pitiful lot of mankind who are 'given no place to rest.'"[27] For Hanslick, the manner in which Brahms deals with Hölderlin's stark contrast between imperfect reality and the ideal is of secondary importance. Indeed, he considers Brahms to be "unswayed by the ideas of the great and immortal," implying, rather, that it is mortals with whom he is concerned. Brahms's postlude of purely instrumental music reveals to his audience the "whole transfiguring power of music."[28] He considers this postlude to go beyond—and to fulfill—the expressive potential announced by the poem, yet never within its reach. It is worth quoting Hanslick at length here:

> In this hopelessness the poet finishes—but not so the composer. It is an extremely beautiful poetic turn, which reveals to us the whole transfiguring power of music. Brahms returns, after the final words sung by the choir, to the solemn, slow movement of the opening, and dissolves the confused hardship of human life in a long orchestral postlude, in blessed peace. In a touching and generally accessible way, Brahms conveys this train of thought via pure instrumental music, without the addition of a single word. The instrumental music here replenishes and complements the poem, and it articulates that which can no longer be expressed in words: a remarkable counterpart to the reverse procedure in Beethoven's Symphony No. 9. Brahms's *Schicksalslied* reminds us in style and mood of an after effect of his admirable *German Requiem*, the same Christian outlook, but Greek in form.[29]

Writing more recently, Michael Musgrave has also likened the general sentiment expressed in the *German Requiem*—"comfort, hope, reassurance, and reward for personal effort"—to Brahms's settings of the legends of classical antiquity, including *Schicksalslied, Nänie*, and *Gesang der Parzen*.[30] Hanslick commended the "Christian outlook" in Brahms's *German Requiem* in 1875, a work which is "stripped of every confessional dress, every sacred convenience" on account of Brahms choosing German biblical words in place of the Latin ritual text.[31] Daniel Beller-McKenna has argued that "by emphasizing Brahms's adherence to purely musical laws and effects, Hanslick sought to decontextualize (or at best recontextualize) op. 45," so that "in Hanslick's view, the piece functions less like sacred music and more like absolute music."[32] I dispute Beller-McKenna's assertion by arguing that Hanslick recontextualized the piece to function not as sacred music, but as a source of comfort for a secularized society. It would have been no coincidence that Hanslick singled out the fifth movement—the soprano aria "Ihr habt nun Traurigkeit"—as a means to illustrate the expressive potential of this requiem. Whereas those who are bereaved would not "remain dry-eyed through the overwhelming, touching sounds of the soprano's aria," he wrote, they would "experience how transfiguring and strengthening the purest comfort is that flows from this music."[33] Michael Musgrave has observed that the fifth and sixth movements of the Requiem "offer the most striking examples of [biblical] meanings changed through selection." He recognizes in this fifth movement "a personal hymn to consolation and comfort which removes the words from a Christian context, the voice of a God figure, or of Christ."[34]

It is noteworthy that it is Brahms's music—in the context of its relationship to the text—that Hanslick recognizes as the "purest comfort." For Hanslick, for those who "now have sorrow," it is Brahms's music (the product of a human spirit and not the utterance of a sacred one) that will provide comfort. Likewise, in *Schicksalslied*, it is "pure instrumental music, without the addition of a single word" that brings "blessed peace," yet this too is dependent on the text, in that it "replenishes and complements the poem."[35]

It was not only *Schicksalslied* and the *German Requiem* that Hanslick considered to be closely related: he considered these both to be companion pieces to the *Alto Rhapsody*, op. 53. In this work, Brahms provides contrasting musical material for each of the three strophes (5–7) of Goethe's poem "Harzreise im Winter" that are concerned with the portrait of a lonely, misanthropic young man.[36] For Hanslick, "the poem becomes truly musical initially with the closing strophe, which brings comfort and reconciliation," the point in the work where the music modulates to the parallel major (Adagio $\frac{4}{4}$), where the four-part male-voice choir joins in with the contralto in a hymn to the "Father of Love." Hanslick identifies a "peculiar, ethical character which is impressed on us so completely and utterly in Brahms's music" that arises in the *Rhapsody* "in gentle tendentious strength." It is on account of this "ethical character" that Hanslick considers Brahms's music to be "so closely related to Beethoven's music."[37]

There are a number of ways of reading Hanslick's frequent references to Beethoven's "ethical character" and his association of this quality with Brahms's works. Marcia Citron observes that before German unification in 1871, Beethoven was held up as a masculine German icon, with his strong, heroic style being used to represent Germanic ideals. She cites "the 'triumphalism' of the 'Eroica' symphony, the *Brüderlichkeit* in the last movement of the Ninth Symphony or the conquering of 'fate' associated with the Fifth Symphony," all of which she sees as being related to the "concept of *Bildung* central to German Romanticism: a melding of education, socialization and struggle as one became a fully formed individual."[38]

Brahms and Beethoven certainly had in common a broad intellectual curiosity, paramount in which was an interest in philosophical issues. Both read widely, and both kept a log of proverbs and philosophical sayings that were significant to them.[39] Whereas Beethoven and Brahms each nominally subscribed to a religious faith (Catholicism in Beethoven's case, Lutheranism in Brahms's), neither was a regular churchgoer. Hanslick himself acknowledged this as early as 1861 in his review of the *Missa Solemnis*: "Beethoven was never especially attached to the articles of the Catholic faith . . . his belief had rather the character of a liberal (free), law-abiding theosophy."[40] As with Brahms, Beethoven's image of God, as Barry Cooper has observed, "was not based solely on traditional Christian teaching but was drawn from a wide variety of influences including Classical antiquity and oriental religions."[41] The work that epitomizes this approach in Beethoven's music is the Ninth Symphony. In order to embrace the message of this work one need not profess allegiance to one true faith or nation. Rather, the nonspecific religiosity of Schiller's poem is enhanced by Beethoven's music, which, as David B. Levy reminds us, "embraces the 'millions' of the world without the slightest hint of exclusivity."[42]

It is this lack of exclusivity, this absence of discrimination between religious faiths or between the secular and sacred, that Hanslick recognizes as the ethical (one might say humanist) character in Brahms's "musical elegies." Such an approach to these works, moreover, corroborates Mark Burford's argument that Hanslick recognized the ideal content of music, "both music's metaphysical essence and materiality" being "inextricably linked to human intellectual activity."[43]

Brahms's *Nänie*, completed in August 1881, is dedicated to the memory of his friend, the artist Anselm Feuerbach. Feuerbach died in Venice on January 4, 1880. *Nänie* is a setting of Schiller's poem "Auch das Schöne muß sterben!," a lament on the transience of life. Hanslick observes that it is less their shared "love of music that connected Feuerbach and Brahms in friendship and affinity than their similar outlooks on art."[44] He considered them to share an "imperturbable orientation toward the great, the exalted, and the ideal"—characteristics that for both artists lead to "sharp severity and seclusion."[45] Hanslick enlists the words of Feuerbach in relation to the latter's painting *Poetry* to illustrate this affinity between artist and composer: "It is no painting dictated by fashion; it is severe and unadorned. I expect no understanding of it, but I can do nothing else. And whoever takes the trouble to consider it for a long time becomes somewhat overcome, as though the picture were not a picture of our time."[46] These words allude to artistic ideals that Brahms and Feuerbach shared, characteristics that lend themselves to artistic creative excellence and integrity—an aspiration toward truth in their respective art forms that was not dependent on superficial or coloristic means and was indifferent to external opinion.[47]

Like most other commentators who have written on this work, both contemporaneously and more recently, Hanslick notes that Brahms reverts to the penultimate line of Schiller's poem for his ending, rather than finishing the work less optimistically, as Schiller does. "It is appropriate that Brahms does not end with the phrase 'for the ordinary goes down unsung into Orcus,'" he writes, "but rather closes with the previous verse, 'Even to be an elegy in the mouth of the beloved is glorious!'"[48] For Hanslick, the return of the opening musical material, again in D major ($^6_4$), "rounds off the work harmoniously."[49] The meaning of *Nänie* for Hanslick, in keeping with the collective tone of Brahms's "musical elegies," is that despite the inevitability of the transience of beauty and perfection, the aesthetic triumphs over death in the memory of beauty.

Gesang der Parzen, after a poem from one of Goethe's classical dramas *Iphigenie auf Tauris*, was completed in 1882. Brahms's setting is the Song of the Fates that Iphigenie sings in act 4 in her attempt to come to terms with the conflicting demands of "the eternally unspoilt peace of the gods, in comparison with the constant fight of the stressful existence of poor humans."[50] Not only is Brahms's composition at odds with Goethe's play, his music has been largely understood as being at odds with the very section of text he chose to set. The poem is concerned with the hopelessness of man in the face of the gods. The text opens with the lines "In fear of the Gods shall ye dwell, sons of men," as the gods hold dominion over mankind in their eternal hands. It further warns mankind that despite being exalted by the gods, they live in constant peril of being plunged, abused, and shamed into the nocturnal depths. And while mankind remains bound in darkness in the hope of justice being served, the gods turn their blessed eyes away from an entire—once beloved—race of people.

It is Brahms's musical language in the fifth strophe that has elicited most comment in relation to the incongruity between poetry and music. The verse reads: "The rulers turn their eyes away from entire races of people, and they shun in grandchildren the once-beloved, silently speaking features of our ancestors." Brahms introduces the parallel D major tonality to the work for the first time at this peak of ruthlessness, albeit with subtle minor mode tilts to ward off any false sense of security in the major. Gustav Ophüls reports Brahms's comment that "I often hear people philosophizing about the fifth strophe of the *Parzenlied*. I think that, at the mere entry of the major key, the unsuspecting listener's heart must soften and his eyes become wet, only then does the whole misery of mankind take hold of him."[51]

In his 1883 review of *Gesang der Parzen*,[52] Hanslick notes the incongruity of Brahms's musical language in the fifth strophe with the remainder of the piece. To him, "this reconciling, almost transfiguring conclusion is not explainable from the poem itself—it is not necessarily a result of it." The fact that "the gods turned their blessed eyes away from the innocent grandchild of the unfortunate, once-beloved ancestor" in the poem does not signify a softening for Hanslick, "but rather indicates the pitiless persistence of their cruel senses."[53] Hanslick takes a similar approach here to that taken in his review of *Schicksalslied*.[54] He avoids making a value judgment on the text, or indeed, taking a position on whether Brahms has been faithful to it or not in his musical setting. Rather Hanslick's emphasis is on the significance of the text as a stimulus for Brahms's musical needs. Brahms, in Hanslick's view, is neither refuting nor reversing the harshness of the heavenly decree of the gods as expressed in Goethe's poem. For Hanslick, "Brahms's penetrating interpretation" privileges the human position.[55] For humans who, along with Iphigenie, face the conflicting demands of heavenly decree and worldly practicality, there is beauty and comfort to be found in this practicality, in the human endeavor of art and, more specifically, in Brahms's composition.

Brahms's demand in *Parzenlied*—as the piece is often called—as seen through the lens of Hanslick's criticism, seems to be that if there must be destitution, there must also be hope and reconciliation. "Just as Rubens or Rembrandt often need a bright color and, without the compulsion of the subject, use it for individual portions of a painting with a dark background," Hanslick writes, "so, we think, Brahms the musician deemed a more reconciled ending to be essential to this chorus and therefore arranged it so touchingly and beautifully."[56] In Hanslick's opinion, Goethe's "gloomy tones of lament," and the "penetrating cry" of the poem, when taken in isolation, "bring us hopelessly down to earth." But when coupled with Brahms's "beautiful sound," it "rises against this hopelessness."[57] Hanslick, in a manner that recalls the turn-of-the-century humanism of Goethe and Schiller, considers *Gesang der Parzen* "highly important in its perfect union of the severity and simplicity of classical antiquity, with the liveliest, most moving expression of feelings."[58]

The *Weltanschauung* that Hanslick espouses in these works is one that juxtaposes harshness and sorrow with comfort and transfiguration. His reviews draw attention to these qualities in a manner that offers consolation for a secularized public by distancing the work from religious dogma. Hanslick discerned similar qualities in Brahms's orchestral works, specifically the *Tragische Ouvertüre*. It is to this work that we now turn.

From the Sacred to the Secular: Distancing Dogma?

Brahms gave no clues as to the origin of the suggestive title *Tragische Ouvertüre*, op. 81, and left no record of having a specific tragedy in mind. Moreover, he did not even hint that the tragedy was of the literary kind. Several commentators have put forward suggested readings of the overture, from Kalbeck's proposal that its origins are in Goethe's *Faust*[59] to Tovey's comparison with Shakespeare's *Hamlet*.[60]

In the absence of clues to the poetic idea embodied in the work, or how the work embodies the notion of tragedy, Hanslick offers his own suggestion for the significance of the title in his 1880 review. Noting that the overture "deals with independent musical thoughts, themes, from which the composer organically develops the whole, with his characteristic, rigorous logic,"[61] Hanslick accurately records that Brahms has no specific tragedy (*Trauerspiel*) in mind for his overture, "rather a general '*Actus Tragicus*' (just as J. S. Bach's inscription reads)."[62] He ventures that "if we had to call on a tragedy to be introduced by Brahms's overture, we would probably call on *Hamlet*."[63]

Hanslick's use of the term *Trauerspiel* in relation to the overture is noteworthy. Brahms himself had toyed with the idea of giving the work the title "Trauerspiel-Ouvertüre."[64] Walter Benjamin perceives the seventeenth-century *Trauerspiel* as being central to baroque allegorical thought, on account of its "antithetical music-allegorical elements."[65] In John Deathridge's 1996 discussion of Wagner's *Tristan und Isolde* (composed 1857–59), he argues that Isolde's *Liebestod* is reminiscent of a *Trauerspiel* owing to its "chorale-like beginning" and "hymn-like gestures." Here Deathridge draws attention to Benjamin's description of the baroque tragedy (*Trauerspiel*) as "showing an antinomic relation between Lutheranism and the everyday, . . . a process that actively resists the sense of disenchantment brought about by rigorous, anti-Transcendentalist Lutheran dogma."[66] Deathridge reminds us that *Trauerspiel* was linked to Lutheranism, but could also be understood as resisting its dogma. Hanslick's liberal Viennese readership in 1880 would most likely have been aware of such associations. Lest the term *Trauerspiel* alone fail to conjure up such images, Hanslick employs further references to Lutheranism.

Hanslick's allusion to *Actus Tragicus* can be read in a number of ways. The very mention of Bach—the composer revered as a German cultural icon in the nineteenth century—draws attention to the historical lineage of Brahms's music. By referring to a Bach cantata, Hanslick evokes the image of Brahms as a North-German Lutheran. *Actus Tragicus* (BWV 106) was one of the better-known Bach cantatas during the nineteenth century, having appeared in A. B. Marx's 1830 edition of the cantatas, and having received frequent performances.[67] In this work, Bach sets texts chosen from the Old Testament, the New Testament, and Martin Luther's chorale "Mit Fried und Freud' ich fahr dahin."[68] Eric Chafe points out that the *Actus Tragicus* differs from its sister genre, the *biblical historia*, in having a more meditative and less purely narrative emphasis.[69] He argues that BWV 106 goes much further than "the confrontation of Old and New Testament texts or of Law and Gospel," and explores both the "doctrinal element" and the "personal, individual and subjective side of faith."[70] The subject of meditation in this cantata, he states, "is the understanding of death according to the stages of salvation history."[71] These stages encompass "the history of Israel to the coming of Christ, his death on the cross, and the era of the Christian church." He also suggests that the sequence can be read "as an internal progression from fear of death and acceptance of its inevitability to faith in Christ and in the promise of the Gospel, and, finally, to the willingness of the believer to die in Christ and his church."[72] In other words, the theme of *Actus Tragicus*, a work steeped in Christian dogma and Lutheran theology, can be understood as the inevitability of death, or, as Beller-McKenna understands it, as "a sequence of ideas that progress towards an acceptance of death."[73]

Whereas Hanslick evokes Lutheran dogma in his review of the *Tragische Ouvertüre*, op. 81, he also distances his review from such dogma, not only by referring to BWV 106, but also in his reference to *Hamlet*. A sequence of ideas that progress toward an acceptance of death is a good description of what happens in *Hamlet*, in particular in the air of resignation we find in the last act.[74] We witness the character's progression from a state of depression in act 1, to that of an exemplary Shakespearean villain, with an over-reliance on reason and a strong belief in a free will, in act 2. By the last scene, Hamlet seems to have become indifferent to death, neither desiring it nor fearing it: "We defy augury. There is special providence in the fall of a sparrow. If it be now, 'tis not to come; if it be not to come, it will be now; if it be not now, yet it will come—the readiness is all. Since no man of aught he leaves knows, what is't to leave betimes?"[75] This is indicative of a state of stoical detachment. Moreover, despite the fact that Hamlet has now come to put his trust in providence, it seems his attitude toward death is not that of a devout Christian. Hamlet shows no particular concern to repent of his sins, for example, as a devout Christian should in the same circumstances.

Of course there is no way of knowing for certain why Hanslick (or indeed, later Tovey) considered *Hamlet* to be a poetic counterpart to the *Tragische Ouvertüre*. Nevertheless, the references to BWV 106 and *Hamlet* taken together illuminate one another, juxtaposing a sequence of ideas steeped in Christian dogma and Lutheran theology and progressing toward an acceptance of death, with a secular counterpart. This reading is in keeping with Hanslick's description of the work as being "filled throughout with a pathetic seriousness that sometimes touches the severe, but never the horribly distorting 'tragic.'"[76] If we are to understand the work in terms of Brahms's musical thoughts and themes, as Hanslick suggests we ought, there is a direct musical analogy in the inability of the theme to articulate the tonic. As James Webster observes, the struggle brought about by this tragic element is evident throughout the overture, but reaches a powerful culmination in the coda. Webster speaks of a "last defiant gesture" (m. 379) as the coda moves toward its relentless close. It is in the passage that follows that the work takes on all of the struggles that have gone before, and thrashes them out in a formidable finale.[77] The work ends with a stoical acceptance of its fate; to invoke Shakespeare: "the readiness is all." Hanslick's reading, therefore, can be interpreted not as suggesting a program for the work, but as providing the reader with a number of ways of understanding the work spiritually. His proposal of literary adjuncts for the work is entirely compatible with this understanding of the work's "characteristic, rigorous logic."[78] I would argue that Hanslick sees Brahms universalizing the spiritual message that he considers the work to embody.

Evidence of Brahms's critics interpreting such universal or humanitarian messages in any of Brahms's works other than the *German Requiem* is scant. Yet as Margaret Notley aptly notes, "beginning with Kalbeck, who referred to the composer as a 'heretic,' Brahms's biographers have usually regarded him as having been an unobservant Christian in his adult years, to have become a liberal like Hanslick in this respect."[79] Notley further argues that among Hanslick's liberal propensities was a tendency to be an unobservant Christian, to view Biblical stories as valuable lessons in moral conduct, regardless of the specific faith of the reader. It is in this context that Hanslick recalls his childhood relationship to religion: "The essence and foundation of religion should be only ethics; all faiths with the same moral principles were of equal worth. We became acquainted with the Biblical stories only from their amiable, tenderhearted, and poetic side, with the 'miracle' only as allegories."[80]

The *Tragische Ouvertüre* was composed in the summer of 1880. On a number of occasions during this period, Brahms expressed his dissatisfaction with his lot as a composer of spiritual music, and explicitly stated his wish to find heathen texts to set. Thus his letter of July 14, 1880, to Elisabet von Herzogenberg: "I am quite willing to write motets, or anything for chorus (I am heartily sick of everything else!); but won't you try and find me some words? One can't have them made to order unless one begins before good reading has spoilt one. They are not heathen enough for me in the Bible. I have bought the Koran but can find nothing there either."[81] In August 1882 Brahms laments to Herzogenberg, "Shall I never shake off the theologian!"[82] Most likely referring to *Gesang der Parzen*, he writes: "I have just finished [a psalm] which is actually heathenish enough to please me and to have made my music better than usual I hope."[83] Kalbeck adds a footnote to his edition of the correspondence at this point to contextualize Brahms's comment: "He had always taken pleasure in hunting up 'godless' texts in the Bible. Nothing made him angrier than to be taken for an orthodox Church composer on account of his sacred compositions."[84] Along the same lines, Beller-McKenna understands the observation made by Clara Schumann that "Brahms was no churchgoer, yet he was of a deeply religious nature" to indicate Brahms's "private versus public relationship to religion."[85]

Whereas it is likely that what I suggest as Hanslick's reading of the *Tragische Ouvertüre* was not indicated by Brahms himself, I propose that Hanslick was open to viewing the work in this manner due to his awareness of both Brahms's position on matters of faith, and the liberal *Weltanschauung* that he shared with him. Hanslick distances dogma from the fundamental message he understands the work to convey and ascribes to this overture a secular view of man's ultimate fate. Given the evidence for Brahms's search for heathen texts and his attitude toward religion, it is likely that this subject may have been discussed with other members of his intimate circle of friends. Notwithstanding the absence of documentary evidence that such a conversation took place (and bearing in mind that absence of evidence is not evidence of absence), Hanslick's discussion of the *Tragische Ouvertüre* presents the listener with alternative ways of understanding the work's spiritual message—one bound to its religious context, the other not. Such a reading is consonant with the spirit of Brahms's musical elegies, and would, moreover, have been readily understood by the secularized public for whom Hanslick wrote.

Hanslick's View of Brahms: A Reconsideration

The *Weltanschauung* that Hanslick distils from Brahms's music is consonant with Schiller's formulation in *Über naïve und sentimentalische Dichtung*, in which he juxtaposes an object of sadness and an object of joy.[86] Hanslick's discussion of these works in this context provides evidence of how a member of Brahms's intimate circle of friends responded to such deeply felt and spiritual works. For that reason they form an integral part of the reception history of Brahms's music. This is all the more important because compared with Brahms's instrumental music, the *Alto Rhapsody, Schicksalslied, Nänie,* and *Gesang der Parzen* have been given scant attention in scholarly writings. Yet they are—as Michael Musgrave attests—among Brahms's most moving and characteristic works.[87]

In the literature concerning Hanslick and Brahms, Hanslick has frequently been accused of seeing a confirmation of his own aesthetic theory in Brahms's works, and of exploiting this confirmation for his own formalist ends.[88] Constantin Floros, for instance, makes two principal claims regarding Hanslick's image of Brahms: the first is that Hanslick saw in Brahms's works "models of the 'pure, absolute music' he tirelessly promoted," asserting that Hanslick recognized in these works "a posterior and unexpected confirmation of the aesthetic theory" he proposed in 1854.[89] The second—an extension of the first—is that Hanslick's "doctrine of Brahms as a prototype of the 'absolute' musician does not do justice to his music. For it simply ignores the considerable share of the poetic and autobiographic in the work of this great composer. In this respect, Hanslick's Brahms interpretations have done great harm and have obstructed the view for a truly differentiated investigation."[90]

Hanslick used the term "pure, absolute music" only once in *Vom Musikalisch-Schönen*, and never in his writings on Brahms. The single instance in the monograph occurs in chapter 2, titled "The Representation of Feeling Is Not the Content of Music." Here Hanslick has "deliberately chosen instrumental music" for his examples. He maintains that "whatever can be asserted of instrumental music holds good for all music."[91] In other words, whether or not a piece of music has a poetic heading, a literary adjunct, or a prescriptive program, the music must remain intelligible in its own right, and not depend on its extramusical adjunct for its comprehensibility: "If some general definition of music be sought, something by which to characterize its essence and nature, to establish its boundaries and purpose, we are entitled to confine ourselves to instrumental music. Of what *instrumental music* cannot do it ought never be said that *music* can do it, because only instrumental music is music purely and absolutely."[92] Burford understands Hanslick to articulate the link he perceives between essence and individuation clearly in this passage. "Both the Romantic and idealist views of art," he argues, "tended to embrace the notion of a *species*-essence—the 'poetic' and 'Spirit' respectively—whereas Hanslick argued for music's individual essence ('musically beautiful,' the 'specifically musical,' etc.)."[93] Hanslick's opposition is not to vocal music, program music, or music with any kind of autobiographical or literary allusion, as Floros falsely asserts. Rather it is to music that seeks to be understood in terms of its extramusical content, and not its musical content—that is its tones, latent within which are the ideal content or spiritual substance (*geistiger Gehalt*), and thereby music's metaphysical status. To this end Hanslick writes, "Where it is a matter of the 'content' [*Inhalt*] of music, we must reject even pieces with specific titles or programs. Union with poetry" he claims, without denouncing such a union, "extends the power of music, but not its boundaries."[94] In other words, we must reject works that have their specific title or program as the content, or spiritual substance, of the piece.[95]

A 1997 essay by Hans Joachim Hinrichsen, "'Auch das Schöne muß sterben' oder Die Vermittlung von biographischer und ästhetischer Subjektivität im Musikalisch-Schönen. Brahms, Hanslick und Schillers *Nänie*"[96] is noteworthy, because Hinrichsen is one of the few commentators who seek to recover Hanslick and his "much abused little book" from the formalist arena to which they have been assigned.[97] However, at the same time he reinforces the view of Hanslick as the formalist champion of Brahms the "absolute" by focusing only on *Vom Musikalisch-Schönen* and not considering Hanslick's critical writings on *Nänie* and a number of other pertinent works.

Hinrichsen attributes the formalist reception of *Vom Musikalisch-Schönen* to a lack of clarity in Hanslick's explication of his concept of "form imbued with meaning" evident in all ten editions, and not to a formalist agenda in the book itself. He considers Hanslick's "famous formulation of 'tönend bewegte Formen' as the only content of music"—the most oft-quoted excerpt from his book, usually cited out of context—to have been "intended as a paradox and received as a tautology." Hinrichsen notes that "form in Hanslick's aesthetics is 'not merely acoustic beauty,' but a carrier and representative medium of the 'spiritual content.'" For Hinrichsen, the difficulty in understanding Hanslick's aesthetic ideals is that whereas Hanslick made it easy for his detractors to reduce his aesthetic theory to a "formalistic exterior," he did not make it easy for his readers to distinguish between "autonomy and objectivity."[98]

Hinrichsen then considers Brahms's compositional process in relation to Hanslick's aesthetic arguments. He makes the case that Brahms's *Tragische Ouvertüre* and *Akademische Festouvertüre* should not be understood as a pair, as the two often are.[99] Rather, he proposes that the *Tragische Ouvertüre* and *Nänie* are a pair because one perceives in both works together the "peculiar ambivalence, above all the radicalism, in Schiller's view of lost beauty," which Hinrichsen identifies as "mourning and tragedy on the one hand, comfort and transfiguration on the other."[100] He considers this to be a "characteristically Brahmsian mode of 'speaking' or 'expressing' in music."[101] Such a reading of opp. 81 and 82 is certainly insightful, taking into consideration not only Brahms's but also Schiller's artistic tendencies.

However, Hinrichsen asserts that Hanslick would not have been amenable to viewing the *Tragische Ouvertüre* and *Nänie* as a pair. These works would actually be separated in principle, he suggests, in the aesthetics of Hanslick due to their *Gattungszugehörigkeit* (the one being considered pure absolute music, the other vocal music).[102] Yet, what is remarkable about Hinrichsen's own reading of these works is how closely aligned it is with Hanslick's view of op. 81 and op. 82 and of Brahms's "musical elegies" considered above. Whereas Hanslick does not go so far as to view these two works as a pair, he identifies strongly with what Hinrichsen deems to be a "Brahmsian mode of 'speaking' or 'thinking' in music."[103] The writings of both authors are comparable in that each distils from Brahms's music the notion of mourning and tragedy on the one hand, comfort and transfiguration on the other.

Noticeable by its absence in Hinrichsen's article is any discussion of Hanslick's critical writings, despite the fact that Hanslick reviewed all of the works to which Hinrichsen refers. In making a case for his own aesthetic reading of Brahms's works, Hinrichsen argues that "the musical poetics and aesthetics of a composer who only expresses himself in a taciturn manner—like Johannes Brahms—are to be deduced predominantly from the compositions themselves."[104] Yet he disregards Hanslick's reviews of these very works. Hanslick is represented once again only by the polemical monograph of his youth, with the critical writings of his maturity being overlooked. This leads Hinrichsen to such claims as, "Only in the instrumental music, as is well known, does Hanslick see music completely fulfilling the term as pure, absolute music; general conclusions about the poetic and compositional concept that are drawn from a piece of vocal music would be, accordingly, of limited stylistic range."[105]

The weakness in Hinrichsen's argument becomes more apparent when he broadens the discussion to include *Schicksalslied*. He suggests that the orchestral postlude in this work can be understood as being contrary to Hanslick's notion of pure instrumental music as espoused in *Vom Musikalisch-Schönen*.[106] As we saw above, however, the spiritual substance of the orchestral postlude in *Schicksalslied*, as Hanslick understands it, is inextricably bound up with—and would not have been conceived were it not for—Hölderlin's poetic text. Hanslick explicitly refers to this postlude as "pure instrumental music."[107] His argument is that Brahms's postlude expresses that which cannot be expressed in words, that which is, arguably, more definite than words, and can in this sense be seen to exemplify what John Daverio refers to as the "leap over the abyss separating the manifest content of a poetic text and its spirit or aesthetic quality."[108]

Brahms's liberalism and humanism are abundantly evident in a number of his works that question the nature of human existence, and are preoccupied with death, fate, suffering, and the human condition. His "musical elegies," being the deeply spiritual works that they are, perhaps reveal this to us more powerfully than any of his other works. Here Brahms provides a source of comfort and glimpses of transient beauty for his fellow human beings. Such music resonates with audiences and performers, regardless of their faiths or beliefs. I argue that Hanslick was acutely aware of this aspect of Brahms's artistic persona and that he sought to convey this in his rich and multifaceted, if at times complex, reviews of Brahms's works. To mistake Hanslick's appreciation of Brahms's "thinking in tones" for a dismissal of anything that lies outside of these tones, and for a disregard for the poetic and autobiographic in the work of this great composer, amounts to a distortion and misrepresentation of Hanslick's writings. Notwithstanding some evidence in the *Brahms Briefwechsel* that points to a liberal and humanist approach to Brahms's works, and given the fact that Brahms is renowned for his reticence in his letters and correspondence, Hanslick's critical writings are key in documenting this aspect of the critical reception of Brahms's œuvre. Elisabet von Herzogenberg, one of Brahms's closest friends, and one whose advice Brahms eagerly and regularly sought on his compositions, was well placed, therefore, to appreciate the value in Hanslick's writings on Brahms, as she did in 1882 in the quotation given as the epigraph for this essay.

Notes

1. Translation taken from Kevin C. Karnes's introduction to Hanslick's writings on Brahms in *Brahms and His World*, ed. Walter Frisch and Kevin C. Karnes (Princeton: Princeton University Press, 2009), 218. "St. John visage" refers to Robert Schumann's comparison of Brahms to John the Baptist in his 1853 paean to Brahms. See Robert Schumann, "Neue Bahnen," *Neue Zeitschrift für Musik* 39 (October 28, 1853): 185–86.

2. As early as 1863 Brahms shared the familiar *du* with Hanslick. See Johannes Brahms, *Johannes Brahms: Life and Letters*, trans. Josef Eisinger and Styra Avins, selected and annotated by Styra Avins (Oxford: Oxford University Press, 1997), 283–84. We know from Hanslick's autobiography that he considered himself, Billroth, and Brahms as the "closest musical threesome" (Den engeren musikalischen Dreibund aber doch wir Drei: Billroth, Brahms und ich.) Hanslick, *AML*, 2:273.

3. Solomon Wank has neatly positioned the political bent of the *Neue Freie Presse* in his formulation that it "spoke for the German-Austrian liberal bourgeoisie, in whose interest it was to maintain Austria as a German-led centralized state in which the German language was, de facto if not de jure, the language of state." Solomon Wank, *In the Twilight of Empire: Count Alois Lexa von Aehrenthal (1854–1912), Imperial Habsburg Patriot and Statesman* (Vienna: Böhlau, 2009), 114.

4. Mark Burford, "Hanslick's Idealist Materialism," *19th-Century Music* 30, no. 2 (2006): 166–81.

5. Ibid., 171.

6. See Carl E. Schorske, *Fin-de-siècle Vienna: Politics and Culture* (New York: Vintage Books, 1981), 5–10; for an in-depth study of the vicissitudes of liberalism and nationalism in Austria during this time, see Pieter Judson, *Exclusive Revolutionaries: Liberal Politics, Social Experience, and National Identity in the Austrian Empire, 1848–1914* (Ann Arbor: University of Michigan Press, 1996), particularly chapters 5, 6, and 7. See also the introduction to William J. McGrath, *Dionysian Art and Populist Politics in Austria* (New Haven, CT: Yale University Press, 1974), particularly 7–13; and Margaret Notley, *Lateness and Brahms: Music and Culture in the Twilight of Viennese Liberalism* (Oxford: Oxford University Press, 2007), particularly 15–21, and 207–16.

7. Judson, *Exclusive Revolutionaries*, 120–21. The legally recognized religions were Catholicism, Calvinism, Greek Orthodox Christianity, Judaism, and Lutheranism.

8. Schorske, *Fin-de-siècle Vienna*, 6.

9. Notley, *Lateness and Brahms*, 16–17.

10. Leon Botstein, "Brahms and His Audience: The Later Viennese Years 1875–1897," in *The Cambridge Companion to Brahms*, ed. Michael Musgrave (Cambridge: Cambridge University Press, 1999), 72.

11. Botstein, "Brahms and His Audience," 74.

12. Tony Davies, *Humanism* (New York: Routledge, 1997), 10.

13. John Addington Symonds, *The Renaissance in Italy: The Fine Arts* (London: Smith Elder, 1898), 52, as cited in Davies, *Humanism*, 22.

14. Schiller (1796) as cited in Patrick H. Vincent, *The Romantic Poetess: European Culture, Politics, and Gender, 1820–1840* (Hanover, NH: University Press of New England, 2004), 32.

15. Svetlana Boym, *The Future of Nostalgia* (New York: Basic Books, 2001), xviii and 13.

16. Davies, *Humanism*, 10.

17. Mark-Daniel Schmid, *The Richard Strauss Companion* (Westport, CT: Greenwood, 2003), 65.

18. Ludwig Curtius as cited in Fritz Stern, *The Politics of Cultural Despair: A Study in the Rise of the Germanic Ideology* (Berkeley: University of California Press, 1989), 12.

19. Botstein, "Brahms and His Audience," 75.

20. Patrick H. Vincent, *The Romantic Poetess*, 32.

21. It is worth noting that these apparently liberal values are also wholly in keeping with Richard Wagner's values. This suggests that the aesthetic divides between Brahms and Wagner do not map neatly onto social ideologies or cultural divisions. For a lucid and engaging revision of the view of Wagner as a kind of antithesis to Viennese liberalism, see Kevin C. Karnes, "Wagner, Klimt, and the Metaphysics of Creativity in *fin-de-siècle* Vienna," *Journal of the American Musicological Society* 62, no. 3 (2009): 647–97. For a reconsideration of such aesthetic divides in late nineteenth-century Vienna, see Leon Botstein, "Music in History: The Perils of Method in Reception History," *Musical Quarterly* 89 (2007): 1–16. Marcia Citron has broached the question of whether "Hanslick's masculine images in Brahms reviews is a polemical response to Wagner's theories." She writes: "On the one hand, absolute music is supposed to entail the highest levels of *Geistigkeit*, or intellectuality, and transcend mundane matters, such as gender. On the other hand, invoking the masculine to describe a type of music reinforces the notion of mind, as per the longstanding mind-body dualism coded as masculine versus feminine. In short, Hanslick's gendered language reinforces the philosophical basis of absolute music at the same time as it threatens to undercut its meaning. Furthermore, by using masculinity for the rationalist side of Brahms's music, Hanslick is putting down the emotional, or feminine, style of Anton Bruckner, who was considered Brahms's antithesis

in Vienna." Marcia Citron, "Gendered Reception of Brahms: Masculinity, Nationalism and Musical Politics," in *Masculinity and Western Musical Practice*, ed. Ian D. Biddle and Kirsten Gibson (Aldershot, UK: Ashgate, 2009), 153.

22. Margaret Notley notes that the Marxist musicologist Georg Knepler also "interprets Brahms as having clung to the *bürgerlich* humanism of the Josephinist era that had also inspired Beethoven even after Joseph II's death in 1790." See Notley, *Lateness and Brahms*, 75. See also Georg Knepler, "Brahms historische und aesthetische Bedeutung [1961]," repr. in *Johannes Brahms oder die Relativierung der "absoluten" Musik*, ed. Hanns-Werner Heister (Hamburg: von Bockel Verlag, 1997), 37–80, particularly 50–55.

23. This subtitle, "Gegenstand der Trauer oder Gegenstand der Freude," as it reads in the original German, is a passage from Schiller's *Über naïve und sentimentalische Dichtung* (1795–96). See Johann Christoph Friedrich von Schiller, *Schillers sämmtliche Werke in zwölf Bänden*, vol. 12 (Stuttgart: J. G. Cotta'scher Verlag, 1838), 212.

24. Angelika Horstmann, *Untersuchungen zur Brahms-Rezeption der Jahre 1860–1880* (Hamburg: Karl Dieter Wagner, 1986), 196.

25. Ibid., 197. John Daverio surveys the contemporary and recent reception of *Schicksalslied* in "The 'Wechsel der Töne' in Brahms's 'Schicksalslied,'" *Journal of the American Musicological Society* 46, no.1 (1993): 84–113.

26. "Die beiden ersten Strophen des Gedichtes preisen die selige Ruhe der olympischen Götter, welche droben im Licht schicksalslos athmen; der Chor singt diese Strophen in einem edel und breit ausklingenden Adagio." Hanslick, "Brahms *Triumphlied* und *Schicksalslied*," in *Concerte, Componisten und Virtuosen*, 53.

27. "Die dritte Strophe des Gedichtes schildert als Gegenbild das beklagenswerte Los der Menschen, denen es gegeben ist, auf seiner Stätte zu ruh'n." Ibid., 53.

28. "Es ist eine überaus schöne poetische Wendung, welche uns die ganze verklärende Macht der Tonkunst offenbart." Ibid., 54.

29. "In dieser Trostlosigkeit schließt der Dichter—nicht so der Componist. Es ist eine überaus schöne poetische Wendung, welche uns die ganze verklärende Macht der Tonkunst offenbart, daß Brahms nach den letzten Worten des Chors zu der feierlich langsamen Bewegung des Anfanges zurückkehrt und in einem längeren Orchesternachspiel das wirre Mühsal des Menschenlebens in seligen Frieden auflöst. In ergreifender, allen verständlicher Weise vollzieht Brahms diesen Gedankengang durch reine Instrumental-Musik, ohne Hinzufügung eines einzigen Wortes. Die Instrumental-Musik tritt also hier ergänzend und vollendend hinzu und spricht aus, was sich in Worte nicht mehr fassen läßt: ein merkwürdiges Gegenstück zu dem umgekehrten Vorgang in Beethovens Neunter Symphonie. Brahms Schicksalslied gemahnte uns in Styl und Stimmung wie ein Nachklang seines bewunderungswürdigen Deutschen Requiems, dieselbe christliche Anschauung, nur in griechischer Form." Ibid., 54.

30. Michael Musgrave, *Brahms: A German Requiem* (Cambridge: Cambridge University Press, 1996), 21.

31. "Ja, unserem Herzen steht letzteres noch näher, schon deshalb, weil es jedes confessionelle Kleid, jede kirchliche Convenienz abstreift, statt des lateinischen Ritualtextes deutsche Bibelworte wählt." Hanslick, "Brahms: 'Deutsches Requiem' und 'Rhapsodie,'" in *Concerte, Componisten und Virtuosen*, 135. This review of the Requiem was originally published as Ed. H., "Concerte," *Neue Freie Presse* (March 4, 1875): 1–3.

32. Daniel Beller-McKenna, "How *deutsch* a Requiem? Absolute Music, Universality, and the Reception of Brahms's *Ein deutsches Requiem*, op. 45," *19th-Century Music* 22, no. 1 (1998): 16.

33. "Wer hingegen ein theures Wesen betrauert, der vermesse sich nicht, bei den überwältigend rührenden Klängen der Sopran-Arie trockenen Auges zu bleiben. Aber er wird erfahren, wie verklärend und stärkend der reinste Trost aus dieser Musik fließt." Hanslick, *Concerte, Componisten und Virtuosen,* 136.

34. Musgrave, *Brahms: A German Requiem,* 22.

35. Hanslick, *Concerte, Componisten und Virtuosen,* 54.

36. "Der mittelere Theil von Goethes 'Harzreise im Winter' (das von Brahms componirte Fragment) beschäftigt sich mit dem Bilde des einsamen, menschenscheuen Jünglings und hat diesem zur Unsterblichkeit verholfen." Hanslick, "Brahms, 'Deutsches Requiem,' op. 45 und 'Rhapsodie,'" in *Concerte, Componisten und Virtuosen,* 138. This review of the *Alto Rhapsody* was originally published as Ed. H., "Theater und Musik," *Neue Freie Presse* (January 12, 1875): 1–3. In his review of the *Alto Rhapsody,* Hanslick makes no reference to this being Brahms's so-called *Brautgesang,* or to the fact that it was largely understood by his contemporaries as a 'confessional' on Brahms's part with regard to his disappointment and loneliness in his unrequited love for Julie Schumann. The seeds for this view of the work seem to have been planted by Brahms himself. For a detailed discussion see Aubrey S. Garlington Jr., *"Harzreise als Herzreise:* Brahms's Alto Rhapsody," *Musical Quarterly* 69, no. 4 (Autumn 1983): 527–42, especially 530–33. See also John Daverio, *"Wechsel der Töne,"* 111. For an alternative reading of the Rhapsody see James Webster, "The *Alto Rhapsody:* Psychology, Intertextuality, and Brahms's Artistic Development," in *Brahms Studies* 3, ed. David Brodbeck (Lincoln: University of Nebraska Press, 2001), 19–46.

37. "Der eigenthümlich ethische Charakter, welcher der Brahmsschen Musik im großen und ganzen aufgeprägt ist und sie in so nahe Verwandtschaft mit Beethoven bringt, tritt in der 'Rhapsodie' mit fast tendenziöser Stärke auf und läßt sie als ein Seitenstück zu seinem 'Schicksalslied' erscheinen." Hanslick, *Concerte, Componisten und Virtuosen,* 136.

38. See Citron, "Gendered Reception of Brahms," 147.

39. With regard to Beethoven, such quotations can be found in his *Tagebuch* of 1812–18. See Barry Cooper, "Beethoven's Beliefs and Opinions," in *The Beethoven Compendium: A Guide to Beethoven's Life and Music,* ed. Barry Cooper (London: Thames & Hudson, 1991), 142. With regard to Brahms, such quotations and writings were kept in his *Deutsche Sprichworte,* found in the composer's apartment after his death. For an introduction to, and translation of, these German Proverbs, see George Bozarth, "Johannes Brahms's Collection of *Deutsche Sprichworte* (German Proverbs)," in *Brahms Studies,* vol. 1, ed. David Brodbeck (Lincoln: University of Nebraska Press, 1994), 1–29. In his baptismal 1833 Lutheran Bible, Brahms underlined passages and recorded his comments in the margins. See Hanns Christian Stekel, *Sehnsucht und Distanz: Theologische Aspekte in den wortgebundenen religiösen Kompositionen von Johannes Brahms* (Frankfurt: Peter Lang, 1997), 65–69. He also had a handwritten pocket notebook of biblical passages, and an 1899 eleventh edition of Gottfried Büchner's popular Bible concordance, with copious marginal annotations and marks. See Daniel Beller-McKenna, *Brahms and the German Spirit* (Cambridge, MA: Harvard University Press, 2004), 35–36.

40. "Wir erinnern daran, daß Beethoven zu den Satzungen des Katholicismus kein inneres Verhältniß gewonnen hatte, daß sein Glaube vielmehr den Charakter eines freien, nur dem Gebet der Sittlichkeit gehorchenden Theismus trug." Hanslick, "Beethoven's große Festmesse," *Sämtliche Schriften* 1/5, 343. This translation amended from *Vienna's Golden Years of Music: 1850–1900,* trans. and ed. Henry Pleasants (New York: Simon and Schuster, 1950), 72.

41. Cooper, "Beethoven's Beliefs and Opinions," 145.//
42. David B. Levy, *Beethoven: The Ninth Symphony* (New Haven, CT: Yale University Press, 2003). 8. Here I refer to the nonspecific religiosity of Schiller's poem and Beethoven's music. As Arnold Whittall reminds us, in addressing only the "Brüder" of the world, it both expresses and casts doubt upon the ideals of universal brotherhood and joy." See Arnold Whittall, "Against the Operatic Grain: *Fidelio* in History and Theory," in *Beethoven Forum* 8, ed. Lewis Lockwood, Christopher Reynolds, and Elaine Sisman (Lincoln: University of Nebraska Press, 2000), 198. Fred Everett Maus discusses Hanslick's account of an ethical character in Beethoven's works in the 1861 review of the *Missa Solemnis*. See Fred Everett Maus, "Hanslick's Composers," in the current volume.

43. Burford, "Hanslick's Idealist Materialism," 177.

44. "Doch war es weniger diese Musikliebe, als vielmehr die Ähnlichkeit in der ganzen Kunstanschauung, was Feuerbach mit Brahms in Freundschaft und Seelenverwandschaft verband." Hanslick, "Nänie," in *Concerte, Componisten und Virtuosen*, 346. The review of *Nänie* was originally published as Ed. H., "Musik," *Neue Freie Presse* (January 12, 1882): 1–3.

45. "dieselbe unerschütterliche Richtung auf das Große, Erhabene und Ideale, die oft bis zur herben Strenge und Abgeschlossenheit führte." Hanslick, *Concerte, Componisten und Virtuosen*, 346.

46. "Es ist kein Bild nach der Mode; es ist streng und schmucklos. Ich erwarte kein Verständniß dafür, aber ich kann nicht anders. Und wer sich die Mühe nimmt, es lange aufzusehen, den wird etwas daraus anwehen, als ob das Bild kein Bild aus unserer Zeit sei." Ibid.

47. These artistic ideals shared by Brahms and Feuerbach would have been understood by Hanslick's readership as contrasting with those of Wagner and Makart. Hans Makart (1840–84), one of Wagner's favorite painters, was Feuerbach's nemesis in Vienna, with the roots of this rivalry, as Leon Botstein notes, being in the "social and political divisions that developed in the 1870s." As Botstein further observes, "Feuerbach's contempt for Makart paralleled Brahms's differences with Wagner." See Leon Botstein, "Brahms and Nineteenth-Century Painting," *19th-Century Music* 14, no. 2 (1990): 154–68 (158 and 162). Hanslick played on this comparison; for instance in his review of Brahms's *Tragische Ouvertüre* he describes the Vorspiel from *Tristan und Isolde* as "this virtuoso orchestral work, which is painted with Makart colors." Hanslick, "Brahms 'Tragische Ouvertüre,'" in *Concerte, Componisten und Virtuosen*, 280–81.

48. "Es ist ein sinniger Zug, daß Brahms das letzte Wort nicht dem 'Gemeinen, das klanglos zum Orcus hinabgeht,' beläßt, sondern mit dem vorletzen Verse schließt 'Ein Klagelied zu sein im Mund der Geliebten ist herrlich—herrlich!'" *Concerte, Componisten und Virtuosen*, 347. The translation of the excerpts from *Nänie* is taken from the sleeve notes to *Johannes Brahms, Werke für Chor und Orchester*, Deutsche Grammophon 449 6651 2.

49. "Die Musik nimmt hier den Anfangs- und Hauptsatz in D-dur (Sechsviertel-Tact) wieder auf, das Ganze zu harmonischen Ring abrundend." Hanslick, *Concerte, Componisten und Virtuosen*, 347.

50. Hanslick, "Gesang der Parzen," in *Concerte, Componisten und Virtuosen*, 374.

51. Johannes Brahms as cited in Gustav Ophüls, *Erinnerungen an Johannes Brahms* (Berlin: Verlag der Deutschen Brahms Gesellschaft, 1921), 280. This translation is taken from Eftychia Papanikolaou, "Brahms, Böcklin, and the *Gesang der Parzen*," *Music in Art: International Journal for Music Iconography* 30, no. 1–2 (2005): 162.

52. Hanslick, *Concerte, Componisten und Virtuosen*, 372–74.

53. "Dieser versöhnende, fast verklärte Abschluß ist aus dem Gedichte selbst nicht recht erklärlich; mit Notwendigkeit ergibt er sich jedenfalls nicht daraus; denn daß die

Götter ihr segnendes Auge noch von dem schuldlosen Enkel des unglücklichen, ernst geliebten Ahnherrn abwenden, bedeutet kein Erweichen, sondern ein erbarmungsloses Fortleben ihres grausamen Sinnes." Hanslick, *Concerte, Componisten und Virtuosen*, 373.

54. Ibid., 51–54.

55. "Brahms tiefsinnige Deutungen." Ibid., 373.

56. "Wie Rubens oder Rembrandt oft eine hellere Farbe braucht und, ohne Nöthigung vom Sujet aus, anwendet für einzelne Partien eines dunkel gehaltenen Gemäldes, so, denken wir uns, hat Brahms, der Musiker, ein versöhnteres Ausklingen seines Chors für unentbehrlich erachtet und dasselbe so rührendschön gestaltet, daß auch wir es fortan nicht entbehren könnten. Brahms' 'Gesang der Parzen' ist hochbedeutend in seiner vollkommenen Vereinigung von antiker Strenge und Einfachheit mit dem lebendigsten ergreifendsten Ausdrucke der Empfindungen." Ibid.

57. "Es bricht der Zwist aus, dumpfe Klagetöne und ein durchdringender Schrei wie aus der Tiefe verkünden den Sturz in den Tartarus, als glänzender Gegensatz, von Wohllaut erfüllt, erhebt sich dagegen die Strophe: 'Sie aber, sie bleiben in ewigen Festen.'" Ibid.

58. "Brahms Gesang der Parzen ist hochbedeutend in seiner vollkommenen Vereinigung von antiker Strenge und Einfachheit mit dem lebendigsten ergreifendsten Ausdrucke der Empfindungen." Ibid.

59. Max Kalbeck, *Johannes Brahms*, 4 vols. (Vienna: Wiener Verlag, 1904), 3:258–60.

60. The piece "is certainly not written at the dictation of any one tragedy," Tovey writes. Rather, he considers any tragic characters of which we may be reminded in the work to be "our own illustrations of its meaning." It is on this basis that Tovey makes a legitimate comparison between "Brahms's energetic but severely formal conclusion with Shakespeare's Fortinbras, not as a course of events, but as an aesthetic fact." Donald Francis Tovey, *Essays in Musical Analysis: Symphonies and Other Orchestral Works* (London: Oxford University Press, 1981), 152.

61. "Sie stellt selbstständige musikalische Gedanken, Themen hin, aus welchen mit der den Componisten charakterisirend strengen Logik das Ganze sich organisch entwickelt." Hanslick, "Brahms: 'Tragische Ouvertüre,'" in *Concerte, Componisten und Virtuosen*, 280.

62. "Brahms hat für seine *Tragische Ouvertüre* kein bestimmtes Trauerspiel als 'Sujet' im Sinne gehabt, sondern einen '*Actus Tragicus*' (wie eine Seb. Bachsche Aufschrift lautet) überhaupt." Ibid., 280. Hanslick is referring to Bach, "Gottes Zeit ist die allerbeste Zeit," BWV 106.

63. "Wenn wir uns durchaus für eine Tragödie entscheiden müßten, welche mit Brahms' Ouvertüre einzuleiten wäre, so würden wir wohl 'Hamlet' nennen." Hanslick, *Concerte, Componisten und Virtuosen*, 281. Hanslick is not the only critic who mentions *Hamlet* in relation to opus 81. Kalbeck critiques Hanslick's discussion of *Hamlet* as a program, finding it not entirely suitable. See Kalbeck, *Johannes Brahms* 3:259. Kalbeck may have missed the point here: Hanslick is not suggesting Brahms had *Hamlet* in mind as a program. Rather he is suggesting a poetic counterpart to the piece in conjunction with Cantata BWV 106.

64. Dillon Parmer, "Brahms the Programmatic: A Critical Assessment" (PhD diss., Eastman School of Music, University of Rochester, 1995), 54.

65. Walter Benjamin, quoted in Eric Chafe, "The 'Symbolism' of Tonal Language in the Bach Canons," *Journal of Musicology* 3, no. 4 (1984): 345.

66. John Deathridge, "Post-mortem on Isolde," *New German Critique* 69 (Autumn 1996): 120. The *Vorspiel* and *Liebestod* from Wagner's *Tristan and Isolde* were in fact programmed

at this same concert. Hanslick pits these works against Brahms's in the following manner, before going on to deal with Brahms's overture in more detail: "The fourth Philharmonic concert opened with 'Vorspiel und Isoldes Liebestod' from Wagner's *Tristan und Isolde*. Many a youthful, passionate nature goes into raptures from the sounds of the somewhat meaningless words 'Liebestod' alone. One can argue how completely effective the music of Wagner's 'Liebestod' is, a music in which each bar is 'outside itself.' Moreover this virtuoso orchestral work, which is painted with Makart colors, was splendidly performed by the Philharmonic Orchestra. Johannes Brahms's *Tragische Ouvertüre*, performed for the first time, formed an interesting contrast to Wagner's pathological mood music." (Das vierte Philharmonische Concert brachte als Einleitungsstück: "Vorspiel und Isoldes Liebestod" aus Wagners "Tristan und Isolde." Es giebt viele jugendlich schwärmerische Naturen, die schon von dem Klange halb sinnloser Wörter, wie "Liebestod," in Entzücken gerathen; man kann sich vorstellen, wie vollends eine Wagnersche Liebestod Musik, in welcher jeder Tact "außer sich" ist, auf sie einwirkt. Dieses mit Makartschen Farben virtuos gemalte Orchesterbild wurde überdies von den Philharmonikern vortrefflich ausgeführt.) Hanslick, *Concerte, Componisten und Virtuosen*, 280.

67. Daniel Beller-McKenna, "Brahms, the Bible, and Post-Romanticism: Cultural Issues in Johannes Brahms's Later Settings of Biblical Texts, 1877–1896" (PhD diss., Harvard University, 1994).

68. A similar approach is taken by Brahms in his motet "Warum ist das Licht gegeben dem Mühseligen?," op. 74, no. 1. For a discussion of the relationship between Bach BWV 106 and Brahms op. 74, no. 1, see Daniel Beller-McKenna, "The Great *Warum?* Job, Christ, and Bach in a Brahms Motet," *19th-Century Music* 19, no. 3 (1996): 231–51. If Hanslick was aware of the relationship between these two works, he did not mention it in his review of the opus 74 motets in *Concerte, Componisten und Virtuosen*, 222–23.

69. For Chafe's more recent discussion of BWV 106, see Eric Chafe, *Analyzing Bach Cantatas* (New York: Oxford University Press, 2000), 149–60.

70. Chafe, "The Symbolism of Tonal Language," 345.

71. Chafe, *Analyzing Bach Cantatas*, 149–60.

72. Ibid.

73. Beller-McKenna, "Brahms, the Bible, and Post-Romanticism," 53.

74. Ibid., 53.

75. William Shakespeare, *Hamlet, Prince of Denmark*, ed. Philip Edwards (Cambridge: Cambridge University Press, 2003), 246.

76. "Die Ouvertüre fließt in einem ununterbrochenen Zuge, ohne Tact und Tempowechsel dahin, durchwegs erfüllt von einem pathetischen Ernste, der mitunter aus Herbe streift, aber niemals das Tragische ins Gräßliche verzerrt." Hanslick, *Concerte, Componisten und Virtuosen*, 281.

77. James Webster, "Brahms's *Tragic Overture:* The Form of the Tragedy," in *Brahms: Biographical, Documentary and Analytical Studies*, ed. Robert Pascall (Cambridge: Cambridge University Press, 1983), 115.

78. Hanslick, *Concerte, Componisten und Virtuosen*, 280.

79. Notley, *Lateness and Brahms*, 214.

80. "Wesen und Grundlage der Religion sei nur die Moral; bei gleichen moralischen Grundsätzen seien alle Bekentnisse gleichwertig. Die biblischen Geschichten lernten wir nur von ihrer liebenswürdigen, gemütvollen und poetischen Seite kennen; die 'Wunder' nur als Gleichnisse." Hanslick, *AML*, 1:6–7. This translation is from Notley, *Lateness and Brahms*, 209.

81. "Motetten oder überhaupt Chormusik schriebe ich ganz gern (sonst schon überhaupt gar nichts mehr), aber versuchen Sie, ob Sie mir Texte schaffen können. Sie sich fabrizieren lassen, daran muß man sich in jungen Jahren gewöhnen, später ist man durch gute Lektüre zu sehr verwöhnt. In der Bibel ist es mir nicht heidnisch genug, jetzt habe ich mir den Koran gekauft, finde aber auch nichts." Johannes Brahms to Elisabet von Herzogenberg, July 14, 1880, in *Briefwechsel mit Heinrich und Elisabet von Herzogenberg*, 1:123. English translation in *The Herzogenberg Correspondence*, 106.

82. "Den Theologen aber kann ich nicht los werden!" Brahms to Elisabet von Herzogenberg, August 8, 1882. Ibid., 1:199, trans., 174.

83. "Ich habe grade einen geschrieben, der mir, was das Heidentum betrifft, durchaus genügt, und ich denke, das wird auch meine Musik etwas besser als gewöhnlich gemacht haben." Ibid., 1:200, trans., 174.

84. "Es war für Brahms von jeher ein Vergnügen, die Bibel nach 'heidnischen,' 'gottlosen' Stellen zu durchforschen. Nichts Ärgeres konnte ihm, als um seiner geistlichen Musik willen für einen gläubigen Kirchenkomponisten angesprochen zu werden." Kalbeck in *Briefwechsel mit Heinrich und Elisabet von Herzogenberg*, note 1, 1:200. This translation from *The Herzogenberg Correspondence*, 174.

85. Beller-McKenna, *Brahms and the German Spirit*, 31.

86. See note 24.

87. Musgrave, *The Music of Brahms* (Oxford: Clarendon Press, 1985), 168.

88. Beller-McKenna discusses Hanslick's review of the *German Requiem* in such terms, as we saw above. See Beller-McKenna, "How *deutsch* a Requiem?," 16. Another instance is that of Susan McClary's discussion of Brahms, Symphony No. 3. For further discussion of McClary's essay in relation to Hanslick, see the introduction to this volume. Susan McClary, "Narrative Agendas in 'Absolute' Music: Identity and Difference in Brahms's Third Symphony," in *Musicology and Difference: Gender and Sexuality in Music Scholarship*, ed. Ruth Solie (Berkeley: University of California Press, 1993), 326–44.

89. Constantin Floros, *Johannes Brahms: "Free but Alone,"* trans. Ernest Bernhardt-Kabisch (Frankfurt/M: Peter Lang, 2010), 195 and 201 respectively. This is a translation of the essay "Das Brahms-Bild Eduard Hanslicks," first published in *Brahms-Kongress Wien*, ed. Susanne Antonicek and Otto Biba (Tutzing: Hans Schneider, 1988), 155–66, and then in Floros, *Johannes Brahms "Frei aber einsam": Ein Leben für poetische Musik* (Zürich: Arche, 1997), 225–38. I find the claims made in this essay regarding Hanslick and Brahms to be contradictory and diffuse, and highly problematic.

90. Floros, *Johannes Brahms: "Free but Alone,"* 202.

91. Eduard Hanslick, *Vom Musikalisch-Schönen: Ein Beitrag zur Revision der Ästhetik der Tonkunst*, vol. 1, ed. Dietmar Strauß (Mainz: Schott, 1990), 52 (hereafter *VMS*); Translated in Hanslick, *On the Musically Beautiful*, trans. Geoffrey Payzant (Indianapolis: Hackett, 1986), 14 (hereafter *OMB*).

92. *VMS*, 52; *OMB*, 14–15 (Hanslick's italics).

93. Burford, "Hanslick's Idealist Materialism," 175.

94. *VMS*, 58; *OMB*, 15.

95. It is for precisely this reason that Hanslick found Liszt's works so problematic. See Nicole Grimes, "A Critical Inferno: Hoplit, Hanslick, and Liszt's *Dante* Symphony," *Journal of the Society for Musicology in Ireland* 7 (2011–12): 3–22.

96. Hans-Joachim Hinrichsen, "'Auch das Schöne muß sterben' oder Die Vermittlung von biographischer und ästhetischer Subjektivität im Musikalisch-Schönen. Brahms, Hanslick und Schillers *Nänie*," in *Johannes Brahms oder Die Relativierung der "absoluten" Musik*, ed. Hanns-Werner Heister (Hamburg: Von Bockel, 1997), 121–54.

97. Hanslick, *Aus meinem Leben*, ed. and with an afterword by Peter Wapnewski (Kassel: Bärenreiter, 1987), 150.

98. "Hanslicks berühmte Formulierung von den tönend bewegten Formen als einzigem Inhalt der Musik war als Paradox gemeint und wurde als Tautologie rezipiert. 'Form' ist in Hanslicks Ästhetik nicht etwa 'bloß akustische Schönheit,' sondern Trägerin und Darstellungsmedium des 'geistigen Gehalts.' Daß dieser Formbegriff, als Autonomie und Objektivität verbürgender gedacht, in Hanslicks Schrift koextensiv mit der 'Schönheit' erscheint, bezeichnet zwar die klassische Beschränkung seiner Ästhetik." Hinrichsen, "Auch das Schöne muß sterben!," 152–53.

99. The composer himself spoke of them in such terms, claiming that "one cries, the other laughs." Brahms cited in John Daverio, "Brahms's *Academic Festival Overture* and the Comic Modes," *American Brahms Society Newsletter* 12, no. 1 (1994): 3. Max Kalbeck refers to the *Academic Festival Overture*, and "its tragic twin sister" (Ihrer tragischen Zwillingsschwester) in *Johannes Brahms im Briefwechsel mit Elisabet und Heinrich von Herzogenberg*, 133, note 3. Daverio notes that the anonymous reviewer for the *Allgemeine musikalische Zeitung* (after a performance in Leipzig on January 13, 1881) and the author of a short piece for the *Musical Times* (May 1, 1881) "agreed that the *Academic Festival Overture* was a more accessible but less important work than its 'tragic' counterpart." Daverio, "Brahms's *Academic Festival Overture*," 1.

100. "Trauer und Tragik auf der einen Seite, Trost und Transfiguration auf der anderen—möglich also, daß sich nicht so sehr, wie scheinbar nahegeliegend, die beiden Ouvertüren Op. 80 und 81, sondern vielmehr Op. 81 und 82 durch unterschiedliche Behandlung desselben Gegenstands zum Werkpaar ergänzen, zwei Werke mithin, die in der Ästhetik Eduard Hanslicks durch ihre Gattungszugehörigkeit eigentlich prinzipiell voneinander zu scheiden wären. Die eigentümliche Ambivalenz, vor allem aber die Radikalität in Schillers Blick auf die verlorene Schönheit hat man jedenfalls nur in beiden Werken zusammen." Hinrichsen, "Auch das Schöne muß sterben!," 152.

101. "ein charakteristisch Brahmsscher Modus des 'Sprechens' oder 'Meinens' von Musik." Ibid., 152. This is reminiscent of Brahms's claim in a letter to Clara Schumann in September 1868: "In meinen Tönen spreche ich." *Clara Schumann—Johannes Brahms Briefe aus den Jahren 1853–1896*, ed. Berthold Litzmann, 2 vols. (Leipzig: Breitkopf & Härtel, 1927), 1:595. Hinrichsen, therefore, considers both works to be concerned with the death of Feuerbach: "Aus alledem ist natürlich nicht zwingend abzuleiten, daß die Komposition der *Tragischen Ouvertüre* überhaupt mit Feuerbachs Tod zu tun zu haben könnte." Hinrichsen, "Auch das Schöne muß sterben!," 152.

102. Ibid.

103. Ibid.

104. "Die musikalische Poetik und Ästhetik eines Komponisten, der sich—wie Johannes Brahms—über sie nur äußerst wortkarg geäußert hat, ist vorwiegend aus den Kompositionen selbst zu erschließen." Ibid., 121.

105. "Nur in der Instrumentalmusik sieht Hanslick bekanntlich die Musik ihren Begriff als reine, absolute Tonkunst ganz erfüllen; generelle Schlüsse auf das poetische und kompositorische Konzept, die aus einem Stück Vokalmusik gezogen würden, wären hiernach nur von begrenzter systematischer Reichweite." Ibid.

106. Ibid., 131.

107. "Reine Instrumental-Musik." Hanslick, *Concerte, Componisten und Virtuosen*, 54.

108. The phrase is borrowed from Daverio, "The *Wechsel der Töne*, 91.

Part Three

Memoirs and Meaning in Social Contexts

Chapter Nine

The Critic as Subject

Hanslick's Aus meinem Leben *as a Reflection on Culture and Identity*

Lauren Freede

As a genre, musical autobiographies fit comfortably in neither musicological nor literary studies. The vagaries of personal recollection make autobiographical writing problematic as a source of historical information, while the failure of many musical writers to realize that the genre is inherently subjective and highly artificial leads to the condemnation of many musical autobiographies for a lack of literary merit. To play on Goethe, whose own autobiography from 1823 served as a spiritual example for many later artists to follow: musical autobiographies reflect little *Dichtung*, and even less *Wahrheit*.[1]

This is, admittedly, less of an issue when considering autobiographies by critics like Eduard Hanslick, given that their instrument of choice was generally the pen, and they thus display greater awareness of literary techniques. However, the role of the critic raises additional problems. As the achievements—and reminiscences—of creative artists (in this case composers, followed at some distance by performers) are generally favored in the longer term over those of their reporters and assessors, memoirs by critics tend to be mined for accounts of more famous, more "worthy" associates. That autobiographies can rarely be a collection of verifiable facts diminishes the value of texts like *Aus meinem Leben* even further. Hans Lenneberg neatly encapsulates this view: "The memoirs of critics are not nearly as compelling as those of creative artists unless, like Hanslick, they themselves become controversial historical personages and especially when their memoirs include descriptions of many famous contemporaries."[2]

It is certainly true that in *Aus meinem Leben*, Hanslick discusses his encounters with an enormous number of literary and cultural figures, a wide acquaintanceship made possible by both his own travels and the importance of Vienna as a musical centre. Many of his stories prove very entertaining, particularly those from the periphery of the German musical scene. One unlikely example involves a dinner with Jenny Lind in London. After a less-than-promising start to the evening, Hanslick retreated to the garden with Lind's husband and found himself watching the Lind children play cricket with the as-yet-unknown Arthur Sullivan.[3]

Yet Lenneberg's view assumes that these "famous contemporaries" are described accurately, and by extension, that the role of an autobiography is to offer an uncomplicated contribution to the historical record. The former is by no means a given in Hanslick's case. In *Aus meinem Leben*, Hanslick recounts the 1846 visit of Hector Berlioz to Prague in great detail, complete with the piquant anecdote that Berlioz tried to pass his mistress off as his wife, pretending that the (very much alive) Harriet Smithson had died.[4] Hanslick describes the major influence Berlioz had on his Prague circle, explaining that "during his stay in Prague, Berlioz was our only thought, our only occupation,"[5] even if his enthusiasm for the French composer's work would later cool. Yet in *The Memoirs of Hector Berlioz*, Hanslick is not even mentioned—the role of Prague guide and companion is given to the critic A. W. Ambros. Geoffrey Payzant's attempt in *Hanslick and Ritter Berlioz in Prague* to untangle what actually took place reveals a fascinating set of relationships, but also exposes the limits of autobiography as a historical source.[6] Is Hanslick exaggerating his own importance to Berlioz? Has Berlioz simply forgotten that the critic was there? Or is the problem with the very nature of the autobiographical genre?

It is certainly possible to read *Aus meinem Leben* as an entertaining collection of anecdotes, if not as verifiable history. The text reads very much like an extended journey through Hanslick's address book, with the great, good, and indifferent of the era all making an appearance. Appendix 9.1 lists only the figures significant enough to merit a mention in a right-hand page header in the 1894 first edition, while Peter Wapnewski's wish to include a commentary on the various dramatis personae in the 1987 edition had to be abandoned owing to the sheer overabundance of names.[7]

This lengthy series of encounters undoubtedly makes for enjoyable and undemanding reading. If not held to absolute standards of veracity, Hanslick's tales of the underwhelming landscape around operatic diva Adelina Patti's Welsh castle and the pianist and composer Henri Herz's habit of providing autographed photos of his much younger self can be enjoyed as entertainment.[8] However, this view simply reinforces Lenneberg's conviction that Hanslick's autobiography has little value for historians.

This essay reassesses the value of Hanslick's *Aus meinem Leben* by reevaluating Hanslick's memoirs within the context of other contemporary musical autobiographies and literary representations of music. It examines Hanslick's influence on the genre and explores the continuities between Hanslick's text and romantic literature concerning music. It also situates the memoir within wider discussions of historical memory. By viewing *Aus meinem Leben* not only as part of a musicological discourse, but also as a document of the social, political, and religious fabric of *fin-de-siècle* Vienna, it weaves together a number of threads, including the extent to which musical autobiographies contributed to a unified concept of national identity in the Austro-German sphere at the turn of the twentieth century; Hanslick's own identity within this concept; and his attitude toward, and documenting of, the attendant issues with this form of national identity, which included the advent of modernism, anti-Semitism, and pan-Germanism.

Truth, History, and Identity in Autobiography

Though often mined as source material, the principal importance of *Aus meinem Leben* is not its mixed contribution to the historical record. Indeed, the capacity of autobiographies to record historical fact is limited. As Hans Glagau argued in 1903, it is not only a question of "whether an autobiographer *wants* to tell the truth, but if he is even *capable* of doing so."[9] Glagau sees this as a fault, but the "untruth" of life writing can also be a virtue; in reconstructing their lived experience for the page, authors mirror the process through which society and identity are constructed and shaped. The manner of elision and evasion contributes as much to an understanding of the writer's world as do the stories actually recounted, as will be discussed later.

This constructed aspect is central to the autobiographical genre. However, Hanslick's autobiography often fails to be read as such. Given his reputation as the "Bismarck of musical criticism,"[10] his memoir is seen as—or assumed to be—an extended canvas for the same views that he expressed in his critical writing, where judgements are defended and the decision to make or destroy a reputation reinforced. In fact, Hanslick made a point of separating his personal and critical opinions, expressing far more of the former than the latter in *Aus meinem Leben*, even if he acknowledges with resignation that most of his "victims" are unable to make that distinction.[11] In defense of an unfortunate aspect of his profession—that he must condemn friends and praise foes—he poses the rhetorical question: "Who in a long critical career has not had to censure compositions by friendly, likeable people, and conversely, had to admire works by men, whom one has never enjoyed dealing with!"[12] The failure of his "victims" to recognize this unpalatable fact was consistent—so much so, that Hanslick specifically mentions the exceptions, those rare artists who were able to forgive received criticism: Baron Perfall, the artistic director of the Bavarian State Opera and the Italian librettist and composer Arrigo Boito.[13]

Hanslick also emphasizes the reverse of this equation: that a negative critical judgement neither negates his own memory of enjoyable times past, nor makes it impossible to recognize and appreciate personal charm. Meeting Franz Liszt again in 1878 after some years without contact, Hanslick "again experienced ... unchanged the fascinating force of his personality," and was happy to recall a dinner in 1858 when he had successfully kept up with the pianist as the two played a four-hand Schubert duet![14]

Even in the case of Hanslick's most notorious critical verdict, his dismissal of Richard Wagner's mature work, he is eager to emphasize that this was a purely professional decision. Hanslick admits to finding Wagner an extremely uncongenial character, yet argues that this had little impact on his assessment of Wagner's music.[15] He is able to make this argument, which might ring false to many, given the very public nature of the controversy, precisely because it is in his autobiography rather than his critical work. He constructs a scenario in which his more substantive criticisms of Wagner are surrounded by vignettes showing that the relationship was not always antagonistic. His first meeting with Wagner was an entirely private one; the young student meeting the great composer on holiday. After a pleasant introduction at dinner, Hanslick—who knew of the composer even if most of the other guests at the Marienbad spa did not—"did not hesitate to visit Wagner, whose friendly, forthcoming nature made a favorable impression on me. Back then he was not yet God, not even revered."[16] A later encounter in Leipzig was equally genial.[17] Moreover, Hanslick specifically mentions his affection for *Tannhäuser*, an opera that "had a considerable, at times intoxicating effect on me."[18]

This frame seems intended to prove to the reader that Hanslick offered his verdict on Wagner's music in good faith and that there was no inherent animosity in their relationship. After establishing such initial good will, Hanslick has an automatic defense against accusations of irrational bias, and is able to reassess his earlier judgements without appearing vindictive or unreasonable. His tactic is to separate Wagner the musician from Wagner the man. Hanslick thus comments that his increasing knowledge of Wagner's actions and personality led to an increasing lack of respect, but he balances this by emphasizing repeatedly that he has "nothing against Wagner,"[19] and that his personal distaste is entirely separate from any negative verdicts delivered in his role as critic. This equivocation continues. Even though Hanslick feels that Wagner "was Egoism personified, operating tirelessly for himself, unsympathetic and inconsiderate towards others,"[20] he claims that the impression Wagner's operas made on him was independent of the impression made by the man. He does admit that his critical language may have been intemperate at times, but this would never have happened if "the excessive, bordering on the comic, exaggerations of our opponents had not made our hearts beat faster."[21]

Peter Gay considers all this a "dignified defense against Wagnerian malice."[22] Certainly Hanslick's supporters have used his autobiography as a way of defending him against those who doubt his lasting importance. William M. Johnston, for example, had observed: "From 1860 to about 1900 the most feared personage in the musical life of Vienna was Eduard Hanslick (1825–1904). Today he is remembered above all for having belittled Wagner, Bruckner, and

Hugo Wolf."[23] Stuart Deas uses Hanslick's own frame when arguing for his continued worth in the "Wagner" chapter of *In Defense of Hanslick*.[24] Similarly, Eric Sams presents Hanslick as "the perfect anti-Wagnerite," trying to work out how the supporter of *Tannhäuser* could become such a virulent opponent.[25] Both use Hanslick's explanations from *Aus meinem Leben* as a way to show that the criticism of Wagner was both fair and justified, but using an autobiography as a source for such material raises two major problems. First, in defending Hanslick the critic by using other sources to nuance his critiques, it actually reinforces the views of those who think his reviews and encounters are all that made him (temporarily) memorable. This has the effect of once again situating Hanslick in opposition to famous composers and making the Wagnerian conflict the central aspect of his career, instead of considering his own achievements. Second, it assumes that arguments made in a memoir are completely fair and rational, which is a misreading of the genre. This is not to suggest that Hanslick's arguments are unreasonable—Gay observes that he gives cogent reasons for "his detestation of Wagner's character and dislike of Wagner's music"[26]—but rather that they are about defining his own identity, and Wagner is ultimately tangential to that process. Wagner does occupy more pages than other composers maligned in the autobiography, but this is unsurprising, given the very public nature of the controversy, and he is by no means the focus of *Aus meinem Leben*.

Autobiography and National Identity: The Role of Music in the Nation

Through the depth and thematic breadth of his writings, Hanslick created "an almost uninterrupted panorama of cultural life between 1850 and 1900."[27] His autobiography provides a literary snapshot of an era, and it is in a literary context that *Aus meinem Leben* can play a crucial role. Eduard Hanslick was a key figure in an era when the belief that music is central to a sense of Austro-German identity became common currency, and he played a part in the establishment of the classical canon as one both dominated and defined by great Germanic composers. This canonical tradition drew on compositions, but truly flourished in prose, to an extent well beyond the power of the individual reviews for which Hanslick is famous. Topical writings had become so important to those interested in understanding music that as Karen Painter argues, "by 1900 the discourse about music became as important as the music itself."[28] This literary dialogue was crucial in shaping the way audiences heard and understood music. Leon Botstein has observed that musical literacy in the nineteenth century involved "think[ing] of music exclusively in terms of language."[29] The fact that ephemeral listening became subordinate to rational linguistic comprehension made it possible for otherwise abstract musical ideas to develop more concrete historical significance, and for audience members to begin to assimilate them as part of their national identity.[30]

The importance of the public in receiving and disseminating this conception of music is reflected in Hanslick's answer to a question posed by Theodor Billroth as part of the critical dialogue that concludes *Aus meinem Leben*. Billroth apparently asked his friend: "Where does that leave the critic, when you deny his nurturing influence on artists and for good measure, his power to determine their success?" Hanslick's response was directed at the broader public: "'It leaves him,' I responded, 'with his best and for the most part also his only reward, the trust and the grateful endorsement of his readers.'"[31]

Hanslick's direct comments to his readers—sometimes in violation of current and future musicological value judgements as to which composers had talent or which works deserved to remain in the repertoire—are precisely what many would later dismiss him for. Yet his role as an arbiter of public as well as academic taste was crucial in the consolidation of music as an art form central to the development of a sense of coherent national and cultural identity in nineteenth-century Germany and Austria. Celia Applegate and Pamela Potter have noted that this development was "only partially the project of composers themselves, and just as much that of writers, conductors, bureaucrats, organizers, and musical amateurs, making their own creative use of music new and old."[32] Even if it appears in hindsight that Hanslick made a mistake dismissing Bruckner and Wolf, the role music played in public life in Vienna had no absolute correlation with objective quality. Instead, Hanslick was contributing to a particular discourse about the role of music in the nation, which was independent of discussions of purely musical merit.

The national consciousness of the major nineteenth-century German and Austrian composers was varied—from Robert Schumann's diffuse and inconsistent musings, to Richard Wagner's idiosyncratic attempts to create absolute German musical supremacy. Therefore, the singular image of German music embedded in the popular consciousness of listeners today—the reductionist belief that it is a uniquely German art form, simultaneously sublime, apolitical, and "absolute," and manifesting a politically constructed nation—cannot be seen as a reflection of concrete musical achievements.[33] Instead, the image emerged out of other aspects of the growing musical performance culture, through both romantic literary developments that helped inspire popular attitudes to music and the new, structured experience of listening to music, as expressed in reviews and other critical appraisals. This constructed idea of national musical supremacy became a self-perpetuating truth through the efforts of later writers about music to position themselves within this new literary tradition. Musical aesthetics had become driven by the written word to an extent where the resulting ideas could become part of the developing national consciousness without needing a direct counterpart in a musical score. Music could therefore be included much more effectively in the discourse of the emerging nation, because there was now a concrete way of discussing what had previously been an emotional but ephemeral aural experience.[34]

Aus meinem Leben and the Influence of the Romantic Literary Tradition

Aus meinem Leben occupies a pivotal place among the texts fusing romanticism and nationalism, even if the role of such a rational, bourgeois autobiography in this progression is not obvious at first. However, both form and content echo central elements in the literary construction of musical identity. A great deal of romantic music literature operated within a pseudo-biographical framework. Moreover, early romantic literature is a direct response to Viennese musical classicism, and far less divorced from the fundamental affection for Mozart and Beethoven than is often assumed.[35] Hanna Segbauer has commented that romantic literature about music reflects an understanding of music "which is drawn from sources other than contemporary music."[36]

The most direct intersection between literature, autobiography, and the idea of the musician as a literary figure is probably Carl Maria von Weber's unfinished *Bildungsroman, Tonkünstlers Leben* (1819).[37] Weber's fragments emerged in the aftermath of Wilhelm Heinrich Wackenroder and Ludwig Tieck's *Herzensergießungen eines kunstliebenden Klosterbruders* (1797) and Wackenroder's *Phantasien über die Kunst, für Freunde der Kunst* (1799),[38] both of which contained fictive biographical extracts about the musician Joseph Berlinger. Wackenroder provided one of the most powerful avowals of the romantic attitude to music,[39] which was also developed through the works of Jean Paul, Novalis, and E. T. A. Hoffmann. In addition, Hoffmann adopted the biographical form with a slightly fantastical slant in his *Lebensansichten des Katers Murr* (1819/21).[40]

As Mark Evan Bonds has noted, despite the extravagant literary stylings of these authors, they form part of a wider tradition leading to the development of romantic musical aesthetics.[41] Part of a recognized and popular genre of musical novellas,[42] their significance is not in their uniqueness, but in the extent to which the fictional views of the often disparagingly labeled musical "dilettantes" became embedded in the popular imagination. In the early nineteenth century, as public concert life developed and a new audience was drawn to a more autonomous concept of music, "dilettantish musical writing increased in importance."[43] While the idealized musical abstraction represented by Wackenroder and his ilk is removed from the later idea of "absolute music" which became a driving force in musical nationalism, it provided an early ideological impetus that continues in unexpected ways in Hanslick's autobiographical writing, as well as in the more obvious aesthetic discussions of *Vom Musikalisch-Schönen*.

Hanslick's autobiography was not the first to emerge from this tradition. The first sections of Carl Friedrich Zelter's romantic-inflected autobiography *Darstellung seines Lebens* appeared in 1820.[44] A. B. Marx, through whose work as a music writer and teacher Hanslick thought "Germany could only benefit,"[45] published his *Erinnerungen* in 1865. Zelter's and Marx's autobiographies are early examples of the growing fusion between romanticism and the idea of the nation in a more modern sense. Though Hanslick and Wagner would later violently disagree on other matters, they had been equally struck by the works of E. T. A. Hoffmann—there is a distinct overlap between certain Wagnerian motifs and Hoffmann's account of the mines of Falun, the basic story of which epitomizes a romantic myth.[46] While there was another flourish of literary works about music in the mid-nineteenth century, including Franz Grillparzer's *Der arme Spielmann* (1848) and Eduard Mörike's *Mozart auf der Reise nach Prag* (1856),[47] the autobiography was increasingly becoming the most prominent medium for presenting and preserving national musical tropes, particularly by those who were not primarily creative composing artists. Hanslick's *Aus meinem Leben* (1894) was eventually followed by autobiographies produced by his successors in academia and the media, for example, Julius Korngold with *Aufzeichnungen* (1945/1990) and Guido Adler with *Wollen und Wirken* (1935). Later, the critic Hans Heinz Stuckenschmidt would write *Zum Hören geboren* (1982) in the same vein.

With the exception of Thomas Mann, who revived the fictional biography as a carrier of musical meaning with *Dr Faustus*,[48] the aesthetic features from earlier romantic writing thus became increasingly located in autobiographies. This is the arena in which many of the tropes about the connection between music and the German soul (which Mann would condemn as destructive) became fixed.

Hanslick's explicit literary engagement with this tradition is sparing, but its influence on his activities and his remembrance of them is clear. In Prague he had been part of a circle around the writer and critic A. W. Ambros that called itself the *Davidsbund*, emulating the half-fantastic, half-real *Davidsbund* founded by Robert Schumann in Leipzig.[49] Later, in addition to visiting Schumann, Hanslick would also attempt to meet others from the original circle. After asking the composer where he could find members of the Bund in Leipzig, he was able to pass on Schumann's greetings to Professor Wenzel, the "last Davidsbündler," and to "discuss Romantic music's glorious youth."[50]

While preferring realism to romanticism in much of his reading—a passion for Dickens replaced his youthful enthusiasm for Jean Paul[51]—Hanslick's greatest cited influence, albeit indirectly, is the writer Franz Grillparzer, who provides a clear link to the influence of the romantic literary tradition as well as directly to Beethoven. Following Grillparzer as an employee in the customs section of the finance ministry provided consolation for Hanslick in his otherwise unromantic occupation,[52] and one of his greatest regrets was that he had

THE CRITIC AS SUBJECT   195

never found the courage to approach Grillparzer directly, despite seeing him every day during a period spent in Baden.[53] Hanslick was later astonished to discover "how actively Grillparzer concerned himself with musical matters until the end of his life, and that he had also read my reviews regularly."[54]

Hanslick and the Tradition of Autobiographical Writing

Hanslick himself was also a critical reader of other autobiographies. Writing in the shadow of Berlioz's *Memoirs* and Wagner's *Mein Leben*, he was certainly familiar with the former text (he mentions two friends—Berthold Damcke and his wife—whom Berlioz also held dear),[55] although the interrupted publication history of the latter makes it hard to judge how far Hanslick would have been aware of its content. However, his cited autobiographical influences are usually nonmusical. One of these was Jean-Jacques Rousseau. Rousseau's *Confessions* (1782) occupied Hanslick's time while he was waiting for a train back to Vienna from Prussian-occupied northern Bohemia in 1866.[56] The explicit revelations of Rousseau's text did not set a precedent Hanslick was inclined to follow. He argued: "Every soul has its private chamber, its exclusive, most concealed joys and sorrows. We open this chamber at most to old, trusted friends from one's youth, and never to unknown readers. . . . Passing, misguided passions of an evergreen heart and similar extremely private matters—do they belong in the public domain?"[57] Some of Hanslick's contemporaries certainly thought the answer to this was yes. After Theodor Billroth had read the first volume of the critic's memoirs, he complained that his friend had failed to describe his life in enough detail.[58] At Billroth's urging, Hanslick did add an extra confessional section outlining his views on music criticism, but his "privatissima" remain private, and the autobiography for the most part is an external affair.

Hanslick sees this reticence as fundamental to autobiographical writing, arguing that "[the autobiographer] should spare his readers matters which wouldn't interest them, even if they were dear and unforgettable to the writer. It is less difficult to remain silent about painful struggles and sorrowful experiences; it is, I would like to say, a dictate of politeness, a natural consideration."[59] The painful and the tragic have no place in Hanslick's literary vision. Moreover, he is reluctant to provide unnecessary historical background, and draws on what he sees as flaws in other autobiographies to make his point. After being bored by the political context provided in texts by, among others, the German author, translator, and journalist Friedrich Martin von Bodenstedt, Hanslick concludes that "an autobiographer, I believe, should . . . just recount the landmark details which he, and only he, has personally experienced."[60]

Hanslick further frames his selectivity about what to include with practical concerns about manners and posterity, particularly in a text intended for relatively prompt publication: "You could throw off many shackles while writing memoirs only intended for later publication. Then you could express yourself far more freely about good times as well as bad, and divulge your inner self."[61] Since this privilege is not available, Hanslick has opted for the lesser sin of omission. He concedes: "Everything that I discuss here was experienced and felt in its entirety, is literally true. But not everything that I have experienced and felt is discussed."[62]

Such reticence was not entirely without regret. While writing *Aus meinem Leben* in 1894, Hanslick came across comments by the Swiss author Gottfried Keller—of whose literary works he was already an enthusiastic reader[63]—on the pleasures of rereading old diaries. As a result, Hanslick began to doubt an old decision to destroy his own journals. After a lengthy illness he had burned diaries dating back twenty-five years, unwilling to retain painful memories of lost happier times and hoping to keep their contents from posterity.[64] The young Keller's words on the subject, that he kept a diary so he could look back in happy moments as well as in despair,[65] made Hanslick regret his premature *auto-da-fé*. Yet all but certain abbreviated travel diaries were already gone, and he had only himself to blame that in his folly such bittersweet reminiscences were lost to him.[66] However, given Hanslick's determination to maintain his privacy, it is hard to see him including these vanished recollections in *Aus meinem Leben*, even had they been available to him. A deeply awkward incident in 1892, where Hanslick had accidentally sent a private letter from Billroth, in which Billroth complained about their mutual friend Johannes Brahms's lack of upbringing and resultant poor manners, directly to the composer, would have provided further motivation for Hanslick to keep unpleasant memories to himself.[67]

Genuine discretion was clearly one reason for Hanslick to limit personal exposure in his autobiography. Even so, there is more than an admission of selective memory at stake. Adopting the French philosopher Georges Gusdorf's idea that events are both experienced and replayed before they ever come to be written down in autobiographical form,[68] Hanslick's authorial decisions involve creating an image of himself rather than recording an extant persona. Paul Ricoeur has discussed the process by which memory is traditionally archived and has observed that in the transition from testimony to archival source, "the emplotment of a told story . . . reinforces the semantic autonomy of the text."[69] While autobiographies are produced somewhat differently than transcribed testimony—there is no intermediary between the saying and the writing—the same principle is in operation: namely, that the narrator and the narrative can exist independently.[70] The psychology of the testimonial process can inspire errors of recollection,[71] but more than that, the testifier—in this case the autobiographer—can never describe himself from outside the events experienced, and is always making choices as to what is recalled and how it is recounted, while simultaneously hoping the account is understood as "true." Eduard Hanslick as understood by the readers of *Aus meinem Leben* is therefore a construction, even as the text appears as a fair summary of extensive (and authentic) lived experience. Hanslick the "character" does draw on the life of Hanslick the author and critic, but is presented as his creator wants to be seen, down to the smallest detail. Carl Dahlhaus has argued that this tendency to include insignificant events makes a work like Hanslick's into a mere memoir instead of an autobiography, where "almost everything that takes place tends to be symbolic."[72] Yet in Hanslick's case, the wholesale inclusion of people and events is highly significant in defining his personality for the reader—the descriptions may not be historically or musicologically symbolic in and of themselves, but they contribute to the development of an independent autobiographical persona: Hanslick as he wanted his readers to know him.

This conscious selection plays a significant role in shifting *Aus meinem Leben* from a simple account of an eventful life to a place of historical memory. Pierre Nora, who pioneered the term, has observed that memoirs (as the term suggests) can certainly be *lieux de mémoire*. He believes that the life-writing genre "exhibits certain constant and specific features despite variations of the quality of individual texts."[73] These include: an awareness of other autobiographies (which Hanslick certainly displays); that the author is "a man of the pen as well as a man of action" (as Hanslick was); an ability to integrate the events of an individual life as part of a wider narrative (Hanslick presents himself as a representative of a particular era and milieu); and an attempt to correlate personal sensibilities with those of the public (Hanslick consistently strives to keep his own opinions in step with, or at least in service of, his readers).[74] A text that meets this criteria, as Hanslick's does, thus forms part of the "memorial heritage of a community,"[75] not merely as a document which recounts the past, but as a source whose composition and subsequent reception helps shape the way the past is remembered.

Hanslick, Jews, and Other Germans

The Hanslick of *Aus meinem Leben* is a model member of the educated Austrian middle class, a public servant who became a professor. He notes of his own career that "the public service career was by far the most predominant among the educated middle class" since at that point a musical or critical path was an impossible dream.[76] In fact, as Hanslick later observes, it was a common, and logical, step for an impoverished art lover to take. "In Vormärz Austria everyone who had a passion for artistic creativity was a civil servant, as he would not be able to support his passion without the additional, comfortable government position."[77]

This interest in the arts is central to understanding Hanslick's self-image. From his youth he had been socialized in an environment owing much to the aesthetic principles of the educated middle-classes, which helped foster the idea of art as foundational to the nation. In turn, he would later promote Germanic cultural traditions as a national ideal. His autobiography positions him at the center of the establishment, meeting with heads of state at home and representing Austria abroad. However, this is deceptive. *Aus meinem Leben* creates a bourgeois Hanslick out of the figure from Prague, and leaves him as a grand old man representing the establishment in Vienna.

This Hanslick is only half true, based on his father and forefathers—arch Catholic countrymen from a region where Jews were hardly known.[78] Hanslick produces this lineage in response to Wagner's "smuggled" inclusion of him in *Das Judentum in der Musik* in 1869, even though this inclusion was apparently no actual cause for annoyance, and gave him the opportunity to "keep company with Mendelssohn and Meyerbeer on the stake as they were burned by Inquisitor Wagner."[79] Friedrich Blume reinforces this image of the emphatically non-Jewish Hanslick in his article in *Die Musik in Geschichte und Gegenwart*. Blume quotes the explanation given in *Aus meinem Leben* for Wagner's accusation: "Wagner couldn't stand Jews; therefore he was happy to assume that anyone he couldn't stand was a Jew."[80] Henry Pleasants and Hans Lenneberg also take offence on Hanslick's behalf at accusations of Judaism, with the latter noting: "Wagner had even stooped to calling Hanslick a Jew."[81]

However, Hanslick's mother, mentioned in *Aus meinem Leben* without reference to her ethnic identity, was in fact "the baptized daughter of a successful Jewish merchant."[82] She had converted to Christianity upon marriage.[83] This fact is carefully elided in Hanslick's reinvention of himself, and his condemnation of anti-Semitism in others is always for the sake of third parties. There is no hint, in his defense of Giacomo Meyerbeer, or of Hermann Levi, the conductor of *Parsifal*, that Hanslick is also speaking for himself. Even though in this era Jewish and German cultures were by no means mutually exclusive, and being Jewish or of Jewish heritage didn't compromise an "authentic Germanness,"[84] this is not an issue that Hanslick chose to tackle in *Aus meinem Leben*. For a man already publicly identified as "Beckmesser" this may have been a bridge too far, and hiding his Jewish (and parts of his Czech) background was a way to anchor his transformation from provincial obscurity to prominence in the imperial capital in Vienna.[85] In fact, Hanslick even adopted some of the mild anti-Semitism common in Vienna in the late-nineteenth century. This was particularly evident in his interactions with the composer Carl Goldmark, with whom Hanslick shared a similar background. According to Harald Graf: "Both men came during the [eighteen] forties from different parts of Old Austria to the centre of the Empire, its capital Vienna. Goldmark, of west-Hungarian origin, son of a Jewish cantor, was the first to arrive in 1844, Hanslick from Prague in 1846. They had a German-language upbringing in common; both were barely able to speak their respective national languages."[86] Yet it was precisely these exotic elements, long discarded by Hanslick, that he would criticize in Goldmark's work. Not that Goldmark was freely accepted when he adopted traditionally German material; when he composed a work to a text by Luther, Brahms reportedly said to a friend: "Don't you find it strange that a Jew has set a text by Martin Luther?"[87]

Hanslick does his best to leave behind his Jewish connections by ignoring them, and *Aus meinem Leben* establishes a pattern that other autobiographers later adopted. It details his education, focusing on the German literary, musical, and cultural heritage in which his father schooled him in Prague, before exploring his development from law student to civil servant to respected professor, and his marriage to the bourgeois Sophie Wohlmuth, who abandons her budding concert career to marry Hanslick.[88] His successors both in critical and academic life would also emphasize their connection to the Germanic cultural center, and downplay their undesirable roots.

Julius Korngold, Hanslick's successor at the *Neue Freie Presse*, had a less cultured childhood than Hanslick, and was thus forced to be even more assiduous in getting himself (and later his son) established in mainstream culture. He adopted the same tactics in his memoirs, recounting his education, career progression, and encounters with the great and the good of musical and cultural life. In spite of his efforts to be known as the embodiment of Germanic traditions, he was overtaken by events and was forced to leave Vienna as the Nazis came to power. While maintaining his own identity, he had been forcibly divorced from the culture around which he had shaped his identity and career—and his autobiographical writings are very much about creating rather than reporting a sense of self.[89]

Guido Adler also presents himself as someone from a simple background who educated himself into the center of the Austro-Hungarian Empire only to find in his declining years that his own fusion of Jewish and Germanic culture would no longer be countenanced in changing political times. This is reflected in his autobiography. With each round of editing his "other" identity became less and less visible,[90] until the published *Wollen und Wirken* begins with his own declaration of religion, actually a fusion of unnamed faith and distinct pride in the nation "to which I belong according to birth and culture."[91]

Ironically, almost fifty years later, the critic Hans Heinz Stuckenschmidt would apply the same framework in reverse. While Hanslick at times used his writings to become part of the establishment, Stuckenschmidt, who had an establishment background, emphasized his roots as a member of the educated bourgeoisie in order to support his work as a critic. Stuckenschmidt encouraged modernist music instead of merely propagating the canon of figures that Hanslick had helped to form. Hanslick wanted to establish and then reinforce the German musical and cultural tradition; Stuckenschmidt makes an explicit connection with it in order to prove his credentials for a professional life devoted first to rattling canonic and conservative musical foundations, and later, after World War II, attempting to dismantle them entirely.[92]

Musical and Literary Culture as Expressions of Pan-German Identity

Hanslick, Korngold, Adler, and Stuckenschmidt all share a sense of the importance of German cultural traditions. While the first three reinvented themselves in life and text as archetypal representatives and supporters of German music, it is hard to pin down precisely what this meant. One curiosity of the romantic-inspired idea of music as a German art form is the somewhat nebulous understanding of the term "German" displayed by both musicians and writers. Does it encompass all German-speaking territories, including the Austro-Hungarian Empire? Does it refer only to post-1871 unified Germany? Do Berlin and Vienna represent the same musical culture?

Hanslick's own position on these questions and their implications for personal identity was never fixed. Having grown up in Prague, he was a figure from the periphery who came to embody the cultural and political establishment of the Vienna that became his home, and also supported a pan-German sense of culture. Though not particularly political himself—in contrast to more activist fellow students in Vienna in 1848, he experienced the uprisings "not as an active participant, but as a very engaged sympathizer and observer"[93]—he would later express deep satisfaction over the foundation of the German Reich in 1871. Hanslick "rejoiced over the German victory and the foundation of the German Empire," writing, "that Alsace had become German again—a deep wish since my childhood—made me as happy as if I had been personally granted a kingdom."[94] Although Austria had remained publicly neutral, her German population—of which Hanslick clearly counts himself a member—"felt unashamedly national and expressed the greatest joy over Germany's victories."[95]

This might appear to indicate that the Prague-born Austrian was in fact a German nationalist. Yet Hanslick's enthusiasm for the new Germany was not absolute. Some of this is simple regret over the loss of past cooperation—for example, over the fact that the Austrian and Prussian troops, the friendly relations between whose officers he had witnessed during a visit to their shared garrison at Rastatt in 1855, would end up facing each other only ten years later as enemies when the brief but decisive Austro-Prussian war erupted in 1866.[96] However, it is also a reflection of the emphasis Hanslick continued to place on Vienna as an *Austrian* city, particularly when describing newcomers to the city in his autobiography. When Brahms and Wagner arrive in 1862, they do so as "German composers";[97] when Theodor Billroth wins the general admiration and love of the Viennese, it is particularly notable for someone hailing from northern Germany.[98] Austria is also the natural home for true musical talent; after observing the conductor Wilhelm Jahn in Wiesbaden, Hanslick's first response is: "Indeed, the man must be won for Vienna. . . . To spend his whole life in Wiesbaden means artistic abdication."[99]

Moreover, part of Hanslick's reinvention as the quintessential Austrian insider meant establishing a deep respect for the royal family. Despite his experiences in 1848 and 1871, the worst tragedy he experienced in Vienna was the death of Crown Prince Rudolf in 1889. As Hanslick recounted: "It vibrates in me like a burning physical pain whenever I am reminded of it. On the afternoon of January 30, 1889, a rumor ran through the city: the Crown Prince was dead!.... I have experienced the saddest catastrophes in Vienna: revolutions, disastrous campaigns, lost provinces, massive devastation through water and fire—none of these could be compared in the slightest with that harrowing January 30."[100]

This apparently incompatible mixture of German and Austrian identity finds a resolution in culture. According to Hanslick, he had found his spiritual home on a visit to Weimar. In fact, as he said: "Here in Weimar it seems to me as if I have found my spiritual Fatherland. I was completely at home in Weimar's classical period, familiar with all its people and places, and clung to Goethe and Schiller as I had to the guides and ideas of my youth with my entire heart—more deeply than I did to Mozart and Beethoven!"[101] This reflects a concept of the nation that is built in "universal, nonterritorial, and largely cultural terms," representing a positive force and a universal culture into which others should be educated.[102] Hanslick's regard for Weimar also reflects his own affection for a range of German-language literature and his sense of representing this literary tradition as much as the musical one with which he is most often associated—he is as happy to have Grillparzer's respect as that of Brahms.

While certain elements of culture are distinctly German or Austrian (with, for example, Johann Strauss and his waltzes belonging clearly to the latter), for Hanslick, culture in general is Germanic in a wider sense. Thus his approval of a speech made at a cultural festival in Salzburg in 1862, when Minister of State Anton von Schmerling discussed the little-raised topic of "the meaning of art for the state and the spiritual dominance of the German element in Austria," is at first glance contradictory, given the way Hanslick presents his personal and political identity so intensely as Austrian rather than German.[103] Yet Schmerling's speech reflects Hanslick's own secondary conviction, that the art so important to the Austrian state is intrinsically German-inflected and not confined to national borders.

This German element extends across both countries, both before and after the unification of Germany. "Musical nationalism" cuts across political definitions of the nation, leaving culture as the only way to find some sort of compromise position.[104] Hanslick certainly has a specific idea of what this means as far as musical culture is concerned. It is one of his most controversial conclusions, but it also epitomizes the nineteenth-century contribution of music to the development of a sense of pan-German identity. For Hanslick, this means emphasizing the modern over the historical, that which reflects culture today over legends of the past. Hanslick's credo is formulated as follows: "For Goethe's *Faust* I would abandon all of Sophocles; for *Hermann and Dorothea*, Milton's *Paradise* and Klopstock's *Messias*; for Schiller's *Tell* or *Wallenstein*, all of Racine's tragedies; for Dickens, Gottfried Keller, Paul Heyse, Alphonse Daudet, and Turgenev, I would abandon all the fiction of the seventeenth and eighteenth centuries."[105] In matters musical, Hanslick is equally willing to sacrifice the past, turning exclusively (though not without a slight hint of apology) to modern German artists: "I would rather see the complete works of Heinrich Schütz burn than the *German Requiem*; rather Palestrina's works than Mendelssohn's, preferably all the concertos and sonatas of Bach over Schumann's or Brahms' quartets. For one *Don Giovanni*, *Fidelio*, or *Freischütz* I would happily abandon all of Gluck."[106] Ultimately, for Hanslick "the history of our living music begins with Bach and Handel." Yet "in his heart it only begins with Mozart, and reaches its peak in Beethoven, Schumann, and Brahms."[107] This is not just an expression of Hanslick's personal taste, but is also the canon often attributed to the German nation. Wagner's own worldview, for the condemnation of which Hanslick has often suffered, does not in fact dominate the popular understanding of German music in the twentieth century. Instead, it operates in parallel with the images conjured by Beethoven and Brahms without overshadowing them. The latter composers have more currency in the popular imagination, but Wagner's self-contained musical and historical imagery has its own independent power. That Hanslick can both recognize and to some extent shape popular conceptions of music is also the endpoint of the transformation presented in *Aus meinem Leben*, through which he describes and reconstructs his identity as an independent agent, operating at the top of the Austrian establishment and thereby representing a wider sense of German cultural identity, one which he had a hand in creating as well as observing.

Given its anecdotal character, *Aus meinem Leben* has not traditionally been read as a foray into the establishment of a national culture in Germany and Austria in which music played a central role. Hanslick's wide circle of acquaintances exposed him to a broad range of musical developments, both within and without Austria, but his work in describing musical life can often seem more descriptive than constructive. Equally, his reputation as a powerful music critic, prone to controversial judgements about major figures like Wagner, has made it difficult to see Hanslick's autobiography as more than a collection of idiosyncratic opinions overtaken by other, more pervasive critical judgements. However, this view overlooks both the process of self-creation inherent in autobiographical writing and the recognition by modern scholars that the foundation of the musical nation was laid as much by writers as it was by practicing musicians. Canonical composers gained prominence in tandem with contemporary literary and political support, yet writers were not without self-interest in offering this support, as their choices contributed to the development of a particular type of self-image.

Hanslick's preference for Mozart, Beethoven, and Brahms over Palestrina and Gluck and for Goethe's *Faust* over Racine's tragedies may well reflect personal taste and preferences, but it is impossible to ignore the impact of these ostensibly private judgements, which on the one hand contributed to the formation of a closed national musical canon, and on the other established Hanslick's credentials as an archetypal supporter of Germanic musical primacy. The biographical elisions practised by Hanslick in *Aus meinem Leben* serve to position a figure originally from the geographical and ethnic periphery at the very center of Austrian society and culture, thus justifying and reinforcing the critical power he wielded. His apparently straightforward biographical narrative is actually a self-aware and self-conscious framing of the nineteenth-century bourgeois ideal, and *Aus meinem Leben* has an important role to play in our understanding of the way in which society, nation, and culture coalesced around classical and romantic music.

Appendix 9.1: People Listed as Page Headers in *Aus meinem Leben*

Ambros, A. W.[108]
Archduke Johann of Austria
Artôt, Désirée
Auber, Daniel
Auerbach, Berthold
Benedict, Julius
Berlioz, Hector
Billroth, Theodor
Brahms, Johannes
Crown Prince Rudolf of Austria
Crown Princess Stéphanie of Austria[109]
Czarvady (Szarvady), Friedrich
Délibes, Leon
Dessauer, Josef
Dessoff, Felix Otto
Dickens, Charles
Dumas, Alexander
Dumba, Nicolaus
Dvořák, Antonín
Engelsberg[110]
Esser, Heinrich
Favre, Jules

Franz, Robert
Gade, Niels
García, Manuel
Geibel, Emanuel
Goethe, Walther[111]
Goethe, Wolfgang[112]
Gounod, Charles
Hauck, Minnie
Haufer, Franz
Hauptmann, Moritz
Heller, Stephen
Herz, Henri
Heyse, Paul
Hiller, Ferdinand
Jahn, Wilhelm
King Oskar II of Sweden
Kossak, Ernst
Lachner, Franz
Lanner, Joseph
Laube, Heinrich
Lewald, Fanny
Lind, Jenny

Liszt, Franz
Lucca, Pauline
Marx, A. B.
Mascagni, Pietro
Meyerbeer, Giacomo
Moscheles, Ignaz
Mosenthal, Salomon
Mozart, Karl
Nohl, Ludwig
Offenbach, Jacques
Paladilhe, Emilie
Patti, Adelina
Patti, Carlotta
Pauer, Ernst
Rastner, Georges
Rinkel, Gottfried
Roger, Gustave
Rossini, Gioacchino
Rubinstein, Anton
Scherer, Wilhelm

Simrock, Fritz
Spitzer, Daniel
Steinway, Theodor
Steub, Ludwig
Strauß, Johann
Tagliana, Emilia
Thiers, Adolphe
Thomas, Ambroise
Ullmann, Bernhard
Unger, Dr Joseph
Verdi, Giuseppe
Volkmann, Robert
von Herbeck, Johann
von Hornstein, Robert
von Köchel, Dr Ludwig
von Schwind, Moritz
Wagner, Richard
Wilbrandt, Adolf
Wilt, Marie
Wohlmuth, Sophie

Notes

1. Johann Wolfgang von Goethe, *Aus meinem Leben: Dichtung und Wahrheit*, ed. G. von Loeper (1811; Berlin: F. Dümmlers, 1876). All translations are my own unless otherwise stated.

2. Hans Lenneberg, *Witnesses and Scholars. Studies in Musical Biography* (New York: Gordon & Breach, 1988), 150.

3. Eduard Hanslick, *Aus meinem Leben* (1894; edited and with an afterword by Peter Wapnewski, Kassel: Bärenreiter, 1987), 220 (hereafter cited as *AML/W*).

4. Hanslick, *AML/W*, 41.

5. "Während seines Prager Aufenthaltes war Berlioz unser einziger Gedanke, unsere einzige Beschäftigung." Hanslick, *AML/W*, 41. Compare Hector Berlioz, *The Memoirs of Hector Berlioz*, trans. and ed. David Cairns (London: Everyman, 2002), 420–23.

6. Geoffrey Payzant, *Eduard Hanslick and Ritter Berlioz in Prague: A Documentary Narrative* (Calgary, AB: University of Calgary Press, 1991). See especially chapter 3.

7. Peter Wapnewski, "Eduard Hanslick als Darsteller seiner selbst: Der Kritker und die Nachwelt," in Hanslick, *AML/W*, 514.

8. Hanslick, *AML/W*, 376–8 and 334.

9. "Es handelt sich für uns nicht nur darum, ob der Selbstbiograph die Wahrheit sagen *will*, sondern ob er sie überhaupt uns zu sagen *vermag*." Hans Glagau is quoted in Martina Wagner-Egelhaaf, *Autobiographie*, 2nd ed. (Stuttgart: J. B. Metzler, 2005), 42.

10. Hanslick's own account: "stellte mich Verdi als 'il Bismarck della critica musicale' vor." Hans Lenneberg takes this as his starting point for the article "Il Bismarck della Critica Musicale: The Memoirs of Eduard Hanslick," *Opera Quarterly* 2:1 (2004): 29–36.

11. Hanslick notes that even when a man relents and acknowledges the critique was justified, his wife will never forgive. "Denn, wenn auch vielleicht der Mann, dem die abfällige Kritik gegolten, im Stillen ihre Gerechtigkeit einsieht und nach und nach verzeiht – seine Frau verzeiht nie! Der frühere freundschaftliche Verkehr ist abgebrochen. Der vordem hochgeschätzte Kritiker ist fortan ein unwissender oder parteiischer Mensch." Hanslick, *AML/W*, 402.

12. "Wer hätte in einem langen Kritikerleben nicht Kompositionen befreundeter, liebenswürdiger Menschen tadeln müssen und umgekehrt, die Werke von Männern bewundert, mit denen er im Leben nicht gern zu tun gehabt!" Hanslick, *AML/W*, 222.

13. "Daß ein Künstler empfangenen Tadel uns nicht nachtrage, gehört zu den größten Seltenheiten." Ibid., 402–3.

14. "Nach Jahren der Entfernung erfuhr ich unverändert wieder die faszinierende Gewalt seiner Persönlichkeit." Ibid., 332–33. Markus Gärtner provides further evidence that Liszt and Hanslick had a cordial relationship, while also noting that in a memoir written for publication Hanslick may well have spared Liszt certain criticism. See Markus Gärtner, *Eduard Hanslick versus Franz Liszt: Aspekte einer grundlegenden Kontroverse* (Hildesheim: Georg Olms, 2005), 48. For details of this 1858 encounter between Hanslick and Liszt, see also Chantal Frankenbach, "Waltzing around the Musically Beautiful: Listening and Dancing in Hanslick's Hierarchy of Musical Perception" in the current volume.

15. Hanslick, *AML/W*, 221.

16. "Ich zögerte nicht, Wagner zu besuchen, dessen freundliches, mitteilsames Wesen mir einen günstigen Eindruck machte. Er war damals noch nicht Gott, nicht einmal vergöttert." Ibid., 46.

17. Ibid., 48–49.

18. "Die Oper übte auf mich eine bedeutende, stellenweise berauschende Wirkung aus." Ibid., 49.

19. Ibid., 220.

20. "Er war der personifizierte Egoismus, rastlos tätig für sich selbst, teilnahmslos, rücksichtslos gegen andere." Ibid., 221.

21. "Wahrscheinlich würden ich und manche meiner Gesinnungsgenossen in ruhigerem Ton über Wagner geschrieben haben, wenn nicht die maßlosen, ans Lächerliche grenzenden Übertreibungen der Gegner unsern Puls beschleunigt hätten. Ich will gerne zugestehen, daß mir das zeitweilig passiert sein mag." Ibid., 360–61.

22. Peter Gay, *Freud, Jews and Other Germans: Masters and Victims in Modernist Culture* (New York: Oxford University Press, 1978), 264.

23. William M. Johnston, *The Austrian Mind: An Intellectual and Social History, 1848–1938* (Berkeley: University of California Press, 1983), 132.

24. Stewart Deas, *In Defence of Hanslick*, rev. ed. (Westmead: Gregg International Publishers, 1972), 10–23.

25. Eric Sams, "Eduard Hanslick, 1825–1904: The Perfect Anti-Wagnerite," *Musical Times* 116 (1975): 867–68.
26. Gay, *Freud, Jews and Other Germans*, 264.
27. "[Hanslicks] Bedeutung beruht zum einen auf der Fülle und der thematischen Breite seiner Schriften, die ein fast lückenloses Panorama des kulturellen Lebens zwischen 1850 und 1900 entwerfen." Christian Wildhagen, "Bismarck und Beckmesser: Der Musikkritiker Eduard Hanslick aus heutiger Sicht," *NZZ Online*, August 7, 2004, http://www.nzz.ch/aktuell/startseite/article9RHJD-1.289153.
28. Karen Painter, *Symphonic Aspirations: German Music and Politics, 1900–1945* (Cambridge, MA: Harvard University Press, 2007), 269.
29. Leon Botstein, "Listening through Reading: Musical Literacy and the Concert Audience," *19th-Century Music* 16, no. 2 (1992): 144. See also Leon Botstein, "Music and Its Public: Habits of Listening and the Crisis of Musical Modernism in Vienna, 1870–1914" (PhD diss., Harvard University, 1985).
30. Ibid., 130.
31. Billroth: "Was bleibt dem Kritiker, wenn Du ihm den erziehenden Einfluß auf den Künstler absprichst und obendrein die Macht über den Erfolg?"
Hanslick: "'Es bleibt ihm,' erwiderte ich, 'als schönster, meistenteils auch einziger Lohn das Vertrauen und die dankbare Zustimmung seines Leserkreises.'" Hanslick, *AML/W*, 401.
32. Celia Applegate and Pamela Potter, "Germans as the 'People of Music': Genealogy of an Identity," in *Music and German National Identity*, ed. Potter and Applegate (Chicago: University of Chicago Press, 2002), 12.
33. Celia Applegate, "What Is German Music? Reflections on the Role of Art in the Creation of the Nation," *German Studies Review* 15 (1992): 27.
34. Celia Applegate, "How German Is It? Nationalism and the Idea of Serious Music in the Early Nineteenth Century," *19th-Century Music* 21, no. 3 (1998): 279.
35. Romantic literature and music do overlap, but, according to Carl Dahlhaus (among others), the literary aesthetic developed before the musical one. See Carl Dahlhaus, "Romantische Musikästhetik und Wiener Klassik," *Archiv für Musikwissenschaft* 29, no. 3 (1972): 167–81.
36. Hanna Segbauer, *Die Akustik der Seele* (Göttingen: Vandenhoeck & Ruprecht, 2006), 10.
37. Carl Maria von Weber, *Writings on Music*, translated by Martin Cooper, edited with an introduction by John Warrack (Cambridge: Cambridge University Press, 1981), document 125.
38. Wilhelm Heinrich Wackenroder and Ludwig Tieck, *Herzensergießungen eines kunstliebenden Klosterbruders*, text based on 1797 ed. (Stuttgart: Reclam, 2005), and Wilhelm Heinrich Wackenroder, *Phantasien über die Kunst, für Freunde der Kunst*, ed. Ludwig Tieck, text based on 1799 ed. (Stuttgart: Reclam, 2005).
39. Linda Siegel, "Wackenroder's Musical Essays in *Phantasien über die Kunst*," *Journal of Aesthetics and Art Criticism* 30, no. 3 (1972): 352.
40. E. T. A. Hoffmann, *Lebensansichten des Katers Murr*, text based on 1st ed. (Düsseldorf: Patmos, 2006).
41. Mark Evan Bonds, "Idealism and the Aesthetics of Instrumental Music at the Turn of the Nineteenth Century," *Journal of the American Musicological Society* 50, nos. 2–3 (1997): 405.
42. Applegate, "What Is German Music?," 30.

43. Karlheinz Schlager, "Der Fall Berglinger. Stufen einer romantischen Biographie am Beispiel Wackenroder," *Archiv für Musikwissenschaft* 29, no. 2 (1972): 115.

44. However, the first publication of the complete manuscript was in 1931. Carl Friedrich Zelter, *Carl Friedrich Zelters Darstellungen seines Lebens* (Weimar: Schriften der Goethe-Gesellschaft 44, 1931).

45. "Marx hat sich erst spät 'mit bittern Schmerzen' entschlossen, seine Tätigkeit als Komponist vollständig mit der eines Musikschriftstellers und Lehrers zu vertauschen. Deutschland konnte dabei nur gewinnen, denn Marx' Lehrbücher... haben überall großen Nutzen gestiftet." Hanslick, *AML/W*, 159.

46. John Neubauer, "The Mines of Falun: Temporal Fortunes of a Romantic Myth of Time," *Studies in Romanticism* 19, no. 4 (1980): 489–94. See also Linda Siegel, "Wagner and the Romanticism of E. T. A. Hoffmann," *Musical Quarterly* 51, no. 4 (1965): 597–99.

47. Franz Grillparzer, *Der arme Spielmann*, text based on 1848 1st ed. (Munich: dtv, 1997), and Eduard Mörike, *Mozart auf der Reise nach Prag*, text based on 1856 ed. (Munich: dtv, 2004).

48. Thomas Mann, *Dr Faustus/Die Entstehung des Doktor Faustus*, 1947 ed. (Frankfurt/M.: S. Fischer, 1994).

49. The Prague circle had been established "in Nachahmung des von Robert Schumann (mehr in dessen Phantasie als in der Wirklichkeit) gestifteten 'Davidsbundes' junger musikalischer Fortschrittler in Leipzig." Hanslick, *AML/W*, 31. The extent to which the original *Davidsbund* was a concrete concept is explored in Bernhard Appel, "Schumanns Davidsbund: Geistes- und sozialgeschichtliche Voraussetzungen einer romantischen Idee," *Archiv für Musikwissenschaft* 38, no.1 (1981): 1–23.

50. "Da konnte ich denn dem wackeren, geistreichen Mann die Größe Schumans überbringen und mit diesem letzten der Leipziger Davidsbündler über die glorreiche Jugendzeit der romantischen Musik sprechen." Hanslick, *AML/W*, 50.

51. Ibid., 36.

52. Ibid., 127.

53. Ibid., 184.

54. "Wie lebhaft Grillparzer bis an sein Lebensende sich um musikalische Dinge bekümmert, auch regelmäßig meine Kritiken gelesen hat." Hanslick discovered Grillparzer's enthusiasm for his work several years after a missed encounter in May 1869. Ibid., 184.

55. "Diesen [B. Damcke] und seine Frau, deren Herzengüte und gastliche Aufnahme, hat Berlioz auch in seinen 'Memoirs' dankbar erwähnt." Ibid., 310.

56. Ibid., 238.

57. "Jede Seele hat ihr Privatkämmerlein, ihre alleinigen, verschwiegensten Freuden und Leiden. Wir öffnen es höchstens einem alten, treuen Jugendfreunde, niemals fremden Lesern.... Vorübergehende thörichte Herzensneigungen eines immergrünen Herzens und ähnliche Privatissima—gehören die vor das Publikum?" Ibid., 284.

58. Ibid., 284.

59. "[Der Selbstbiograph] soll seine Leser mit Dingen verschonen, die sie nicht interessieren und welche doch ihm selbst teuer und unvergeßlich sind. Schmerzliche Kämpfe, traurige Erlebnisse zu verschweigen, das fällt weniger schwer; es ist, ich möchte sagen, ein Gebot der Höflichkeit, eine natürliche Rücksicht." Ibid., 130.

60. Hanslick's conclusion in full reads: "Die Fehler anderer sollen meinen Lesern zum Vorteil gedeihen. Es hat mich nämlich sehr gelangweilt, in mancher neueren Selbstbiographie, z. B. der von Bodenstedt, die politischen Ereignisse des Jahres 48, die ganze Entwicklung der Märzbewegung u.s.w ausführlich geschildert zu finden, als wären

das lauter neue Dinge und nicht in jedem moderen Geschichtswerke nachzulesen. Ein Autobiograph, glaube ich, sollte aus jenem, allen Zeitgenossen so geläufigen Jahr lediglich erzählen, was er persönlich, und nur er, an charakteristischen Einzelheiten erlebt hat." Ibid., 82.

61. "Man könnte manche Fesseln abwerfen, wenn man Memoiren schreibe, die erst später veröffentlicht werden. Mann könnte dann sich selbst im Guten wie im Schlimmen freier geben, sein innerstes Innere preisgeben." Ibid., 283.

62. "Alles, was ich hier erzähle, ist vollständig so erlebt und gefühlt, ist buchstäblich getreu. Aber nicht alles, was ich erlebt und empfunden habe, erzähle ich." Ibid., 283. Hanslick does show more self-awareness with this admission than many other musical figures who took to autobiography—the conductor Karl Böhm, for instance, would call his memoir *Ich erinnere mich ganz genau* without apparent irony. See Karl Böhm, *Ich erinnere mich ganz genau*, ed. Hans Weigel (Vienna: Fritz Molden, 1974).

63. Hanslick, AML/W, 160.

64. Hanslick's explanation in full: "Nach einer längeren Krankheit vernichtete ich alle meine Tagebücher, die ich von meinem fünfzehnten Jahre an durch volle fünfundzwanzig Jahre mit liebevoller Sorgfalt geführt hatte. Wozu diese schmerzliche Erinnerung an entschwundene glücklichere Zeiten? Und sollten sie, wenn ich stürbe, in fremde Hände fallen?" Ibid., 284.

65. Hanslick, quoting Gottfried Keller: "Nicht bloß in Tagen der Mutlosigkeit, nein!, auch in Tagen der festlichen Freude will ich stille Momente verweilen und ausruhen im traulichen Schmollwinkel meines Tagebuchs. . . . So will ich mich in meinen letzten Erdentagen erfreuen an den Bildern entschwundener Freuden." Ibid., 284.

66. Hanslick continues: "So verbrannte ich denn einen Band nach dem andern und schaute mit schmerzlichem Behagen in das Kaminfeuer, wie die geliebten Blätter rasch aufflammten und sich dann zu schwarzen funkendurchsprengten Schichten zusammenballten. Nur meine Reisetagebücher wurden verschont; sie bestanden bloß aus kurzen täglichen Notizen. Wie oft, wie schwer habe ich dieses voreilige Autodafé bereut!" Ibid., 284.

67. Brahms's reply to Hanslick is included in *Johannes Brahms: Life and Letters*, ed. Styra Avins, trans. Josef Eisinger and Styra Avins (New York: OUP, 1997), 700–701. Brahms advised Hanslick not to say anything—advice which Hanslick apparently followed, even though it soured Billroth's final musical evening.

68. Georges Gusdorf, quoted in Martina Wagner-Egelhaaf, *Autobiographie*, 2nd ed. (Stuttgart: J. B. Metzler, 2005), 48.

69. Paul Ricoeur, *Memory, History, Forgetting*, trans. Kathleen Blaney and David Pellauer (Chicago: University of Chicago Press, 2004), 166.

70. Ibid., 166.

71. Ibid., 172. Ricoeur is discussing the work of Marc Bloch here.

72. "[eine Autobiographie unterscheidet sich] von bloßen Memorien, in denen Menschen und Vorkommnisse durchaus um ihrer selbst willen geschildert werden können. In einer Autobiographie ist demnach, pointiert ausgedrückt, nahezu alles, was geschieht, tendenziell symbolisch." Carl Dahlhaus, "Wagners Inspirationsmythen," in *Gesammelte Schriften*, ed. Hermann Danuser (Laaber: Laaber, 2004): 465.

73. Pierre Nora, *Realms of Memory: Rethinking the French Past*, ed. Lawrence D. Kritzman, trans. Arthur Goldhammer, 3 vols. (New York: Columbia University Press, 1996), 1:17.

74. Ibid., 17.

75. Ibid., xvii.

76. "Die Beamtenkarriere war die weitaus vorherrschende im gebildeten Mittelstand." Hanslick, *AML/W*, 27.

77. "Im vormärzlichen Österreich war jedermann Beamter, den die Liebe zu künstlerischem Schaffen verzehrte, während er selbst nichts zu verzehren gehabt hätte ohne ein nebenbei betriebenes, gemütliches Staatsamt." Ibid., 67.

78. Ibid., 220.

79. "Daß mich Wagner später, 1869, in sein 'Judentum' eingeschmuggelt hat, das konnte mich noch weniger kränken. . . . Es würde mir nur schmeichelhaft sein, auf ein und demselben Holzstoß mit Mendelssohn und Meyerbeer von Pater Arbuez Wagner verbrannt zu werden." Ibid., 220.

80. "Wagner mochte keinen Juden leiden; darum hielt er jeden, den er nicht leiden konnte, gern für einen Juden." Hanslick, quoted in Friedrich Blume, "Hanslick, Eduard," *Die Musik in Geschichte und Gegenwart*, vol. 12 (Kassel: Bärenreiter, 1956), 1486. Peter Gay views Blume's emphatic defense of Hanslick's non-Jewishness with extreme discomfort, wondering about its necessity. See Gay, *Freud, Jews, and Other Germans*, 264. Indeed, Werner Abegg's article on Hanslick in the 2002 MGG edition completely omits any mention of religion. Werner Abegg, "Hanslick, Eduard," *Die Musik in Geschichte und Gegenwart* (Kassel: Bärenreiter, 2002), Personenteil, vol. 8, 667–72.

81. Lenneberg, "Il Bismarck della Critica Musicale," 29. See also the introduction to Eduard Hanslick, *Vienna's Golden Years of Music: 1850–1900*, trans. and ed. Henry Pleasants (London: Gollancz, 1951), where Pleasants mentions the lack of evidence in support of Hanslick's Judaism. On the details of Hanslick's Jewish heritage, see Jitka Ludvová, "Zur Biographie Eduard Hanslicks," *Studien zur Musikwissenschaft* 37 (1986): 37–46.

82. David Brodbeck, "Hanslick's Smetana and Hanslick's Prague," *Journal of the Royal Musical Association* 134, no. 1 (2009): 11. Eric Sams had previously mentioned Hanslick's "much loved Jewish mother" without further specifics. Sams, "Eduard Hanslick, 1825–1904: The Perfect Anti-Wagnerite," 868.

83. Wapnewski, in Hanslick, *AML/W*, 512.

84. Gay, *Freud, Jews, and Other Germans*, 99–100.

85. David Brodbeck discusses the Czech aspects of Hanslick's transformation extensively in "Hanslick's Smetana and Hanslick's Prague."

86. "Beide kamen in den 40er Jahren des vorigen Jahrhunderts aus unterschiedlichen Teilen Altösterreichs ins Zentrum des Reiches, in die Hauptstadt Wien. Goldmark, westungarischer Provenienz, Sohn eines jüdischen Kantors, erstmals 1844, der Prager Hanslick 1846. Gemeinsam war ihnen eine deutschsprachige Erziehung, ihrer jeweiligen Landessprache waren beide kaum mächtig." Harald Graf, "Carl Goldmark. Beziehung zu den Zeitgenossen," *Studia Musicologica Academiae Scientiarum Hungaricae* 38, no. 3–4 (1997): 374. See also David Brodbeck, "'Poison-Flaming Flowers from the Orient and Nightingales from Bayreuth': On Hanslick's Reception of the Music of Goldmark" in the current volume.

87. Graf tells the story as follows: Soll Brahms Ignaz Brüll gegenüber im Zorn geäußert haben: 'Finden Sie es nicht sonderbar, daß ein Jude einen Text von Martin Luther komponiert?'" Graf, "Carl Goldmark," 387. The incident itself is recorded in Carl Goldmark's autobiography, *Erinnerungen aus meinem Leben* (Vienna-Leipzig: Rikola, 1922), 87.

88. Hanslick, *AML/W*, 322.

89. The most accessible, though somewhat condensed version of Julius Korngold's memoirs is Julius Korngold et al., *Die Korngolds in Wien: Der Musikkritiker und das Wunderkind*. Aufzeichnungen von Julius Korngold (Zürich: M & T Verlag, 1991).

90. Barbara Boisits, "Autobiography and Its Hidden Layers: The Case of Guido Adlers *Wollen und Wirken*," unpublished conference paper, presented at the conference (Auto)Biography as a Musicological Discourse, Department of Musicology and Ethnomusicology, Faculty of Music, University of Arts, Belgrade, April 21, 2008.

91. Guido Adler, *Wollen und Wirken* (Vienna: Universal, 1935), 1.

92. H. H. Stuckenschmidt, *Zum Hören geboren. Ein Leben mit der Musik unserer Zeit* (Kassel: Bärenreiter, 1982).

93. "Ich habe die ganze Bewegung zwar nicht als aktiver Teilnehmer, doch als sehr erregter Mitempfinder und Beobachter durchgemacht." Hanslick, *AML/W*, 82.

94. "Ich jubelte über die Siege der Deutschen und die Gründung des neuen Reichs. Daß Elsaß wieder Deutsch geworden—ein Herzenswunsch schon meiner Kindheit—machte mich glücklich, als wäre mir persönlich ein Fürstentum geschenkt worden." Ibid., 282.

95. "Österreich verhielt sich bekanntlich neutral zwischen den beiden kriegführenden Mächten, unsere deutsche Bevölkerung hingengen fühlte unverblümt national und äußerte die lauteste Freude über Deutschlands Siege." Ibid., 282.

96. Hanslick is referring to a visit to the fortress of Rastatt, where his sister Lotti's husband Moritz von Fialka was stationed. Ibid., 167. The Rastatt Fortress became (in)famous in 1849, when its troops mutinied in support of the democratic regime in Baden. The fortress was handed over after a three-week siege on July 23 in order to prevent a civilian massacre, and nineteen of the mutineers were executed. Hanslick is recalling a more peaceful past before the dissolution of the German League.

97. "Das Jahr 1862 führte zwei *deutsche* Tondichter nach Wien, große und eigenartige Erscheinungen; dabei einander so unähnlich als möglich: Johannes Brahms und Richard Wagner." Emphasis mine. Ibid., 215.

98. "Ich wüßte keine Persönlichkeit, namentlich keine aus *Norddeutschland* herübergekommene, zu nennen, die in Wien eine so allgemeine Verehrung und Liebe genossen hätte wie Billroth." Emphasis mine. Ibid., 274.

99. "Gewiß, der Mann mußte für Wien gewonnen werden! . . . Sein Leben lang in Wiesbaden verbleiben, heißt, Künstlerisch abdizieren." Ibid., 352–53.

100. "Aber Österreich war ein noch größerer Verlust beschieden. Es durchzuckt mich wie ein brennender physischer Schmerz, sooft ich daran erinnert werde. Am Nachmittag des 30. Januar 1889 durchlief ein Gerücht die Stadt: der Kronprinz sei tot! . . . Ich habe in Wien die traurigsten Katastrophen erlebt: Revolutionen, unglückliche Feldzüge, verlorene Provinzen, mörderische Verheerungen durch Wasser und Feuer—nichts von alledem war diesem grauenvollen 30. Januar entfernt zu vergleichen." Ibid., 370.

101. "Hier in Weimar schien mir's, als hätte ich mein geistiges Vaterland gefunden. War ich doch in Weimars klassischer Zeit vollkommen zu Hause, mit all ihren Personen und Örtlichkeiten vertraut und hing an Goethe und Schiller, als an den Führern und Idealen meiner Jugend mit meinem ganzen Herzen—inniger als an Mozart und Beethoven!" Ibid., 168.

102. Pieter M. Judson, "Rethinking the Liberal Legacy," in *Rethinking Vienna 1900*, ed. Steven Beller (Berghahn, New York and Oxford, 2001), 66–67. This passage is quoted in Brodbeck, "Hanslick's Smetana and Hanslick's Prague," 4.

103. "Der September des Jahres 1862 versammelte in Salzburg die deutschen und österreichischen Künstler zu einem dreitägigen Künstlerfest. Die Rede des Staatsministers Schmerling beim Festmahl wurde als ein Ereignis gefeiert. Die beiden Themen, welche Schmerling in langer freier Rede entwickelte, waren: Die Bedeutung der Kunst im Staate und die geistige Herrschaft des deutschen Elementes in Österreich. Selten

hat ein österreichischer Staatsmann diese beiden Momente mit solcher Freiheit und Entschiedenheit entwickelt." Hanslick, *AML/W*, 187.

104. Applegate, "What Is German Music?" 30.

105. "Für Goethes 'Faust' gebe ich den ganzen Sophokles hin, für 'Hermann und Dorothea' Miltons 'Paradies' samt der 'Messiade' von Klopstock, für Schillers 'Tell' oder 'Wallenstein' alle Tragödien von Racine, für Dickens, für Gottfried Keller, Paul Heyse, Alphonse Daudet, Turgeniew die gesamte Belletristik des siebzehnten und achtzehnten Jahrhunderts." Hanslick, *AML/W*, 405.

106. "Nicht anders ergeht es mir im Bereich der Musik; ich kann nichts dafür. Ich würde lieber den ganzen Heinrich Schütz verbrennen sehen als das 'deutsche Requiem,' lieber Palestrinas Werke als die Mendelssohns, lieber alle Konzerte und Sonaten von Bach als Schumanns oder Brahms' Quartette. Für den einen 'Don Juan.' 'Fidelio' oder 'Freischütz' gebe ich mit Freuden den ganzen Gluck hin." Ibid., 405.

107. "Für die Geschichte beginnt mir unsere lebendige Musik mit Bach und Händel. Für mein Herz beginnt sie erst mit Mozart, gipfelt in Beethoven, Schumann und Brahms." Ibid., 407.

108. Information taken from Hanslick, AML. Names have been completed and alternative spellings noted as necessary. (Duplicate figures are only listed once.)

109. Princess Stéphanie of Belgium.

110. Eduard Schön.

111. Goethe's grandchild.

112. Goethe's grandchild.

Chapter Ten

"Faust und Hamlet in Einer Person"

The Musical Writings of Eduard Hanslick as Part of the Gender Discourse in the Late Nineteenth Century

Marion Gerards

Reading Hanslick's autobiography *Aus meinem Leben* (1894), one could be forgiven for thinking that both a public discourse on gender and the women's movement were completely absent in Vienna during the latter part of the nineteenth century;[1] for nowhere does Hanslick refer to this socially and politically rousing topic.[2] Events such as the Prater massacre in August 1848, which witnessed the brutal suppression of a protest by female workers against a 25 percent pay cut, go completely unmentioned. Had this been pointed out to Hanslick, presumably he would have retorted that his job as music critic had nothing to do with the gender debate; his task was to comment on and judge musical compositions, concerts, and performing artists rather than sociopolitical issues. In other words, his area of responsibility was not politics, but the music and arts pages.[3] As Carl Dahlhaus has pointed out, however, "literature about music is no mere reflection of what happens in the musical practice of composition, interpretation, and reception," but rather the material that is perceived acoustically only becomes an actual aesthetic event (i.e., music) by virtue of its reception—by being discussed.[4] I would apply this further and argue that the reception of and writing about music are constitutive elements of music. The extent to which the discussion of music is affected by contemporary thought processes is something that Dahlhaus explains elsewhere: "The general level of knowledge of a particular period affords the author several different formulations, and these are no less important for the content and validity of his insights than for his observations on the music itself. The selection, accentuation and interpretation of the facts from which a theory is 'deduced'—allegedly via simple induction—is by and large contingent on the linguistic categories of the age that restrict thought."[5] The terms used to reflect on music and talk about musical meaning refer to categories governing relevant societal discourses. Given that gender is regarded to be a central structuring mechanism in the formation of society, and given that Eduard Hanslick, the most influential music critic of the period and an advocate of aesthetic formalism, does not consciously reflect on or mention the women's movement in his autobiography, this article examines whether Hanslick's music-critical writings were influenced by the gender debate and its accompanying connotations. A brief historical overview is necessary to chart the gender debate in Austria in the second half of the nineteenth century and to show its impact on Hanslick's life and work. Following this, and by drawing on a number of examples in their sociohistorical context, I aim to show how the discourses on gender and music are interconnected in Hanslick's writings.

The Women's Movement in Vienna between 1850 and 1900

In the nineteenth century, gender theories[6] proceeded from the assumption that the sexes were polarized "by nature" and that men and women were to be seen as "immutable beings by virtue of their specific gender":[7] the man was seen to be inherently active, strong, daring, rational and independent, while the woman was passive, emotional, weak and dependent. The binary nature of the bourgeois gender system—present in countless other dichotomies such as nature/culture, feeling/reason—posits fundamental categories of perception and thought.[8] This dichotomous hierarchy of gender characteristics possessed discursive agency as an ideological and ordered construct. At the same time, there were both individual deviations from the norm and criticisms of this construct, especially during the bourgeois debates on equality and freedom when the calls for equal rights for women became ever more persistent.

During the revolutions of 1848 Austria experienced the first stirrings of a women's movement. One of its pioneers was Karoline von Perin (1808–88) who founded the "Wiener demokratischer Frauenverein" (Viennese Democratic Women's Society) and who was closely linked with the Viennese musical writer Alfred Julius Becher. Becher later rose to the position of leader of the Viennese radicals. Hanslick discussed his subsequent fate in some detail in his autobiography.[9]

During the following years the women's movement in Austria become increasingly inactive, and it was only in the wake of the economic crisis of 1866 that the Wiener Frauenerwerbsverein (Viennese Society for Working Women) was founded. Initially, this society established sewing and knitting circles; in the 1870s, it founded liberal arts colleges and even a commercial college for women to prepare impoverished, widowed or unmarried middle-class women to earn a living. One of the few jobs available to women at that time was teaching the piano. Many women who could play the piano (even if only at a preliminary level) gave piano lessons, however modest the resulting income might be.[10] Hanslick was wont to complain about the "ever-growing numbers of proletarian piano teachers and virtuosos, in particular those of the fairer sex," and also mocked the "horde of women pianists, singers, violin-playing fairies and witches,"[11] all of whom wanted to be heard and judged, as a favorable review from Vienna meant that they could go on to teach or give recitals in the provinces. Clearly, the terms "violin-playing fairy" or "violin-playing witch" are derogatory, implying criticism of the women's musical capabilities and artistic claims. Hanslick does not comment at all, however, on the precarious social situation facing unmarried middle-class women who were denied educational and professional opportunities by virtue of their gender.

It was not until 1878 that young Austrian women were granted the right to take the final school exam [*Matura*], studying for this by way of private tuition. Moreover, the *Matura* did not automatically admit them to third-level studies, as they were denied matriculation (the so-called *Reifeklausel* or maturity clause). Consequently, Hanslick's lectures in the history of music at the University of Vienna (from October 1856 on) could only be attended by male students. He was, however, asked—"by ladies especially (who were excluded from attending university lectures)"[12]—whether he could open up his lectures to a nonstudent audience. In 1858 he held the first cycle of eight lectures on "The History of Music up to Beethoven," which he continued in 1859 with "The History of Music from Beethoven to the Present," and in 1860 with "The History of Opera."[13] This series marked the start of more popular and accessible academic lectures.

The real start of the women's movement in Austria dates from 1888, when self-employed women in Lower Austria were stripped of their right to vote for the state parliament—a right they had held since 1861. Auguste Fickert, Marie Lang, and Rosa Mayreder founded the Allgemeiner Österreichischer Frauenverein (General Society for Women in Austria) in 1893 and called for complete equality for women, admittance to all institutes of education, equal job prospects with equal pay conditions, and general, equal and direct suffrage (although this was not granted until 1918).[14]

In the discursive media of the age—in newspapers, literature, theater, painting, educational manuals, theological, philosophical, legal, medical or sociological publications,[15] at public gatherings and protests—the women's campaign for emancipation, educational prospects, and the right to vote was hotly debated on a daily basis, and went hand in hand with a controversial discussion about "natural" gender qualities. But as Peter Gay has pointed out, what these debates actually contributed to "the bourgeois experience retains much of its mystery, buried as feelings often were in intimate correspondence and private jottings."[16] However, they did impact on writings and reflections on music. These will now be examined more closely with respect to the music reviews and other writings of Eduard Hanslick.

Public Discourses: Music and Concert Reviews

In the second half of the nineteenth century, reports and reviews served the needs of continually expanding concert audiences for information about music and musical life in their own and other cities. Indeed, the middle of the 1860s witnessed a veritable explosion in the number of newspapers and journals (both titles and print runs) by comparison to 1848, when the main Viennese post office recorded 3.5 million annual newspaper deliveries; this number had risen to 20.5 million by 1868 and 51 million by 1887,[17] when every leading daily newspaper carried articles on musical life. By the middle of the 1880s, there were more than 500 journals in circulation in Vienna, of which twenty were dedicated to the arts.[18]

Music reviews in journals or concert guides document an author's subjective reaction to the music; thus they are a contemporary verdict and address a specific readership. Such reviews translate musical perception into accessible language; the musical experience is given literary expression, while the vocabulary and kind of commentary influence the aural expectations of the concert-going audience:

> Reading about music and adopting the language of description and judgment influenced the aural expectations of the audience and their sense of what constituted coherence, form, beauty, symmetry, and the logic of musical argument and speech. The audience ... listened to music through the medium of prose translations of the musical experience which helped define the emotional and intellectual meaning of the music heard by the audience in concert.[19]

Eduard Hanslick, the foremost critic of the nineteenth century and founder of the music pages in the papers, wrote his reviews chiefly for the *Neue Freie Presse*, the most important and also the largest daily paper in Vienna. His judgment could influence the acceptance or rejection of a work. Between 1870 and 1900, his collected reviews appeared in compilations, supplemented toward the end of the 1860s by his two-volume history of Viennese concert life. In addition, his polemical treatise *Vom Musikalisch-Schönen* (*On the Musically Beautiful*) appeared in 1854, in which he developed his principles of music aesthetics. According to these, "every art has as its goal to externalize an idea actively emerging in the artist's imagination. In the case of music, this idea is a tonal idea, not a conceptual idea which has first been translated into tones." And assuming that the tones take up the idea of the artist, "the spiritual energy and distinctiveness of each composer's imagination make their mark upon the product as character." This means that it is justified to talk of "a musical theme as majestic, graceful, tender, dull, hackneyed, but all these expressions describe the musical character of the passage." Hanslick goes on to say that although "we often choose terms from the vocabulary of our emotional life: arrogant, peevish, tender, spirited, yearning . . . we can also take our descriptions from other realms of appearance, however, and speak of fragrant, vernal, hazy, chilly music."[20] Within the context of this basic premise of music aesthetics, it is apposite to ask from which "realms of appearance" Hanslick takes his concepts when writing about music in his reviews, as they show up the categories and gender connotations through which musical meaning is communicated.

Masculinity as Sign of Quality in Music and Musicians

In the first movement of Symphony No. 1 in C Minor, op. 68, by Johannes Brahms, Hanslick identifies passionate pathos and a Faustian struggle; in the *Andante* a long, drawn-out and noble song is heard, while in the *Scherzo*, melodic and rhythmic charm is absent. In the slow introduction to the fourth movement, "from darkening clouds the song of the woodland horn rises clear and sweet above the tremolo of the violins. All hearts tremble with the fiddles in anticipation."[21] Overall, his assessment of Brahms's foray into the genre of the symphony is expressed as follows: "Brahms recalls Beethoven's symphonic style not only in his individually spiritual and supra-sensual expression, the beautiful breadth of his melodies, the daring and originality of his modulations, and his sense of polyphonic structure, but also—and above all—in the manly and noble seriousness of the whole."[22]

In addition to specific structural features such as melodic shape, modulations, and polyphony, Hanslick describes the character of the symphony using terms that are borrowed from the emotional sphere (e.g., the Greek *pathos* connotes suffering, pain, passion, or solemn emotion)[23] or employ natural and mythological concepts (e.g., thunderstorms, Faust), thus imbuing the description with poetic content. In specifying his overall judgment, Hanslick later opts for the term *Ernst* (seriousness or earnestness) derived from the Middle-High German noun *ernest* and signifying something like "combat, steadfastness, and sincerity."[24] The positive meaning of the term *Ernst* is further underscored by two interrelated adjectives: the adjective *männlich* (male) with its connotations of strength and rationality in accordance with the perceived order of the sexes at that time, and the adjective *hoch*, used here in the sense of "exalted" or "superior," to express the notion of rank and dignity. Crowning it all is the comparison with Beethoven, by means of which Hanslick attaches the concepts of musical quality and aesthetic value to the symphony. This example shows quite strikingly how structural listening and associative or emotional listening can influence each other, thus contradicting Hanslick's own request for a formal and structural mode of receiving the work, that is, one that should "continuously follow and anticipate the composer's designs," and result in a mode of aesthetic listening that yields "unemotional yet heartfelt pleasure."[25]

Hanslick uses similar metaphors and concepts in his review of Brahms's Symphony No. 2 in D Major, op. 73. For example, "Its essential characteristics can best be defined as serene cheerfulness, at once manly and gentle, animated alternately by jolly good humor and reflective seriousness."[26] The adjective *manly* is used in combination with *serene* and *cheerfulness* in order to highlight the carefree nature of the music. *Cheerfulness* suggests a bright mood that takes a two-pronged approach in the symphony: one being a playful mood,[27] going in the direction of increasing gaiety and even arriving at humor, the other geared toward the more sober emotional sphere of seriousness and thoughtfulness, a cheerful serenity in the face of the inadequacies in the world.[28] The chosen adjectives show up quite clearly the contrast to the first symphony: in place of passion, pathos, or temerity we have calm, gentleness, bright disposition, and cheerful composure. The adjective *manly* in conjunction with the reference to thoughtful seriousness makes it clear that this is not about superficial feelings or flirtations. The overall meaning of masculinity or manliness thus ensures the lasting compositional and poetic value of the symphony.

In his review of Brahms's Symphony No. 3, op. 90, Hanslick once again falls back on concepts of masculinity, for instance, in describing the prevailing mood of this symphony as the embodiment of self-assured and active energy, even if the heroism is free of warlike connotations. Two resounding forte chords in the brass open the first movement, and are followed by the "belligerent theme."[29] Here Hanslick avoids explicit reference to masculinity, although the adjectives and concepts ("self-confident," "active," "strength," "heroic," "belligerent") hint at a connection. In the case of Brahms's Violin Concerto in D Major, op. 77, Hanslick alludes unequivocally to the masculinity concept of his age, describing the concerto as a "work of elevated and powerful stature, yet also exhibiting that calm and genuinely male cheerfulness which to our joy gains momentum in the mind of the composer."[30]

In his 1974 dissertation on the music aesthetics and criticism of Eduard Hanslick, Werner Abegg points out that particularly when reviewing works by Johannes Brahms, Hanslick does not restrict himself to tracing musical forms or describing the musical material; rather, he writes about feelings in music or even ascribes extramusical content to music.[31] The expressive meaning of music to be found in its formal composition is not adequately described by analytical or technical terminology. What Hanslick instead tries to do is to capture the musical "idea" via concepts and adjectival terms, metaphors, and associations. In this, he was reliant on prevailing concepts and formulations that would both express his views and be familiar to the general public. As is clear from the examples quoted above, one of these was the meaning implicit in masculinity that enabled certain male qualities (in accordance with the prevailing concept of gender) to be applied to the character of the music. The relevance of gender for the discourse on music is reflected in Hanslick's decision to choose gender connotations as conceptual categories with which to describe and evaluate music—connotations that corresponded to nineteenth-century bourgeois notions of masculinity. According to Hanslick, Brahms's "masculine" compositions are characterized by attributes such as seriousness, boldness, strength, rationality, logic, and dignity. They correspond to the catalogue of male virtues laid down by the "Order of the Sexes."[32] Thus, masculinity is an unequivocal sign of quality and one which Hanslick only confers on Brahms and a few other composers and their works—one such person being his teacher, Václan Jan Tomášek (1774–1850),

> the "musical pope" or "musical Dalai Lama" of Prague, . . . an established composer, who was innovative, prolific and disciplined. His music was always masculine and full of character and intimacy, his songs not at all sentimental but full of wit and life, his piano pieces without coquettishness, and his church music dignified and glorious. If anything was lacking in his music, one would have to mention mellifluousness and sensual attractions.[33]

Accordingly, Tomášek's *Rhapsodies* were praised highly: "Such nourishing and healthy food! The volume is an example of Tomášek's artistic autonomy, which has led him to create new and unheard of forms, and is also testimony to the occasionally bitter, but always masculine and powerful spirit of his music."[34]

Another example is Franz Liszt, whom Hanslick visited in 1846 during one of the latter's stays in Vienna: "I met the celebrated composer in his hotel; at that time he was bursting with vigor and youthful, male charm. . . . I don't need to say much about Liszt's playing here. Suffice to say: it made an enormous impression on me, as it does on everyone. I have still to hear a more brilliant, bold and polished performance: it was incredible."[35] To describe a male artist as not masculine is a damning judgment, as can be seen in Hanslick's assessment of Johann Friedrich Kittl (1806–68), director of the Prague Conservatory:

> Though a composer and conductor of considerable talent, Kittl always came across as lacking in male dignity, and as someone who was ingratiating, petty and vain. His outward appearance seemed to confirm this; he was a rotund youth, boasting an oily double chin and indistinct facial expressions. As the *enfant gâté* of the aristocracy, especially of ladies, he owed his directorship of the conservatoire—from a young age—to their protection of him; he succeeded Dionys Weber, who was a man of years, dignified, and pedantic.[36]

Hanslick used the adjective *masculine* not only for composers and their works, but also to describe performance skills and abilities—for example, Brahms's piano technique: "His technique can be compared to a strong, tall man, who walks around somewhat aimlessly and who takes little pride in sartorial matters."[37] Or, in another example, Brahms is "a piano virtuoso with panache, whose brilliant, manly recitals scale interpretative heights while demonstrating superlative technique."[38] In his description of Brahms's personal style Hanslick invokes yet another gendered simile when, with reference to Beethoven, he compares the music of Brahms and Schubert:

> Whereas Schubert took up and made his own out of the gentle, girlish (Schumann's words), "Provençal element" in Beethoven's music, Brahms adopted the manly, impassioned, Germanic element of his master. Schubert is far more charming, melodic, sensual than Brahms, and as a result more direct; but in Brahms's large-scale compositions there is more of the unified energy and strictly logical thought progression that give Beethoven's creations their sense of inner necessity.[39]

At the end of the nineteenth century, Beethoven was generally hailed as the most masculine of all composers,[40] and yet Hanslick credits him with male and female qualities, concepts that he distinguishes in terms of gender in the music of Brahms and Schubert. Gentle, girlish, charming, sensual, and melodic—this is how he views Schubert's music;[41] while Brahms's is masculine, impassioned, energized, and logical. This quotation is also interesting for its linking of musical gender coding with cultural attributes. Female and sensual music à la Schubert is seen as the prerogative of a Provençal-Mediterranean cultural circle, while the music of Brahms with its energetic, masculine, and logical principles embodies the northern-Germanic values of the national German culture. In other words, in the discourse on music, gender connotations are used not just to make musical judgments on specific works or composers, but also (by means of these judgments) to comment on the musical styles of different cultural spheres. The gendered discussion of music was therefore anchored in both the discourse on the sexes and in the formation and demarcation of cultural identity. Regarding the link between masculinity and nationalism in Brahms-reception, Marcia Citron makes the following comment:

> In this light, it is striking that Brahms's symphonies all appeared *after* unification. Do they represent the "perfected" masculinist trajectory of nationalism and a triumph over the "feminine" symphonies of Romantic predecessors? Perhaps Hanslick's comment that the First Symphony "is a possession of which the nation may be proud" is meant to show that the work supplants the earlier, feminine attempts at the symphony—by Mendelssohn, Schumann, and others—and their potential status as representatives of Germanness. Constructing a seductive Trinity of Brahms's Symphony, unified nation, and masculinist trajectory, Hanslick has the masculinity of the First Symphony express the strength of the new German nation.[42]

Hanslick contends that heightened masculinity is necessary if someone is interested in writing a symphony, as this can only be achieved by someone who feels like "Faust and Hamlet in one and the same person."[43] Faust is the prototype of the person in search of knowledge while transcending his own limitations: the larger-than-life Titan personality who is striving for self-realization; Hamlet, by contrast, is a man destroyed by a sacred duty he can "neither fulfill nor shake off."[44] And Hanslick continues: this person does not just have to be the reincarnation of Faust and Hamlet rolled into *one*, but must also be affected by the suffering and misery of the whole of humankind.[45] With that, the personal premises of the composing (and receiving) subject have to realign themselves to notions of grandeur that are hard to surpass.

"Feminine" Response to Music and Pathological Listening

In contrast to the positive qualities implicit in the concept of masculinity, femininity is unequivocally negatively charged. Rather than associating this second meaning with Brahms, Hanslick links it to Wagner: "The music of *Lohengrin* [is] gentle, spineless, and often affected," and only the "unmusical and sentimental souls" get excited about *Lohengrin*, the opera that is "the favorite of all sensitive ladies." *Tannhäuser*, by contrast, is "more powerful, masculine, and natural."[46] Hanslick never refers explicitly to "feminine" or "not masculine" music; while he opts for the comparative form "more masculine" [*männlicher*] to refer to *Tannhäuser*, the music of *Lohengrin* is still described as "masculine," albeit less so than *Tannhäuser*. However, the adjectives *gentle, spineless* and *affected*, in conjunction with the reference to the sensitive female lovers of this music, carry negative connotations, thereby devaluing the work as a whole.

Pertinent here is Nietzsche's verdict on Brahms in *The Case of Wagner*, in which he alleges Brahms exhibits "the melancholy of incapacity. . . . In particular, he is the musician for a certain type of dissatisfied women."[47] Nietzsche's polemical treatise on Wagner was written in 1888. Disappointed with the first Festspiele at Bayreuth in 1876, Nietzsche became ever more estranged from Wagner and accused him of having poisoned [*krank gemacht*] music. He felt that Wagner's music was putting a large strain on the nerves of its listeners, which was a possible explanation for its appeal to women.[48] And yet, in the second postscript he comes to the conclusion that there is no alternative to Wagner, there being no one strong and self-assured enough to halt music's demise. Not even Brahms, according to Nietzsche, is able to compose music that is any better than Wagner's—it is just more trivial, appealing to a certain class of persons, namely dissatisfied women. Wagner's music is also more appreciated by women, but the female Wagnerite is, in Nietzsche's opinion, more interesting and more charming than the female Brahmsian. In other words, being listened to and appreciated by a female audience is an indication of the diminished quality of a work or a composer. Nietzsche and Hanslick are of one mind here, even if they end up criticizing two composers representing polar opposites in the "War of the Romantics."[49]

As mentioned earlier, Hanslick wrote of Brahms's Symphony No. 1 that at the sound of the alpine-horn melody in the fourth movement, all hearts tremble in anticipation.[50] This formulation appears again, almost word for word, in the correspondence between the surgeon and amateur musician Theodor Billroth and his friend Brahms: "At the horn solo, all hearts trembled in anticipation with the fiddles," wrote Billroth, specifying the gender of the hearts: "I felt how all hearts near me, especially those of the women, trembled with the violins and the muted tone."[51] Billroth's description must have been in circulation amongst Brahms's acquaintances, eventually finding its way into Hanslick's review. Even without the unambiguous gendered designation, the subtle criticism is clear. In the gender dichotomy of the time, the heart was synonymous with love and feelings and was thus feminine, its opposite being masculine reason and rationality. A feminine response to music, or rather, an effusive and emotional response on the part of female listeners, points to a music that is intensely (perhaps too much so) emotional and sensual. A brief look at Hanslick's *Vom Musikalisch-Schönen* sheds light on the meaning and context here.

In the fifth chapter, "Musical Perception: Aesthetic versus Pathological," Hanslick deals with the perception of music, contrasting the "aesthetic" with the "pathological," where the "elemental in music, i.e., sound and motion" is perceived in "passive receptivity." This mode of listening—"a constant twilight state of sensation and reverie, a drooping and yearning in resounding emptiness"[52]—is, according to Hanslick, pathological, and is contrasted with conscious listening, which "is the only artistic, true form; the raw passion of savages and the gushing of the music-enthusiast can be lumped together in a single category contrary to it."[53] Hanslick recognizes that only the musically educated are capable of listening aesthetically.[54] Rationality, reason, knowledge, education, and an active understanding of the formal requirements of music are necessary in order to be able to practice the aesthetic listening stipulated by Hanslick. Simply responding with feeling, enthusiasm, and musical illiteracy leads to pathological listening. Consequently, Hanslick lists "the musical explosions"[55] of Bettina von Arnim as an example of pathological listening and describes this "music-besotted lady" as the "prototype of all vague enthusiasm."[56] The "rotten aesthetic of emotions"[57] reveals itself in an effusive, emotional, and associative musical response, that is, where there is an emotional reaction rather than an intellectual and rational debate about music. The term "feminine" is apt here, as this type of passive and emotional listening without any kind of active, rational, and intellectual engagement can also be observed in the male sex—and Hanslick even detects it in a musical nation: "Like many individual persons, some nations are able to give over to it only with great difficulty. The tyranny of the upper vocal part among the Italians has one main cause in the mental indolence of those people, for whom the sustained penetration with which the northerner likes to follow an ingenious web of harmonic and contrapuntal activity is beyond reach."[58] Taking into account the personal requirements on the part of the listeners (male and female) and noting that Hanslick describes music in Germanic and masculine terms and as suitable to be confronted only by "Faust and Hamlet in one and the same person," it can be assumed that in his opinion, it is German males, above all, who are in a position to respond appropriately to music; a positive male response is a measure of the aesthetic merits of a composition. Conversely, an effusive and emotional response to a composition by a woman, or by women, is an indicator of the formal weakness of a composition. Accordingly, if sentimental ladies, above all, are in raptures about Wagner's *Lohengrin*, and (female) hearts beat faster on hearing the horn solo in the fourth movement of Brahms's Symphony No. 1, then this music speaks "only" to those who respond emotionally to music, while those who are capable of engaging with it critically and rationally remain unmoved.

A similarly derogatory opinion can be detected in Hanslick's assessment of a song collection popular at the time which, in keeping with the very basic musical skills required for performances in the home, is rejected as a "musical, sentimental commodity for our suburban Fräuleins."[59] His reviews of piano recitals by some female pianists—which may be read in the context of the hierarchy of the sexes at that time—also contain negative comments on the physical and intellectual capabilities of women: "Miss Nanette Falk (women are taking over on the piano front) gave a well-attended second recital in the hall of the Musikverein. She played the familiar *Rondo capriccioso* (Op. 14) by Mendelssohn very nicely indeed; its delicate flippancy suits female virtuosity perfectly."[60] If a female pianist dared to perform a somewhat less "delicate" piece—one by Liszt, for example—one reads: "Only the most powerful and courageous performers emerge unscathed from the glorious combat with Liszt's dramatic "Hungarian Rhapsody." Tender hands, such as those belonging to our recitalist [Fräulein Fritz] are best advised to stay well away; it is quite frightening to watch a panther being attacked with a knitting-needle."[61] In this example, Hanslick picks up on gendered topoi that serve to make his derogatory criticism all the clearer: the delicate hands of the pianist are able to manage knitting needles and are thus perfectly adequate for a housewife and mother, but as pianist's hands they simply cannot get such an ambitious work under control. Admittedly, Hanslick criticizes elsewhere the piano playing of some male pianists[62] and acknowledges the artistry of Clara Schumann.[63] However, the above two examples highlight the reception problems facing many female pianists who, by daring to appear in public as performing artists, were seen to have overstepped the mark. Moreover, they performed canonical works already considered gendered, and their physical presence on the stage was under gendered observation.[64]

Bearing this in mind, Hanslick's description of the singer Sophie Wohlmuth, whom he got to know in his capacity as music critic, and subsequently married on April 29, 1876, when he was fifty-one years old, is most interesting. Hanslick was moved by her warm voice and deeply felt performance: "It wasn't just her talent, but her whole being that interested me: she was modest, reticent, shy, yet when she sang she blossomed unexpectedly."[65] She turned down a contract with the municipal theater in Leipzig, but as Hanslick explained: "My wife has renounced the stage, but not art per se.... She has appeared incognito in public when she enhanced my lectures in Pest, Prague, and Graz by illustrating them with songs." He adds that Professor Woltmann of Prague put it beautifully when he admired "the idea of the selfless subordination of a female artist to an academic cause, which is twice as moving and beautiful when evidence of the love of a woman for her husband."[66]

This is the "ideal woman" then, who, in accordance with the gender expectations of the age, gives up her own career and uses her musical talent to further the academic career of her husband. In short, it is clear that both in the description of his spouse and in the writing of his music reviews Hanslick was influenced by the gender discourse of his time.

Gender Connotations in Musical Narratives

The literary analogies to and personification of music take center stage in many of Hanslick's reviews. A good example of this is to be found in Hanslick's review of Brahms's Double Concerto for Violin and Cello, op. 102:

> A double concerto may be compared to a play that has not one, but two heroes, both of whom evoke our sympathy and admiration, but who also get in the way of one another. If there is one particular musical genre that can be said to rest on the superiority of its victorious hero, it is the concerto. Is painting not similar in this respect? Artists rail against double portraits, as they don't like having to immortalize a man and woman side by side on canvas. Two identical instruments ... blend ... better in a concerto than these two principals of such contrasting pitch: the violin and cello.... In the same way ... we get the impression of a play in which every character speaks in a sophisticated and witty manner, but where there is no sign of a plot.[67]

Hanslick devises a narrative scheme in keeping with the meaning of the Italian "concertare." He views the concerto as a drama in which the solo instrument is personified as a hero competing against the orchestra or—to put it more neutrally—as an animated conversion between the two. The plot of the double concerto (so to speak) is analogous to a drama involving two different heroes—or a hero and heroine, given the gendered double portrait and the respective registers of the instruments. However, the presence of two solo instruments ultimately leads to structural complications, which Hanslick describes as the action coming to a standstill. For Hanslick, therefore, music can be experienced as a narrative, or plot. In his discussion of Hanslick's *Vom Musikalisch-Schönen*, Fred Everett Maus comes to a similar conclusion: "Hanslick attributes a story-like quality to music.... These descriptions depict music ... as sound that is understood the way one understands other people, by attributing thoughts and by following a succession of responses to situations."[68] A final example of Hanslick's gendered attitude toward music is a review of Beethoven's *Eroica*:

> For my feelings, the "heroic symphony" is not heroic at all when considered in its totality, though it is at certain isolated moments. It is *lofty*, and could with reason have been characterized as such, just as the celebrated C minor sonata is. But, heroic, belligerent, victorious—the "Eroica" is none of these, if the terms are applied conventionally, e.g., to the entry of a triumphant general. There are only very few isolated flashes of *military* strength and grandeur. The start of the first movement is the most powerful: the main motif, a pure triad, makes an energetic entry as if announcing the arrival of the hero. However, just four bars later the confident tone has grown weak, with mournful chords suggesting private grief. ... Yes, the hero enters, but he is already bleeding to death.[69]

Hanslick was not the only music critic to rely on the implications of gender distinctions in order to more precisely formulate his musical judgment, narrativize musical action by means of plot, and personify musical motives as heroes. It is striking how many reviews of the time are replete with images of gender dichotomy, and thus semantically laden. Two examples follow, this time from reviews of Brahms.[70]

In an article on new pieces by Brahms, Hermann Kretzschmar looks closely at Brahms's Piano Concerto No. 1 in D Minor, op. 15. Adopting a style characteristic of his (later) concert guides, he gives a narrative interpretation reminiscent of epic theater. He focuses on the first movement in particular:

> The orchestra is completely frantic, with warriors screaming violently.... One particular moment [the chain of trills in the strings] is unforgettable; and whoever has read "Beowulf" is bound to think of this scene where the terrible beast of the bog appears in the mead hall. ... It appears like words of the most furious determination. ... Again and again, the sinister hero stands before us, singing these first, horror-filled bars, violent and yet utterly fearless, albeit of gloomy disposition, his steely eye fixed on the unending wretchedness of human existence. He hears the good-natured melodies, and sees the loving and attractive pictures: but when he decides to linger a moment, the warning voices are to be heard. ... Listening to this movement many conjure up images of Cain, the furies, and other such things.[71]

By describing the first movement of the piano concerto in terms of the legend of Beowulf,[72] Kretzschmar personalizes the music material by creating a male protagonist and aligning the musical form and structure with the battle fought by the hero. This hero has to fulfill all that is demanded of him, and not be led astray by amiable, tender, and enticing temptations. In the concerto these are heard in the lyrical episodes (e.g., mm. 26–62) or in the piano solo after the orchestral exposition (from m. 91 onward). A narrative structure is evident here, like those forming the basis of Max Kalbeck's accounts of Brahms's music.

Kalbeck was another noted music critic in Vienna, where he had been resident since the 1880s, and, like Hanslick, was a member of Brahms's inner circle.[73] His biography of the composer marks the culmination of a gendered interpretation and contextualization of Brahms's music. The biography contains numerous detailed poetic interpretations; for example, of the first movement of Symphony No. 3, op. 90, he writes that the actual opening motif seems to "lure the hero away from the fairy-tale Romantic forest into the snares of game and battle,"[74] who on his adventures encounters a

> pleasant and pretty girl, able to win over any male heart! She seems to be the embodiment of innocence and nature. . . . Just look and see how she dances and sways, how she twists and turns, how every graceful movement makes her supple body ever more attractive! . . . This masterfully drawn portrait shows characteristic traits of the female par excellence. The gynaecophile will adore her, the misogynist ask offensively whether the beautiful shepherdess is perhaps not a hay-scented urban lady in disguise. . . . The delightful temptress only needs to give a swish of her skirts, and the lovesick fool will be enchanted by her curtseying.[75]

Kalbeck goes on to describe how the lovesick fool is prevented in the nick of time from agreeing to marry the savvy seductress: "His broken heart mends and he is receptive to more ideal gratification."[76] Kalbeck thus focuses on the threats to male identity posed by the seductive wiles of the female. His interpretation is a prime example of how a narrative based on the pronounced gender typology of the nineteenth century can be applied to absolute music. This constitutes the triumph of the heroic male over the seductive female—a "tonal battle of the sexes."[77]

Motivation and Purpose

What does it mean when Hanslick and his colleagues personify music as a relatively famous hero, or when they talk about "the Faustian struggle,"[78] impassioned battles[79] or dangerous, seductive females in the music? The possible interpretations inherent in any composition regarded as an "open work of art"[80] mean that Hanslick and all other recipients have to rely on their respective modes of thinking and valuation. The chosen interpretative approach and terminology have to do with the recipients' own categories of thinking. Thus, by opting for gendered concepts and metaphors Hanslick has made a specific interpretative decision and ascribed extramusical meaning to music against a gendered backdrop. In musical terms, then, he wants to narrow down and clearly justify his own aesthetic judgment. Reverting to the masculine/feminine hermeneutic only makes sense when the preconceived ideas of gender, including the positive and negative connotations associated with this, are universally intelligible. The use of gender connotations is thus an indication that the male/female-dichotomy was indeed relevant for Hanslick and his readers—even if in his autobiography Hanslick does not enter into the topical gender debate.

By comparison with the interpretations of his colleagues Kretzschmar and Kalbeck, Hanslick's music reviews are certainly less affected by contemporary gender bias, yet they, too, are anchored in the gender discourse of the age. And because music cannot indicate extramusical themes in a precise manner—but instead leaves interpretive spaces for listeners to fill with their own ideas, topics, associations and concepts[81]—it is (also) possible within the musical discourse to assign concepts of masculinity and femininity to music and, in so doing, define or codify them. In this way, instrumental music functions as a screen upon which the topics within the discourse on gender can be projected. Viewed as such, the perception and public reception of music becomes a discursive medium of communication, precisely because musical structures are devoid of specific meaning and are (at least initially) gender neutral.[82] In the second half of the nineteenth century, the voices and narratives taking part in the public discourse on music were largely male;[83] in other words, it was an androcentric discourse, as men were prescribing the images and ideas influencing the way music was received. Within the public discourse on music, these men defined their own masculine identity by leaning on those concepts of femininity prevalent in the gender discourse of the time.

Because reception is always embedded in a sociocultural context—a context, moreover, that influences individual perception—cultural and historical parameters must always be taken into consideration. Individual perception is in turn dependent on the musical knowledge and skills, the fundamental aesthetic outlook, and the integration of the individual into social discourses. These external factors definitively determine the musical perception and general discussion of the music of the time. The cultural and historical context influences the reception and methods of reflecting on music, whose concepts (masculine/feminine) are adopted to justify an aesthetic value judgment, and whose ideas and thoughts, pictures, and narratives are associated with music.

One particular sociological aspect relating to the function of gender connotations in reviews of concerts frequented by the middle classes is worth noting: "Every people [sic] who comes together with a common . . . purpose to share an aesthetic experience generally constitutes a 'socialization' of private persons. It is ... a voluntarily conducted 'collectivization,' bound up within a non-obligatory *ad hoc* meeting."[84] And yet if a contemporary concertgoer, prior to attending a particular concert, had read a review by Hanslick (or by another critic) commenting on the "masculine and exalted seriousness" or "Faustian struggle" expressed in the symphony, then the formal characteristics of the piece being performed would be imbued with a set of gender images that could certainly have a socializing effect. Dotted and rising melodies, major tonalities, broken triadic motion, a forte dynamic, counterpoint, alternating themes, and tonal contrasts are just some of the musical structures considered to be masculine in Hanslick's time. If music is heard under these auspices, it attests to a masculine image characterized by power, energy, or even aggressiveness. Alternatively, certain narratives can be attributed to the music, where male heroes have to triumph in battle and resist female charms. Gendered analyses and reviews of concerts, which are an integral part of the public discourse on music, clearly do more than provide information on the aesthetic value of musical compositions—they are also socializing in the context of the gender debate.

Hanslick saw his role as music critic as "having a gradual and formative influence on the concertgoing public,"[85] and by this he meant the musical education of the concertgoers (male and female), rather than the socializing effect of his gendered observations on music. However, because his observations were embedded in the prevailing cultural context and gender discourse, they had a social and discursive impact, as Sara Mills pointed out with reference to Foucault: "The way in which we interpret things and events and position them within our frame of reference depends ... on the discursive structures. According to Foucault, these structures determine how things and events appear to us in real and material terms."[86] It is seen that discourses contain a significant and not-to-be underestimated frame of reference and influence; Judith Butler assigns them even a materializing force, as they influence our thought and actions, structure our perception and interpretation of reality, and shape our identity.[87]

In conclusion, the gender connotations in the music reviews of Eduard Hanslick possessed discursive significance within the cultural practice of the age; they influenced the way in which music in performance was thought of, interpreted, and received. The reviews must be understood in the context of the socially-established thought systems, one of these being the gender dichotomy in the latter half of the nineteenth century. In other words, Hanslick's gender-laden music reviews are not just part of the discourse on music, they are also inextricably linked to the contemporary discourse on gender. As such, they are part of the constant and unavoidable process of "doing gender."

Translated by Siobhán Donovan

Notes

All translations are by Siobhán Donovan unless otherwise stated.

1. Eduard Hanslick, *Aus meinem Leben*, ed. And with an afterword by Peter Wapnewski. (Kassel: Bärenreiter, 1987) (hereafter, *AML/W*).

2. The following discussion is taken in part from my published doctoral dissertation, *Frauenliebe—Männerleben: Die Musik von Johannes Brahms und der Geschlechterdiskurs im 19. Jahrhundert* (Cologne: Böhlau Verlag, 2010). I am grateful to the Böhlau publishing house for permitting me to quote excerpts in English translation.

3. Hanslick had been music critic in Vienna since 1846, first for the *Allgemeine Wiener Musikzeitung*, and then for the *Wiener Zeitung* (from 1847); from 1855 to 1864 for the *Presse* and from 1864 for the *Neue Freie Presse*. See Werner Abegg, "Hanslick, Eduard," in *Musik in Geschichte und Gegenwart*, ed. Ludwig Finscher, 2nd rev. ed., "Personenteil," vol. 8 (Kassel: Bärenreiter/Metzler, 2002), col. 667–72; Rudolf Bockhold, "Hanslick, Eduard," in *Allgemeine Deutsche Biographie und Neue Deutsche Biographie (Digitale Register)*, vol. 7 (Berlin: Duncker & Humblot 1966), 637–39.

4. See Carl Dahlhaus, *Die Idee der absoluten Musik* (Kassel: Bärenreiter, 1994), 66–67. This English translation taken from Carl Dahlhaus, *The Idea of Absolute Music*, trans. Roger Lustig (Chicago: University of Chicago Press, 1989), 63.

5. "Die in der allgemeinen Bildung einer Epoche bereitliegenden Formulierungsmöglichkeiten, über die ein Autor verfügt, sind für den Sach- und Wahrheitsgehalt der Einsichten, zu denen er gelangt, kaum weniger bedeutsam als seine Beobachtungen an Notentexten. Die Auswahl, Akzentuierung und Interpretation der Tatsachen, von denen eine Theorie—mit dem Anschein schlichter Induktion—'abgeleitet' wird, ist weitgehend von den Kategorien abhängig, die in der Sprache eines Zeitalters enthalten sind und den Horizont des Denkens begrenzen." Carl Dahlhaus, "Ästhetische Prämissen der 'Sonatenform' bei Adolf Bernhard Marx," *Archiv für Musikwissenschaft* 41 (1984): 73–85, repub. in Dahlhaus, *Klassische und romantische Musikästhetik* (Laaber: Laaber Verlag, 1988), 352.

6. For a good overview, see *Philosophische Geschlechtertheorien. Ausgewählte Texte von der Antike bis zur Gegenwart*, ed. Sabine Doyé, Marion Heinz, Friederike Kuster (Stuttgart: Reclam, 2002); Ute Frevert, "Bürgerliche Meisterdenker und das Geschlechterverhältnis. Konzepte, Erfahrungen, Visionen an der Wende zum 18. und 19. Jahrhundert," in *Bürgerinnen und Bürger: Geschlechterverhältnisse im 19. Jahrhundert*. ed. Ute Frevert, Kritische Studien zur Geschichtswissenschaft 77 (Göttingen: Vandenhoeck & Ruprecht, 1988), 17–48; Claudia Honegger, *Die Ordnung der Geschlechter. Die Wissenschaften vom Menschen und das Weib 1750–1850*, 1st ed. (Frankfurt/M.: Campus-Verlag, 1991); Ute Frevert, "*Mann und Weib, und Weib und Mann.*" *Geschlechterdifferenzen in der Moderne*, Beck'sche Reihe 1100 (Munich: Beck, 1995).

7. "Als in ihren Geschlechtseigentümlichkeiten unveränderliche Wesen." Frevert, *Mann und Weib*, 56.

8. Thomas Kühne, "Männergeschichte als Geschlechtergeschichte," in *Männergeschichte—Geschlechtergeschichte. Männlichkeit im Wandel der Moderne*, ed. Thomas Kühne, Reihe Geschichte und Geschlechter 14 (Frankfurt/M.: Campus-Verlag, 1996), 11.

9. Hanslick, *AML/W*, 92–94. Both she and Becher were captured after the suppression of the revolution and the *Frauenverein* folded. Becher was sentenced and executed, but Perin managed to emigrate to Munich. However, she lost custody of her three children, and her estate and assets were confiscated.

10. On piano teaching for women, see Claudia Schweitzer, "*ist übrigens als Lehrerinn höchst empfehlungswürdig.*" *Kulturgeschichte der Clavierlehrerin*, Schriftenreihe des Sophie Drinker Instituts 6 (Oldenburg: BIS-Verlag der Carl von Ossietzky Universität, 2008).

11. "Furchtbar anwachsende Proletariat der Klavierlehrer und Klaviervirtuosen, insbesondere weiblichen Geschlechts"; "die Schar der Pianistinnen, der kleinen Sängerinnen, Geigenfeen und Geigenhexen." Hanslick, *AML/W*, 399. On the reception of female pianists in French music criticism, see Katharine Ellis, "Female Pianists and Their Male Critics in Nineteenth-Century Paris," *Journal of the American Musicological Society* 50, no. 2–3 (1997): 353–85.

12. "Insbesondere von Damen (sie waren damals von den Universitätsvorlesungen ausgeschlossen)." Hanslick, *AML/W*, 174.

13. Ibid., 174–75. Not until 1897 were women admitted to study philosophy, and in the winter semester three regular auditors enrolled at the University of Vienna; 1900 saw the awarding of the first doctorates to women in philosophy and science.

14. On reaching the age of twenty-one, women were able to cast their vote in elections, but it was not until they turned twenty-nine that they were eligible to run as candidates. In 1907 universal male suffrage was introduced in Austria.

15. An example of this is the most famous emancipatory work of its time, *The Subjection of Women*, by Harriet Taylor Mill and John Stuart Mill, 1869, in which the supposedly "natural" characteristics of gender were analyzed as a social rather than natural fact. The German translation appeared in the same year.

16. Peter Gay, *Education of the Senses*, vol. 1 of *The Bourgeois Experience: Victoria to Freud* (New York: Oxford University Press, 1984), 172.

17. Leon Botstein, "Music and its Public: Habits of Listening and the Crisis of Musical Modernism in Vienna, 1870–1914" (PhD diss., Harvard University, 1985), 874.

18. Ibid., 863, 874.

19. Ibid., 878.

20. Hanslick, *Vom Musikalisch-Schönen: Ein Beitrag zur Revision der Ästhetik der Tonkunst*, vol. 1, ed. Dietmar Strauß (Mainz: Schott, 1990), 80–81 (hereafter *VMS*); Hanslick, *On the Musically Beautiful*, trans. Geoffrey Payzant (Indianapolis: Hackett, 1986), 31–32 (hereafter cited as *OMB*).

21. Eduard Hanslick, "Brahms. Erste Symphonie," in *Concerte, Componisten und Virtuosen der letzten fünfzehn Jahre. 1870–1885. Kritiken von Eduard Hanslick*, 3rd ed. (Berlin: Allgemeiner Verein für Deutsche Litteratur, 1896), 166. This translation taken from Hanslick, *Vienna's Golden Years of Music*, ed. and trans. Henry Pleasants (New York: Simon and Schuster, 1950), 134.

22. Hanslick, "Brahms. Erste Symphonie," 168; this translation from *Vienna's Golden Years*, 136.

23. *Herkunftswörterbuch: Etymologie der deutschen Sprache*, 3rd rev. and ext. ed. (Mannheim: Dudenverlag, 2001), 593–94.

24. Ibid., 186.

25. Hanslick, *VMS*, 133; *OMB*, 64.

26. Hanslick, *Concerte*, 225. This translation slightly amended from *Vienna's Golden Years*, 176.

27. Jacob Grimm and Wilhelm Grimm, *Deutsches Wörterbuch*, vol. 10 (Leipzig: S. Hirzel, 1877), col. 1907.

28. *Herkunftswörterbuch*, 349.

29. Hanslick, "Brahms: Dritte Symphonie in F-Dur," in *Concerte, Componisten und Virtuosen*, 362–63. This translation taken from *Vienna's Golden Years*, 39.

30. "Werk von hohem, starkem Wuchs, dabei von jener ruhigen, echt männlichen Heiterkeit, die zu unserer Freude immer mehr Boden gewinnt im Gemüte des Komponisten." Hanslick, "Virtuosen, Brahms' Violin-Concert (gespielt von Joachim)," in *Concerte, Componisten und Virtuosen*, 265–68.

31. Werner Abegg, *Musikästhetik und Musikkritik bei Eduard Hanslick* (Regensburg: Gustav Bosser Verlag, 1974), 64–67.

32. Honegger, *Ordnung der Geschlechter*.

33. "der 'Musikpapst' oder 'Musik-Daleilama' von Prag . . . ein bedeutender Komponist, erfindungsreich, fruchtbar, von strenger Schulung. Seine Musik ist immer männlich und charaktervoll; innig, ohne Weichlichkeit in den Liedern, geistreich, lebendig, ohne Koketterie in seinen Klavierstücken, würdevoll, auch prächtig in den Kirchenkompositionen. Wenn ihr eine Eigenschaft abging, so war es das Einschmeichelnde, sinnlich Reizende." Hanslick, *AML/W*, 21.

34. "Welch kräftige, gesunde Kost! Das Heft ist ein Beispiel von der künstlerischen Selbständigkeit, mit der Tomaschek sich neue, damals unerhörte Formen schuf, und von dem mitunter herben, aber stets männlich-kraftvollen Geist seiner Musik." Eduard Hanslick, *Sämtliche Schriften* 1/4, 395.

35. "Ich traf den Gefeierten, welcher damals in vollster Frische und männlich jugendlicher Anmut prangte, in seinem Hotel. . . . Über Liszts Spiel brauche ich mich hier nicht auszusprechen. Es machte mir, wie allen, den Eindruck des Außerordentlichen. Nie wieder habe ich genialer, kühner, glänzender, unbegreiflicher spielen gehört." Hanslick, *AML/W*, 54–55.

36. "Als Komponist und Dirigent von entschiedener Begabung, war Kittl im Leben ohne männliche Würde, schmeichlerisch und kleinlich eitel. Sein Äußeres stimmte dazu; ein dicker Jüngling mit einem fetten Doppelkinn und verschwommenem Gesichtsausdruck. *Enfant gâté* der Aristokratie, insbesondere der Damen, war er durch deren Protektion in jungen Jahren Direktor des Konservatoriums geworden; als Nachfolger des alten, würdevoll pedantischen Dionys Weber." Ibid., 44 (emphasis in original).

37. "Seine Technik ist wie ein kräftiger, hochgewachsener Mann, der aber etwas schlendernd und nachlässig gekleidet einhergeht." Eduard Hanslick, *Aus dem Concertsaal. Kritiken und Schilderungen aus den letzten 20 Jahren des Wiener Musiklebens nebst einem Anhang: Musikalische Reisebriefe aus England, Frankreich und der Schweiz* (Vienna: Wilhelm Braumüller, 1870), 258.

38. "Ein Klaviervirtuose in großem Stil, dessen männlicher, geistvoller Vortrag sich frei über einer riesigen Technik erhebt." Hanslick, *AML/W*, 222.

39. "Allein während Schubert das Weiche, Mädchenhafte (nach Schumanns Ausdruck) das 'provençalische Element' Beethovens selbständig weitergebildet hat, hält sich Brahms an die männliche, pathetische Seite, an das germanische Element des Meisters. Schubert ist ungleich reizvoller, melodiöser, sinnlicher als Brahms, er wirkt viel unmittelbarer; hingegen waltet in den großen Compositionen von Brahms mehr von jener zusammenhaltenden Kraft und strengen Logik der Gedanken, welche Beethovens Schöpfungen den Charakter innerer Nothwendigkeit ausgeprägt." Hanslick, "Brahms Clavierconcert in D-moll," in *Concerte, Componisten und Virtuosen*, 111.

40. See Beatrix Borchard, "Beethoven: Männlichkeitskonstruktionen im Bereich der Musik," in *Kunst, Geschlecht, Politik. Männlichkeitskonstruktionen und Kunst im Kaiserreich und in der Weimarer Republik*, ed. Martina Kessel (Frankfurt/M.: Campus-Verlag, 2005), 65; Scott Burnham, *Beethoven Hero* (Princeton, NJ: Princeton University Press, 1995); Robin Wallace, "Myth, Gender, and Musical Meaning. The *Magic Flute*, Beethoven, and 19th-Century Sonata Form Revisited," *Journal of Musicological Research* 19, no. 1

(1999): 1–25; Sanna Pederson, "Beethoven and Masculinity," in *Beethoven and His World*, ed. Scott Burnham and Michael Steinberg (Princeton, NJ: Princeton University Press, 2000), 313–31.

41. On Schubert, see Marie Agnes Dittrich, "Kein grollender Titan. Franz Schubert, der Österreicher," *Hamburger Jahrbuch für Musikwissenschaft* 15 (1998): 191–201.

42. Marcia Citron, "Männlichkeit, Nationalismus und musikpolitische Diskurse. Die Bedeutung von Gender in der Brahmsrezeption," in *History / Herstory. Alternative Musikgeschichten*, ed. Annette Kreutziger-Herr und Katrin Losleben (Köln: Böhlau-Verlag, 2009), 364, emphasis in original. The translated Hanslick quotation is from *Vienna's Golden Years*, 127–28. Citron's essay appears in English as "Gendered Reception of Brahms: Masculinity, Nationalism and Musical Politics," in *Masculinity and Western Musical Practice*, ed. Ian D. Biddle and Kirsten Gibson (Aldershot, UK: Ashgate, 2009), 150–51.

43. "Faust und Hamlet in Einer Person." Hanslick, *Aus dem Concertsaal*, 260.

44. "Weder tragen noch abwerfen kann." This characterization is to be found in Johann Wolfgang Goethe's *Wilhelm Meisters Lehr- und Wanderjahre* (book 4, chapter 13).

45. "The plight of the whole of humankind" (Der Menschheit ganzer Jammer) is a quotation from Goethe's *Faust I*, lines 4405–8. In the prison scene, Faust meets Margaret for the last time, and even at the prison door is struck by the cruelty of the institution: "I shudder once again, / The plight of the whole of humankind grips me. / She is living here, behind these damp walls, / Her crime was really an act of delusion!" (Mich fasst ein längst entwohnter Schauer, / Der Menschheit ganzer Jammer fasst mich an. / Hier wohnt sie, hinter dieser feuchten Mauer, / Und ihr Verbrechen war ein guter Wahn!)

46. "Gegen den 'Tannhäuser,' ist die 'Lohengrin'-Musik weichlich, marklos, oft geziert; sie wirkt wie das weiße Magnesiumlicht, in das wir nicht lange schauen können, ohne daß uns die Augen schmerzen. Dieses weiß flimmernde zuckende Licht ist es eben, wofür die unmusikalisch-sentimentalen Seelen schwärmen. 'Lohengrin' ist die Lieblingsoper aller gefühlvollen Damen. Ich finde den 'Tannhäuser' kräftiger, männlicher, natürlicher." Hanslick, *AML/W*, 217. In 1846 and in the context of his lengthy review of *Tannhäuser*, Hanslick described Wagner as the "most dramatically talented living composer," albeit criticizing him for his lack of melody and for his excessive harmonies. See Hanslick, *Sämtliche Schriften* 1/1, 59. From *Lohengrin* on, Hanslick distanced himself more and more from Wagner. See Dietmar Strauß, "Hanslicks Tannhäuser-Aufsatz im rezeptionsgeschichtlichen Kontext." Hanslick, *Sämtliche Schriften* 1/1, 315–22.

47. *Über Brahms: Von Musikern, Dichtern und Liebhabern. Eine Anthologie*, ed. Renate and Kurt Hofmann (Stuttgart: Reclam, 1997), 117. This translation taken from Friedrich Nietzsche, *The Case of Wagner*, in *Basic Writings of Nietzsche*, ed. and trans. Walter Kaufmann (New York: The Modern Library, 2000), 645.

48. Friedrich Nietzsche, "Der Fall Wagner," in Friedrich Nietzsche, *Der Fall Wagner; Goetzen-Dämmerung: Nietzsche contra Wagner*, ed. Peter Puetz (Munich: Goldmann, 1988).

49. For a more in-depth discussion of Nietzsche's opinion of Brahms, see Marcia Citron, "Gendered Reception of Brahms," 144–47. —Ed.

50. Eduard Hanslick, *Concerte, Componisten und Virtuosen der letzten fünfzehn Jahre*, 166. This translation taken from Pleasants, *Vienna's Golden Years*, 135.

51. "Bei dem Hornsolo zittern alle Herzen mit den Geigen um die Wette"; "Ich sah in meiner Nähe, wie alle zumal weiblichen Herzen mit den sordinierten Violinen um die Wette zitterten." *Billroth und Brahms im Briefwechsel. Mit Einleitung, Anmerkungen und 4 Bildtafeln* (Berlin: Urban & Schwarzenberg, 1935; repr. 1991), 228. Billroth wrote both letters on December 15, 1876, after attending a rehearsal of the symphony for its Viennese première on December 17. This translation taken from Brahms and Billroth,

Johannes Brahms and Theodor Billroth: Letters from a Musical Friendship, trans. and ed. Hans Barkan (Norman: University of Oklahoma Press, 1957), 42.

52. *VMS*, 127–28; *OMB*, 58.

53. *VMS*, 137; *OMB*, 63.

54. See *VMS*, 140; *OMB*, 65.

55. Hanslick is referring here to Goethe, who coined this phrase to describe Bettina von Arnim's letters to him: "I found your explosions on music particularly interesting, by which I mean your little, but intense contemplations, which have the advantage of increasing its appeal" (so waren mir besonders deine Explosionen über Musik interessant, so nenne ich diese gesteigerten Anschauungen deines Köpfchens die zugleich den Vorzug haben auch den Reiz dafür zu steigern). Bettine von Arnim, *Goethe's Briefwechsel mit einem Kinde*, ed. Wolfgang Bunzel (München: Deutscher Taschenbuch Verlag, 2008), 255. However, Hanslick does not acknowledge that this correspondence is largely fictitious—Bettina von Arnim conceived her letters more as a memorial to the poet.

56. *VMS*, 143; *OMB*, 67.

57. The polemical term "verrottete Gefühlsästhetik" is used by Hanslick in the first edition to his treatise. See Eduard Hanslick, *Vom Musikalisch-Schönen. Ein Beitrag zu Revision der Ästhetik der Tonkunst* (1854; repr. Darmstadt: Wissenschaftliche Buchgesellschaft, 1976), V.

58. *VMS*, 138–39; *OMB*, 64.

59. "Musikalischer Sentimentalitäts-Bedarf für unsere Vorstadt-Fräuleins," Hanslick, *Sämtliche Schriften* 1/4, 65. Hanslick is referring to the "Wiener Liederkranz" by [Franz] Glöggl (1853).

60. "Fräulein Nanette Falk (die Frauen herrschen jetzt auf dem Clavier) gab ein besuchtes zweites Concert im Musikvereinssaale. Sehr hübsch gelang ihr das bekannte *Rondo capriccioso* (Op. 14) von Mendelssohn, dessen zierliche Flüchtigkeit vollkommen in das Ressort der Damen-Virtuosität gehört." Ibid., 61.

61. "Mit Liszts effectvoller 'ungarischer Rhapsodie' vollends können nur die Stärksten und Muthigsten einen glorreichen Kampf bestehen. Zarte Arme, wie die unserer Concertgeberin [Frl. Fritz], mögen davon lieber fernbleiben; es ist ein ängstlicher Anblick, jemand mit einer Stricknadel gegen einen Panther losgehen zu sehen." Ibid.

62. See, for instance, his review of Leonard Borwick's interpretation of Brahms's Piano Concerto No. 1 in D minor, op. 15. "How remarkable that Brahms wrote the D Minor Concerto, a work of mature masculinity and mastery, as a young man, and performed it publicly more than thirty years ago in Leipzig. Those who heard the piece by Brahms himself, or by Bülow, would have missed much in the performance by Mr. Leonard Borwick. The young man is still lacking sufficient strength, intellectual as well as physical, for this task. Mr Borwick gets little tone from the piano, his touch is dull in the cantabile parts, hard and nevertheless poor in the *forte* passages. Everything was played correctly—which in itself verifies an important technique—but the depth and passion, the burning colors were missing. In this cool, immaculate, inoffensive manner of performing, Mr. Borwick almost seemed to me like an English Gentleman, which indeed he really is." Hanslick, "Brahms D-moll-Concert," in *Aus dem Tagebuch eines Musikers*, 344–45. —Eds.

63. For instance, in a review of Clara Schumann, Hanslick writes: "She is not given to the choice of extremely forceful pieces; but in what she does play she rather shames the brilliant virtuosos of our time, by the masculinity of her playing. There is nothing effeminate and retiring, nor any overabundance of emotion. Everything is distinct, clear, sharp as a pencil sketch. The frequent small accents which she affects differ remarkably

from the stresses which the majority of female pianists use to place a personal emotional imprint upon every single note." Hanslick, "Musikalische Briefe (Clara Schumann)," *Sämtliche Schriften* 1/3, 202. This translation is from *Vienna's Golden Years*, 42. —Eds.

64. For more detail, see Freia Hoffmann, *Instrument und Körper. Die musizierende Frau in der bürgerlichen Kultur* (Frankfurt/M.: Insel Verlag, 1991) and Ellis, *Female Pianists*.

65. "Nicht nur ihr Talent, ihr ganzes Wesen interessierte mich, das, bescheiden, schweigsam, schüchtern, nur im Gesang einen ungeahnten Aufschwung nahm." Hanslick, *AML/W*, 321-22.

66. "Meine Frau hat der Bühne, aber nicht der Kunst entsagt. . . . In die Öffentlichkeit ist sie nur noch inkognito getreten, um meine Vorlesungen in Pest, Prag und Graz durch den Vortrag einiger, den Gegenstand illustrierender Gesangsstücke zu unterstützen. Der frühverstorbene geistvolle Kunsthistoriker Professor Alfred Woltmann in Prag hat damals in einem Toast den Gedanken schön ausgeführt, daß die selbstlose Unterordnung einer Künstlerin unter einen wissenschaftlichen Zweck uns doppelt schön und herzlich anmute, wenn sie zugleich als ein Liebesbeweis der Frau für ihren Mann erscheint." Ibid., 333.

67. "So ein Doppelkonzert gleicht einem Drama, das anstatt eines Helden deren zwei besitzt, welche, unsere gleiche Teilnahme und Bewunderung ansprechend, einander nur im Wege stehen. Wenn man aber von einer Musikform behaupten darf, daß sie auf der Übermacht eines siegreichen Helden beruht, so ist's das Konzert. Haben wir nicht etwas Ähnliches in der Malerei? Die Künstler wehren sich gegen Doppelporträts, mögen nicht gern Mann und Frau auf einer Leinwand verewigen. Gleiche Instrumente . . . fügen sich . . . schon leichter zu einem Konzert als zwei Prinzipalstimmen von so unterschiedlicher Tonhöhe wie Violine und Violoncell. . . . So empfangen wir . . . den Eindruck eines Theaterstückes, in welchem alle Personen sehr gescheit und geistreich sprechen, wo es aber zu keiner Handlung kommen will." Eduard Hanslick, *Aus dem Tagebuche eines Musikers. Kritiken und Schilderungen*, 2nd edn (Berlin: Allgemeiner Verein für Deutsche Literatur, 1892), cited in Hanslick, *Musikkritiken* (Leipzig: Verlag Philipp Reclam, 1972), 290.

68. Fred Everett Maus, "Hanslick's Animism," *Journal of Musicology* 10, no. 3 (1992): 279. He continues: "Hanslick animates musical events, hearing themes, harmony, melody, and interacting lines as characters whose behavior a listener may follow. . . . And his animism is sometimes eroticized, in its references to embodiment or in its descriptions of musical motion" (282).

69. "Nach meinem Gefühle ist die 'heroische Sinfonie' durchaus nicht heroisch in ihrer Totalstimmung, sondern nur nebenbei in einzelnen sich aufraffenden Momenten. Sie ist durchweg *pathetisch* und hätte mit diesem Stichwort ebenso füglich charakterisiert werden können als jene gefeierte c-Moll-Sonate. Heldenhaft, schlachtenfroh, siegreich—dies alles ist die 'Eroica' nicht in dem Sinne, welchen man mit der Vorstellung eines triumphierenden Feldherrn verbindet. Von *militärischer* Kraft und Herrlichkeit blitzen kaum hin und wieder einzelne Strahlen. Am kräftigsten tritt noch der erste Satz auf: Das im reinen Dreiklang fest einherschreitende Hauptmotiv durfte in der Tat einen Helden ankündigen. Allein schon nach vier Takten trübt sich der Ton der Zuversicht, und wehklagende Akkorde sprechen von geheimer Trauer. . . . Der Held tritt schon verblutend auf." Hanslick, *Aus dem Concertsaal*, cited in Hanslick, *Musikkritiken*, 90-91.

70. An overview of the gendered reception of Brahms's music (with plentiful examples) is to be found in chapter 6 of my dissertation *Frauenliebe—Männerleben*.

71. "Alles ist im Orchester ausser sich, Recken schreien in wilder Phrase.... Es ist dies eine Stelle [Trillerkette vom gesamten Streichorchester], die man nie vergessen kann; wer seinen 'Beowulf' gelesen hat, der muss unwillkürlich an die Scene denken, wo das entsetzliche Moorungeheuer in der Methhalle erscheint.... Das sieht aus wie Worte wüthendster Entschlossenheit.... Stets von Neuem steht der finstere Held vor uns, der diese ersten, grausen Takte sang, eine Natur gewaltig und todeskühn, aber mit einem Hang zum Düsteren, das Auge stets gerichtet auf die ewige Erbärmlichkeit des menschlichen Seins. Die freundlichen Weisen, er hört sie, die liebenden und lockenden Bilder, er sieht sie: sobald er aber weilen möchte, da kommen die Mahner.... Kain, Furien und ähnliche Bilder werden Viele beim Hören dieses Satzes begleiten." Hermann Kretzschmar, "Neue Werke von J. Brahms," *Musikalisches Wochenblatt* 5 (1874): 5–7, 19–21, 31–32, 43–45, 58–60, 70–73, 83–85, 95–97, 107–11, 147–50, 164–66; here 5–6.

72. The Anglo-Saxon heroic epic poem dates from the sixth century, and tells the story of the heroic battle of Beowulf, chieftain of the Geats (a tribe from southern Sweden). With the help of fourteen companions he comes to the aid of the Danish king, kills the monster Grendel and, in a second battle, murders his vengeful mother. In the second part of the poem, Beowulf is King of Denmark whose kingdom is threatened by a dragon; he slays the dragon, but dies from his wounds.

73. Max Kalbeck (1850–1921) wrote the first biography of Brahms, a monumental undertaking, the first volume of which was published 1903/04, and was followed by further volumes 1908/09, 1910/12 and 1914. Kalbeck's endeavor heralded the completion of the first phase of research on Brahms's biography and interpretation of his works.

74. "Den Helden aus dem Märchenwald der Romantik ins Leben zu Spiel und Kampf." Max Kalbeck, *Johannes Brahms*, 4 vols. (repr. Tutzing: Verlag Hans Schneider, 1976), 3: 387.

75. "Gefällige Schöne, die jedes Männerherz erobert! Sie scheint ganz Einfalt, ganz Unschuld, ganz Natur.... Seht nur, wie sie tänzelt und schwänzelt, wie sie sich wendet und dreht und bei jeder anmutigen Bewegung ihrem biegsamen Körper neue Reize abgewinnt!... In dem meisterhaft gezeichneten weiblichen Porträt finden wir die Merkmale des Gattungscharakters, das Weib schlechthin. Der Gynäkophile wird es adorieren, der Misogyne die beleidigende Frage stellen, ob die holde Schäferin nicht etwa ein verkleidetes, mit Heugeruch parfümiertes Stadtfräulein sei... Die reizende Verführerin braucht nur mit dem kurzen Röckchen zu schwenken, und der verliebte Tor ist von ihren Knixen so bezaubert." Ibid., 3:387–90.

76. "Die Wunde seines Herzens schließt sich. Idealere Freuden ziehen bei ihm ein." Ibid., 3:393.

77. Freia Hoffmann, "Geschlechterkampf in Tönen? Zur Diskussion über die Konstruktion von Weiblichkeit und Männlichkeit in der Musik," in *Frauen, Körper, Kunst. Frauen- und Geschlechterforschung bezogen auf Musik, Tanz, Theater und Bildende Kunst*, Band 2: *Dokumentation von Gastvorträgen und -kursen 1995–1998*, ed. Martina Peter-Bolaender (Kassel: Furore-Verlag, 1999), 73–92.

78. "Faustische[s] Ringen." Hanslick, *Concerte*, 166.

79. In the context of his review of Brahms's Serenade in D Major, op. 11, Hanslick takes a gendered approach by contrasting the gentle, tender, calm, and airy character of a serenade with the substantive criteria required for symphonies and their calls for "impassioned battles and the most sublime pathos" (das leidenschaftlichen Kämpfen, das erhabenste Pathos). Hanslick, *Aus dem Concertsaal*, 260.

80. Umberto Eco, *Das offene Kunstwerk* (Frankfurt/M.: Suhrkamp Verlag, 1977), 222.

81. The term *Leerstelle* (empty space) comes from reader-response criticism in literary theory, and was coined by Wolfgang Iser. See Meinhard Winkgens, "Leerstelle," in *Metzler Lexikon Literatur- und Kulturtheorie. Ansätze—Personen—Grundbegriffe*, ed. Ansgar Nünning, 3rd rev. ed. (Stuttgart: Metzler, 2004), 377–78.

82. By way of comparison, see Helmut Rösing, "Auf der Suche nach Männlichkeitssymbolen. Beethoven und die Sonaten(hauptsatz)form," in *Der "männliche" und der "weibliche" Beethoven. Bericht über den Internationalen musikwissenschaftlichen Kongress vom 31. Oktober bis 4. November 2001 an der Universität der Künste Berlin*, ed. Cornelia Bartsch, Beatrix Borchard, and Rainer Cadenbach (Bonn: Verlag Beethoven-Haus Bonn, 2003), 5–6. "In music, unlike painting and verbal language, it is all about a nondiscursive medium of communication. . . . With its notes, sounds, noises, harmonies and rhythms, music is one thing above all: gender neutral" (Bei Musik handelt es sich, im Gegensatz zu Bildern und Sprache, um ein nicht-diskursives Kommunikationsmedium. . . . Musik mit ihren Tönen, Klängen, Geräuschen, Harmonien und Rhythmen ist erst einmal und vor allem eins: geschlechtsneutral).

83. Drawing on the private music reception of Clara Schumann and Elisabet von Herzogenberg and the Brahms biographies by Florence May and Marie Lipsius (La Mara), I have shown in my doctoral dissertation how these women described the music they heard less as a narrative and more as an experience of a natural phenomenon or organic development. The whole area of female music reception merits further research.

84. Hiroshi Yoshida, "Eduard Hanslick and the Idea of 'Public' in Musical Culture. Towards a Socio-Political Context of Formalistic Aesthetics," *International Review of the Aesthetics and Sociology of Music* 32, no. 2 (2001): 197, emphasis in original.

85. Eduard Hanslick, *AML/W*, 400.

86. "Die Art und Weise, wie wir Dinge und Ereignisse interpretieren und sie innerhalb unseres Bedeutungssystems positionieren, hängt . . . von diskursiven Strukturen ab. Diese diskursiven Strukturen bestimmen, so Foucault, dass Dinge und Ereignisse uns real und materiell erscheinen." Sara Mills, *Der Diskurs. Begriff, Theorie, Praxis* (Tübingen: A. Francke Verlag, 2007), 54.

87. See Judith Butler, *Körper von Gewicht. Die diskursiven Grenzen von Geschlecht* (Frankfurt/M.: Suhrkamp Verlag, 1997), 35–41.

Chapter Eleven

Body and Soul, Content and Form

On Hanslick's Use of the Organism Metaphor

Nina Noeske

It has been common practice since the early nineteenth century to compare a musical work with a "living organism," a metaphor that Eduard Hanslick—like Richard Wagner, Franz Brendel, and many others—also employed, both in his treatise *On the Musically Beautiful* (1854) and in many of his reviews.[1] That he rarely reflects on this practice is revealing of the underlying assumptions of Hanslick's aesthetic thinking, his musical preferences and antipathies. These unreflected, apparently self-evident paradigms are particularly relevant to the intellectual horizon of an author and his epoch. On the one hand, there is the tradition of German idealism in the wake of Kant, Schiller, Schelling, and Hegel, with its classical concept of "unity in diversity" [*Einheit in der Mannigfaltigkeit*], and its equation of "idea" [*Idee*] with "sensual and corporal phenomena" (i.e., the "content versus form" debate). On the other hand, there is the scientific-physiological thinking around 1830, that in part explicitly distances itself from idealism. This almost inexplicable tension between idealism and positivism/materialism, recently described as "idealist materialism" by Mark Burford,[2] shapes both Hanslick's treatise and his musical preferences (which are inexplicably bound up with one another).[3] The nuances of the organism concept may, however, allow for a new understanding of this matter. As idealist materialism was not only relevant for biology, physiology, medicine, philosophy, and aesthetics, but also for contemporary theories of governance and linguistics,[4] conclusions drawn from an analysis of Hanslick's use of language may afford us an insight that extends beyond purely musical matters.

Following a brief outline of the intellectual discourse in which the notion of "organism" was rooted, this article will explore Hanslick's use of the organism metaphor in his writings.[5] Detailed quotations will show which metaphors were used in what context and to what end. We shall see, for example, that his critique of the composers of the so-called New German School, in particular, is closely linked to this "fascination with the organic,"[6] yet his views on the musical abilities of nations or gender are also based on the organism paradigm, and shall be discussed briefly at the end. It will emerge that Hanslick applied the term "organism" only to compositions he liked; it rarely mattered whether or not there were factual "organic" elements in such compositions. Ultimately, Hanslick viewed the musically beautiful as a healthy—and preferably male—organism. This means that he (along with many other writers on music of his time) was inherently interested in the preservation of a certain societal order, of which music is an important part.

In the nineteenth century it was often claimed that materialist and spiritualist ideas in philosophy and science could be regarded as analogous to the aesthetic debates of the 1850s in music. This essay, however, will conclude that such an equivalence does not exist. Though there are occasional similarities between "formalism" and "idealism" on the one hand and "aesthetics of substance" and "materialism" on the other, these fleeting similarities are not strong enough to warrant speaking of a parallel system.

Materialism and Spiritualism

Any discussion of the organism metaphor must consider not just the term itself but also its underlying concepts. The organic world consists of human and animal bodies as well as plants, which are all made up of specific organs and other parts yet can also join forces to form larger metaorganisms. On account of their metabolism, organisms are alive, they breathe, are relatively autonomous and die as a result of undue force or old age. The "living organism" of a human or animal with its cells, skin, bones and blood cells, is a supremely mysterious unity of intellect and body, and represents a value sui generis, juxtaposed only by "nothingness" or "death" as lifeless matter. This special value has always been enshrined in aesthetics of music as well as music-related value judgments. From the middle of the nineteenth century, sciences such as physiology and aesthetics drew closer together than had previously been the case. The mid- and late 1850s witnessed the climax of the aesthetic battle between supporters of so-called absolute and program music. Furthermore, philosophy and natural science (the latter had received a massive boost during the first half of the century) engaged in a lively and polemical discussion about the interaction of matter, body, soul and intellect. "Life-force or -energy" [*Lebenskraft*]—a term as controversial as it was vague—was a topic of much debate.[7] Science and physiology also focused on how entities in the world interacted, how the world could be understood as an animated whole. This was not confined to a view of the world as the stage for the development of Hegel's concept of *Weltgeist*. Materialism and spiritualism represented polar opposites in this debate: while the former tried to determine matter as the source of being, and from which the intellect had developed, the latter acknowledged the primacy of the immaterial over the material.

It is well known that during Hanslick's time in Prague, a fellow student and later colleague, the philosopher Robert Zimmermann, introduced him to the contemporary philosophical and scientific ideas in vogue there, such as the works of the Kantian Johann Friedrich Herbart and the philosophical ideas of Bernard Bolzano.[8] Mark Burford has pointed out a number of other possible sources of Hanslick's "idealist materialism."[9] It can be assumed that Hanslick was familiar with works like Louis Büchner's highly successful "materialistic" best seller *Kraft und Stoff* and its counterpart, Julius Schaller's *Leib und Seele* (both published in 1855).[10] Although Hanslick never explicitly refers to them, they were well known among intellectuals at the time.[11] So, we can take Büchner literally in the preface to the fifth edition of *Kraft und Stoff*: "The literature on force and matter, body and soul, spirit and matter, faith and knowledge, nature and revelation and similar things, grows by the day."[12] Avoiding this discourse must have been difficult, if not impossible.

Among other things, Hanslick refers in *Vom Musikalisch-Schönen* to important contemporary sources linking philosophy, physics, physiology, psychology, and medicine, such as the third volume of Hans Christian Oersted's *Geist in der Natur* (German edition 1851),[13] the second edition of Karl Rosenkranz's *Psychologie* (1843, first published 1837),[14] Hermann Lotze's *Medicinische Psychologie* (1852),[15] the first volume of Gabriel Gustav Valentin's *Physiologie des Menschen* (second edition, 1847–51),[16] the *Handwörterbuch der Physiologie* in four volumes (1842–53),[17] and Jacob Grimm's classic *Der Ursprung der Sprache* (1851),[18] which features the organism metaphor just as regularly as the other publications do. A footnote in *Vom Musikalisch-Schönen* reveals that Hanslick was at least partly familiar with the writings of Carl Gustav Carus, a multitalented, prolific physician, painter, and writer.[19] Carus promoted a holistic "organic recognition,"[20] which he explained in detail in his books.

These writings are pertinent to the fourth chapter of Hanslick's treatise, in which he discusses the appropriate reception of the musically beautiful. He points out that neither psychology nor physiology can ultimately explain the strong effect music has on the nervous system. While psychologists would not look beyond the "mesmeric compulsion of the impression" and thus the "specific stimulation of the nerves," physiologists focused on sound as such, yet not in a musical context;[21] the result is that psychology is overreliant on spirituality whereas physiology is overreliant on materialism. An interpretation of the effect of music on the listener as a simple interplay of stimulus and reaction, as attempted by "musico-medical" specialists (that is, physiologists) would be wrong, as it does not take into account music as a specifically artistic genre.[22] "That music shares the same material substratum (i.e., sound) with those manifestations in which sounds act so intensely on the nerves will later be seen to have important consequences for us. Here we are emphasizing an antimaterialistic view, that music begins where those isolated effects leave off."[23] Hanslick also rejects the assumption that music directly affects the "soul," as the immaterial and the spiritual. This view could go so far as to deny (contrary to all experience) any physical transmission of "an auditory stimulus to the organism as a whole."[24] This means that neither psychology nor physiology can explain "the particular way in which particular musical factors . . . act upon different nerves"[25] and thus create aesthetic impressions. These are "paraphrases a thousandfold of this one ancient riddle: how the body is connected to the soul."[26]

The sciences named above cannot contribute much to an aesthetics of music, yet according to Hanslick, physiology is still necessary in order to prevent musicology from arriving at wrong conclusions.[27] He points out that two of the most eminent physiologists of the time, Hermann Lotze and Emil Harleß, admitted that we cannot explain the connection between certain acoustic stimuli of the nerves and human emotions, thus a causal link between emotions and music cannot be established. This leads Hanslick to conclude that an aesthetic theory of the beautiful cannot be based on the emotional impact of music. "The aesthetical recipe must show us how the musician produces beauty in music, not how he produces arbitrary effects in the audience."[28]

Hanslick is convinced that "this sphinx"—the relationship between body (matter) and soul (spirit) "will never throw herself off the rock";[29] so the riddle can be expressed only by referring to the notion of "organism" as the concept encompassing both sides. For this reason, the term occupies a key position in Hanslick's aesthetics. Uniting, as it does, body and spirit, it can be explained neither by consistent materialism, which regards everything related to the soul as completely physiological and determinable in matter, nor by spiritualism/idealism (both terms were often used synonymously in the middle of the nineteenth century). The separation of spirit and matter, culminating in the popular postulate of a "life energy" [*Lebenskraft*] that occasionally joins forces with matter, is not an option for Hanslick, as he is convinced that music *always* affects the body as well. According to the public intellectual discourse of the time, we can understand Hanslick's aesthetic position as mediating between polar opposites, a position in many ways close to that of the philosopher and antimaterialist Julius Schaller. Schaller also regards "organism" as the only concept capable of describing appropriately the unity of body and spirit, as he points out in *Leib und Seele*.

> Despite its material and divisible existence in space, the organism in its harmonic unity of its parts as a cohesive whole is non-spatial, indivisible and immaterial. . . . If I regard the soul as a substance, or even as something that perceives sensations, this ultimately means that the soul is something devoid of life that lives, something devoid of sensation that feels. The soul does not perceive, it is the act of perception itself. Precisely this activity, this process, is what gives it substance. The body itself as an active, composed, idealizing whole is soul.

Any attempt to explain the organism through mechanical and chemical processes alone can always be countered by referring to the body that can perceive and has formed a composed whole. As long as this individual, subjective unity is left unexplained, the main point—the aspect specific to organism—remains unexplained. Whatever is created solely by a combination of matter and chemical processes without any other influence is at best a thing, to which we give a name, yet which can never be a unit in its own right, never be a subject.[30]

Replacing just a few terms in this extract would be enough to give quite a pointed synopsis of Hanslick's aesthetics of music: e.g., "music" or "aesthetic experience" instead of "organism," "music" or "form" instead of "soul," "content" instead of "feeling or sensation" or "body," "motion" instead of "process," "feeling/sensation" instead of "thing," "music" or "aesthetic experience" instead of "unity" and "subject." "The content of music is tonally moving forms,"[31] or, to vary Schaller's extract quoted above, "the musical form *has* no content, it *is* in itself the production of content. Precisely this activity, this motion, marks its substantiality. Content as an active . . . whole is form." This "one-to-one substitution, whereby the external conveys the internal,"[32] represents a core component of the living organism, which turns out to be a very suitable metaphor for the phenomenon "music." It is difficult to accuse these formulations (which are equally applicable to organism and music), of "formalism."

Reflecting on the principle of "life" as *the* central aspect of everything organic was thus for many disciplines an obvious alternative to the sole primacy of the Hegelian's *Geist*. The aesthetic "battle" fought between Hanslick on one side and the "New Germans" and Franz Brendel on the other appears to reflect these contemporary discussions between "materialists" and "idealistic" "Old Hegelians" [*Alt-Hegelianer*], yet not as a carbon copy but rather as a model for this kind of argument. Nevertheless it is typical when, for example, August Wilhelm Ambros writes in 1855 (misunderstanding Hanslick): "Like the materialists in the sphere of natural science, the deniers of the subject-matter of music, the estheticians of absolute form-play, are materialists in [the sphere] of philosophy. These intellectual movements are more intimately connected with each other than would appear at first glance, or even than their supporters themselves can divine."[33] And yet, works like those by the physician and physiologist Jacob Moleschott (a prototypical materialist Ambros refers to) were also discussed in Franz Brendel's journal *Anregungen für Kunst, Leben und Wissenschaft*.[34] Even Louis Büchner, who was often denounced as a "vulgar materialist," and who regarded the soul—as he put it in *Kraft und Stoff*—as a mere "product of a specific composition of matter,"[35] contributed to this journal in 1857 and 1861.[36] Conversely, the Baltic natural scientist Karl Ernst von Baer—like many others—used the music metaphor (specifically, rhythm and melody) when attempting to describe the "life process" of organisms in general.

As a materialist one can say melody consists of a succession of notes, i.e., vibrations of the air, and also, speech is a succession of linguistic utterances. Yet it would be wrong to claim that melody consists only of notes, and speech only of linguistic utterances.... Likewise it appears unthinkable to me that that the life process can be understood as a succession of physical or chemical reactions, or that our conscience is a succession of numerous small events.

The individual components of organisms are constructed according to the type and rhythm of the concomitant life process as well as through its effectiveness, so that they could not have the same function in another life process. Hence, I want to call the different processes of life—comparing them in this way to musical thoughts or themes—creative thoughts that create their bodies themselves. What we call harmony and melody in music is type (a combination of components) and rhythm (a succession of forms).[37]

Clearly, it is difficult to link aesthetic positions and specific philosophical ideas, especially in contemporary perception. Both sides used buzzwords like *body, soul, form, content, emotion, life* and *nature*, but sometimes their respective viewpoints differed only minimally.

Hanslick's Use of the Organism Metaphor

In *Vom Musikalisch-Schönen* as well as in Hanslick's reviews, the organism is mentioned several times. In general, we can distinguish two ways in which Hanslick uses the term: he refers either directly to the organism of the human body or metaphorically to the organism of the musical work. Both are important to Hanslick, with the human body functioning as a kind of yardstick with which to determine whether music is perceived aesthetically (sensually and cognitively, as befits music) or pathologically (sensually and bodily, purely passively). Yet only a "healthy" organism is able to pass aesthetic judgment on a musical work, that is, to look at it consciously and without bias:[38] "A purely aesthetic effect addresses itself to the healthy nervous system and does not rely upon any degree of psychological abnormality."[39]

Hanslick may have taken this idea from Johann Heinrich Dambeck's *Vorlesungen über Ästhetik*, which was published by his father's publishing house in 1822.[40] There we read. "People suffering from fever, melancholy, hypochondria, or similar conditions cannot pass reliable judgments on beauty, truth, morality, etc. If the bodily functions and/or the soul do not work properly, it is normal and natural that this will affect all perceptions, so that the judgments of those people can never be assumed to be clear and correct."[41] Apart from those who are ill, "savages" (described as early as 1807 by Peter Lichtenthal, whom Hanslick used as a negative example elsewhere)[42] are particularly susceptible to the "physical effects" of music, as in their case, no guiding spirit is able to exercise control. "The scantier the vestige of refinement, the more powerfully does such influence penetrate. As is well known, music exercises the strongest effect upon savages."[43] A savage, however, does not react appropriately to music as the most intellectual and simultaneously the most sensual of arts: on the one hand, the nerves are "no less obscure organs of the imperceptible telegraph service between body and soul"[44] than the music itself that brings those opposing forces together. Yet, on the other hand, a focus on "such pathological ways of being affected by a piece of music"[45] pushes the barometer too much toward a materialistic position, resulting in a dangerous imbalance, as it ultimately threatens the subject's control over itself. "It is the elemental in music, i.e., sound and motion, which shackles the defenseless feelings of so many music lovers in chains which they rattle quite merrily."[46] A diseased organism, in which emotions are enchained and the subject has lost its moral autonomy,[47] can no longer recognize the beautiful as such. "But the more powerfully an effect from a work of art overwhelms us physically (and hence is pathological), the more negligible is its aesthetic component. (Of course, this proposition cannot be inverted.)"[48] This leads to the object—the musical work—being perceived in a distorted way. If one's own organism is imbalanced, one is—as Hanslick pointed out elsewhere—"tied to the unreliable effects of musical appearances instead of penetrating the inner nature of the works and understanding their content and beauty on the basis of their internal organic structure."[49] Thus, only the interaction of two healthy and autonomous organisms allows for a beautiful and aesthetic experience, or, as Fred Everett Maus puts it: "Hearing music is like being in the presence of a beautiful body."[50]

According to Hanslick, the "beautiful" aesthetic object is a "flourishing organism" [*blühender Körper*].[51] The four movements of a sonata are ideally "organically unified,"[52] while rhythm represents the "regular alternating motion of individual limbs [*Glieder*] within the metric period" and simultaneously the "artery which carries life to music."[53] Ambros also compares music to a body; unlike Hanslick, however, he distinguishes between body and soul, form and content: "In describing the organization of the period-structure, the regular pulse of the rhythm, the inner structure of harmony and the smooth, singing substructure of melody, we have described the *body* of the piece of music. The *body*, however, requires a soul."[54] The plantlike "arabesque"[55] is alive, "not dead and static," and in "continuous self-formation." It evolves "before our eyes"; its "artistic spirit" pours its creativity into the "arteries of this dynamism."[56] Even the famous kaleidoscope metaphor—as the cultural context shows—is linked to plants. Hanslick describes the "musical, audible kaleidoscope" as a "direct emanation of an artistically creative spirit,"[57] and thus ultimately as a living being. *Herders Conversations-Lexikon* from 1855 describes it not only as an "entertaining," but also as indispensible "for those drawing arabesques, patterns," and thus for those producing plantlike objects.[58]

Furthermore, Hanslick calls the motif or theme that provides the starting point of the composer's work a "seed," which "pleases us in itself . . . like products of natural beauty such as leaves and flowers."[59] The composition ideally evolves "in organically distinct gradations, like sumptuous blossoming from a bud."[60] Yet "whatever does not (explicitly or implicitly) lie ready in the theme cannot later be organically developed."[61] Hanslick's most striking comparison between the living body and a "beautiful" musical work is formulated thus: "Thoughts and feelings run like blood in the arteries of the harmonious body of beautiful sounds. They are not that body; they are not perceivable, but they animate it."[62]

By referring to "organism," Hanslick simultaneously allocates "nature" a central position, as another quotation illustrates: "Every particular thing stands in some relationship to nature. This relationship is for each thing the most fundamental, most venerable, and most influential."[63] Accordingly he emphasizes the implicit natural law governing music: "All musical elements have mysterious bonds and affinities among themselves, determined by natural laws." If parts of the "human music" ignore those affinities that exist "instinctively in each cultivated ear," they are dubbed "caprice and ugliness" as the "cultivated" human ear "instinctively" prefers "organic, rational coherence" over "absurdity and unnaturalness."[64] According to Hanslick, one could formulate the equation thus: beautiful = natural = organic = reasonable; ugly = unnatural = inorganic or unhealthy = absurd. Compared to this wealth of biological imagery, Hanslick's description of the musical idea as a crystal is negligible: "It takes shape progressively, like a crystal, until imperceptibly the form of the completed product stands before him in its main outlines."[65] The crystal line, however, can be seen as a transitional step toward the organic. In Karl Rosenkranz's *Psychologie*, from which Hanslick quotes elsewhere, the author explains that "the translucent shine of the crystal" marks the "transition from inorganic to organic nature."[66]

A recurring theme in Hanslick's reviews is the notion of a work that is *not* self-contained, is nonorganic and pieced together, that would in the worst instance aim to produce purely physiological effects of tone and thus damage the organism of the listener. For example, Hanslick criticized Wagner's *Tannhäuser* overture on the basis that it was "motivically assembled rather than organically developed." Passages that tire the listener with their "monotony and noise" render the composition "mortal, or better, already dead artistically."[67] Only occasionally, as Hanslick writes in 1857, "do some melodic buds raise their heads out of the long, thorny undergrowth."[68] In the following year, Hanslick described Wagner's operas in general as "musically infertile," lacking both "the ability to conceive," and consequently the "really beautiful injustice of nature."[69] Lohengrin falls short of what "constitutes the real musical body," namely melody and "independent song."[70]

Any search for a "musical core" is futile in these circumstances.[71] Like Franz Liszt's symphonic poems, Wagner's music—namely his *Faust* overture—"boastfully" relies on "coarse material" effects in order to cover up its artistic "impotence."[72] In 1861 Hanslick comments once again on Liszt's compositions: "Ingeniously combined and colorful impotence remains at the heart of all of Liszt's compositions." Occasionally, here and there, individual melodies "timidly raise their pretty heads only to be crushed immediately."[73] In the symphonic poem *Mazeppa*, the "components are often put together like in a mosaic,"[74] which indicates that they don't come "from the pure well of music" but are instead "artificially distilled water." "In the case of Liszt, musical creation does not come to light in a free and pristine way, but rather by way of reflection."[75] Thus in the *Graner Festmesse* one senses less the "warm breath of religious sentiment" but more the "pondering reflection" that looks "out of every bar with piercing grey eyes."[76] The "intention" places its "barren hand" on "each syllable," "and where once aromatic violets swayed, now does the ghostly pale and deadly tree of knowledge raise its head."[77]

A musical organism, seriously disturbed and imbalanced by both an excess of sensuousness and too much reflection, can even damage the listener's organism in a very literal sense. Hanslick talks of the "torture of the aural nerves";[78] Liszt's *Prometheus* would "ingeniously torture" the listener, with "a musical vulture" pecking "not his liver but instead deep into his ear."[79] The audience emerges from a recital of Liszt's works "bemused and annoyed."[80] In the same way, "every sane and sensible person" would "turn away" from *Mazeppa*.[81] Anton Rubinstein's music too—lacking the "singing soul"—swamps the listener's ear, making it "lethargic" and "apathetic."[82] One reason for this is that, according to Hanslick, Rubinstein's works are "artistic freaks."[83] Jacques Halévy's opera *La Juive*, as the final example, "overstretches" the audience's "nerves,"[84] with its "bizarre melodic lines" betraying an "unhealthy aspiration . . . to achieve what is most uncommon."[85]

According to Hanslick's review from 1857, however, Schubert's "great" C major symphony produces a "veritable stream of strength and health"; its first movement stretching "its young limbs boldly and pugnaciously,"[86] Robert Schumann's D Minor Symphony also represents a "blossoming texture of tones"[87] due to its "inner unity."[88] In this Schumann review—also from 1857—Hanslick insinuates that there is also in "the life of art . . . a continuous process of decay and renewal, a spiritual 'metabolism.'"[89] It is thus not surprising that during his final years, when Schumann was close to death, he was no longer able to breathe new life into his later works. His Sonata for Violin and Piano No. 2 in D major, op. 121, for example, lacks "warm, inner life that should be replaced by external, febrile fervor." The development section is no longer "unspoilt life springing forth from the main subject," the creativity has dried up, its "inner, magnificent blossoming [has] ceased," the music even shows a "pallid death drive."[90] Even Brahms is not safe from Hanslick's negative judgments. The latter describes *Ein Deutsches Requiem* as one of the "ripest fruits that . . . have been growing in the field of sacred music." Yet the B-major Allegro at the end of "Denn alles Fleisch, es ist wie Gras" was a mistake, since it "appears more like an external appendix rather than an organic ending."[91] In the finale of Brahms's String Sextet in G major, "the warm, alive pulse of the music recedes, to be replaced by mechanical and fatiguing gray reflection. This is abstract music-making, a restless combining and brooding to the point of a headache."[92] Josef Rheinberger's symphonic poem *Wallenstein* cannot convince Hanslick, and his reasons sound very familiar: its motives are "put together in the style of a mosaic, rather than developed organically out of each other." To him, only the scherzo is "capable of life [*lebensfähig*]."[93] Inadequate interpretation can destroy an artistic organism as well. The "assiduous, almost timid . . . threading together of notes" by the female pianist "Fräulein Bondy" causes nothing less than the "spiritual death" of Beethoven's Sonata op. 29 [*sic*], "despite its external body appearing quite undamaged."[94] There is no shortage of examples of "biological" metaphors of this kind.

Aspects of Gender

It is not only musical works and their interpretations that Hanslick associates with the concept of "organism." He also writes about the "organism" of a conservatory,[95] the "independent organism" rooted in the conviviality of a male choral society,[96] or the "organism" of musical life; for example he considers it of the "utmost importance" to "nurture" a string quartet as "a musical organism."[97] As Hanslick notes, the English nation has, despite its "outwardly magnificent organism," an "unhealthy core," due to its deeply rooted lack of musical ability.[98] This is based on the "finest organisms of the [English] constitution,"[99] namely their "numbness of the nerves,"[100] as well as their "one-sided interest in the melodramatic," or, in the light of Hanslick's aesthetics, the pathological.[101]

Classifying everything as either "natural" and "unnatural," or "healthy" and "unhealthy," was the nineteenth century's central approach to understanding the world, an approach that is dealt with in detail in Claudia Honegger's book *Ordnung der Geschlechter*.[102] Like most of his contemporaries, Hanslick regards the male organism as dominated by the intellect, thus being much closer than the female organism to the ideal. Not only does he refer in many reviews to the physical shortcomings of female pianists,[103] which do not allow "female artists even of the highest caliber to convey the full effect of the most moving works."[104] He also emphasizes repeatedly, almost in passing and as a matter of course, the "more sensually organized"[105] nature of women. This is fully in line with the gender discourse of his time. For example, in *Vom Musikaslich-Schönen* he notes that it is first and foremost ladies who "at the opera . . . with lively, accessible melodies . . . automatically nod their heads this way and that,"[106] so the "pathological" and related bodily effects of music not only affect ill people and savages but, increasingly, also women.[107] In a review of a concert given by Clara Schumann (an artist he held in high esteem) in 1856, Hanslick mentions the "effeminate" in the same breath as "overcome with pity" and "flooded with emotions":

> Our artist is, incidentally, a long way from selecting excessively virtuosic pieces; she embarrasses the virtuosos of our time by the masculinity of her interpretation. Nothing effeminate, overcome with pity or flooded with emotions can be found in Clara Schumann's playing: everything is definite, clear, precise, like a pencil drawing. The regular little accents she loves are remarkably different from the emphasis with which most female pianists seek to add emotion to every single note; what is in this case affectation of subjective emotion is elsewhere just careful highlighting of rhythmic or harmonic opposition."[108]

Elsewhere Hanslick emphasizes Schumann's "strongly uniform, masculine approach that doesn't interrupt the flow by languishing on every little detail," as one that is extremely rare in other female pianists.[109] In a similar fashion he writes in 1858 of two young violinists, sisters Virginie and Caroline Ferni, that their interpretation reveals "a masculine spirit rejecting all squeamishness and effusiveness."[110] A composition is most likely to appeal to Hanslick if it has "marrow and bone" like Mendelssohn's Symphony No. 4: "Its posture is upright, firm and masculine."[111] Such an artistic organism can only be created by an equally structured human organism, as Hanslick states in December 1855: "Virtually nobody will think of training 'girls to become composers,' even with the necessary restrictions in place that make sense of this."[112] In a review of works by the female composer Louise Adolpha Le Beau, he writes, "In my view, experience shows that women lack the creative imagination, the musical inventiveness and talent, and thus the innate gift and basic requirement for all independent musical activity."[113] Finally, in *Vom Musikalisch-Schönen* he cites the fact that women "have not amounted to much as composers"[114] as an argument against the relevance of "emotion" in composition: if the "strengths and agility of feelings" played a major part, the "complete lack of female composers . . . would be difficult to explain" (würde der gänzliche Mangel von Componistinnen . . . schwer zu erklären sein)[115] as they are by nature dependent on emotion. In composition, however, the "renunciation of subjectivity" is a crucial component, as the musical "ideal" is to be "set forth objectively in order to create pure form."[116]

Here Hanslick refers explicitly to Karl Rosenkranz's elaborations on the female [*Weib*] in the latter's *Psychologie* (rather than—as Felix Printz claims[117]— to the relevant section in Nägeli's *Vorlesungen über Musik*). Rosenkranz also talks about renouncing one's subjectivity [*Entäußerung der Subjectivität*], which was essential particularly for the plastic arts:

As the female is most suitable to malleable activity, she is psychically destined for sentiment and oneness of herself with the world. She is introspective, yet only in an immediate way, as she is open to any impression from the outside world; she gets easily excited and is most receptive to the outward appearance of things and the surface of life.—This high degree of passivity limits a woman's productivity. She cannot achieve anything in the plastic arts, for example, as this would require her to renounce subjectivity, which she is not able to do ... *Music*, namely playing string instruments and singing, is the art suitable for women. Yet women have *created* very little in music.[118]

According to Rosenkranz, in contrast, the "natural constitution" of the male makes him "destined to think by virtue of his advanced nervous system, and destined to project himself externally by virtue of his enhanced muscular strength. In order to be able to act, he has to deal with divisiveness—from within himself, and with the world.... Hence the male is designed for universal productivity and not limited by nature in any aspect of human art, knowledge or action."[119] To put it paradoxically: the "natural" constitution of the male makes it possible for him to rise above "nature" as an autonomous subject. What Hanslick neglects to take into account when criticizing Rosenkranz for being inconsistent is that the "emotion" of the male "goes deeper than that of the female ... as it has to explore deeper abysses that remain invisible to women, as these remain shrouded in mellow mist. It is empty idolization to regard the woman as more emotional than the man.... The woman is, so to speak, emotion, whereas the man has emotions.... Man is expected to transcend himself and his sorrow, engage with the latter and—understanding it—break free of it."[120] According to Hanslick, a similar attitude is necessary to obtain an adequate view of the musically beautiful. Eva Rieger's and Freia Hoffmann's rather vague statement that Hanslick's notion of absolute music comes with specifically masculine connotations[121] can thus be supported by specific quotations and references to Hanslick's "extramusical" sources.

Yet it is not only women who are less well suited to genuine artistic activity because their natural constitution is weaker, supposedly more sensual, and more receptive, and prone to weak nerves, illness, hysteria and fainting.[122] The same applies to the representatives of the "New German School" who ultimately try to hide their "impotence" behind their boastful and showy works. Both assessments are based on the paradigm of the organic, which extends the primacy of nature to historico-cultural phenomena. To give just one of many possible examples, Lorenz Oken's *Lehrbuch der Naturphilosophie* (published 1809–11) states: "Gender stands for ... the opposition of spirit and matter, light and mass, ether and earthly elements, sun and planet, electricism and chemistry as represented in the organism in its totality." Thus gender is "the primeval opposition in the world, spirit and matter cast in an organism.... The reproductive elements of the fruit are called the female, what stirs reproduction, the male. . . . Masculinity stands for the spirit of the world, femininity for the matter that is animated by the former."[123] Hanslick gets closer to a "vulgar materialism" [*Vulgärmaterialismus*] than his aesthetic principles suggest when talking about the genuine creative incapability of the female sex, as he bases his conclusions regarding spiritual/cultural capabilities on physiological attributes. Louis Büchner, for example, explained the alleged lower intelligence of women by simply referring to their lighter brain,[124] while Carl Gustav Carus—clearly navigating "materialist" waters—collected casts of the skulls of famous female and male artists in order to investigate the physiological foundations of human creativity.[125]

The musical work has to resemble as closely as possible the beautiful human (male) form as an ideal synthesis of spirit, soul and body, i.e., as the most highly developed organism. August Wilhelm Ambros points out that ultimately it is man (i.e., the human being) who is the "sole and main object" of art:

> Man desires to behold, *outside of himself*, that which springs from his innermost soul, "condensed into permanent thoughts," embodied in a *beautiful* form; what constituted a part of his Ego is to sink itself in a plastic material, and now—like an individual that bears in itself the rational conditions and limitations of its existence, like something alien—is to stand facing him like a non-ego, something *alien* and yet *his image*—his image in the sense in which man is called an image of Deity. Where an art-work lacks the ideal feature, the interest drawn from man's higher life—not the merely physiologically active life of his corporeal organism, but from his spiritual life—we have no *finished, entire* artwork, but only a phase in its development. The spiritual feature of the art-work, the ideal feature, is the living Promethean spark, fetched from heaven, that alone gives life to the symmetrical, but lifeless, image of clay.[126]

Hanslick's reviews indicate that he finds such ideal formations [*Gebilde*] mainly in Beethoven. Yet he also accepts "plantlike" artistic organisms—perfect as they are on their respective lower levels—while it looks as if he is less convinced by the "animal body" as a musical metaphor.[127] Hanslick rarely refers to artistic-organic models of society, yet Suzanne G. Cusick can still convincingly argue that Hanslick's ideal listener participates "in European ideas of rationality . . . and so can imagine being eligible for inclusion in the category of individuals who can wield political and social power."[128]

There is no doubt that Hanslick's musical and aesthetic views were classicistic. Yet the fact that his unity of content and form is derived from the discussion, prevalent in the 1850s, of the unity of the ideal natural organism, has received scant attention heretofore. This could also help to explain many of Hanslick's preferences and antipathies as a critic. According to Büchner's *Kraft und Stoff*, the "basic principles of the education of body and soul, of organic and inorganic life, are the same everywhere."[129] With this in mind, what would be more obvious than to explain art and society according to those "natural" laws as well?

This essay has traced the popular and aesthetic foundations of Hanslick's organism discourse, focusing on the aesthetic relevance of gender in the context of the contemporary gender discourse. That this approach is governed by an "ideological" dimension is highlighted by the fact that the organism metaphor can be applied only very indirectly to structural aspects of composition.

Further investigation of the metaphorical connections between the "healthy" and "unhealthy" organism in writings on music (which are by no means limited to Hanslick)[130] would be a promising interdisciplinary project. In the context of the history of a discourse, the prominent Viennese critic's much-discussed, metaphorically rich and most pronounced judgments and preferences could provide crucial clues toward what it is that holds a culture together at its core.

Translated by Wolfgang Marx

Notes

All translations are by Wolfgang Marx, unless otherwise stated.

1. See Lothar Schmidt, "Arabeske. Zu einigen Voraussetzungen und Konsequenzen von Eduard Hanslicks musikalischem Formbegriff," *Archiv für Musikwissenschaft* 46, no. 2 (1989): 91–120; Schmidt, however, operates on the basis of "idealistic" presuppositions.

2. Mark Burford, "Hanslick's Idealist Materialism," *19th-Century Music* 30, no. 2 (2006): 166–81.

3. See Christoph Landerer, "Ästhetik von oben? Ästhetik von unten? Objektivität und 'naturwissenschaftliche' Methode in Eduard Hanslicks Musikästhetik," *Archiv für Musikwissenschaft* 61, no. 1 (2004): 43. See also Christoph Landerer, "Aesthetica longa, ars brevis. Vergänglichkeit des Schönen und Zeitlosigkeit der Ästhetik bei Eduard Hanslick," *Musik & Ästhetik* 14, no. 53 (2010): 10–19. Dietmar Strauß also points toward a "gradual transition from German idealism to the natural sciences via Hanslick's concept of the scientific. See Dietmar Strauß, *Vom Musikalisch-Schönen: Ein Beitrag zur Revision der Ästhetik der Tonkunst*, vol. 2 (Mainz: Schott, 1990), 113 (hereafter *VMS/2*).

4. See Ahlrich Meyer, "Mechanische und organische Metaphorik politischer Philosophie," *Archiv für Begriffsgeschichte* 13 (1969): 128–99; *Faszination des Organischen. Konjunkturen einer Kategorie der Moderne*, ed. Hartmut Eggert, Erhard Schütz, and Peter Sprengel (Munich: Iudicium, 1995).

5. Since my focus is not so much on the development of Hanslick's thinking but rather on the influence of "organic concepts in the middle of the nineteenth century, I refer mainly to the first edition of *Vom Musikalisch-Schönen: Ein Beitrag zur Revision der Ästhetik der Tonkunst* (Leipzig: Weigl, 1854). Translator's note: wherever possible, quotations from *Vom Musikalisch-Schönen* are taken from Geoffrey Payzant's translation of Hanslick's treatise, which is based on the eighth edition of 1891. See Hanslick, *On the Musically Beautiful*, trans. Geoffrey Payzant (Indiana: Hackett, 1986), hereafter *OMB*. For references to the original German, see the definitive text that tracks the changes to all ten editions published in Hanslick's lifetime: Hanslick, *Vom Musikalisch-Schönen: Ein Beitrag zur Revision der Ästhetik der Tonkunst*, ed. Dietmar Strauß, vol. 1 (Mainz: Schott,

1990), hereafter *VMS*. Where the first and the eighth edition differ substantially, the translation is my own. In these cases, the footnote refers to the 1854 edition cited above.

6. Eggert, Schütz, and Sprengel, eds., *Faszination des Organischen*.

7. See, for example, Hermann Lotze, "Leben: Lebenskraft," *Handwörterbuch der Physiologie mit Rücksicht auf physiologische Pathologie*, vol. 1, ed. Rudolph Wagner (Braunschweig: Vieweg und Sohn, 1842), 9–58; Julius Schaller, *Leib und Seele. Zur Aufklärung über "Köhlerglauben und Wissenschaft"* (Weimar: Böhlau, 1855), 31.

8. For recent publications see Ines Grimm, *Eduard Hanslicks Prager Zeit. Frühe Wurzeln seiner Schrift "Vom Musikalisch-Schönen"* (Saarbrücken: Pfau, 2003); Kurt Blaukopf, *Pioniere empiristischer Musikforschung. Österreich und Böhmen als Wiege der modernen Kunstsoziologie* (Vienna: Hölder-Pichler-Templsky, 1995).

9. Burford, "Hanslick's Idealist Materialism"; see also Dietmar Strauß, "Vom Kaffeehaus zum Katheder. Hanslicks Musikfeuilletons in der 'Presse' und das Studium der Musikgeschichte," Eduard Hanslick, *Sämtliche Schriften* 1/3, 333–69.

10. Louis Büchner, *Kraft und Stoff: Empirisch-naturphilosophische Studien in allgemeinverständlicher Darstellung* (Frankfurt/M.: Meidinger, 1855); Schaller, *Leib und Seele*.

11. See also Burford, "Hanslick's Idealist Materialism," 167: "The basic tenets underlying scientific materialism and, more generally, the challenge of idealism, were common coin among middle-class Germans—in both popular and scholarly form—at the very time at which Hanslick was writing." See also ibid., 177: "His idealist materialism demonstrated that he was *au courant* with the latest scientific theories. *On the Musically Beautiful* was published in late 1854, shortly before the appearance of *Force and Matter*, when the buzz and controversy surrounding scientific materialism were reaching an apex. In light of this concurrence, we should take Hanslick's analysis of music's materiality more seriously than has typically been the case." Blaukopf pointed out in 1995 that the connection between Hanslick's aesthetics of music and contemporary physiological research is overlooked far too often; see Blaukopf, *Pioniere empiristischer Musikforschung*, 91–92. Dahlhaus and others do indeed focus mainly on Hanslick's background in idealism.

12. "Von Tag zu Tag schwillt die Literatur über Kraft und Stoff, Leib und Seele, Geist und Materie, Glauben und Wissen, Natur und Offenbarung und verwandte Dinge stärker an." Louis Büchner, *Kraft und Stoff. Empirisch-naturphilosophische Studien in allgemein-verständlicher Darstellung* (Frankfurt/M.: Meidinger, 5th ed., 1858), 37.

13. Hans Christian Oersted, *Neue Beiträge zu dem Geist in der Natur*, trans. Karl Ludwig Kannegiesser (Leipzig: Lorck, 1851); see Eduard Hanslick, *VMS*, 97; *OMB*, 41. (Hanslick, however, quotes Oerstedt's treatise—a conversation between music-lovers—out of context and does not do it full justice here). The reference to Oerstedt is also to be found in August Wilhelm Ambros, *Die Grenzen der Musik und Poesie Eine Studie zur Ästhetik der Tonkunst*, reprint of the Leipzig edition of 1855 (Hildesheim: Olms, 1976), 34–35.

14. Karl Rosenkranz, *Psychologie oder Die Wissenschaft vom subjectiven Geist* (Königsberg: Gebrüder Bornträger, 2nd ed., 1843); see Hanslick, *VMS*, 105; *OMB*, 46.

15. Hermann Lotze, *Medicinische Psychologie oder Physiologie der Seele* (Leipzig: Weidmann'sche Buchhandlung, 1852); see Hanslick, *VMS*, 122; *OMB*, 55. Lotze in turn reviewed Hanslick's essay quite positively, despite criticising some detail; see Hermann Lotze, in *Göttingische gelehrte Anzeigen* (1855), 1049–68; reprint in Hermann Lotze, *Kleine Schriften*, vol. 3 (Leipzig: Hirzel, 1891), 200–14; see also Hermann Lotze, *Geschichte der Aesthetik in Deutschland* (Munich: Cotta, 1868), 478–87.

16. Gabriel Gustav Valentin, *Lehrbuch der Physiologie des Menschen. Fuer Aerzte und Studirende*, vol. 1 (Braunschweig: Vieweg, 1847); see Hanslick, *Vom Musikalisch-Schönen* (1854), 65; *VMS*, 121–22.

17. *Handwörterbuch der Physiologie mit Rücksicht auf physiologische Pathologie*, 4 vols, ed. Rudolph Wagner (Braunschweig: Vieweg, 1842–53); see Hanslick, *VMS*, 121; *OMB*, 55. Hanslick here refers to the entry on "Hören" (listening) by Adolf Harleß.

18. Jacob Grimm, *Der Ursprung der Sprache* (Berlin: [no pub.]. 1851); see Hanslick, *VMS*, 150; *OMB*, 71.

19. See Hanslick, *VMS*, 121; *OMB*, 55.

20. Carl Gustav Carus, *Organon der Erkenntniß der Natur und des Geistes* (Leipzig: Brockhaus, 1856).

21. Hanslick, *VMS*, 113; *OMB*, 51.

22. Ibid.

23. Hanslick, *VMS*, 115; *OMB*, 52.

24. Hanslick, *VMS*, 116; *OMB*, 53.

25. Hanslick, *VMS*, 119; *OMB*, 55.

26. Hanslick, *VMS*, 122; *OMB*, 56.

27. Ibid.

28. *VMS*, 125; *OMB*, 57. Hanslick's view that the current lack of knowledge about these matters means they can never be explained by physiology alone is of course questionable. In later editions of his essay, Hanslick revised this passage under the influence of the research into the physiology of tone undertaken by Hermann von Helmholtz: see Strauß, *VMS/2*, 107–9.

29. Hanslick, *VMS*, 122; *OMB*, 56.

30. "Der Organismus ist in der harmonischen Einheit seiner Glieder, als dieses in sich zusammenhängende untheilbare Ganze trotz seiner räumlichen, theilbaren, materiellen Existenz doch unräumlich, untheilbar, immateriell.... Wenn ich die Seele als eine Substanz betrachte, oder gar als ein Etwas, welches Empfindungen hat, so heißt dieses im Grunde nichts anderes als: die Seele ist ein Lebloses, welches lebt, ein Empfindungsloses, welches empfindet. Die Seele hat nicht Empfindung, sondern sie ist der Act des Empfindens selbst. Eben diese Thätigkeit, dieser Proceß ist ihre Substanzialität. Der Leib selbst als thätiges, sich zusammenschließendes, sich idealisirendes Ganze ist Seele.

Dem Versuche, den Organismus auf mechanische und chemische Processe zurückzuführen, ist immer diese Thatsache des sich empfindenden und eben in diesem Act sich zum Ganzen zusammenfassenden Leibes entgegen zu halten. So lange man nicht eben diese individuelle, subjective Einheit mechanisch und chemisch erklärt hat, ist eben die Hauptsache, die specifische, den Organismus charakterisirende Erscheinung nicht erklärt. Was aber nur durch eine äußere Combination von Stoffen und chemischen Kräften entsteht, was nur aus diesen als seinen Ursachen resultirt, ist höchstens ein Ding, welches wir mit Einem Namen benennen, aber nie und nimmermehr eine Einheit für sich, nie und nimmermehr Subject." Schaller, *Leib und Seele*, 140.

31. Hanslick, *VMS*, 75; *OMB*, 29.

32. Christian Kaden, *Das Unerhörte und das Unhörbare. Was Musik ist, was Musik sein kann* (Kassel: Bärenreiter & Metzler, 2004), 257.

33. Wilhelm August Ambros, *The Boundaries of Music and Poetry: A Study in Musical Aesthetics*, trans. J. H. Cornell (New York: Schirmer, 1893), 187.

34. See the anonymous review of *Wissenschaft und Sittenlehre: Briefe an Jacob Moleschott von Mathilde Reichardt* (1856), *Anregungen für Kunst, Leben und Wissenschaft* 1 (1856): 295–301.

35. "Produkt einer eigenthümlichen Zusammensetzung der Materie," Büchner, *Kraft und Stoff* (5th ed.), 130.

36. See Louis Büchner, "Naturwissenschaft. Der Kreislauf des Lebens. Physiologische Antworten auf Liebig's Chemische Briefe. Mainz, v. Zabern. 1st ed. 1852. 2nd ed 1855," *Anregungen für Kunst, Leben und Wissenschaft* 2 (1857): 30–38; Louis Büchner, "Naturwissenschaft. Geist und Körper in ihren Wechselbeziehungen, mit Versuchen naturwissenschaftlicher Erklärung. Von R. Reclam, Docent an der Universität Leipzig. Leipzig und Heidelberg 1859," *Anregungen für Kunst, Leben und Wissenschaft* 6 (1861): 26–31.

37. "Vom materialistischen Standpunkte hat man ein Recht, zu sagen, eine Melodie bestehe aus einer Reihe von Tönen, d. h. Vibrationen der Luft, und ebenso, eine Rede sei eine Reihe von Sprachlauten. Aber man hat Unrecht, wenn man sagt, eine Melodie bestehe nur aus Tönen, eine Rede nur aus Sprachlauten . . . Eben so wenig ist mir denkbar, daß der Lebens-Proceß aus den einzelnen physikalischen und chemischen Vorgängen erwächst, oder daß unser Selbstbewußtsein von unzähligen kleinen Vorgängen zusammengesetzt wird. . . .

In den Organismen sind die einzelnen Theile derselben nach dem Typus und Rhythmus des zugehörigen Lebens-Processes und durch dessen Wirksamkeit gebaut, so daß sie einem andern Lebens-Processe nicht dienen können. Deswegen glaube ich die verschiedenen Lebens-Processe, mit musikalischen Gedanken oder Themeten sie vergleichend, Schöpfungsgedanken nennen zu können, die sich ihre Leiber selbst aufbauen. Was wir in der Musik Harmonie und Melodie nennen, ist hier Typus (Zusammensein der Theile) und Rhythmus (Aufeinanderfolge der Bildungen)." Karl Ernst von Baer, *Reden gehalten in wissenschaftlichen Versammlungen und kleinere Aufsätze vermischten Inhalts, erster Theil: Reden* (St. Petersburg: H. Schmitzdorff, Karl Röttger, 1864), 280–81.

38. Hanslick, *Vom Musikalisch-Schönen* (1854), 77.

39. Hanslick, *VMS*, 112–13; *OMB*, 50. This is to contradict Kurt Blaukopf, when he wants to make a clear distinction between Hanslick's concept of the "pathological" (understood neutrally as the "immediate bodily influence on the organism including the effect on the nervous system" [unmittelbar körperlichen Einfluß auf den Organismus unter Einschluß der Wirkung auf das vegetative Nervensystem]) and the associations of illness. He does this by pointing to the historical use of the term. See Blaukopf, *Pioniere empiristischer Musikforschung*, 101.

40. Dambeck's influence on Hanslick is discussed in Grimm, *Eduard Hanslicks Prager Zeit*, 12 and 35–36.

41. "Fieberkranke, Melancholische, der Hypochonder u. dgl. können eben so wenig über Schönheit als über Wahrheit, Sittlichkeit u. s. w. ein zuverlässiges Urtheil fällen. Waltet Störung in den körperlichen Funkzionen [*sic*] ob, ist die Seele verstimmt, so ist es wenigstens ein eben so natürlicher als gewöhnlicher Fall, daß diese Umstände nachtheilig auf die Empfindung einwirken, und daher läßt sich das Urtheil solcher Menschen nie für zuverlässig r e i n und r i c h t i g annehmen." Johann Heinrich Dambeck, *Vorlesungen über Aesthetik*, vol. 1, ed. Joseph Adolph Hanslik (Prague: Carl Wilhelm Enders, 1822), 318.

42. Peter Lichtenthal, *Der musikalische Arzt, oder: Abhandlung von dem Einflusse der Musik auf den Körper, und von ihrer Anwendung in gewissen Krankheiten. Nebst einigen Winken, zur Anhörung einer guten Musik* (Vienna: Wappler and Beck, 1807), 100–104. See Hanslick, *OMB*, 52.

43. Hanslick, *VMS*, 133–34; *OMB*, 61.

44. Hanslick, *VMS*, 113; *OMB*, 51.

45. Hanslick, *VMS*, 137; *OMB*, 63.

46. Hanslick, *VMS*, 127; *OMB*, 58.

47. See Tobias Plebuch, "Vom Musikalisch-Bösen. Eine musikgeschichtliche Annäherung an das Diabolische in Thomas Manns 'Doktor Faustus,'" in *Thomas Mann: Doktor Faustus 1947–1997*, ed. Werner Röcke (Bern: Peter Lang, 2001), 252: "Hanslick's defence of aesthetic autonomy was in reality more a defence of moral autonomy." "Hanslicks Ehrenrettung der ästhetischen Autonomie galt eigentlich der moralischen."

48. Hanslick, *VMS*, 126; *OMB*, 57.

49. "Klebt" man "an der unsichern Wirkung musikalischer Erscheinungen anstatt in das Innere der Werke zu dringen und aus den Gesetzen ihres eigenen Organismus zu erklären, was ihr Inhalt ist, worin ihr Schönes besteht." *VMS*, 35; Hanslick, *Vom Musikalisch-Schönen* (1854), 7.

50. Fred Everett Maus, "Hanslick's Animism," *Journal of Musicology* 10, no. 3 (1992): 280. His deconstructive "close reading" of Hanslick's aesthetics yields the following additional insight: "Such a figure carries the possibility of a sexual quality in musical experience."

51. Hanslick, *VMS*, 50; *OMB*, 14.

52. Hanslick, *VMS*, 89; *OMB*, 37.

53. Hanslick, *VMS*, 74. This translation amended from *OMB*, 28.

54. Ambros, *The Boundaries of Music and Poetry*, 31.

55. Contemporary encyclopedias note that its pattern is reminiscent of certain plant shapes. See, for example, the article "Arabesken," in *Herders Conversations-Lexikon*, vol. 1 (Freiburg i. Br.: Herder, 1854), 227. Nägeli also bases his comparison of music and the arabesque on the latter's organic nature. See Hans Georg Nägeli, *Vorlesungen über Musik mit Berücksichtigung der Dilettanten (1826). Mit einem Vorwort zum Neudruck von Martin Staehelin* (Darmstadt: Wissenschaftliche Buchgesellschaft, 1983), 45. See also Schmidt, "Arabeske."

56. Hanslick, *VMS*, 75; *OMB*, 29.

57. Hanslick, *VMS*, 76; *OMB*, 29.

58. "Kaleidoskop," in *Herders Conversations-Lexikon*, vol. 3 (Freiburg i. Br.: Herder, 1855), 528.

59. Hanslick, *VMS*, 80–81; *OMB*, 32. The reference to the seed is ongoing in the chapter.

60. Hanslick, *VMS*, 167; *OMB*, 81.

61. Hanslick, *VMS*, 168; *OMB*, 82.

62. Hanslick, *VMS*, 169; *OMB*, 82. This leads Maus to conclude that the most fitting physiological analogy of a composition (according to Hanslick) would be an "erect penis which, like the composition, owes its condition to the fluid that engorges it; Hanslick's previous eroticized descriptions of interacting lines facilitate this association." Maus, "Hanslick's Animism," 281.

63. Hanslick, *VMS*, 145; *OMB*, 68.

64. Hanslick, *VMS*, 78–79; *OMB*, 31. See Peter Wapnewski, "Eduard Hanslick als Darsteller seiner selbst. Der Kritiker und die Nachwelt," in Hanslick, *Aus meinem Leben*, ed. and with an afterword by Peter Wapnewski (Kassel: Bärenreiter, 1987), 509: "The aesthetician does not recognize that the definition of art results in its un-naturalness." (Der Ästhetiker verkennt, daß die Definition von Kunst eben auf deren Un-Natur hinausläuft.) See also Werner Abegg, *Musikästhetik und Musikkritik bei Eduard Hanslick* (Regensburg: Gustav Bosse, 1974), 80: "If a work of art is original, it appears natural. To appear artificial is detrimental for a work of art." (Ein Kunstwerk, das originell erfunden ist, hat den Anschein des Natürlichen. Künstlich zu wirken, ist demnach für ein Kunstwerk verhängnisvoll.)

65. Hanslick, *VMS*, 85; *OMB*, 35.
66. Rosenkranz, *Psychologie*, 83. See Hanslick, *VMS*, 105; *OMB*, 46.
67. "Der Theil, wo die Ouverture sterblich oder besser: künstlerisch schon todt ist... Die Ouverture wird musivisch zusammengesetzt, anstatt organisch entwickelt." Eduard Hanslick, *Geschichte des Concertwesens in Wien* (Hildesheim: Olms, 1979), 2:62. (For the incorrect "musivisch," read "motivisch.")
68. "aus langem, dornigen Gestrüpp hie und da einzelne melodiöse Knöspchen hervor." Eduard Hanslick, "'Tannhäuser' von Richard Wagner," *Sämtliche Schriften* 1/4, 160.
69. "Was gegen die vermeintlich absolute Größe der Wagner'schen Opern entscheident bleibt, ist ihre musikalische Unfruchtbarkeit. Es fehlt ihnen, was sich nicht erwerben und nicht entbehren läßt: die göttliche Mitgift, die zeugende Kraft, der angeborene Reichthum,—kurz die ganze schöne Ungerechtigkeit der Natur." Hanslick, "Die Oper 'Lohengrin,'" *Sämtliche Schriften* 1/4, 336.
70. "Was den 'eigentlichen musikalischen Körper bildet,' nämlich an 'Melodie' und 'selbstständige[m] Gesang.'" Ibid., 344.
71. "Musikalische Kern." Ibid., 346.
72. "Was aber diesen Bau ausfüllt, ist eine Impotenz, die trotz ihres prahlerischen Gebahrens wahrhaftes Mitleid erweckt... so roh materiellem Sinne." Hanslick, *Geschichte des Concertwesens*, 2: 230. This wording appears to confirm Maus's reading; see Maus, "Hanslick's Animism," 281.
73. "Geistreich combinirende und colorirende Impotenz bleibt doch überall der Kern Liszt'scher Compositionen.... Eine einzelne Melodie steckt hin und wieder furchtsam ihr hübsches Köpfchen heraus, um sofort in wüstem Gedränge unterzugehen." Ibid., 224.
74. "Bestandtheile oft mosaikartik aneinander gereiht," Hanslick, "'Les préludes,' Symphonische Dichtung für großes Orchester von Franz Liszt," *Sämtliche Schriften* 1/4, 50.
75. "Die Hauptsache, an der dir Kritik festhalten muß, bleibt aber doch immer, daß alles, was an den Liszt'schen Symphonien das Publicum fesselt und den Musiker interessirt, nicht aus dem reinen Quell der Musik fließt, sondern künstlich gebranntes Wasser ist. Die musikalische Schöpfung drängt sich bei Liszt nicht frei und ursprünglich ans Licht, er setzt sie auf dem Wege der Reflexion zusammen." Ibid., 52.
76. "fühlte man durch das Ganze den warmen Athemzug religiöser Empfindung wehnen. Allein die grübelnde Reflexion schaut mit stechend gruen Augen aus jedem Tact heraus." Hanslick, "Die 'Graner Messe' von Liszt," *Sämtliche Schriften* 1/4, 264.
77. "Auf jede Sylbe legt sie ihre dürre Hand, und wo sich sonst duftige Veilchen wiegten, da entsteigt nun gespensterbleich der tödtliche Baum der Erkenntniß." Ibid., 265.
78. "Tortur der Gehörsnerven," Ibid., 264.
79. "Es glich dabei selbst einem anständig duldenden Prometheus, dem ein musikalischer Geier zwar nicht in die Leber, aber desto tiefer in's Ohr hackt." Hanslick, *Geschichte des Concertwesens*, 2: 199.
80. "betäubt und verstimmt." Ibid., 224.
81. "Jeder Mensch mit gesunden Sinnen wird sich von dem dissonirenden Geheul, das einen so wesentlichen Theil der 'Mazeppa-Symphonie' bildet, abwenden." Hanslick, "Les préludes," *Sämtliche Schriften* 1/4, 49.
82. "Allein, daß seiner Musik die singende Seele fehlt... das Ohr des Hörers wird dadurch überschwemmt, stumpf, theilnahmslos." Hanslick, "Musikalische Briefe," *Sämtliche Schriften* 1/3, 52.
83. "Künstlerische Mißgeburten," ibid., 52.

84. "als seine Nerven überspannen." Hanslick, "Musikalische Briefe (Die 'Jüdin' von Halevy)," *Sämtliche Schriften* 1/3, 139.
85. "Bizarre Melodieführung . . . oft krankhaftes Bestreben verrathen, das Ungewöhnlichste zu erreichen." Ibid., 141.
86. "Ein wahrer Strom von Kraft und Gesundheit . . . einem ersten Satz, der keck und kampflustig die jungen Glieder regt." Hanslick, "Concerte," *Sämtliche Schriften* 1/4, 39.
87. "Inneren Einheit," Hanslick, "Concerte," *Sämtliche Schriften* 1/4, 68.
88. "Blühendes Tongewebe," Ibid., 69.
89. "Auch im Leben der Kunst webt ein fortwährender Verbrennungs- und Erneuerungsproceß, ein geistiger 'Stoffwechsel.'" Ibid., 71.
90. "Es fehlt dem Werk das warme, innere Leben; eine äußere, fieberische Leidenschaftlichkeit soll es ersetzen . . . Solche Durchführung ist nicht mehr urwüchsig aus dem Hauptgedanken quellendes Leben . . . der fühlt in der D-*moll*-Sonate schon die allmälige Vertrocknung der Phantasie; er erkennt den fahlen Todeszug in dem gewaltsam aufgeregten Antlitz. Das innere wunderbare Blühen, das früher bei Schumann so ganz einzig, hat hier aufgehört." Hanslick, "Musik," Ibid., *Sämtliche Schriften* 1/4, 19.
91. Hanslick, "Es dünkt uns als eine der reifsten Früchte, welche . . . auf dem Felde geistlicher Musik hervorgewachsen . . . das angefügte B-dur-Allegro: 'Die Erlösten des Herrn' erscheint mehr wie ein äußerlicher Anhang, als wie ein organischer Abschluß." *Geschichte des Concertwesens*, 2:426.
92. "Im Finale vollends tritt der warme, lebendige Pulsschlag der Musik zurück, und an seiner Stelle hämmert mechanisch und ermüdend die graue Reflexion. Da ist ein abstractes Musiciren, ein ruheloses Combiniren und Grübeln bis zum Kopfschmerz." Ibid., 428.
93. "Ferner sind die Motive mehr mosaikartig zusammengesetzt, als organisch aus sich heraus entwickelt . . . halten wir für eigentlich lebensfähig daran nur das Scherzo." Ibid., 450.
94. "Solch emsiges, fast ängstliches Zusammenfädeln der Töne ist geistiger Tod für Beethoven's Musik, und war es selbst für dessen *G-dur* Sonate (op. 29)." Hanslick, "Musikalische Briefe. (Frln. Bondy. Zweite Quartett-Production)," *Sämtliche Schriften* 1/3, 313. Beethoven's op. 29 is the String Quintet in C major, and not a piano sonata.
95. "Organismus," Hanslick, *Geschichte des Concertwesens*, 1:164.
96. "Selbstständiger Organismus," Hanslick, *Geschichte des Concertwesens*, 2:458.
97. "Die Pflege des Streich-Quartettes ist in einem musikalischen Organismus von hoher Wichtigkeit." Ibid., 2:45.
98. "Ungern, schließe ich meine 'englischen Suiten' mit einem Blicke in den kranken Kern dieses äußerlich so großartigen Organismus." Ibid., 2:517.
99. "Feinsten Organismen der Physis." Ibid., 2: 512.
100. "Stumpfheit der Nerven." Ibid., 2:514.
101. "So hat der Engländer eine sehr einseitige Neigung für das Pathetische." Ibid., 2:512.
102. Claudia Honegger, *Die Ordnung der Geschlechter. Die Wissenschaften vom Menschen und das Weib 1750–1850* (Frankfurt/M.: Campus, 1991). A good summary of the biases of the late nineteenth century can be found in Robert Weininger, *Geschlecht und Charakter* (Vienna: Braumüller, 1903).
103. See, for example, Hanslick's review of Nanette Falk in "Concerte," *Sämtliche Schriften* 1/4, 61–62.
104. "Wir haben bei Besprechung mehr als einer andern Pianistin hervorgehoben, wie schon dieser Mangel an Muskelkraft an sich weit über seine materielle Bedeutung

hinaus in das Aesthetische des Vortrags greift und selbst Künstlerinnen ersten Ranges die volle Wirkung großartig erschütternder Tonstücke versagt." Ibid., 43.

105. Hanslick, *Geschichte des Concertwesens*, 2:179–80; Hanslick compares Goethe and Schiller here: "The more sensual, effeminate Goethe was closer to music, even though he preferred to focus on its rational aspects" (Der sinnlicher organisirte, weiblichere Göthe stand der Musik näher, obwohl er sich vorzugsweise an das verständige Element in ihr hielt).

106. Hanslick, *VMS*, 120; *OMB*, 54.

107. See also Maus, "Hanslick's Animism," 286.

108. "Unsere Künstlerin ist übrigens weit entfernt, sich übermäßige Forcestücke auszuwählen; sie beschämt lieber die Kraftvirtuosen der Neuzeit durch Männlichkeit des Vortrages. Nichts Weibisches, Zerflossenes, Gefühlsüberschwengliches herrschte in dem Spiel Clara Schumanns: es ist alles bestimmt, klar, scharf, wie eine Bleistiftzeichnung. Die häufigen kleinen Accente, die sie liebt, unterscheiden sich merkwürdig von dem Nachdruck, mit welchem die meisten Pianistinnen in jede einzelne Note ein eigenes Gefühl zu legen suchen; was hier Affectation der subjectiven Empfindung, ist dort stets nur sorgfältiges Beleuchten rhythmischer oder harmonischer Gegensätze." Hanslick, "Musikalische Briefe (Clara Schumann)," *Sämtliche Schriften* 1/3, 202.

109. "Einen weiteren, ganz speciellen Vorzug der Schumann, der insbesondere bei Damen zu höchsten Seltenheiten gehört, ist ihre streng einheitliche, männliche Auffassung, die das Ganze nicht durch schmachtendes Verweilen auf den kleinlichsten Einzelheiten unterbricht." Hanslick, "Concerte," *Sämtliche Schriften* 1/4, 377.

110. "Allein der Vortrag selbst dieser Sächelchen zeugte von einem männlicheren Geist der jede affectirte Zimperei und Ueberschwenglichkeit verschmäht." Hanslick, "Musik (Die Schwestern Ferni . . .)," *Sämtliche Schriften* 1/4, 357.

111. "Die A-*dur*-Symphonie hingegen hat mehr Mark und Knochen, ihre Haltung ist aufrecht, fest und männlich." Hanslick, "Musikalische Briefe," *Sämtliche Schriften* 1/3, 322.

112. "Mädchen 'zu Componistinnen bilden' zu wollen, wird selbst mit der Beschränkung, in welcher dieser Ausdruck Sinn hat, kaum jemand beifallen." Hanslick, "Musikalische Briefe," *Sämtliche Schriften* 1/3, 179.

113. Quoted in Abegg, *Musikästhetik und Musikkritik*, 67.

114. Hanslick, *VMS*, 105; *OMB*, 46.

115. Hanslick, *VMS*, 105; Translator's note: this is my own translation. This passage is not in the 8th edition of 1891 upon which Payzant based his translation. See *OMB*, 46 for the context of this deleted passage.

116. Hanslick, *VMS*, 105; *OMB*, 46.

117. Felix Printz, *Zur Würdigung des musikästhetischen Formalismus Eduard Hanslicks* (Borna-Leipzig: Noske, 1918), 14–15.

118. "Da im Weibe die plastische Thätigkeit vorherrscht, so ist es psychisch zum Gefühl und zur Einheit mit sich und der Welt bestimmt. Es ist also nach Innen gerichtet, allein nur auf unmittelbare Weise, insofern es für jeden Eindruck von Außen offen ist; es wird leicht erregt und hat für den Schein der Dinge, für die Oberfläche des Lebens, die zarteste Empfänglichkeit.—Durch die große Passivität ist aber die Productivität des Weibes beschränkt. Es vermag z. B. in den plastischen Künsten nichts, weil diese eine Entäußerung der Subjectivität fordern, deren es nicht fähig ist. . . . Musik, namentlich die Behandlung der Saiteninstrumente und Gesang, ist die dem Weibe zusagende Kunst. . . . Erfunden haben die Frauen in der Musik allerdings nur wenig." Rosenkranz, *Psychologie*, 60. (Emphasis is mine.)

119. "Durch seine natürliche Organisation mittelst der größeren Ausbildung des centralen Moments des Nervensystems zum Denken und mittelst der stärkeren Muskelkraft zur Wirkung nach Außen bestimmt. Um zur That zu gelangen, muß er in die Entzweiung mit sich und der Welt sich einlassen. . . . Der Mann ist daher zur universellen Productivität organisirt und in keinem Zweige menschlicher Kunst und menschlichen Wissens und Handelns durch die Natur beschränkt." Ibid., 61.

120. "Weil es in größere Abgründe sich stürzen muß, welche dem Weibe ewig mit lieblichen Nebeln verdeckt bleiben. Es ist eine leere Vergötterung des Weibes, es für gefühlvoller als den Mann zu halten . . . Das Weib ist, so zu sagen, Gefühl, während der Mann Gefühle hat. . . . Vom Mann fordert man, daß er über sich, über seinen Schmerz hinauskomme, ihn sich zum Gegenstand mache, ihn begreifend die Freiheit von ihm erlange." Ibid., 61.

121. See Eva Rieger, *Frau, Musik und Männerherrschaft. Zum Ausschluß der Frau aus der deutschen Musikpädagogik, Musikwissenschaft und Musikausübung* (Frankfurt a. M., Berlin and Wien: Ullstein, 1981), 147. ["Absolute Musik bedeutet mehreres: zum einen das Ahnen des Absoluten, also Metaphysischen; zum anderen das Hinüberwechseln aus der Sphäre des Gefühls in die der 'reinen' Idee. Beides enthält abgrenzende Elemente der Frau gegenüber . . . Absolute Musik bedeutete aber auch durch die Kultivierung der 'reinen Geistigkeit, eine Verabsolutierung männlicher Eigenschaften, da seit alters her die Körperhaftigkeit und Sinnlichkeit in der männlichen Imagination als weibliches Merkmal fungiert."] Freia Hoffmann argues similarly (yet is slightly vaguer and thus somewhat misleading) in *Instrument und Körper. Die musizierende Frau in der bürgerlichen Kultur* (Frankfurt/M.: Insel, 1991), 236–37. See also Maus, "Hanslick's Animism," 287–88.

122. This matter will be explored further in my forthcoming study "Liszt—Faust—Diskurs," a study devoted to Liszt's working of the Faust legend.

123. "Das Geschlecht ist . . . der Gegensatz zwischen Geist und Materie, zwischen Licht und Masse, zwischen Aether und den irdischen Elementen, Sonne und Planet, zwischen Electrismus und Chemismus dargestellt im Organismus als Totalität." Das Geschlecht sei mithin "der Urgegensatz der Welt, des Geistes und der Materie organisch dargestellt. . . . Das Producierende der Frucht heißt das Weibliche; das was die Production weckt, das Männliche. . . . Männlichkeit ist der Geist der Welt, Weiblichkeit die Materie, welche von jenem belebt wird" Lorenz Oken, *Lehrbuch der Naturphilosophie* (Jena: Friedrich Frommanu, 3rd ed. 1843), 221. See also, among others, Wilhelm von Humboldt, "Ueber den Geschlechtsunterschied und dessen Einfluß auf die organische Natur," *Die Horen* I/1.2 (1795): 99–132.

124. Büchner, *Kraft und Stoff* (5th ed.), lviii.

125. See for example Carl Gustav Carus, *Lebenserinnerungen und Denkwürdigkeiten*, part III (Leipzig: F. A. Brockhaus, 1866), 182; there Carus compares the skull of the composer Niels Gade with other skulls.

126. Ambros, *The Boundaries of Music*, 20–21.

127. See Strauß, *VMS/2*, 103–4.

128. Suzanne G. Cusick, "Gender, Musicology, and Feminism," in *Rethinking Music*, ed. Nicholas Cook and Mark Everist (Oxford: Oxford University Press, 2001), 496. See also Maus, "Hanslick's Animism," 287, who reads the imaginary link between "creative spirit" and "listener" as "homosocial bond between men, constructed as identification rather than desire, based on shared recognition of their desire for and control over women." Among other things this means that "Hanslick's account of active listening creates a comfortably masculine position for the listener."

129. "Grundprincipien körperlicher und geistiger Bildung, organischen und unorganischen Lebens überall dieselben," Büchner, *Kraft und Stoff* (5th ed.), 48.

130. See, for example, Ambros, *The Boundaries of Music*, 161, where he describes the Queen Mab episode in Berlioz's *Romeo et Juliette* as a "minor incident that has expanded and turned into a principal episode, as if in a healthy body some unessential gland should swell up to a morbid monstrosity." Richard Wagner's writings offer many more examples.

Part Four

Critical Battlefields

Chapter Twelve

Hanslick and Hugo Wolf

Timothy R. McKinney

Hugo Wolf spoke with the voice of both artist and critic. The reviews he wrote for the *Wiener Salonblatt* in 1884–87 before achieving lasting success as a composer of lieder provide fascinating glimpses into the concert life and musical politics of contemporary Vienna; they also provide rich insight into the relationship between composer and critic. By promoting the music of the New German School, Wolf placed himself squarely in opposition to Eduard Hanslick and Viennese cultural conservatism, thus joining in a larger struggle between proponents of traditionalism who championed Brahms and a stridently progressive faction that elevated Wagner to near godlike status. In this larger conflict, political maneuvering along party lines drove the rhetorical and tactical engines of war, and both camps made exaggerated claims about the lack of artistic worth and aesthetic insight of the other. Subsequent commentators suggested that as critics Hanslick and Wolf are known to history largely for judging the artistic hero of the other side too harshly: Hanslick for a few "mistakes" he made about Wagner, Wolf for a few "foolish things" he said about Brahms.[1] My purpose in the current essay is to look beyond the sometimes ridiculous invective and examine the subtext of the quarrel between Wolf the artist and Hanslick the critic,[2] a quarrel that manifested itself in Wolf's music as well as his criticism, and in Hanslick's autobiography, *Aus meinem Leben*.[3]

Due to his evolving and novel academic position at the university,[4] his widely read and frequently reissued treatise on music aesthetics,[5] and his commanding critical voice in the *Neue Freie Presse* and other journals, Hanslick had been an icon of aesthetic authority in Vienna for three decades before Wolf launched his Wagnerian counterattack.[6] As became widely known, Wagner himself toyed with the idea of giving Hanslick's name to the stodgy town clerk and song judge Sixtus Beckmesser in *Die Meistersinger von Nürnberg*, whose hidebound pedantry in criticism would stifle progressive art if left unchecked, and whose inept bungling in his own artistic efforts clearly symbolized the contempt Wagner held for his critics in general: they criticize that which they cannot do.[7] Certainly Wolf, who once likened critics discussing music to the blind discussing color,[8] knew the connection well; in his review of *Die Meistersinger* on September 20, 1885, he wrote, "The world has only one Beckmesser, and if the world would like to meet him, the world must come to Vienna."[9] Conversely, in Hanslick's view, Wagner and the New German School were taking music down the wrong path by focusing on extramusical meaning and undermining conventional tonal structures when music's beauty should depend on purely musical meaning; i.e., on its *tönend bewegte Formen*.[10] While acknowledging Wagner's genius, Hanslick also expressed very serious concerns on both musical and dramatic grounds about the "formless" nature of his later works, their "endless melody," restless harmony, rigid declamation, overbearing orchestra, and unnatural and unwieldy plots and poetry.[11] For the young Wagnerian firebrand Wolf, Hanslick's denouncements of Wagner's ideals were nothing short of blasphemy against the true artistic faith, prompting a visceral response. As we shall see, Hanslick and Wolf were as different in their motivations and methodologies for criticism as in their ideologies of musical art.

Wolf: Aspiring Composer and Reluctant Critic

Wolf arrived in Vienna in the fall of 1875 at the age of fifteen in order to enter the conservatory, and immediately immersed himself in the musical life of the city.[12] Soon thereafter he encountered Wagner's music during the latter's extended visit to the city in November and December to supervise productions of *Tannhäuser* and *Lohengrin*. Wolf wrote home: "I am quite beside myself because of the music of this great master and have become a Wagnerian."[13] In current parlance we would say the young Wolf "stalked" Wagner until he obtained an interview, during which he sought the master's opinion on some early compositions. Wagner encouraged him without really examining his work, and the two never established a personal relationship. Wolf's temperamental personality and lack of academic discipline led to his dismissal from the conservatory and his return home in March 1877. He contrived to return to the city after eight months, and managed to eke out a living by giving a few music lessons, accompanying, and receiving support from family and friends, all the while continuing to compose on his own.

Despite his Wagnerian allegiance, the young Wolf also expressed appreciation for several of Brahms's works, and in 1879 sought Brahms's opinion on his compositional skills as well.[14] Though primarily only biased, secondhand anecdotal evidence of the nature of the interview remains, given Brahms's often caustic personality and Wolf's impetuosity and petulance, it would have been surprising had Wolf left with his feelings intact.[15] However, we can gather from Wolf's family correspondence that Brahms suggested Wolf study counterpoint with Gustav Nottebohm, and that Wolf went so far as to inquire about his fee.[16]

Wolf's first recorded interaction with Hanslick was amiable enough. Sometime before February 1, 1883, Wolf apparently shared some of his early songs with Hanslick in order to obtain his opinion of them, for on that date Hanslick replied in a short letter:

> Although it was not easy for my eyes to master the miniature writing of your manuscripts, yet I owe to them the acquaintance of a new, very promising talent and have the honor to return your sensitive, interesting songs with best thanks,
>
> Yours sincerely,
> Dr. Eduard Hanslick.[17]

After further consultation, it seems Hanslick recommended Wolf submit his compositions to Simrock, Brahms's publisher, for publication consideration. However, on February 13, less than two weeks after Hanslick's letter to Wolf, Wagner died in Venice, a heavy blow for the twenty-two-year-old Wolf. This tragedy led Wolf to submit his compositions to Schott, publisher of many of Wagner's works, on February 18.[18] Though Schott would later publish Wolf's mature works, they were not interested in these early songs, despite the support Wolf had procured from the conductor Felix Mottl, to whom he reported: "Schott refuses in the politest manner the publication of my songs and regrets the rejection all the more since you pressed my affairs so warmly upon them. I will now try my luck with Breitkopf & Härtel, since I cannot make up my mind, in spite of Hanslick's recommendation, to offer my compositions to Simrock."[19] His reluctance to try Brahms's publisher did not prevent him from leveraging Hanslick's influence for his sales pitch to Breitkopf & Härtel in his cover letter of May 28: "Perhaps Eduard Hanslick's enclosed letter will assist my request; however favorable his opinion of my abilities, however much you, Sirs, may be convinced by his view—is this a reason, a sufficient reason to publish the manuscript?"[20] Breitkopf & Härtel did not think so, as Wolf complained in a letter to his father. Here he also indicates that he eventually did send his manuscripts to Simrock, who also rejected them.[21]

Failing to secure a publisher for his music in 1883, in January 1884 Wolf became the music critic for the *Wiener Salonblatt*, a weekly society magazine.[22] Wolf succinctly described his journalistic mission and method several years later in a letter to his new friend Dr. Oskar Grohe on May 2, 1890: "Hanslick and the whole Viennese [establishment] sharply attacked—for that reason now banished. No regrets, however."[23] Just nineteen days later, while writing to another new friend and supporter, Dr Emil Kauffmann, he again referred to his tenure as a critic while explaining his dislike for Brahms's music:

> If I am concisely and briefly to say what I think of Brahms, then permit me to cite Friedrich Nietzsche's familiar words: "Brahms's creativity is the

melancholy of impotence." I fully endorse these words that are spoken from the soul. I also advocated this opinion most emphatically at that time as a reporter for a Viennese weekly paper and thereby made friends of neither Brahms nor Hanslick, which was never my intention.[24]

By his tenth review on March 23, 1884, Wolf had indeed disparaged Brahms and made thinly veiled references to what he perceived to be Hanslick's abuse of his critical authority:

> What we have heard of Brahms' recent works has left us rather cold. Some of it has been absolutely repulsive, especially the symphonies, which have been canonized by certain critics in such a manner that one could only regret their bad taste, their blindness, if one did not know that "personality" constitutes the spectacles through which a work of art is viewed, and according to which it is assessed. It is well to distinguish whether the works of a living composer are regarded by a benevolent or a hostile eye. The critic is, after all, only human, and subject to personal influences. But in the end he is still a critic, and as such he has no business expressing his friendship for the author by immoderate praise of his tortured products while inversely, and from contrary motives, smearing inspired composition with odious slander.[25]

To objective eyes, Wolf, of course, is as guilty of slander against Brahms as he implies Hanslick is against Wagner. Prompted by what struck him as the adulatory tone of Hanslick's review of the Viennese première of Brahms's Fourth Symphony in January of 1886,[26] Wolf moved beyond sniping at an anonymous "clever" (*geistreicher*) or "'famous' and 'feared'" (*berühmten' und 'gefürchteten*) critic[27] and began to attack Hanslick sarcastically by name: "Herr Hanslick is, as everybody knows, a very unbiased critic, as amply demonstrated on the one hand by his reviews of Richard Wagner, and on the other hand by his reviews of Brahms."[28] In the remainder of this review, Wolf makes some of his most famous and most scathing remarks about Brahms, claiming that he has mastered the art of composing without ideas, asserting that in his symphonies the fundamental tone alternates between "can't do" (*Nichtkönnen*) and "wish I could" (*Gernwollen*), and glossing and sharpening Nietzsche's barb about compositional impotence that he later quoted to Emil Kauffmann: the melancholy of impotence (*Melancholie des Unvermögens*) becomes the most intense musical impotence (*der intensivsten musikalischen Impotenz*).[29]

By the final season of his critical career, Wolf's gloves are completely off, and he directly questions Hanslick's integrity in the wake of the latter's attempt to explain the cool reception given to the second Viennese performance of Brahms's Fourth Symphony.[30] Wolf ascribes to Hanslick the motives and methods of the shady politician, the card shark, the illusionist: "May one perceive in these concessions made to truth nevertheless only a political dodge by my illustrious colleague, in any case he will now have to shuffle his cards more carefully if he wants to successfully display the semblance of objectivity strived for through his political dealing."[31] Wolf's assault on what he viewed as the oppressive nature of the Viennese establishment would continue unabated until his regular contributions to the *Wiener Salonblatt* ceased on April 24, 1887, under circumstances that remain unclear.[32]

Aside from its famous polemical tone, though, Wolf's critical writing also resonates with the dissonance he felt between his intense desire to achieve success as a composer and the bitter reality of being known as a critic. He explicitly expresses his discontent early in his second year, in an article that appeared on January 18, 1885:

> To a professional musician concerned primarily with the vocal art of the performer, Herr Vogl's convulsive blinking would be a matter of indifference. In the opinion of the music critic *Dp* this lamentable circumstance "proved insuperable to this performer's considerable artistry."
>
> The professional musician, destined by a dire fate to be a music critic, too, will stick to what is relevant and pertinent, in contrast to our esthetically cultivated music critics who indulge themselves so happily in abstract hairsplitting.[33]

Wolf clearly distances himself from the professional critic, styling himself as a musician instead, an artist forced by unfortunate circumstance to assume the duties of a lesser calling, a Wolf in sheep's clothing, as it were, or, perhaps more appropriately, an artistic lamb in the clothing of the vicious wolf-critic. His disassociation with the critical profession resurfaces in an article dated October 23 of the same year, after his unpublished string quartet had been refused a performance by the Rosé Quartet.[34] Wolf entitled the article "Musik?" and devoted it entirely to a sardonic soliloquy on rejection and the unanimous verdict rendered by the quartet; the fact that Wolf had earlier ridiculed in print the compositions of the group's violist, Siegmund Bachrich, certainly did not support his cause, and that he would submit his music to the group after publicly mocking one of its members leads one to question his grasp of the political realities his critical pronouncements might impose on his quest for artistic recognition and success.[35] Though Wolf couched his complaint in sarcastic humor, one nonetheless hears the voice of the wounded artist cry out, not only over the rejection of his piece (which was more than enough to set him off), but also over the cruel irony of his current lot in life:

> There is hardly anything more depressing than never to be able to see an ever-so-modest wish fulfilled; and yet nothing preoccupies a man more than anxiety or confidence about the fulfillment of his hopes and wishes. In the process one turns into the fool, the drunkard, the misanthropist, the astrologer,

the starveling, the treasure hunter, the habitual debtor, the exorcist, the lyric poet, the loafer, the unsuccessful lover, yes, even the critic (as with me, for example), and God knows what else that is useful and pleasing.[36]

Yet Wolf's dissatisfaction with his employment as critic was not due to any reluctance on his part to be critical. He was all too happy to expound upon his favorite partisan themes, to deride the concert-going public in Vienna for what he claimed to be their ignorance, their senseless lack of taste, and their willingness to be swayed by the pronouncements of "powerful" critics rather than thinking for themselves, to mock the artistic directors of the principal performing organizations for their programming choices, and to brazenly challenge the acumen and integrity of other critics, with Hanslick becoming his most frequent target. In a vivid—if dated—turn of phrase, Wolf biographer Ernest Newman describes the entrance of Wolf's brash and acerbic criticism into the pages of a polite society journal tailored largely toward women as "rather like the irruption of a fanatical dervish into a boudoir."[37] For Wolf, there were no half-measures in dealing with matters of art, as he stated in an oft-quoted letter to Emil Kauffmann in 1890: "To me, the most important principle in art is rigid, harsh, inexorable truth, truth unto cruelty."[38]

Hanslick: Music Critic and Music Historian

Hanslick held a greatly divergent view of the critical profession and of the relationship of the critic to artist and public, and took a vastly different approach to his critical writing. Whereas Wolf's rough edges show at nearly every turn and his sometimes shrill rhetoric and attempts at humor can come off as sophomoric despite his keen musical insights and critical acumen, Hanslick's writing is polished, erudite, historically informed and informative, and reflective of his superior educational and cultural background, as befitted the standards of the *Neue Freie Presse*, the leading Viennese newspaper of his day.[39] His critical reproaches, which can be searing, generally are delivered with the decorum he believed appropriate for one who respects his calling and his readership. Wolf fires off opinion and dispenses judgment while usually giving little context outside the concert attended unless required by partisan politics. By contrast, Hanslick often describes the genesis, performance history, and reception history of musical works or discusses biographical details of composers or performers at length, regardless of the side of the ideological fence upon which they sit. Hanslick, in short, reads more like a professional music historian, albeit a biased one, while Wolf reads more like a scrappy aficionado. Wolf, for all his public attacks on Hanslick, nonetheless privately showed some respect for his writing, and purportedly remarked to his young admirer and future editor Heinrich Werner that "only those have the right to write who can do so with distinction, who can write like Nietzsche—or Hanslick, perhaps."[40] It is telling that Wolf resisted having his *Salonblatt* criticisms republished during his lifetime, not because of the opinions he expressed, but because of his dissatisfaction with stylistic characteristics of his writing.[41] Hanslick, however, published topical collections of his own selected reviews in order to record and preserve his "living history" of Viennese musical culture.[42]

Hanslick's criticism brought him much renown and authority, allowed him to rub elbows with high society and royalty and to interact with artistic giants, and garnered invitations from far and wide to consult on musical matters; his pride in this regard is immediately evident from his autobiography. In stark contrast to Wolf, who saw himself as a creative artist and chafed in the critic's role, Hanslick enjoyed and received fulfillment from his critical activities and was content to see himself and be seen by others as no more than an amateur musician. He believed the music critic should engage in practical musicianship in order to enhance his critical craft, such as knowing from personal experience, for instance, which intervals and syllables are difficult or uncomfortable to sing.[43] He was a competent pianist who frequently played chamber works or four-hand arrangements in private gatherings within his circle of friends, which included Brahms, and on occasion in similar settings with other luminaries such as Franz Liszt.[44] He tried his hand at composing in his younger days, and five of his songs were published many years later in 1882 with the assistance of Brahms.[45] We can imagine how galling it must have been for Wolf to see the critic's songs in print when his own songs would not begin to be published until 1888, especially so because Brahms aided Hanslick, yet in Wolf's view did little for Wolf himself. Exacerbating his frustration would be Hanslick's self-deprecating remarks about the collection in a *feuilleton* of January 29, 1884, just nine days after Wolf's first review appeared. Hanslick's comments, prompted by a performance of one of the songs at a concert under review, refer to the songs' old-fashioned style and melodious naivety, and imply that they are not worthy of public presentation.[46]

Despite Hanslick's early experimentation with composition, or perhaps more correctly because of it, in his autobiography he declares his personal preference for the critic's life over that of the creative artist:

> Since my youth, I have always regarded, next to a professorship, the activity of a music critic in a distinguished major paper as the most desirable. Above the poet who depends upon his own invention, the critic enjoys the advantage that the flow of new material continually gives him. No year passes without the sometimes intermittent, but never depleted source of artistic production supplying us some grains of gold. Beside worthless works that absolutely impose silence, works of originality and excellence also emerge. Not only excellence, however, also pretentious ugliness, self-assertive eccentricity provokes and occupies the critic.[47]

Hanslick freely admits that he relies on the creative invention of others rather than his own to provide the raw material for his work, yet turns this inevitable charge into an "advantage."[48] In a similar vein his pride in the critic's role emerges from the manner in which he relates the story in his autobiography about playing duets with Liszt. According to Hanslick, at an informal dinner in Vienna in 1858 Liszt extended an open invitation for someone to join him at the piano to play Schubert's *Divertissement à la Hongroise*, but received no takers until Hanslick stepped forward. Hanslick records Liszt's response to his venture as "Bravo, . . . but criticism only comes second to production, do you not agree? Therefore, play the *secondo!*"[49] Although Liszt's remark puts Hanslick and criticism in their places relative to the artist and artistic creation, Hanslick included this in his autobiography to demonstrate that he was recognized by the most famous artist in Europe at that time for his role as a critic.

Yet, more importantly, Hanslick extols the altruistic belief that his critical expertise influences the overall course of artistic development by educating the public, even if he claims to have little immediate influence on artists or works of art.[50] He maintains that he addresses his critical writing to the public, not the artist, and that artists rarely take any advice he might offer them. He dismisses the notion that he could control the career of an artist, asserting instead that he could not sway the opinion of the public against its will, and that the public is mostly correct in its assessment. Artists determine their own fates, each according to his or her worthiness.

Hanslick goes on to say that he wields the most influence when the public is not certain how something should be received, and that he can obtain his goal of educating the public only by having gained the confidence and agreement of his readership, which can only be accomplished through genuine means; that he was able to do so he considered his greatest treasure.[51] In other words, Hanslick believes that proper criticism serves a vital function in musical society that outweighs its seeming lack of creativity, and believes that he has not merely fed off the artistry of others, but has earned his success and deserves the stature that comes with it. This is because as a critic, like the artists he judges, he has had to win the trust and approval of the public through his own merit. Had he not possessed the acumen, insight, aptitude, and knowledge needed to excel at his craft and to become Vienna's leading authority in musical matters, he would not have been able to do so.

Wolf's *Abschied* to Criticism and to Hanslick

While Hanslick took pride in his critical career and believed it provided a valuable service to society, we can be sure Wolf was all too happy to abandon the critical profession, regardless of how he came to part ways with the *Salonblatt* in April of 1887.[52] Things began to change dramatically for Wolf just months later in early 1888, when his creative talent finally erupted in full force and presented him with more than ninety songs in that year alone. Almost from the beginning of this artistic awakening, Wolf was occupied with personifying in his music the inevitable struggle between the conflicting demands of received tradition and artistic growth that every artist faces, the same struggle with which so much of his and Hanslick's criticism was preoccupied. This struggle comes to the forefront in his famous setting of Mörike's "Abschied," completed on March 8, in which he takes Mörike's explicit critique of criticism, enriches it, and makes it his own. In a review published almost two years earlier, Wolf had paraphrased a line from "Abschied" without attribution.[53] Clearly he already was engaged with this text, but perhaps did not yet feel up to the task of setting it, not only because of insecurity about his creative powers, but also because of the anxiety of being currently cast in the critic's role himself. Any such reservations were swept away by his flood of inspiration in 1888, and Wolf's life experiences as both artist and critic channeled that flood into a brilliant musical reading.[54] The poem and translation are as follows:

Unangeklopft ein Herr tritt abends bei mir ein:
"Ich habe die Ehr', Ihr Rezensent zu sein."
Sofort nimmt er das Licht in die Hand,
Besieht lang meinen Schatten an der Wand,
Rückt nah und fern: "Nun, lieber junger Mann,
Sehn Sie doch gefälligst mal Ihre Nas' so von der Seite an!
Sie geben zu, dass das ein Auswuchs is."
—Das? Alle Wetter—gewiss!
Ei Hasen! ich dachte nicht,
All mein Lebtage nicht,
Dass ich so eine Weltsnase führt' im Gesicht!!
Der Mann sprach noch Verschiedenes hin und her,
Ich weiss, auf meine Ehre, nicht mehr;
Meinte vielleicht, ich sollt' ihm beichten.
Zuletz stand er auf; ich tat ihm leuchten.
Wie wir nun an die Treppe sind,
Da geb' ich ihm, ganz froh gesinnt,
Einen kleinen Tritt,
Nur so von hinten aufs Gesässe, mit—
Alle Hagel! ward das ein Gerumpel,
Ein Gepurzel, ein Gehumpel!
Dergleichen hab' ich nie gesehn,
All mein Lebtage nicht gesehn
Einen Menschen so rasch die Trepp' hinabgehn![55]

[Without knocking a man enters my room one evening:
"I have the honor to be your critic."
At once he takes the lamp in hand,

Inspects at length my shadow on the wall,
Marches near and far: "Now, my dear young man,
Kindly look at your nose just so from the side!
You will grant, that that is an excrescence."
—"That? Good heavens—certainly!"
Gadzooks! I never thought,
Never in all my days,
That I bore such a world-size nose in my face!!
The man spoke more about this and that,
I remember, on my honor, nothing more;
Perhaps he thought I should confess to him.
At last he stood up; I lit the way for him.
When we were at the top of the stairs,
There I gave him, entirely merrily minded,
A small kick
Just so from behind on his seat—
By thunder! what a rumbling,
A tumbling, a stumbling,
I have never seen the like,
In all my days have never seen
A person go down the stairs so fast!]

In both the poem and Wolf's setting of it we must distinguish between the voice of the critic as a character in the drama and the critical mode of the authorial voice. Given Wolf's obsessive public vilification of Hanslick, there can be little doubt that the voice of the critic in Mörike's poem would be attributed to Vienna's foremost *feuilletonist* in Wolf's mind, despite the fact that Hanslick had not actually reviewed Wolf at that time, nor even responded in print to his harangues. We must also recognize that the subtle interplay of the artist's and the critic's voices in Wolf's song goes far beyond anything in Mörike's poem. A close reading of the music itself supports my suggestion that Wolf had Hanslick centered in his crosshairs.

The uninvited critic and his motive enter first. As seen in example 12.1, he has no substance, which is why Wolf paints him with a unison line shared between voice and piano. The critic announces himself in measures 5–8 with a classical cadential progression, the type of structural closure Hanslick decried the lack of in Wagner,[56] in the key of C minor, the key of Beethoven's Fifth Symphony and Brahms's First, a key in which Hanslick would have felt very much at home. The chords are hammered out with accented grace notes; although the poem describes the critic as entering without knocking, Wolf presents him as being as abrasive and jarring as any unexpected knock.

The critic's motive returns in measure 14 as he prepares to pronounce his verdict on the shadow of the artist's nose in the borrowed light of the artist's lamp (because he does not have the vision to judge the artist himself nor the ability to illuminate anything on his own). As seen in example 12.2, the largely

Example 12.1. Hugo Wolf, *Abschied* from *Gedichte von Eduard Mörike*, mm. 1–9

unison texture erupts into a succession of augmented triads as he declares: "Sie geben zu, dass das ein Auswuchs is," introducing a progressive harmonic technique Arnold Schoenberg called "suspended tonality."[57] Yet here the symmetrical sonorities that threaten traditional tonality are associated with the critic, the traditionalist, rather than the artist, the progressive. I suggest this association stems intentionally from Wagner's association of augmented triads with Beckmesser in *Die Meistersinger*,[58] representative instances of which are shown in example 12.3. Given Wagner's and Wolf's explicit identification of Beckmesser with Hanslick, the shared use of augmented triads to depict inept criticism in *Meistersinger* and *Abschied* directly ties Hanslick to Mörike's critic in Wolf's song. The essential irony of Mörike's poem, in which the critic seeks to judge the artist yet unwittingly passes judgment on himself, thus draws from Wolf musical irony: the intentionally "bad" progression indeed represents an artistic "Auswuchs"—of the namer, not of the named object. When the artist speaks in the following line, he achieves tonal clarity by measure 40 in the relative key of E-flat major, the alter ego of the critic's C minor. In a dual role reversal, aberration represents tradition, while the traditional represents the progressive. The critic speaks his nonsense through a musical language made

Example 12.2. Wolf, *Abschied*, mm. 32–40

Example 12.3. Richard Wagner, *Die Meistersinger von Nürnberg*, act 2; first excerpt, act 2, scene 2, mm. 120–21; second excerpt, act 2, scene 4, mm. 236–37.

Example 12.4. Wolf, *Abschied*, mm. 64–68

possible only by the progressive artist, just as criticism depends upon art for its substance. The artist conversely represents the verity of his own artistic vision through traditional means and thus resembles Harold Bloom's strong poet, able to appropriate tradition and bend it to his own purposes, and thus overcome it.[59]

Wolf returns quite subtly to hints of augmented triads in measures 63 to 68 at "meinte vielleicht, ich sollt' ihm beichten" (see ex. 12.4), where the B-flat with the first syllable of *beichten* (confess) forms an augmented triad before resolving to A. Wolf here uses the B-flat augmented triad Wagner frequently used in *Die Meistersinger*, even placing it in first inversion as Wagner did at some of the more salient references to Beckmesser (ex. 12.3).[60] The harmonic and contrapuntal motion from the augmented sixth between E-flat and C-sharp to the third (D) of the augmented triad in measures 64 to 65 of Wolf's song is found repeatedly with Beckmesser as well, as exemplified in the third and fourth measures of example 12.3. Wolf repeats the musical figure of measures 64 to 65 in measures 67 to 68, now placing the augmented triad on *leuchten* and thus "illuminating" the critic for what he is.

Example 12.5. Wolf, *Abschied*, mm. 78–80

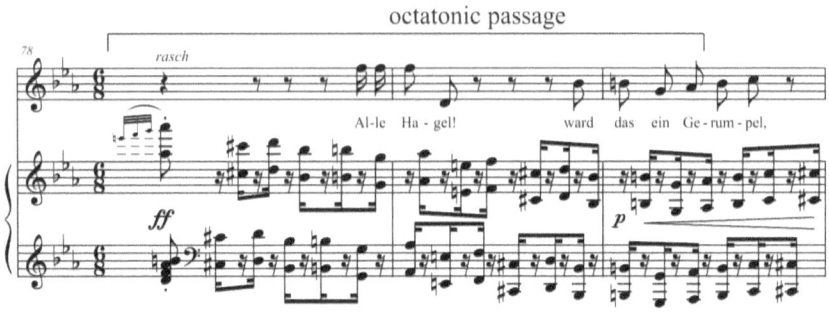

Example 12.6. Wolf, *Abschied*, mm. 99–1

The critic's motive returns again as he prepares to go, becoming impish as the artist hatches his scheme to help the critic down the stairs, and tumultuous as the critic tumbles to the bottom to the accompaniment of a thunderous octatonic passage in the piano (see ex. 12.5). Wolf here again uses a symmetrical structure (the octatonic scale) capable of threatening traditional tonality in association with the critic, yet in this instance the point is not to depict the critic through the progressive device so much as it is to defeat him by it. As seen in example 12.6, the role reversal continues in the closing waltz that follows, which twirls through purely traditional harmony in the key of B-flat major; Wolf boasting that he knows tradition better than the traditionalist. In this celebratory waltz, one hears the Wolf of early 1888 exult in the certain knowledge that through his newly-created Mörike songs he has achieved artistic success, and that the aberration of having to live as a critic himself has been booted down the stairs along with Mörike's critic and, in effigy, Hanslick as well. Finally, by choosing for his victory dance the waltz—that quintessentially Viennese genre—Wolf claims triumph over the Viennese establishment itself. Wolf had yet to convince the world, however. And one wonders how well the young man understood the lasting effect of his critical barbs on their targets, and appreciated the import they would have for his future.[61]

Hanslick on Wolf

Although Wolf occasionally responded to specific reviews by Hanslick, Hanslick did not reply overtly in kind in the pages of his critical writings. The reason can be surmised from his assessment of a controversial event during a series of concerts in Vienna by Hans von Bülow and the Meiningen Court Orchestra in 1884. The orchestra's performance of Beethoven's *Egmont* Overture in their first concert received harsh criticism from Ludwig Speidel, which prompted Bülow to deliver a petulant rejoinder from the stage during a later concert.[62] Although Hanslick was not present to hear Bülow's speech, he addressed it in his *feuilleton* of December 4, 1884:

> It remains absolutely tactless and impolite, if an artist reacts personally to unfavourable criticism levied against him in the press, all the more so if he addresses this to an audience assembled for a completely different purpose. He acts most appropriately and most nobly by calmly leaving the final judgment over an alleged unfairness to public opinion. Personal recriminations, like Bülow's latest, do not harm anybody except himself. Whoever knows Bülow, knows that his harangues are not to be taken too seriously, and he himself certainly knows this. It is not so much insulted artistic pride or animosity that drives him to it, as rather a strange desire for the dust it whirls up, in which he seems to feel at home, possibly like a warhorse in gunsmoke.[63]

By not responding directly to Wolf's personal attacks, Hanslick took not only the moral high ground but also his own advice, letting public opinion decide who was being fair and recognizing that Wolf's attacks only harmed Wolf himself.

He did respond indirectly in his critical writing by addressing in subsequent reviews some of the aesthetic issues Wolf raised, if not his ad hominem attacks, yet a fuller exegesis of the subtle dialogue that emerges when Hanslick's reviews are placed alongside Wolf's would have to be taken up in a subsequent study. In any event, Hanslick comes closest to speaking directly about Wolf's critical deportment in *Aus meinem Leben*, particularly in the concluding chapter, "Ein Gespräch über Musikkritik" (A conversation about music criticism).[64] Though he does not name Wolf, when we read his comments in the context of the current study, we see how apropos they are to his relationship with Wolf.[65] Hanslick proffers this conversation as the transcription of one that took place in the fall of 1893 between himself and Theodor Billroth, the famous surgeon and music buff who was friend to both Hanslick and Brahms. Whether or not the conversation actually took place as recorded, Hanslick follows an ancient tradition of using dialogue for didactic purposes, or as a medium for debating issues of philosophy. He thereby gains the advantage of getting his points across while having the other interlocutor either raise the issues he wishes to discuss or hand down judgments on those issues; as recorded by Hanslick, it is even Billroth who suggests their conversation appear in the autobiography.

In the course of the discussion, Hanslick discloses that he was not overly troubled by the inevitable animosity toward the critic aroused in artists who have been weighed and found wanting, but he admits that in earlier times he had been offended by continued and systemic attacks coming from another source, attacks which seemed strange to him.[66] We pick up the dialogue with Billroth's question concerning the source of these attacks:

B: Certainly from Wagnerians?

H: O no! The Wagnerians must let loose on me; as with a party they are sworn to that and have had it drilled in to them. Wagner—each word and each note of Wagner—is their religion, the defense and propagation of him their only pathos. In this sense their attacks are nevertheless something else and better than personal malice. I have assiduously shot at the other side, and thus must let the return fire fall upon me. I do not even want to begrudge these gentlemen the poisoned arrows; though I have been greatly pestered by them, I also have not died from their poison. Their opposition does not cause me pain. What I mean is the methodically continued maliciousness of 'colleagues' whom I never attacked with a word, indeed to whom I proved myself helpful when they started out.

B: That explains everything! A vulgar character cannot bear to owe someone thanks. It is an eternal type:
"He hates the rescuer most from that hour forth,
When he no longer requires the helping hand."
I know these people. Scientific debate is not the discourse of a straightforward objective interest. They only want to provoke the older, better-known writers to a polemic which would drag them out from the twilight of their newspaper into a brighter light. I am pleased that you never could be driven to a rejoinder, as much as your fingers might itch you.

H: And I owe a debt of gratitude to you, that you always have held me from it.[67]

Hanslick's reference to "colleagues" (i.e., other critics) who conducted continual and systemic attacks against him, his assertion that he had never attacked these antagonists with his own words, and his claim to have worked on their behalf at the beginning of their careers, all apply directly to Wolf, as we have seen.[68] By using the dialogic format, Hanslick finds a solution to a vexing conundrum that he had faced for the past decade. Though Hanslick could forgive Wolf's Wagnerian polemics, he was hurt by the personal nature of Wolf's assault and would have liked to defend himself publicly, but did not want to dignify Wolf's accusations with a response. Even though he stuck to his philosophy of letting the public decide for itself which party was being fair, it rankled to leave Wolf's charges unanswered. In his memoirs he can no longer remain silent; he wishes to set the record straight and make it known that he took the moral high road all along. He has Billroth commend him for his restraint, and continues to cling to the high road by letting Billroth diagnose Wolf's motivation as hoping to elicit a response from the widely read critic in order to thrust himself before the public eye from the relative obscurity of his own paper.

When Hanslick finally did mention Wolf in the *Neue Freie Presse*, it was not until the close of 1894, the year in which *Aus meinem Leben* had appeared, and then for the purpose of reviewing a performance of Wolf's music. Regardless of the political animosity generated by Wolf's *Salonblatt* criticism of 1884–87, Hanslick would not have reviewed any of Wolf's early compositions in those years because they remained unpublished and largely unnoticed before 1888.[69] But even though 1888 brought Wolf some public support from performers and the Wagner-Verein, and even though some of Wolf's early songs were finally published in March and his mature songs began to appear in print in 1889, to my knowledge it was not until two of Wolf's works were performed at a concert of the prestigious *Gesellschaft der Musikfreunde* on December 2, 1894, that Hanslick felt compelled to review him. Wolf's supporters alleged that by 1890, as his works were gaining recognition, performers were discouraged from presenting his works in Vienna by threat of boycott from the critical establishment against which Wolf had railed.[70] Partisan critic Max Graf claimed Wolf had been silenced in Vienna, and that Hanslick put him "under the great ban and Wolf's name disappeared from the columns of Hanslick's paper."[71] Yet regardless of exactly where the truth lies relative to these charges, the facts remain that Wolf's music was not performed in venues Hanslick felt compelled to review before 1894, and that when it was he immediately critiqued it with grudging respect:[72]

> Two choruses with orchestral accompaniment by Hugo Wolf, *Elfenlied* and *Der Feuerreiter*, have met with great approval and are also the best that I know from this infinitely prolific composer in tightly confined domains. Hugo Wolf pursues song composition on a grand scale, not in booklet, but in volume form, therein a rival of the ballad manufacturer Martin Plüddemann

of Graz, who rants in his own brochure against the mean publishers, whose caution forced him to initiate a provisional subscription for his next large ballad volume. Hugo Wolf composes not simply poems, but, whole poets, so to speak. A volume of Goethe, 51 poems (price 25 marks), a volume of Mörike, 53 poems (price 25 marks), and so forth. Our composer dearly loves to make the piano accompaniment the main thing, the voice an appendage, every now and then the accompaniment is also a kind of sarcastic troublemaker to the singing part. Like every self-confident and revolutionary emerging young talent, Wolf, the alleged inventor of the "symphonic song," has a small, enthusiastic following. This following sees in Hugo Wolf the Richard Wagner of the song, as in Bruckner the Richard Wagner of the symphony. The fame of these two newer ones, if we understand it correctly, thus should be attributed to the fact that each makes something from his artistic genre (song, symphony) that it should not be. With the two above-mentioned choral compositions Wolf takes the first step, if not toward larger form (for both pieces were originally published for a single voice with piano accompaniment), then toward richer means. His attempt is successful. Both pieces belong to that descriptive, pictorial kind, which most willingly comes to meet the talent of this composer. The well-declaimed and for the most part vocally idiomatic, modest choir part moves over a brilliant, refined orchestra full of effects. In *Elfenlied* the subtlest, in *Der Feuerreiter* the most blaring tricks of the modern art of orchestration are summoned up with success. In many places in *Der Feuerreiter* the orchestral noise unfortunately grew so over-abundantly loud that one could not understand a word, which certainly is not completely indifferent in the ballad. In the Gesellschaft concert Mr Hugo Wolf has for the first time successfully presented himself to a larger, not exclusively Wolfian public. Unquestionably a man of spirit and talent, he has only to guard against arrogance and "good friends."[73]

Wolf was quite pleased with the performance and ostensibly with Hanslick's review, as well. He wrote to amateur pianist Heinrich Potpeschnigg on December 16:

You seem to have heard absolutely nothing of the musical coup d'etat which I achieved on 2 December in the second Gesellschaft concert over the conservative gang of the gentlemen of the *Gesellschaft der Musikfreunde*, since you mention not a word about the same. On that day my *Elfenlied* from the *Midsummer Night's Dream* and *Der Feuerreiter* for choir and orchestra were played with great success and acknowledged nearly unanimously by the critics (including Hanslick). If you have not yet read Hanslick's review, I can forward the same to you.[74]

Heinrich Werner's Wolf diary records Wolf's delight over the widespread recognition he expected to gain from the critical acknowledgment of his work by Hanslick: "Wolf most pleased about Hanslick's critique, as the *Neue Presse* is seen by the whole world and so the not ill-intentioned words find at any rate wide dissemination."[75]

Wolf would not have been entirely pleased with the review, however, as he hints in a letter to Baroness Frida von Lipperheide written on the following January 8: "From all sides I was congratulated on my 'sensational' success, chiefly because of Hanslick's review, which everybody who is conversant with the conditions found 'quite wonderful.' Finally, I myself also found the said review 'wonderful' though I had some doubts about its 'wonderfulness.'"[76] Wolf does not elaborate, but a careful reading of Hanslick's critique viewed in light of the two men's relationship over the years shows that Hanslick's praise was not as high as it might seem at first blush. Each positive comment tends to be qualified by a more negative one, some obviously, others more subtly, at least for a modern reader. Among the former would be the observations that Wolf has achieved fame, but only among a small following and only by making the song something it should not be, and that he has spirit and talent, yet arrogance may bar his way to greater success. Among the latter would be the comment that the piano part is often a sarcastic troublemaker; while this is an apt turn of phrase that reveals Hanslick's familiarity with Wolf's style well beyond the confines of this particular concert, when viewed in the light of Wolf's earlier critical assault, we can be sure that Hanslick expected his readers to recall Wolf himself as a sarcastic troublemaker even as he warns him against further arrogance. Wolf would not have been happy about the comparison to Plüddemann, nor did Hanslick intend for him to be. Another critic had compared the two earlier in the same year, which drew the following response from Wolf in a letter to Frieda Zerny: "O these music critics! Plüddemann, just so you know, is considered a musical camel [i.e., idiot], which naturally does not prevent another camel from drawing a parallel between him and me."[77] Though in some senses Wolf might like being called the Richard Wagner of the song, he knew Hanslick did not mean it as a compliment, and it is well known that Wolf fretted over being recognized only as a master of song, a miniature genre, aspiring as he did to be an opera composer. Hanslick made sure to point out that although Wolf had written for larger performing forces in this concert, he had not achieved success in larger forms thereby, since all he had done was orchestrate a couple of his songs (and not without some problems of balance). Hanslick takes shots at Wolf's followers as well, cautioning Wolf about his own friends and referring to his "*wölfisch*" public, an adjective with pejorative overtones, meaning "Wolfian" to be sure, yet also "wolfish."

Nonetheless, Wolf and his followers celebrated Hanslick's review for what it was, a concession if not a capitulation. It is clear from Wolf's comments that the reception of his music at the Gesellschaft concert provided him with just the sort of victory over Hanslick that he had dreamed of almost seven years earlier as he set "Abschied"; it came none too soon, as syphilis would claim Wolf's mind in 1897 and his life in 1903. Though Hanslick acknowledged no such victory, after a lifetime of inveighing against *Zukunftsmusik* he would write "Now, at the beginning of a new century, it is advisable to reiterate every time in relation to the novelties of the musical 'secession' (Mahler, Richard Strauss, Hugo Wolf, etc.): it is very possible that the future belongs to them."[78] Should the future take this undesired turn, however, Hanslick would see no tangible defeat therein; it merely would provide more grist for the mill of the critic and the historian.

Notes

All translations are my own unless otherwise stated.

1. *The Music Criticism of Hugo Wolf*, trans. and ed. Henry Pleasants (New York: Holmes & Meier, 1978), xi. Pleasants, a critic himself, translated all of Wolf's published critical writing and a small sampling of Hanslick's; he attributes the reference to Hanslick's mistakes about Wagner to Ernest Newman. For a far harsher assessment of Hanslick's critical work sparked by Pleasants's translation, see Joseph Kerman, "Hanslick's Critics," *Hudson Review* 4, no. 4 (1952): 607–11.

2. For a fuller picture of Wolf's music criticism, see especially Leopold Spitzer, "Hugo Wolf (1860–1903) als Musikkritiker im *Wiener Salonblatt*," in *Skizzen einer Persönlichkeit: Max Kalbeck zum 150. Geburtstag: Breslau 4. Jänner 1850–Wien 4. Mai 1921: Symposion, Wien 21.–24. Mai 2000: Bericht*, ed. Uwe Harten (Tutzing: Hans Schneider, 2007), 362–69; Andreas Dorschel, "Arbeit am Kanon: Zu Hugo Wolfs Musikkritiken," in *"Wahrheit bis zur Grausamkeit": Bericht über das internationale Hugo Wolf Symposion Graz / Slovenj / Ottawa, November 2003. Musicologica Austriaca* XXVI, ed. Barbara Boisits and Cornelia Szabó-Knotik (Vienna: Österreichische Gesellschaft für Musikwissenschaft, 2007), 43–52; and the recent study by Benjamin Korstvedt listed in the bibliography.

3. Eduard Hanslick, *Aus meinem Leben*, 2 vols. (Berlin: Allgemeiner Verein für Deutsche Litteratur, 1894; repr., Farnborough: Gregg, 1971).

4. First engaged at the University of Vienna as an unpaid lecturer, Hanslick later became one of the first professors of music history and aesthetics.

5. Hanslick, *Vom Musikalisch-Schönen: Ein Beitrag zur Revision der Ästhetik der Tonkunst* (Leipzig: Weigl, 1854). It is interesting that both Brahms and Wolf dismissed Hanslick's treatise in their letters, Brahms saying he could not finish it because he found in it "so viel Dummes," Wolf saying he turned to it only in desperation as a mental emetic (*Brechmittel*) during a fallow compositional period. See *Clara Schumann, Johannes Brahms: Briefe aus den Jahren 1853–1896*, ed. Berthold Litzmann, 2 vols. (Leipzig: Breitkopf & Härtel, 1927), 1:168; and *Hugo Wolfs Briefe an Oskar Grohe*, ed. Heinrich Werner (Berlin: Fischer, 1905), 78–79. Brahms later expressed a far more favorable opinion on the treatise when writing to Hanslick himself in 1863. See *Johannes Brahms: Life and Letters*, ed. Styra Avins (Oxford: Oxford University Press, 1997), 284. I am grateful to Nicole Grimes for bringing this later reference to my attention.

6. Wolf's first music criticism appeared in the *Wiener Salonblatt* on January 20, 1884.

7. In his autobiography Hanslick defended himself against his likening to Beckmesser by Wagnerians by asserting that he criticized Wagner only on general aesthetic and stylistic principles, not on nitpicking details and petty rule-breaking in matters of harmony and melody in the manner of Beckmesser. He in turn accuses the Wagnerians of being "adoration-Beckmessers" who will not rest until they "have rummaged

out the most insignificant note, the most ordinary phrase, the most innocent sixteenth rest and glorified it as an incomparable work of genius" (die unbedeutendste Note, die allergewöhnlichste Phrase, die unschuldigste Sechzehntelpause hervorgestöbert und als unerreichbares Geniewerk verherrlicht haben). Hanslick, *Aus meinem Leben*, 2:227–34; the relevant passage of the autobiography appears in English translation in Eduard Hanslick, *Vienna's Golden Years of Music 1850–1900*, trans. and ed. Henry Pleasants (New York: Simon & Schuster, 1950), 330–35. For a reconsideration of Wagner's treatment of Hanslick in *Die Meistersinger*, see Thomas Grey, "Masters and Their Critics: Wagner, Hanslick, Beckmesser, and *Die Meistersinger*," in *Wagner's "Meistersinger": Performance, History, Reception*, ed. Nicholas Vazsonyi (Rochester, NY: University of Rochester Press, 2002), 165–89.

8. "Rezensenten reden von der Musik wie der Blinde von der Farbe." Hugo Wolf, letter to Hugo Faißt in 1896 in *Hugo Wolfs Briefe an Hugo Faißt*, ed. Michael Haberlandt (Stuttgart: Deutsche Verlags-Anstalt, 1904; repr. Leipzig: Breitkopf & Härtel, 1911), 124.

9. "die Welt hat nur einen Beckmesser und wenn sie den kennen will, muß sie nach Wien kommen." Hugo Wolf, "Hofoper: *Die Meistersinger von Nürnberg*," *Wiener Salonblatt* (hereafter *WS*), September 20, 1885; repr. in critical edition in *Hugo Wolfs Kritiken im Wiener Salonblatt*, 2 vols., ed. Leopold Spitzer with Isabella Sommer (Vienna: Musikwissenschaftlicher Verlag, 2002), 1:114; as translated in *The Music Criticism of Hugo Wolf*, 154. Wolf later mentions in a letter of October 22, 1890, to Melanie Köchert that he had been shown that day a sketch of *Die Meistersinger* in which the character was named Veit Hanslick; see Hugo Wolf, *Briefe an Melanie Köchert*, ed. Franz Grasberger (Tutzing: Hans Schneider, 1964), 29; or *Letters to Melanie Köchert*, trans. Louise McClelland Urban (New York: Schirmer Books, 1991), 31.

10. This phrase comes from the most frequently cited sentence in Hanslick's *Vom Musikalisch-Schönen*. In the first three editions this reads: "Tönend bewegte Formen sind einzig und allein Inhalt und Gegenstand der Musik." Thereafter it reads "Der Inhalt der Musik sind tönend bewegte Formen." The first can be rendered in English as "Tonally moving forms are the one and only content and subject matter of music." Geoffrey Payzant translates the second as "The content of music is tonally moving forms." Hanslick, *Vom Musikalisch-Schönen: Ein Beitrag zur Revision der Ästhetik der Tonkunst*, vol. 1, ed. Dietmar Strauß (Mainz: Schott, 1990), 75 (hereafter *VMS*); Hanslick, *On the Musically Beautiful*, trans. Geoffrey Payzant (Indianapolis: Hackett, 1986), 29. —Eds.

11. See, for example, Hanslick's review of the Vienna première of *Tristan und Isolde*: Ed. H., "'Tristan und Isolde' von Richard Wagner, I," *Neue Freie Presse* (October 5, 1883): 1–3; Ed. H., "'Tristan und Isolde' von Richard Wagner, II" (October 9, 1883): 1–3, just three months before Wolf began writing for the *Wiener Salonblatt*; repr. in *Musikalisches Skizzenbuch, Der "Modernen Oper*," vol. 4 (Berlin: Allgemeiner Verein für Deutsche Litteratur, 1888), 3–28; as translated in *Hanslick's Music Criticisms*, trans. and ed. Henry Pleasants (Mineola, New York: Dover, 1988), 214–27. Because Hanslick signed his byline in the *Neue Freie Presse* as "Ed. H.," it will be retained here in citations of his articles from that newspaper. See also his reviews of *Die Meistersinger von Nürnberg*, the *Ring* cycle, and *Parsifal* gathered in this latter source. It also has been suggested, of course, that Hanslick's attacks on Wagner were exacerbated by Wagner's anti-Semitism (Hanslick's mother was of Jewish descent, yet converted to Catholicism before marrying Hanslick's father); Eric Sams, "Eduard Hanslick, 1825–1904: The Perfect Anti-Wagnerite," *Musical Times* 116/1592 (October 1975): 867–68.

12. For the details of Wolf's life story, see especially Frank Walker, *Hugo Wolf: A Biography*, rev. ed. (London: Dent, 1968).

13. "Ich bin durch die Musik dieses großen Meisters ganz außer mir gekommen und bin ein Wagnerianer geworden." Hugo Wolf, *Hugo Wolf: Eine Persönlichkeit in Briefen: Familienbriefe*, ed. Edmund von Hellmer (Leipzig: Breitkopf & Härtel, 1912), 9–10.

14. Even in his *Salonblatt* criticism, Wolf spoke well of Brahms's String Sextet in G, op. 36; *Alto Rhapsody*, op. 53; String Quintet in F, op. 88; and song *Von ewiger Liebe*, op. 43, no. 1.

15. The principal account of the meeting has been that by the critic and Brahms biographer Max Kalbeck, an ally of Hanslick and determined foe of Wolf. Kalbeck's account, which alleges the meeting took place in the year 1881 or 1882, places Wolf in an unfavorable light and is highly discounted by Wolf biographers; see Max Kalbeck, *Johannes Brahms*, 4 vols., vol. 3/2, *1881–1885* (Berlin: Deutsche Brahms-Gesellschaft, 1912), 409–12.

16. See Wolf, *Familienbriefe*, 42; see also Walker, *Hugo Wolf*, 84–85. The Brahms camp attributed Wolf's later antipathy toward Brahms to his comments in this meeting. In his reviews, Wolf frequently made sarcastic references to Brahms's penchant for counterpoint.

17. As translated in Walker, *Hugo Wolf*, 138.

18. Ibid., 138–39.

19. Letter of February 26, 1883, as translated in Walker, *Hugo Wolf*, 139. The original is cited in Ernst Decsey, *Hugo Wolf*, 4 vols. (Leipzig: Schuster & Loeffler, 1903–6), 1:119–20. Mottl at this time was a rising star among conductors of a Wagnerian stripe. Wolf had met and befriended Mottl, four years his senior, during his days at the conservatory.

20. "Vielleicht unterstützt mein Ansinnen beiliegender Brief Ed. Hanslicks; so günstig jedoch auch seine Meinung über meine Fähigkeit lautet, so sehr auch Euer Wohlgeboren von der Richtigkeit seiner Ansicht überzeugt sein mögen—ist dies ein Grund, ein hinlänglicher Grund das Manuskript zu verlegen?" Wolf's letter is printed along with a partial facsimile in Wolfgang Schmieder, *Musikerhandschriften in drei Jahrhunderten* (Leipzig: Breitkopf & Härtel, 1939), 47 and 72.

21. Wolf, *Familienbriefe*, 60–61. Wolf had also tried Breitkopf & Härtel and others in 1878, without success.

22. The younger Viennese critic and Wolf advocate Max Graf said the *Salonblatt* was "filled with news of the court and the aristocracy—accounts of the parties, the engagements, the marriages, the hunts, the dances of the eighty families who, according to Napoleon, ruled Austria." Graf, *Composer and Critic: Two Hundred Years of Musical Criticism* (New York: W. W. Norton, 1946), 275. Sandra McColl characterizes the *Salonblatt* as "not so much a newspaper as a women's magazine" that focused on the "lifestyles of the rich, noble, and/or famous" and was politically neutral because women did not have the right to vote. McColl, *Music Criticism in Vienna 1896–1897: Critically Moving Forms* (New York: Oxford University Press, 1996), 18.

23. "Auch Hanslick und das ganze Wiener[—]scharf attakiert—deshalb jetzt in Acht und Bann getan. Bereue jedoch nichts." *Wolfs Briefe an Grohe*, 18.

24. "Soll ich kurz und bündig sagen, wie ich über Brahms denke, so gestatten Sie mir das geflügelte Wort Friedr. Nietzsche's anzuführen. 'Brahms' Schaffen ist die Melancholie des Unvermögens.' Ich unterschreibe diese mir aus der Seele gesprochenen Worte mit meinem vollen Namenszug. Auch habe ich diese Ansicht seinerzeit als Referent eines Wiener Wochenblatts auf das entschiedenste vertreten und mir dadurch

weder Brahms noch Hanslick zu Freunden gemacht, was allerdings auch nie in meiner Absicht liegen konnte." Hugo Wolf, *Hugo Wolf's Briefe an Emil Kauffmann*, ed. Edmund von Hellmer (Berlin: Fischer, 1903), 9. Wolf paraphrases Nietzsche's comment from *Der Fall Wagner*. See Friedrich Nietzsche, *Sämtliche Werke* (Munich: Deutscher Taschenbuch Verlag, 1980), 6:47.

25. "Was wir von Brahms in der letzteren Zeit seines Producirens gehört, hat uns ziemlich kalt gelassen, vieles davon geradezu abgestoßen, so namentlich seine Symphonien, die von gewissen Kritikern in einer Art verhimmelt werden, daß man ihren schlechten Geschmack, ihre Blindheit bedauern müßte, wüßte man nicht, daß zumeist "Persönlichkeit" die Brille ist, durch die ein Kunstwerk geschaut und darnach beurtheilt wird. Es ist wohl zu unterscheiden, ob man die Werke eines lebenden Componisten mit dem Auge des Wohlwollens oder dem der Mißgunst ansieht. Der Kritiker ist eben auch nur ein Mensch und persönlichen Einflüßen zugänglich. Aber zuletzt ist er doch Kritiker und als solcher steht es ihm nicht an, seiner persönlichen Freundschaft für den Autor Ausdruck zu verleihen, indem er dessen auf der Folterbank gezeugte Producte über alle Maßen verherrlicht, während er umgekehrt geniale Compositionen aus entgegengesetzen Gründen mit übelrichendem Geifer beschmutzt." Hugo Wolf, "Oper und Concerte," *WS*, March 23, 1884; *Kritiken* 1:24; as translated in *The Music Criticism of Hugo Wolf*, 28.

26. For Hanslick's review of Brahms's Symphony No. 4, see Ed. H., "Concerte," *Neue Freie Presse* (January 19, 1886): 1–3; repr. in *Aus dem Tagebuch eines Musikers, Der "Modernen Oper,"* vol. 6 (Berlin: Allgemeiner Verein für Deutsche Litteratur, 1892), 203–6; abridged translation in *Hanslick's Music Criticism*, 243–45.

27. See *Kritiken*, 1:76 and 92; as translated in *The Music Criticism of Hugo Wolf*, 100 and 123.

28. "Herr Hanslick bekanntermassen ein sehr unparteiischer Kritiker ist, wie seine Recensionen einerseits über Rich. Wagner und anderseits über Brahms zur Genüge beweisen." Wolf, "Concerte," *WS*, January 24, 1886; *Kritiken*, 1:137; as translated in *The Music Criticism of Hugo Wolf*, 185.

29. Wolf, *Kritiken*, 1:138.

30. Hanslick and *Vom Musikalisch-Schönen* figure prominently in a lengthy portion of Wolf's review of January 9, 1887, that was excised by the editor; the unpublished material appears in *Kritiken*, 2:108–10. See also Clemens Höslinger, "Hugo Wolf's Brahms-Kritiken: Versuch einer Interpretation," in *Brahms-Kongress, Wien, 1983: Kongressbericht*, ed. Susanne Antonicek and Otto Biba (Tutzing: Hans Schneider, 1988), 266–68.

31. "Mag man in diesem, der Wahrheit gemachten, Zugeständnisse immerhin nur einen politischen Kunstgriff meines illustren Collegen erblicken, jedenfalls wird er jetzt sorgfältiger die Karten zu mischen haben, wenn er den, durch sein politisches Verfahren angestrebten, Schein der Objectivität mit Erfolg zur Schau tragen will." Wolf, "Concerte," *WS*, January 23, 1887; *Kritiken*, 1:186.

32. Wolf continued to attack Hanslick in his letters.

33. "Einen Musiker von Fach, dem es hauptsächlich um die Gesangskunst des Darstellers zu thun sein könnte, mögen Herrn Vogl's unfrei hin und her zuckende Wimpern, welcher fatale Umstand, nach dem Dafürhalten des Herrn Musik-Referenten Dp., 'der bedeutenden Kunst des Darstellers unüberwindlich bleiben mußte,' immerhin gleichgiltig lassen. Der Musiker von Fach, hat ihn ein leidiges Schicksal auch noch zum Kritiker bestimmt, hält sich gern an das zur Sache gehörige Hauptsächliche im Gegensatze zu unsern ästhetisch gebildeten Musik-Recesenten, die sich so gern in abstracten Tüfteleien ergehen." Hugo Wolf, "Oper und Concerte," *WS*, January 18, 1885; *Kritiken*,

1:79; as translated in *The Music Criticism of Hugo Wolf*, 105. Heinrich Vogl (1845–1900), a tenor at the Hofoper in Munich, was famous for performing Wagnerian roles. "*Dp*" was Gustav Dömpke (1851–1923), a Hanslick ally who wrote for the *Wiener Allgemeine Zeitung*.

34. Spitzer states the *Salonblatt* for October 25 was printed with the erroneous date October 23; *Kritiken*, 2:76.

35. He received the following snub in reply: "We have attentively played through your D minor Quartet and unanimously resolved to leave the work for you with the doorkeeper of the Court Opera. Will you have the kindness to send for it as soon as possible? He could easily mislay it." Translated in *The Music Criticism of Hugo Wolf*, 159–60, n. 1.

36. "Es gibt wohl kaum etwas Betrübenderes, als einen noch so bescheidenen Wunsch nie erfüllt sehen zu können; und doch beschäftigt den Menschen nichts so sehr, als das Bangen oder die Zuversicht auf Erfüllung seiner Wünsche und Hoffnungen. Man wird darüber zum Narren, zum Trunkenbold, zum Misanthropen, zum Sterndeuter, zum Hungerleider, zum Schatzgräber, zum Schuldenmacher, zum Teufelsbeschwörer, zum lyrischen Dichter, zum Bummler, zum unglücklichen Liebhaber, ja sogar zum Recensenten (wie z. B. ich) und Gott weiß zu was Allem Nützlichen noch und Angenehmen." Hugo Wolf, "Musik?" *WS*, October 23, 1885; *Kritiken*, 1:117.

37. Ernest Newman, *Hugo Wolf* (London: Methuen & Co., 1907; repr., New York: Dover Publications, 1966), 29. Max Graf put it rather differently: "Hugo Wolf's criticism was about as much at home in this journal as a pure and pious youth would be in a brothel." *Composer and Critic*, 275.

38. "Oberstes Prinzip in der Kunst ist mir strenge, herbe, unerbittliche Wahrheit, Wahrheit bis zur Grausamkeit." Wolf, *Briefe an Emil Kauffmann*, 13.

39. See McColl, *Music Criticism in Vienna*, 15–16.

40. As cited and translated in Frank Walker, "Conversations with Hugo Wolf," *Music & Letters* 40, no. 1 (1960): 9. Werner further reports Wolf's recognition of Hanslick's stature in comparison to other critics: "Wolf scandalized by [Theodor] Helm, who now always writes with 'I' and 'my,' whereas earlier he at least employed only the modest 'we.' Hanslick had the right to employ the 'I' form, because he is a personality. But Helm?"

41. Walker, *Hugo Wolf*, 162.

42. In his autobiography Hanslick referred to his collections of concert reviews as "eine lebendige Geschichte des neueren Wiener Konzertwesens" (a living history of recent Viennese concert life); Hanslick, *Aus meinem Leben*, 2 vols. (Berlin: Allgemeiner Verein für Deutsche Litteratur, 1894), 1:245 (hereafter *AML*); as translated by Kevin C. Karnes, *Music, Criticism, and the Challenge of History: Shaping Modern Musical Thought in Late Nineteenth-Century Vienna* (Oxford: Oxford University Press, 2008), 58.

43. Hanslick, *AML*, 1:74. Werner Abegg suggests that in the continuation of this passage Hanslick was speaking of Hugo Wolf when he complained of modern composers of vocal music who wrote unsingable music and implied that they did so because they had not studied singing; Abegg, *Musikästhetik und Musikkritik bei Eduard Hanslick* (Regensburg: Gustav Bosse Verlag, 1974), 126.

44. Hanslick, *AML*, 2:187. References to Hanslick's performance activities are scattered throughout his autobiography and in his correspondence with Brahms, Billroth, and others.

45. *Lieder aus der Jugendzeit* (Bonn: Simrock, 1882). Wolf poked fun at the collection in his *Salonblatt* article of February 14, 1886: "Herr Götze . . . lent his Faust so indignant and defiant a tone as if from spite he was determined, for example, to sing Hanslick's songs from his golden-haired youthful years to Herrn Dömpke without interruption until his old age." (Herrn Götze . . . seinem Faust einen so unwilligen und trotzigen

Ton verlieh, als ob er zum Aergsten entschlossen sei, z. B. Hanslick's Lieder aus dessen goldlockiger Jugendzeit Herrn Dömpke bis an seinem Lebensabend ununterbrochen vorzusingen.) *Kritiken*, 1:141.

46. "Schließlich sang Herr Adolfi abermals einige Lieder, worunter meine in schwärmerischen Studentenjahren componi[e]rte 'Serenade Paul Clifford's.' Es hätte ihm leicht etwas Gescheiteres einfallen können. Nachdem auch schon andere Sänger und Sängerinnen einigen meiner Lieder die Ehre öffentlicher Ausgrabung erwiesen haben, so darf ich wo[h]l mit der Bermerkung herausrücken, daß diese in ihrer melodiösen Naivetät völlig altmodischen Herzensergüsse einem großen Publicum unmöglich Vergnügen bereiten können, am wenigsten mir selbst, der ich als Componist nicht die geringsten Ansprüche habe oder mache." Ed. H., "Concerte," *Neue Freie Presse* (January 29, 1884): 1–3.

47. "Von Jugend auf habe ich, nächst einer Professur, stets die Thätigkeit des Musikkritikers in einem vornehmen, großen Blatt für die begehrenswerteste gehalten. Vor dem auf eigenes Erfinden angewiesenen Dichter genießt der Kritiker den Vorteil, daß ihm fortwährend neuer Stoff zuströmt. Kein Jahr vergeht, ohne daß die manchmal intermittierende, aber niemals versiegende Quelle der künstlerischen Produktion uns einige Goldkörner zuführt. Neben wertlosen, absolut Schweigen auferlegenden Werken taucht sicher auch Eigenartiges, Vortreffliches auf. Aber nicht blos das Vortreffliche, auch das anspruchsvoll Häßliche, selbstbewußt Verschrobene reizt und beschäftigt den Kritiker." Hanslick, *AML*, 2:293.

48. Oscar Wilde expatiated wittily on this same essential theme in his dialogic essay "The Critic as Artist," first published in *The Nineteenth Century* in July and September of 1890, later revised and published along with other essays in his book *Intentions* (London: James R. Osgood, McIlvaine, 1891).

49. "Bravo," rief Liszt, "aber der Kritik gebührt neben der Produktion doch nur die zweite Rolle, nicht wahr? Spielen Sie also den Sekond!" Hanslick, *AML*, 2:187.

50. Ibid., 2:295–96.

51. Ibid., 2:298–99. Hanslick's turns from aesthetic theory toward the eventual merging of his critical and scholarly enterprises are examined in Karnes, *Music, Criticism, and the Challenge of History*, Part I, "Eduard Hanslick and the Challenge of *Musikwissenschaft*."

52. The precise circumstances leading to Wolf's departure from the *Salonblatt* have not come to light. Leopold Spitzer notes that the young Wolf experimented with many compositional genres, and that during his years as a critic he wrote but one song in 1884, none in 1885, and three in 1886, yet seven in the first four months of 1887. Spitzer suggests Wolf began to feel his future lay as a song composer, and that this led to the abandonment of his career as a critic. See Spitzer, "Hugo Wolf (1860–1903) als Musikkritiker im *Wiener Salonblatt*," in *Skizzen einer Persönlichkeit: Max Kalbeck zum 150. Geburtstag: Breslau 4. Jänner 1850–Wien 4. Mai 1921: Symposion, Wien 21.–24. Mai 2000: Bericht*, ed. Uwe Harten (Tutzing: Hans Schneider, 2007), 362–63.

53. Wolf, "Oper und Concerte," *WS*, April 18, 1896; *Kritiken*, 1:152.

54. For other discussions and various critical opinions of Wolf's *Abschied*, see Walker, *Hugo Wolf*, 238; Mosco Carner, *Hugo Wolf Songs* (London: British Broadcasting Corporation, 1982), 31–32; Eric Sams, *The Songs of Hugo Wolf*, 2nd ed. (London: Eulenburg, 1983), 145–48; Kurt Honolka, *Hugo Wolf: Sein Leben, sein Werk, seine Zeit* (Stuttgart: Deutsche Verlags-Anstalt, 1988), 148; Susan Youens, *Hugo Wolf: The Vocal Music* (Princeton: Princeton University Press, 1992), 79, 86, and 88–92; Stéphane Goldet, *Hugo Wolf* (Paris: Librairie Arthème Fayard, 2003), 574–77; and Andreas Dorschel, "Arbeit

am Kanon: Zu Hugo Wolfs Musikkritiken," in *"Wahrheit bis zur Grausamkeit": Bericht über das internationale Hugo Wolf Symposion Graz / Slovenj / Ottawa, November 2003. Musicologica Austriaca* 26, ed. Barbara Boisits and Cornelia Szabó-Knotik (Vienna: Österreichische Gesellschaft für Musikwissenschaft, 2007): 43.

55. Eduard Mörike, *Sämtliche Werke*, 2 vols. (Munich: Winkler-Verlag, 1967), 1:869.

56. See, for example, "Die Meistersinger von Richard Wagner," in *Kritiken und Studien, Die moderne Oper*, vol. 1 (Berlin: Allgemeiner Verein für Deutsche Litteratur, 1875), 303; translated in *Hanslick's Music Criticisms*, 119–20.

57. Arnold Schoenberg, *Harmonielehre* (Vienna: Universal Edition, 1911); trans. Roy E. Carter as *Theory of Harmony* (Berkeley: University of California Press, 1978), 384.

58. Similarly, Thomas Grey notes that Wagner has Beckmesser speak with the very music he is meant to oppose; "Masters and their Critics: Wagner, Hanslick, and Beckmesser," 175.

59. Harold Bloom, *The Anxiety of Influence: A Theory of Poetry* (Oxford: Oxford University Press, 1973), 5.

60. Eric Sams notes that the "rasping interjections after 'beichten' recall the critical motif of Beckmesser in *Die Meistersinger von Nürnberg*." *The Songs of Hugo Wolf*, 148.

61. See the accounts of the disastrous reading of his symphonic poem by Hans Richter and the Vienna Philharmonic in Walker, *Hugo Wolf*, 183; and Kalbeck, *Johannes Brahms*, 3/2:404.

62. For more details on the incident, see Alan Walker, *Hans von Bülow: A Life and Times* (Oxford: Oxford University Press, 2010), 312–13.

63. "Es bleibt unbedingt tactlos und unfein, wenn ein Künstler persönlich Antikritik übt gegen ihm missfällige Journal-Urtheile, vollends wenn er damit ein zu ganz anderem Zweck versammeltes Auditorium apostrophirt. Er wird stets am zweckmässigsten und am vornehmsten handeln, indem er das Endurtheil über eine vermeintliche Ungerechtigkeit ruhig der öffentlichen Meinung überlässt. Persönliche Recriminationen, wie Bülow's jüngste, schaden Niemandem, ausser ihm selbst. Wer übrigens Bülow kennt, der weiss, dass seine Standreden nicht allzu ernst zu nehmen sind, wie er dies ja selber thut. Es ist nicht sowo[h]l gekränkter Künstlerstolz oder Feindseligkeit, was ihn dazu treibt, als vielmehr eine sonderbare Lust an dem davon aufgewirbelten Staub, in welchem er sich so wohl zu fühlen scheint, wie irgend ein Haudegen im Pulverdampf." Ed. H., "Concerte," *Neue Freie Presse* (4 December 1884): 1–3. The war imagery here may well refer to Bülow's pseudonym, Peltast (a species of troops between heavy-armed and light-armed, furnished with a pelta (or light shield) and short spear or javelin. See for instance Bülow's "Die Opposition in Süddeutschland," *Neue Zeitschrift für Musik* 39, no. 22 (November 25, 1853): 229–30; no. 23 (December 2): 240–43; no. 24 (December 9): 252–55; no. 25 (December 16): 265–66; and 26 (December, 23): 276–79. —Eds.

64. Hanslick, *AML*, 2:292–309.

65. See also Varges, *Der Musikkritiker Hugo Wolf*, 32.

66. Hanslick, *AML*, 2:301.

67. "Gewiß von Wagnerianern?" "O nein! Die Wagnerianer müssen gegen mich losgehen; darauf sind sie als Partei eingeschworen und einexerzirt. Wagner—jedes Wort und jede Note von Wagner—ist ihre Religion, die Verteidigung und Ausbreitung derselben ihr einziges Pathos. In diesem Sinne sind ihre Angriffe doch etwas anderes und besseres, als persönliche Gehässigkeit. Ich habe fleißig hinübergeschossen und muß mir also das Herüberschießen gefallen lassen. Auch die vergifteten Pfeile will ich diesen Herren nicht verübeln, habe ich sie doch weidlich geärgert, bin auch an ihrem Gift nicht gestorben. Ihre Gegnerschaft tut mir nicht weh. Was ich meinte, sind die methodisch fort-

gesetzten Bosheiten von 'Kollegen,' die ich nie mit einem Worte angegriffen, ja denen ich in ihren Anfängen mich hülfreich erwiesen habe." "Das erklärt alles! Gemeine Naturen vertragen es nicht, jemandem Dank schuldig zu sein. Es ist ein ewiger Typus: 'Er haßt den Retter meistens von der Stunde an, Wo er den Helferarm entbehren kann.' Ich kenne diese Leute. Von einem aufrichtig sachlichen Interesse, wissenschaftlichem Streit ist da nicht die Rede. Sie wollen den älteren, bekannteren Schriftsteller nur zu einer Polemik reizen, die sie aus dem Halbdunkel ihrer Zeitung in ein helleres Licht hervorzöge. Es ist mir lieb, daß Du Dich niemals zu einer Erwiderung hast hinreißen lassen, so sehr Dir die Finger jucken mochten." "Und ich bin Dir Dank schuldig, daß Du mich immer davon abgehalten hast." Ibid., 2:301-2.

68. Another candidate would be Robert Hirschfeld, a student of Hanslick who developed a strong interest in early music and sought to revive it in the concert hall. In his critical writing, Hanslick questioned the wisdom of doing so, because this music could no longer speak to modern audiences as powerfully as it could to audiences of its own day or as powerfully as could music of recent times; he thought it more properly placed in the purview of the music historian than of the impresario. Hirschfeld responded with an attack on Hanslick's critical methodology and historical bias in the pamphlet *Das kritische Verfahren E. Hanslicks*. Though Hanslick may well have had Hirschfeld in mind as he penned his dialogue, the fact that Hirschfeld turned against Hanslick in direct response to Hanslick's criticism does not square precisely with Hanslick's claim in the dialogue that he had not attacked the protagonists to which he refers. Wolf remains the most likely candidate, and frequently had referred derisively to Hanslick as his colleague in his reviews of 1887 (see above). For more on the conflict between Hanslick and Hirschfeld, see Leon Botstein, "Music and Its Public: Habits of Listening and the Crisis of Musical Modernism in Vienna, 1870-1914" (PhD. diss., Harvard University, 1985), especially 889-900; and Karnes, *Music Criticism*, 67-75.

69. The first public performance of any of Wolf's songs took place on March 2, 1888, in the Bösendorfersaal. They appeared there again on December 15, but had by then been performed in private gatherings and the Wagner-Verein.

70. See Walker, *Hugo Wolf*, 224-25.

71. Graf, *Composer and Critic*, 23 and 278. See also Karl Kraus's similar accusations concerning Wolf's treatment by the Viennese critical establishment in Sandra McColl, "Karl Kraus and Music Criticism: The Case of Max Kalbeck," *Musical Quarterly* 82, no. 2 (1998): 279-308.

72. That Wolf did not expect a good reception is evident from a letter to Hugo Faißt of October 12, 1894, in which he predicted the "dear Viennese" would be greatly dismayed and the criticism would be abusive: "Am 2. Dezember wird mein *Elfenlied* und *Feuerreiter* in Wien im Gesellschaftskonzerte gemacht. Zum erstenmal, daß mir diese Ehre widerfährt. Die lieben Wiener werden groß dreinschauen, und die Kritik wird mich nicht wenig verschimpfieren. Glückerweise bin ich an den Ton bereits gewöhnt." Cited in *Hugo Wolfs Briefe an Hugo Faißt*, 48.

73. "Zwei Chöre mit Orchesterbegleitung von Hugo Wolf, Elfenlied und Der Feuerreiter, haben grossen Beifall gefunden und sind auch das Beste, was ich von diesem auf eng begrenztem Gebiete unendlich fruchtbaren Komponisten kenne. Hugo Wolf betreibt die Lieder-Komponisten im grossen, nicht heft-, sondern bandweise, darin ein Rivale des Grazer Balladenfabrikanten Martin Plüddemann, welcher in einer eigenen Broschüre gegen die schnöden Verleger wettert, deren Zurückhaltung ihn nötige, für seinen nächsten grossen Balladenband eine vorläufige Subskription einzuleiten. Hugo Wolf komponiert nicht bloss Gedichte, sondern so zu sagen ganze Dichter. Ein Band

Goethe, 51 Gedichte (Preis 25 Mark), ein Band Mörike, 53 Gedichte (Preise 25 Mark) u. s. w. Unser Komponist liebt es leidenschaftlich, die Klavierbegleitung zur Hauptsache, den Gesang zum Anhängsel zu machen, mitunter auch die Begleitung zu einer Art bissigem Störenfried der Gesangspartie. Wie jedes selbstbewusst und revolutionär auftretende junge Talent verfügt Wolf, der angebliche Erfinder des "symphonischen Liedes," über eine kleine enthusiastische Partei. Sie erblickt in Hugo Wolf den Richard Wagner des Liedes, wie in Bruckner den Richard Wagner der Symphonie. Der Ruhm dieser beiden Neuerer soll also, wenn wir es recht verstehen, darin liegen, dass jeder aus seiner Kunstgattung (Lied, Symphonie) etwas macht, was sie nicht sein soll. Mit den zwei obengenannten Chor-Kompositionen vollzieht Wolf den ersten Schritt, wenn auch nicht zu grösserer Form (denn beide Stücke sind ursprünglich für eine Singstimme mit Klavierbegleitung erschienen), so doch reicheren Mitteln. Sein Versuch ist geglückt. Beide Stücke gehören jener schildernden, malenden Gattung an, welche dem Talent dieses Komponisten am willigsten entgegenkommt. Die gut deklamierte und meistens stimmgemäss gesetzte Chorpartie bewegt sich über einem blendenden, raffiniert effektvollen Orchester. Im *Elfenlied* sind die subtilsten Künste, im *Feuerreiters* die grellsten der modernen Instrumentierungskunst mit Erfolg aufgeboten. An manchen Stellen des *Feuerreiters* überwuchert leider der Orchesterlärm so stark, dass man kein Wort versteht, was doch gerade in der Ballade nicht ganz gleichgültig ist. Im Gesellschaftskonzert hat Herr Hugo Wolf sich zum ersten Male einem grösseren, nicht ausschliesslich wölfisch gesinnten Publikum mit Glück vorgestellt. Unzweifelhaft ein Mann von Geist und Talent, hat er sich nur zu hüten vor Überhebung und vor "guten Freunden." Ed. H., "Concerte," *Neue Freie Presse* (December 5, 1894): 1–2; repr. in *Fünf Jahre Musik [1891–1895], Der "Modernen Oper,"* vol. 8 (Berlin: Allgemeiner Verein für Deutsche Litteratur, 1896), 270–72. See also Youens, *Hugo Wolf: The Vocal Music*, 181 and 347–49, n. 70.

74. "Du scheinst von dem musikalischen Staatsstreich, den ich am 2. Dezember im zweiten Gesellschaftskonzerte über die konservative Bande der Herren von der Gesellschaft der Musikfreunde errungen, absolut nichts erfahren zu haben, da Du mit keinem Worte desselben gedenkst. An jenem Tage wurde mein Elfenlied aus dem Sommernachtstraum und der Feuerreiter für Chor und Orchester mit großem Erfolg gespielt und von der Kritik fast einstimmig (inclusive Hanslick) anerkannt. Wenn Du Hanslicks Kritik noch nicht gelesen, kann ich Dir dieselbe zuschicken." Hugo Wolf, *Briefe an Heinrich Potpeschnigg*, ed. Heinz Nonveiller (Stuttgart: Union Deutsche Verlagsgesellschaft, 1923), 65–66.

75. As translated in Walker, "Conversations with Hugo Wolf," 8–9.

76. As translated in Karl Geiringer, "Hugo Wolf and Frida von Lipperheide: Some Unpublished Letters," *Musical Times* 77/1123 (September 1936): 794.

77. "O diese Musikrezensenten! Plüddemann, daß Du's nur weißt, gilt als ein musikalisches Kameel, was natürlich ein anderes Kameel nicht hindert zwischen ihm und mir eine Parallele zu ziehen." Wolf, *Briefe an Frieda Zerny*, ed. Ernst Hilmar and Walter Obermaier (Vienna: Musikwissenschaftlicher Verlag, 1978), 31.

78. "Jetzt, am Beginne eines neuen Jahrhunderts empfiehlt es sich, den Novitäten der musikalischen 'Secession' (Mahler, Richard Strauß, Hugo Wolf u.) jedesmal nachzusagen: Es ist sehr möglich, daß ihnen die Zukunft gehört." Hanslick, *Aus neuer und neuester Zeit, Der modernen Oper*, vol. 9 (Berlin: Allgemeiner Verein für Deutsche Litteratur, 1900), 77.

Chapter Thirteen

Battle Rejoined

Hanslick and the Symphonic Poem in the 1890s

David Larkin

> Antonín Dvořák and Richard Strauss arm in arm—a right queer sight.
> —Theodor Helm

As an observer of late nineteenth-century Viennese cultural life, Eduard Hanslick towers above all other journalists and writers who attempted to map the changing face of music in this period.[1] He has been typecast as the archenemy of musical progress, a foe to any who questioned the sacred tenets of "absolute" music, of which he was alleged to be a seminal theorist and tireless propagandist.[2] His championing of Brahms, as guardian of what he considered the legitimate compositional tradition, is as celebrated as his opposition to Liszt, Wagner, and their ilk, is notorious. Even when it was fashionable to point up his short-sightedness in this latter area, Hanslick's critical pronouncements still continued to be invoked, arguably as much for their eloquence and acumen as out of the need to cite a representative view of misguided conservatism. As a result of the disciplinary upheavals which musicology has undergone over the last twenty-five years, Hanslick's star is again in the ascendant; his judgments have been rehabilitated and reopened to scrutiny in tandem with the dismantling of the idea of "musical progress" as an unquestioned article of faith. Reading through his concert reports offers a glimpse into the contested musical politics of the later nineteenth-century Germanic lands, a world in which old certainties were crumbling, with his being one of the few voices to offer a coherent aesthetic picture, albeit one shaped by certain contestable ideological premises. These presuppositions, most clearly articulated in *Vom Musikalisch-Schönen*, need to be taken into consideration if one is to arrive at a true estimation of Hanslick's pronouncements in any individual case. The fact remains that, whether or not one agrees with his stance on program music and similar issues, Hanslick's critical writings offer some unrivalled insights into the music that came within his ambit; indeed, he often proves to be most discerning where he most opposes the work under scrutiny.

As one of the representative genres of the progressive *neudeutsche Schule*, the symphonic poem was never going to be entirely to Hanslick's taste. In fact, he regarded the Lisztian invention as "having succeeded more completely than anything heretofore in getting rid of the autonomous significance of music," and thus representing a position antithetical to his own belief that "the beauty of a piece of music is specifically musical."[3] According to Detlef Altenburg, Hanslick's hostility toward the despised "aesthetic of feeling" (*Gefühlsästhetik*) contributed to a broad misunderstanding of Liszt's purposes in writing his symphonic poems.[4] Hanslick's 1857 review of the first nine symphonic poems was openly hostile. The specific points of his critique will be amply illustrated later, but a sampling of his gibes is perhaps appropriate: he speaks of the "falsity" of Liszt's "abusive" method, the "atrociousness of such content as there is," and characterizes the composer as one of "those ingenious but barren temperaments."[5] Nor did his opposition to the Lisztian synthesis of poetic content and music decrease over time: his 1887 piece on the *Faust* Symphony exudes the same overt dislike.[6] The conclusion that Hanslick was implacably hostile to anything designated as a "symphonic poem," or anything that shared its aesthetic premises, is tempting, but is, in fact, demonstrably false. Considering Hanslick's attitudes toward Smetana's *Má Vlast* cycle, David Brodbeck has noted that the critic found something to like in each of the four works he heard, and even urged the performance of the last two symphonic poems.[7] Was his distaste therefore directed toward Liszt's art in particular; or (since the four Smetana reviews date from the 1890s) might it be that Hanslick had made his peace with the genre at this point?

In light of the foregoing remarks, the present study of Hanslick's engagement with the symphonic poem in the final decade of the nineteenth century explores some important and hitherto neglected terrain. For several reasons, I have decided to focus on his responses to Antonín Dvořák and Richard Strauss. These were the two best-known composers to produce a series of new symphonic poems (in Strauss's case, under the cognate term "tone poems") over the course of the 1890s. Hanslick's critiques of their symphonic poems have certainly not passed unnoticed, but the decision to set the two sets of critical responses side by side is new and brings several significant benefits.[8] Despite their shared cultivation of the symphonic poem, Strauss and Dvořák were poles apart in almost every other respect, including Hanslick's estimation of them. Strauss was one of the leaders of the emerging new wave of composers: a brash, pioneering modernist whose aesthetic credo clashed at virtually every point with that of the elderly critic. Dvořák, by contrast, belonged to an older generation, and had long enjoyed Hanslick's support. Where Strauss was a self-confessed disciple of Wagner, Dvořák was a friend and colleague of

Brahms. However, it is these very differences between the two that will enable us to gain new insights into the critic's attitudes to the symphonic poem *qua* genre. We can set aside any suspicion of negative prejudice when reading Hanslick's reviews of Dvořák's symphonic poems, and equally, his reports of Strauss's works will be free of positive bias. Any common issues of contention that emerge in the essays, therefore, will relate to those core aspects of the symphonic poem to which Hanslick impersonally objected. Moreover, by looking at those cases where his displeasure at some aspect of Strauss's music is tempered in his criticisms of Dvořák's works, we will get a sense of how far his objective standards could be swayed by personal factors.

Insightful Antipathy: Criticizing Strauss's Tone Poems

In 1908, four years after Hanslick's death, Strauss made the following wry observation: "To me there is nothing more stimulating that [*recte:* than] the criticism of a deadly enemy who has listened with the preconceived notion of picking holes in the work wherever possible. The more acute his intelligence, the less likely will he be to let pass even the least apparent weaknesses which the enthusiast or even the sympathetic listener is bound consciously or unconsciously to overlook."[9] Although Hanslick is not mentioned explicitly, Strauss may well have intended his words as a posthumous tribute to one of his most outspoken and yet insightful opponents. Their "deadly enmity" was a foregone conclusion, even before Hanslick unleashed his first critical salvos on Strauss in the early 1890s. In fact, Hanslick's earliest recorded opinion of Strauss's music was a positive one: in 1882 he described the violin concerto as the work of "a talent out of the ordinary."[10] Admittedly this work, though accomplished, is hardly what we would consider echt-Straussian in style. The emergence of a recognizably Straussian voice by the end of the decade occurs in tandem with his final "conversion" to the New German aesthetic position.[11] By the late 1880s, Hanslick had become the totemic representative of all that was conservative and anti-Wagnerian in the public mind, and as such, he was inevitably going to be something of a hate-figure for Strauss, who described himself as "a young progressive musician of the most extreme left."[12] In a letter he sent Hans von Bülow in August 1888, a document which is an unofficial manifesto of his new compositional direction, Strauss summarily noted that "of course, purely formalistic, Hanslickian music-making will no longer be possible."[13] Hanslick's most famous soundbite—which equates the content of music with "tonally moving forms" (*tönend-bewegte Formen*)[14]—was repeatedly used by Strauss as a shorthand for what he perceived as an outmoded, sterile retention of classical formal principles. In an exchange with the conductor and composer Johann Bella from 1890, this is particularly clear: "*Those others* for whom music is "sounding form" (*tönende Form*) (or rather, not form, but instead the formula of the classical figures quietly and thoughtlessly retained) base the work they are to compose on some general mood and develop the themes which have emerged according to an external *musical* logic which I no longer can accept, since I now only recognize *poetic* logic."[15] Despite his fundamental disagreement with Hanslick's principles, Strauss nonetheless seems to have appreciated the value of such a pithy slogan, and regularly represented his own position as upholding the doctrine of "music as expression" in direct opposition to "Hanslickian 'sounding form.'"[16]

It was almost a decade after his brief review of the violin concerto that Hanslick resumed his public commentary on Strauss: in 1892, his piece on *Don Juan* appeared, and thereafter he reviewed all the major Viennese premières of Strauss's works up to *Also sprach Zarathustra*. Sadly, the "out of the ordinary [talent]" was now characterized as "a splendid instrumental virtuoso, lacking only in musical ideas."[17] Strauss's declared allegiances were clear for all to see: in his choice of genre (the Lisztian symphonic poem), cultivated by Strauss with an especially pointed narrative focus; in his focus on instrumental color rather than clearly delineated formal procedures; and in his use of a post-Wagnerian harmonic syntax. All these become objects of grievance in Hanslick's reviews, which are addressed thematically rather than chronologically in what follows.

Inevitably, the fact that Strauss had chosen to write program music came repeatedly to the fore in Hanslick's reviews. "With Liszt's symphonic poems began the modern tendency of scrounging the content and meaning of a symphony from literature, and using these extorted alms in place of its own musical coinage."[18] Hanslick bemoaned the fact that "most of our younger composers think in a foreign language (philosophy, poetry, painting), and translate their thought into music," an accusation he levelled directly at the composer of *Tod und Verklärung*.[19] Strauss's peculiarly realistic brand of programmaticism inspired a plethora of vivid metaphors: "compromized literature,"[20] "musical tracings of painting and poetry,"[21] "emancipated naturalism,"[22] and "a boundless and aimless succession of scenes [*Bilderjagd*]."[23] Hanslick even compared *Tod und Verklärung* to a magic lantern, with the composer's colored glass pieces alternately showing delightful enamels or flaming blazes.[24] Surely the critic's fantasy here has been inflamed *malgré lui* by Strauss's music, rising to new imaginative heights? In fact, this review as a whole shows us Hanslick at his most perceptive. From the nature of the programmaticism here, with the music following the prefatory poem "step by step, as if it were a ballet libretto," Hanslick was able to predict Strauss's eventual move into opera.[25] *Guntram*, which appeared in 1894, does seem like the answer to this prophecy, although Strauss had been working on it since 1887.

One of the consequences of working "with poetic rather than with musical elements" was a regrettable "emancipation from musical logic."[26] Needless to say, the lack of traditional *Formenlehre* structures in the tone poems perturbed the critic considerably. In one review, Strauss and Bruckner were together chided for the "absolute freedom of their instrumental work which seems like a masterless rambling of their fantasy, mocking at organic coherence and gladly surrendering itself to the infinite."[27] In *Don Juan*, "tatters of Wagnerian motives fly around helplessly," leaving Hanslick "waiting in vain for the development of musical ideas."[28] Essentially the same protest was restated in the review of *Till Eulenspiegel*, where he noted the "many quaint, witty inspirations in it; but there is not even one that escapes being immediately set on by another and having its neck broken." In the most vividly pictorial of these complaints, Hanslick describes the "Funiculì" tune in the finale of *Aus Italien* as being "torn to pieces by polyphonic wild beasts: a pair of little feathers float up in the end, telling of the wretched fate of the poor little creature."[29]

In *Vom Musikalisch-Schönen*, Hanslick differentiated between an "aesthetic" mode of listening to music (based on the appreciation of themes, harmonies, and formal processes), and an unreflective wallowing in its emotional effects; the latter type of listening is described as "pathological."[30] This epithet recurs in his review of *Tod und Verklärung*, condemning this product of the "most sophisticated *Überkultur*" for exerting a "sensual pathological effect" through its "merciless depiction."[31] The *fin-de-siècle* rhetoric of degeneracy recurs time and again: *Don Juan* is a "musical narcotic" which gives rise to "voluptuous shudders";[32] *Till Eulenspiegel* is a "product of the most refined decadence";[33] and even the early *Aus Italien* shows an "uneasy, nervous talent."[34]

While deprecating the results, Hanslick at the same time is clearly fascinated by Strauss's technical skill in creating his effects. "The composer is like a practiced chemist," he claimed, "who knows how to mix all the elements of musical-sensual stimulation with extreme skill to obtain a stunning *Lustgas* [aphrodisiac gas]."[35] Strauss's genius as an orchestral colorist is fully acknowledged, although Hanslick tuts over the more general trend in music composition whereby color is given precedence over ideas.[36] At times, indeed, it seems as if the elderly critic is almost in danger of succumbing to the seductions of Strauss's kaleidoscopic surfaces. On one occasion, he calls the composer a "splendid virtuoso of style. His special talents embellish *Till Eulenspiegel* also. It is extravagant in sound effects, piquant in its surprising contrasts, full of contrapuntal art-pieces, idiosyncratic rhythms and witty modulations; everything terribly witty and madly beautiful."[37] To be sure, the tone here is one of ironic exaggeration, but nevertheless one feels that beneath this lurks a genuine if reluctant admiration. Elsewhere, it is not the beauty but rather the ugliness of Strauss's music that Hanslick identifies, calling him a "talent for false music, for the musically ugly."[38] The fact that Strauss's music could give rise to both ravishment and repugnance was seen as a direct consequence of the "tyranny of music as expression" (a deliberate reference to Strauss's credo), leading to the dominance of the characteristic at the expense of the beautiful.[39] For Hanslick, the Keatsian equation of truth and beauty still held, whereas Strauss is more of a post-Baudelairean realist, able to embrace the deliberately ugly for the sake of conveying truth as he saw it. The generational gulf between them was never so apparent.

Hanslick professed to finding himself puzzled by the success which greeted Strauss's works, although in his theoretical treatise he had noted that the layman is more likely to engage with music pathologically.[40] While reporting the positive response of the majority of the public (as well as carefully noting the protests of the minority), he ungenerously ascribed the applause to the presence of a pro-Straussian claque,[41] or saw it as acknowledging the heroic efforts of the orchestra rather than the work itself. As he wrote after *Also sprach Zarathustra*: "I can hardly believe that our public really gained pleasure and excitement from this hollow witches' cauldron."[42] At such moments, it must have required all his inner assurance in the rightness of his views to maintain stoutly that "a healthy reaction must come" to vindicate his stance.[43]

This confidence in the judgment of history was actually something which critic and composer shared, although naturally they differed in their opinions as to what posterity's ultimate verdict would be. Sustained by the belief in his ultimate vindication, Strauss was able to bear Hanslick's sophisticated denunciations with an amused shrug, for the most part.[44] He awaited the review of *Don Juan* with no more than mild interest, knowing what he could expect from a critic of Hanslick's proclivities. Needless to say, when the review appeared, containing epithets such as "half-Bacchanale, half witches' Sabbath," it lived up to his expectations.[45] In a letter to his parents, Strauss implicitly contrasted Hanslick's likely reaction with that of Mahler's nineteen-year-old brother, who wrote at length and with deep understanding about the work.[46] With younger, open-minded listeners on his side, Strauss could tolerate the gibes of the elderly critic. His belief that over time a work would get the reception it deserved, whether it was initially greeted with praise or censure, was founded in large measure on the *per ardua ad astra* trajectory of Wagner's career. "What a lot of nonsense was written at the time about the damage Hanslick's pamphlets on Wagner were supposed to have wrought," Strauss once exclaimed.[47] In fact, to have aroused Hanslick's ire to such a marked extent was, in a way, a matter for self-congratulation—Strauss was well aware of the publicity value of becoming a subject of contention in the musical press.

This did not necessarily entail passive endurance of whatever mud was flung at him: "Des Heldens Widersacher" ("the hero's detractors"), the satirical portrait of his critics in *Ein Heldenleben* shows that he was willing to return fire with fire (ironically—just as in the case of Beckmesser in *Die Meistersinger*—this had the side-effect of immortalising his opponents.) On another occasion, Strauss ventured in print to praise the critics of Graz at the expense of those in Vienna: "In the capital, sadly, eternal laws of beauty still prevail, which we should like to see spelled out just once; but until now they remain mysterious secrets hidden in the bosoms of Herr Hanslick and company."[48] In response, Hanslick cited the works of Mozart and Beethoven, Schubert, Mendelssohn and Schumann,

Brahms and Dvořák, all of whom "were innovators in comparison with their precursors—but they made music in their symphonies, not picture puzzles."[49] The critic went on to show the kind of penetrating wit that made him, in his seventies, still a daunting adversary. Taking up on Strauss's known interest in Nietzsche, Hanslick pretended to have thought that "the famous author of so many symphonic picture-books has for a long time been beyond praise and blame" in the manner of the Nietzschean superman. That Strauss should have praised the friendly reports of Graz at the expense of the more critical ones from Vienna was "human, all too human."[50]

More in Sorrow than in Anger: Scrutinizing Dvořák's Symphonic Poems

The history of the relations between Hanslick and Dvořák before 1890 is a rich one, and detailed treatment lies outside the scope of this article.[51] Suffice it to say that Hanslick's reviews of the Czech composer's music were hugely positive in tone, as this excerpt from his 1883 piece on the Sixth Symphony indicates: "In our time of reflection, which is poor in production, we are pleased to encounter a naturally feeling, happily productive talent such as Dvořák, who has grown into the highest forms of instrumental music and who with pronounced singularity has remained faithful to the ideals of our classical period."[52] Such warm approbation was matched on Dvořák's side by genuine appreciation for the critic; in a letter he wrote to Hanslick three days after the appearance of the above review, Dvořák hoped to visit Vienna soon: "My first trip always takes me to you and Brahms, and God willing, it will always remain so in the future!"[53] So confident had he become of the critic's approval by 1896 that Dvořák even expressed the wish that Hanslick should attend the private première of his first three symphonic poems, which took place in Prague. The plan never came to fruition, perhaps fortunately, given Hanslick's eventual reaction to these works.[54]

Taking Hanslick's remarks on Dvořák as a whole, it is clear that the critic regarded the composer as one of the bulwarks against the rising New German tide. Any characteristics of his music which others might regard as musico-politically neutral or even potentially consonant with the Wagnerian way are stridently proclaimed to embody true classical virtues. Thus his approval of Dvořák's "splendid" instrumentation in the symphonies comes with a rider emphasizing how it differed from "the newest German manner, which makes sound effects the main concern."[55] Even the *Husitska* Overture, a work that might have seemed dangerously close to the sort of thing being produced by Lisztian disciples, is firmly reclaimed by Hanslick for the anti-Wagnerian, but still truly German camp: "Dvořák does not fall back into formlessness and the search for false contrasts which repulse us in the 'dramatic' symphonies of so many New German composers. This Slav knows his Beethoven better than many Germans, and the *Coriolan* and *Egmont* [Overtures] were not without effect on the *Husitska* [Overture]."[56] His earliest reservations are found in the 1895 review of Dvořák's trio of overtures: *V přírodě* [*In Nature's Realm*], *Karneval* [*Carnival*] and *Othello*, opp. 91–93. The first two are both warmly received, possessing the same "joy in sweet sounds, the same melodic freshness, immediacy and naturalness."[57] However, *Othello*, "an introduction or a poetic retelling of the Shakespearean tragedy," is another matter entirely. Dvořák is accused of "wearing a mask, which at times recalls Liszt, at times Wagner."[58] Hanslick ascribed this unaccustomed lapse from stylistic independence to the dissonance between the tragic subject matter and Dvořák's nature, "to which the destructive dramatic conflict, the self-laceration and spilling of blood is foreign."[59] The problematic character of the work is principally due to its attempt "to replicate the dramatic course of the tragedy, dwelling in horrible detail on the strangling of Desdemona. Dvořák displays at the wrong place that he is a dramatic composer; however, he is not really a dramatic composer in an exalted sense; he ought to have demonstrated this in the right place, in his operas, which sparkle only for their lyrical beauty, especially their expressive and cheerful moods."[60] The three overtures were followed shortly afterward by a series of symphonic poems Dvořák wrote inspired by the poetry of his fellow Czech, Karel Jaromír Erben: *Vodník* (*The Water Goblin*), *Polednice* (*The Noon Witch*), *Zlatý kolovrat* (*The Golden Spinning Wheel*) and *Holoubek* (*The Wood Dove*). Three of these four were reviewed by the critic, as was the fifth and final symphonic poem, *Píseň bohatýrská* (*A Hero's Song*).

The two aspects of *Othello* which most vexed Hanslick—the gruesome subject matter, and its excessively detailed portrayal—were issues that resurfaced repeatedly in his criticisms of the symphonic poems. In his review of Dvořák's first symphonic poem (*The Water Goblin*), he expresses bafflement as to why anyone would select "such horrible material that revolts every finer feeling" for musical representation.[61] This repulsion was intensified after *The Noon Witch*: "Strange, this passion of Dvořák's, giving himself now to the horrible, the unnatural, the ghostly, which so little corresponds to his real musical sensibility or his amiable character,"[62] and the issue continues to exercise him in his review of *The Wood Dove*. The idea that Dvořák's music exemplifies naturalness, naivety, cheerfulness, and lack of artifice, a view which Hanslick repeatedly propagated, has continued to be an important one down to the present. However, rather than representing transgressions of this norm, the Erben symphonic poems perhaps demonstrate the limitations of these critical tropes.

Another, related source of Hanslick's discontent with Dvořák's Erben symphonic poems was the level of correspondence that existed between music and paratext. "We do not want our ears and imagination to be stuck following along one particular route," he complained on one occasion.[63] Hanslick felt that a simple title such as *The Water Goblin* would have sufficed "to give definite stimulation to the poetic and pictorial imaginative powers of the listeners."[64] Unhappily, as he saw it, both composer and listener were forced to follow the prefatory tale step by step.[65] Moreover, while in the program the different scenes were clearly separated from each other, the preponderance of the first theme associated with the Water Goblin melded them together in the musical realisation. Dvořák, thus, is "an interesting composer, but a bad story-teller,"[66] who is judged to have fallen for the "mad fashion of no longer making music with tones, but of wanting to tell stories and paint pictures."[67] When it came to *The Noon Witch*, Hanslick was still less impressed by Dvořák's approach: the crying of the infant, which might have been a witty gesture the first time around, became tasteless when repeated. He conceded the appeal of some ingenious tone painting ("from the childlike, merry sound-pictures in Haydn's *Creation* and *Seasons*, to the inspired tone-pictures of the Romantics and Wagner's captivating Magic Fire music"), but the illustrations of Erben's verse were not acceptable.[68] Where the music of *The Water Goblin* was splendid enough to gain Dvořák an acquittal, here Hanslick can find no mitigation.

The 1899 review of *The Wood Dove* is in many ways the most enlightening of all as regards Hanslick's views on program music. The critic claimed that "it was not necessary for Dvořák to go soliciting poetry (and what 'poetry'!) for his music [as] his rich musical invention does not need any loans, any crutch, any instruction manual."[69] So, if the obvious explanation of the extramusical as covering a poverty of musical thought (a charge he had leveled at many other programmatic composers) does not hold here, why should Dvořák have embarked on this course? The only answer he can give is that the Czech composer had a penchant for the "depiction of the different voices of nature."[70] However, "if, for a change, he feels impelled to move from wordless instrumental music to real shapes," Dvořák was encouraged to turn to opera, just as was Strauss.[71] And once again, Hanslick's exhortation seems prophetic, with *Rusalka* being completed the following year. This was perhaps less startling than his forecasting the appearance of Strauss's *Guntram*, as Dvořák had been active as an opera composer throughout his career. Nonetheless, there does seem to be a distinct correlation between his focus on programmatic orchestral writing and his increased operatic activities in the 1890s: not only did he revise two earlier stage works during this decade (*Dimitri*, 1882, rev. 1894; *The Jacobin*, 1888, rev. 1897), but he also produced two original works (*The Devil and Kate*, 1899; *Rusalka*, 1900).

With *A Hero's Song*, Hanslick was able once again to approve of a work that he felt was no more programmatic than the similarly named *Eroica* Symphony of Beethoven. Unlike the earlier symphonic poems he had reviewed previously, the critic noted that in this case Dvořák did not impose any "detailed operating instructions" on his listeners, an element that was sadly indispensible for the full comprehension of its precursors. *A Hero's Song* was "mainly comprehensible and effective as music," although Hanslick recognized that this would not prevent exegetes from trying to interpret it, as had been done *ad nauseum* in the case of the *Eroica*.[72] Following the cues in the "authentic communication" of the concert program, Hanslick reports that the hero is less a military man than a Slavic bard or rhapsodist.[73] This "tone poem" thus commemorates the fate or the development of a spiritual hero, but the changing moods do not replicate specific events.[74] This is vital in legitimizing it in Hanslick's eyes.

This section would not be complete without a brief mention of Dvořák's orchestration, which has already been touched on at various points. Hanslick continued to appreciate the inventiveness of Dvořák's sonic palette; crucially, the cultivation of sound still remained subordinate to what he considered more fundamental musical parameters (such as formal and harmonic clarity). He may have felt that the patriotic overture *Husitska* perhaps pushed the boundaries—there is more than a touch of disapproval for a work that "sounds so fanatical, as though in parts it had been orchestrated with hatchets, scythes, and cudgels"—but given the title, this could be a recognition of its potency in expressing the subject matter.[75] In the symphonic poems, even when he finds it impossible to approve of the nature of the subject matter or the replication of the details in music, he is able to admire the "dazzling, wholly new orchestral effects." This sample comment comes from a review of *The Water Goblin*, a work in which the new sonorities initially seemed to serve appropriate "poetic" ends.[76] Hanslick is here referring to the use of tone painting in the depiction of "natural" phenomena, such as the undulating wave motion in the composition. Since such effects are hallowed by tradition, they are legitimate in his eyes, or rather in his ears and mind.

Principled Objections: Judging Hanslick's Judgments

As Strauss and Dvořák were the principal composers to cultivate the symphonic poem in this decade, it comes as no surprise that Hanslick should have been moved to compare the two directly on a number of occasions. In his report on *The Water Goblin*, having deprecated the overly close musico-poetic correspondence this work displays, the critic lamented "I fear that with this detailed program music Dvořák has embarked on a precipitous path, which will eventually lead to—Richard Strauss."[77] Among the regrettable similarities to Strauss's tone poems he cited were the stringing-up of Till Eulenspiegel on the scaffold, and the passage in *Tod und Verklärung* where the shudders of the dying man extinguish the night lamp.[78] This morphed into a tirade on Strauss's *Also sprach Zarathustra*, of which Hanslick only knew the title at the time. After this digression, Hanslick concluded that Dvořák should not be classified with Strauss: the former was, after all, "a real musician, who has shown hundreds of times that he needs no programs and no inscriptions in order to enchant us with pure, nonrepresentational music."[79] The comparison, which Hanslick (perhaps anxiously) rejected in the end, was intended as a "friendly warning."[80]

On November 19, 1899, Gustav Mahler conducted a concert that included the first Viennese performances of Strauss's *Aus Italien* and Dvořák's *The Wood Dove*.[81] These premières were reviewed by the semi-retired Hanslick—a fortunate circumstance, as the direct comparison enables more accurate assessment of the relative standing of the two composers in his mind. Ironically, Dvořák was the greater transgressor here in the matter of explicit extramusical correspondence, one of Hanslick's main gripes. Where Strauss's early four-movement symphonic fantasy merely "paints Italian landscape and Italian country-life," Dvořák "recounts a varied tale" in his symphonic poem: for Hanslick, this amounted to a distinction between semi-veiled and totally blatant programmaticism.[82] (Admittedly, *Aus Italien* was unrepresentative of the later works of "the leader of our musical secessionists" in this regard.)[83] Hanslick went on to praise the "exquisite orchestral effects in Strauss's symphonic fantasy" (a constant in his reviews, as we have seen), but even these could not reconcile him to the work.[84] He complained of the lack of "Italian color and Italian mood: everything sounds so laboriously German! In the blurry, turgid melodies there is no drop of Italian blood."[85] Admittedly, this Teutonic character could hardly be otherwise, given the lineage he deduced for Strauss: "Visibly inspired by Berlioz, working with Wagnerian combinations, Strauss is nonetheless unashamed to borrow from Mendelssohn on occasion." *Aus Italien* is summed up as the work of "an ingenious, skilfully theatrical artist, more poetically inspired than musically creative."[86]

In comparison with Strauss, Dvořák is judged to possess a "musically stronger and more original nature," on the basis of his "naïve sentiments and melodic richness."[87] Hanslick concedes that *The Wood Dove* goes beyond *Aus Italien* in terms of programmaticism, but concludes that where the latter work "unites beautiful inscriptions with ugly music, Dvořák [unites] beautiful music with an ugly text."[88] Once again, there is a venting of critical bewilderment at Dvořák's recent exploitation of horrifying subject matter (Hanslick specifically refers back to *The Water Goblin* and *The Noon Witch* here). However, even less to Hanslick's taste than the nature of the poems is the fact that the listeners are constrained "to compare the music every step of the way with the tale forced upon it,"[89] something which detracts from "the agreeable grace and naïvety of the music."[90] Not only does the excessive correspondence affect the esthesic dimension, it also impacts unfavorably on the poietic process: "Music always suffers when a detailed program crushes the freedom of the composer or the listeners."[91] Dvořák's music is compared to a fair prisoner chained to guards and constrained to follow their path. The program is doubly unfortunate, because it can be misunderstood, and because it is indispensable. By the latter admission, Hanslick recognizes that the sequence of musical events, with all the changes of mood and so forth, cannot be understood away from the program. He explicitly contrasted this with cases where the extramusical content is indicated solely by a title (such as Strauss's *Aus Italien*), giving the listener sufficient freedom.

Having been forced to the unpalatable conclusion that Dvořák's programmaticism here is more prescriptive than Strauss's, Hanslick cast about for reasons for this new turn in his erstwhile favorite's output. "What may have tempted him from the kingdom of absolute music, of which he has been ruler since Brahms's death, is obviously the imitation of the voices of nature"—a skill which Hanslick conceded was perfectly acceptable, pointing with approval to various instances in Dvořák's symphonic poems.[92] Hanslick was able to console himself further with the thought that *Holoubek* grips and delights uninterruptedly, thanks to its magical sounds and realistic traits, which, despite their boldness, never touch on the ugly.

Conclusions

When one considers this dual review in tandem with those summarized earlier, several conclusions can be drawn about Hanslick's aesthetic stance toward the symphonic poem. First, he is clearly fascinated by the textural and orchestral inventiveness of both Strauss and Dvořák; he cannot gainsay the sheer sensuous impact of these sound worlds, pathological though this kind of listening would be if surrendered to, or indulged in isolation from the intellectual faculties. The aesthetician in him frequently disapproved of the uses to which this inventiveness was put, and he certainly deprecated the increasing prominence given to texture over aspects of symphonic composition traditionally considered more important, but the sonic thrill is undeniable, and (presumably) helped him rationalize the attraction Strauss's work had for the ordinary concertgoer.

Second, the nature of the subject matter and its treatment is clearly of crucial importance to the critic. The gruesome violence of the Erben-inspired symphonic poems and the abstruseness of a tone poem based on Nietzsche's philosophical text were both repugnant to him. Even the relatively unobjectionable schema found in *Tod und Verklärung*—the well-known *Kampf und Sieg*, "through struggle to victory" trope prominent in Beethoven's works and elsewhere—becomes problematic when realized in excessive detail. The constraint an overly close relationship between music and paratext puts on both composer and listener is something to which Hanslick had strong objections (ones shared by certain figures on both sides of the musico-political divide in the later nineteenth century).[93] In an attempt to counter the well-known argument that would justify program music on the grounds of music's increasing narrative and depictive potency, the critic asked why such detailed programs were still necessary: if the expressive potential of instrumental music had developed so radically since Berlioz's time, it should be possible to convey all through the music itself without resorting to verbal aids.[94] Hanslick is even able to quote one of Nietzsche's aphorisms to justify his stance: "In comparison with music all verbal communication is shameless;

words dilute and addle, words depersonalize, words make the uncommon commonplace."[95] The one symphonic poem of which he warmly approved, Dvořák's *A Hero's Song*, is praised for avoiding such minute correspondence. This work is also described as having the "form of a 'symphonic poem' in Liszt's sense, a continuous movement that contains several sections contrasting in tonality, tempo and expression and that are not sharply demarcated from each other."[96] Thus the apparent heterogeneity of the musical surface and the concomitant freedom of musical structure were not aspects which, for Hanslick, deserved automatic condemnation. Despite his strictures against Straussian formal confusion, the critic is less dogmatic on this point than might have been imagined.

Ultimately, it is difficult to account for the disparity in Hanslick's judgment of the two composers in terms of either the subject matter or the textural resources used. So why the discrepancy? Might it be merely 'human bias'—Hanslick going easy on a friend while unleashing broadsides at an opponent? While this very human motivation cannot be entirely discounted, it still leaves unaddressed just *why* he was riled by Strauss's music: there was nothing in their personal history to explain it. It must have been something internal to Strauss's tone poems themselves that aroused his antagonism and led him to conclude that Strauss wrote ugly music, and Dvořák beautiful music. Although it receives little mention in the reviews, I posit that the answer lies in their respective treatment of tonal syntax. Dvořák's melodic gifts, underpinned as they are by a harmonic palette that is traditional without ever losing freshness, would certainly have been more to Hanslick's taste than Strauss's far richer chromatic vocabulary and his preference for polyphonically constructed rather than melodically dominated textures. Moreover, Strauss was influenced by the aperiodicity of Wagner's musical prose, and is generally less regular and foursquare in his phrase construction than Dvořák. Thus I would argue that Hanslick's attitudes toward their symphonic poems were vitally shaped by his taste or distaste for endemic stylistic features characteristic of each composer, even if these receive little explicit comment.

What emerges from this study, therefore, is the picture of a critic who, in keeping with his aesthetic dogma, has principled objections to excessive narrative in instrumental music and dislikes sensational subject matter; who, despite his aesthetic prescriptions to the contrary, betrays a weakness for the textural and orchestral inventiveness of both Dvořák and Strauss; and who displays a predictable fondness for overt melodism and tonally circumscribed harmonic and formal patterning. It is only in the last of these that Dvořák and Strauss differ noticeably. This, when taken in the context of their opposing positions on the musico-political spectrum, goes some way toward explaining the disparity between Hanslick's gentle reproaches of Dvořák and his acerbic disapproval of Strauss.

Through analysing critiques of individual works we have been able to map Hanslick's attitudes toward the symphonic poem genre in the 1890s in some detail. I would like to close with a nod to the reverse approach, by acknowledging that the declared generic affiliation must have influenced in advance how the critic would respond to the specific works. The horizon of expectations aroused by the use of the term 'symphonic poem' was the background against which Strauss and Dvořák were asking to be judged, and Hanslick was openly hostile to the Lisztian exemplars, as we saw. The whole idea of a "generic contract" between producer and listener inevitably involves an element of prejudging (not to say prejudice) on the part of the culturally attuned receiver. Qua genre, Hanslick was opposed to the symphonic poem. He would rather have seen a clear distinction between opera and other dramatic works on the one side and the purely instrumental symphony on the other, so inevitably his appreciation for that in-between genre, the symphonic poem, was never going to be more than lukewarm. Nonetheless, in spite of this prejudice (or these preconceptions, if one prefers), his criticisms of Dvořák and Strauss are varied and nuanced, and amply demonstrate the combination of insight and wit that has led to our continuing interest in his opinions more than a century after they were written.

Notes

Portions of this paper were presented at the conference "Eduard Hanslick: Aesthetic, Critical, and Cultural Contexts," which took place at University College Dublin in June 2009. The author would like to thank the editors of this volume, in particular Dr. Nicole Grimes, as well as the anonymous readers for many helpful comments and suggestions, and would also wish to acknowledge the support of a research fellowship from the Irish Research Council for the Humanities and Social Sciences (IRCHSS) from 2007 to 2009, during which the research for this paper was partly carried out.

Epigraph: Theodor Helm, Review of *The Noon Witch*, in *Deutsche Zeitung* (December 25, 1896); cited in translation in Sandra McColl, *Music Criticism in Vienna, 1896–1897: Critically Moving Forms* (Oxford: Clarendon Press, 1996), 193.

1. The present volume testifies to the continuing interest in, and perhaps unfair dominance of Hanslick's views in discussion of music reception in late nineteenth-century Vienna. In her study of the entire Viennese critical landscape over the years 1896–97, Sandra McColl has tried to correct this imbalance, announcing programmatically that "it is time Hanslick was given his context." McColl, *Music Criticism*, vii. Much more wide-ranging chronologically than McColl, and with a focus equally nonexclusive, is Leon Botstein's gigantic study of the culture of listening in Vienna between 1870 and 1914. Leon Botstein, "Music and Its Public: Habits of Listening and the Crisis of Musical Modernism in Vienna, 1870–1914" (PhD diss., Harvard University, 1985).

2. For a recent discussion of "absolute" music and the assertion that it is a myth that Hanslick championed the term, see Sanna Pederson, "Defining the Term 'Absolute Music' Historically," *Music and Letters* 90, no. 2 (2009): 240–62, especially 250–53. This demythologizing might itself be open to question: Hanslick does make one specific use of this term in relation to Dvořák's music (see note 92 below).

3. Hanslick, *On the Musically Beautiful*, trans. Geoffrey Payzant (Indianapolis: Hackett, 1986), xxiii (hereafter, *OMB*). In the introduction at this point he specifically mentions getting to know "Liszt's so-called 'program symphonies'" while he was revising *Vom Musi-*

kalisch-Schönen (*VMS*) for a second edition (1858). The works in question were in fact the first nine symphonic poems: see Hanslick's 1857 review in which he referred to Liszt's "nine symphonies, or, as he calls them, 'symphonic poems.'" Eduard Hanslick, *Music Criticisms 1846–1899*, trans. Henry Pleasants, rev. ed. (London: Penguin, 1963), 54.

4. Detlef Altenburg, "Vom poetisch Schönen: Franz Liszts Auseinandersetzung mit der Musikästhetik Eduard Hanslicks,' in *Ars musica, musica scientia: Festschrift Heinrich Hüschen zum fünfundsechzigsten Geburtstag am 2. März 1980*, ed. Detlef Altenburg (Cologne: Gitarre & Laute, 1980), 2.

5. Hanslick, *Music Criticisms*, 55, 56.

6. This was, in fact, the second time he reviewed the work. Eduard Hanslick, *Aus dem Tagebuche eines Musikers*, Der "Modernen Oper" VI. Theil (Berlin: Allgemeiner Verein für Deutsche Litteratur, 1892), 238–41. For Hanslick's first review of the *Faust Symphony*, written in 1863, see Hanslick, "Liszt's Faust-Symphonie," in *Aus dem Concertsaal: Kritiken und Schilderungen aus den letzten 20 Jahren des Wiener Musiklebens* (Wien: Braumüller, 1870), 290.

7. David Brodbeck, "Hanslick's Smetana and Hanslick's Prague," *Journal of the Royal Musical Association* 134, no. 1 (2009): 6.

8. Hanslick's criticisms of Strauss were first considered in Max Steinitzer's early life-and-works study of the composer: Max Steinitzer, *Richard Strauss* (Berlin: Schuster & Loeffler, 1911), 226–28. The best and most recent study of Hanslick's reception of Dvořák's music is David Brodbeck, "Dvořák's Reception in Liberal Vienna: Language Ordinances, National Property, and the Rhetoric of *Deutschtum*," *Journal of the American Musicological Society* 60, no. 1 (April 2007): 71–132. In addition to the studies by McColl and Botstein referred to in note 1, other useful items include Kevin C. Karnes, *Music, Criticism, and the Challenge of History: Shaping Modern Musical Thought in Late Nineteenth-Century Vienna* (Oxford: Oxford University Press, 2008); Wolfgang Dömling, "Mit und ohne Programm: Dvořák und die Idee der Symphonischen Dichtung," in *The Work of Antonin Dvořák (1841–1904): Aspects of Composition—Problems of Editing—Reception*, ed. Jarmilla Gabrielova and Jan Kachlik (Prague: Akademie Věd České Republiky Praha, 2007), 78–81; Marc Niubo, "The Wild Dove Op. 110 and the Reception of Dvořák's Symphonic Poems in Bohemian Lands," in Gabrielova and Kachlik, *The Work of Antonin Dvořák*, 299–309; Erich Wolfgang Partsch, "Gustav Mahler dirigiert Antonín Dvořák in Wien: ein Beitrag zur frühen Dvořák-Rezeption," *Hudební věda* 43/1 (2006): 15–26; Mark-Daniel Schmid, "The Tone Poems of Richard Strauss and Their Reception History from 1887–1908" (PhD diss., Northwestern University, 1997); Karen Stöckl-Steinebrunner, "The Uncomfortable Dvořák: Critical Reactions to the First Performances of Symphonic Poems in German-Speaking Lands," in *Rethinking Dvořák: Views from Five Countries*, ed. David Beveridge (Oxford: Clarendon Press, 1995), 201–10; Leon Botstein, "Strauss and the Viennese Critics (1896–1924)," in *Richard Strauss and His World*, ed. Bryan Gilliam (Princeton: Princeton University Press, 1992), 311–71; John Clapham, "Dvořák's relations with Brahms and Hanslick," *Musical Quarterly* 57 (1971); 241–54.

9. "Ich kenne nichts Förderlicheres als die Kritik eines Todfeindes, der von vornherein mit der Absicht zugehört hat, aus welchem Grunde auch immer, dem Autor am Zeuge zu flicken, wo er kann! Je schärfer seine Intelligenz ist, desto weniger werden ihm auch die verborgensten Schwächen entgehen, die der Begeisterte oder auch nur sympathisch Wohlwollende bewußt oder unbewußt übersieht." Richard Strauss, *Betrachtungen und Erinnerungen*, 2nd ed. (Zurich: Atlantis, 1957), 23; trans. as *Recollections and Reflections*, trans. of first ed. by L. J. Lawrence (London: Boosey & Hawkes, 1953), 19 (hereafter, Strauss, *Betrachtungen*, 23/E19).

10. "ein nicht gewöhnliches Talent." Ed. H. [Eduard Hanslick], "Concerte," *Neue Freie Presse* (December 12, 1882): 1–3; also quoted in Steinitzer, *Richard Strauss*, 29. Because Hanslick signed his byline in the *Neue Freie Presse* as "Ed. H.," it will be retained here in citations of his articles from that newspaper. See Strauss's own recollection of this incident (*Betrachtungen*, 205/E135). The violin concerto was premièred on December 5, 1882.

11. Strauss's embrace of the New German position has been analysed in David Larkin, "Reshaping the Liszt-Wagner Legacy: Intertextual Dynamics in Strauss's Tone Poems" (PhD diss., University of Cambridge, 2007), chapter 2. Charles Youmans has problematized the notion of Strauss's "conversion" to an unproblematic Wagnerian discipleship in *Richard Strauss's Orchestral Music and the German Intellectual Tradition: The Philosophical Roots of Musical Modernism* (Bloomington: Indiana University Press, 2005), 29–58.

12. "einen jungen musikalischen Fortschrittler (äußerste Linke)." Letter from Strauss to Hans von Bronsart, February 9, 1889, in *Lieber Collega!: Richard Strauss im Briefwechsel mit zeitgenössischen Komponisten und Dirigenten*, ed. Gabriele Strauss, Veröffentlichungen der Richard-Strauss-Gesellschaft vol. 14 (Berlin: Henschel, 1996), 125.

13. "Ein rein formales, Hanslicksches Musizieren ist dabei allerdings nicht mehr möglich." Letter from Strauss to Hans von Bülow, August 24, 1888; Strauss, *Lieber Collega!*, 83.

14. Hanslick, *OMB*, 29; see also 101–2 for a discussion of the difficulties in translating this phrase.

15. "*Die anderen*, denen die Musik 'tönende Form' ist, d. h. sie legen dem zu componierenden Werke (die Form d. h. nicht mehr *Form* sondern Formel der Classiker ruhig gedankenlos beibehaltend), irgend eine allgemeine Grundstimmung unter und entwickeln diese entsprungenen Themen nach einer ganz äußerlichen, *musikalischen* Logik, für die mir heute, da ich nur mehr eine *dichterische* Logik anerkenne, schon jedes Verständnis fehlt." Letter from Strauss to Johann L. Bella, March 3, 1890; in Dobroslav Orel, *Ján Levoslav Bella: k. 80. narozeninám seniora slovenské hudby* (Bratislava: Philosophy Faculty of the Comenius University of Bratislava, 1924), 570.

16. See, inter alia, the letter from Strauss to Bella, December 2, 1888, and various late autobiographical essays such as "On Inspiration in Music" and "Recollections of My Youth and Years of Apprenticeship" (Strauss, *Betrachtungen*, 167/E117, 210/E138–9). The phrase "music as expression" is a reference to Friedrich von Hausegger's *Musik als Ausdruck* (Vienna: Konegen, 1885) published in the same year, the same year that saw the appearance of the seventh edition of Hanslick's *Vom Musikalisch-Schönen*.

17. "Der Komponist des 'Don Juan' bewährt sich hier [in *Tod und Verklärung*] neuerdings als ein glänzender Orchester-Virtuose, dem es nur an musikalischen Gedanken fehlt." Hanslick, "Richard Strauß: 'Tod und Verklärung,'" in *Fünf Jahre Musik*, 219. This review was originally published as Ed. H., "Concerte," *Neue Freie Presse* (January 27, 1893): 1–3.

18. "Mit Liszts symphonischen Dichtungen begann die modernste Tendenz, Inhalt und Bedeutung einer Symphonie von der Litteratur zu erbetteln und durch dieses abgedrungene Almosen den Mangel an eigenem musikalischen Bargeld zu ersetzen." Eduard Hanslick, "'Zarathustra' von Richard Strauß," in *Am Ende des Jahrhunderts*, 265. This review was originally published as Ed. H., "Concerte (Philharmonisches Concert)," *Neue Freie Presse* (March 23, 1897): 1–2.

19. "Das Unglück ist, daß die meisten unserer jüngeren Komponisten in einer fremden Sprache denken (Philosophie, Poesie, Malerei) und das Gedachte erst in die Muttersprache übersetzen." Hanslick, *Fünf Jahre Musik*, 181. He repeats the accusation at 221.

20. "komprimierte Litteratur." Hanslick, "'Zarathustra' von Richard Strauß," in *Am Ende des Jahrhunderts*, 270.

21. "musikalischen Nachmalens, Nachdichtens." Hanslick, "Richard Strauß: 'Don Juan,'" in *Fünf Jahre Musik*, 178. Originally published as Ed. H., "Concerte," *Neue Freie Presse* (January 12, 1892): 1–2.

22. "emanzipierten Naturalismus in der Instrumentalmusik." Hanslick, "Richard Strauß: 'Don Juan,'" in *Fünf Jahre Musik*, 180.

23. "diese maß- und meisterlose Bilderjagd." Hanslick, "Klavier-Concert von E. Schütt. 'Eulenspiegel' von R. Strauß. Vorspiel zu 'Parsifal' von Wagner," in *Am Ende des Jahrhunderts*, 199. Originally published as Ed. H., "Philharmonische Concerte," *Neue Freie Presse* (January 9, 1896): 1–2.

24. "Er schiebt in seine Zauberlaterne verschiedene bunte Gläser, deren abwechselnd reizender Schmelz oder flammende Glut unsere Sinne beschäftigt." Hanslick, "Richard Strauß: 'Tod und Verklärung,'" in *Fünf Jahre Musik*, 219.

25. "Die Musik folgt ihr Schritt für Schritt wie einem Ballett-Libretto. . . . Die Art seines Talents weist den Komponisten eigentlich auf den Weg zum Musikdrama." Ibid., 219.

26. "Das Charakteristische des Symphonikers Strauß besteht darin, daß er mit poetischen, anstatt mit musikalischen Elementen komponiert und durch seine Emanzipation von der musikalischen Logik eine Stellung mehr neben, als in der Musik einnimmt." Ibid., 221.

27. "Die absolute Freiheit der Instrumental-Komposition erscheint bei Strauß und Bruckner als ein meisterloses Schweifen der Phantasie, welche, des organischen Zusammenhanges spottend, sich gern ins Ungemessene verliert." Hanslick, "'Wanderers Sturmlied' von Richard Strauß," ibid., 204.

28. "Dazwischen fliegen kleine Melodie-Ansätze, Fetzen Wagnerscher Motive ratlos umher; wir warten vergebens auf eine Entwickelung musikalischer Ideen." Hanslick, "Richard Strauß: 'Don Juan,'" ibid., 180–1.

29. "Wieviel hübsche, witzige Einfälle tauchen darin auf; aber nicht ein einziger, dem nicht sofort ein anderer auf den Kopf spränge, ihm das Genick zu brechen. Ein paar Federchen fliegen ganz zuletzt noch auf und melden das schnöde Ende des armen Tierchens." Eduard Hanslick, ". . . 'Eulenspiegel' von R. Strauß . . . ," in *Am Ende des Jahrhunderts*, 199 (ellipses in the original).

30. See Hanslick, *OMB*, chapter 5 "Musical Perception: Aesthetic versus Pathological," 58–67.

31. "so gehört auch 'Tod und Verklärung' zu den Erzeugnissen der raffinierten Überkultur unserer Musik. . . . Dadurch erklärt sich auch die starke sinnlich-pathologische Wirkung, welche ein so unbarmherziges Nachtgemälde auf die Zuhörer ausübt." Hanslick, "Richard Strauß: 'Tod und Verklärung,'" in *Fünf Jahre Musik*, 220.

32. "musikalische Narkosen"; "ein wollüstiger Schauer." Hanslick, "Richard Strauß: 'Don Juan,'" ibid. 180, 179.

33. "ein Produkt der raffiniertesten Décadence." Hanslick, ". . . 'Eulenspiegel' von R. Strauß . . . ," in *Am Ende des Jahrhunderts*, 199.

34. "Strauß' unruhiges, nervöses Talent." Hanslick, "Neue Orchesterwerke, 'Aus Italien' von R. Strauß. 'Die Waldtaube' von Dvořák," in *Aus neuer und neuester Zeit*, 81. Originally published as Ed. H., "Concerte," *Neue Freie Presse* (December 5, 1899): 1–2.

35. "Der Komponist gleicht da einem routinierten Chemiker, der alle Elemente musikalisch-sinnlicher Aufreizung äußerst geschickt zu einem betäubenden 'Lustgas' zu mischen versteht." Hanslick, "Richard Strauß: 'Don Juan,'" in *Fünf Jahre Musik*, 180.

36. Hanslick, "'Zarathustra' von Richard Strauß," in *Am Ende des Jahrhunderts*, 269 (where, after praising Strauss's legendary instrumental technique, he predictably laments the confusion of ends and means); see Hanslick, "Richard Strauß: 'Don Juan,'" in *Fünf Jahre Musik*, 179.

37. "wir nennen ihn als einen glänzenden Virtuosen der Mache.... Es ist verschwenderisch in Klangeffekten, pikant in seinen überraschenden Kontrasten, voll contrapunktischer Kunststücke, origineller Rhythmen und witziger Modulationen; alles furchtbar geistreich und wahnsinnig schön." Hanslick, "... 'Eulenspiegel' von R. Strauß ...," in *Am Ende des Jahrhunderts*, 201.

38. "Ein großes Talent für falsche Musik, für das musikalisch Häßliche." Hanslick, "Richard Strauß: 'Don Juan,'" in *Fünf Jahre Musik*, 180.

39. "Die Tyrannei der 'Musik als Ausdruck.'" Hanslick, "... 'Eulenspiegel' von R. Strauß ...," in *Am Ende des Jahrhunderts*, 200.

40. "The person who wallows in feeling is in most instances untrained in the aesthetical comprehension of the musically beautiful. The layman is most likely to 'feel' when he listens to music; the trained artist is least likely to do so." Hanslick, *OMB*, 65.

41. "War es doch vorauszusehen, daß zwei nachfolgende Nummern allermodernsten Stils einen organisierten Beifallssturm entfesseln würden." Hanslick, "... 'Eulenspiegel' von R. Strauß ...," in *Am Ende des Jahrhunderts*, 198.

42. "ich kann mir kaum denken, daß unser Publikum wirklich Genuß und Begeisterung aus diesem wüsten Hexenkessel geschöpft habe." Hanslick, "'Zarathustra' von Richard Strauß," in *Am Ende des Jahrhunderts*, 271; see also Hanslick, "Neue Orchesterwerke, 'Aus Italien' von R. Strauß. 'Die Waldtaube' von Dvořák," in *Aus neuer und neuester Zeit*, 82–83.

43. "[es wird] gewiß aber eines Tages eine gesunde Reaktion hervorrufen." Hanslick, "Richard Strauß: 'Tod und Verklärung,'" in *Fünf Jahre Musik*, 221; see also Hanslick, "Richard Strauß: 'Don Juan,'" Ibid., 181.

44. "die sehr amüsante Kritik von Hanslick schicke ich nächstens!" Letter from Strauss to his parents, February 13, 1893; Richard Strauss, *Briefe an die Eltern*, ed. Willi Schuh (Zürich: Atlantis Verlag, 1954), 164.

45. "halb Bacchanale, halb Walpurgisnacht." Hanslick, "Richard Strauß: 'Don Juan,'" in *Fünf Jahre Musik*, 179.

46. See his letter to his parents, January 31, 1892; Strauss, *Briefe an die Eltern*, 148.

47. "Was hat man seinerzeit nicht von dem Unheil gefabelt, das die Hanslickschen Pamphlete über Wagner angerichtet haben?" Strauss, *Betrachtungen*, 24/E19.

48. "In der Hauptstadt herrschen leider noch die ewigen Schönheitsgesetze, die unsereins auch gern einmal zu Gesichte bekäme, die aber bis heute als rätselhafte Geheimnisse im Busen der Herren Hanslick und Genossen schlummern." Cited in Hanslick, "'Es war einmal' von Zemlinsky," in *Aus neuer und neuester Zeit*, 49; also (with minor orthographic differences) in Steinitzer, *Richard Strauss*, 165, who incorrectly dates it to the aftermath of the 1905 *Tonkünstlerversammlung*. Given that Hanslick died in 1904 and still managed to respond to Strauss's remark (which Steinitzer paraphrases), it must have been a few years earlier, possibly when Strauss was in Graz in 1903 (March 5–7).

49. "Jeder von ihnen, wohlgemerkt, war ein Neuerer gegen seine Vorgänger—sie alle haben in ihren Symphonien Musik gemacht und nicht Bilderrätsel." Hanslick, "'Es war einmal' von Zemlinsky," in *Aus neuer und neuester Zeit*, 49.

50. "Ich war fest überzeugt, der berühmte Autor so vieler symphonischer Bilderbücher stehe längst jenseits von Lob und Tadel und blicke auf vereinzelte nicht zustimmende Kritiker mit dem Gleichmut des richtigen Übermenschen herab. Nach dem Erlaß an seine getreue Hauptstadt Graz scheint dies jedoch nicht ganz der Fall zu

sein. Freundlich lobt er, die ihn loben, und bitter tadelt er die Tadler. Das ist ja 'menschlich, allzumenschlich.'" Ibid., 50. The critic is indulging in word play on Nietzsche's titles: *Jenseits von Gut und Böse* (1886), and *Menschliches, Allzumenschliches* (1878).

51. See Brodbeck, "Dvořák's Reception," in which the author contextualizes Hanslick's aesthetic judgments by exploring the complicated political situation in later nineteenth-century Vienna, in particular the stew of linguistic and national interests involving Bohemia, on which turns the larger question of Czech versus German identity.

52. "Freuen wir uns, in unserer productionsarmen, reflectirten Zeit noch einem naiv empfindenden, fröhlich schaffenden Talent wie Dvorak zu begegnen, das in die höchsten Formen der Instrumental-Musik sich hineingewachsen und bei ausgesprochener Eigenthümlichkeit dem Ideale unserer classischen Periode die Treue bewahrt hat." Eduard Hanslick, *Concerte, Componisten und Virtuosen der letzten fünfzehn Jahre, 1870–1885*, 3rd ed. (Berlin: Allgemeiner Verein für Deutsche Litteratur, 1896), 371.

53. "Mein erster Weg führt mich immer zu Ihnen und Brahms und soll es auch für alle Zukunft so Gott will so bleiben!" Letter from Dvořák to Hanslick, February 23, 1883; John Clapham, "Dva neznámé Dvořákovy dopisy E. Hanslickov," *Hudební věda* 17, no.2 (1980): 155.

54. "Die Aufführung der sinf[onischen] Dicht[ungen] wird Ende d[ieses] M[onats] sein. Könnte Hanslick kommen?" Letter from Dvořák to Fritz Simrock, May 10, 1896; *Antonín Dvořák: Correspondence and Documents*, vol. 4: 1896–1904: *Correspondence Dispatched*, ed. Milan Kuna (Prague: Bärenreiter Suprahon, 1995), 28.

55. "Die ungemein interessante Symphonie [No. 9], welche glänzend instrumentiert, doch keineswegs nach jüngstdeutschen Manieren die Klangeffekte zur Hauptsache macht." Hanslick, "E-moll Symphonie und 'Der Wassermann' von A. Dvořák," in *Am Ende des Jahrhunderts*, 215. Originally published as Ed. H., "Concerte," *Neue Freie Presse* (December 8, 1896): 1–2.

56. "Dvořák verfällt nicht in die Formlosigkeit und die Jagd nach falschen Kontrasten, die uns in den 'dramatischen' Symphonien so vieler neudeutscher Komponisten abstößt. Dieser Slave kennt gründlicher als mancher Deutsche seinen Beethoven, dessen Coriolan und Egmont nicht ganz ohne Einwirkung auf die 'Husitska' geblieben sind." Hanslick, "Dvořák: Orchester-Suite und 'Husitska,'" in *Fünf Jahre Musik*, 190.

57. "Aber beide beherrscht dieselbe Freude am schönen Klang, dieselbe melodische Frische, Unmittelbarkeit und Natürlichkeit." Hanslick, "Dvořák: Drei Ouvertüren," in *Fünf Jahre Musik*, 298. Originally published as Ed. H., "Concerte," *Neue Freie Presse* (February 5, 1895): 1–2.

58. "eine Einleitung oder Nachdichtung des Shakespeareschen Trauerspieles . . . im 'Othello' trägt er eine Maske, die bald an Liszt, bald an Wagner erinnert." Hanslick, "Dvořák: Drei Ouvertüren," in *Fünf Jahre Musik*, 298, 299.

59. "da seiner Natur der vernichtende dramatische Konflikt, das Selbstzerfleichen und Blutvergießen ferne liegt." Ibid., 299.

60. Die 'Othello' Ouverture sucht den dramatischen Verlauf der Tragödie nachzubilden und verweilt mit grausamer Ausführlichkeit bei dem Erwürgen der Desdemona. Dvořák kehrt hier am unrechten Ort den dramatischen Komponisten hervor; er ist aber kein dramatischer Komponist im eminenten Sinne; das hätte er am rechten Ort, in seinen Opern, zeigen müssen, welche nur durch ihre lyrischen Schönheiten, vorzüglich in gemütvoller und heiterer Stimmung glänzen." Ibid.

61. "Wie man einen so gräßlichen, jedes feinere Gefühl empörenden Stoff zu musikalischer Darstellung sich wählen könne, ist mir nicht recht begreiflich." Hanslick,

"E-moll Symphonie und 'Der Wassermann' von A. Dvořák," in *Am Ende des Jahrhunderts*, 216–17.

62. "Seltsame Passion Dvořáks, sich jetzt dem Gräßlichen, Widernatürlichen, Gespenstischen hinzugeben, das seinem echt musikalischen Sinne, seiner liebenswürdig menschlichen Natur so wenig entspricht!" Hanslick, "'Die Mittagshexe,' von Dvořák." Ibid., 226. Originally published as Ed. H., "Concerte," *Neue Freie Presse* (December 22, 1896): 1–3.

63. "Wir wollen unser Ohr und unsere Phantasie nicht in eine gebundene Marschroute zwängen lassen." Hanslick, "E-moll Symphonie und 'Der Wassermann' von A. Dvořák," in *Am Ende des Jahrhunderts*, 217.

64. "Die einfache Überschrift, 'Der Wassermann' hätte vollkommen genügt, um der poetischen und malerischen Einbildungskraft des Zuhörers eine bestimmte Anregung zu geben." Ibid.

65. "Aber das Unglück ist, daß der Komponist, sowie der Hörer einer vorgedruckten Erzählung Schritt für Schritt folgen muß." Ibid.

66. "Das ist alles interessant musiziert, aber schlecht erzählt." Ibid.

67. "diese tolle Mode, die mit Tönen nicht mehr musizieren, sondern erzählen und malen will." Ibid., 218.

68. "Dem Reiz einer geistreichen Tonmalerei widersteht niemand, von den kindlich heiteren Klangbildern in Haydns 'Schöpfung' und 'Jahreszeiten' angefangen bis zu den genialen Tongemälden der Romantiker und Wagners berückendem Feuerzauber." Hanslick, "'Die Mittagshexe,' von Dvořák." Ibid., 226.

69. "Dvořák hat es nicht nötig, für seine Musik bei der Dichtkunst (und welcher 'Dichtkunst'!) betteln zu gehen. Seine reiche musikalisch Erfindung bedarf keiner Anleihe, keiner Krücke, keiner Gebrauchsanweisung." Hanslick, "Neue Orchesterwerke, 'Aus Italien' von R. Strauß. 'Die Waldtaube' von Dvořák," in *Aus neuer und neuester Zeit*, 86.

70. "die Nachbildung der verschiedenen Naturstimmen." Ibid.

71. "drängt es ihn aber, zur Abwechslung, heraus aus der wortlosen Instrumentalmusik zu realen Gestalten, dann steht ein weit offenes Thor einladend vor ihm: die Oper." Ibid.

72. "Eigentliche Programm-Musik ist das 'Heldenlied' ebensowenig wie Beethovens Eroica, an die es durch seinen Namen erinnert. Dvořák zwingt dem Hörer keine detaillierte Gebrauchsanweisung auf, wie bei seinen symphonischen Dichtungen 'Wassermann,' 'Mittagshexe,' 'Spinnrad,' welche diesen Notbehelf leider nicht entbehren können. Das 'Heldenlied' ist in der Hauptsache rein musikalisch verständlich und wirksam . . . Auslegerkünste werden sich wohl auch an dem 'Heldenlied' zu schaffen machen—wie viele Erklärungen hat nicht schon die 'Eroica' erlebt und erlitten!" Hanslick, "Brahms und Dvořák," in *Am Ende des Jahrhunderts*, 312. Originally published as Ed. H., "Musik. Philharmonisches Concert. Brahms und Dvořák," *Neue Freie Presse* (December 6, 1898): 1–2.

73. "Nach einer 'authentischen Mitteilung' des Concertprogramms haben wir bei dem 'Heldenlied' . . . weniger an einen Kriegshelden, als an eine slavischen Rhapsoden oder Barden zu denken." Hanslick, *Am Ende des Jahrhunderts*, 312.

74. "Die Tondichtung gemahnt also an die Schicksale oder die Entwickelung eines Geisteshelden, ohne daß die wechselnden Stimmungen bestimmte Vorgänge wiederspiegeln müßten." Ibid.

75. "Das Stück klingt so fanatisch, als wenn es stellenweise mit Äxten, Sensen und Morgensternen instrumentiert wäre." Hanslick, "Dvořák: Orchester-Suite und 'Husitska,'" in *Fünf Jahre Musik*, 189–90.

76. "Die Komposition selbst ist bewunderungswürdig durch ihre blendenden, ganz neuen Orchester-Effekte, ihre originelle, im Anfang auch sehr poetische Tonmalerei." Hanslick, "E-moll Symphonie und 'Der Wassermann' von A. Dvořák," in *Am Ende des Jahrhunderts*, 217.

77. "Ich fürchte, Dvořák hat mit dieser detaillierten Programm-Musik eine abschüssige Bahn betreten, welche am Ende direct zu—*Richard Strauß* führt." Ibid.

78. "Dieser Tonmaler [Strauss] läßt uns bekanntlich in seinem 'Eulenspiegel' hören, wie der Vagabund auf den Galgen hinaufgezogen wird, in 'Tod und Verklärung,' wie dem im Todeskampf Zuckenden das Nachtlicht verlöscht u. s. w." Ibid.

79. "Es kann mir nicht beikommen, Dvořák ... mit Richard Strauss auf eine Linie zu stellen; er ist ein echter Musiker, der hundert Mal bewiesen hat, daß er keines Programms und keiner Aufschrift bedarf, um uns durch reine gegenstandslose Musik zu entzücken." Ibid., 219.

80. "Aber eine leise freundschaftliche Warnung kann ihm nach dem 'Wassermann' vielleicht nicht schaden." Ibid.

81. Date according to Franz Trenner, *Richard Strauss: Chronik zu Leben und Werk*, ed. Florian Trenner (Vienna: Verlag Dr. Richard Strauss, 2003), 189. Hanslick's review came out two weeks later on December 5, 1899. See Ed. H., "Concerte," *Neue Freie Presse* (December 5, 1899): 1–2. Reprinted as Hanslick, "Neue Orchesterwerke, 'Aus Italien' von R. Strauß. 'Die Waldtaube' von Dvořák," in *Aus neuer und neuester Zeit*, 80–87.

82. "*Aus Italien* ist halbverhüllte, *Die Waldtaube* ganz unverhüllte Programmmusik. In vier großangelegten Symphoniesätzen malt Richard Strauss italienische Landschaft, italienisches Volksleben: Dvorak erzählt in einem Satz eine ganze wechselvolle Geschichte." Hanslick, *Aus neuer und neuester Zeit*, 80.

83. "der Führer unserer musikalischen Secessionisten." Ibid.

84. "Blendende Instrumentalwitze ziehen unsere Aufmerksamkeit vom Ganzen ab." Ibid., 81.

85. "Ja, wir vermissen darin sogar ... italienische Farbe, italienische Stimmung! Wie klingt das alles so deutsch umständlich! In diesen verschwommenen, dickflüssigen Melodien rinnt kein italienischer Blutstropfen." Ibid., 81–82.

86. "Die ganze symphonische Phantasie interessiert stellenweise als das Produkt eines geistreichen, effektkundig, mehr poetisch angeregten als musikalisch-schöpferischen Künstlers. Sichtlich von Berlioz inspiriert, mit Wagnerschen Kombinationen arbeitend, verschmäht es Strauss trotzdem nicht, einigemal von Mendelssohn zu borgen." Ibid., 82.

87. "Neben R. Strauss ist Dvořák unstreitig die musikalisch stärkere, ursprünglichere Natur; in naïvem Empfinden und melodischem Reichtum diesem unendlich überlegen." Ibid., 83.

88. "Diese bringt schöne Aufschriften zu unschöner Musik, Dvořák schöne Musik zu unschönem Texte." Ibid.

89. "die fortwährende Nötigung des Zuhörers, die Musik schrittweise mit der ihr aufgezwungenen Erzählung zu vergleichen." Ibid., 84.

90. "Dabei ist die Musik von einer liebenswürdigen Anmut und Naivetät." Ibid.

91. "Die Musik leidet immer darunter, wenn ein detailliertes Programm die Freiheit des Komponisten wie des Hörers vernichtet." Ibid., 84–85.

92. "Was ihn weggelockt haben mag aus dem Reiche der absoluten Musik, das er seit Brahms' Heimgang als Erster beherrscht, ist offenbar die Nachbildung der verschiedenen Naturstimmen. Darin schafft Dvořák ganz Unvergleichliches, Wunderbares." Ibid., 86. This use of the phrase "absolute music" problematizes Pederson's recent claim that the popular conception of Hanslick as an "advocate of absolute music" is a "myth."

While his usage of the term (as opposed to the constellation of ideas it represented) may indeed have been infrequent, the foregoing instance is not cited in her article (see note 3 above).

93. Other figures who expressed disquiet over detailed musico-programmatic correspondences include Wagner, Franz Brendel, W. A. Ambros, and Felix Weingartner. For a discussion of the extent to which Hanslick's views on program music are in keeping with these writers, see Nicole Grimes, "A Critical Inferno: Hoplit, Hanslick and Liszt's *Dante Symphony*," *Journal of the Society for Musicology in Ireland* 7 (2011–12): 3-22.

94. Hanslick, *Aus neuer und neuester Zeit*, 86.

95. "Im Verhältnis zur Musik ist alle Mitteilung durch Worte von schamloser Art; das Wort verdünnt und verdummt, das Wort entpersönlicht, das Wort macht das Ungemeine gemein." Hanslick, "'Es war einmal' von Zemlinsky." Ibid., 49–50. The quotation is from *Aus dem Nachlaß der Achtzigerjahre*, in Friedrich Nietzsche, *Werke in drei Bänden*, vol. 3 (Munich: Beck, 1956), §14, no. 810.

96. "Der Form nach ist es eine 'symphonische Dichtung' im Sinne Liszts und spielt sich in Einem fortlaufenden Satze ab, welcher mehrere in Tonart, Tempo und Ausdruck kontrastierende Teile ohne scharfe Abgrenzung in sich faßt." Hanslick, "Brahms und Dvořák," in *Am Ende des Jahrhunderts*, 312.

Chapter Fourteen

On "Jewishness" and Genre

Hanslick's Reception of Gustav Mahler

David Kasunic

Hanslick De-Formalized

The historian Peter Gay concludes his 1978 book *Freud, Jews and Other Germans: Masters and Victims in Modernist Culture* with a chapter entitled "For Beckmesser: Eduard Hanslick, Victim and Prophet." What is remarkable about the chapter is Gay's studied avoidance of the issue of anti-Semitism as it relates to arguments about *Die Meistersinger* or Hanslick, or both. In a book that elsewhere addresses issues of anti-Semitism, this last chapter fashions Hanslick as one of the "other Germans" of its title. The issue of anti-Semitism, however, is picked up in two of the chapter's footnotes. Footnote fourteen cites Friedrich Blume's encyclopedia entry for Hanslick in the 1956 *Musik in Geschichte und Gegenwart*, calling it "an authoritative treatment, though somewhat marred by an unnecessary 'defense' against the 'charge' that Hanslick was of Jewish descent."[1] Here, Gay signals his own reason for sidestepping the issue of Hanslick's Jewish descent. Footnote forty-three, a long footnote coming almost at the end of the chapter and hence the book, explains why:

> In one rather wry way, one can define Hanslick as a "modern" through his presumed Jewishness, since to anti-Semites, Jews were the "moderns." As Hanslick noted in his autobiography, Wagner "accused" him of being Jewish, in the second edition of his *Judentum in der Musik* (1869), in which Wagner calls *Vom Musikalisch-Schönen* "a lampoon, written with extraordinary cleverness, in the interest of music-Jewry." Hanslick professes to be flattered at the chance of being burned at the same stake with Mendelssohn and Meyerbeer, but denies Wagner's charge by referring to his father's family as "arch-Catholic peasants." ... He says nothing of his mother's family, and the notion that Hanslick was half-Jewish remains a staple. (Thus William M. Johnston, *The Austrian Mind: An Intellectual and Social History 1848–1938* (1972), 132–33;

and see above, note 14.) Whatever the truth, I am constrained to ask, as I did in some earlier essays, Does it matter? Did it stamp his work?[2]

Coming from a scholar as curious and as psychologically keen as Gay, these questions register as defensive. Yes, Gay is perhaps being humane in wishing Hanslick's Jewishness not to matter, as Hanslick did not wish it to matter. But to relegate this issue to a footnote at the end of a book that has "Jews" in the title speaks to something more. Gay, like many others who have written about Hanslick, has allowed the celebrated formalist aesthetics of Hanslick's 1854 *Vom Musikalisch-Schönen (On the Musically Beautiful)* to subsume Hanslick himself, such that the "form" that is the treatise determines the "content" of the essentialized critic. In this way, any identification of a Hanslick self not contained by the aesthetics becomes, necessarily, ad hominem. Carl Dahlhaus, for another example, in his frequent mentions of Hanslick over the course of *Die Idee der absoluten Musik (The Idea of Absolute Music)*, fashions Hanslick as no more than the views put forth in his early treatise. The recent work of Kevin Karnes has used this well-worn fixation on Hanslick's treatise as the productive starting point for drawing our attention to Hanslick's vast body of subsequent writing as a music critic, writing that complicates our formalist picture of the man. Indeed, Hanslick's music reviews project a more complexly human figure, one whose reviewing hand may be aesthetically guided by miscellaneous human concerns and feelings (conscious and not) and by the force of individual performances and performers. As Hanslick himself reminds us, in an 1899 review of a Philharmonic Concert in which Mahler has the whole string section play Beethoven's Quartet in F minor, op. 95—a programming decision that baffled and disturbed many and that Hanslick alone defended—Hanslick would not "refuse for pedantic reasons a new impression, an unusual pleasure."[3]

Indeed, Hanslick was perhaps least the pedant where Mahler was concerned. In Mahler, Hanslick was confronted with a fellow Bohemian musician of Jewish descent who championed Wagner and purveyed program music—for Hanslick, an obviously thorny mix of identity and aesthetics. Hanslick's reception of Mahler the conductor and, later, of Mahler the composer, humanely registers this complexity. In the case of Hanslick's Mahler reception, and in response to Gay's above questions, Hanslick's Jewish descent *does* matter, and it *did* stamp his work, in ways that have shaped the subsequent reception of Mahler to the present day.

The two Hanslick reviews that are the reason for this essay, and thus its ultimate focus, are his reviews of concerts conducted by Mahler and featuring Mahler's compositions: the January 16, 1900, review of the Vienna Philharmonic concert in which Mahler first introduced his orchestral *lieder* to Vienna, and the November 20, 1900, review of the Philharmonic concert that included the Vienna première of Mahler's Symphony No. 1. Aside from Mahler's completion of Carl Maria von Weber's comic opera *Die drei Pintos* (discussed below), the only Mahler compositions that Hanslick reviewed were five of his orchestral *lieder* and his First Symphony, toward the end of his long reviewing career. But Hanslick reviewed many performances of Mahler as a conductor prior to reviewing Mahler as a composer. The work of K. M. Knittel has deepened our understanding of the critical response to Mahler in *fin-de-siècle* Vienna, especially the response to Mahler as a conductor.[4] The focus of Knittel's work, however, has been the anti-Semitic response to Mahler, thus she reasonably gives Hanslick light treatment. In her monograph *Seeing Mahler: Music and the Language of Antisemitism in Fin-de-Siècle Vienna*, Knittel limits her consideration of Hanslick to his review of Mahler's Symphony No. 1, as part of a broader consideration of "absolute music" versus "program music."[5] Here, she effectively invokes the work of Sanna Pederson, who has persuasively argued that "it was the idea of a German musical culture that—gradually and against resistance—became the paradigm of absolute music in the nineteenth century."[6] For Pederson, "'the idea of absolute music' arises primarily out of the correlation of two systems of differences: one of function (music for its own sake as opposed to other kinds of music); the other of nation (German music as opposed to that of other countries)."[7] The symphony was the genre most charged with this German nationalist agenda.

Grouping Hanslick with the chorus of critics who are vexed by Mahler's First Symphony mutes the distinctiveness of Hanslick's response to Mahler as a composer. By instead considering Hanslick's review of Mahler's First Symphony both alongside his review of Mahler's orchestral lieder and as an extension of an already-forged disposition to Mahler as a conductor, we will better understand the intersection of ideas about genre with ideas about being Jewish in the Viennese critical response to Mahler. In order to do so, we must begin not with *what* is being said (the reviews themselves), but with *who* is saying it: Hanslick. After first assessing Hanslick's broad philosophical position regarding Mahler, we will consider Wagner's making-public of Hanslick's Jewish ancestry, before touching on Karnes's recent work on Hanslick's historiography in order to entertain how the beginning of his new critical enterprise after 1869 likely served as a response to Wagner. We will then review Hanslick's championing of Mahler the conductor, before considering Hanslick's two reviews of Mahler's compositions from a renewed perspective.

My contention throughout is that Hanslick's Jewish lineage "matters" to the extent that it mattered to Wagner and to the anti-Semites, mentioned by Gay, who regarded Jews as being "modern." But where Gay regards Hanslick as an accidental modern because of his Jewish lineage and a modernist *avant la lettre* because of his "commitment to the idea of aesthetic autonomy," Hanslick's Wagner-inspired awareness of his Jewishness prompted a philosophical response that is modernist *not* in its formalist regard for the musical work (*à la On the Musically Beautiful*), but in its deliberate and ritual insistence on the musical performance, comprised as it is of performing bodies, as the constructor of musical meaning.

Wagner versus Berlioz: German National Identity and Generic Contracts

I use "philosophical" with intended force. For while Dahlhaus casts the Hanslick of the 1854 aesthetics treatise as Hegel's metaphysical stepson,[8] Hanslick in his music criticism is more Friedrich Nietzsche's kindred spirit, especially in that both Hanslick, in his reviews of Mahler's compositions, and Nietzsche, in *The Case of Wagner* (1888), suggest a French-derived musical modernism that sidesteps Wagner. The similarity is not accidental: the recent work of Dieter Borchmeyer, Christoph Landerer, and Manfred Eger has revealed Nietzsche's indebtedness to Hanslick's music criticism in the former's critique of Wagner.[9] Being musically "modern" then meant being Wagnerian, and attempts to define "musical modernism" since have devolved on the influence of Wagner.[10] In their critical work, Nietzsche and Hanslick resist that Wagnerian juggernaut, and both, in their later writings, respond to a German idealist co-opting of musical experience that denies the presence of physical bodies. At issue was the "idea of absolute music"—"the idea that music," as Dahlhaus writes, "is a revelation of the absolute, specifically because it 'dissolves' itself from the sensual, and finally even from the affective sphere."[11] (Such idealizing has been the critical tendency of hermeneutics in general. As David E. Wellbery points out in his discussion of the work of Friedrich Kittler, Kittler's posthermeneutics are inspired by Nietzsche, who punned that the father of hermeneutics, Friedrich Schleiermacher, was just that—a maker (*Macher*) of veils (*Schleier*).)[12] This "dissolv[ing] itself from the sensual" is precisely what Nietzsche claims that Wagner, reflexively channeling Schopenhauer, does to Brünnhilde over the course of writing the *Ring*: "Brünnhilde was initially supposed to take her farewell with a song in honor of free love, putting off the world with the hope of a socialist utopia in which 'all turns out well'—but now gets something else to do. She has to study Schopenhauer first; she has to transpose the fourth book of *The World as Will and Representation* into verse. *Wagner was redeemed.*"[13] This idealization will, from there, subsume all of Wagner's (understanding of his) music: "[Wagner] invented a style for himself charged with 'infinite meaning'—he became the *heir of Hegel.*—Music as 'idea.'"[14]

At the beginning of *The Case of Wagner*, Nietzsche famously, rapturously puts forth the earthbound Carmen, from Bizet's *Carmen*, as the antidote to the idealized Brünnhilde.[15] As Nicole Grimes has drawn to our attention, while Hanslick's final assessment of Bizet's opera is tepid, he is smitten by the character of Carmen to such an extent that, in a move rare for him, he forsakes contemplating the music to instead record its *physical* effects: "It is only with the appearance of Carmen," he writes, that "the blood of the composer and the listener begins to surge in their veins."[16] But the non-German body that will "matter" (retaining Gay's word) for Hanslick where Mahler is concerned is not Carmen's or Bizet's, but Berlioz's.[17] Geoffrey Payzant has shown Hanslick's youthful enthusiasm for and deep engagement with the music of Berlioz when he was part of a group arranging for Berlioz to visit Prague, in 1846.[18] Hanslick's admiration for Berlioz, however, does not wholly evaporate with his youth, even though, reviewing a Mahler-conducted concert over fifty years later, he sees Berlioz's *Symphonie fantastique* as having "the decisive influence on our latest program music."[19] For in this same review, Hanslick will boast about his personal acquaintance with Berlioz, relating how in 1845 he not only saw Berlioz conduct this symphony but also attended all of Berlioz's rehearsals of the work.[20] Hanslick's reminscences of Berlioz in *Aus meinem Leben* go still further to underscore that, while Hanslick's sympathy for Berlioz's music may have faded just as it did for Wagner's, his fondness for Berlioz the person stayed with him, as if it were only yesterday that they were walking together.[21] And while Hanslick knows that Berlioz, like Wagner, was not indifferent to his published criticisms, he insists that Berlioz was the "more noble figure, [possessing a] far more sympathetic nature than Wagner."[22] With Berlioz, just as with Wagner, Hanslick conjures up the *person* as standing there before him. Unlike with Wagner, however, Hanslick cherishes those memories of Berlioz.[23]

So, although Hanslick's recalling Berlioz upon seeing Mahler conducting Berlioz's work in 1898 is unremarkable in itself, this linking of Berlioz to Mahler will, nevertheless, frame Hanslick's reception of Mahler's compositions. For what Berlioz represents for Hanslick is a non-German composer (thus *not* Wagner) of a music embraced by the so-called New German School. In being a French exponent of what will be claimed as a German musical practice, Berlioz presents Hanslick with a model of a musical belonging-while-not-belonging— not unlike that experienced by the Bohemian-Jewish Mahler upon his return to Vienna in 1897, to assume the directorship at the Hofoper.

The climate for Jews in the Vienna to which Mahler returned would have been less welcoming than the Vienna of his student days in the 1870s. Steven E. Aschheim's work has charted the change wrought by the beginning of the pogroms in 1881, the year that "heralded the great demographic redistribution of the Jewish People from East to West."[24] As Germany and Austria were the gateways for this exodus, German and Austrian Jews shouldered the burden of its physical reality, at the very time that organized political anti-Semitism in those countries was on the rise.[25] While assimilated Jews regarded the increasing presence of the *Ostjuden* as a threat to their "own project of assimilation,"[26] increasingly it was the "modern" Jew who was vilified by both anti-Semites and other assimilated Jews. As Aschheim observes in a chapter titled "Caftan and Cravat: 'Old' Jews, 'New' Jews, and Pre–World War I Anti-Semitism," a so-called new (read "assimilated") Jewish writer like Walther Rathenau (1867–1922), in his tract "Höre Israel" (1897), "regarded the restless, rootless parvenu spirit as the most distasteful aspect of contemporary German Jewish behavior."[27] In Aschheim's formulation, then, the "modern" Jew would be even newer (in manner, if not in age) than the assimilated Jew, who is "new" by comparison to the "old" Jews, "the *Urjuden*, [who are] intent on maintaining traditional, unethical ghetto practices and unwilling to change their national loyalties and dubious values."[28] As a composer of music and writer of texts that gave voice to this "restless, rootless" spirit, Mahler was perceived as a modern, and as such, was tarnished by the wide anti-Semitic brush of not only what Aschheim refers to as the (non-Jewish) "Volkish critics of 'Jewish modernism,'"[29] but by Viennese Jewish writers as well. For instance, the philosopher Otto Weininger (1880–1903) in *Sex and Character* (1903) "depicted Jews as essentially amoral, cynical, skeptical, lacking in warmth and emotion," a depiction that the Jewish philosopher and historian Hans Kohn (1891–1971) argues stems from Weininger's acquaintance "with only the superficial, inauthentic, and assimilated 'coffee-house' Jews of Vienna."[30]

Hanslick's viewing Mahler through a Berlioz lens thus does not skew Hanslick's perception so much as it enables him to identity with Mahler and, thereby, to register Mahler's "modern" musical achievement, as alien as that achievement may have been to the elderly Hanslick. To say that Hanslick would "identify" with Mahler is not to go too far: as a practitioner of Austrian culture at a time when a Jewish-tolerant political liberalism yields to an anti-Semitic ethnic nationalism,[31] and when because of "*successful* Jewish acculturation . . . 'race' became an effective explanation of 'Semitic-Aryan' difference,"[32] Hanslick's performing (listening, writing) Jewish body will *matter* as much for ethnic nationalists as will Dvořák's Czech body or Mahler's Jewish body.

Yet where Dvořák largely composed pieces that Hanslick could aesthetically endorse and in a Germanic style, such that Hanslick will "distance Dvořák from the cause of Czech nationalism by implying that the composer was, in effect, 'one of us'—a German,"[33] Mahler composed orchestral lieder that the late-in-life Hanslick could not call *lieder* and a symphony that he could not call music.[34] Both are arguably the two genres bound up most with a German nationalist agenda. What matters, in this regard, is that Hanslick does not identify these works so much as *failed* lieder and a *failed* symphony, but as neither lieder nor symphony. Mahler has stretched the formal expectations of a "symphony" and "lieder" to the extent that Hanslick believes that Mahler has broken their generic contracts.[35] As we shall see, this is where Hanslick sympathetically tempers his expectation of that music in order to try to come to terms with the modernist rethinking of inherited genres that is at the heart of Mahler's compositional project. As such, Hanslick's questioning aloud fits the ambitions of Mahler's music. For while Hanslick will not claim Mahler as a German, per se, he will, in a way that converts the ad hominem arguments of the anti-Semites into a source of existential promise, claim the Mahler who is speaking to him in these performances as a modernist prophet for the new century.

Wagner Responds to Hanslick, and Hanslick to Wagner

The reason Hanslick fashions Mahler not as an apostate but as a prophet stems from Hanslick's own treatment at the hands of Wagner. Like Nietzsche's early embrace of Wagner, Hanslick's embrace soon turned cold, and the chill was aesthetic and personal. In order to appreciate how Wagner's public attack on Hanslick occasioned a shift in Hanslick's critical practice, we must survey relevant events in the evolution of this relationship, starting with Hanslick's 1846 review of *Tannhäuser*. Expanding on Jens Malte Fischer's work, Thomas Grey draws our attention to "Hanslick's central position in the 1869 'afterword' to *Jewishness in Music* [*Das Judenthum in der Musik*],[36] and how that reflects Wagner's ongoing preoccupations during the writing, composition, and production of *Die Meistersinger*."[37] Both Fischer and Grey, unlike Gay, take Hanslick's Jewish lineage as a given. Their focus is Wagner's response to Hanslick, and they contend that for Wagner, in the case of both the 1850 version of his *Jewishness in Music* essay, published at that time anonymously, and the 1869 version of the essay, now with Wagner's name attached, "a longer-brewing period of rancor against supposed Jewish competitors and adversaries is finally ignited by a specific event or factor."[38] Synthesizing the conclusions reached by Fischer and Grey, we are able to construct the following timeline:

1846   Hanslick's long and enthusiastic review of the Dresden production of *Tannhäuser* appears, in twelve installments, in the *Wiener allgemeine Musik-Zeitung*. This same year, Wagner, in his "program" for Beethoven's Ninth Symphony, coins the term "absolute music."[39]

1850   Ludwig Bischoff's laudatory article on the opera then sweeping through Europe, Meyerbeer's *Le Prophète*,[40] appears in the first volume of *Rheinische Musikzeitung*. This article serves as the immediate catalyst for the first version of Wagner's *Jewishness in Music*, published under the pseudonym "K. Freigedank" in the *Neue Zeitschrift für Musik*,[41] and targeting Jewish composers.

1854   Hanslick's *Vom Musikalisch-Schönen* is published. In it, Hanslick adopts Wagner's term "absolute music" in order to oppose the kind of music espoused by Wagner and his followers.

1861   Promoted to the rank of tenured professor at the University, Hanslick quits his job at the Ministry of Education, thereby permitting him to pursue journalism full time. And late in this year, Wagner produces the prose sketch of the scenario for *Die Meistersinger*, with "Veit Hanslich" as the name of the Marker.

1862 Both Wagner and Hanslick attend a gathering at the home of the physician Dr. Joseph Standhartner, at which a dramatic reading of the *Meistersinger* libretto is given.

Early 1860s Hanslick likely confides to Wagner information about his family background, during a meeting arranged by Luise Dustmann to reconcile the two men. (As Grey notes, a "diary entry by Cosima from 27 June 1870 strongly suggests this, as well as suggesting that Wagner was quite deliberately aiming to 'out' Hanslick's Jewish background in the 1869 afterword, in a gesture he regarded as well-deserved retribution: [Cosima writes] 'At lunch he [R.W.] tells us about Hanslick (his mother a Jewess) and Herr Ambros, who allowed himself to be bought by the *Neue Freie Presse* (against R.), how both of them had approached him, made admissions to him, and then, reckoning on his good manners like the miserable creatures they are, had no fear that he would one day tell what he knew.'")[42]

1868 *Die Meistersinger* premières on June 21 in Munich, and Hanslick writes a mostly unfavorable review of the opera.

1869 Wagner reissues *Jewishness in Music* as a signed pamphlet with a new afterword railing against his alleged Jewish critics, mentioning Hanslick by name.

In this afterword, on the heels of a discussion of how his idea of "Artwork of the Future" had been twisted by critics, Wagner makes clear that he is targeting Hanslick in particular. Parodying the critic, he writes that "my music must be as abominable as my Theory." Wagner attributes this view to "a Viennese jurist, a great friend of Music's and a connoisseur of Hegel's Dialectics, who moreover was found peculiarly accessible through his—albeit charmingly concealed—Judaic origin."[43] Wagner "outs" Hanslick with purpose: he wants to show how the esteem that Hanslick gained through writing *Vom Musikalisch-Schönen* permitted Hanslick perhaps to "succeed in doing a thing by all means harder, namely in establishing modern Jewish music as the sterling 'beautiful' music."[44] But it didn't stop there for Wagner. Hanslick was now, by turning to music criticism, starting to use what was for Wagner a bully pulpit to damn all of Wagner's "artistic doings" as worthless. "Through his ingenious booklet the author rooted himself in general respect, and had thereby gained a position which gave importance to him when, as a bewondered aesthete, he now appeared as a reviewer, too, in the best-read political paper, and straightaway pronounced myself and my artistic doings completely null and void."[45] For Wagner, this was deeply personal, because Hanslick set the tone for a much broader response to Wagner's project, and thereby distracted people away from the issue at hand—Jewishness in music:

[Hanslick] thus succeeded (or others succeeded through him, if you will) in getting just this tone [*Ton*] about me adopted as the fashion [*Styl*], at least so far as newspapers are read throughout the world—this tone which it has so astonished you, most honoured lady, to meet where'er you go. Nothing but my contempt for all the great masters of Tone, my warfare against Melody, my horrible mode of composition, in short "The Music of the Future," was thenceforth the topic of everybody's talk: about that article on "Judaism in Music," however, there never again appeared a word.[46]

In a subsequent footnote Wagner made it clear that he was referring specifically to *Meistersinger*, and that he perceived the resistance to and difficulties in producing this work in Vienna and Berlin to be a consequence of the press it received.[47]

Jacob Katz has gone further to show that Wagner, as revealed by his correspondence from late 1868 and early 1869, was not republishing his essay simply to create desired controversy, as some have speculated, but had been particularly exercised by the Viennese press's response to *Meistersinger*.[48] As Wagner wrote to Karl Tausig, in April 1869, "The unheard-of insolence of the Viennese press on the occasion of the 'Meistersinger,' the constant spinning of lies about me . . . finally induced me to take my reckless step."[49] That this was personal for Wagner is borne out by his remark in a letter to Julius Lang, in February 1869: "I have now decided to confront the effronteries even where my own person is concerned."[50] Wagner's principal target in his afterword being Hanslick, we must not overlook the fact that, for Wagner, Hanslick's being Jewish was racial. Wagner makes this point by pitting Hanslick's body against a German body, in the only time he writes Hanslick's name: "But that above-named pamphlet of Dr Hanslick of Vienna . . . had also been brought with hottest haste into such celebrity that one can scarcely blame a blond German Aesthetician, Herr Vischer . . . if he associated himself, for convenience and safety's sake, with the so very much belauded Vienna Music-aesthete."[51] Wagner's ad hominem attack is deliberate: it is because Hanslick has a Jewish body that he writes and thinks the way he does, regardless of what Hanslick may claim, regardless of how he was raised. Wagner makes this clear already in the 1850 essay, in a long passage on the "cultured" (read "assimilated") Jew: "The cultured Jew has taken the most indicible pains to strip off all the obvious tokens of his lower coreligionists: in many a case he has even held it wise to make a Christian baptism wash away the traces of his origin."[52] Wagner's views thus adumbrate the radical racializing of Jewishness that will increasingly take place in the last decades of the century.[53]

Both Katz and Michael Saffle have brought to our attention responses to the reissue of *Jewishness in Music* that were published later in 1869.[54] This same year plays a prominent role in the history of Hanslick's career. On the basis of *Vom*

Musikalisch-Schönen the University of Vienna hires Hanslick in 1856, after which he abandons a systematic study of aesthetics for a series of publishing ventures, beginning with his 1869 *History of Concert Life in Vienna* and *History of Concert Life*, that compiles his previously published reviews and fashions them as a "living history" (*lebendige Geschichte*)—Hanslick's phrase—of Viennese musical life.[55] What is significant here is Hanslick's decision to compile his previous criticism in book form in this very year. Karnes classifies Hanslick's approach to the writing of music history as a "particularist historiography," borrowing Leo Treitler's phrase.[56] For Treitler, particularist historiography "is the conception of history as critical engagement with the object that directs attention to the individual and to the particular."[57] As Wagner directed our attention to Hanslick and his Jewish lineage, so, I argue, will Hanslick direct our attention away from Mahler's Jewish lineage and toward his achievements as a conductor, then composer, in large part *because* of Hanslick's appreciation of, if not empathy for, Mahler's being Jewish.

On Mahler the Conductor

Thus, starting with the *History of Concert Life*'s foreword, the date for which Hanslick gives as the Christmas season of 1869, Hanslick's new critical path responds to Wagner's own particularist history—his ad hominem attack against Hanslick and public outing of Hanslick's Jewish lineage. Hanslick's new path similarly privileges the subjective, the contingent, and the present—the *who* is speaking and to *whom*—and, as such, anticipates Nietzsche's critique of Wagner.[58] In their shared rejection of the neo-romantic musical metaphysics revived by what Dahlhaus calls the "Schopenhauerian renaissance, brought about by Wagner, starting in the 1860s,"[59] Hanslick comes across as Nietzsche's philosophical (and lapsed Wagnerian) kin. We are thus left to ponder the potential connection between Hanslick's critical practice *cum* particularist historiography and Nietzsche's happy embrace of the informal fallacy—the ad hominem argument. For a particularist historiographic approach—a focus on the moment, the substance, and the context of the music at hand, as well as on the governing theme, character, or idea of that music—invariably leads to a greater appreciation of *who* is responsible for the music we hear (not just how that music behaves), as in the present case of Hanslick's reception of Mahler. By the same token, as in our attempt to understand Hanslick himself, what he writes constitutes a *who*, an uttering subject. In reading Hanslick, we develop a relationship with him, and we may come to feel that we "know" him, that we even trust his judgments. This does not give Hanslick carte blanche, but it does encourage us to value what he says because it is *he* who is saying it.

As much as Hanslick does say about Wagner—and he says much, writing more on Wagner than on any other composer (and not all of it negative)—

we still do not know how the Wagner and Wagner-inspired anti-Semitic attacks against his person made him feel. In his review of Wagner's pamphlet and in his autobiography, Hanslick responds to the claim that he has Jewish roots by denying it. Thanks to the recent work of Jitka Ludvová, we have a clearer sense of Hanslick's Prague upbringing, specifically where his Jewish background is concerned.[60] Hanslick's mother, Karolina, was born in 1795 in Prague's Jewish ghetto, to Salomon Abraham Kisch and his wife, Rebeka.[61] Kisch was a banker and businessmen,[62] and not an Orthodox Jew.[63] Thus, after Karolina's birth, the Kisches took steps toward greater assimilation: they moved out of the ghetto,[64] and Abraham sought the society of Christians.[65] Karolina converted to Catholicism upon marrying Hanslick's father.[66] In 1833, the family moved into shared accommodation, so that from the time Hanslick was eight years old, he lived with his maternal grandparents, enjoying their company on a daily basis.[67]

Were Hanslick to have responded to Wagner's attack by acknowledging his Jewish roots, even in a qualified way, he would have provided the public face for Wagner's rabid caricature, which would have amounted to an undoing of the assimilation his grandparents had accomplished in just one generation. While this may account for Hanslick's denial, perhaps unanswerable questions still remain, and they are, how did Wagner's attacks make Hanslick feel? Did they cause him any private grief? Given the role that his grandparents played in his upbringing, would Hanslick not have felt at least for them, if not for his mother or himself? I do not presume to know how Hanslick felt. But I ask these questions out of a desire to humanize the great critic, and because it is on a human level that Hanslick's responses to Gustav Mahler, first as a conductor and then, late in life, as a composer, impress, for their sensitivity, their occasional self-questioning hesitancy, and their empathy. Hanslick does, after all, register the worsening climate for composers of Jewish origin, as when, in 1899, writing appreciatively on the topic of Mendelssohn's music, he observes the following: "In more recent times, elements from the outside have been used against Mendelssohn—the Wagnerians and anti-Semites united in hate and presumption. We allow them this sad business."[68] It thus may be in Hanslick's prolonged response to Mahler that we sense, obliquely, the anger or annoyance or hurt that he may have felt yet rarely voiced directly. Regardless, in being aware of Hanslick's experiences with anti-Semitism in the 1860s especially, one can hear their echoes in Hanslick's late-in-life championing of a conductor and composer whose tastes and compositions were cut from a Wagnerian cloth. With Mahler, Hanslick responds with an indulgence that suggests the empathetic stamp of a fellow Bohemian musician of Jewish descent.

What is extraordinary about Hanslick's relationship to Mahler the composer, in comparison with the other composers Hanslick reviewed, is that Hanslick had a long musical acquaintance with him prior to hearing his compositions. Guided largely by Henry-Louis de La Grange's biography and

Hanslick's reviews, these next few paragraphs will highlight key moments in the history of Hanslick's reception of Mahler the conductor.

In the fall of 1879, Mahler registered for Hanslick's university lectures on the history of music from the death of Beethoven to the present; we do not know if Hanslick was aware of Mahler then.[69] According to Mahler, Hanslick, along with Brahms, Goldmark, and Richter sat on the 1881 committee for the Beethoven Prize of the Gesellschaft der Musikfreunde, which rejected his submission of the cantata *Das klagende Lied*, but here, Mahler's version of events do not neatly square with all we know.[70] We do know that Hanslick was certainly aware of Mahler by the time he favorably reviewed Mahler's completed version of Weber's comic opera *Die drei Pintos*, first sung in Vienna on January 19, 1889.[71] Here, Hanslick first reveals the forbearance and even indulgence that will characterize his subsequent reception of Mahler. While Hanslick questions the enterprise of completing an opera he thinks would have been better left as a fragment, he maintains that "if it had to be completed, then Mr. Mahler has done so with undeniable historicity."[72] As Hanslick would later endorse Mahler's having an entire orchestral string section realize a Beethoven string quartet, because doing so suited the space in which the "quartet" was being performed, he endorsed those Mahler orchestrations in *Pintos* that were anachronistic. He argued that Mahler "orchestrated for the public of today, not for [that of] the [eighteen] twenties."[73] And Hanslick even endorsed the orchestration of the entr'acte to the opera's Second Act, which "waxed Wagnerian."[74] Thus, Hanslick's early reception of Mahler's work as a conductor and composer-arranger was quite flattering.

Seven years later, in the spring of 1896, when Wilhelm Jahn announced he would be resigning from the directorship of the Hofoper, Hanslick was famously thrown into direct advocacy of Mahler's cause.[75] Only two names were put forth for this position, Mahler and Felix Mottl, the non-Jewish Wagner acolyte and conductor.[76] Mottl had the support of Princess Metternich. So Hanslick, breaking form, offered Baron Bezecny, Director of the Court Theaters, some unsolicited advice, affirming Mahler's balanced programming and preservation of the "classical tradition" in Prague and Hamburg, and warning of a potential "disaster" were Mottl to become director:

> The reason for my letter is not a personal concern; it is one of interest to all friends of the opera. I have just learned that Jahn's resignation is said to be an accomplished fact; that would be a disaster. The only candidates mentioned to succeed him are Mottl and Mahler. In my modest opinion, it might be a disaster if Mottl were to become director. It is known from his activity in Karlsruhe that he loves and conducts only the works of Wagner and his horrible epigoni. . . . To judge by what Mahler has accomplished in Prague and Hamburg, he on the contrary would give our opera new life without violating its classical tradition.[77]

But repertoire ultimately was not the issue. For this public pitting of two Wagnerites against one another only served to underscore Mahler's primary stumbling block, his being Jewish. Raised in an assimilated German-speaking Jewish community, Mahler was forced to acknowledge that the way he saw himself was not the way that others did. As de La Grange has observed, "[Mahler] considered himself above all Austrian and Viennese and only became really conscious of his origins between 1894 and 1897, when his race appeared to be an insurmountable obstacle to his career."[78] Thus, in order to secure the deal, on February 23, 1897, Mahler is baptized into the Roman Catholic Church. But certainly, by this late date in Vienna, such conversions would have been mere theater.[79]

Indeed, in the years following his conversion, Mahler's Jewishness would only become more of an issue for the Viennese. Take, for example, the publication of the stunningly virulent anti-Semitic article in the *Deutsche Zeitung* entitled "The Jewish Regime at the Opera," submitted anonymously by a group of musicians intent on having Mahler ousted from the opera—two days before Mahler was to conduct his first concert with the Vienna Philharmonic, on November 6, 1898.[80] On musical matters, these anonymous writers were most enraged by Mahler's tinkering with Beethoven's score, adding an E-flat clarinet here, doubling a section there, and so on. But upon reviewing this concert, Hanslick makes no mention of any of these adjustments, Wagnerian in their approach though they were. (As we saw in the case of *Die drei Pintos*, Hanslick could appreciate, where Mahler was concerned, a "Wagnerian sound" even when it was out of place.) In a roundly glowing review that, as such, parts with those of his critic colleagues, Hanslick draws greatest attention to Mahler's subdued approach to Mozart's Symphony in G Minor (K. 550) only then to defend it, saying that it was Mahler's design, in order to throw the two Beethoven "volcanoes" that framed it (the *Coriolanus* Overture and the *Eroica* Symphony) into bolder relief.[81]

In his performances of Mozart and Beethoven, Hanslick saw Mahler breathing fresh air into a repertoire cherished by the Austrian public. That public was still wary of Berlioz's *Symphonie fantastique* at the turn of the century. Reviewing Mahler's performance of that work, Hanslick appreciates that wariness, and despite his preference for Mahler cutting the whole of the Finale (the performance of which he calls "always a dangerous experiment") Hanslick continues his advocacy of Mahler even in that movement, conceding that as a "sensitive and impulsive" conductor, Mahler "brought [the Finale] back to life." Hanslick here likens Mahler to the "singer or actor [who] has to go back to the original text," which Mahler does with a "blend of ingenuity and diligence.[82]

These examples of Hanslick's critical forbearance with Mahler as a conductor portray a side of Hanslick that is all the more remarkable if we consider the Viennese Jewish writer Stefan Zweig's recollection of the "anti-youth, repressively adult culture of his own schooldays and its shock at the appointment of so young a man as Mahler (aged thirty-seven) to the directorship of the *Hofoper* in 1897."[83] Hanslick, Mahler's most influential advocate, was then seventy-two years old. Given what Hanslick had witnessed with Mahler in those last years of the nineteenth century—the anti-Semitism Mahler was subjected to, the self-imposed trials Mahler endured because of his exacting standards, his obsessive involvement in his music making—Hanslick knew that Mahler could not detach himself from the music he produced, whether as a conductor or as a composer. Before a note of Mahler's music sounded for Hanslick, he must have anticipated that Mahler, who was always putting his stamp on whatever he conducted and who had already put his stamp on his completion of Weber's opera, would have done the same with his compositions. And being Jewish *and* Bohemian in the cultural and political climate of *fin-de-siècle* Vienna, Mahler could perhaps compose a "symphony," but not a symphony; "lieder," but not lieder. These were, after all, musical genres central to the German nationalists' cultural imagining of a German nation.

On Mahler the Composer

As complexly engaged with and adoring of the music of both Beethoven and Wagner as he was, it is unsurprising that Mahler would compose symphonies and lieder that responded to both composers. While at work on the cantata *Das klagende Lied* in 1879, Mahler turns to writing the libretto for an opera, *Rübezahl*, which he does not complete and for which the music is lost. He toils with this opera until 1883, at which point he turns to writing the words and music for *Lieder eines fahrenden Gesellen*; themes and images from the opera's libretto surface in the *Gesellen* texts. The connection between these songs and the First Symphony is well known. What has not been acknowledged is that Mahler was effectively retracing Wagner's path: Wagner's "sketch" for *Tristan*, the song "Träume," existed first as a piano-vocal lied (1857, published in 1862), then as an orchestral lied that Wagner himself orchestrated, and finally as the climax of the act 2 *Liebesnacht* of *Tristan* ("O sink' hernieder, Nacht der Liebe"), the music-drama that Wagner regarded as his "most symphonic" conception and *the* Wagner work that most consumed Mahler (not to mention much of his generation).[84] The pivotal difference in Mahler's path is that it neither began nor ended with a music drama. Yet Mahler's conception of both the lied and the symphony, beginning with his *Lieder eines fahrenden Gesellen* and the First Symphony, owes as much to the genre of the music drama as it does to that of lied or symphony.

How then did Hanslick perceive these early Mahler works? Let us first turn to Hanslick's review of the Philharmonic concert on January 14, 1900,[85] which included, for the first time before the Viennese public, a selection of Mahler's orchestral lieder: three selections from the *Des Knaben Wunderhorn* orchestral settings, and the second and fourth songs from *Lieder eines fahrenden Gesellen*, the two songs that feature prominently in Mahler's Symphony No. 1, "Ging heut' Morgen über's Feld" and "Die zwei blauen Augen." Hanslick begins the review by dispensing with the other pieces on the program, a well-played Schumann Fourth Symphony and a performance of Berlioz's *Carnaval romain*, similarly well executed but, "for all its splendor, essentially impoverished music," an impression that, for Hanslick, becomes more and more the case with each hearing of this piece.[86] He then proceeds to devote the rest of the review to Mahler's "five songs with orchestral accompaniment" (*Fünf Gesänge mit Orchesterbegleitung*). Upon remarking on Mahler's "modesty bordering on self-denial in holding back his own compositions from performance in Vienna, however favorably they may have been received in other towns," Hanslick signals to the reader that "something new and individual has come to be expected of [Mahler]."[87] It is here that Hanslick's having first referred to the mix of songs on the program as *Gesänge*, which had seemed appropriate, takes on greater meaning:

> In the songs we heard yesterday, too, he proclaims himself an enemy of the conventional and the customary, a "chercheur," as the French would say, without implying any derogatory criticism by the use of this term. The new "songs" are difficult to classify: neither lied nor aria, nor dramatic scene, they possess something of all these forms. More than anything, their form recalls that of Berlioz's songs with orchestral accompaniment, "La captive," "Le chasseur danois," and "Le [jeune] pâtre Breton."[88]

While the anti-Semitic press will deny Mahler's "songs" being classified as "lieder," Hanslick does the same, obviously not for German nationalist reasons, but to carve out a distinct generic, non-Wagnerian space for Mahler's works. Hanslick achieves this by making both Mahler (a "chercheur") and his songs *French*. Hanslick knew that the proper and obvious model for Mahler's orchestral lieder was not Berlioz's *Nuits d'été*, but Wagner's *Wesendonck-Lieder*. Indeed, given the connection of two of the *Wesendonck-Lieder* ("Träume" and "Im Treibhaus") to *Tristan*, Hanslick's claim that these difficult-to-classify new "songs" are "neither lied nor aria, nor dramatic scene [but] possess something of all these forms" rings truer for Wagner's lieder than for Berlioz's songs. Only "Träume" was orchestrated by Wagner; this orchestral version first became a birthday present for Mathilde Wesendonck and preserves the orchestration for its corresponding *Tristan* music, "O sink hernieder" from the Liebesnacht. Here is the rub: the other four songs were orchestrated by none other than Felix Mottl, the non-Jewish Wagner acolyte routinely pitted against Mahler. Mahler knew these Wagner lieder well: at the Weimar première of Mahler's Symphony No. 1 on June 3, 1894 (the second concert at the Thirtieth Festival of the Allgemeiner Deutscher Musikverein), Mahler conducted all of the *Wesendonck-Lieder*.[89]

What is remarkable about Hanslick's Berlioz deflection is that it was perpetuated throughout the twentieth century, and a long line of commentators continuing to the present day link Mahler's orchestral lieder to Berlioz's songs, not to Wagner's lieder.[90] As an almost-dying act, Hanslick attempts to save Mahler from both Mottl and Wagner, and the persistent (though wrong-headed) linking of Berlioz's songs to Mahler's lieder speaks to the success of Hanslick's rescue effort.

In reviewing these so-called Berlioz-styled orchestral lieder, Hanslick names Mahler as "one in the forefront of modernism," noting how Mahler goes beyond the lied in assigning a "sumptuous accompaniment" not to the piano, but to the orchestra, resulting in a "contradiction, a dichotomy, between the concept of the 'folk song' and this artful, superabundant orchestral accompaniment." "Yet," Hanslick continues, "Mahler has pursued this venture with extraordinary delicacy and masterly technique." And then, placing Mahler in context and assuming a prophetic stance, Hanslick intones the following: "As we stand at the beginning of a new century, we are well advised to say of each new work produced by the musical 'Sezession' (Mahler, Richard Strauss, Hugo Wolf, etc.): 'It may very well be that the future lies with them.'"[91] By grouping Mahler with the German Strauss and the Austrian Wolf, Hanslick's "musical Secesssion" is Austro-Germanic and stylistic.[92] What Hanslick cites is a musical modernity that would seem obviously born of Wagner. Yet with Mahler, in his orchestral lieder, Hanslick sees a musical modernity born of Berlioz. And with Strauss and Wolf being embraced as German and thus potential heirs to Wagner—recall, here, Hanslick's line (in his letter to Baron Bezecny) about "Wagner and his horrible epigoni," the latter including Mottl but not Mahler—Mahler effects a secession redoubled: by virtue of being Jewish and Bohemian, Mahler must bodily secede from the German body, thereby charting a space of musical belonging-while-not-belonging.

Our sense of Mahler charting this space is most acute with his First Symphony, with its unorthodox form not explained by a program. Having heard Mahler's orchestral lieder and having read reports of his Second Symphony, Hanslick was, given his tastes, disposed to dislike Mahler's First Symphony prior to hearing it. After all, this was the *symphony*, the genre that Hanslick, in his 1886 review of Brahms's Fourth Symphony, calls "the instrumental composer's severest test and highest calling."[93] And dislike this First Symphony Hanslick does, when he first hears it on November 18, 1900.[94] But what is striking about his review of it is the extent to which he goes out of his way to qualify his response to Mahler's opus as that of an outlier, as if Hanslick is now conceding, ten months after his review of Mahler's orchestral lieder, that the future does, indeed, lie with Mahler and his ilk. In that light, the "genuine modesty" (*ehrliche Bescheidenheit*) that Hanslick claims at the beginning of his review comes across not as rhetorical, but as genuine: "'One of us must be crazy, and it is not I!' This is how one of two stubborn scholars ended a long argument. It probably is I, I thought with genuine modesty, after recovering from the horrific Finale of Mahler's D Major Symphony."[95] What annoys and confounds Hanslick most about the symphony is his knowledge that it had a program and now does not, as though Mahler were undertaking a stealth campaign similar to what Schumann claims Chopin was trying to do with his Sonata in B-flat Minor, op. 35—"[Chopin] has simply bound together four of his most reckless children; thus under his name smuggling them into a place into which they could not else have penetrated."[96] For Hanslick, this meant that Mahler was calling a "symphony" a piece that really should not be called a symphony at all, for it was "the kind of music which for me is not music."[97] Such a qualifying "for me" is nowhere to be found in Schumann's summary pronouncement of Chopin's "sonata." Hanslick is, unlike Schumann, unusually chastened by the aesthetic quandary in which he finds himself, and wrestles aloud with whether Mahler's symphony would have been better with a program or not:

> As a sincere admirer of the conductor Mahler, to whom the Opera and the Philharmonic Orchestra are so deeply indebted, I do not want to be hasty in my judgment of his strange symphony. On the other hand I owe sincerity to my readers and thus must sadly admit that the new symphony is the kind of music which for me is not music. Perhaps I would have developed a closer relationship (if hardly one of love) to the piece had its origin and meaning not remained secret. At its première in Weimar the symphony was called "Titan" and had a detailed program; critics found these "abstruse"; and, as a result, both were removed. Generally such poetic user manuals are partly annoying and partly suspect: our symphonic masters, from Haydn and Mozart to Brahms and Dvořák, have let us into their heaven without admission tickets. Mahler's symphony would hardly have pleased us more with a program than without. But we cannot remain indifferent to knowing what an ingenious man like Mahler had in mind with each of these movements and how he would have explained their puzzling incoherence. Thus we lack a guide to show the correct path in the darkness. What does it mean when a cataclysmic Finale suddenly breaks forth, or when a Funeral march on the old student canon "Frère Jacques" is interrupted by a section entitled "parody"? To be sure, the music itself would have neither gained nor lost anything with a program; still, the composer's intentions would have become clearer and the work therefore more comprehensible. Without such aid, we had to be satisfied with some witty details and stunningly brilliant orchestral technique.[98]

Hanslick's frustration is fundamental. Were he to have heard at the same concert *Lieder eines fahrenden Gesellen* and then the First, which is how the lieder were premièred in Berlin in 1896, Hanslick may have been able to make better sense of the implied program of Mahler's symphony, but then that would have only come at the likely expense of confirming a Wagnerian, not Berliozian, compositional trajectory of subsuming orchestral lieder into a larger musical-dramatic genre.[99] To believe that a program mattered to Mahler in the ways that they matter to Hanslick is to persist in seeing Mahler through a Berlioz lens. Were Hanslick to have heard Mahler's other symphonies, he would not have been assuaged. While by the Fourth Symphony, as Adorno has observed, the "composition has swallowed the programme,"[100] Hanslick would have remained perplexed, throughout Mahler's œuvre. For Hanslick brings to the listening table central expectations about how instrumental music should behave, and Mahler's symphonies, by increasingly moving away from a program at the same time they set a course of formal exploration, would have dogged Hanslick at every turn.

Hanslick ends his review of the First by noting how the others *liked* the symphony: "The applause was enthusiastic—at least from the younger audience. Crammed into the standing room and the gallery, they could not stop calling Mahler back onstage again and again."[101] He then returns to the self-qualifying place from which he began the review and admits that his review is more "confession than judgment" (*mehr Beichte als Urtheil*) and, in his final sentence, he admits that at present he lacks "a full appreciation of what at times this most intelligent composer lacks: the grace of God."[102] In this last sentence, then, Hanslick finds common ground with Mahler in their shared human frailty—in the subjective contingency of their aesthetic perspectives. The future may lie with Mahler, but Hanslick will not be a part of it.

Otherness, Belonging, and Genre

In the *pas de deux* that is Mahler's music and Hanslick's response to it, we approach Hermann Danuser's notion of *Weltanschauungsmusik*: "In the nineteenth and twentieth centuries, a particular strain of *Weltanschauungsmusik* developed out of this tradition of musical autonomy. The symphony and, in particular, large-scale vocal works that took on the ideals of symphonic music, and were through their texts capable of world-view constructions, served as paradigms of an aesthetic world created with musical means."[103] While the post-Wagnerian "large-scale vocal works" that Danuser has in his view are Schoenberg's *Gurrelieder* and Mahler's *Das Lied von der Erde*, the interplay that Mahler constructs between his *Lieder eines fahrenden Gesellen* and his First Symphony establishes the standard and, arguably, the point of his existentialist musical œuvre: it hovers, amid genres, amid styles, amid forms, amid words, amid representations—the musical expression of Mahler's belonging-while-not-belonging. While that hovering unsettled Hanslick, he recognized it for what it is.

This subjectivity *in extremis* becomes the modern condition of the early twentieth century. Mahler thus gives musical voice to an enduring concern that is at once philosophical, cultural, psychological, and ethical. As Julia Kristeva has movingly reminded us in her historical meditation on otherness that is *Strangers to Ourselves*, it is at the time of Mahler and Hanslick that their fellow Viennese Sigmund Freud locates the other within us—our self-otherness—which becomes the precondition for a modern conception of self, and of coexisting selves:

> With Freud indeed, foreignness, an uncanny one, creeps into the tranquility of reason itself, and, without being restricted to madness, beauty, or faith anymore than to ethnicity or race, irrigates our very speaking-being, estranged by other logics, including the heterogeneity of biology.... Henceforth, we know that we are foreigners to ourselves, and it is with the help of that sole support that we can attempt to live with others.[104]

The foreignness of which Kristeva speaks is our own foreignness, and what Freud locates—"discovers"—is the unconscious, a concept first put forth by Nietzsche:[105]

> With the Freudian notion of the unconscious the involution of the strange in the psyche loses its pathological aspect and integrates within the assumed unity of human beings an *otherness* that is both biological *and* symbolic and becomes an integral part of the *same*. Henceforth the foreigner is neither a race nor a nation. The foreigner is neither glorified as a secret *Volksgeist* nor banished as disruptive of rationalist urbanity. Uncanny, foreignness is within us: we are our own foreigners, we are divided.[106]

Thus in a chain reaction that starts with Wagner outing Hanslick as having Jewish descent, Hanslick's otherness gives way to a recognition of the otherness in Mahler, an otherness that is at once musical (generic) and physical (racial, bodily). Mahler's musical belonging-while-not-belonging (writing lieder and symphonies within an Austro-Germanic art music tradition that confound the formal expectations of those genres) converges with his physical belonging-while-not-belonging (being a Bohemian Jew in Vienna) such that Mahler's life amounts to a contemporaneous external *performance* of Freud's foreignness-within-us.

Hindsight permits us to see Mahler composing at a pivotal time in Western music history. We now see that his rendering of the inherited genres of the lied and the symphony constituted a profound and visionary shift in musical practice.[107] Leonard Bernstein benefits from such hindsight in casting Mahler as a musical and moral prophet for the new century, anticipating in his music that century's crises, despair, and its ultimate promise of rejuvenation.[108] Bernstein casts him as such because Mahler's musical language was, for its time, often abstruse and elliptical, thus befitting oracular pronouncements.

Hanslick did not have the benefit of Bernstein's hindsight in writing his reviews of Mahler's orchestral lieder and First Symphony, yet his reviews' rhetorical squirming (their ambivalence, restraint, and questioning) and their oracular tone indicate the scale of Mahler's achievement. Even if Hanslick's genre taxonomies repeatedly come up short in assessing Mahler's music, Hanslick appreciates, in a profound way, the eventual reach of that music. He knows that Mahler has something important to say, but cannot get at what that something is. Hanslick was a cautious and candid prophet.

Notes

1. Peter Gay, *Freud, Jews and Other Germans: Masters and Victims in Modernist Culture* (New York: Oxford University Press, 1978), 264.

2. Ibid., 275.

3. "Aber sollen wir aus Pedanterie uns um einen neuen Eindruck, einen auserlesenten Genuss bringen?" Ed. H. [Eduard Hanslick], "Theater- und Kunstnachrichten," *Neue Freie Presse* (January 17, 1899): 7. "Ed. H." is Hanslick's characteristic identifying signature in the *Neue Freie Presse* and will be retained here in citations to his articles in that newspaper. Discussion of Hanslick's and other reviews of this concert found in Henry-Louis de La Grange, *Gustav Mahler, Volume 2: Vienna: The Years of Challenge (1897–1904)* (Oxford: Oxford University Press, 1995), 136–39.

4. K. M. Knittel, "'Ein hypermoderner Dirigent': Mahler and Antisemitism in 'Fin-de-siècle' Vienna," *19th-Century Music* 18, no.3 (1995): 257–76; and in *Seeing Mahler: Music and the Language of Antisemitism in Fin-de-siècle Vienna* (Farnham, UK: Ashgate, 2010).

5. Knittel, *Seeing Mahler*, 78.

6. Sanna Pederson, "A. B. Marx, Berlin Concert Life, and German National Identity," *19th-Century Music* 18 (1994): 89.

7. Ibid.

8. Carl Dahlhaus, *The Idea of Absolute Music*, trans. Roger Lustig (Chicago: Chicago University Press, 1989), see especially 108–13.

9. Eger's work is especially useful in providing a laundry list of Nietzsche's likely semantic and conceptual borrowings from Hanslick's criticism. See Dieter Borchmeyer, "Hanslick und Grillparzer—'oder über die Grenzen der Musik und Poesie'"; Christoph Landerer, "Eduard Hanslick und Bernard Bolzano: Ästhetisches Denken in Österreich in der Mitte des 19. Jahrhunderts"; and Manfred Eger, "Nietzsches Ausfälle mit Hanslicks Einfällen: Fakten und Fatalitäten um den 'Fall Wagner,'" in *Eduard Hanslick zum Gedenken: Bericht des Symposiums zum Anlass seines 100. Todestages*, ed. Theophil Antonicek, Gernot Gruber, and Christoph Landerer (Tutzing: Hans Schneider, 2010), 113–22, 55–63, and 103–12, respectively.

10. See, for example, Leon Botstein, "Modernism," *The New Grove Dictionary of Music and Musicians*, ed. Stanley Sadie and John Tyrrell, vol. 16 (London: Macmillan, 2001), 868–75.

11. Dahlhaus, *Absolute Music*, 17. Dahlhaus's remarks here accord with Daniel Chua's take on "absolute music" in *Absolute Music and the Construction of Meaning* (Cambridge: Cambridge University Press, 1999).

12. David E. Wellbery, in the foreword to Friedrich Kittler, *Discourse Networks: 1800/1900*, trans. Michael Metteer, with Chris Cullens (Stanford, CA: Stanford University Press, 1990), ix.

13. Friedrich Nietzsche, *The Case of Wagner*, trans. Walter Kaufmann (New York: Vintage Books, 1967), 164.

14. Nietzsche, *The Case of Wagner*, 178.

15. Ibid., 155–60. Manfred Eger suggests that Nietzsche was so faithful in following Hanslick's lead that he even adopts (whether deliberately or not) Hanslick's errors, as in writing "Brunhilde" instead of "Brünnhilde." Eger, "Nietzsches Ausfälle mit Hanslicks Einfällen," 105.

16. "Aber erst mit dem Auftreten Carmen's geräth das Blut des Componisten und der Zuhörer in Wallung." Ed. H., "Feuilleton, 'Carmen,'" *Neue Freie Presse* (October 26, 1875): 2. Cited in Nicole Grimes, "'Ein Ausdruck zugleich von Wollust und von Grausamkeit': Hanslick's Review of Bizet's *Carmen* in 1870s Vienna," paper presented at the Association for German Studies in Great Britain and Ireland Conference, University of Reading, March 20, 2010. I wish to thank the author for sharing this paper with me.

17. Taken together, my retaining Gay's verb "matter" and my insistence on the physical presence of human bodies, be they conductors or composers, rather than the abstraction that is "Mahler" or "Berlioz," results in the accidental semantic invocation of Judith Butler's book title *Bodies that Matter: On the Discursive Limits of Sex* (New York: Routledge, 1993). While I am not, in this essay, interested in Butler's theories of gender and sexuality, I do see how Butler's overall sense of the performative could guide a reading of the performances of Jewish identities in Vienna circa 1900, though that, too, lies beyond the purview of this essay.

18. Geoffrey Payzant, *Eduard Hanslick and Ritter Berlioz in Prague: A Documentary Narrative* (Calgary, AB: University of Calgary Press, 1991).

19. "Der entscheidende Einfluss dieser Symphonie auf unsere neuesten Programm-Musiker." Ed. H., "Feuilleton: Chor- und Orchesterconcerte," *Neue Freie Presse* (November 22, 1898): 1.

20. "Einen einzigen Vortheil habe ich—leider!—vor ihm voraus: ich habe als Student im Jahre 1845 die 'Fantastique' noch unter Berlioz eigener Leitung gehört und allen Proben beigewohnt." Ibid.

21. "Als wäre es gestern, sehe ich mich mit Berlioz in sonnig glitzerndem Wintermorgen über die Moldaubrücke wandern, jenseits welcher der Generalbaß in Person residierte. Berlioz hatte sich fest in mich 'eingehängt'; ich litt unter dem vernichtenden Bewußtsein dieser Auszeichnung so sehr, daß ich förmlich fürchtete, Bekannten zu begegnen." Eduard Hanslick, *Aus meinem Leben*, ed. Peter Wapnewski (Kassel: Bärenreiter, 1987), 41 (hereafter cited as *AML/W*).

22. "Als Berlioz 1866 in Wien erschien, um daselbst seine 'Damnation de Faust' aufzuführen, war ich bei dem ihm zu Ehren gegebenen Bankett, sprach ihn aber nicht an, da ich von Pariser Freunden wußte, daß Berlioz sich über meine späteren, stark abgekühlten Berichte verletzt geäußert. Trotz aller vorgeblichen Gleichgültigkeit war Berlioz doch keineswegs—wenigstens nicht ausnahmslos—unempfindlich gegen Kritiken, ebensowenig wie Richard Wagner, mit dem mir später Ähnliches bevorstand. Berlioz war eine edlere Erscheinung, ein mir weit sympathischerer Charakter als Wagner." Ibid., 44.

23. "Ich habe seiner echten, tiefen Künstlernatur, seinem warmen, trotz unsäglichen Leidens und zunehmender Verbitterung echten, ehrlichen Gemüt ein pietätvolles, dankbares Andenken bewahrt." Ibid.

24. Steven E. Aschheim, *Brothers and Strangers: The East European Jew in German and German Jewish Consciousness, 1800–1923* (Madison, WI: University of Wisconsin Press, 1982), 32.

25. Ibid.
26. Ibid., 41. This perceived threat is the subject of the second chapter of Aschheim's book, "The Ambivalent Heritage: Liberal Jews and the Ostjuden, 1880–1914" (32–57).
27. Ibid., 74.
28. Ibid., 59.
29. Ibid., 74. Aschheim discusses Volkish ideology later in his book, in the context of early German Zionism: "There is no doubt that much of the thinking about Jewish national regeneration was influenced by German Volkish ideas. Volkish ideology was not a purely right-wing affair. The stress on 'community' and 'organicism' was shared by many on the Left who were disenchanted with liberalism and the impersonal, fragmented experience of living in the *Kaiserreich*. The common denominator of the Volkish approach was its disaffection from bourgeois conventions and capitalist impersonality. All sought ways of creating 'rooted' communities capable of engendering profound personal ties which they felt were conspicuously absent in an increasingly atomized modern Germany. Emphasis shifted from the formal institution of the state to the primal, enduring *Volksgeist* and its capacity for regeneration." Ibid., 102–3.
30. Ibid., 75.
31. David Brodbeck, "Dvořák's Reception in Liberal Vienna: Language Ordinances, National Property, and the Rhetoric of *Deutschtum*," *Journal of the American Musicological Society* 60, no. 1 (2007): 116.
32. Aschheim, *Brothers and Strangers*, 76.
33. Brodbeck, "Dvořák's Reception in Liberal Vienna," 83.
34. This is unlike his response to the work of, say, Bruckner, whose symphonies could at times displease Hanslick without their running the risk of ceasing to be music: "Bruckner's B-dur-Symphonie (Nr. 5), eine Novität bei den Philharmonikern, war uns bereits aus einer früheren Wiener Aufführung bekannt. Es will bei bestem Willen uns nicht glücken, viel Neues über diese 'Fünfte' vorzubringen die Bruckner'schen Symphonien sehen einander so ähnlich, daß auch die Kritiken sich ziemlich gleichen müssen. Wie in den anderen Symphonien von Bruckner, so wechseln auch in dieser Fünften kühne, originelle Einzelheiten mit leeren, trockenen, auch brutalen Stellen, oft ohne erkennbaren Zusammenhang. Wie helle Blitze leuchten hier vier, dort acht Tacte in eigenartiger Schönheit auf; dazwischen verwirrendes Dunkel, müde Abspannung, fieberhafte Ueberreizung. Auch in der B-dur-Symphonie vermissen wir das logische Denken, den geläuterten Schönheitssinn, den sichtenden und überschauenden Kunstverstand. Sie hat, meines Erachtens, weniger sinnlichen Reiz und Originalität als die Siebente Symphonie in E-dur; weniger Gesang und tiefe Empfindung als (namentlich im Adagio) die Dritte in D-moll. Nur in Einem Punkte dürfte sie ihre Schwestern noch übertreffen; in ihrer ermüdenden Länge. Director Mahler, ein warmer Anhänger Bruckner's, doch kein so blinder wie unsere Wiener Fanatiker, hat an der Partitur sehr einschneidende Kürzungen vorgenommen." Ed. H., "Feuilleton: Musik," *Neue Freie Presse* (March 5, 1901): 1.
35. Here I use the sense of "generic contract," where genre is construed as an "invitation to form," as elaborated by Jeffrey Kallberg in "The Rhetoric of Genre: Chopin's Nocturne in G Minor," *19th-Century Music* 11, no. 3 (Spring 1988): 238–61.
36. While William Ashton Ellis famously translated "Judenthum" as "Judaism" (*Richard Wagner's Prose Works, vol. 3: The Theatre*, trans. William Ashton Ellis [London: Kegan Paul, Trench, Trübner, 1907]), such that that translation has stuck for subsequent English-language writers, "Jewishness" is the more accurate translation and thus the one I use.

37. Jens Malte Fischer, "Richard Wagners 'Das Judentum in der Musik': Entstehung—Kontext—Wirkung," in *Richard Wagner und die Juden,* ed. D. Borchmeyer, A. Maayani, and S. Vill (Stuttgart: J. B. Metzler, 2000), 35–54; Thomas Grey, "Masters and Their Critics: Wagner, Hanslick, Beckmesser, and *Die Meistersinger,*" in *Wagner's Meistersinger: Performance, History, Representation,* ed. Nicholas Vazsonyi (Rochester, NY: University of Rochester Press, 2002), 165–89.

38. Grey, "Masters and Their Critics," 168.

39. For the original *Tannhäuser* review, see Eduard Hanslick, "Richard Wagner und seine neueste Oper 'Tannhäuser,'" *Sämtliche Schriften* 1/1, 57–94. For Wagner's "program" on Beethoven's Ninth Symphony, see Richard Wagner, *Sämtliche Schriften und Dichtungen* (Leipzig: Breitkopf & Härtel, 1911–16), 2: 61. This program note is translated by Thomas Grey in *Wagner and His World,* ed. Thomas Grey (Princeton, NJ: Princeton University Press, 2010), 481–90.

40. Ludwig Bischoff, "Der Prophete von Scribe und Meyerbeer," *Rheinische Musik-Zeitung* 2, no. 1 (July 13, 1850): 9–11; 3, no. 1 (July 20, 1850): 17–20; 1, no. 5 (August 3, 1850): 33–37; 1. no. 8 (August 24, 1850): 57–60; 1, no. 12 (September 21, 1850): 92–95; 1, no. 13 (September 28, 1850): 97–100; 1, no. 16 (October 19, 1850): 121–23; 1, no. 19 (November 9, 1850); 145–49. It is likely that Bischoff was, in turn, responding to the articles published by Theodor Uhlig on *Le Prophète* which contained anti-Semitic comments on Meyerbeer. See Theodor Uhlig, "Der Prophet von Meyerbeer," *Neue Zeitschrift für Musik* 32, no. 11 (February 5, 1850): 49–52; and "Noch einmal der Prophet von Meyerbeer," *Neue Zeitschrift für Musik* 32, no. 17 (February 26, 1850): 81–84.

41. Karl Freigedank [Richard Wagner], "Das Judenthum in der Musik," *Neue Zeitschrift für Musik,* 33 (September 3, 1850): 101–7, 109–12.

42. Grey, "Masters and Their Critics," 182.

43. Richard Wagner, "Appendix to 'Judaism in Music,'" in *Richard Wagner's Prose Works, vol. 3: The Theatre,* trans. William Ashton Ellis, 104.

44. Ibid., 105.

45. Ibid.

46. Ibid., 105–6.

47. Ibid., 111.

48. Jacob Katz, *The Darker Side of Genius: Richard Wagner's Anti-Semitism* (Hanover, NH: University Press of New England, 1986), 70–71.

49. Ibid., 70.

50. Ibid.

51. Wagner, "Appendix to 'Judaism in Music,'" in *Richard Wagner's Prose Works, vol. 3: The Theatre,* 113. In attempting to capture the spirit of Wagner's words, Ellis translates "blonden deutschen Aesthetiker" as "blond and pure-bred German Aesthetician"; I have omitted "and pure-bred." I have, however, preserved Ellis's translation of "Musikaesthetiker" as "Music-aesthete" because Wagner's larger discussion of Vischer makes clear that Wagner praises the scope of Vischer's project—a systematic study of aesthetics, which is what Hanslick had initially intended as the follow-up on his treatise—at the expense of the narrowness of Hanslick's project in *Vom Musikalisch-Schönen,* which for Wagner is no more than an exposition on "die musikalische Jüdenschönheit."

52. Wagner, "Judaism in Music," 87.

53. Aschheim, *Brothers and Strangers,* 76–79.

54. Katz, *Darker Side of Genius,* 74–77; and Michael Saffle, *Richard Wagner: A Guide to Research* (New York: Routledge, 2002), 398.

55. Kevin C. Karnes, *Music, Criticism, and the Challenge of History: Shaping Modern Musical Thought in Late Nineteenth-Century Vienna* (Oxford: Oxford University Press, 2008), 21–75.

56. Ibid., 12, 63–65.

57. Ibid., 64.

58. See, again, the recent work of Dieter Borchmeyer, Christoph Landerer, and Manfred Eger, in *Eduard Hanslick zum Gedenken*, cited in note 9.

59. Dahlhaus, *Absolute Music*, 17.

60. Jitka Ludvová, "Einige Prager Realien zum Thema Hanslick," in *Eduard Hanslick zum Gedenken: Bericht des Symposiums zum Anlass seines 100. Todestages*, ed. Theophil Antonicek, Gernot Gruber, and Christoph Landerer (Tutzing: Hans Schneider, 2010), 163–79.

61. Ibid., 164–65.

62. Ibid., 164.

63. Ibid., 166.

64. Ibid., 165.

65. Ibid., 166.

66. Ibid., 167.

67. Ibid., 166.

68. "Seine 'Walpurgisnacht,' seine Symphonien in A-dur und A-moll (Werke eines zweiundzwanzigjährigen Jünglings!), seine Concert-Ouvertüren, endlich sein 'Paulus' und 'Elias' wirken trotzdem noch mit unversehrter Frische und Macht. 'Ewig' ist ein leeres Wort für musikalische Schöpfungen—aber auf sehr, sehr lange hinaus werden sie alle Freunde edler, ernster Kunst erquicken und erheben. In neuerer Zeit haben auch Elemente von außen her sich gegen Mendelssohn gekehrt: die in Haß und Überhebung vereinigten Wagnerianer und Antisemiten. Gönnen wir ihnen das traurige Geschäft." Hanslick, "Zur Erinnerung an Felix Mendelssohn," in Hanslick, *Am Ende des Jahrhunderts, 1895–1899: Musikalische Kritiken und Schilderungen* (Berlin: Allgemeiner Verein für Deutsche Litteratur, 1899), 416–17. Cited and translated by Nicole Grimes in her "'Wordless Judaism, Like the Songs of Mendelssohn'? Hanslick, Mendelssohn and Cultural Politics in Late Nineteenth-Century Vienna," in *Mendelssohn Perspectives*, ed. Nicole Grimes and Angela R. Mace (Aldershot, UK: Ashgate, 2012), 61. I am most grateful to the author for sharing the typescript of this essay with me.

69. Herta Blaukopf, "The Young Mahler, 1875–1880: Essay in Situational Analysis after Karl R. Popper," in *Mahler Studies*, ed. Stephen E. Hefling (Cambridge: Cambridge University Press, 1997), 20.

70. Henry-Louis de La Grange, *Gustav Mahler: Volume 1* (Garden City, NY: Doubleday, 1973), 78–81.

71. Ibid., 192.

72. "Wenn schon bearbeitet werden musste, Herr Mahler hat es mit unleugbarer Geschichtigkeit gethan." Ed. H., "Feuilleton," *Neue Freie Presse* (January 20, 1889): 3. Hanslick adds, "Seine Instrumentirung verräth einen seinen Sinn für Orchesterwirkung und klingt im Grossen und Ganzen verwandt an Weber an."

73. "Er instrumentirte eben für das Publicum von heute, nicht für das der Zwanziger-Jahre." Ibid., 3. Hanslick's review of January 17, 1899, of Mahler's Beethoven adaptation is cited above. See note 3.

74. "Sehr stimmungsvoll und fein instrumentirt—schon mit einer Vorausnahme Wagner'schen Klanges—ist Mahler's Zwischenactmusik vor dem zweiten Aufzuge." Ibid., 3.

75. de La Grange, *Mahler: Volume I*, 393.
76. Ibid.
77. Ibid.
78. Ibid., 412.
79. As Tatjana Buklijas has observed, "Yet economic growth was cut short by the crisis that followed the 1873 stock-market crash. As unemployment grew and wages fell, anti-Jewish feelings, dormant for some decades, re-emerged with full force. This time racial antisemitism replaced old attitudes grounded in religious intolerance. Rapid assimilation and conversion to Christianity now mattered little." Tatjana Buklijas, "Surgery and National Identity in Late Nineteenth-Century Vienna," *Studies in History and Philosophy of Biological and Biomedical Sciences* 38, no. 4 (2007): 766. And Jeremy King, writing about Austria in the mid-1880s, notes that "German National parties soon began excluding Jews, even baptized ones." Jeremy King, *Budweisers into Czechs and Germans: A Local History of Bohemian Politics, 1848–1948* (Princeton, NJ: Princeton University Press, 2002), 71.
80. de La Grange, *Mahler: Volume 2*, 118–21. In addition to the work of K. M. Knittel cited above, Edward F. Kravitt fleshes out the particular strains of and contexts for this newly resurgent anti-Semitism. See Kravitt, "Mahler, Victim of the 'New' Anti-Semitism," *Journal of the Royal Musical Association* 127, no. 1 (2002): 72–94.
81. "Mahler's oberstes Bestreben, jedes Musikstück auf einen herrschenden Grundton zu stimmen, in seinem eigensten Styl zu bewahren, zeigte sich am deutlichsten in der Mozart'schen G-moll-Symphonie, wo Manche vielleicht energischere Accente, glühendere Farben gewünscht hätten. Aber nur so und nicht anders dachte Mahler dieser lichten, fleckenlosen Grazie zwischen den zwei Beethoven'schen Vulcanen ihre Individualität zu wahren. Die Wirkung der Coriolan-Ouvertüre und vollends der heroischen Symphonie lässt sich nicht schildern. So klar und anschaulich in ihrem feinsten Gewebe, dabei so überwältigend gross und machtvoll im Totaleindruck haben wir diese Tondichtungen kaum jemals gehört. Das Publicum des Philharmonie-Concerte—es ist an das Beste gewöhnt—ließ nach jedem Stück, ja nach jedem Satz der 'Eroica,' seiner Begeisterung freien Lauf und wurde nicht müde, den neugewonnenen Feldherrn unserer altbewährten Elitetruppe immer und immer wieder hervorzurufen Anfang gut, Alles gut." Ed. H., "Theater- und Kunstnachrichten," *Neue Freie Presse* (November 7, 1898): 2.
82. "Die Aufführung dieses Finales bleibt jederzeit ein gefährliches Experiment; man unterzieht sich ihm von Zeit zu Zeit, mehr aus historischem Interesse als zu musikalischem Vergnügen. Director Mahler, ein beherzter Mann, lässt die 'Walpurgisnacht' wieder aufleben. Er hat sie, die er schön nicht machen konnte, wenigstens so interessant und effectvoll als möglich gemacht und die stachelige Aufgabe als eminent feinfühliger und impulsiver Dirigent gelöst . . . Der Dirigent ebenso wie der Sänger und der Schauspieler darf und muss auf den Urtext zurückgehen. Und diesen hat Mahler mit der ihm eigenen Mischung von Genialität und Gewissenhaftigkeit aufgefaßt und ausgelegt." Ed. H., "Feuilleton: Chor- und Orchesterconcerte," *Neue Freie Presse* (November 22, 1898): 1.
83. Peter Franklin, *Mahler: Symphony, No. 3* (Cambridge: Cambridge University Press, 1991), 9. Franklin cites both Zweig's *The World of Yesterday: An Autobiography*, 3rd ed. (London: Cassell & Co., 1943), 37, and William McGrath, *Dionysian Art and Populist Politics* (New Haven, CT: Yale University Press, 1974), 20.
84. David Kasunic, "Wagner's 'Träume' and the Rise of the Orchestral *Lied*," paper given at the Annual Meeting of the American Musicological Society, Los Angeles, November 2006.

85. Ed. H., "Theater- und Kunstnachrichten," *Neue Freie Presse* (January 16, 1900): 8. The translation of this review cited here is from appendix G of Donald Mitchell, *Gustav Mahler: The Wunderhorn Years* (Boulder, CO: Westview Press, 1975), 430–31. For full concert information, see Knud Martner, *Mahler's Concerts* (New York: Overbrook Press, 2010), 145–46.

86. "Den Anfang machte Schumann's anmuthige D-moll-Symphonie, herrlich gespielt und begeistert aufgenommen. Trotz gleich virtuoser Ausführung erzielte Berlioz' 'Römischer Carneval' doch nicht denselben Eindruck; das Aeußerliche, Raffinirte, bei Allem Prunk doch innerlich Arme dieser Musik wird uns bei jeder Wiederholung derselben auffallender." Ibid., 8.

87. "Director Mahler hat bis jetzt mit einer an Selbstverleugnung streifenden Beschiedenheit seine eigenen Compositionen für Wien versteckt gehalten, so günstigen Erfolg dieselben in anderen Städten davon getragen. Von ihm stand Neues, Eigenartiges zu erwarten." Ibid., 8.

88. "Auch aus dem gestern gehörten Gesängen spricht der Feind des Hergebrachten und Gewöhnlichen, der 'Chercheur,' wie die Franzosen sagen, ohne mit dem Worte eine abschätzige Kritik zu verbinden. Die neuen 'Gesänge' sind schwer zu classificiren: weder Lied noch Arie, noch dramatische Scene, haben sie von alledem etwas. Sie erinnern der Form nach am ehesten an die Gesänge mit Orchester-Begleitung von Berlioz: 'La captive,' 'Le chasseur danois,' 'Le pâtre breton.'" Ibid., 8.

89. Martner, *Mahler's Concerts*, 95–97.

90. Kasunic, "Wagner's 'Träume.'" So influential were Hanslick's initial words on these lieder, that this linking of Mahler to Berlioz persisted even after Mahler friend and musicologist Guido Adler takes aim, in his 1916 monograph on Mahler, both at the anti-Semitism that drove Mahler from Vienna and at the purported Mahler-Berlioz connection by linking Mahler's art to not only Wagner's in general, but to *Tristan* by name: "Mahler stands on the firm soil of German culture, like the masters already cited who preceded him. His Jewish lineage may perhaps explain the occasionally pronounced over-sharpening of expressive force and the fanatical exaggeration in the re-creation of his spiritual impulses. But whether this tendency can be traced back exclusively to lineage remains an open question, for it is also perceptible in thoroughly German masters. Thus Richard Wagner, who, as he 'only felt himself well, when he was beside himself,' heightened expression to the extreme, to the greatest extreme. And just there is his power at its greatest, as in *Tristan*. To term Mahler a follower of Berlioz is also stylistically a bad mistake, both with regard to the nature of Mahler's voice-leading and with regard to his aesthetic attitude; for just as he was far-removed from the programmatic, he never considered sonority an end in itself and used it merely as a means. To be sure, Mahler did learn from this master of sound. That he resembles Berlioz in coloristic mastery is a phenomenon that results from the expressive power of Mahler's art and from the master's sense of sonority. Like every true art, that of Mahler directs itself to all musically civilized cultures and also has the power gradually to conquer them." Guido Adler, *Gustav Mahler*, trans. Edward R. Reilly in his *Gustav Mahler and Guido Adler: Records of a Friendship* (Cambridge: Cambridge University Press, 1982), 42–43.

91. "Mahler, als der Modernsten Einer, mochte sich, wie das oft geschieht, gern in das Extrem flüchten, in die Naivetät, die ungebrochene Empfindung, die knappe, ja ungefüge Sprache des älteren Volksliedes. Diese Gedichte mit der schlichten Anspruchslosigkeit früherer Componisten zu behandeln, widerstrebte aber seiner Natur. Dem volksthümlich gehaltenen Gesang unterlegte er eine üppige Begleitung von geistreicher Beweglichkeit und scharfer Modulation und gab sie nicht dem Clavier, sondern

dem Orchester. Für Volkslieder ein ungewöhnlich reiches, ja raffinirtes Aufgebot: drei Flöten, Piccolo, drei Clarinetten, Bassclarinette, Englischhorn, vier Hörner, zwei Harfen. Ein Widerspruch, ein Zwiespalt zwischen dem Begriffe 'Volkslied' und dieser kunstvollen, überreichen Orchesterbegleitung ist nicht wohl wegzuleugnen. Aber Mahler hat dieses Wagestück mit ausserordentlicher Feinheit und meisterlicher Technik ausgeführt. Jetzt, am Beginne eines neuen Jahrhunderts empfiehlt es sich, den Novitäten der musikalischen 'Secession' (Mahler, Richard Strauss, Hugo Wolf, usw.) jedesmal nachzusagen: Es ist sehr möglich, das ihnen die Zukunft gehört." *Neue Freie Presse* (January 16, 1900): 8. This translation from appendix G of Mitchell, *Gustav Mahler: The Wunderhorn Years*, 430–31.

92. Hanslick seems to use the term not as writers like Herman Bahr took to using it, but as Carl Schorske has argued, as an "indictment of materialistic liberalism as the source of the degeneration of art, [thereby showing] an affinity to the explicitly political 'secessionists' from the liberal camp who led the new mass movements." Carl E. Schorske, "Cultural Hothouse," *New York Review of Books*, December 1, 1975, http://www.nybooks.com/articles/archives/1975/dec/11/cultural-hothouse/?pagination=false#fnr1-119575867.

93. "Die Symphonie verlangt vollendete Meisterschaft; sie ist der unerbittlichste Prüfstein und die höchster Weihe des Instrumental-Componisten." Ed. H., "Feuilleton," *Neue Freie Presse* (January 19, 1886): 1–3 (2).

94. Preceding the symphony on the program (and before intermission) are Beethoven's *Prometheus* Overture and Schumann's *Manfred* Overture. For full concert information, see Martner, *Mahler's Concerts*, 157–58.

95. "'Einer von uns Beiden muss verrückt sein—ich bin es nicht!' Damit endete einer der beiden eigensinnigen Gelehrten den langen Streit. Wahrscheinlich bin ich es, dachte ich mit ehrlicher Bescheidenheit, nachdem ich von dem Schreckensfinale der Mahler'schen D-dur-Symphonie mich erholt hatte." Ed. H., "Theater- und Kunstnachrichten," *Neue Freie Presse* (November 20, 1900): 7–8. The English translation used here is from "Mahler's German-Language Critics," ed. and trans. Karen Painter and Bettina Varwig, in *Mahler and His World*, ed. Karen Painter (Princeton, NJ: Princeton University Press, 2002), 289–90.

96. Throughout the 1830s, Schumann's reviews of Chopin's compositions urge Chopin to forego small forms (such as the *étude*) for larger forms. But when Chopin finally does essay the genre of the piano sonata, Schumann denies it being called a "sonata," saying that doing so is a "caprice, if not a jest, for [Chopin]," and continues as cited above. See Robert Schumann, *On Music and Musicians*, ed. Konrad Wolff, trans. Paul Rosenfeld (New York: Pantheon Books, 1946), 136–42.

97. "Die neue Symphonie zu jener Gattung Musik gehört, die für mich keine ist." Ed. H., "Theater- und Kunstnachrichten," *Neue Freie Presse* (November 20, 1900), 7.

98. "Als aufrichtiger Verehrer des Directors Mahler, dem die Oper wie das Philharmonische Concert so tief verpflichtet sind, möchte ich nicht eilfertig über seine wunderliche grosse Symphonie urtheilen. Anderseits schulde ich meinem Lesern Aufrichtigkeit, und so gestehe ich denn betrübt, dass die neue Symphonie zu jener Gattung Musik gehört, die für mich keine ist. Vielleicht hätte ich doch ein näheres Verhältnis (wenn auch kein Liebesverhältniss) zu ihr gewonnen, wäre uns ihre Herkunft und Bedeutung nicht verheimlich worden. Bei ihrer ersten Aufführung in Weimar hiess die Symphonie 'Titan' und war von einem ausführlichen Programm begleitet. Die Kritiker fanden es 'abstrus,' und so tilgte der Componist sowol den Titel als die Erklärung. Im Allgemeinen sind dergleichen poetische Gebrauchsanweisungen theils lästig, the-

ils verdächtig. Unsere symphonischen Meister von Haydn und Mozart bis auf Brahms und Dvorak nehmen uns ohne solches Entrée-Billet in ihren Himmel auf. Schwerlich hätte auch Mahler's Symphonie uns mehr erfreut mit einem Programm, als ohne solches. Aber gleichgiltig [*sic*] war es uns nicht, zu erfahren, was ein geistreicher Mann wie Mahler sich bei jedem dieser Sätze vorgestellt und wie er ihren uns räthselhaften Zusammenhang erklärt hätte. Und so fehlte uns doch ein Führer, der in diesem Dunkel, den rechten Weg weisen könnte. Was hat dieses plötzlich einbrechende Weltuntergangs-Finale zu bedeuten, was der Trauermarsch mit dem alten Studentencanon 'Bruder Martin,' was die mit 'Parodie' bezeichnete Unterbrechung desselben? Die Musik selbst hätte mit einem Programm an Reiz weder gewonnen noch verloren, gewiss, aber die Absichten des Componisten wären uns deutlicher und damit das Werk verständlicher geworden. So mussten wir uns denn an manchen gestreichen Einzelheiten und der verblüffend glänzenden Orchestertechnik genügen lassen." Ibid., 7; English trans. in Painter and Varwig, "Mahler's German-Language Critics," 289.

99. Here, Wagner's advocacy of program music should be noted. See Carl Dahlhaus, "Wagner and Program Music," *Studies in Romanticism* 9, no. 1 (1970): 3–20. For the program of the March 16, 1896, world première of *Lieder eines fahrenden Gesellen*, with the Berlin Philharmonic, see Martner, *Mahler's Concerts*, 113 and 115.

100. Cited in Donald Mitchell, "'Swallowing the Programme': Mahler's Fourth Symphony," in *The Mahler Companion*, ed. Donald Mitchell and Andrew Nicholson (Oxford: Oxford University Press, 1999), 188.

101. "Bewunderungswürdig war die Ausführung dieser unerhört schwierigen Novität, enthusiastisch der Beifall, wenigstens von Seite der Jugend, die, eingepfercht im Stehparterre und auf der Galerie, nicht aufhören konnte, Mahler immer von neuem hervorzurufen." Ed. H., "Theater- und Kunstnachrichten," *Neue Freie Presse* (November 20, 1900), 8; English trans. in Painter and Varwig, "Mahler's German-Language Critics," 290.

102. Ich hoffe, diese kurze Notiz—mehr Beichte als Urtheil—einmal gelegentlich einer Wiederholung der Symphonie weiters ausführen zu können. Vorläufig fehlt mir zu ihrer vollen Würdigung, was mitunter auch den gestreichsten Componisten im Stiche lässt: 'Die Gnad' von Gott.'" Ibid., 8; Painter and Varwig, 290.

103. Hermann Danuser, "Musical Manifestations of the End in Wagner and in Post-Wagnerian 'Weltanschauungsmusik,'" *19th-Century Music* 18, no. 1 (1994): 64–82; and his recent book on the topic, Danuser, *Weltanschauungsmusik* (Schliengen: Edition Argus, 2009).

104. Julia Kristeva, "Might Not Universality Be . . . Our Own Foreignness?" (ellipsis in original) in *Strangers to Ourselves*, trans. Leon S. Roudiez (New York: Columbia University Press, 1991), 170.

105. See chapter 2, "The Unconscious and the Conscious," in Paul-Laurent Assoun, *Freud and Nietzsche*, trans. Richard L. Collier Jr. (New York: Continuum Books, 2000), 107–19; and A. H. Chapman and M. Chapman-Santana, "The Influence of Nietzsche on Freud's Ideas," *British Journal of Psychiatry* 166 (1995): 251–53.

106. Kristeva, "Might Not Universality Be," 181.

107. Subsequent works that similarly hover amid genres, like Schoenberg's *Erwartung* (1909), arguably are the progeny of Mahler's musical experiments.

108. Leonard Bernstein, "The Twentieth Century Crisis," in *The Unanswered Question: Six Talks at Harvard* (Cambridge, MA: Harvard University Press, 1981), 263–374. Bernstein puts it starkly at first: "Ours is the century of death, and Mahler is its musical prophet" (313).

Selected Bibliography

A full bibliography for this volume is far too wide-ranging to include here. We have therefore chosen to include only a selected one. This comprises primary sources on Hanslick, secondary sources dealing explicitly with Hanslick, and only those sources on broader topics in nineteenth-century music that deal extensively with Hanslick.

Abegg, Werner. *Musikästhetik und Musikkritik bei Eduard Hanslick.* Regensburg: Gustav Bosse, 1974.

Altenburg, Detlef. "Vom poetisch Schönen: Franz Liszts Auseinandersetzung mit der Musikästhetik Eduard Hanslicks." In *Ars musica, musica scientia: Festschrift Heinrich Hüschen zum fünfundsechzigsten Geburtstag am 2. März 1980,* edited by Detlef Altenburg, 1–9. Cologne: Gitarre & Laute, 1980.

Anon. "Dr. Eduard Hanslick Dead: Austrian Musical Critic Once Was a Bitter Opponent of Wagner." *New York Times,* August 8, 1904, 7.

Anon. "Eduard Hanslick." *Der Kunstwart* 17 (1904): 488.

Antonicek, Theophil, Gernot Gruber, and Christoph Landerer, eds. *Eduard Hanslick zum Gedenken: Bericht des Symposiums zum Anlass seines 100. Todestages.* Tutzing: Hans Schneider, 2010.

Blume, Friedrich. "Hanslick, Eduard." In *Die Musik in Geschichte und Gegenwart.* Kassel: Bärenreiter, 1956, 1482–93.

Bonds, Mark Evan. "Aesthetic Amputations: Absolute Music and the Deleted Endings of Hanslick's *Vom Musikalisch-Schönen.*" *19th-Century Music* 36, no. 1 (2012): 3–23.

———. "Idealism and the Aesthetics of Instrumental Music at the Turn of the Nineteenth Century." *Journal of the American Musicological Society* 50, nos. 2–3 (1997): 387–420.

———. *Music as Thought: Listening to the Symphony in the Age of Beethoven.* Princeton, NJ: Princeton University Press, 2006.

Botstein, Leon. "Listening through Reading: Musical Literacy and the Concert Audience." *19th-Century Music* 16, no. 2 (1992): 129–45.

Brodbeck, David. "Dvořák's Reception in Liberal Vienna. Language Ordinances, National Property, and the Rhetoric of *Deutschtum.*" *Journal of the American Musicological Society* 60, no. 1 (April 2007): 71–132.

———. "Hanslick's Smetana and Hanslick's Prague." *Journal of the Royal Musical Association* 134, no. 1 (2009): 1–36.

Burford, Mark. "Hanslick's Idealist Materialism." *19th-Century Music* 30, no. 2 (2006): 166–81.

Carpenter, Patricia. "Musical Form and Musical Idea: Reflections on a Theme of Schoenberg, Hanslick, and Kant." In *Music and Civilization: Essays in Honor of Paul Henry Lang*, edited by Edmond Strainchamps and Maria Rika Maniates in collaboration with Christopher Hatch, 394–427. New York: Norton, 1984.

Clapham, John. "Dvořák's Relations with Brahms and Hanslick." *Musical Quarterly* 57 (1971): 241–54.

Cook, Nicholas. *The Schenker Project: Culture, Race and Music Theory in Fin-de-Siècle Vienna*. New York: Oxford University Press, 2007.

Dahlhaus, Carl. *Die Idee der absoluten Musik*. Kassel: Bärenreiter, 1978.

———. *The Idea of Absolute Music*. Translated by Roger Lustig. Chicago: University of Chicago Press, 1989.

———. "Eduard Hanslick und der musikalische Formbegriff." *Musikforschung* 20 (1967): 145–53.

Deas, Stewart. *In Defence of Hanslick*. London: Williams & Norgate, 1940. Revised edition, Farnborough: Gregg, 1972.

Deaville, James. "The Controversy Surrounding Liszt's Conception of Programme Music." In *19th-Century Music: Selected Proceedings of the Tenth International Conference*, edited by Jim Samson and Bennett Zon, 98–124. Aldershot, UK: Ashgate, 2002.

Frankenbach, Chantal. "Disdain for Dance, Disdain for France: Choreophobia in German Musical Modernism." PhD diss., University of California Davis, 2012.

Gay, Peter. *Freud, Jews and Other Germans: Masters and Victims in Modernist Culture*. New York: Oxford University Press, 1978.

Gärtner, Markus. *Eduard Hanslick versus Franz Liszt: Aspekte einer grundlegenden Kontroverse*. Hildesheim: Olms, 2005.

Gooley, Dana. "Hanslick and the Institution of Criticism." *Journal of Musicology* 28, no. 3 (2011): 289–324.

Grey, Thomas. "Masters and Their Critics: Wagner, Hanslick, and Beckmesser." In *Wagner's Meistersinger: Performance, History, Representation*, edited by Nicholas Vazsonyi, 165–89. Rochester, NY: University of Rochester Press, 2003.

Grimes, Nicole. "A Critical Inferno: Hanslick, Hoplit, and Liszt's *Dante* Symphony." *Journal of the Society for Musicology in Ireland* 7 (2011–12): 3–22.

———. "'Wordless Judaism, Like the Songs of Mendelssohn'? Hanslick, Mendelssohn and Cultural Politics in Late Nineteenth-Century Vienna." In *Mendelssohn Perspectives*, edited by Nicole Grimes and Angela R. Mace, 49–62. Aldershot, UK: Ashgate, 2012.

Grimm, Ines. *Eduard Hanslicks Prager Zeit. Frühe Wurzeln seiner Schrift "Vom Musikalisch-Schönen."* Saarbrücken: Pfau, 2003.

Hall, Robert. "Hansick and Musical Expressiveness." *Journal of Aesthetic Education* 29/3 (1995): 85–92.

Hall, Robert W. "On Hanslick's Supposed Formalism in Music." *Journal of Aesthetics and Art Criticism* 25, no. 4 (1967): 433–36.

Hanslick, Eduard. *Am Ende des Jahrhunderts (1895–1899): Musikalische Kritiken und Schilderungen*. Berlin: Allgemeiner Verein für Deutsche Litteratur, 1899. Reprint, Farnborough: Gregg, 1971.

———. *Aus dem Concertsaal. Kritiken und Schilderungen aus den letzten 20 Jahren des Wiener Musiklebens nebst einem Anhang: Musikalische Reisebriefe aus England, Frank-*

reich und der Schweiz. Vienna: Wilhelm Braumüller, 1870 & 1897. Reprint, Farnborough: Gregg, 1971.

———. *Aus dem Opernleben der Gegenwart: Neue Kritiken und Studien*. Berlin: Allgemeine Verein für Deutsche Litteratur, 1884. Reprint, 1889. Reprint, Farnborough: Gregg, 1971.

———. *Aus dem Tagebuche eines Musikers: Kritiken und Schilderungen*. Berlin: Allgemeiner Verein für Deutsche Litteratur, 1892. Reprint, Farnborough: Gregg, 1971.

———. *Aus neuer und neuester Zeit: Musikalische Kritiken und Schilderungen*. Berlin: Allgemeiner Verein für Deutsche Litteratur, 1900. Reprint, Farnborough: Gregg, 1971.

———. *The Beautiful in Music: A Contribution to the Revisal of Musical Aesthetics*. Translated by Gustav Cohen. London and New York: Novello, 1891. Reprint, New York: Da Capo Press, 1974.

———. *Concerte, Componisten und Virtuosen der letzten fünfzehn Jahre 1870–1885*. Berlin: Allgemeiner Verein für Deutsche Litteratur, 1886. 3rd ed.; Berlin: Allgemeiner Verein für Deutsche Litteratur, 1896. Reprint, Farnborough: Gregg, 1971.

———. *Die moderne Oper: Kritiken und Studien*. Berlin: Allgemeiner Verein für Deutsche Litteratur, 1875. Reprint, 1885. Reprint, Farnborough: Gregg, 1971.

———. *Fünf Jahre Musik (1891–1895). Kritiken*. Berlin: Allgemeiner Verein für Deutsche Litteratur, 1896. Reprint, Farnborough: Gregg, 1971.

———. *Geschichte des Concertwesens in Wien*. 2 vols. Vienna: W. Braumüller, 1869. Reprint, Farnborough: Gregg, 1971; Hildesheim: Olms, 1979.

———. *Music Criticisms, 1846–99*. Translated and edited by Henry Pleasants. Harmondsworth: Penguin Books, 1963.

———. *Musikalische Stationen*. Berlin: Allgemeiner Verein für Deutsche Litteratur, 1880. Reprint, 1885. Reprint, Farnborough: Gregg, 1971.

———. *Musikalisches und Litterarisches: Kritiken und Schilderungen*. Berlin: Allgemeiner Verein für Deutsche Litteratur, 1889. Reprint, Farnborough: Gregg, 1971.

———. *Suite. Aufsätz über Musik und Musiker*. Vienna: Prochaska, 1884.

———. *Vienna's Golden Years of Music: 1850–1900*. Translated and edited by Henry Pleasants. New York: Simon and Schuster, 1950.

Hinrichsen, Hans-Joachim. "'Auch das Schöne muß sterben' oder Die Vermittlung von biographischer und ästhetischer Subjektivität im Musikalisch-Schönen. Brahms, Hanslick und Schillers *Nänie*." In *Johannes Brahms oder Die Relativierung der "absoluten" Musik*, edited by Hanns-Werner Heister, 121–54. Hamburg: Von Bockel, 1997.

Hilmar, Ernst. "Hanslick, Eduard." *Hugo Wolf Enzyklopädie: 518 Einzelartikel zu Leben und Werk, Umfeld und Rezeption*. Tutzing: Hans Schneider, 2007.

Hirschfeld, Robert. *Das kritische Verfahren E. Hanslicks*. Vienna: R. Löwit, 1885.

Hostinský, Otakar. *Das Musikalisch-Schöne und das Gesammtkunstwerk vom Standpunkte der formalen Ästhetik*. Leipzig: Breitkopf & Härtel, 1877.

Karnes, Kevin C. "Eduard Hanslick's History: A Forgotten Narrative of Brahms's Vienna," *American Brahms Society Newsletter* 22, no. 2 (2004): 1–5.

———. *Music, Criticism, and the Challenge of History: Shaping Modern Musical Thought in Late Nineteenth-Century Vienna.* New York: Oxford University Press, 2008.
Kivy, Peter. *Antithetical Arts: On the Ancient Quarrel between Literature and Music.* New York: Oxford Clarendon Press, 2009.
———. *New Essays on Musical Understanding.* Oxford: Oxford University Press, 2001.
Korngold, Julius. "Eduard Hanslick." *Neue Freie Presse*, Abendblatt (8 August 1904): 1–4.
Korstvedt, Benjamin M. "Reading Music Criticism beyond the *Fin-de-siècle* Vienna Paradigm." *Musical Quarterly* 94, no. 1–2 (2011): 156–210.
Kralik, Heinrich. *Aus Eduard Hanslicks Wagner-Kritiken.* Vienna: Europa-Verlag, 1947.
Landerer, Christoph. "Aesthetica longa, ars brevis. Vergänglichkeit des Schönen und Zeitlosigkeit der Ästhetik bei Eduard Hanslick." *Musik & Ästhetik* 14, no. 53 (2010): 10–19.
———. "Ästhetik von oben? Ästhetik von unten? Objectivität und 'naturwissenschaftliche' Methode in Eduard Hanslicks Musikästhetik." *Archiv für Musikwissenschaft* 60, no. 1 (2004): 38–53.
———. *Eduard Hanslick und Bernard Bolzano: Ästhetisches Denken in Österreich in der Mitte des 19. Jahrhunderts.* Sankt Augustin: Academia, 2004.
Lange, Otto. "Musik-Literatur: Dr. Eduard Hanslick, Vom Musikalisch-Schönen . . . ," *Neue Berliner Musikzeitung* 9, no. 42 (October 17, 1855): 330.
Laurencin, Ferdinand Peter Graf von. *Dr. Hanslick's Lehre vom Musikalisch-Schönen: Eine Abwehr.* Leipzig: Heinrich Matthes, 1859.
Lenneberg, Hans. "Il Bismarck della Critica Musicale. The Memoirs of Eduard Hanslick." *The Opera Quarterly* 2:1 (2004): 29–36.
Ludvová, Jitka. "Zur Biographie Eduard Hanslicks." *Studien zur Musikwissenschaft* 37 (1986): 37–46.
Maus, Fred Everett. "Hanslick's Animism." *Journal of Musicology* 10, no. 3 (1992): 273–92.
McColl, Sandra. *Music Criticism in Vienna 1896–1897: Critically Moving Forms.* Oxford: Clarendon Press, 1996.
Payzant, Geoffrey. *Eduard Hanslick and Ritter Berlioz in Prague.* Calgary, AB: University of Calgary Press, 1991.
———. "Hanslick, Heinse, and the 'Moral' Effects of Music." *Music Review* 49, no. 2 (1988): 126–33.
———. Hanslick on Music as Product of Feeling." *Journal of Musicological Research* 9, no. 2/3 (1989): 133–45.
———. *Hanslick on the Musically Beautiful: Sixteen Lectures on the Musical Aesthetics of Eduard Hanslick.* Christchurch, NZ: Cybereditions, 2003.
———. "Hanslick, Sams, Gay, and 'Tönend Bewegte Formen.'" *Journal of Aesthetics and Art Criticism* 40, no. 1 (1981): 41–48.
Pederson, Sanna. "Defining the Term 'Absolute Music' Historically." *Music and Letters* 90, no. 2 (2009): 240–62.
Printz, Felix. *Zur Würdigung des musikästhetischen Formalismus Eduard Hanslicks.* Borna-Leipzig: Noske, 1918.
Sams, Eric. "Eduard Hanslick, 1825–1904: The Perfect Anti-Wagnerite." *Musical Times* 116 (1975): 867–68.

Schäfke, Rudolf. *Eduard Hanslick und die Musikästhetik*. Leipzig: Breitkopf & Härtel, 1922.
Schmidt, Lothar. "Arabeske. Zu einigen Voraussetzungen und Konsequenzen von Eduard Hanslicks musikalischem Formbegriff." *Archiv für Musikwissenschaft* 46, no. 2 (1989): 91–120.
Schrader, Bruno. "Eduard Hanslick." In *Bremers Handlexikon der Musik*. Leipzig: Reclam, 1905.
Sponheuer, Bernd. *Musik als Kunst und Nicht-Kunst: Untersuchungen zur Dichotomie von 'hoher' und 'niederer' Musik im musikästhetischen Denken zwischen Kant und Hanslick*. Kassel: Bärenreiter, 1987.
Strauß, Dietmar, ed. *Eduard Hanslick: Vom Musikalisch-Schönen. Ein Beitrag zur Revision der Ästhetik in der Tonkunst*. 2 vols. Mainz: Schott, 1990.
———. "Hanslicks Tannhäuser-Aufsatz im rezeptionsgeschichtlichen Kontext." In Hanslick, *Sämtliche Schriften: Historisch-kritische Ausgabe*. Vol. 1/1, *Aufsätze und Rezensionen 1844–1848*, edited by Dietmar Strauß, 315–22. Vienna: Böhlau, 1993.
———. "Vom Davidsbund zum ästhetischen Manifest: Zu Eduard Hanslicks Schriften 1844–1854." In Hanslick, *Sämtliche Schriften: Historisch-kritische Ausgabe*. Vol. 1/1, *Aufsätze und Rezension 1844–1848*, edited by Dietmar Strauß, 271–99. Vienna: Böhlau, 1993.
———. "Vom Kaffeehaus zum Katheder. Hanslicks Musikfeuilletons in der 'Presse' und das Studium der Musikgeschichte." In Hanslick, *Sämtliche Schriften: Historisch-kritische Ausgabe*. Vol. 1/3, *Aufsätze und Rezensionen 1855–1856*, edited by Dietmar Strauß, 333–69. Vienna: Böhlau, 1995.
Tschulik, Norbert. ed. *Also sprach Beckmesser: Aus den Schriften von Eduard Hanslick*. Vienna: Bergland Verlag, 1965.
Wapnewski, Peter. "Eduard Hanslick als Darsteller seiner selbst: Der Kritiker und die Nachwelt." In Eduard Hanslick, *Aus meinem Leben*, edited and with an afterword by Peter Wapnewski, 487–515. Kassel and Basel: Bärenreiter, 1987.
Wildhagen, Christian. "Bismarck und Beckmesser: Der Musikkritiker Eduard Hanslick aus heutiger Sicht." *NZZ Online*, August 7, 2004. http://www.nzz.ch/aktuell/startseite/article9RHJD-1.289153.
Yoshida, Hiroshi. "Eduard Hanslick and the Idea of 'Public' in Musical Culture. Towards a Socio-Political Context of Formalist Aesthetics." *International Review of the Aesthetics and Sociology of Music* 32, no. 2 (2001): 179–99.
Youmans, Charles. *Richard Strauss's Orchestral Music and the German Intellectual Tradition: The Philosophical Roots of Musical Modernism*. Bloomington: Indiana University Press, 2005.

Contributors

DAVID BRODBECK is professor of musicology and the Robert and Marjorie Rawlins Chair of Music at the University of California, Irvine. He has published on a wide range of topics related to Brahms and other nineteenth-century German composers. His current research focuses on the intersection of liberal ideology and constructions of social identity in the reception of new music in late Habsburg Vienna. His article "Hanslick's Smetana and Hanslick's Prague" (*Journal of the Royal Musical Association*) was awarded the H. Colin Slim Prize by the American Musicological Society. Other recent publications include "Dvořák's Reception in Liberal Vienna: Language Ordinances, National Property," and "'*Ausgleichs-Abende*': The First Viennese Performances of Smetana's *Bartered Bride*" (in a special volume of *Austrian Studies* titled *Word and Music*).

JAMES DEAVILLE is professor of music at the School for Studies in Art and Culture at Carleton University. He has lectured and published on Wagner, Mahler, Richard Strauss, Reger, Liszt and his circle in Weimar, music criticism, music and gender, television and film music, and music and race. He is the editor of *Music in Television: Channels of Listening* (2011); coeditor and cotranslator, with George Fricke, of *Wagner in Rehearsal, 1875–1876: The Diaries of Richard Fricke* (1998); and has contributed to *Liszt and His World* (Princeton, NJ: Princeton University Press, 2006) and *Wagner and His World* (Princeton, NJ: Princeton University Press, 2009). He is currently editing a volume titled *Liszt's Legacies* for Pendragon Press.

SIOBHÁN DONOVAN is a college lecturer in German at the School of Languages and Literatures at University College Dublin, and a graduate of Trinity College Dublin. She is the author of *Der christliche Publizist und sein Glaubensphilosoph: Zur Freundschaft zwischen Matthias Claudius und Friedrich Heinrich Jacobi* (Würzburg: Königshausen & Neumann, 2004), and is editor, together with Robin Elliott, of *Music and Literature in German Romanticism* (Rochester, NY: Camden House, 2004). She has published articles on German-language literature of the eighteenth and nineteenth centuries. Current areas of research include word and music studies (especially operas of German literary origin) and contemporary Swiss-German women writers.

CHANTAL FRANKENBACH is a graduate student at the University of California, Davis, where she is completing her dissertation, "Disdain for Dance, Disdain for France: Choreophobia in German Musical Modernism." A former dancer, Frankenbach received her Bachelor of Arts in dance from the University of California, Irvine. She has received numerous grants and fellowships, including the Mabelle McLeod Lewis Grant in Aid of Scholarship (2009), the Phi Beta Kappa Graduate Scholarship (2010), and the Alvin H. Johnson AMS 50 Dissertation Fellowship (2012). She currently teaches at California State University, Sacramento.

LAUREN FREEDE studied German and history at the University of Sydney, and is completing a PhD in German at the University of Edinburgh. Her dissertation looks at the role of musical autobiographies in identity formation in postwar West Germany and Austria. Her research moves between history, musicology, and literary studies, with further research interests including the role of music in national identity since the nineteenth century, as well as the process of denazification and coming to terms with the past among German musical institutions such as the Berlin Philharmonic. Her research has been supported by a number of awards from both Australia and the United Kingdom, and she has presented papers in the United Kingdom, Ireland, and Serbia. She is working as a *Lektorin* (foreign language lecturer) at the Carl von Ossietzky University Oldenburg.

MARION GERARDS is professor of music and social work at the University of Applied Sciences, Hamburg. Following her studies in social pedagogy, she trained in the social psychiatric area, then studied musicology, sociology, and pedagogy at the University of Cologne, leading to doctoral studies with Freia Hoffmann at the University of Oldenburg. Her doctoral dissertation, "The Music of Johannes Brahms in the Context of the Gender Discourse at Its Time of Origin," was published under the title *Frauenliebe—Männerleben: Die Musik von Johannes Brahms und der Geschlechterdiskurs im 19. Jahrhundert* (Cologne: Böhlau Verlag, 2010). Between 2001 and 2010 she lectured at various universities and was Research Assistant at the Sophie Drinker Institute, Bremen.

DANA GOOLEY is associate professor of music at Brown University. His publications focus on Franz Liszt, the cult of the virtuoso, music criticism, and the role of charisma in the public sphere of nineteenth-century Europe. His article "Hanslick and the Institution of Criticism" appeared in *Journal of Musicology* in 2011. He is the author of *The Virtuoso Liszt* (2004) and coeditor of *Franz Liszt and His World* (2006). He has published in *19th-Century Music*, *Musical Quarterly*, *Musiktheorie*, and *Performance Research*, and numerous edited publications including, most recently, *Camille Saint-Saëns and His World* (2012). Forthcoming articles will appear in *Taking it to the Bridge: Music and Performance*, ed. Nicholas Cook and Richard Pettengill (2013) and *The Oxford Companion to Critical Improvisation Studies* (2013). He is currently writing a book on improvisation and improvisational aesthetics in nineteenth-century music.

CONTRIBUTORS 347

NICOLE GRIMES is a Marie Curie Fellow (2011–14) with joint affiliation at the University of California, Irvine, and University College Dublin (UCD). She was awarded a PhD at Trinity College Dublin in 2008 for her dissertation on Johannes Brahms, and has carried out postdoctoral research at Humboldt University Berlin (DAAD-funded) and UCD (IRCHSS-funded). She has published articles on Brahms, Schumann, Mendelssohn, and Hanslick in various journals, most recently in *Music Analysis*. She is the editor, with Angela R. Mace, of *Mendelssohn Perspectives* (Aldershot, UK: Ashgate, 2012). She is currently working on a monograph on the reciprocal relationship between Brahms's music and the Austro-German intellectual tradition.

DAVID KASUNIC is assistant professor of music history at Occidental College, having received his doctorate from Princeton in 2004 with a dissertation on Fryderyk Chopin's compositional and commercial relationship to vocal music in relation to the aesthetic, scientific, literary, and philosophical reception of singing in 1830s and 1840s in Paris. He has published several related articles, and more recently has written on the legacy and reception of Chopin's keyboard technique in relation to nineteenth-century ballet and the writings of Heinrich Schenker. Other primary research interests are opera, the history of aesthetics, and Mahler. Current projects include an article on Mahler's compositional relationship to opera, and two book projects: one on the history of the relationship of music and food, and the other on Chopin, for which he received a 2011 research fellowship from the University of California Humanities Research Institute.

DAVID LARKIN (University of Sydney/Sydney Conservatorium of Music) read music at University College Dublin, before pursuing doctoral studies at the University of Cambridge, where he was awarded his PhD in 2007 for a dissertation entitled "Reshaping the Liszt-Wagner Legacy: Intertextual Dynamics in Strauss's Tone Poems." He has published articles on Strauss's orchestral works in the *Musical Quarterly* and *The Cambridge Companion to Richard Strauss*, and has reviewed print and sound materials for *Nineteenth-Century Music Review*, *Music and Letters*, *Notes: Quarterly Journal of the Music Library Association*, and the *Musicology Review*. Currently in preparation are articles on Strauss's *Don Quixote* and Strauss's understanding of history, Dvořák's programmatic orchestral music, and Liszt's *Mephisto Waltz*. He is also working on a book-length study of the Liszt-Wagner relationship.

WOLFGANG MARX is senior lecturer at the School of Music, University College Dublin. He was awarded a PhD in Hamburg in 2002 for his dissertation, subsequently published as *Klassifikation und Gattungsbegriff in der Musikwissenschaft* [Classification and the concept of genre in musicology] (Hildesheim: Olms, 2004). He is the editor, with Louise Duchesneau, of *György Ligeti: Of Foreign*

Lands and Strange Sounds (Woodbridge, UK: Boydell & Brewer, 2011). He has served as coeditor of the online journal *Frankfurter Zeitschrift für Musikwissenschaft* since 2002, and from 2004 to 2012 was an editor of the *Journal of the Society for Musicology in Ireland*. His research interests include the music of György Ligeti, the representation of death in music, and the theory of musical genres.

FRED EVERETT MAUS is associate professor of music theory at the University of Virginia. He has published widely on theory and analysis, gender and sexuality, popular music, aesthetics, and the dramatic and narrative aspects of instrumental music. In 2010 he served as a fellow of the Mannes Institute on Musical Aesthetics. He has published widely on topics such as masculine discourse in music theory (*Perspectives of New Music*, 1993), Eduard Hanslick (*Journal of Musicology*, 1992), and the Pet Shop Boys (*Popular Music*, 2001).

TIMOTHY R. MCKINNEY is professor of music theory at Baylor University. He received his PhD in music theory from the University of North Texas in 1989 with a dissertation on the songs of Hugo Wolf. His primary research interests include the relationship between words and music, the history of music theory, recent theories of musical form, and analysis of sixteenth-century and late nineteenth-century music. His articles and reviews appear in the *Musical Quarterly, Early Music, Music Theory Spectrum, Music Review*, and other journals and edited volumes. His book *Adrian Willaert and the Theory of Interval Affect: The Musica nova Madrigals and the Novel Theories of Zarlino and Vicentino* appeared from Ashgate in 2010.

NINA NOESKE is assistant professor of musicology at the University of Salzburg. She was awarded a PhD at the Institute for Musicology Weimar-Jena in 2005, which she published in 2007 as *Musikalische Dekonstruktion: Neue Instrumentalmusik in der DDR*. In 2006 she led a research group on the New German School and was involved with the new edition of Franz Liszt's complete writings in Weimar. She is coeditor of *Zwischen Macht und Freiheit: Neue Musik in der DDR* (2004), *Jahrbuch Musik und Gender* (2009 and 2010), *Musikwissenschaft und Kalter Krieg: Das Beispiel DDR* (2010), and *Musik und Popularität. Eine Kulturgeschichte zwischen 1500 und heute* (2011). From 2007 to 2011 she was lecturer at the University of Music, Drama, and Media in Hannover. In 2012 she was deputy professor both in Hannover and at the University of Music and Drama in Hamburg.

ANTHONY PRYER is programme director of the MA in the Music Department of Goldsmiths' College, University of London. Research interests include medieval music, Monteverdi, Mozart, and historiography. His editions of the three earliest Monteverdi printed collections have recently been published as volume 1 in the collected works issued by the Fondazione Claudio Monteverdi of Cremona. He also publishes on the philosophy of music, and is currently working on a joint project on art and nature with the Japanese artist Shuji Okada and the British Sound Artist John Drever, funded by the Daiwa Foundation. He served as an elected member of the executive committee of the British Society of Aesthetics (2001–7), was appointed a trustee of the Accademia Monteverdiana (2005), and was a jury member on the BBC Classical Music Awards panel in 2007 and again in 2011.

FELIX WÖRNER is lecturer and researcher at Basel University (Switzerland). His research focuses on the history of music theory and aesthetics in the nineteenth and twentieth centuries. His publications include a monograph on the early twelve-tone works of Anton Webern (Berne, 2004) and the coedited volume (with Philipp Rupprecht and Ullrich Scheideler) *Tonality 1900–1950: Concept and Practice* (Stuttgart, 2012). Currently he is working on a project titled "Imagining Form in Music: Investigations in German Music Theory (1850–1950)."

Index

Abegg, Werner, 25, 28, 209n80, 217
absolute instrumental music, 80–81
absolute music, 4, 15, 25, 28, 75, 81, 102, 165, 173, 175, 193, 225, 247, 289, 300, 309–10n92, 313, 314, 317. *See also* pure absolute music; pure instrumental music; pure music
Actus Tragicus, 170
Adler, Guido, 24, 71, 194, 199
Adorno, Theodor Wiesengrund, 24, 25, 328
Aeschylus, 144
Alboni, Marietta, 24
Allgemeines Bürgerliches Gesetzbuch (1812), 56
Altenburg, Detlef, 290
Ambros, August Wilhelm, 17, 18, 20, 72, 75–77, 188, 194, 203, 240, 242, 248, 318
anaesthetics, 118
ancient Germanic law, 57
Anregungen für Kunst und Wissenschaft, 19, 240
anti-Jewishness, 323
anti-Semitism, 23, 102, 141, 162, 189, 198, 311, 313, 315–17, 321, 323–25
antiliberal opposition, 94
Applegate, Celia, 192–93
Aristotle, 66n13
Arnim, Bettina von, 221
Artôt, Désirée, 203
Aschheim, Steven E., 315–16
Auber, Daniel, 120, 203
Auerbach, Berthold, 203
Austrian legal system, 56, 58
Austrian Finance Ministry, xiii, 194
Austrian Landesgericht, 53

Austrian Ministry of Education, xiii, 73, 317
Austro-German identity, 5, 187–203
Austro-Prussian War (1866), 200

Bach, Johann Sebastian, 54, 57, 120, 121, 202; *Actus Tragicus*, BWV 106, 170–71; "Ich hatte viel Bekümmernis," BWV 21, 133; *St Matthew Passion*, BWV 244, 42
Bachrich, Siegmund, 265
Baer, Karl Ernst von, 240
Baudelaire, Charles, 293
Bayreuth Festspiel, 220
Bayreuther Blätter, 24
Becher, Alfred Julius, 213
Beckmesser, Sixtus, 22, 23, 198, 261, 271, 273, 294, 312,
Beethoven, Ludwig van, 20, 42–44, 57, 120, 125, 164, 166–67, 193–94, 201, 202, 214, 216, 219, 245, 248, 270, 294, 300, 322, 323–24; *Coriolan Overture*, op. 62, 143, 296, 323; *Egmont Overture*, op. 84, 143, 275, 296; and *Fidelio*, 202; and masculinity, 219, 226; *Missa Solemnis*, op. 123, 42–43, 167; overture to *The Creatures of Prometheus*, op. 43, 43, 56; String Quartet No. 11 in F minor, op. 95, 312; Symphony No. 3 in E flat major (*Eroica*), op. 55, 59, 166, 221, 297, 323; Symphony No. 5 in C minor, op. 67, 166, 270; Symphony No. 9 in D minor, op. 125, 165–66, 317, 322
Behr, François, xiii
Beiblätter zu Ost und West, xiii
Bella, Johann, 291

Beller-McKenna, Daniel, 165, 170, 172
Benedict, Julius, 203
Benjamin, Walter, 170
Beowulf, 224–25
Berlin, 20, 21, 28, 200, 319, 327
Berlinger, Joseph, 193
Berlioz, Hector, 188, 195, 203, 299, 300, 314–16, 325–28; *Le Carnaval romain*, 325; *Harold Symphony*, 15, 19; *Mémoirs*, 188, 195; *Nuits d'été*, 325; in Prague, 188, 315–16; *Symphonie Fantastique*, 315, 323
Bernstein, Leonard, 329
Bettelheim, Caroline, 135, 137, 139
Bezecny, Baron, 322, 326
Bible, 172; New Testament, 170; Old Testament, 140, 170
Bildung, 7, 95, 142, 162, 164, 166
Billroth, Theodor, 6, 120, 143, 161–62, 192, 195–96, 200, 203, 221, 276–77; in dialogue with Hanslick (*Aus meinem Leben*), 276–77
Bischoff, Ludwig, 317
Bizet, Georges, 314–15
Bloom, Harold, 273
Blume, Friedrich, 27, 198, 311
Bodenstedt, Friedrich Martin von, 195
Boito, Arrigo, 189
Bolzano, Bernard, 238
Bonds, Mark Evan, 2, 161, 193
Botstein, Leon, 162, 191, 215
Boym, Svetlana, 163
Brahms, Johannes, 4, 6–8, 22, 25, 42, 120–22, 147, 160–76, 196, 198, 200–203, 216–24, 244–45, 261–64, 267, 276, 289, 291, 295, 300, 322, 326–27; *Academic Festival Overture*, op. 80, 173; *Alto Rhapsody*, op. 53, 162–3, 166, 174; and Bible, 172; Double Concerto for Violin and Cello, op. 102, 223; *Ein deutsches Requiem*, op. 45, 164–66, 171, 202, 245; *Gesang der Parzen*, op. 89, 162–63, 165, 167–68, 173; on Hanslick, *Vom Musikalisch-Schönen*, 121, 280n5; as heathen, 172; *Liebeslieder Waltzes*, op. 52, 121; *Nänie*, op. 82, 162–63, 165, 167–68, 173–75; Piano Concerto No. 1 in D minor, op. 15, 224; and religion, 167, 172; *Schicksalslied*, op. 54, 162–66, 168–69, 173, 175; Sixteen Waltzes, op. 39, 120–22; String Sextet in G major, op. 36, 245; Symphony No. 1 in C minor, op. 68, 42, 162, 216, 219, 221–22, 270; Symphony No. 2 in D major, op. 73, 217; Symphony No. 3 in F major, op. 90, 217, 225; Symphony No. 4 in E minor, op. 98, 264, 326; *Tragic Overture*, op. 81, 162, 169, 172, 174–75; Violin Concert in D major, op. 77, 217
Breitkopf & Härtel, 263
Brendel, Franz, 17, 19, 20, 236, 240
Brodbeck, David, 5, 93, 102, 121, 290
Bronsart, Hans von, 20
Bruckner, Anton, 16, 22, 25–27, 190, 192, 278, 292
Büchner, Ludwig, 60, 161, 238, 240, 248
Bülow, Hans von, 275, 291
Burford, Mark, 2, 3, 161, 167, 173, 236, 238
Butler, Judith, 227, 331n17

Canon Law, 57
Carltheater, Vienna, 110, 134
Carpenter, Patricia, 5, 25
Carriére, Moriz, 17, 18
Carus, Carl Gustav, 238, 248
Casuistics, 56
Catholicism, 6, 161–62, 167, 321, 323
Cavell, Stanley, 49
Chafe, Eric, 170
Chamberlain, Houston Stewart, 26
Charles University, Prague, 71
Chopin, Fryderyk, 327; Piano Sonata No. 2 in B flat minor, op. 35, 327
Christianity, 161, 164–67, 170, 198, 319, 321
Citron, Marcia, 166, 219
Cohen, Gustav(e), 37n111, 126n3

INDEX 353

Cold War, 3, 4, 28
Cologne, 20
Cone, Edward T., 49
Cook, Nicholas, 2, 5, 20, 25, 109
Cooper, Barry, 167
Cornelius, Peter, 17, 19
Crittenden, Camille, 101
Csáky, Moritz, 102
Curtius, Ludwig, 163
Cusick, Suzanne G., 248
Czarvady (Szardavy), Friedrich, 203

Dachs, Josef, 135
Dahlhaus, Carl, 3, 4, 28, 70, 197, 212, 312, 314, 320
Dambeck, Johann Heinrich, 241
Damcke, Berthold, 195
Danuser, Hermann, 328
Daudet, Alphonse, 201
Daverio, John, 175
Davidsbund (Prague), 194
de La Grange, Henry-Louis, 321, 323
Deas, Stewart, 27, 191
Deaville, James, 6
Délibes, Leo, 203
Dessauer, Josef, 203
Dessoff, Otto, 138, 203
Deutschtum, 133
Dickens, Charles, 147, 194, 201, 203
Die österreichische-ungarische Monarchie in Wort und Bild, xiv
Dömpke, Gustav (Dp), 6, 162, 265
Duke Ellington, 15
Dumas, Alexander, 203
Dumba, Nicolaus, 203
Dustmann, Luise, 23, 318
Dvořák, Anton: *Carnival*, op. 92, 296; *The Devil and Kate*, op. 112, 297; *Dimitri*, op. 64, 297; *Golden Spinning Wheel*, op. 109, 296; *Hero's Song*, op. 111, 296–97, 301; *Husitska Overture*, op. 67, 295–96, 298; *In the Realm of Nature*, op. 91, 296; *The Jacobin*, op. 84, 297; *Noon Witch*, op. 108, 296, 297, 299; *Othello*, op. 93, 296; *Rusalka*, op. 114, 297; Symphony No. 6 in D major, op. 60, 295; *Water Goblin*, op. 107, 296–99; *Wood Dove*, op. 110, 296–97, 299, 300
Dwight, John Sullivan, 23, 24
Dwight's Journal of Music, 23

economic crisis of 1866, 213
Eger, Manfred, 314
Ehlers, Paul, 27
Ehrlich, Heinrich, 18
Elssler, Fanny, 119
Engels, Friedrich, 60
Enlightenment, 142
English law, 57
entartet art, 27
Epstein, Julius, 135
Erben, Karel Jaromir, 296–97, 300
Esser, Heinrich, 203
ethics, 43, 92, 164, 166–67, 172, 328
Étienne, Michael, 138
European-Occidentalism, 141

Fabbri-Mulder, Inez, 24
Falk, Nanette, 222
Favre, Jules, 203
Ferni, Caroline, 246
Ferni, Virginie, 246
Feuerbach, Anselm, 167
Feuerbach, Ludwig, 60, 161
Fichte, Johann Gottlieb, 77
Fickert, Auguste, 214
Fischer, Jens Malte, 317
Floros, Constantin, 4, 173–74
Flotow, Friedrich von, 101, 102
formalism, 2, 18, 25, 27, 38, 40, 59, 71, 174, 213, 237, 240
Foucault, Michel, 227
Franco-Prussian War (1871), 162, 166, 200
Franz, Robert, 203
Franz Joseph of Austria, Emperor, 101
Freud, Sigmund, 311, 329
Fickert, Auguste, 214
Fuchs, Christian, 18

Gade, Niels, 203
Garcia, Manuel, 203
Gärtner, Markus, 29

Gay, Peter, 190–91, 214, 311–13, 315, 317
Gefühlsästhetik, 290
Geibel, Emanuel, 203
gender, 7–8, 212–27, 236–49
generic boundaries, 92–97, 122–24, 279, 302, 316
genre and nationalism, 166, 324,
Gerigk, Herbert, 25
German Democratic Republic, 3, 28
German idealism, 5, 161, 236
German national identity, 219, 314–17
German unification (1871), 162, 166, 200
Gesamtkunstwerk, 6, 70–82
Gesellschaft der Musikfreunde, Vienna, 98, 134–35, 138, 277–79, 322
Glagau, Hans, 189
Glasenapp, Carl Friedrich, 26
Gluck, Christoph Willibald, 56–57, 202; "Che farò senza Euridice," 56
Goebbels, Josef, 25–26
Goethe, Johann Wolfgang, 7, 161–64, 166, 168–69, 188, 201–3; *Dichtung und Wahrheit*, 187; *Faust*, 169; *Hermann und Dorothea*, 201; *Iphigenie auf Taurus*, 162, 168
Goethe, Walther, 203
Goldmark, Carl, 7, 101, 132–48, 198, 322; *Der gefesselte Prometheus*, op. 38, 144–45; *Das Heimchen am Herd*, 133, 147–48; "*Im Frühling*" Overture, op. 36, 143; *Die Kriegsgefangene* (*Achilles*), 101; *Die Königin von Saba*, 132–34, 136, 138, 139–42, 146–48; *Merlin*, 141; *Penthesilea Overture*, op. 31, 143–44; Piano Trio No. 1 in B flat, op. 4, 135; *Sakuntala Overture*, op. 13, 136–37, 146; *Sappho Overture*, op. 44, 145–46; String Quartet in B flat major, op. 8, 135; String Quintet in A minor, op. 9, 135; *Sturm und Drang*, nine characteristic pieces, op. 5, 135; Suite for Violin and Piano in D major, op. 11, 135
Gounod, Charles, 203
Graf, Harald, 198

Graf, Max, 277
Greco-Roman civilization, 163
Grey, Thomas, 23, 317, 318
Grillparzer, Franz, 145–46, 194–95, 201
Grimm, Jacob, 238
Grohe, Oskar, 263
Gusdorf, Georges, 196
Gutt, Bernhard, 53
Gyrowetz, Adalbert, 123

Halévy, Jacques, 244
Hamburg, 322
Handel, Georg Frideric, 56–57, 202; *Messiah*, 56
Hanslick, Eduard: *Aus meinem Leben*, xiv, 2, 7, 29, 187–204, 212, 276, 277, 315; and "Beckmesser," 22–23, 198, 261, 271, 273, 294, 311; on Brahms as pianist, 219; as composer, xiii, 53, 267; on dance, 6, 92–100, 103, 108–26, 141; in dialogue with Billroth (*Aus meinem Leben*), 276–77; doctorate in law (1849), xiii, 53; and Judaism, 23–27, 198–99, 311–30; on listening, 2, 6, 38–49, 52, 55, 60, 62, 65, 96–97, 108–10, 113–20, 122–26, 143, 191–92, 215–17, 220–24, 226, 238, 241, 243–45, 293–94, 300, 328; on Liszt as pianist, 218; "living history," 1, 267, 320; on March 1848 revolution, 100; as "Veit Hanslich," 317; reception of *Vom Musikalisch-Schönen*, 15–29, 70–71; and religion, 172; on role of critic, 267–68; *Vom Musikalisch-Schönen*, xi, xiii, 1–2, 4–6, 15–25, 27–29, 60, 70, 73, 82, 96, 108, 114–18, 161, 173–76, 193, 215, 221, 224, 238, 241, 246, 293, 312, 317–18
Hanslik, Joseph Adolph
Hanslik, Karolina Katharina (née Kisch), xii, 321
Hartmann, Eduard von, 18
Hauck, Minnie, 203
Haufer, Franz, 203
Hauptmann, Moritz, 203
Hausegger, Friedrich von, 18, 20, 27

Haydn, Joseph, 101, 123, 297, 327; *The Creation*, 297; *The Seasons*, 297
Hegel, Georg Wilhelm Friedrich, 29, 53, 77, 161, 236, 237, 240, 314, 318; *Lectures on Aesthetics* (1818), 77. *See also* Old Hegelians; Young Hegelians
Heidegger, Martin, 82
Heller, Stephen, 203
Hellmesberger, Josef, 135
Hellmesberger Quartet, 135
Helmholtz, Hermann von, 18
Hepokoski, James, 3–4, 28
Herbart, Johann Friedrich, 29, 53, 73, 78–79, 238
Herbeck, Johann von, 137–38, 204
Herz, Henri, 188
Herzogenberg, Elisabet von, 160, 172, 176
Heuberger, Richard, 101
Heyse, Paul, 201, 203
Hiller, Ferdinand, 203
Hinrichsen, Hans Joachim, 174–75
Hirschfeld, Robert, 20, 22
Hitler, Adolf, 26
Hoffmann, Albert, 21
Hoffmann, E. T. A., 193–94
Hoffmann, Freia, 247, 346
Hoffmeister, Franz Anton, 123
Hohenlohe of Germany, Prince, 138
Hölderlin, Friedrich, 7, 161–65, 175
Honegger, Claudia, 218, 245
Hornstein, Robert von, 204
Horton, Julian, 26
Hostinský, Ottakar, 6, 18, 20, 70–82
Humboldt, Wilhelm von, 163
Humperdinck, Engelbert, 22

Idealism, 3, 5, 18, 161, 236–37, 239
idealist materialism, 236, 238

Jahn, Wilhelm, 200, 203, 322
Jewishness and modernism, 313–14
Jewish pogroms (1881), 315
Jewish-Orientalism, 139, 140–42, 146, 148
Johann of Austria, Archduke, 203
Johnston, William M., 190, 311

Judaism, 198, 311–30
Judson, Pieter, 93, 162
Jůzl, Miloš, 71

Kalbeck, Max, 6, 121, 162, 169, 171–72, 225–26
Kālidāsa, 136
Kant, Immanuel, 18, 29, 53, 76–77, 80, 236; *Critique of Judgment*, 76–77, 80
Karlsruhe, 322
Karnes, Kevin, 1, 5, 22–23, 93, 113, 312–13, 320
Katz, Jacob, 319
Kauffmann, Emil, 263–64, 266
Keats, John, 293
Keller, Gottfried, 196, 201
Kerman, Joseph, 3
King Oscar II of Sweden, 203
Kisch, Rebeka, 321
Kisch, Salomon Abraham, 321
Kittl, Johann Friedrich, 218
Kittler, Friedrich, 314
Kleist, Heinrich von, 143
Knepler, Georg, 28
Knittel, K. M., 313
Köchel, Ludwig von, 204
Kocka, Jürgen, 96, 102
Kohn, Hans, 316
Koran, 172
Korngold, Julius, 24, 194, 199
Kossak, Ernst, 203
Köstlin, Heinrich Adolf, 18
Köstlin, Karl Rheingold, 18
Kralik, Heinrich, 24
Kramer, Lawrence, 3
Kretzschmar, Hermann, 224–26
Kristeva, Julia, 328–29
Krüger, Eduard, 18, 94
Kullak, Adolf, 7, 9, 17, 20, 25
Kunstverein, 74, 78–82
Kunstwart, Der, 24

Lachner, Franz, 203
Lamb, Andrew, 121–22
Landerer, Christoph, 314
Lang, Julius, 319
Lang, Marie, 214

Lange, Otto, 19
Lanner, Joseph, 94, 97, 99, 100, 103, 120, 203
Laube, Heinrich, 203
Laurencin, Ferdinand Peter Graf von, 17–18, 20–21, 72
Lazarus, Moritz, 18
Le Beau, Louise Adolpha, 246
Lebenskraft, 237, 239
Lecoq, Alexandre Charles, 98
legal systems, 56–8
Leipzig, 28, 94, 110, 190, 194, 223
Leipziger Repertorium der deutschen und ausländischen Literatur, 19
Lenneberg, Hans, 187, 198
Lessing, Gotthold Ephraim, 78
Levi, Hermann, 198
Lewald, Fanny, 203
liberalism, 2, 5–7, 21, 43, 72, 91–103, 133–34, 141, 160–64, 167, 170, 172, 176, 213, 316
Lichtenthal, Peter, 241
Liebmann, Otto, 18
Lind, Jenny, 24, 188, 203
Lipiner, Siegfried, 141
Lipperheide, Baroness Frida von, 279
Liszt, Franz, 8, 15, 16, 17, 19, 20, 22, 24, 42, 63, 134, 136, 145, 189, 204, 218, 222, 244, 267–68, 289, 290, 292, 295, 296, 301, 302; *Dante* Symphony, 145; *Faust* Symphony, 290; *Graner Festmesse*, 244; *Hungarian Rhapsodies*, 222; *Mazeppa*, 244; *Les Préludes*, 134; *Prometheus*, 244
Lobe, Johann Christoph, 18
Lortzing, Albert, 92, 101–2
Lotze, Hermann, 18, 238, 239
Lucca, Pauline, 204
Ludvová, Jitka, 321
Lueger, Karl, 161
Luther, Martin, 198
Lutheranism, 167, 170, 171

Maecenas, 135
Mahler, Gustav, 8, 280, 294, 299, 311–30; appointment to *Hofoper*, 324; arr. of Beethoven, String Quartet No. 11 in F minor, op. 85, 312, 323; baptism, 323; as conductor, 312–3, 320–24, 327; completion of Weber's opera, *Die drei Pintos*, 313, 322, 323; *Fünf Gesänge mit Orchesterbegleitung*, 325; as Hanslick's student, 322; *Das klagende Lied*, 322, 325; *Das Lied von der Erde*, 328; *Lieder eines fahrenden Gesellen*, 324–28; *Rübezahl*, 324; Symphony No. 1 in D major, 312–13, 325; Symphony No. 2 in c–E flat, 326
Malibran, Maria, 24
Mann, Thomas, 194
March revolution, 94, 95, 99–100, 102, 124, 133
Maria Theresa, Empress of the Holy Roman Empire, 56
Marx, Adolph Bernhard, 170, 194, 204
Marxist musicology, 3, 28
Mascagni, Pietro, 204
masculinity, 216–22, 226, 227, 237
materialism, 3, 60, 161, 236–39, 248
Maus, Fred Everett, 224, 242–43
Mayreder, Rosa, 215
McClary, Susan, 4
McColl, Sandra, 23
Meiningen Court Orchestra, 275
Mendelssohn, Felix, 25, 125, 198, 219, 222, 246, 294, 299, 311, 321; *Rondo capriccioso*, op. 14, 222; Symphony No. 4 in A major, op. 90 ("Italian"), 246
Metternich of Austria, Princess Pauline Clémentine von, 203, 322
Meyerbeer, Giacomo, 91, 98, 139, 140, 198, 204, 317; *Les Huguenots*, 91; *Le Prophète*, 317
Millenkovich-Morold, Max von, 26
Milton, John, 201
Moleschott, Jacob, 240
Mörike, Eduard, 8, 194, 269, 270, 271, 275, 278
Moscheles, Charlotte, 109
Moscheles, Ignatz, 109, 204
Mosenthal, Salomon Hermann, 132–33, 137, 139, 204
Moser, Hans-Joachim, 27
Mottl, Felix, 263, 322, 325, 326

Mozart, Wolfgang Amadeus, 54, 57, 193, 201–2, 294, 323, 327; *Don Giovanni*, 202; *Musical Joke, A*, K 522, 54; Symphony No. 40 in G minor, K 550, 323
Mozart, Karl, 204
Munich, 71, 318
municipal theater, Leipzig, 223
Musgrave, Michael, 165–66
music and the body, 41, 46–47, 112, 116–19, 239–43, 315
Music of the Future, 26, 122–24, 139, 319
musical coherence, 115, 215, 243, 293
musical modernism, 125, 314
musical narrative, 49, 223–27, 292, 300
musical secession, 280, 299, 326

Nachmärz, 100, 102
Nägeli, Carl, 246
national identity, 7, 71, 134, 189, 191–93, 219
nationalism, 71, 134, 146, 193, 201, 219, 316, 324
national socialism, 25–27, 199
neoabsolutism, 94
Neudeutsche Schule, 290. *See* New German School
Neue Berliner Musikzeitung, 16, 19
Neue Freie Presse, xiii, xiv, 2, 6, 21, 23, 24, 27, 94, 112, 133, 138, 160, 162, 199, 215, 261, 266, 277, 318
Neue Zeitschrift für Musik, 17, 19, 94, 317
New German School, 8, 16, 18, 25, 123, 236, 247, 262, 315
New Humanism, 7, 161, 163–64, 169
New Musicology, 3–4
New York Times, 24
Newman, Ernest, 23, 266
Newton, Isaac, 55
Nietzsche, Friedrich, 220, 221, 263–64, 267, 295, 300, 314, 317, 320, 329; on Brahms, 220; *The Case of Wagner*, 220, 263–64, 314; influence of Hanslick on, 267, 314, 320

Nohl, Ludwig, 204
Nora, Pierre, 197
Notley, Margaret, 6, 93, 102, 171–72
Nottebohm, Gustav, 262
Novalis (Friedrich von Hardenberg), 193
Oersted, Hans Christian, 238
Oesterreichische Blätter für Literatur und Kunst, 16, 17, 18
Offenbach, Jacques, 92, 93, 98–99, 101, 204
Oken, Lorenz, 247
Old Hegelians, 240
Ophüls, Gustav, 168
Oppenheim, Joseph, 112–13
orchestral lied, 312
Oriental music, 136, 141, 146
Ostjuden, 315

Paddison, Max, 25
Painter, Karen, 191
Palacký, František, xii
Paladilhe, Emilie, 204
Palestrina, Giovanni Pierluigi da, 202
Pan-German identity, 189, 199–201
Paris, 92–93
Patti, Adelina, 24, 120, 188, 204
Patti, Carlotta, 204
Pauer, Ernst, 204
Payzant, Geoffrey, 1, 5, 8, 29, 61, 118, 188, 315
Pederson, Sanna, 28, 313
Perfall, Baron, 189
Perin, Karoline von, 213
Pleasants, Henry, 3, 25, 27, 198
Pleyel, Ignatz, 123
polka, 92–93, 97–98, 120
Plüddemann, Martin, 277, 279
Pohl, Richard, 20
Potpeschnigg, Heinrich, 278
Potter, Pamela, 192
Prague, xii–xiii, 29, 53, 71, 124, 134, 188, 194, 198–200, 223, 238, 295, 315, 321, 322
Prague Conservatory, 218
Prater massacre, Vienna (1848), 212
Printz, Felix, 246

358　INDEX

program music, 2, 4, 5, 8, 19, 25, 71, 136, 142–45, 174, 237, 289, 292, 297, 298, 300, 312-13, 315
proximate cause, 54–56, 58, 61–62
Prussia, 161, 195, 200
pure absolute music, 173, 175
pure instrumental music, vii, 4, 75, 80, 145, 165, 166, 173, 175
pure music, 41, 75, 80, 143, 192, 236, 262
Purkyně, Jan Evangelista, xii

Racine, Jean, 201–2
Rappoldi, Eduard, 134
Rastner, Georges, 204
Rathenau, Walther, 315
Redoutensaal, Vienna, 43
religion, xii, 142, 162, 167, 172, 199, 276, 319
Rembrandt, 169
Rheinberger, Josef, 245
Rheinische Musik-Zeitung, 16, 317
Richter, Hans, 322
Richter, Jean Paul, 193, 194
Ricoeur, Paul, 196
Rieger, Eva, 247
Riemann, Hugo, 4, 28
Rinkel, Gottfried, 204
Rochlitz, Johann Friedrich, 57
Roger, Gustave, 204
Roman Law, 57
romantic literary tradition, 188, 193–95
romantic music aesthetics, 193
Rosé Quartet, 265
Rosenkranz, Karl, 238, 246–47
Rosetti, Francesco Antonio, 123
Ross, Alex, 15
Rossini, Giachino, 120, 204
Rousseau, Jean-Jacques, 195
Rozenblit, Marsha, 142
Rubens, Peter Paul, 169
Rubinstein, Anton, 204, 244
Rudolf, Crown Prince of Austria, 200, 203

Saffle, Michael, 319
Sams, Eric, 191
Schäfke, Rudolf, 25, 70

Schaller, Julius, 238–39, 240
Schelling, Friedrich Wilhelm Joseph, 236
Schenker, Heinrich, 4, 5, 24–25
Scherer, Wilhelm, 204
Scherwatzky, Robert, 26
Schiller, Friedrich von, 7, 125, 161–64, 167, 169, 173–75, 201, 236
Schir Zion (*Song of Zion*), 141
Schleiermacher, Friedrich, 314
Schmerling, Anton von, 201
Schoenberg, Arnold, 3, 5, 24–25, 271, 328
Schopenhauer, Arthur, 29, 314, 320
Schorske, Carl, 93, 162
Schott publishing, 263
Schrader, Bruno, 25
Schubert, Franz, 41–44, 48–49, 121, 190, 219, 244, 268, 294; *Divertissement à la Hongrois*, D. 818, 268; Symphony No. 8 in B minor ("Unfinished"), 41–42, 48; Symphony No. 9 in C major ("The Great"), 244
Schumann, Clara, 172, 222, 232–33n63, 246
Schumann, Robert, 192, 194, 202, 219, 244, 294, 325, 327; Sonata for Violin and Piano No. 2 in D minor, op. 121, 244; Symphony No. 4 in D minor, op. 120, 244, 325
Schütz, Heinrich, 202
Schwind, Moritz von, 204
secession. *See* musical secession
Segbauer, Hanna, 193
Seidl, Arthur, 18, 20–21
Shakespeare, William, 125, 169, 171, 296; *Othello*, 296; *The Tragedy of Hamlet, Prince of Denmark*, 169, 171
Shostakovich, Dmitri, 54
Shreffler, Anne, 3, 4, 28
Sibelius, Jean, 15
Simrock publishing, 204, 263
Slonimsky, Nicholas, 16, 21
Smetana, Bedřich, 72, 134, 145, 146, 158, 290; *The Bartered Bride*, 72; *Dalibor*, 72; *Má Vlast*, 290; *Vyšehrad*, 145–46

INDEX 359

Smithson, Harriet, 188
Socrates, viii
Sonntagsblätter, xiii
Sophocles, 201
Soukoup-Botschon, Cecilie, xiii
Specht, Richard, 120–21
Speidel, Ludwig, 6, 162, 275
spiritualism, 237
Spitta, Philipp, 57
Spitzer, Daniel, 204
Stachel, Peter, 141
Stade, K., 18, 72
Ständetheater, Prague, xiii
Standhartner, Joseph, 318
Steinway, Theodor, 204
Stengel, Theo, 25
Stéphanie, Crown Princess of Austria, 203
Steub, Ludwig, 204
Stimmung, 71, 76–82
stock-market crash (1873), 93
Strauß, Dietmar, 5
Strauss, Johann, Jr. (Strauss II): *Die Fledermaus*, 98; *Indigo*, 97–98, 100; *Der Karneval in Rom*, 98; "King of Waltz," 100; *Der lustige Krieg*, 91, 99; *Ritter Pásmán*, 101, 103; *Simplicius*, 101; *Der Zigeunerbaron*, 101
Strauss, Johann, Sr. (Strauss I), 94–97, 99, 103, 109–10, 122
Strauss, Richard: *Also sprach Zarathustra*, 292, 294, 298; *Aus Italien*, 293, 299; "Des Helden Widersacher," 294; *Don Juan*, 292–94, 292; *Guntram*, 292, 297; *Ein Heldenleben*, 294; *Till Eulenspiegel*, 293, 298; *Tod und Verklärung*, 292–93, 298, 300; Violin Concerto in D minor, op. 8, 291–92
Stuckenschmidt, Hans Heinz, 194, 199
Sullivan, Arthur, 188
Sulzer, Salomon, 141
Suppé, Franz von, 92
symphonic poem, 8, 20, 42, 134, 136, 145–46, 244–45, 289–302. *See also* tone poem
symphonic song, 278. *See also* orchestral lied

Tagliana, Emilia, 204
Tappert, Wilhelm, 16, 26
Tausig, Karl, 319
Tchaikovsky, Pyotr Ilych, 15–16, 22; Violin Concerto in D major, op. 35, 15
Thayer, Alexander Wheelock, 24
theosophy, 167
Thiers, Adolphe, 204
Third Reich, 25–28
Thomas, Ambroise, 137, 204
Thomson, Virgil, 15
Tieck, Ludwig, 193
Tomášek, Václav Jan, xii, 218
tone poems, 25, 290–92, 298, 300–301. *See also* symphonic poem
Trauerspiel, 169–70
Treitler, Leo, 320
Turgenev, Ivan, 201

Ullmann, Bernhard, 204
Unger, Joseph, 204
University of Vienna, xiii, xiv, 1, 120, 135, 214, 320
Urjuden, 316

Valentin, Gabriel Gustav, 238
Verdi, Giuseppi, 91, 204
Vienna, xiii, xiv, 1–2, 5–7, 16, 20, 21, 23–25, 43, 53, 55, 71, 91–95, 98–102, 109, 113, 116, 120–21, 123–24, 126, 132–38, 141, 142–45, 160–62, 187, 189–90, 192, 195, 198–200, 212, 213–15, 218, 225, 261–62, 266, 268, 270, 275, 277, 294–95, 312–13, 315–16, 319, 320, 322–25, 329
Vienna Conservatory, 135, 262
Vienna Court Opera (*Hofoper*), 132, 136–37, 315, 322, 324
Vienna Philharmonic Orchestra, 136, 138, 143, 145, 312, 323–24, 327
Viennese cultural conservatism, 261
Vischer, Friedrich Theodor, 17–18, 53, 72–73, 319
Vogl, Heinrich, 265
Volkmann, Robert, 204
Volkstümlichkeit, 92–95, 100, 103
Vormärz, 93, 100–102, 124, 197

Wackenroder, Wilhelm Heinrich, 193
Wagner, Cosima, 318
Wagner, Richard, xiii, 6, 8, 15–20, 22–28, 63, 70–71, 81, 94, 98, 100–102, 123–24, 139–41, 143–44, 147, 170, 190–92, 194–95, 198, 200, 202, 204, 220, 222, 236, 243–44, 261–64, 270–73, 276–79, 289–95, 297, 299, 301, 311–15, 317–29; *The Flying Dutchman*, 63; *Das Judenthum in der Musik*, 23, 317–18; as "Karl Freigedank," 317; *Lohengrin*, 25, 220, 222, 243, 262; *Mein Leben*, 23, 195; *Die Meistersinger von Nürnberg*, 22–23, 261, 271–73, 294, 311, 317–19; and racial anti-Semitism, 319; *Rienzi*, 63; *Der Ring des Nibelungen*, 101; *Tannhäuser*, xiii, 139, 190–91, 220, 243, 262, 317; *Tristan and Isolde*, 170, 324–25; *Wesendonck Lieder*, 325
Wagnerian School, 139
Wagnerism, 94, 100–103
Wagner-Verein, 277
Walker, Alan, 20
Walton, Kendall, 49
waltz, 92–100, 102–3, 108–26, 201, 274–75
Wapnewski, Peter, 188
Weber, Carl Maria von, 125, 193, 313, 322, 324
Weber, Dionys, 218
Webster, James, 171
Weimar, 16–17, 123, 201, 325, 327
Weininger, Otto, 316
Wellbery, David, 76–77, 314
Weltgeist, 327
Wenzel, Johann, 194. *See also* Johann Stamitz

Werner, Heinrich, 266, 278
Wesendonck, Mathilde, 325
Wiener Allgemeine Musik-Zeitung, xiii, 317
Wiener demokratischer Frauenverein, 213
Wiener Frauenerwerbsverein, 213
Wiener Salonblatt, 261, 263, 265, 267–68, 277
Wiener Zeitung, xiii
Wilbrandt, Adolf, 204
Willner, A. M., 147
Wilt, Marie, 204
Wohlmuth, Sophie, xiv, 199, 204, 223
Wolf, Hugo, 8, 22, 191–92, 261–88, 326; on Brahms, 262–64; *Elfenlied*, 277–78; *Die Feuerreiter*, 277–78; *A Midsummer Night's Dream*, 278
Woltmann, Alfred, 223
Wolzogen, Hans von, 26
women's movement in Vienna, 212–15
Wranitzky, Paul, 123
Wrbna-Freudenthal, Count Eugen, 137–39
Würst, Richard, 27

Yoshida, Hiroshi, 27
Young Hegelians, 60

Zelter, Carl Friedrich, 194
Zerny, Frieda, 279
Zimmermann, Robert, 17–18, 29, 53, 73, 77, 238
Zukunftsmusik, 280. *See also* Music of the Future
Zweig, Stefan, 323

www.ingramcontent.com/pod-product-compliance
Lightning Source LLC
Chambersburg PA
CBHW032012300426
44117CB00008B/998